Thomas CONSTABLE'S NOTES on the Bible

Volume V Hosea – Malachi

Thomas L. Constable

Thomas Constable's Notes on the Bible
Volume V: Hosea – Malachi
(print edition)
©2014 Tyndale Seminary Press
Fort Worth, TX

ISBN13 – 978-1-938484-12-4

All rights reserved. No part of this publication may be reproduced, stored in a retrieval system, or transmitted in any form or by any means except by brief quotation, without the prior permission of the publisher.

For electronic access to notes from Dr. Thomas L. Constable, visit **www.soniclight.com**

This volume is dedicated to serious students of the Bible around the world, for whom I have written these notes, especially my students at Dallas Theological Seminary. Many of them have taught me much - as they have asked questions about various passages of Scripture - that have led me to try to help them.

Contents

Thomas Constable's Notes on the Bible
Volume V: Hosea – Malachi

Constable's Notes on Hosea……………………………………………………………………………..7

Constable's Notes on Joel………………………………………………………………………………49

Constable's Notes on Amos……………………………………………………………………………..71

Constable's Notes on Obadiah………………………………………………………………………..109

Constable's Notes on Jonah…………………………………………………………………………..127

Constable's Notes on Micah…………………………………………………………………………..157

Constable's Notes on Nahum………………………………………………………………………….187

Constable's Notes on Habakkuk……………………………………………………………………...209

Constable's Notes on Zephaniah……………………………………………………………………..231

Constable's Notes on Haggai………………………………………………………………...……….251

Constable's Notes on Zechariah……………………………………………………………………...269

Constable's Notes on Malachi………………………………………………………………………...327

Constable's Notes
on Hosea

Introduction

Title and Writer
The prophet's name is the title of the book. The book claims to be "the word of the LORD" that "Hosea" received (1:1). Thus he appears to have been the writer.

Unity
Historically almost all Jewish and Christian scholars have regarded the whole book as the product of Hosea. Some critics, however, believe later editors (redactors) added the prophecies concerning Judah (e.g., 4:15; 5:5, 10, 12-14; 6:4, 11; et al.), since most of the book contains prophecies against Israel, the Northern Kingdom.[1] Yet there is no good reason to deny Hosea the Judean prophecies.[2] All the other eighth-century B.C. prophets also spoke about Judah, including Amos, who ministered to the Northern Kingdom at this time. Some critics say the salvation passages in Hosea (e.g., 11:8-11; 14:2-9) are so different from the judgment passages that someone else must have written them. However, the mixing of judgment and salvation messages is very common in all the prophets.

Date
Hosea's ministry spanned the reigns of four Judean kings (Uzziah, Jotham, Ahaz, and Hezekiah; cf. Isa. 1:1) and one Israelite king (Jeroboam II; 1:1). King Uzziah (Azariah) of Judah began reigning in 792 B.C., and King Hezekiah of Judah stopped reigning in 686 B.C., spanning a period of 107 years. Probably Hosea's ministry began near the end of Jeroboam II's (793-753 B.C.) and Uzziah's (792-740 B.C.) reigns, and ended in the early years of Hezekiah's sole reign (715-686 B.C.). Hezekiah evidently reigned for 14 years as co-regent with his father Ahaz (729-715 B.C.; cf. 2 Kings 18:1). This would mean that the prophet's ministry lasted perhaps 45 years (ca. 760-715 B.C.). It also means that Hosea's ministry extended beyond the fall of Samaria in 722 B.C., since Hezekiah began ruling in 715 B.C. Hosea did not date any of his prophecies. Other possible dates are between 760 and 753 to 715 B.C. (38 to 45 years),[3] 760 to 720 B.C. (38 years),[4] 760 to sometime during Hezekiah's reign (715-686 B.C., about 45 years,[5] over half a century,[6] and about 60 or 65 years.[7]

There were six other kings of Israel who followed Jeroboam II that Hosea did not mention in 1:1 that ruled during the reigns of the four Judean kings he named. They were Zechariah (753 B.C.), Shallum (752 B.C.), Menahem (752-742 B.C.), Pekah (752-732 B.C.), Pekahiah (742-740 B.C.), and Hoshea (732-723 B.C.). Hosea evidently prophesied during the reigns of more kings of Israel and Judah than any other prophet, probably eleven. It seems unusual that Hosea would mention four Judean kings and only one Israelite king, especially since he ministered primarily to the Northern Kingdom. He may have done this because the six Israelite kings named above were less significant in Israel's history than the other kings Hosea did mention. Another possibility is that Hosea did this because he regarded the Judean kings as Israel's legitimate kings in contrast to those of the North. He may have mentioned Jeroboam II because he was the primary king of the Northern Kingdom during his ministry, or because he was the strongest king of that kingdom during that period.

Historical Background
Hosea began ministering near the end of an era of great material prosperity and military success for both Israel and Judah (cf. 2 Kings 14:25-28; 2 Chron. 26:2, 6-15). In the first half of the eighth-century B.C., Assyrian influence in the west had declined temporarily, allowing both Jeroboam II and Uzziah to flourish. However, under Tiglath-Pileser III (745-727 B.C.), Assyria began to grow stronger and to expand westward again. In 734 B.C. the Northern Kingdom became a puppet nation within the Assyrian Empire (2 Kings 15:29). After Israel tried to revolt, Assyria defeated Samaria, the capital of the Northern Kingdom, in 722 B.C., and deported the people of Israel into captivity (2 Kings 17:1-6; 18:10-12). Judah also became a vassal state in the Assyrian Empire during Hosea's ministry (2 Kings 16:5-10).

Hosea's prophecy reflects conditions of economic prosperity, religious formalism and apostasy, and political stability that marked Jeroboam II's reign. The historical background of the Book of Amos is almost identical.

---

[1] E.g., W. R. Harper, *A Critical and Exegetical Commentary on Amos and Hosea*, pp. clix-clxii; H. W. Wolff, *Hosea*, pp. xxix-xxxii.
[2] For discussion of the Judean passages, see R. K. Harrison, *Introduction to the Old Testament*, pp. 868-70; John Bright, *A History of Israel*, p. 280.
[3] Leon Wood, "Hosea," in *Daniel-Minor Prophets*, vol. 7 of *The Expositor's Bible Commentary*, p. 163, and idem, *The Prophets of Israel*, p. 276.
[4] Douglas Stuart, *Hosea-Jonah*, p. xliii.
[5] Hobart E. Freeman, *An Introduction to the Old Testament Prophets*, p. 175.
[6] Charles Lee Feinberg, *Hosea*, p. 10.
[7] C. F. Keil, "Hosea," in *The Twelve Minor Prophets*, 1:15.

Place of Composition

Besides the fact that Hosea ministered to the Northern Kingdom, his reference to the king of Samaria as "our king" (7:5) seems to make his residence in Israel certain. The book never states the location of any of his preaching, however.

Audience and Purpose

Hosea, like Amos, addressed the Northern Kingdom of Israel primarily. Their contemporaries, who were Isaiah and Micah, ministered primarily to the Southern Kingdom of Judah. Some scholars believe that Amos preceded Hosea slightly.[8] But this seems impossible to prove conclusively since we have so little information about exactly when these prophets wrote. Hosea's purpose was to announce that because the nation had broken Yahweh's covenant (the Mosaic Covenant), judgment was coming (cf. Deut. 28:15-68). His purpose was, therefore, similar to Jeremiah's in that both prophets announced and witnessed the downfall of their respective nations. One writer referred to Hosea as the Jeremiah of Israel.[9] The people needed to repent and return to the Lord and His covenant. If they did, they might avoid His judgment. However, the prophet announced that the nation as a whole would not repent, though individuals could, so judgment was coming. Hosea also reaffirmed God's promise to bless His people Israel eventually, in the distant future (cf. Deut. 30:1-10).

> "Understanding the message of the book of Hosea depends upon understanding the Sinai covenant. The book contains a series of blessings and curses announced for Israel by God through Hosea. Each blessing or curse is based upon a corresponding type in the Mosaic law."[10]

Theology

The major biblical doctrines that Hosea stressed were sin, judgment, salvation, and the loyal love of God.

Regarding sin, the prophet stressed the idolatry of the Israelites, which he compared to spiritual adultery. Israel had turned from Yahweh to worship Baal, the Canaanite god of fertility. The Lord told Hosea to marry a woman who would prove to be unfaithful to him, so he could appreciate and communicate how the Lord felt about His wife's (Israel's) unfaithfulness to Him. Hosea also pointed out other sins that the Israelites needed to forsake: violent crimes (4:2; 6:9; 12:1), political revolt (7:3-7), foreign alliances (7:11; 8:9), spiritual ingratitude (7:15), social injustice (12:7), and selfish arrogance (13:6).

Hosea called for repentance, but he was not hopeful of a positive response because most of the people did not want to change. God's judgment would, therefore, descend in the form of infertility, military invasion, and exile. Hosea stressed the fact that God was just in sending judgment on the Israelites. He would do it by making their punishments match their crimes.

The prophet assured the Israelites that God would not abandon them completely. After judgment would come salvation. Eventually the people would return to Yahweh, as Hosea's wayward wife would return to him. In Hosea, passages on salvation follow sections announcing judgment, though there are more predictions of punishment than promises of deliverance.

Judgment	Restoration
1:2-9	1:10—2:1
2:2-13	2:14—3:5
4:1—5:14	5:15—6:3
6:4—11:7	11:8-11
11:12—13:16	ch. 14

The outstanding revelation concerning God that this book contributes is the loyal love of Yahweh for His own.

> "In no prophet is the love of God more clearly demarcated and illustrated than in Hosea."[11]

> "Nowhere in the whole range of God's revelation do we find more beautiful words of love than in Hosea 2:14-16; 6:1-4; 11:1-4, 8, 9; 14:4-8."[12]

---

[8] E.g., Wood, "Hosea," pp. 162, 163; Stuart, p. xliii; and H. L. Ellison, *The Prophets of Israel*, p. 95.
[9] Freeman, p. 177. Cf. Wood, *The Prophets . . .*, p. 282.
[10] Stuart, pp. 6-7.
[11] Walter C. Kaiser Jr., *Toward and Old Testament Theology*, p. 197.
[12] Feinberg, pp. 10-11.

"Every page of the prophecy keeps declaring God's love for Israel."[13]

The great illustration of how committed God is to His people is how He instructed Hosea to relate to his unfaithful wife. The Lord will not forsake those with whom He has joined in covenant commitment, even if they become unfaithful to Him repeatedly. He will be patient with them and will eventually save them (cf. 11:1-4; 14).

"The Lord's covenantal relationship with His people Israel is central to the messages of the eighth-century prophets Hosea, Amos, and Micah. Each of these prophets accused God's people of violating the obligations of the Mosaic Covenant and warned that judgment was impending. Despite painting such a bleak picture of the immediate future, these prophets also saw a bright light at the end of the dark tunnel of punishment and exile. Each anticipated a time when the Lord, on the basis of His eternal covenantal promises to Abraham and David, would restore Israel to a position of favor and blessing. In fact, the coming judgment would purify God's people and thus prepare the way for a glorious new era in Israel's history."[14]

Themes

"The major truths of the book are: (1) God suffers when His people are unfaithful to Him; (2) God cannot condone sin; and (3) God will never cease to love His own and, consequently, He seeks to win back those who have forsaken Him."[15]

Wood identified five basic themes that recur throughout the book. Israel continued to break the covenant that God had made with her. The broken marriage covenant of Hosea and Gomer illustrated Israel's sin. In spite of Israel's unfaithfulness, God remained faithful to her. The Israelites could expect severe punishment for breaking the covenant. And yet Israel would again enjoy gracious benefits from God, including future restoration.[16]

Genre and Literary Forms

Hosea consists of prophetic oracles, most of which are in poetic form.[17] Silva regarded Hosea as essentially a covenant enforcement document. He identified the following subgenres or literary forms in Hosea: the prophetic judgment speech, the covenant lawsuit speech (or *rib* oracle), the oracle of salvation, the prophetic call or commission, the symbolic action, proverbs and wisdom sayings, calls to alarm or battle warnings, the woe oracle, rhetorical questions, a penitential song, a divine lament, an admonition or exhortation to repent, and a love song.[18]

"Hosea was a master literary craftsman. His work is so elevated in style that it is often difficult to distinguish between his use of poetry and prose."[19]

"The single most striking feature of the poetic/literary nature of the book is its use of metaphor and simile."[20]

Text

Hosea contains the highest proportion (not number) of textual problems of any Old Testament book except possibly Job.[21]

Outline

I. Introduction 1:1
II. The first series of messages of judgment and restoration: Hosea's family 1:2—2:1
    A. Signs of coming judgment 1:2-9
    B. A promise of restoration 1:10—2:1

---

[13]Ibid., p. 16.
[14]Robert B. Chisholm Jr., "A Theology of the Minor Prophets," in *A Biblical Theology of the Old Testament*, p. 398.
[15]*The New Scofield Reference Bible*, p. 919.
[16]Wood, *The Prophets . . .*, pp. 282-83.
[17]Tremper Longman III and Raymond B. Dillard, *An Introduction to the Old Testament*, p. 403.
[18]Charles H. Silva, "Literary Features in the Book of Hosea," *Bibliotheca Sacra* 164:653 (January-March 2007):34-48.
[19]Richard D. Patterson, "Portraits from a Prophet's Portfolio: Hosea 4," *Bibliotheca Sacra* 165:659 (July-September 2008):294-308.
[20]Longman and Dillard, p. 405.
[21]F. I. Andersen and D. N. Freedman, *Hosea: A New Translation, Introduction and Commentary*, p. 66.

III.   The second series of messages of judgment and restoration: marital unfaithfulness 2:2—3:5
- A.   Oracles of judgment 2:2-13
  1. Judgment on Gomer as a figure of Israel 2:2-7
  2. Judgment on Israel 2:8-13
- B.   Promises of restoration 2:14—3:5
  1. Renewed love and restored marriage 2:14-20
  2. Renewed fertility and restored favor 2:21-23
  3. The restoration of Hosea's and Yahweh's wives ch. 3

IV.   The third series of messages on judgment and restoration: widespread guilt 4:1—6:3
- A.   The judgment oracles chs. 4—5
  1. Yahweh's case against Israel ch. 4
  2. The guilt of both Israel and Judah ch. 5
- B.   The restoration promises 6:1-3

V.   The fourth series of messages on judgment and restoration: Israel's ingratitude 6:4—11:11
- A.   More messages on coming judgment 6:4—11:7
  1. Israel's ingratitude and rebellion 6:4—8:14
  2. Israel's inevitable judgment 9:1—11:7
- B.   Another assurance of restoration 11:8-11

VI.   The fifth series of messages on judgment and restoration: historical unfaithfulness 11:12—14:8
- A.   Judgment for unfaithfulness 11:12—13:16
  1. The deceitfulness of Israel 11:12—12:14
  2. Israel's impending doom ch. 13
- B.   Restoration in spite of unfaithfulness 14:1-8
  1. An appeal for repentance 14:1-3
  2. A promise of restoration 14:4-8

VII.   Conclusion 14:9

Message

The Book of Hosea is an unusually powerful book, because the prophet ministered out of his deep personal emotions. His intellectual appeals to the Israelites in his day, and to us in ours, arose out of great personal tragedy in his own life. We might say that he cried out as he bled. Hosea appreciated the pain that God felt over His people's apostasy, as no other prophet did, because he felt the intense pain of his wife's unfaithfulness. Hosea could speak of the deepest things in the economy of God because he entered into fellowship with God in God's sufferings (cf. Phil. 3:10). That is one reason this book is so appealing and so powerful.

The permanent values of this book are its revelations of sin, judgment, and love. Hosea reveals what sin is at its worst. It also reveals the nature of judgment. Third, it reveals the unconquerable force of true love.

With regard to sin, Hosea reveals the very nature of sin, what makes it so appalling, not just the various forms of sin. Hosea was able to penetrate to the very heart of sin. What made the sin of the Israelites so great was the fact that they had sinned against light and love.

The more light (revelation from God) that people have, the greater is their responsibility (cf. Amos; Rom. 1—3). What made the Israelites' sin so bad was that they were the Chosen People of God, the people of all peoples on earth who enjoyed the most revelation of the gracious person and the loving plans of Yahweh for their blessing. They had the Law, they had God's presence among them, and they had God's covenant promises (cf. Rom. 9). Yet they rebelled against Him and chose to walk in darkness rather than light.

Furthermore, they had sinned against God's love. They had experienced Yahweh's election, His provisions, His protection, and more of His blessings than any other people on the earth, but they had walked away from Him and spent His gifts to them to satisfy their lewd desires. They had not only committed spiritual adultery, but they had become spiritual prostitutes. They had sinned against His love as well as against His light.

In one respect, all sins are equally bad in that they are all offenses against God. But in another sense, some sins are worse than others, because people who have experienced much of God's light and love have greater responsibility to respond to that light and love, than people who have fewer of these blessings. In Romans 2, Paul explained that God will judge people according to the light that they had (cf. James 3:1). The Israelites had much light, and they had experienced much love. This made their sin especially heinous.

Hosea declared that the human marriage relationship symbolized the relationship that existed between Yahweh and His people. Israel had become unfaithful to God. God taught Hosea the seriousness of this unfaithfulness and how He felt about it through the prophet's own marriage relationship. Hosea experienced the tragedy and heartbreak of an unfaithful wife, not just an adulteress, which is bad enough, but an adulteress turned prostitute—which enabled him to enter into the fellowship of God's sufferings over the behavior of His "wife," Israel. Hosea's heart was broken, and he felt the most unutterable sorrow that a man can feel, when he feels his wife abandon him. He learned how God felt, and he denounced kings, priests, and people out of that broken heart that mirrored the broken heart of God. Hosea, then, revealed the deepest nature of sin, namely: infidelity to the elective grace of God. The worst thing in the realm of sin is apathy to the love of God. The opposite of love is not hate but apathy.

Hosea also revealed the nature of judgment. In view of the essential nature of sin, namely: violation of covenant love, judgment will inevitably fall, unless there is genuine repentance. In view of their sin, the Israelites had no basis for hoping that God would pardon them. Hosea referred to the past love of God for Israel, His present love, and His future love for His Chosen People. Interspersed between these reminders of God's love through the book we have Hosea's tracing of Israel's history downward to the place where judgment was inevitable. Such great sinners against God's light and love had no reason to expect divine mercy. No one can see this as clearly, or feel it so intensely, as the person who has been sinned against as long and persistently as Hosea had been. Hosea felt the divine justice in God's action, so he could announce it in the clearest and most forceful terms, as this book shows.

Nevertheless, in spite of the great revelations of sin and judgment that this book contains, its greatest revelation is that of love, divine love. In the midst of Hosea's personal overwhelming sorrow, because of Gomer's infidelity, God told him to seek out his sinning wife, to go after her and bring her back, first into a wilderness seclusion for a while, but then back into a place of love and privilege at his own side. Through his wife's unfaithfulness Hosea learned the awfulness of sin, and in obedience to God's command to seek out and accept his traitorous wife, he learned God's love in spite of sin.

These three great revelations—sin, judgment, and love—constitute the living message of the Book of Hosea. These are the great lessons that we as Christians must apply to ourselves and to those to whom we minister. We need a constant re-emphasis of each of these truths, because we tend to get away from them, both individually, and corporately as the church. We fail to appreciate the love of God, because we fail to appreciate the essential nature of our sin, and that it makes judgment inevitable. Jesus said that the person who is most impressed with his or her own sin is the person who is most impressed with God's love for him or her (Luke 7:47).

Hosea teaches that the most heinous and damnable sin of which people are capable is infidelity to love. This is the sin that damns unbelievers; they fail to respond to the love of God that reaches out to them. It is also the sin that will bring judgment on believers who are apathetic to the love of their Savior. Apathy toward divine love, if unchecked, will inevitably lead to spiritual adultery. Compared to this, the animalism and violence of the heathen are as nothing. It would be better not to have the light, or to have known divine love, than to have them and then to be unfaithful to them (cf. 2 Pet. 2:21).

Hosea also teaches that divine judgment is the fruit of sin. Infidelity to love can lead only to degradation. Israel thought she was repenting, but this prophet pointed out that her repentance was only superficial (6:4; 13:3). Just as faithfulness to the covenant brought blessing, so unfaithfulness brought discipline, and discipline in proportion to the light and love violated.

Hosea teaches, too, that true love will triumph over unfaithfulness. Though unfaithfulness inevitably results in chastening, and unfaithfulness to divine light and love leads unquestionably to the worst kind of misery, true love does not forsake the one loved. In fact, true love bears the judgment, the heartache, and the suffering that the unfaithful lover causes. It takes this judgment on itself so that final restoration can be possible. This book closes with the Lord saying at last, "I will heal their apostasy; I will love them freely" (14:4). God will not cast off those who sin against Him, even those who sinned in the most heinous way. He will disciple them, but He will not cast them away from His presence. He will give them a new heart of faithfulness to Himself eventually (Jer. 32:39). This revelation supports the doctrine of eternal security.

The application of the message of Hosea to our generation touches both the church and the individual Christian. It is a message to God's people, not to unbelievers, primarily. It is a message to those who walk in great light and enjoy great love: to all those who are "married" to God.

Like Israel of old, the modern church has become apathetic to the love of God and has wandered away from Him, has become unfaithful to Him, and has even prostituted herself to the world to find satisfaction and approval. The evidence of spiritual adultery in our time is worldliness: the paganism of our day that is part of church life. The church is going after the things that the world values at the expense of faithfulness to the Word and will of God. This is due, ultimately, to our dissatisfaction with God's love. We take the resources that God has given us and spend them to satisfy unworthy ambitions and pleasures. We are enflaming ourselves with carnality under every "green tree," as Israel did. Consequently, we are failing to bear the testimony to the light and love of God that we as the church should be proclaiming, and unbelievers are not taking God seriously. One of the greatest hindrances to evangelism today is the behavior of Christians.

Hosea spoke of God's judgment coming on His people in three figures.

He said God would weaken His people's strength, as a moth and rottenness weaken clothing (5:12). That judgment is evident in the church today. We see it in the church's lack of influence in the world, the lack of conversions as the gospel is preached, and the world's indifference to the church's testimony, for example. This is because the church has turned to other sources of strength beside the Lord, as Israel turned to Egypt and Assyria, and like Gomer turned to her lovers. The church, like Israel, has only repented superficially. This judgment is already taking effect.

Second, Hosea said judgment would come like a young lion and a bear (11:10; 13:7-8). This is a manifestation of the fiercer anger of the Lord. This form of judgment is also evident in some churches. They have lost their testimony completely. They have no spiritual impact, because they have abandoned the Lord. They have rejected His Word and His will to pursue other interests, like a prostitute.

The third form of judgment is God's withdrawal from His own people (5:6). When they call on Him, He does not answer them because they have refused to listen to Him for so long (cf. Jer. 7:13-15; 14:11-12). His presence and blessing have departed from them, and there is no more indication that they even belong to Him. Of course, God will not fully abandon His own, but He will remove His presence from them to such an extent that they are without His help. God did this to Israel when He allowed them to go into captivity.

Nevertheless, after all the failure, heartbreak, and desolation caused by the unfaithfulness of God's people, He will gather them to Himself. As He promised to restore and revive Israel's love for Himself, so He has promised to take the church to abide forever with Himself one day (John 14:3). What God will do for Israel at the Second Coming, He will do for the church at the Rapture. These restorations are in spite of, not because of, His people's responses to His light and love. They are due to the love of God, a love that remains committed to those whom He has chosen, regardless of their commitment to Him. May His love for us move us to remain faithful to Him, and to practice that kind of love toward those who have been unfaithful to us as well. God's unconditional love should be our model in our relationship with those in covenant relationship with us (e.g., our spouses).[22]

The Minor Prophets

Hosea is the first of the so-called "Minor Prophets." The Minor Prophets are called Minor Prophets because they are shorter than the Major Prophets. Hosea and Zechariah, which may appear longer than Daniel, because they have 14 chapters each, compared with Daniel's 12, are really shorter than Daniel. Hosea has 197 verses, and Zechariah has 211, whereas Daniel has 357.

There are 12 Minor Prophets in the Hebrew Bible, and they are called "The Twelve." These books were originally copied on one scroll, whereas the Major Prophets required a whole scroll for each book. The Twelve include Hosea, Joel, Amos, Obadiah, Jonah, Micah, Nahum, Habakkuk, Zephaniah, Haggai, Zechariah, and Malachi. The 12 "Minor Prophets" in our English Old Testaments are exactly the same as "The Twelve," the shorter prophets in the Hebrew Bible.

Lamentations and Daniel were put in the Hagiographa—or Writings—section of the Hebrew Bible, not the Prophets section. Lamentations was placed there because it is a book of poetry, and Daniel was placed there because it is a book of history primarily, though it contains prophecy. In the Hebrew Bible, there are only three Major Prophets: Isaiah, Jeremiah, and Ezekiel. Also, Daniel was not officially a prophet.

Exposition

I. INTRODUCTION 1:1

This verse introduces the whole book. The word of Yahweh came to Hosea, the son (possibly descendant) of Beeri, during the reigns of Uzziah, Jotham, Ahaz, and Hezekiah, kings of Judah (cf. Isa. 1:1). It also came to him during the reign of Jeroboam II of Israel (cf. Amos 1:1). As explained above under "Date," Hosea's ministry probably extended from about 760 to 715 B.C. Hosea's name means "He [Yahweh] has saved" and is a variation of "Joshua" (cf. Num. 13:8, 16; Gr. Jesus). We know nothing else about Beeri ("my wellspring"), or any of Hosea's other ancestors, or his hometown.

II. THE FIRST SERIES OF MESSAGES OF JUDGMENT AND RESTORATION: HOSEA'S FAMILY 1:2—2:1

Though we know nothing of Hosea's personal life before he began prophesying, we do know about a crisis that arose in his family while he ministered. This personal tragedy and its happy ending proved to be a lesson to the people of Israel. This lesson corresponds to and illustrated the other messages of judgment and restoration that follow. Other prophets also experienced personal problems that the Lord used to teach His people (e.g., Isa. 20:1-4; Ezek. 4:1—5:4).

---

[22]Adapted from G. Campbell Morgan, *Living Messages of the Books of the Bible*, 1:2:165-79.

The major themes of the book come into view in this opening section: Israel's unfaithfulness to Yahweh, His judgment of her, and His later restoration of her.

A. SIGNS OF COMING JUDGMENT 1:2-9

The Lord used Hosea's family members as signs to communicate His message of coming judgment on Israel.

1:2 At the beginning of Hosea's ministry, Yahweh commanded him to take "a wife of harlotry" and to have "children of harlotry." The reason the Lord gave for this unusual command was that the land of Israel (i.e., the people of the Northern Kingdom, cf. 4:1) were committing flagrant harlotry in the sense that they had departed from the Lord to pursue other loves. The Lord used personification to picture the land (i.e., the people of the land) as a woman acting like a prostitute.

Students of this book have understood the phrase "a wife of harlotry" (Heb. *'esheth zenunim*) to mean one of four things. These major views fall into two groups: non-literal and literal interpretations.

First, some believe the text means that God gave Hosea a vision or that He told him an allegory in which his wife was or would become a harlot.[23] This view avoids the moral problem of God commanding His prophet to marry a woman who was already or would become a harlot. However, there is no indication in the text that this was a visionary experience or an allegorical tale, and there are many details that point to it being a real experience. For example, Hosea recorded the name of his wife and her father's name (1:3). He also named the exact amount that he paid for her (3:2).

Second, some interpreters believe that Hosea's wife became "a wife of harlotry" because she was already or became a worshipper of a false god; her harlotry was spiritual rather than physical. A related view is that she was a spiritual harlot merely by being an Israelite since the Israelites had been unfaithful to Yahweh.[24] Again the details of the story as it unfolds argue for literal sexual unfaithfulness.

Third, it is possible that Hosea's wife was sexually promiscuous before he married her.[25] Some have even suggested that she may have been a temple prostitute. One writer suggested that she had participated in a Canaanite rite of sexual initiation in preparation for marriage, but this would not likely have made her a harlot.[26] If the Lord meant that Hosea was to marry a harlot, it would have been more natural for Him to say "take to yourself a harlot" (Heb. *zonah*) or "prostitute." The biggest problem with this view is ethical. It seems very unlikely that God would command His prophet to marry a woman who was already a harlot.

Fourth, the preferred view seems to be that Hosea's wife became unfaithful to him after they got married, and that Yahweh told him that she would do this before they got married.[27] Similarly, God told Moses that Pharaoh would harden his heart and not allow the Israelites to leave Egypt before Moses first went into Pharaoh's presence (Exod. 3:19). This view posits a situation that was most similar to the relationship that existed between Yahweh and Israel, which Hosea's marital relations illustrated (cf. 2:2, 4; 4:12; 5:4). Israel became unfaithful to Yahweh after previous faithfulness; Israel was not unfaithful when Yahweh married her (at Sinai). She was a brand new bride freshly redeemed out of Egyptian slavery (cf. Jer. 2:2-3). This parallelism suggests that the woman whom Hosea loved again (ch. 3) was Gomer, his original wife. Another view is that two wives are involved, one in chapter 1 and a different one in chapter 3. Discussion of this issue follows under chapter 3.

Another difficulty is the meaning of "children of harlotry." Were these children that Gomer already had?[28] Were they children that Hosea would have by Gomer that would prove unfaithful like their mother?[29] Or were they born to Hosea and Gomer after she became unfaithful?[30] Probably the phrase means "children of a wife who is marked by harlotry."[31] It seems to me that the children in view were the children born to Hosea and Gomer, and they became known as "children of harlotry" when their mother became a harlot.

---

[23]E. J. Young, *Introduction to the Old Testament*, pp. 245-46.
[24]Stuart, pp. 26-27.
[25]Keil, 1:29, 37; T. E. McComiskey, "Hosea," in *The Minor Prophets*, pp. 11-17; J. L. Mays, *Hosea: A Commentary*, p. 26; Longman and Dillard, p. 402; and Warren W. Wiersbe, "Hosea," in *The Bible Exposition Commentary/Prophets*, p. 316.
[26]Wolff, pp. 14-15.
[27]Andersen and Freedman, p. 162; Harper, p. 207; Wood, "Hosea," p. 166; idem, *The Prophets . . .*, p. 279; Robert B. Chisholm Jr., *Handbook on the Prophets*, p. 337; Freeman, pp. 181-82; and Kaiser, p. 197.
[28]Keil, 1:29.
[29]Wood, "Hosea," p. 171.
[30]McComiskey, pp. 15-16.
[31]Andersen and Freedman, p. 168; and Kaiser, p. 197.

"In ancient Israelite society harlots were chiefly foreigners."[32]

1:3-4   Hosea obediently married Gomer (probably meaning "completion"), the daughter of Diblaim ("fig cakes"). She bore Hosea a son whom the Lord told the prophet to name "Jezreel." The Lord also prescribed the names of Isaiah's sons (Isa. 7:3; 8:3-4), Messiah (Isa. 7:14; 9:6), and many other individuals. He also assigned the symbolic names "Oholah" and "Oholibah" to Samaria and Jerusalem (Ezek. 23). The name "Jezreel" means "God sows" (by scattering seed), but it was not just the meaning of the name that was significant in this case, but also the associations with the town in Israel that bore that name.

Each section on Hosea's children (vv. 3-5, 6-7, 8-9) contains a birth notice, a word of instruction from the Lord about the child's name, and an explanation of the meaning of the name. The names of Hosea's children all reminded everyone who heard them of the broken relationship that existed between Yahweh and Israel, and each one anticipated judgment.

It was at Jezreel that King Jehu of Israel (841-814 B.C.) had massacred many enemies of Israel, including King Ahab and Queen Jezebel of Israel, King Jehoram of Israel, and many prophets of Baal, which was good (cf. 2 Kings 9:6-10, 24; 10:18-28, 30). But he also killed King Ahaziah of Judah and 42 of his relatives, which was bad (2 Kings 9:27-28; 10:12-14). Ahaziah and his relatives did not die in Jezreel, but their deaths were part of Jehu's wholesale slaughter at Jezreel. Jehu went too far and thereby demonstrated disrespect for the Lord's commands (cf. 2 Kings 10:29-31).

Because of Jehu's atrocities that overstepped his authority to judge Israel's enemies, God promised to punish his house (dynasty).[33] The fulfillment came when Shallum assassinated King Zechariah, Jeroboam II's son and the fourth king of Jehu's dynasty, in 753-752 B.C. This death ended Jehu's kingdom (dynasty) forever (2 Kings 15:10). Another view is that the reference to putting an end to the kingdom of the house of Israel refers to the demise of the Northern Kingdom in 722 B.C.[34] It is very difficult to determine if the word rendered "kingdom" should be translated "kingdom" (Heb. *mamlekat*) or "kingship" (*mamlekut*). When Hosea wrote, the Hebrew alphabet only had consonants, no vowels.

1:5   This name of Hosea's first son would also point to a future judgment that would also take place in the valley near Jezreel. It would happen on "that day," namely, a future unspecified day. Yahweh promised to break Israel's military strength, symbolized by an archer's "bow," there and then. The Assyrian king Tiglath-Pilesar III fulfilled this prophecy when he invaded and defeated Israel there in 733 B.C. (2 Kings 15:29; cf. 2 Kings 17:3-5). Gideon had defeated the Midianites in this valley (Judg. 6:33; 7), the Philistines had defeated the Israelites under Saul's leadership there (1 Sam. 29:1, 11; 31), and Pharaoh Neco II defeated Josiah there after the Assyrians attacked (2 Kings 23:29-30).

1:6   After some time, Gomer bore Hosea a daughter. Some scholars believed that Hosea fathered only the first child and that Gomer's other children were born of fornication.[35] The Lord told Hosea to name this girl "Lo-ruhamah," meaning, "Not Loved," because He would not have compassion on Israel to forgive her for her sins. This was an outrageous name for a daughter. Yahweh had been very compassionate toward Israel in the past, but her persistent unfaithfulness to Him and His covenant with her made continuing compassion impossible.

1:7   In contrast, the Lord would have compassion on the Southern Kingdom of Judah and deliver her from such a fate. He said He would do this by Yahweh their God, perhaps using His own name this way to impress on the Israelites who their true God was. He said He would not do this in battle, however. The Israelites relied on human arms and alliances, but the Judahites trusted in the Lord, generally speaking, so He delivered the Judahites supernaturally. He did it in 701 B.C. by killing 185,000 Assyrian soldiers in one night while they slept encamped around Jerusalem (2 Kings 19:32-36; Isa. 37). Jerusalem was the only great city that did not fall to the Assyrians during this invasion of Syria-Palestine. Judah's sins were not as great as Israel's at this time. Judah enjoyed a succession of four "good" kings (Joash, Amaziah, Uzziah, and Jotham), and Hosea may have received this prophecy when Uzziah or Jotham was reigning.

> "The northern kingdom had arrogated the name of Israel to itself. It clung obstinately to the belief that its greater riches, area and strength showed that it was the true representative of God's people. The mention

---

[32]McComiskey, p. 19.
[33]Ibid., p. 20.
[34]Wood, "Hosea," p. 171.
[35]E.g., Charles H. Dyer, in *The Old Testament Explorer*, p. 725; and F. F. Bruce, *The Letter of Paul to the Romans: An Introduction and Commentary*, pp. 184-85.

of Judah underlines the vital truth that the rejection of the North in no way involved God's complete repudiation of Israel's sonship."[36]

1:8-9   Two or three years later, after Gomer had weaned Lo-ruhamah (cf. 1 Sam. 1:23; 2 Macc. 7:27), she bore Hosea another son. The reference to weaning is a detail that would seem superfluous if this were an allegory or vision. This time the Lord told Hosea to name the boy "Lo-ammi," meaning "Not My People." The Lord no longer regarded the kingdom of Israel as His people or Himself as their God. He did not mean, of course, that He would break His unconditional promises to His people (e.g., Exod. 6:7; Lev. 26:12; Deut. 26:17-18), but that the relationship that they had enjoyed so far would come to an end. The last phrase of verse 9 literally is "I [am] not I AM ['ehyeh] to you" (cf. Exod. 3:14). The Lord would withdraw the covenant He had so dramatically made with the revelation of this same name. He would remove protection that He had formerly provided and allow another nation to invade and discipline His people.

This passage contains four symbolic names: the names of Hosea's three children and Yahweh's new name, "not your I AM," indicating His rejection of Israel. Positive names were the rule in the ancient Near East, yet the last three of these names are bluntly negative. The collective impact of these four names is the message of this pericope: Israel's unfaithfulness had become so obnoxious to Yahweh that He would not tolerate her any longer.

HOSEA'S CHILDREN		
Name	**Meaning**	**Purpose**
Jezreel	God plants (scatters)	God would scatter His people.
Lo-Ruhamah	No compassion	God would no longer show compassion by rescuing Israel from destruction.
Lo-Ammi	Not my people	God would sever His relationship because of Israel's disobedience.

"Hos 1:2-9 functions as a summarizing preface to the entire book. It presents an overview, in stark and moving terms, of the prophet's proportionately dominant message: God has given up his people. The theme of restoration after this judgment then follows immediately in 2:1-3 [in the Hebrew Bible, 1:10—2:1 in the English versions]."[37]

B. A PROMISE OF RESTORATION 1:10—2:1

A wonderful promise of future restoration immediately follows this gloomy revelation of judgment. It provided encouragement to Hosea's audience by assuring a glorious and secure future for Israel eventually.

1:10   This verse begins chapter 2 in the Hebrew Bible. Despite the judgment promised, Yahweh revealed that the number of the Israelites would be as the "sand" grains of the sea (i.e., innumerable, cf. Gen. 22:17; 32:12). He also said that in the same place where they heard His word of rejection (v. 9) they would hear His word of acceptance, namely, in the land of Israel. They would again be sons of the living God. This family terminology points to the restoration of intimate covenant relationship and privilege. The "living God" title recalls Joshua 3:10, where Joshua told the Israelites that they would know that the living God was among them when they saw Him defeat their enemies in the Promised Land. In this future day the Israelites would again see that Yahweh was the only living God (true God), when He defeated their enemies and led them in victory.

> "Hosea's words here are crucial to an understanding of his theology of hope. His prophetic oracles appear to presage absolute judgment, but that was so only for his unbelieving generation. The nation's unfaithfulness to God and their trust in Assyria would be their downfall, but God would preserve a people, and out of them would spring an innumerable multitude."[38]

---

[36]Ellison, p. 105.
[37]Stuart, p. 35.
[38]McComiskey, p. 29.

1:11   The Northern and Southern Kingdoms would reunite, and they would have only one king instead of two (cf. 3:5; 2 Sam. 7:11-16; Isa. 9:6-7; Ezek. 37:22; Amos 9:11; Mic. 5:2). They would also go up from the land, probably in the sense of growing strong in the land, as a plant.[39] When this happens, it will be a great day for Jezreel. As Jezreel was a place of former victory for Israel (Judg. 7), so it would be again in the future (cf. Isa. 9:4-7; 41:8-16; Joel 3:9-17; Amos 9:11-12; Rev. 19:11-21). The leader in view is probably Jesus Christ (cf. 3:5; Jer. 30:21), so this is probably a messianic prophecy.

2:1   The Lord instructed future representatives of the restored nation to announce to their fellow Israelites—then—that they were again "My (God's) people," and that they were again Yahweh's "loved one" (cf. Deut. 30:1-9; Rom. 11:25-32).

> "Just as no other prophet pronounces doom alone upon Israel without a promise of future blessing, so Hosea follows his dark predictions with words of great comfort. In verses 1:10 through 2:1 the prophet promises five great blessings to Israel: (1) *national increase* (1:10a); (2) *national conversion* (1:10b); (3) *national reunion* (1:11a); (4) *national leadership* (1:11b); (5) *national restoration* (2:1)."[40]

The fulfillment of this prophecy has not come yet, so we look forward to the regathering of Israel, rule by David's descendant, and Israel flourishing in her land in the future. Amillennial interpreters believe the church replaces Israel in the promises of God and that Jesus began the day of Jezreel at His first advent.[41]

III. THE SECOND SERIES OF MESSAGES OF JUDGMENT AND RESTORATION: MARITAL UNFAITHFULNESS 2:2—3:5

These messages develop more fully the comparison between Hosea's relationship with his adulterous wife and Yahweh's relationship with unfaithful Israel. In both relationships, restoration follows judgment.

A. ORACLES OF JUDGMENT 2:2-13

Two judgment oracles follow. In the first one, Hosea and Gomer's relationship is primarily in view, but the parallels with Yahweh and Israel's relationship are obvious. In the second one, it is almost entirely Yahweh and Israel's relationship that is in view. In both parts the general form of the messages is that of the lawsuit or legal accusation (Heb. *rib*) based on (Mosaic) covenant violation.

1. Judgment on Gomer as a figure of Israel 2:2-7

In this message, the Lord described Israel's unfaithfulness to Him in terms similar to those that a husband would use to describe his wife's unfaithfulness to him. The whole message appears to be one that Hosea delivered to his children, but it really describes Israel as the unfaithful "wife" of Yahweh. As explained above (cf. 1:2), the evidence suggests that Hosea's wife really was unfaithful to him; this is not just an allegory in which God projected His relationship with Israel onto Hosea and his wife for illustrative purposes.

2:2   Hosea called on his children to act as witnesses against the conduct of their mother. She was not acting like a true wife, so he could not be a true husband to her. Perhaps they had separated. She needed to stop practicing harlotry and adultery.

In the figure Yahweh used, He called on the Israelites to contend with their mother, a figure for the nation as a whole.

> "Israel's one hope is that her own sons should stand up in accusation against her, as Ezekiel was later to do with Judah (cf. chs. 16, 20, 23), rebuking her not for her faults but for her fundamental unfaithfulness."[42]

"Contend" (Heb. *rib*) often refers to a legal accusation. Yahweh was bringing legal charges against Israel that could stand up in court. The legal charge was not a formal declaration of divorce, however, because He wanted to heal the relationship, not terminate it (cf. vv. 6-7, 14-23). The relationship between Yahweh and Israel was not what it should have been because Israel had become a spiritual harlot.[43] She had stopped worshipping and serving Yahweh exclusively and had worshipped and served other gods. This was spiritual adultery. Under the Mosaic Law, a husband could have his wife stoned for being unfaithful (Lev. 20:10; Deut. 22:22), but this was not God's intention for Israel.

---

[39]See Robert B. Chisholm Jr., "Hosea," in *The Bible Knowledge Commentary: Old Testament*, pp. 1381-82.
[40]Feinberg, p. 20.
[41]E.g., Stuart, p. 41.
[42]Ellison, p. 106.
[43]Cf. D. Kidner, *Love to the Loveless: The Message of Hosea*, p. 27.

"Marriage is one of many figures used in Scripture to emphasize the relationship of God to men. This illustration is used in both O.T. and N.T. to picture love, intimacy, privilege, and responsibility. In the O.T., as here in vv. 16-23, Israel is described as the wife of the LORD, though now disowned because of disobedience. Nevertheless eventually, upon repentance, Israel will be restored. This relationship is not to be confounded with that of the Church to Christ (Jn. 3:29). In the mystery of the divine Trinity both are true. The N.T. speaks of the Church as a virgin espoused to one husband (2 Cor. 11:1-2), which could never be said of an adulterous wife restored in grace. Israel is, then, to be the restored and forgiven wife of the LORD; the Church is the virgin wife of the Lamb (Jn. 3:29; Rev. 19:6-8). Israel will be the LORD's earthly wife (ch. 2:23); the Church, the Lamb's heavenly bride (Rev. 19:7)."[44]

2:3   If she did not respond appropriately, Hosea threatened to strip her as naked as when she was born, to expose her to shame and helplessness. Stripping naked like a prostitute was a metaphor used to describe the punishment due a covenant breaker in the ancient Near East.[45] Gomer had exposed herself to her lovers (v. 2), and now her husband would expose her for all to see. He would also make her like a desert wilderness in that she would become sterile and incapable of bearing other children. Her insistence on having sexual relations with many men would result in her not being able to bear the fruit of sexual relations, children. Even though she thirsted for children, she would bear no more.

The threat to Israel involved, first, making the nation an object of shame and ridicule in the world (cf. v. 10; Ezek. 16:35-43). Second, Yahweh would remove all her powers of fertility. Her flocks and herds would not flourish, her fields would become unproductive, and her women would be unfruitful.

2:4   Furthermore, Hosea threatened to have no compassion on the children that Gomer had given birth to in her harlotry, children of other fathers. These appear to be children in addition to the three named earlier, but they could refer to the last two named.

For Israel, this signified that Yahweh would not recognize as His own, and love as His own, the descendants that the Israelites bore. He would regard them as the offspring of others, not Himself.

Rather than slaying the guilty, steps would follow to restore the fallen to their former state.

2:5   The reason for Hosea's lack of compassion for these children was that Gomer had shamelessly played the harlot and had conceived them in adultery. She had brazenly sought out lovers who promised to provide money adequate to take care of her needs and wants.

Israel pursued other gods (Baals) because she believed they could take care of her better than Yahweh. Trade agreements required acknowledging foreign gods.[46]

2:6   Hosea said he would oppose Gomer as though he put a hedge of thorns or a wall across her path so she would turn aside from her ways.

Yahweh would make it perilously difficult for Israel to pursue idols.

2:7   Consequently, Gomer would pursue her lovers but not be able to catch up with them. She would seek them but not find them. Out of frustration she would give up pursuing them and return to her husband. She would conclude that she was better off with him than with them.

Out of frustration Israel would turn back to Yahweh.

2. Judgment on Israel 2:8-13

In the section that follows, the relationship between Israel and Yahweh becomes even clearer. The mention of Baals and Israel's feasts makes this obvious. Hosea's relationship with Gomer recedes into the background.

2:8   Israel failed to acknowledge that it was Yahweh who had provided for her and had given her all she needed when she was pursuing pagan gods (cf. Deut. 7:13; 11:14; 26:10). The Israelites used the silver and gold that the Lord had bestowed on them to make idols of Baal, which they credited with their agricultural blessings.

---

[44] *The New Scofield . . .*, p. 920.
[45] D. Hillers, *Treaty Curses and the Old Testament Prophets*, pp. 58-59.
[46] Wood, "Hosea," p. 176.

Hosea spoke frequently of knowledge. He traced Israel's declension back to her lack of knowledge about Yahweh's bounty in this verse. In the future the Israelites would know the Lord (v. 20). The prophet bemoaned the lack of knowledge of God that presently existed in the land (4:1). The Israelites' destruction was due to this lack of knowledge (4:6). The fact that they had not known the Lord stood in the way of their return to Him (5:4). But when repentance came, they would know and follow on to know the Lord (6:3). They would learn that knowledge of the Lord is more important to Him than burnt offerings (6:6). The last verse in the book calls on the wise to know these things (14:9).[47]

2:9 Therefore the Lord would withdraw the blessings of fertility that He had formerly provided for Israel. Covenant curses would take their place (cf. Lev. 26:3-39; Deut. 28).

2:10 He would also expose Israel to shame (Heb. *nabluth*, a withered state) in the sight of those with whom she had committed adultery. No one would be able or willing to save her from this punishment.

2:11 Yahweh would also put an end to all of Israel's happy yearly, monthly, and weekly celebrations. In the time of Jeroboam II, the Sabbath was apparently a feast day (cf. Amos 8:5). Idolatry had so corrupted Israel's sacred feasts that Yahweh no longer wanted His people to observe them.

2:12 The Lord would also destroy the vines and fig trees, the sources of Israel's finest products. Israel regarded these trees as pay from her lovers, but Yahweh would turn these groves of fruit trees into wild forests, and wild beasts would destroy the trees and their fruit. This suggests that there would no longer be Israelites in the land to care for these crops (cf. Isa. 5:5-6; 7:23-25; 17:9; 32:9-14; Mic. 3:12).

2:13 Yahweh would also punish Israel for observing sacred days in honor of the Baals and offering sacrifices to them. "Baal" means "lord." The Canaanites considered that there were many local representations (Baals) of the one deity (Baal). The Israelites had worshipped at many different shrines to Baal—they had pursued the Baals—as a harlot pursues many lovers. Israel had gotten dressed up to impress her idols and to celebrate these occasions, but she had forgotten Yahweh, in the sense that she had refused to acknowledge Him (cf. Deut. 4:9; 8:11; Judg. 3:7; 1 Sam. 12:9-10; Ps. 78:9-11; Jer. 23:27).

B. PROMISES OF RESTORATION 2:14—3:5

Three messages of restoration follow the preceding two on coming judgment. They assured Israel that Yahweh would remain faithful to His promises to His people—even though they were unfaithful to Him and incurred His punishment (cf. 1:10—2:1; 2 Tim. 2:13).

1. Renewed love and restored marriage 2:14-20

The emphasis in this message is on the fact that God would renew His love for Israel and would restore their "marriage" relationship.

2:14 Following Israel's decision to return to Yahweh after her punishment (v. 7), the Lord promised to woo her back to Himself. He would appeal to her with tender and attractive words, lead her into a place where there would be few distractions (cf. 13:5; Jer. 2:2-3), and speak kindly to her heart. This verse presents the Lord as wooing Israel back to Himself.[48]

> "As . . . God persuaded Israel to leave Egypt, go out into the desert, and move on finally to the Promised Land; so in the final day he will persuade her to leave the Egypt of spiritual declension, go out into the wilderness of fellowship alone with God, and move on to the Promised Land of blessed rest."[49]

2:15 The Lord promised that He would restore the blessings of "vineyards" to the Israelites. He would turn "the valley of Achor" (lit. Trouble, the site of Achan's sin, Josh. 7:24-26) into "a door of hope" (cf. 1:11). This memorial site would no longer remind the Israelites of past sins but would appear to them as the gateway to a new and better future in the land. She would sing again, as the Israelites did when they had crossed the Red Sea (Exod. 15). It is as though Israel would start over as a nation, as she did when she came out of Egypt and the wilderness into the Promised Land.

2:16-17 In that coming day of restoration, the Israelites would call Yahweh *Ishi*, "my Husband," and would no longer refer to Him as *Baali*, "My Lord" or "My Master." "Baali" would recall the Baals of Israel's past, which the Lord would remove from her heart and mouth. They would not even mention the name of Baal by referring to Yahweh as their Baali.

---

[47] Harold P. Barker, *Christ in the Minor Prophets*, pp. 10-11.
[48] See Mays, pp. 44-45.
[49] Wood, "Hosea," p. 179.

2:18	"In that day," the Lord promised, He would also make the animals in the Promised Land safe and secure (cf. v. 12; Lev. 26:5-6, 22). He would make it safe for the animals to live there by removing war from the land. This is a way of saying that the Israelites, and even the animals in Israel, would dwell in peace and security. Attacks from wild animals and destruction from war were prominent motifs employed in the curses threatened in ancient Near Eastern treaties.[50]
2:19-20	It would be as though Yahweh and Israel began life anew as husband and wife.[51] They would return to the courtship days and start again as an engaged couple. In the ancient Near East, a man paid a price to seal the agreement when he became engaged (cf. 2 Sam. 3:14), and people regarded the couple as good as married in the eyes of the law. What the Lord vowed to give Israel to seal this nuptial agreement was: righteousness (what was right), justice (fair treatment), loyal love (unswerving commitment), compassion (tender affection), and faithfulness (dependability). This was God's marriage vow for Israel. In response, Israel would recognize her special relationship to Him and show this by faithfully obeying Him (cf. Jer. 31:31-34).

2. Renewed fertility and restored favor 2:21-23

This message stresses the renewed fertility and restored favor that Israel could anticipate because Yahweh would reach out and save her in the future.

2:21-22	In that coming day of blessing, the Lord would restore agricultural productivity to the land. He would respond to the heavens, personified as crying to Him to send rain. The cry of the heavens would be in response to an appeal that the earth made to it to send rain. The earth would ask for rain because the grain, new wine, and oil had told the earth they needed rain. These crops would appeal to the earth because Jezreel had appealed to the earth, too. Jezreel ("God Plants" or "God Sows") here personifies the nation of Israel as a whole, though its area was also the traditional "breadbasket" of the Northern Kingdom. Israel in the past had cried to Baal, the Canaanite god of rain and fertility, but he had not helped. Having returned to the Lord, the Israelites would now appeal to Him as the true God of fertility, and He would respond by sending rain.
2:23	The Lord would also plant Israel in the Promised Land; He would plant her there securely where she would grow under His care and blessing. He would show compassion to the people whom He formerly said were "not loved," and He would reclaim as His own the people whom He formerly called "not my people" (cf. 1:6, 9). They would then acknowledge Yahweh as their God, not Baal. The names of all three of Hosea's children come together again in verses 22-23.

> "Hosea 2:23, along with 1:10, is quoted in Romans 9:25-26 and 1 Peter 2:10. Paul quoted those Hosea passages to say that both Jews and Gentiles will be converted during the Church Age (cf. Rom. 9:24). This does *not* mean, however, that he equated the Gentiles with Israel and regarded the conversion of Gentiles as a direct fulfillment of Hosea's prophecy. Paul clearly taught that national Israel would be saved as well (Rom. 11). Rather, Paul extracted from Hosea's prophecy a principle concerning God's gracious activity . . ."[52]

3. The restoration of Hosea's and Yahweh's wives ch. 3

Like the first section in this series of messages that develop the figure of marital unfaithfulness (2:2-8), this last section also blends the prophet's personal experience with that of Yahweh. This is the strongest affirmation of Gomer's and Israel's restorations. Chapter 3 is probably a separate cycle of judgment and restoration speeches from 2:2-23.[53]

The restoration of Hosea's wife 3:1-3

3:1	Yahweh told Hosea to seek out in love the woman whom he formerly loved, Gomer, even though she was an adulteress. Stuart held that this second woman was not Gomer but an adulteress, probably a prostitute, with whom Hosea never consummated his (second) marriage.[54] He believed there is no evidence that Gomer was ever unfaithful to Hosea. Most scholars regard the wife in chapter 1, Gomer, as the same wife in chapter 3, and I agree. The basis for this is that both women were unfaithful to Hosea.

---

[50]Hillers, pp. 54-56.
[51]Cf. Kidner, p. 34.
[52]Chisholm, "Hosea," p. 1387.
[53]Charles H. Silva, "The Literary Structure of Hosea 1—3," *Bibliotheca Sacra* 164:654 (April-June 2007):181-97.
[54]Stuart, pp. 64-68.

	Hosea's action would be similar to that of the Lord Himself, who loved the Israelites even though they had become spiritually unfaithful to Him. They had turned from following Him to worship other gods, and they loved the raisin cakes that were evidently part of their worship (cf. Jer. 7:18; 44:19).
3:2	Hosea obeyed the Lord and sought out his wife. He had to pay 15 shekels of silver and an homer and a half of barley (about 9 bushels), since she had apparently become the property of someone else. Fifteen shekels of silver was half the price of a dead slave (Exod. 21:32), and barley was cattle food. An homer and a half cost about 15 shekels of silver.[55] So Hosea evidently paid the price of a dead slave for his wife.
3:3	After Hosea had brought Gomer home, he told her to stay with him from then on. She was his by right of marriage and by right of purchase. She was not to play the harlot or to have a lover any longer. He also promised to be faithful to her. Keil argued that Hosea meant that they would have no intimate relations.[56] But this goes beyond what the text says.

The restoration of Yahweh's wife 3:4-5

3:4	The Lord explained that the Israelites would remain for a long time separated from their idolatrous practices. During this time they would not have a king or leader (i.e., enjoy national sovereignty), sacrifices or sacred pillar (or stone, i.e., engage in formal religious activity), ephod or household idols (Heb. *teraphim*, i.e., use methods of divination, cf. Judg. 18:27-31). Large stone pillars often stood at Canaanite shrines and were probably symbolic of deity. The Mosaic Law banned these standing stones (Deut. 16:22), but the Israelites ignored the prohibition. They would have none of the things that marked them as God's people or that they had used to worship idols.
3:5	After this period of cleansing, the Israelites would return to the Lord. They would seek Him as their God and a Davidic king as their ruler (cf. 2:7; 5:15; Deut. 4:29). They would approach the Lord with a healthy sense of fear because of His rich blessings. This would happen "in the last days," namely, the days of Israel's national restoration (i.e., the Millennium; cf. Deut. 4:30; Isa. 2:2; Mic. 4:1).

> "The reference to 'David their king' should not be understood in an overly literalistic manner. The prophets view the ideal Davidic ruler of the future as the second coming of David (see Isa. 11:1-10; Mic. 5:2) and even call him 'David' on occasion (see Jer. 30:9; Ezek. 34:23-24; 37:24-25). This 'David' carries out royal functions that cannot be distinguished from those assigned to the messianic king. Other texts make it clear that this 'David' is actually a descendant of David (see Jer. 23:5-6; 33:15-16) who comes in his ancestor's spirit and power, much like John the Baptist came in the spirit and power of Elijah and thus fulfilled the prophecy of Malachi 4:5 (see Matt. 11:10-14; 17:11-12; Mark 1:2-4; Luke 1:17, 76; 7:27)."[57]

This appears to be another messianic prophecy (cf. 1:11).

"Chapter 3 is one of the classic O.T. passages describing Israel's past, present, and future. Her idolatrous past is illustrated by Gomer's unfaithfulness to Hosea (vv. 1-2), despite which Hosea is commanded to love her and buy her back 'according to the love of the LORD toward . . . Israel,' a love which led Him to pay the purchase price of the blood of the cross to redeem Israel, the basis of her restoration. The present condition of Israel is illustrated and plainly prophesied in vv. 3-4. Her future is declared in v. 5, showing her repentance toward God who, in His faithfulness, will restore her."[58]

"To summarize [chapters 1—3]:

"God is gracious, and no matter what 'name' our birth has given to us, He can change it and give us a new beginning. Even the 'valley of trouble' can become a 'door of hope.'

"God is holy and He must deal with sin. The essence of idolatry is enjoying the gifts but not honoring the Giver. To live for the world is to break God's heart and commit 'spiritual adultery.'

"God is love and promises to forgive and restore all who repent and return to Him. He promises to bless all who trust him [*sic* Him]."[59]

---

[55]Wolff, p. 61.
[56]Keil, 1:69-70.
[57]Chisholm, *Handbook on . . .*, p. 348. Cf. Kaiser, p. 198.
[58]*The New Scofield . . .*, p. 921.
[59]Wiersbe, p. 320.

IV. THE THIRD SERIES OF MESSAGES ON JUDGMENT AND RESTORATION: WIDESPREAD GUILT 4:1—6:3

The remaining messages that Hosea recorded in this book continue to expound the themes introduced in the first two series (chs. 1—3). All five series of messages major on Israel's guilt and coming judgment, but all conclude on a positive note promising restoration in the future.[60]

> "At this point we leave the account of Hosea's marriage and begin a new section, which extends to the end of the book and contains oracles of doom and hope. Even in this section, however, we are never far from Hosea's marriage, for it is always in the background and is the catalyst for his message to his people. We see it in the references to the nation as mother and children, as well as in the numerous allusions to spiritual harlotry and adultery."[61]

Chapters 4—14 contain speeches that Hosea probably gave at various times in his long prophetic career.

A. THE JUDGMENT ORACLES CHS. 4—5

Chapters 4 and 5 contain more messages of judgment. Chapter 4 focuses on the sins of the Northern Kingdom. Chapter 5 describes the guilt of all the Israelites in both the Northern and Southern Kingdoms and announces judgment on both groups.

1. Yahweh's case against Israel ch. 4

This chapter exposes Israel's sins more particularly than we have seen so far. The Northern Kingdom had broken covenant with Yahweh. Her priests (religious leaders) were especially guilty, but the idolatrous citizens also deserved divine judgment, and they would receive it.

Israel's breach of covenant 4:1-3

The Lord brought a legal charge against the Israelites for breaking the Mosaic Covenant (cf. Isa. 1). Again the literary form of this section is a legal confrontation (Heb. *rib*, cf. 2:2). Scholars therefore often refer to these courtroom type charges as "*rib* oracles," pronounced "reeve." Waltke called these messages oracles of reproach in the form of a lawsuit.[62] The Lord stated His charges against Israel in 4:1-3 and then developed these charges in reverse order.

God's Lawsuit against Israel		
The charges	**Stated**	**Developed**
No faithfulness (trustworthiness)	4:1	11:12—13:16
No love (kindness)	4:1	6:1—11:11
No acknowledgment of God	4:1	4:4—5:15

4:1   Hosea called on the Israelites to listen to a message from Yahweh because He was charging them with serious crimes (cf. Isa. 1:2). Yahweh was taking the Israelites to court. The basic accusation is that there was no faithfulness (truth, trustworthiness), kindness (loyalty, Heb. *hesed*), or (evidence of) knowledge of God in the land. The Israelites failed to acknowledge Yahweh as their God (cf. 2:20). These were all things that God had ordered His people to pursue when He covenanted with them at Sinai.

4:2   Instead of these virtues, He observed swearing (cursing others by misusing oaths and imprecations), deception, murder, stealing, adultery, violence, and continual bloodshed. An imprecation is a formal curse made in the name of some deity in which one person calls down calamity on another (cf. Job 31:29-30). These were things He had forbidden in His covenant. He identified violations of at least five of the Ten Commandments (numbers 3, 9, 6, 8, and 7). Violent crimes were so common that they seemed to follow one another without interruption.

4:3   Therefore God was not blessing Israel, but instead was bringing curses on the land, so that every part of the Northern Kingdom suffered—every living thing. Drought seems to be the primary form of chastisement in view (cf. Lev. 26:19; Deut. 28:23-24).

---

[60] See Charles H. Silva, "The Literary Structure of Hosea 4—8," *Bibliotheca Sacra* 164:655 (July-September 2007):291-306.
[61] McComiskey, p. 56.
[62] Bruce K. Waltke, *An Old Testament Theology*, p. 836.

The guilt of Israel's priests 4:4-10

In this pericope, God addressed the Israelites as a whole, but identified sins of their priests in particular.

4:4   Israel's guilt was so clear that the Lord forbade the people from denying His charge against them. As judge, He silenced them in His court. In defying Him, they were like witnesses who brazenly defied their authority on earth: "the priest."

4:5   Because of this rebellion, the people would have great difficulty and would stumble as they walked through life. Their false prophets would also err. Both types of spiritual leaders, priests and (false) prophets, were guilty before God. The Lord also promised to destroy the "mother" of the Israelites, probably another reference to the nation as a whole (cf. 2:2).

4:6   God would destroy the Israelites because of their lack of knowledge of Himself. That is, they failed to acknowledge Him as their God (cf. v. 1). God would reject them as His priests on the earth, whose task it was to mediate the knowledge of God to the nations (Exod. 19:6), because they rejected the knowledge that He gave them in His law. He would abandon (forget) their children because they had abandoned (forgotten) His law.

> "To the modern Western mind, it might seem unfair that the priests' mothers and children should be punished for their sins. But the concept of corporate guilt and punishment was common in ancient Israel and is frequently reflected in the Hebrew Bible."[63]

4:7   God had blessed the Israelites by increasing their numbers, but their response to this blessing had been to increase their sinning against Him. Consequently He would change their glory, a large population (or perhaps Yahweh Himself), into shame; He would reduce their numbers (and withdraw from them).

4:8   Israel's priests were feeding on the sin offerings that the people brought to their pagan shrines. Yet since these offerings were *also offered* to idols, it was as though the priests actually fed on the people's sins. The priests desired these offerings, which meant they wanted the people to practice idolatry so they would bring more sacrifices. King Jeroboam I had appointed as priests people from any tribe and all walks of life in Israel (1 Kings 12:31; 13:33).

4:9   God would, therefore, punish the unfaithful priests of Israel as He would punish the unfaithful people of Israel. Both groups were sinning, so God promised to punish them for their sinful ways and to repay them for their idolatrous works.

4:10   They would eat, "but not have enough," because the Lord would send drought and scarcity of food as punishment (cf. v. 3). They would act like harlots by committing fornication with pagan temple prostitutes, but their numbers would not increase because Yahweh would reduce their fertility. He would do this because they had stopped listening to and obeying Him by observing His law.

The guilt of Israel's idolatrous citizens 4:11-14

The following section is a general indictment of the people of Israel for their idolatry.

4:11   The practice of idolatry (spiritual harlotry), with its emphasis on drinking wine, had turned the hearts of the Israelites from Yahweh. Along with their heart for God went their realistic understanding of what was best for them, which He had revealed.

4:12   God's people consulted wooden idols and sought revelations using a diviner's rod. Their spirit of harlotry led them astray from the true God and His Word. They behaved like harlots departing from the authority of their true husband, Yahweh.

4:13   They worshipped their idols on the tops of hills and under trees because they enjoyed worshipping at their convenience (cf. 2 Kings 17:10-11). This was as bad as the daughters of the Israelites practicing harlotry and adultery with male cult prostitutes (cf. Deut. 23:17-18; 1 Kings 14:24).

> "Faithlessness toward God always results in faithlessness to the most sacred ties of earth."[64]

4:14   However, Yahweh would not punish only the females in Israel, because the males were just as guilty. The females were unfaithful to their husbands, but their husbands were also engaging in immoral acts with pagan temple prostitutes. Stuart believed that homosexual prostitution was also involved.

---

[63]Chisholm, *Handbook on . . .*, p. 349.
[64]Feinberg, p. 39.

"For homosexuals, homosexual prostitutes were provided (1 Kgs 14:24; 15:12; 22:46; 2 Kgs 23:7)."[65]

Thus, this people marked by lack of understanding, would come to ruin when God humbled them with punishment.

Judgment on the idolatrous worship 4:15-19

4:15 The Lord warned the Israelites not to pollute their brethren in the Southern Kingdom with their unfaithfulness. He also warned them not to go to the pagan shrines and take an oath in His name since they did not really worship Him. This was pure hypocrisy. Gilgal and Beth-aven were representative pagan cultic sites (cf. 9:15; 12:11; Amos 4:4). The prophet had come to refer to "Bethel" ("House of God") by the name "Beth-aven" ("House of Wickedness"), because it had become one of the main centers of idolatry in Israel since the time of Jeroboam I (cf. 10:5; Amos 5:5). The use of one site's name to represent a different though similar place is a figure of speech called *atbash*. Another view is that Beth-aven was a town east of Bethel.[66]

> "The site served as a boundary mark for Benjamin's allotment (Jos. xviii. 12). In Hosea (iv. 15, v. 8, x. 5) the name may be a derogatory synonym for Bethel, 'House of the false (god)'."[67]

4:16 The Lord asked, rhetorically, if He could continue to guide Israel as its Shepherd, since it was not behaving like a compliant heifer or lamb, but had become stubborn and obstinate. No, He could not.

4:17 Since Ephraim (lit. fruitful), the largest tribe in the Northern Kingdom that stood for the whole nation, had abandoned his Shepherd for idols, He called for others to leave him alone also. He would abandon him to the judgment that would come inevitably from pursuing sin (cf. Rom. 1:18-32). Ephraim had become incorrigible.

> "By referring to the North as Ephraim Hosea reminds Israel that, as we saw in the story of Jeroboam I, it owed its very existence to Ephraim's jealousy of Judah with its God-given institutions of the Jerusalem temple and the Davidic monarchy."[68]

4:18 Even when the Israelites were not under the influence of liquor (cf. v. 11), they still played the harlot continually. The rulers of the people, who were to be as shields protecting the general populace, also loved the sins that brought shame on the nation.

4:19 God would blow Israel away in judgment as though "the wind" wrapped the nation in "its wings." When judgment came, the Israelites would finally feel shame for sacrificing to idols.

"God's covenant people are called to court, found to be in violation of the stipulations of his covenant, and sentenced to destruction.

"The passage details a long series of crimes against the divine law, all related to the catalog of blessings and curses found in Deut 28—33. The sins of omission and commission pictured so relentlessly throughout the chapter make up a remarkably complete picture of the depths of Israel's apostasy."[69]

2. The guilt of both Israel and Judah ch. 5

The general pattern of accusation of guilt followed by announcement of judgment, that marked the messages in chapter 4, is also evident in chapter 5. One significant difference, however, is that in chapter 5 Judah falls under the prophet's condemnation, though the primary object of the prophet's criticism continues to be Israel.

A warning to the priests, people, and royal family of Israel 5:1-7

The target audience of this warning passage was originally the leaders as well as the ordinary citizens of Israel.

5:1 Hosea called on the Israelite priests, the whole population of Israel, and the royal household to hear this message from Yahweh (cf. 4:1). The following word of judgment applied to all of them because they had been as a bird "snare" to people in the Northern Kingdom. Their policies and practices had trapped many people in idolatry and its consequent bondage and destruction. There was an Israelite Mizpah in Gilead (Judg. 10:17; 11:29) and one in the territory of Benjamin (1 Sam. 7:5;

---

[65] Stuart, p. 83.
[66] Feinberg, p. 40.
[67] *The New Bible Dictionary*, s.v. "Beth-aven," by R. J. Way.
[68] Ellison, p. 115.
[69] Stuart, p. 86.

10:1). It is probably the one in Gilead that is in view here. Mt. Tabor stood in the Jezreel Valley in northern Israel. Probably these hunting sites represent the whole nation (by merism), from north to south or east to west. These may also have been the locations of important worship sites in the north.[70] The point is that the leadership was corrupting the people everywhere.

5:2   Those who had revolted against Yahweh's covenant had gone deep into depravity, as though they waded through much carnage, to continue the hunting imagery. Yet the Lord promised to chasten all of them so they would return to Him.

5:3   Yahweh knew Israel well; He had not been deceived and fallen into a trap, as the Israelites had. Ephraim had played the harlot against her husband, the Lord, and had defiled herself by doing so (cf. Lev. 18:20, 24; Num. 5:20, 27-28). Ephraim was the largest tribe in Israel and so, frequently, was a synonym for the Northern Kingdom (e.g., 4:17). Hosea may have referred to it here because this tribe was foremost in idolatry.[71] It was part of the priests' responsibility to distinguish between clean and unclean (Lev. 10:10), but they had not done their job, so Israel had defiled herself.

5:4   The cultic practices of the Israelite idolaters had ensnared them so they could not return to their real God. The spirit of a harlot had taken them over; they had become sin addicts. Consequently they did not acknowledge (know) Yahweh.

5:5   The self-exalting arrogance of the Israelites gave evidence of their guilt and caused them to stumble as they pursued iniquity (cf. Prov. 16:18). With their proud noses high in the air, they frequently stumbled as they walked. Judah had also stumbled in some of the same sins.

5:6   The guilty might seek the Lord, bringing their animal sacrifices to Him, but they would not find Him because He had withdrawn from them. Whereas holiness makes fellowship with God possible, sin and hypocrisy rule it out. He would withdraw His help and blessing from them.

5:7   They had dealt treacherously against the Lord by being unfaithful to their natural and contractual (covenant) responsibilities to Him. In this they were like an unfaithful wife who had given birth to illegitimate children, the natural result of unfaithfulness. Probably many illegitimate children who were the products of Israelites and temple prostitutes populated the Northern Kingdom. Participation in apostate religious festivals would only hasten their destruction, not avert it. Perhaps sexually transmitted diseases were taking their toll on the Israelites. Their lands would also experience destruction when enemy invaders overran Israel.

A warning to Ephraim and Judah 5:8-15

This warning confronted the tribe of Ephraim, or perhaps the whole Northern Kingdom, and the Southern Kingdom of Judah.

5:8   Blowing trumpets in cities announced the coming of an invader. Throughout Israel's towns the sentries would blow alarms: in Gibeah and Ramah in northern Judah and in Beth-aven (Bethel) in southern Israel. Throughout the territory of Benjamin, which was home to all these towns at one time or another, news of war would come. Rather than leading Ephraim into battle, as the tribe of Benjamin did in Deborah's day (Judg. 5:14), the invader would pursue Benjamin as it did Ephraim. Benjamin should have been particularly watchful because of its close geographical proximity to Israel.

> "This verse describes an invasion of the territory of Benjamin from the south, i.e., from Judah. The enemy is portrayed as advancing along the main mountain road from Jerusalem through Bethel and thereafter into the heart of Ephraim. Gibeah, only three miles north of Jerusalem, is the first to be attacked; then Ramah, five miles north of Jerusalem; and finally Bethel, eleven miles north of Jerusalem, on the northern border of Benjamin."[72]

5:9   When the Lord rebuked Ephraim for his sins, he would become desolate throughout his tribal territories. The Lord promised that this would surely happen (cf. Lev. 26:32-35).

5:10 The leaders of Judah had also broken covenant with the Lord (cf. Isa. 5:8; Mic. 2:1-2), as those who move boundary markers. Judah had re-annexed Benjamite territory, thus violating the terms of the Mosaic Covenant regarding tribal allotments (cf. Deut. 19:14; 27:17).[73] Consequently God's wrath would rain down on them. The boundaries that the leaders of Judah had moved were not just physical but also spiritual. They had moved the boundaries between right and wrong, true and false religion, and the true God and idols.

---

[70]Ellison, p 116.
[71]Wood, "Hosea," p. 190.
[72]Stuart, p. 102
[73]Ibid., p. 104.

5:11	Ephraim would experience crushing judgment by an enemy invader because he determined to follow false gods rather than divine commands (cf. Deut. 4:3; 6:14; 8:19; 28:14; Jer. 2:5). The human command in view is probably Jeroboam I's institution of calf worship at altars in Bethel and Dan (1 Kings 12:27-30).
5:12	Yahweh would consume the Northern Kingdom as a moth eats cloth or as rot causes bones to decay. He was behind the enemy invasion.
5:13	Both Israel and Judah appealed to the king of Assyria for help, but he was unable to save them. King Ahaz of Judah did this (2 Kings 16:5-9), and so did King Menahem of Israel (2 Kings 15:19-20) and King Hoshea of Israel (cf. 2 Kings 17:3). Rather than assisting, the Assyrians attacked both nations. King Jareb ("The Avenging" or "The Great") probably refers to Tiglath-Pileser III, with whom both Israel and Judah made alliances.
5:14	However, it would be Yahweh, not the Assyrians, who was ultimately responsible for the discipline of these kingdoms (cf. v. 12). As a lion, He would tear them to pieces and carry them away in judgment, and there would be no one who could deliver them. Israel fell to the Assyrians, in 722 B.C., after two previous Assyrian invasions (in 743 and 734-32 B.C.). Judah escaped Assyria in 701 B.C., due to King Hezekiah's trust in the Lord, but Babylonia finally fulfilled this prophecy to her in 586 B.C.
5:15	As a lion returning to its lair, Yahweh would go away and leave His people until they bore their punishment and sought His forgiveness. When they felt their affliction, moved by His Spirit, they would seek Him earnestly (cf. v. 6; Deut. 4:29).

> "The language would appear to reach into the Millennium, when the Israelites will indeed repent before God and seek his face (cf. 1:10-11; 2:14-23)."[74]
>
> "Taken with Mt. 23:37-39, this passage gives in broad outline the course of Israel's future restoration to God."[75]

The last statement of this verse provides a transition from the messages of judgment in chapters 4 and 5 to the promises of restoration in 6:1-3.

B. THE RESTORATION PROMISES 6:1-3

This first part of chapter 6 envisions Israel's repentance. The prophet predicted the words that the penitent generation of Israelites would say when they sought the Lord (5:15). The message contains two cycles, each containing an exhortation (vv. 1a, 3a) and a motivating promise (vv. 1b-2, 3b).[76]

> "Some of the most gracious calls to repentance in all Scripture are found in 6:1-3 and 14:1-3."[77]

6:1	The repentant Israelites would encourage each other to return to Yahweh because they believed He would heal them (as a shepherd, cf. 5:13) even though He had torn and wounded them (as a lion, cf. 5:14). They would recognize that their punishment had come from Him, not just from a foreign enemy (cf. Deut. 32:39).
6:2	He would revive them after a relatively brief period of judgment (two days; cf. Job 5:19; Prov. 6:16; 30:15, 18; Amos 1:3, 6, 9, et al.) and restore them to life and usefulness. He would do this so they might enjoy His fellowship and serve Him. The fact that Jesus Christ was in the tomb two days and arose on the third day is only a coincidental parallel. It is, however, one of many similarities between Christ and Israel.
6:3	Such a hope would motivate this revived generation of Israelites to encourage themselves to pursue intensely knowing (acknowledging) Yahweh as the true God and as their God (cf. 4:1, 6; 5:4). They would be confident of His restoration because of His character, His faithfulness to His promises (e.g., 5:15), and His power. His return to bless them would be as certain and as life-giving as the sunrise. He would bring refreshment and fertility back to the nation (cf. Deut. 11:13-15). No more would they look to Baal for these blessings.

Corporate Israel has never prayed like this. The fulfillment must still be future, at the beginning of Christ's millennial reign.

---

[74]Wood, "Hosea," p. 192.
[75]*The New Scofield . . .*, p. 922.
[76]Chisholm, "Hosea," p. 1393.
[77]Kaiser, 197.

V. THE FOURTH SERIES OF MESSAGES ON JUDGMENT AND RESTORATION: ISRAEL'S INGRATITUDE 6:4—11:11

This section of the book contains another series of messages that deal, first, with the judgment coming on Israel and, second, the restoration that will follow. There are three major addresses in this section, each introduced by a direct address (6:4; 9:1; 11:8).

A. MORE MESSAGES ON COMING JUDGMENT 6:4—11:7

The subject of Israel's ingratitude is particularly prominent in these messages. Each of the two major messages of judgment ends with a reference to Israel returning *to* Egypt (8:13; 11:5). The message on restoration that follows these two (11:8-11) refers to the Israelites returning *from* Egypt (11:11).

1. Israel's ingratitude and rebellion 6:4—8:14

Two oracles of judgment compose this section. Each one begins by referring to Israel's breach of covenant (6:7; 8:1), and each one contains a reference to Egypt near the end (7:16; 8:13).

Accusations involving ingratitude 6:4—7:16

The Lord accused the Israelites of being ungrateful for His many blessings in the past and therefore being disloyal to Him and His covenant with them. The section primarily enumerates and illustrates these accusations, but it closes with an announcement of coming judgment (7:12-13, 16).

Lack of loyalty 6:4-11

This section stresses Israel's covenant disloyalty to Yahweh.

6:4 The Lord twice asked rhetorically what He should do with Ephraim and Judah. The questions express frustration, helplessness, and despair more than inquiry. The loyal love (Heb. *hesed*, cf. 2:19; 4:1) of these elect nations, expressed in their obedience to Yahweh's covenant, was as short-lived as the morning fog or as dew. Both disappear quickly, especially in the hot Palestinian sun.

6:5 Therefore the Lord had sent messages of condemnation through His prophets that had the effect of mowing His people down. These messages had been as destructive as lightning bolts (cf. Amos 4:6-11).

6:6 God's preference is that His people love Him faithfully more than that they offer Him other types of sacrifices. He wanted the Israelites to acknowledge (know) Him rather than bringing burnt offerings to their altars (cf. 2:20; 4:1, 6). Sacrifices were meaningless, even offensive, unless offered out of a heart of love that demonstrated obedience to God's Word (cf. 1 Sam. 15:22; Isa. 1:11-17; Amos 5:21-24; Mic. 6:6-8; Matt. 9:13; 12:7).

6:7 Like Adam, the first and typical man in an endless stream of human beings, the Israelites had violated God's loving directions even though His blessings had been abundant. The AV translation "like men" (Heb. *'adam*) highlights Adam's typical significance. The covenant that Adam transgressed was not the Mosaic Covenant, which the Israelites and Judahites had violated. It was the arrangement with Adam that God had specified for life within the Garden of Eden, the Adamic Covenant (Gen. 2:16-17). Ever since Adam, all people, including God's people, dealt treacherously with Him by trying to seize the sovereignty from God—because they doubted His love for them.

6:8 The Lord viewed Gilead, a region of Israel east of the Jordan River, as a city. Perhaps He meant that the whole area was similar to a city in which violence and murder were so widespread that one could see bloody footprints in the streets. He may have been referring to a particular city named Gilead (Ramoth-Gilead?) in the region of Gilead where those conditions prevailed (cf. Gen. 31:47-48; Judg. 10:17). In any case, the point is clear. Evidence of gross violence against one's neighbors demonstrated lack of love for Yahweh and lack of respect for His covenant.

6:9 Whether priests were really murdering travelers as they approached the Israelite town of Shechem is uncertain. Perhaps they were. Shechem was a major religious and political center in Israel. On the other hand, this may simply be another (hyperbolic) way of describing the perverse behavior of even those who should have been closest to God. Shechem and Ramoth-Gilead were cities of refuge where people could supposedly flee for safety (cf. Josh. 20:1-2, 7-8), but they had been contaminated by blood.. Shechem stood on the route between Samaria and Bethel, so many pilgrims traveled through Shechem. The Hebrew word translated "crime," (*zimmah*) refers to the vilest sexual sins elsewhere (e.g., Lev. 18:17; 19:29; Judg. 20:5-6; Job 31:9-11). Such behavior by priests, who should have been serving the people by leading them to Yahweh, was vile to God.

6:10 The Lord had observed a horrible thing. The Israelites as a whole had practiced harlotry by going after pagan gods and had thus made themselves unclean. Religious apostasy involved sexual immorality, so both forms of harlotry are doubtless in view.

6:11 Judah also had sinned horribly and could anticipate a harvest of judgment. This would come when the Lord paid back His people for their sins. Yet the hope of eventual restoration was clear. This would be another type of harvest, a harvest marked by blessing and restoration, and that is the one primarily in view here. Reference to restoration concludes this brief message as it does the major series of messages on judgment.

The mention of Judah at the beginning and at the end of this message proves again that both kingdoms were guilty of disloyalty to God, though Israel was the worse offender.

Internal corruption 7:1-7

This section focuses on Israel's domestic sins.

7:1 The Lord longed to heal Israel, but when He thought about doing so, new evidences of her sins presented themselves. The prophets He sent to them were mainly ineffective in stemming the tide of rebellion. Most people's reaction to their messages was rejection and further heart-hardening. The people lied to one another and stole from each other. These two crimes are a synecdoche for civil and social injustices in general.

7:2 The Israelites apparently hoped that the Lord would not hold some of their sins against them, but He remembered all their wickedness. Their evil deeds surrounded them like a wall, so they were constantly before His eyes. They reminded Him of their sins whenever He looked in their direction.

7:3 Their political leaders rejoiced in the wickedness of the people because that made it easier for them to get away with sinning. These leaders, of course, should have opposed all forms of ungodliness since they were Yahweh's representatives on earth.

7:4 The Israelites as a whole were all adulterers, both physically and spiritually. Their passion for wickedness was like the fire in a baker's oven: very hot and constantly burning.

> "The oven was so hot that a baker could cease tending the fire during an entire night—while the dough he had mixed was rising—and then, with a fresh tending of the fire in the morning, have sufficient heat for baking at that time."[78]

7:5 Verses 5-7 describe the assassination of one or more of Israel's kings, an example of the passion for wickedness just illustrated. The political leaders became drunk on a particular festive occasion that honored the king. The king himself joined in scoffing at what was holy.

7:6 The princes eagerly plotted to overthrow the king. Their anger with him smoldered for a long time and was not obvious to him, like a fire hidden in an oven (v. 4), but at the proper time it flared up and consumed him and his supporters. Hosea saw this happen four times. Shallum assassinated Zechariah, Menahem assassinated Shallum, Pekah assassinated Pekahiah, and Hoshea assassinated Pekah (2 Kings 15:10, 14, 25, 30).

7:7 All of Israel's past kings had fallen. All the Israelite kings who followed Jeroboam II suffered assassination except Menahem and Hoshea (cf. 2 Kings 17:3-6). The Israelites murdered their leaders, leaving themselves like a ship without a rudder. A continuing dynasty, as existed in Judah, never succeeded in the North. The reason was that none of the Israelites sought the Lord. Since this prophecy is undated we do not know when Hosea gave it, but it must have been during the tumultuous times when Israel's final kings reigned (ca. 752-722 B.C.).

> "So blinded had the people become that they did not realize that even though their kings had been of their own making, in destroying them they were destroying God's order (Rom. 13:1)."[79]

---

[78]Wood, "Hosea," pp. 196-97. See Stuart, p. 119, for a fuller description of the bread-baking process.

"Like every revolutionary state that has no faith in anything beyond itself, Israel was burning up in its own anger."[80]

Reliance on foreigners 7:8-16

This pericope condemns Israel's foreign policy.

7:8   Ephraim had mixed itself with the pagan nations like unleavened dough mixed with leaven. She had done this by making alliances with neighbor nations, as well as by importing heathen customs and pagan gods into Israel.

> "Hoshea's lurching foreign policy is illustrative. In 732 B.C., Hoshea, after killing Pekah, suddenly shifted from alliance with Egypt, Philistia, and Aram-Damascus to alliance with Assyria. A few years later he broke that alliance, and coming virtually full circle, again sought alliance with Egypt. These confused policies are caricatured in the figurative sense of 'mixed up.'"[81]

Ephraim had become like all the other nations rather than distinctive, as Yahweh intended (Exod. 19:6). To use another figure, Ephraim was similar to a pancake that the cook had not turned over, all burnt and black on one side and soggy and runny on the other. In other words, she was only half-baked, worthless, not what God intended or what could nourish others. She was crusty toward Yahweh but soft toward other nations.

> "It is so easy for us all to become a cake unturned. We may have much of doctrine and little of deed, much of creed and little of conduct, much of belief and little of behavior, much of principle and little of practice, much of orthodoxy and little of orthopraxy."[82]

7:9   Foreign alliances had sapped Ephraim's strength rather than adding to it, but the Israelites were ignorant of this. They thought they were as strong as ever. Tribute payments to allies constantly drained the nation's wealth and weakened its economy (cf. 2 Kings 15:19-20; 17:3). Israel was unaware of its real condition, as when a person's hair becomes gray but he does not notice it. Others can sense the approach of death, but he does not. Israel was dying in the late 730s and early 720s, but its own people did not know it.

> "Are there gray hairs here and there in your spiritual life and you know it not? Prayerlessness, lack of fervor, no passion for the lost, distaste for the worship of God's house, no delight in the study of the word, no desire for fellowship with the Lord, and no interest in God's missionary plan which burns in the heart of the Lord Jesus for Jew and Gentile as a never-dying flame?"[83]

7:10   Despite Israel's weakness, the nation was too proud to return to Yahweh and seek His help. Israel seems to have been living in the past glory days rather than in the present. The years following the reign of King Jeroboam II saw the weakening of Israel that this whole section of the book pictures.

7:11   Ephraim was behaving like a dove, a bird known for its silliness and naiveté (cf. Matt. 10:16). Expediency and human wisdom, marked by vacillation, had guided Israel's foreign policy for years—rather than the will of God. This was "bird-brained" diplomacy. Emissaries had fluttered off to Egypt (2 Kings 17:3-4) and Assyria (2 Kings 15:29), seeking aid without realizing the danger that these nations posed (cf. 11:11). Finally, because Israel turned from Assyria to Egypt for help against Assyria, Assyria captured and destroyed the Northern Kingdom.

7:12   Yahweh promised to bring Israel under His control and to subdue it, as when a hunter throws a net over birds. He would chasten His people in harmony with what He had earlier proclaimed to them when He gave them the Mosaic Covenant (cf. Lev. 26:28).

> "Vv 8-12 would appear to refer to Hoshea's desperate, inconsistent attempts at foreign alliances. He came to power submitting to Assyrian hegemony, paying tribute, and thus preserving the central-southern

---

[79]Ellison, p. 124.
[80]Mays, pp. 106-7.
[81]Stuart, p. 121.
[82]Feinberg, p. 57.
[83]Ibid., p. 58.

	portions of the nation not yet controlled by Assyria. Within a few years (i.e., sometime in the mid-720s) he stopped tribute payments to Assyria and appealed for support to a temporarily resurgent Egypt (1 [*sic* 2] Kgs 17:2-4). This was the 'mixed up' foreign policy 'among the nations' (v 8) of a dying people (v 9)."[84]
7:13	The Lord pronounced doom on the Israelites because He would judge them for straying from Him like sheep from their Shepherd. Destruction would be their punishment because they rebelled against Him. His desire was to redeem them from destruction, but they only spoke lies about His desire and ability to redeem them. That is why they made foreign treaties: to defend themselves since they thought Yahweh would or could not.
	"The God of the Exodus is unchanged in His will, but because of Israel's lies there will be no 'exodus' from the Assyrian danger."[85]
7:14	When the people cried out, it was not in prayer to God but out of self-pity over their miserable condition. These tears did not impress Him. They assembled (or gashed themselves, maybe both) to obtain food and drink from their idols. Crying out, wailing, and slashing oneself were all aspects of the self-destructive Canaanite worship style that the Israelites adopted (cf. 1 Kings 18:28). They turned away from Yahweh, the only One who could provide their needs, like stubborn children.
	"According to Canaanite religious beliefs, prolonged drought was a signal that the storm god Baal had been temporarily defeated by the god of death and was imprisoned in the underworld. Baal's worshipers would mourn his death in hopes that their tears might facilitate his resurrection and the restoration of crops."[86]
7:15	It was Yahweh who had taught His people how to be strong. He had also made them strong militarily (cf. Ezek. 30:24-25), for example, during Jeroboam II's reign (cf. 2 Kings 14:25-28). Yet they had used what He had given them to sin against Him (cf. Gen. 50:20). They treated Him as their enemy. This was further evidence of their ingratitude.
7:16	They had looked around to other nations for help, but they had not turned their hearts and eyes to heaven to seek the Lord's help. They had become like a warped bow in Yahweh's hands. Rather than shooting His enemies, they shot their own leaders and slew them (e.g., Zechariah, Shallum, Pekahiah, and Pekah). In the days of Jeroboam II, the Israelites had even boasted insolently to the Egyptians about not needing Yahweh. But the Egyptians, their treaty partner on several occasions, would deride them for their weakness.

"As we review these images, we might take inventory of our own devotion to the Lord. How lasting is it? How deep is it? How strong is it? How serious is it? How dependable is it?"[87]

Accusations involving rebellion ch. 8

Judgment would also come on Israel because God's people had rebelled against Yahweh. In the previous section (6:4—7:16), accusations were more common than promises of judgment. In this one judgment becomes more prominent, though accusations continue.

Making idols 8:1-7

8:1	The Lord commanded Hosea to announce coming judgment by telling him to put a trumpet to his lips. The blowing of the shophar announced that an invader was coming (cf. 5:8). Israel's enemy would swoop down on the nation as an eagle attacking its prey (cf. 5:14; Deut. 28:49). The "house of the LORD" refers to the people of Israel, His household. The reason for this judgment was Israel's transgression (overstepping) of Yahweh's covenant (the Mosaic Covenant) and the nation's rebellion against His Law (the Mosaic Law; cf. 7:13).
8:2	The Israelites claimed that they acknowledged (knew) the authority of their God, but their transgressions and rebellion proved that they did not (cf. 4:1, 6; 5:4). Their knowledge of Him was only historical and traditional (cf. John 8:33).
8:3	Because Israel had rejected the good (i.e., the Lord's moral and ethical requirements), an enemy would pursue him (cf. Deut. 28:45).
8:4	One example of Israel's rebellion was the setting up of kings and other leaders without consulting Yahweh.

---

[84]Stuart, p. 117.
[85]Mays, p. 111.
[86]*The Nelson Study Bible*, p. 1455.
[87]Wiersbe, p. 324.

> "Yahweh *alone* determines who can be king either by charismatic gifts or by direct revelation through a prophet. He *gives* kings to the nations (e.g., 1 Kgs 19:15-16); they do not decide who their kings will be.... The king was Yahweh's representative or regent, not the people's choice."[88]

The making of idols was another example of rebellion. The result of this rebellion was that God would cut Israel off (separate Israel from its land and people).

8:5   The Lord rejected the calf idol, that had come to represent Israelite worship, ever since Jeroboam I first set up images of calves at Dan and Bethel (1 Kings 12:28-30). "He" refers to Yahweh (cf. 1:7; 2:23; 4:6, 10, 12; 8:13), and "Samaria" again represents the whole Northern Kingdom, by metonymy. Hosea spoke to the people about Yahweh in the third person here. The Lord also said His anger burned against the Israelites because of this idolatry. He lamented that they persisted in uncleanness, asking them rhetorically how long they would be incapable of "innocence" (purity).

8:6   From Israel, of all people, had come the pagan idol. A human craftsman had fashioned it, so the idol was not the true God (cf. Isa. 40:18-20; 44:9-20). When Jeroboam I originally presented these idols to the people of Israel, he said, "Behold your gods, O Israel" (1 Kings 12:28; cf. Exod. 32:4). These idols, represented here as the calf of Samaria, would be broken to pieces, demonstrating the impotence of the gods.

8:7   Normally farmers sowed seed and reaped grain, but Israel had sowed "the wind," something foolish and worthless (cf. Job 7:7; Prov. 11:29; Eccles. 1:14, 17), namely: idolatry. Consequently, instead of reaping something beneficial and nourishing, he would reap a "whirlwind," something equally vain but also destructive. "Sowing the wind and reaping the whirlwind" may have been a proverb in Israel.[89] The literal seed the Israelites sowed would grow up but not produce any grain, only bare stalks without heads. If the land *did* yield some grain, strangers would confiscate it and the Israelites would not benefit from it.

Making treaties 8:8-10

8:8   The prophet looked ahead to the time of Israel's judgment. The nation would be swallowed up, as when someone eats grain (v. 7). Israel would become a part of the nations, having gone into captivity and lost its own sovereignty—and even its identity. It would be like an earthenware pot that no one wanted because it was broken (cf. Jer. 22:28; 48:38).

8:9   Ephraim (Israel) had made treaties with Assyria to help protect her from her enemies (cf. 7:11), but the Assyrians would turn and devour Israel. Wild donkeys were notorious for their willfulness and being difficult to control (cf. Jer. 2:24), and so was Israel. Ephraim was also like a harlot, *but even worse* in that he paid others to love him, rather than receiving pay from them (cf. 2:5; Jer. 2:23-25). Yahweh had promised to care for the nation because He loved it.

8:10   Hiring allies among the pagan nations by making treaties with them would not work. Yahweh Himself would gather them up to judge them. He would use as His instrument of judgment "the king of princes," namely, the king of the Assyrian Empire, the very king to whom the Israelites appealed for protection (cf. 10:6; Isa. 10:8). The result would be the diminution of the nation of Israel.

Making altars, palaces, and fortified cities 8:11-14

8:11   In rebellion against Yahweh's covenant, the Israelites had also built many altars (Deut. 12). They built them to offer many sin offerings, but since God had not authorized these altars they became places for sinning rather than places for worshipping. More altars simply meant more sinning.

8:12   Yahweh had been very specific about His demands in the Mosaic Covenant, but the Israelites treated them as something foreign to their lives. Ironically, they had treated God's laws as foreign, but they had imported foreign idols and practices and followed them. "Ten thousand precepts" looks at the abundant detail that God had provided His people so they would know just what to do, not at the literal number of His commands.

8:13   They offered the sacrifices prescribed in the Law, but the Lord looked at them as *only* meat; they had no sacrificial value to Him. The Hebrew word *basar*, translated "meat," is in the emphatic position before the verb. God regarded the sacrifices as nothing more than meat. He took no delight in these sacrifices because the people mixed them with rebellion. Consequently He would call them into judgment for their sins and punish them. He would send them back "to Egypt," where they used to live as slaves before He redeemed them in the Exodus (cf. 9:3). Josephus wrote that the Roman general, Titus, who destroyed

---

[88]Stuart, p. 131.
[89]Dyer, p. 732.

Jerusalem in A.D. 70, sent many of the Jews as prisoners to the Egyptian mines.[90] Perhaps the Lord also meant that He would send them to an *Egypt-like place*, which Assyria proved to be (cf. 11:5; Deut. 28:68).[91]

> "In the deliverance from Egyptian bondage Israel had experienced God's grace. Having spurned that grace, she would return to slavery."[92]

8:14   Both Israel and Judah had forgotten (turned away from) their Creator. Instead of continuing to trust and obey Him, the people had put their confidence in their own ability to provide for themselves. This attitude of self-reliance manifested itself in building palaces and fortified cites as places of prominence and protection. Palaces and fortified cites are not wrong in themselves, but in this context, set against remembering Yahweh, they were expressions of self-trust. In judgment, the Lord would burn down their palaces and fortified cities. He would remove the objects of their confidence and teach the people their personal inadequacy. Tiglath-Pileser III did this when he destroyed Samaria and the other Israelites cities, and Sennacherib did it when he attacked all the fortified cities of Judah (2 Kings 17:6; 18:13).

To summarize, five types of sin stand out in this section as reasons for Israel's punishment: Israel had usurped Yahweh's sovereign authority to lead the nation (v. 4), and had worshipped idols (vv. 4-6). Israel depended on foreign treaties rather than God (vv. 9-10), and had adopted and perpetuated a corrupt cult (system of worship, vv. 5, 6, 11, 13). And Israel arrogantly disregarded Yahweh's Law (vv. 1-3, 5, 12, 14).

2. Israel's inevitable judgment 9:1—11:7

This section of prophecies continues to record accusations against Israel, but the emphasis on the inevitability of coming judgment increases. Also in contrast to chapter 8, this section is not a speech by Yahweh but one that Hosea delivered about Him.[93]

Israel's sorrow 9:1-9

Israel would sorrow greatly because of her sins. Description of her sorrow precedes the explanation for it.

The result: termination of festivals 9:1-6

9:1-2   The Lord told Israel not to rejoice like other nations at the prospect of an abundant harvest; that would not be her privilege. He promised to remove her grain and wine. These were threatened curses for covenant unfaithfulness (cf. Deut. 28:30, 38-42, 51). Her unfaithfulness to Him had precluded further blessing. She had credited Baal with providing the blessings that she enjoyed rather than Yahweh. The prophet envisioned Israel as a harlot committing adultery on a threshing floor by worshipping idols there. Threshing floors and winepresses were common places where ritual prostitution took place. It was through these rites that the worshippers sought to stimulate the gods to engage in sex and so bestow fruitfulness on them and their land.

9:3   Israel would not remain in the Promised Land but would go into captivity (cf. Deut. 11:8-21). Assyria, likened here to Egypt (cf. 7:16; 8:13; 11:5), would be the place the Israelites would eat unclean food (i.e., no longer be independent; 2 Kings 17:6; Ezek. 4:13; Amos 7:17). She would eat defiled food in a defiled land because she had defiled herself with sin.

> "The place of their captivity was first called 'Egypt' (cf. 8:13) in order to show its general character; then Assyria was named as the actual place the people would be taken to (cf. 11:5)."[94]

"Egypt" is a metonymy for exile because it was the original place of Israel's captivity (cf. Deut. 28:68).

9:4   Opportunities for legitimate worship would end in exile since Israel had corrupted legitimate worship in the land. Drink offerings of wine, which accompanied certain sacrifices, would cease (cf. Num. 15:1-12), and sacrifices offered there would be unacceptable to Yahweh. They would be similar to the bread that mourners ate, namely, ceremonially unclean because of contact with dead bodies (cf. Num. 19:14-15, 22). Such bread might be suitable for human consumption, but it was unacceptable as an offering to God. Cultic celebration would give way to disease and death.

9:5   Consequently the Israelites would have nothing to offer the Lord when their annual feasts rolled around. These feasts centered on offerings to the Lord, but those offerings would be unacceptable in exile.

---

[90]Flavius Josephus, *The Wars of the Jews*, 6:9:2.
[91]See McComiskey, p. 117.
[92]Chisholm, "Hosea," p. 1397.
[93]See Charles H. Silva, "The Literary Structure of Hosea 9—14," *Bibliotheca Sacra* 164:656 (October-December 2007):435-53, for a literary analysis of this section of Hosea.
[94]Wood, "Hosea," p. 204.

9:6   The Israelites would leave their land because of the destruction Yahweh would send. Egypt and Memphis, as two undertakers, would bury the exiles. Memphis (near modern Cairo) was an Egyptian city famous as a burial site because of the pyramid tombs there. Back in the land weeds would overgrow the Israelites' abandoned treasures, and thorns would take over their houses (cf. Deut. 28:36-46).

The cause: opposition to prophets 9:7-9

9:7   Israel was to know that the days of her punishment and retribution were imminent because the nation's iniquity was fat and its hostility to the Lord was great. Another reason for her judgment was that the Israelites had regarded the prophets whom the Lord had sent to them as demented fools (cf. 2 Kings 9:11; Jer. 29:26-27). This probably included Hosea.

> "The prophet represents Yahweh as saying that the captivity was a payment for the sin of the nation. One of the primary themes of this prophecy is the stark truth that sin demands requital, and Israel was soon to know that by experience. The present respite from national calamity was not to last forever."[95]

9:8   Ephraim tried to function as a prophet of God warning others of approaching danger. But Ephraim had tried to entangle the prophets God had sent the people, like a hunter catches birds in a net. Thus there was nothing but hostility in the land of Israel between the Ephraimites and the true prophets of Yahweh. Ephraim saw nothing as a prophet and criticized the prophets for preaching what they saw, namely: coming judgment.

9:9   The Israelites had delved deep into depravity, as when the men of Gibeah raped and murdered the visiting Levite's concubine (Judg. 19). This was another occasion in which the Israelites punished one of their own rather than protecting her. The Lord would remember their iniquities and punish their sins. This sin had resulted in war in Israel and almost the obliteration of the tribe of Benjamin (Judg. 20). War would come again, and God would almost entirely obliterate all the Israelites for their sins.

Israel's humiliation 9:10-17

This section is one in a series that looks back on Israel's previous history, and its reflective mood colors its prophecies (cf. 10:1-8, 9-15; 11:1-7).

> "Divine speech and prophetic speech combine in this passage to pronounce upon the disobedient Israelites the fulfillment of the curses for disobedience contained in the Mosaic covenant. Here for the first time Hosea himself calls down the wrath of God upon his own compatriots (vv 14, 17). He is thus both announcer and imprecator of punishment."[96]

Diminished fruitfulness 9:10-14

"The gloomy, foreboding atmosphere of verses 1-9 changes now to one of pathos. The words here are at once tender and loving."[97]

9:10   In the early days of Israel's history in the wilderness, the Lord took great delight in His people, as one rejoices to find grapes in a desert or the first figs of the season. However, when they came to Baal-Peor, where they worshipped Baal and committed ritual sex with the Moabite and Midianite women (Num. 25), they became as detestable to Yahweh as the idols they loved. This first instance of Baal worship set the pattern of Israel's idolatry that followed in the land and resulted in her present judgment.

9:11   The glory of the Ephraimites, their numerous children, would fly away like a bird, quickly and irretrievably. There would be few births, or even pregnancies, or even conceptions. There is a play on the name "Ephraim" here, which sounds somewhat like the Hebrew word meaning "twice fruitful." The Ephraimites had looked to Baal for the blessing of human fertility, but Yahweh would withhold it in judgment. Ephraim, the doubly fruitful, would become Ephraim, the completely fruitless.

9:12   Most of the children born would die prematurely, and few of them would remain, probably because of the coming invasion (cf. Deut. 32:25). When Yahweh withdrew His protection from His people, their doom would be great. He would no longer multiply the nation.

---

[95]McComiskey, p. 144.
[96]Stuart, p. 155.
[97]McComiskey, p. 148.

9:13   Yahweh saw that Ephraim had been fertile in the past, comparable to the prosperity of Tyre. Yet in the future, Ephraim's sons were destined to become prey to the enemy. Ephraim's punishment would be similar to Tyre's.

9:14   Hosea called on Yahweh, after reflecting on her punishments, to disappoint Ephraim's hopes concerning descendants and the inability to sustain their children. The combination of "womb" and "breasts" is a pairing that describes human fruitfulness (cf. Gen. 49:25).

Expulsion from the land 9:15-17

"The previous section (vv. 10-14) began with a tender expression of Yahweh's love. This section (vv. 15-17) begins with an affirmation of his hatred. The previous section looked back to the wilderness; this section looks back to Gilgal. Hosea views God as acting in history; thus historical events and the geographical sites where they occurred become vehicles of divine truth. The events of the exodus from Egypt spoke volumes about God, as did the events that took place in the wilderness and at Gilgal. To Hosea God's response to the people at those places forever remains as crystallized truth about the nature of God."[98]

9:15   What the Israelites did at Gilgal caused the Lord to hate them. This is covenant terminology meaning He opposed them; personal emotion is not the main point. At Gilgal the Israelites practiced the pagan fertility cult (cf. 4:15; 12:11). Gilgal epitomized the syncretistic worship of Hosea's day. Yahweh would drive His people out of the land, as He had expelled Adam and Eve and the Canaanites, because they had sinned and had adopted the ways of sinners. He would love (choose to bless) them no more, as He had in the past, because all their leaders rebelled against Him.

     Even though God loves (chooses) all the elect (Eph. 1:4), He has a special affection for those who comply with His will (cf. John 15:14). The Israelites had stopped being compliant and had been rebellious.

9:16   The Lord had struck the very roots of the nation so that it would dry up and bear no fruit (cf. Mal. 4:1). This probably refers to human barrenness, agricultural unfruitfulness, and animal infertility. Even though the people bore children that were precious to them, the Lord would slay them.

9:17   Hosea's God would cast the Ephraimites out of the land because they proved unresponsive to Him (cf. Deut. 28:62-64). They would end up wandering among the other nations of the world. Because they had wandered from the Lord, they would wander in the earth, like Cain whom the Lord also cursed (cf. Gen. 4:12).

Israel's vulnerability 10:1-8

The allusion that opens this series of messages is similar to the ones in 9:10, 10:9, and 11:1, in that it refers to Israel's early history. A mood of loss of confidence and protection marks this section. As so often occurs in Hosea, evidences of covenant unfaithfulness begin the section followed by announcements of punishment for unfaithfulness. In this one: announcement of the fate of the nation's cultic symbols (altars, idols, sacred standing stones, and high places) gives way to announcement of judgment on Israel's political symbol (the king).

Judgment on Israel's cultic symbols 10:1-2

10:1   Hosea compared Israel to a luxuriant (degenerate) vine; the people enjoyed great economic prosperity. The grapevine was a common figure for Israel. Yahweh had planted Israel in Canaan as a vine and had blessed it with fruitful prosperity (cf. Ps. 80:8-10; Jer. 2:21; Ezek. 19:10-11). Yet the more the Lord blessed Israel, the more the Israelites multiplied altars and sacred pillars to honor idols. They worshipped pagan gods in response to Yahweh's blessing.

10:2   Such behavior indicated an unfaithful (Heb. *halaq*, flattering, hypocritical, lit. slippery) heart that rendered the Israelites guilty before God. He would do away with the altars and pillars that they had erected.

Judgment on Israel's political symbol 10:3-8

10:3   When the Lord brought destruction, the people would realize that their self-appointed king had failed them and that they did not respect the Lord. They would acknowledge that no human king could help them. Hoshea would prove to be Israel's last king, and perhaps he was already on the throne when Hosea gave this prophecy.

---

[98]Ibid., p. 154.

10:4	The people had not been true to their word. They had broken covenants they made with one another. Consequently, God's judgment was as inevitable as poisonous weeds growing in the furrows of their fields and choking out the crops. His judgment would slay the people just as surely as poisonous hemlock weeds kill those who eat them. God's judgments would replace His blessings. Another view is that the weeds represent perverted justice, and true justice would have been as wheat.[99]
10:5	When God destroyed Israel's altars (v. 2), specifically the golden calf at Beth-aven (i.e., Bethel, cf. v. 8; 4:15; 5:8), the Israelites who lived in Samaria, Israel's capital, would fear. "Beth-aven" may stand not merely for Bethel, but also for the entire official, semi-pagan religious set-up in Israel.[100] The people would mourn, and the idolatrous priests (Heb. *kemarim*; cf. 2 Kings 23:5; Zeph. 1:4) who served there would bewail the demise of this altar, since its glory had departed from the land.
10:6	The Assyrians would carry the golden calf to their land in honor of their king (cf. 8:10). Israel would then feel great shame because the Israelites had decided to trust in a foreign alliance with the Assyrians for their security (cf. 5:13; 7:8-9, 11; 8:9-10).

> "For us alliances between nations are such a commonplace of life that we can hardly imagine a nation standing alone . . .
>
> "It should have been fundamental, however, for Israel that no foreign alliances were possible. The reason was quite simply that in those days the secular state did not exist, and so in practice it was impossible to distinguish between a state and its gods. In an extant treaty of peace between Rameses II of Egypt and Hattusilis the Hittite king it is a thousand of their gods on either side who are the witnesses to and guarantors of it.[101] So even a treaty on equal terms with a neighbouring country would have involved for Israel a recognition of the other country's deities as having reality and equality with Jehovah. To turn to Assyria or Egypt for help implied of necessity that their gods were more effective than the God of Israel."[102]

10:7	The Assyrians would also remove the Israelites (Samaria) along with their king. They would be swept away like a twig floating on the surface of a fast-moving stream. They would be helpless, totally at the mercy of the Assyrians.

> "The three centers of authority in the North were king, cult, and capital city. The final two verses of the passage announce the fulfillment of covenant sanctions against each of these, beginning in v 7a with the capital."[103]

10:8	The Assyrians would also destroy the sites of the idolatrous shrines at "Aven" (wickedness, i.e., Bethel [or Beth-aven, cf. v. 5]), where the Israelites had sinned. Ironically, when the Israelites had entered the Promised Land, the Lord had commanded them to destroy such places (Num. 33:52; Deut. 12:2-3). Since they had not obeyed, the Lord would use the Assyrians to fulfill His command. The pagan altars there would become overgrown with wild thorns and thistles. The Israelites would then express their terror over this judgment by calling on the mountains and hills to cover them (cf. Luke 23:30; Rev. 6:16). They would prefer death to life (cf. Jer. 8:3; Rev. 9:6).

Israel's coming war 10:9-15

This section also opens with a reference to an event in Israel's past history (cf. 9:10; 10:1; 11:1). Announcements of war punishment (vv. 9-10, 14-15) bracket Yahweh's indictment of His people for their sins (vv. 11-13).

An initial announcement of war 10:9-10

10:9	The Israelites had sinned consistently since the days of the atrocity at Gibeah (Judg. 19—20; cf. 9:9; Isa. 1:10). The prophet depicted them as warriors standing at Gibeah. He asked rhetorically if the Lord's battle against them would not be victorious at this site of their early sinning. He would indeed defeat these people so long associated with iniquity.
10:10	At the Lord's chosen time, He would chasten (punish, discipline, cf. 5:2) His people by binding them as prisoners, harnessing them to their sins (cf. v. 11). Other peoples would oppose them in battle when the Lord had bound them up for being twice guilty. The double guilt in view is probably their original guilt because of their sin at Gibeah and their present guilt because of

---

[99]Ibid., p. 164.
[100]Ellison, p. 128.
[101]Footnote 1: James B. Pritchard, ed., *Ancient Near Eastern Texts Relating to the Old Testament*, pp. 200-201.
[102]Ellison, p. 131.
[103]Stuart, p. 162.

their sin at Bethel.[104] Another view is that it refers to the sin of forsaking God and the sin of forsaking His appointed Davidic kings.[105]

A confirming announcement of war 10:11-15

10:11 Hosea compared Ephraim to a heifer that enjoyed threshing.

> "Threshing was a comparatively light task, made pleasant by the fact that the creature was unmuzzled and free to eat . . . as it pulled the threshing sledge over the gathered corn."[106]

Ephraim had abandoned this comparatively light service in preference for becoming yoked to sin (v. 10). As punishment, Yahweh would yoke the people of both Northern and Southern Kingdoms to an enemy who would greatly restrict their movements and force them to do hard work. "Judah" refers to the Southern Kingdom and "Jacob" to the Northern, using the name of the patriarch that stresses this ancestor's rebelliousness. Or possibly "Jacob" refers to all 12 tribes.[107]

10:12 The prophet appealed to the Israelites to repent. They should cultivate righteousness with a view to reaping the Lord's kindness (Heb. *hesed*). Breaking up fallow ground is what a farmer does when he plows land that has remained untouched for a long time, even forever (cf. Jer. 4:3). This is a figure for confessing sins and exposing them to God when they have remained unconfessed under the surface of life for a long time. It was time for the people to seek Yahweh, whom they had failed to seek in repentance for so long. They should confess and repent until the Lord sent the blessings of righteousness (deliverance, cf. 2:19) on them like rain (cf. 6:3).

This well-known verse is a good summary of what all Israel's prophets appealed to God's people to do throughout their history (cf. 2 Cor. 6:2).

10:13 Instead of plowing righteousness and reaping loyal love (v. 12), the Israelites had plowed wickedness and reaped injustice. Instead of eating the fruit of righteousness, they had eaten the fruit of lies. They had done this because they trusted in themselves and in their own military might.

10:14 Because the Israelites trusted in their own army, turmoil rather than tranquility would mark their life. Their fortresses would suffer destruction, rather than protecting the Israelites from destruction. Hosea compared this future loss to one in Israel's past, but what past event is uncertain.

"Shalman" may refer to King Shalmaneser III, an Assyrian who conducted campaigns in the West in the ninth century B.C. Another identification of "Shalman" is King Salamanu, a Moabite ruler who was a contemporary of King Hoshea of Israel, whose name appears in a list of kings who paid tribute to the Assyrian king Tiglath-Pileser III.[108] A third possibility is the Assyrian king, Shalmaneser V, who prepared the way for Israel's captivity by invading the land (cf. 2 Kings 17:3-6).[109] "Beth-arbel" could refer to the town of Arbela about 18 miles southeast of the Sea of Chinnereth (Galilee), or to Mt. Arbel two miles west of that sea. In any case, the battle had been a bloody one that the Israelites of Hosea's day remembered vividly. The enemy had slaughtered mothers and their children without mercy.

10:15 The Israelites would suffer a similar slaughter at Bethel because of their great wickedness. "Bethel" here may refer to the town or to the whole nation of Israel (by metonymy, cf. v. 7).

> "Since her destruction would occur 'when that day dawns' (meaning the very beginning of the day of battle), it is noteworthy that Israel's final king, Hoshea, was taken captive by the Assyrian conqueror Shalmaneser V before the actual siege of Samaria began."[110]

---

[104]Wolff, p. 184.
[105]Keil, 1:133.
[106]Kidner, pp. 97-98.
[107]Wood, "Hosea," p. 211.
[108]Ellison, pp. 140-41.
[109]See Harper, p. 358.
[110]Wood, "Hosea," p. 211.

Israel's rebelliousness 11:1-7

Again this section, which is all divine speech, begins with a reference to something in Israel's history to contrast the past with the present (cf. 9:10; 10:1, 9).

> "The passage at its outset has similarities to the form of the legal complaint made by parents against a rebellious child (Deut 21:18-21; cf. Isa 1:2-20 where hope is held out that the child [Israel] may yet repent and receive compassion rather than death)."[111]

Proof of rebelliousness 11:1-4

11:1   The Lord reminded His people that when Israel was in its early days as a nation, like a youth, He loved the nation (cf. Exod. 4:22-23). As often is the case, loving refers to choosing (cf. Gen. 12:2-3). God chose Israel for special blessing among the world's nations and in this sense loved him. He called and led His "son" Israel out of bondage in Egypt (cf. Deut. 14:1; 32:6; Isa. 1:2-20; Jer. 3:19, 22; 4:22; 31:9, 20).

> "We need not find the slightest difficulty in Israel's being called Jehovah's son and not His wife. In a book of so many brief and normally unconnected oracles, with their wealth of metaphors and pictorial imagery, it is worse than pedantic to see a contradiction."[112]

Matthew wrote that Jesus Christ fulfilled this verse (Matt. 2:15). Jesus did so in that, as the Son of God in another sense, God the Father called and led Him out of Egypt when He was a child. Matthew did not mean that Hosea had Jesus Christ in mind or was predicting His exodus from Egypt when he wrote, but that Jesus' experience corresponded to what Hosea had written about Israel. He saw the experience of Jesus as analogous to that of Israel. Jesus' experience completed the full meaning of Hosea's statement and in this sense fulfilled it.[113]

> "This is a reference not only to the exodus of Israel from Egypt but also to the fact that all of God's dealings with Israel were based upon the love that He would show in calling His Son, the Lord Jesus Christ, back from the comparative safety of Egypt in order that He might suffer and die to accomplish His great redemptive work."[114]

11:2   God continued to call the Israelites after they left Egypt. He did so through His prophets. But the more the prophets appealed to the people to follow the Lord, the more the people turned aside from following Him. They kept sacrificing to Baal and kept burning incense to idols (cf. Judg. 2:11-13).

11:3   Israel demonstrated this ungrateful apostasy even though it was Yahweh who taught His son Israel to walk (behave, cf. Deut. 1:31; Isa. 1:2), provided tender loving care, and healed him when he needed restoration.

11:4   The restraints that the Lord had placed on Israel in its youth were cords of love, designed to protect and preserve the people, rather than robbing them of freedom. The Lord freed them from oppressive bondage and made special provision to feed them. The image of a loving herdsman taking care of his animal is in view here. Often a cattleman would lift the yoke from an ox's shoulders, so that when it bent over to eat, the yoke would not slide down over its face and impede its feeding.[115]

Punishment for rebelliousness 11:5-7

11:5   Because Israel refused to "return" (Heb. *shub*) to Yahweh after so many appeals by His prophets (v. 2), He would "return" (Heb. *shub*) the nation to captivity. Yet the place of exile would not be Egypt but Assyria. In other messages, Hosea identified Egypt as the place of Israel's future exile (cf. 8:13; 9:3, 6), but here it becomes clear that he was only using "Egypt" as a metaphor for a *place of captivity*. Assyria would be the geographical location of Israel's exile. Thus "Egypt" is an *atbash* for Assyria (cf. 4:15).

11:6   Enemy soldiers would swarm around Israel's cities and break down the gate bars that secured them against foreign attack. They would consume the Israelites because of the decisions the Israelites had made to depart from the Lord (cf. Mic. 6:16). These were the result, in part, of false prophets' advice. Yahweh had fed His people (v. 4), but now the sword would feed on them (cf. Isa. 1:19-20).

---

[111] Stuart, p. 175
[112] Ellison, p. 143.
[113] See Dyer, pp. 733-34, for several comparisons and contrasts between the history of Israel and the history of Jesus Christ.
[114] *The New Scofield . . .*, p. 925.
[115] Wood, "Hosea," pp. 212-13.

11:7	The Israelites' resolve to abandon Yahweh was firm. In spite of the prophets' appeals to return to Him, none of them exalted the Lord by doing so. The Hebrew text of the last part of verse 7 is very difficult to understand. The NIV translators thought it meant God refused to hear the desperate cry of His people.

B. Another assurance of restoration 11:8-11

As previously, a series of messages assuring Israel's judgment (6:4—11:7) ends with assurance of future restoration. God would definitely bring devastating judgment on Israel, but His compassion for the nation and His promises to the patriarchs required final blessing after the discipline (cf. Deut. 4:25-31).

> "These verses are like a window into the heart of God. They show that his love for his people is a love that will never let them go."[116]

11:8	The Lord asked four rhetorical questions that reveal how hard it was for Him to turn Israel over to an enemy for punishment. They are strong expressions of divine emotion, specifically, *love*, for His chosen people. "Admah" and "Zeboiim" were cities that God annihilated along with Sodom and Gomorrah (cf. Gen. 10:19; 14:2,8; Deut. 29:23). God could not bring Himself to deal with the cities of Israel as He had with those towns. He would not totally destroy them. His heart of judgment was turned upside down into a heart of compassion. All His compassion flamed up in Him as judgment emotions had done before.

> "Israel will not be completely 'overturned' as the cities mentioned here; rather, there will be an 'overturning,' that is, a change, in Yahweh's heart."[117]

11:9	God did not change His mind about bringing judgment on Israel, but He promised not to apply the full measure of His wrath or to destroy Ephraim again in the future. He would show restraint because He is God, not a man who forgets his promises, is arbitrary in his passions, and might be vindictive in his anger (cf. 1 Sam. 15:29). He was the Holy One in the midst of the Israelites, so He would be completely fair with His people. He would not descend on them with unbridled wrath.

> "Some theologians argue that God does not possess emotions. Of course, to make such an assertion they must dismiss as anthropopathic the many biblical texts that attribute emotions to God. Hosea 11:9 demonstrates that this view of God's nature is erroneous and unbiblical. God, like human beings whom he made in his image, is capable of a wide range of emotions, but God, unlike human beings, expresses his emotions in perfect balance. The distinction between God and human beings does not lie in some supposed absence of divine emotion, but in God's ability to control his emotions and express them appropriately."[118]

11:10	In the future, the Israelites would follow the Lord (cf. vv. 2, 5). He would again announce His intentions like a roaring lion (cf. 5:14; 13:7; Amos 1:2; 3:8). However, this time it would not be as a lion about to devour its prey, but as a lion leading its cubs to safety. The Israelites would follow Him, "trembling from the west" (cf. 3:5; Exod. 19:16).

Since Assyria lay to Israel's east, it seems that this reference to regathering from the west does not refer to return from Assyrian captivity. Apparently it refers to return from another worldwide dispersion. Presently the Israelites live dispersed all over the world. This verse then probably alludes to a still future restoration from our perspective in history. It may refer to the restoration that Antichrist will encourage (Dan. 9:27), but it probably refers to the streaming of Israel back into the land following Jesus Christ's return to the earth (cf. Isa. 11:11-12).

11:11	The idea of a universal return finds support in the references here to return from both Egypt (the symbolic place of exile) and Assyria (the literal place; cf. Zech. 10:10-11). Yahweh promised to settle the Israelites in their houses, namely, in the places that they formerly left, in the land of Israel. The Israelites had been as silly as doves seeking foreign alliances (7:11), but now they would return as vulnerable and as swift as doves to the land (cf. Ps. 55:6-7; Isa. 60:8).

VI. THE FIFTH SERIES OF MESSAGES ON JUDGMENT AND RESTORATION: HISTORICAL UNFAITHFULNESS 11:12—14:8

A tone of exhortation and instruction marks this fifth and last collection of messages.

---

[116]Ibid.," p. 214.
[117]Wolff, p. 201.
[118]Chisholm, *Handbook on . . .*, p. 362.

A. JUDGMENT FOR UNFAITHFULNESS 11:12—13:16

Hosea again established Israel's guilt and predicted her punishment. Israel's unfaithfulness to God receives special emphasis (cf. ch. 3).

1. The deceitfulness of Israel 11:12—12:14

Several comparisons of Israel and the patriarch Jacob point out the deceitfulness of the Northern Kingdom in this apparent mosaic of messages. Israel had cheated on its covenant with Yahweh. The form of the passage is again that of a lawsuit in which the Lord brought charges against Israel (the *rib* oracle) and concluded by announcing its doom.

An introductory accusation and announcement of judgment 11:12—12:2

11:12   This is verse 1 of chapter 12 in the Hebrew Bible. The Lord complained that Ephraim (Israel) had consistently lied and tried to deceive Him. He described Himself as surrounded and under attack by His own people. Wherever He looked, all He saw was cheaters. Deception (Heb. *mirmah*, unfaithfulness) had also marked Israel's ancestor, Jacob (cf. 12:3-4, 12; Gen. 27:35). But the kingdom of Judah had also been unruly (Heb. *rud*, wayward) in its relationship with "the Holy One (cf. v. 9) who is faithful." Yahweh was always faithful to His covenant promises, even though these groups of His people had wandered from Him and sought out Baals and foreign allies. Both kingdoms had been unfaithful to the covenant the Lord had made with them.

12:1   Describing Ephraim feeding on wind pictures the nation pursuing vain efforts that do not satisfy (cf. 8:7; 13:15). Reference to the "east wind" suggests the hot desert wind that no one in his right mind would pursue. Ephraim also multiplied "lies and violence," evidences of internal social injustice (cf. 4:2; 7:1). She made covenants (treaties) with Assyria and Egypt rather than trusting in God (cf. 5:13; 7:8, 11; 8:8-9; 2 Kings 17:3-4; 18:21; Isa. 30:7). Carrying "oil to Egypt" probably pictures Ephraim fulfilling a covenant obligation to her treaty partner.

12:2   The Lord also had a charge (Heb. *rib*, cf. 2:2) to bring against Judah, and promised to punish Jacob in harmony with his sins. "Jacob" may represent the Northern Kingdom here in contrast to Judah, the Southern Kingdom, or "Jacob" may represent both kingdoms since both descended from him (cf. 10:11).

> "Israel is not a 'chip off the old block' but a nation *unlike* its eponymous ancestor, in that it refuses to acknowledge Yahweh as its sole God."[119]

A lesson from Jacob's life 12:3-6

The Lord proceeded to teach His people the need to repent by reminding them of the experience of their forefather Jacob.

12:3   The Lord described the ancestor of these kingdoms further. Jacob grasped his brother's heel while he was still in the womb of his mother Rebekah (Gen. 25:26). This was a preview of the grasping character that marked him all his life (cf. Gen. 27:35-36). In later life he also continued to contend with God. These references to the early and later life of Jacob picture him as being a contentious person all his life.[120] Other interpreters thought Hosea used this characteristic of Jacob as a positive example for his hearers and readers.[121] They took it as an indication of Jacob's desire to obtain the promised blessings.

12:4   One important instance of Jacob contending with God was when he wrestled with the angel at Peniel and prevailed over him by weeping and pleading with him to bless him (Gen. 32:22-32). This event was a turning point in Jacob's life because he finally realized that he could not succeed simply by manipulation and trickery. He recognized his need for God's help and turned to Him in desperation. It was the occasion of Jacob's repentance. God had prepared Jacob for this event by allowing him to experience several years of conflict with his uncle Laban (cf. Gen. 31:42).

> "Making no mention of an angel, the Genesis account refers to Jacob's foe as 'a Man'" (Gen. 32:24 reflects Jacob's initial perspective), but then indicates that Jacob wrestled with God Himself (see Gen. 32:28, 30). Since vv. 4, 5 seem to place *God* and the Angel in parallel, some understand the Angel of the Lord to be in view here. This angel is sometimes equated with God in the Old Testament (see Gen. 16:9-13; Judg. 6:11-14; 13:20-22)."[122]

---

[119]Stuart, p. 190.
[120]See Harper, p. 379; and Chisholm, "Hosea," p. 1404.
[121]Keil, 1:146; Stuart, p. 197; and Wood, "Hosea," p. 216.
[122]*The Nelson . . .*, p. 1460.

Another significant event in Jacob's life was when he returned to Bethel, where God had appeared to him in a dream years earlier (Gen. 28:10-22). This return to Bethel, and the act of worship Jacob performed there, were in obedience to God's instruction to him to go there and fulfill his former vow (Gen. 35:1-14). This, too, was an act of submissive obedience and resulted in God changing Jacob's name to Israel (prince with God), blessing him yet again, and renewing the Abrahamic Covenant with him.

It is ironic that the place where Jacob got right with God was Bethel, since *Bethel* was the place where the Israelites had gotten wrong with Him by worshipping idols. Jacob's return to God at Bethel provided a good example for the Israelites to get right with Him, there, too.

12:5   Yahweh, the Almighty God of armies, even Yahweh, spoke to all the Israelites when He spoke to Jacob at Bethel. He did this in that He intended the Israelites to learn from the experience of the patriarch.

12:6   The lesson was that, like Jacob, the Israelites should return to their covenant God. They should practice loyal love and justice in dealing with one another, rather than being like the old Jacob. And they should commit to waiting in faith for God to act for them, rather than seizing control of the situation, as Jacob so often had done.

The pride of Israel that needed humbling 12:7-11

12:7-8   A merchant who used dishonest scales loved to oppress his customers. Similarly, Israel's oppression of others was traceable to pride in her riches. Much of Israel's dealings with the nations involved trading contaminated by deceit. The Israelites considered their wealth a blessing from God that they interpreted as due to their cleverness and His approval of their lifestyle. Instead, it was due to His grace, and in spite of their sins.

> "The word *Canaanite* also means 'merchant.' Here the word may allude to Israel's dishonest economic activities."[123]

12:9   Yahweh reminded His people that He had been their God since before the Exodus. He was able to make them revert to a humble wilderness lifestyle again, which their yearly Feast of Booths (Tabernacles) reminded them about (cf. Lev. 23:33-43). This is clearly an allusion to the coming captivity of Israel.

12:10   The Lord also reminded them that He had spoken to them through prophets many times (cf. 9:7; 11:2). He had given the prophets visions, and they had taught their lessons to the Israelites. Nevertheless, in spite of so many exhortations to return to the Lord, the people had not responded.

12:11   What was going on in Gilead was an example of Israel's depravity (cf. 6:8-9). In Gilgal, too, worthless Israelites were sacrificing bulls, expensive offerings, on numerous altars that they had built there. The use of Gilead, on the west side of the Jordan, and Gilgal, on the east side, did not just represent the whole nation. It also provided a rhetorical parallelism since the two names sound similar (assonance). The number of the pagan altars at Gilgal was as great as the piles of stones that the farmers gathered beside their furrows. These altars would become simply piles of stones. There is a play on the name "Gilgal," which sounds like the Hebrew word *gallim*, meaning "pile of stones."

The land that Israel occupied had very stony ground, and when farmers plowed they often hit stones that they had to remove from the fields. Evidently they would pile these stones beside their furrows.

Another lesson from Israel's history 12:12-14

12:12   The Lord reminded the Israelites again of their humble origins. Jacob was a refugee who migrated to the land of Aram. There he had to work to pay for a wife, and he did so by tending sheep, a very humble occupation (cf. Deut. 26:5).

12:13   Later the Lord brought the Israelites out of Egypt and kept them alive during their wilderness wanderings by using a prophet—Moses (cf. Deut. 18:18). The Israelites, as well as Jacob, had experienced hardship while in a foreign land. By implication they should not, therefore, have despised the prophets that Yahweh had sent them since Moses (cf. v.10). Furthermore, they should remember that they could return to these conditions if they were not careful.

12:14   In spite of these mercies, the Israelites had provoked the Lord to bitter anger with their idolatry (cf. Deut. 4:25; 9:18; 31:29; 32:16, 21; Judg. 2:12; 1 Kings 14:9, 15). Consequently, He would not remove the guilt of their sins by forgiving them, but would pay them back with punishment and shame. This was the sentence of their divine Judge.

---

[123]Ibid.

2. Israel's impending doom ch. 13

Again Hosea charged Israel with covenant unfaithfulness that called for destruction. Here he graphically portrayed the impending doom of the nation.

> "In this passage Hosea brings to a close via climactic crescendo the predictions and warnings that comprise the bulk of the book."[124]

Israel's sin against privilege 13:1-3

13:1   When members of the tribe of Ephraim spoke, the other Israelites trembled because they looked to Ephraim for leadership (cf. Judg. 8:1-3; 12:1-6). Jacob had prophesied that Ephraim would lead (Gen. 48:13-20), and the first king of the Northern Kingdom, Jeroboam I, had come from the tribe of Ephraim (1 Kings 11:26; 12:25). The Ephraimites "exalted" (strengthened) themselves in the north as well. Yet they were also the leaders in Baal worship. Therefore they were as good as dead since God would judge idolaters.

13:2   The Ephraimites, and the other Israelites, had continued to sin more and more by making molten images and carved idols of silver (cf. Exod. 20:4-5; 34:17; Deut. 5:8-9). They took great pains to make beautiful idols by employing skilled craftsmen for their construction. They also required that those who made sacrifices to them profess their devotion and homage by kissing the images. The NIV translation "they offer human sacrifice" is literally "sacrificers of men kiss calves." Human sacrifice is probably not in view here. There is no other indication that the Israelites practiced human sacrifice at Bethel or Dan at this time. (They evidently *did* practice human sacrifice later, during the reign of Israel's last king, Hoshea [cf. 2 Kings 17:16-17].) The idea is that those among the people (men) who sacrificed to idols kissed the images. How doubly ironical it was that they should worship things that they had created and that they should kiss images of animals!

13:3   Because they did this, the Ephraimites would soon vanish from their land. They would disappear like fog or dew in the morning, and like chaff from a threshing floor or smoke from a chimney, that the wind blew away. Judgment would come swiftly and surely.

The perversity of Israel's idolatry 13:4-8

13:4   Yahweh had been Israel's God since the Israelites had lived in Egypt. Israel first became a nation in Egypt. Before that, the Israelites were just a large family (Gen. 46:3). He had commanded the Israelites not to acknowledge any other gods besides Himself, because He was the only God who could save them (cf. Deut. 11:28; 32:17; Jer. 9:2; 31:34). For them to become idolaters would only be frustrating and futile. To abandon the only Savior is to doom oneself to no salvation.

13:5   The Lord also was the One who cared for the Israelites in the wilderness, and who kept them alive in that barren wasteland. His provisions of manna and water are only two examples.

13:6   When they entered the Promised Land and began to enjoy rich pastures, they soon became self-satisfied, proud, and forgot their God. Prosperity is often a greater temptation to depart from conscious dependence on God than adversity is, and Israel fell into that trap.

13:7-8   In view of Israel's behavior, the Lord promised to become as an enemy of His people, like a lion or leopard that laid in wait to attack a sheep grazing in rich pasture (v. 6). He would confront them as a mother bear crazed by the loss of her cubs (cf. 2 Sam. 17:8; Prov. 17:12). He would tear them open like a bear and consume them like a lioness. The lion, leopard, and bear were all wild animals native to Canaan that were notorious for their relentless manner of killing prey.

Israel's misplaced confidence 13:9-11

13:9   By turning against the Lord who only desired to help them (cf. v. 4), the Israelites had done something that would result in their own destruction. How ironic it was that Israel's helper would become her destroyer!

13:10   The people had formerly asked their leaders to give them a king like all the other nations. They hoped that their king and his princes would provide deliverance for them. God had given them kings: first Saul (1 Sam. 8:4-9; 12:12), and more recently the kings of Israel that were not of David's line but were kings of the people's own choosing (1 Kings 12:16-20). Yet all these kings had proved ineffective in saving the Israelites. Only Yahweh was their Savior (v. 4).

---

[124]Stuart, p. 200.

13:11	God conceded to His people's request for a king (Saul and or Jeroboam I), but it made Him angry because it expressed their reluctance to trust and obey Him. When these kings proved ineffective, since they did not trust in Yahweh, the Lord removed them, which also made Him angry. King Hoshea was the last of the Northern Kingdom kings. The Lord had removed the Ephraimite kings because they followed the pattern of Saul, and He would continue to do so until none were left. The sins and bad times, that all these Northern Kingdom kings' reigns brought on Israel, were unnecessary and displeasing to the Lord—who wanted His people to enjoy peace and prosperity.

Israel's stubbornness and its consequences 13:12-14

13:12	God would not forget Israel's sins. Its iniquities were rolled up (Heb. *sarar*) in a bundle, like a scroll, and stored up (Heb. *sapan*) like a treasure. They stood as hard evidence that condemned the nation.
13:13	Israel was like a baby that refused to come out of its mother's womb, in the sense that it refused to leave its comfortable sin. Despite the mother's (God's) strenuous efforts to bring the child into freedom, Israel refused to repent. This was evidence that Israel was a foolish child. She would sooner die, rather than leave her sins, apparently feeling that the proper time for repenting was not yet.
13:14	The Lord asked, rhetorically, if He would buy the Israelites back out of Death's hand. Would He pay a price for their redemption? No, compassion would be hidden from His sight; He would have no pity on them. He appealed for Death (like a thornbush) to torment the Israelites, like thorns tearing their flesh. He called on the Grave (as a hornet) to sting them fatally.

Later in history, God did provide a ransom for His people from the power of the grave, and He redeemed them from death. He did this when Jesus Christ died on the cross and rose again. God's future redemptive work for His people meant that death would not be the end for Israel, even though judgment in the near future was inevitable.

The Apostle Paul quoted the famous couplet in this verse in 1 Corinthians 15:55, and applied it to the resulting effect of Christ's redemption on all of God's people. Death and the grave are not the final judgment and home of the believer, because God *did* provide a ransom and redeemed His people. God has a glorious future beyond His punishment for sin—for His own people—both for national Israel and for Christians. Paul's use of this passage does not support the view that the church fulfills God's promises concerning Israel. Here in Hosea, the promise is that Israel would indeed suffer death and the grave, not that she would escape it. Paul turned the passage around and showed that Jesus Christ's resurrection overcame the judgment and death that are inevitable for sinners.[125]

Covenant unfaithfulness punished 13:15-16

13:15	With the removal of God's compassion (v. 14), Israel's prosperity would end. Hosea described that change as a hot eastern desert wind sweeping over Israel and drying up all its water sources. Israel had flourished among its neighbors, as a plant does when it grows in shallow water among reeds. Like a sirocco, Assyria would sweep over Israel from the east and cause the nation of Israel to wither. The Assyrians would plunder everything valuable in the land.
13:16	This verse begins chapter 14 in the Hebrew Bible, but its connection is clearly with the preceding verse rather than with those that follow. Yahweh would hold Samaria, a metonymy for Israel, guilty for rebelling against Him: her *covenant lord* and God (cf. 7:13; 8:1). Israel's soldiers would die in battle (cf. Lev. 26:25), her children would suffer unmerciful executions (cf. Deut. 28:52-57; 32:25), and the Assyrians would even cut open her pregnant women with their swords (cf. 2 Kings 15:16; Amos 1:13). This gruesome form of execution killed both the mother and the unborn child, making it impossible for the coming generation to rise up eventually and rebel against the conqueror. These were curses that the Lord warned would follow rebellion against the terms of His covenant (cf. Lev. 26:25; Deut. 28:21; 32:24-25; Amos 4:10).

B. RESTORATION IN SPITE OF UNFAITHFULNESS 14:1-8

As usual in the major sections of Hosea, promises of restoration follow announcements of judgment. This final section of restoration promises begins with an appeal for repentance and closes with the prospect of full and complete restoration.

> "In beauty of expression these final words of Hosea rank with the memorable chapters of the OT. Like the rainbow after a storm, they promise Israel's final restoration. Here is the full flowering of God's unfailing love for his faithless people, the triumph of his grace, the assurance of his healing—all described in imagery that reveals the loving heart of God."[126]

---

[125]See Chisholm, *Handbook on . . .*, p. 366.
[126]Wood, "Hosea," p. 223.

"In many ways the last chapter of Hosea is the most beautiful in the entire prophecy and forms a fitting close to the series of prophetic discourses."[127]

1. An appeal for repentance 14:1-3

"As we move toward the conclusion of Hosea's prophecy, the thundering voice of the prophet becomes a tender whisper as he pleads lovingly with Israel."[128]

14:1   Hosea appealed to Israel to return to Yahweh her God because her iniquities had caused her to stumble in her history as a nation. We know from Israel's history that Hosea's generation of Israelites did not repent, but nevertheless, God's invitation was open and genuine.

14:2   The prophet counseled the people to return to the Lord with "words" (not animal sacrifices) that expressed their repentance. They should acknowledge their sins and ask Him to remove their iniquity (cf. 1 John 1:9). They should also ask Him to receive them graciously, with a view to their praising Him with their "lips" (not offerings).

14:3   They should renounce confidence in "Assyria" (a synecdoche for political alliances) and war "horses" (military might) for their security and victory. They should also promise not to call their hand-made idols their gods (heterodox worship). And they should acknowledge that only from Him could vulnerable, dependent orphans such as themselves find mercy. They were orphans in that they had no other means of deliverance and support.

"If their hearts were broken, their relationship to God would be mended."[129]

2. A promise of restoration 14:4-8

14:4   When Israel repented, the Lord promised to heal the apostasy of the Israelites that had become a fatal sickness for them (cf. 6:1). He also promised to bestow His love on them generously, because then He would no longer be angry with them.

"When a person collapses with sickness, it's usually the result of a process that's been working in the body for weeks or months. First an infection gets into the system and begins to grow. The person experiences weariness and loss of appetite, then weakness, and then the collapse occurs. When sin gets into the inner person and isn't dealt with, it acts like an insidious infection: it grows quietly; it brings loss of spiritual appetite; it creates weariness and weakness; then comes the collapse."[130]

14:5   The Lord would descend on Israel with blessing "like the dew." Instead of being dry and withered (13:15), Israel would "blossom like the" prolific spring "lily" (or crocus, cf. Song of Sol. 2:2). The Israelites would become as "beautiful" as an "olive tree" (v. 6), that is not only attractive but the source of beneficial products (cf. Ps. 52:8; Jer. 11:16). Israel would "take root" and grow strong, like a cedar of "Lebanon" (cf. Song of Sol. 4:11).

14:6   Israel would become productive and attractive to the eye and nose, namely: totally appealing. "Shoots" imply *stability*, "beauty" suggests *visibility*, and "fragrance" connotes *desirability*.

14:7   Other nations would also flourish as they benefited from Israel's good influence. The Israelites would again grow grain, a sign of covenant blessing (cf. 2:21-23; Deut. 28:4, 8, 11; 30:9; Amos 9:13-15). The nation would be like a fruitful vine that produced the best wine, no longer like a scraggly vine in the wilderness (10:1).

14:8   Ephraim would repudiate her dealings with idols (cf. 2:8; 4:17; 8:4-6), and the Lord would respond with a commitment to care for her. Formerly He lay in wait (Heb. *shur*) for Israel like a leopard ready to pounce on her in judgment (13:7), but now He would care (Heb. *shur*) for her. He would be the source of her fruit, like a cypress or pine tree that bears cones.

"Hosea closes his book with the heartening word of forgiveness. When Israel responds to the LORD's loving plea to return to Him (vv. 1-3), then will follow the gracious healing of their backsliding, the free bestowal of His love, the turning away of His anger, the future blessing of their restoration, and their final repudiation of idolatry (vv. 4-8)."[131]

---

[127] Feinberg, p. 111.
[128] McComiskey, p. 229.
[129] Ibid., p. 237.
[130] Wiersbe, pp. 329-30.
[131] *The New Scofield . . .*, p. 927.

The Israelites have not yet met these conditions for restoration, and restoration has not yet come to them. Fulfillment awaits the return of Christ to the earth and His millennial reign that will follow. Then Israel will be blessed and will become a source of blessing for all the other nations of the world, as the prophet predicted.

VII. CONCLUSION 14:9

Hosea added a conclusion to his prophecies that is a word of wisdom for the discerning reader. One should learn three things from this book. First, the Lord's "ways" (covenant commands) are the "right" (correct and therefore, best) ways. Second, righteous people will choose to walk in the Lord's ways and to keep His covenant commands because that results in blessing. Third, transgressors (rebels) will stumble over His ways and bring destruction on themselves for their disobedience. Their downfall results from their failure to obey His commands, to walk in His ways.

This is an unusual closing verse in a Bible book, in that it applies the teaching of the whole Book of Hosea to the reader.

Bibliography

Andersen, Francis I., and David Noel Freedman. *Hosea: A New Translation, Introduction and Commentary*. Anchor Bible commentary series. Garden City, N.Y.: Doubleday & Co., 1980.

Barker, Harold P. *Christ in the Minor Prophets.* New York: Loizeaux Brothers, n.d.

Bright, John. *A History of Israel.* Philadelphia: Westminster Press, 1959.

Bruce, Frederick F. *The Letter of Paul to the Romans: An Introduction and Commentary*. Tyndale New Testament Commentary series. Revised ed. Leicester, England: InterVarsity Press, and Grand Rapids: Wm. B. Eerdmans Publishing Co., 1985.

Chisholm, Robert B., Jr. *Handbook on the Prophets.* Grand Rapids: Baker Book House, 2002.

_____. "Hosea." In *The Bible Knowledge Commentary: Old Testament*, pp. 1377-1407. Edited by John F. Walvoord and Roy B. Zuck. Wheaton: Scripture Press Publications, Victor Books, 1985.

_____. "A Theology of the Minor Prophets." In *A Biblical Theology of the Old Testament*, pp. 397-433. Edited by Roy B. Zuck. Chicago: Moody Press, 1991.

Dyer, Charles H., and Eugene H. Merrill. *The Old Testament Explorer.* Nashville: Word Publishing, 2001. Reissued as *Nelson's Old Testament Survey*. Nashville: Thomas Nelson Publishers, 2001.

Ellison, H. L. *The Prophets of Israel: From Ahijah to Hosea.* Exeter, Eng.: Paternoster Press, 1969; American ed., Grand Rapids: Wm. B. Eerdmans Publishing Co., 1974.

Feinberg, Charles Lee. *Hosea.* The Major Messages of the Minor Prophets series. New York: American Board of Missions to the Jews, N.d.

Freeman, Hobart E. *An Introduction to the Old Testament Prophets.* Chicago: Moody Press, 1968.

Harper, William Rainey. *A Critical and Exegetical Commentery on Amos and Hosea.* International Critical Commentaries series. Edinburgh: T. & T. Clark, 1905.

Harrison, R. K. *Introduction to the Old Testament.* Grand Rapids: Wm. B. Eerdmans Publishing Co., 1969.

Hillers, D. *Treaty Curses and the Old Testament Prophets.* Biblica et orientalia 16. Rome: Pontifical Biblical Institute, 1964.

Josephus, Flavius. *The Works of Flavius Josephus.* Translated by William Whiston. London: T. Nelson and Sons, 1866; reprint ed. Peabody, Mass.: Hendrickson Publishers, 1988.

Kaiser, Walter C., Jr. *Toward an Old Testament Theology.* Grand Rapids: Zondervan Publishing House, 1978.

Keil, Carl Friedrich. *The Twelve Minor Prophets.* 2 vols. Translated by James Martin. Biblical Commentary on the Old Testament. Reprint ed. Grand Rapids: Wm. B. Eerdmans Publishing Co., 1949.

Kidner, Derek. *Love to the Loveless: The Message of Hosea.* The Bible Speaks Today series. Downers Grove, Ill.: InterVarsity Press, 1981.

Longman, Tremper, III and Raymond B. Dillard. *An Introduction to the Old Testament.* 2nd ed. Grand Rapids: Zondervan, 2006.

Mays, James Luther. *Hosea: A Commentary.* The Old Testament Library series. Philadelphia: Westminster Press, 1969.

McComiskey, Thomas Edward. "Hosea." In *The Minor Prophets: An Exegetical and Expositional Commentary*, 1:1-237. 3 vols. Edited by Thomas Edward McComiskey. Grand Rapids: Baker Books, 1992, 1993, and 1998.

Morgan, G. Campbell. *Living Messages of the Books of the Bible.* 2 vols. New York: Fleming H. Revell Co., 1912.

The Nelson Study Bible. *Edited* by Earl D. Radmacher. Nashville: Thomas Nelson Publishers, 1997.

The New Bible Dictionary, 1962 ed. S.v. "Beth-aven," by R. J. Way.

The New Scofield Reference Bible. Edited by Frank E. Gaebelein, William Culbertson, et al. New York: Oxford University Press, 1967.

Patterson, Richard D. "Portraits from a Prophet's Portfolio: Hosea 4." *Bibliotheca Sacra* 165:659 (July-September 2008):294-308.

Pritchard, James B., ed. *Ancient Near Eastern Texts Relating to the Old Testament*. 3rd ed. Princeton, N.J.: Princeton University Press, 1969.

Silva, Charles H. "Literary Features in the Book of Hosea." *Bibliotheca Sacra* 164:653 (January-March 2007):34-48.

_____. "The Literary Structure of Hosea 1—3." *Bibliotheca Sacra* 164:654 (April-June 2007):181-97.

_____. "The Literary Structure of Hosea 4—8." *Bibliotheca Sacra* 164:655 (July-September 2007):291-306.

_____. "The Literary Structure of Hosea 9—14." *Bibliotheca Sacra* 164:656 (October-December 2007):435-53.

Stuart, Douglas. *Hosea-Jonah*. Word Biblical Commentary series. Waco: Word Books, 1987.

Waltke, Bruce K., with Charles Yu. *An Old Testament Theology: an exegetical, canonical, and thematic approach*. Grand Rapids: Zondervan, 2007.

Wiersbe, Warren W. "Hosea." In *The Bible Exposition Commentary/Prophets*, pp. 315-32. Colorado Springs, Colo.: Cook Communications Ministries; and Eastbourne, England: Kingsway Communications Ltd., 2002.

Wolff, Hans Walter. *Hosea*. Translated by Gary Stansell. Philadelphia: Fortress Press, 1974.

Wood, Leon J. "Hosea." In *Daniel-Minor Prophets*. Vol. 7 of *The Expositor's Bible Commentary*. 12 vols. Edited by Frank E. Gaebelein and Richard P. Polcyn. Grand Rapids: Zondervan Publishing House, 1985.

_____. *The Prophets of Israel*. Grand Rapids: Baker Book House, 1979.

Young, Edward J. *An Introduction to the Old Testament*. Revised ed. Grand Rapids: Wm. B. Eerdmans Publishing Co., 1960.

Constable's Notes
on Joel

Introduction

Title

The title of this book is the name of its writer, as is probably true of all the prophetical books of the Old Testament.

We know little about Joel, whose name means "Yahweh is God." He was the son of Pethuel, who does not appear to have been an especially famous person. Eleven other individuals in the Old Testament bore the name Joel (1 Sam. 8:2; 1 Chron. 4:35; 5:4; 7:3; 11:38; 15:7; 26:22; 27:20; 2 Chron. 29:12; Ezra 10:43; Neh. 11:9).

Unity

All the extant Hebrew manuscripts and the ancient versions of Joel attest to the unity of the book. Critics who deny its unity and argue for two different writers do so on the basis of supposed literary and conceptual differences, usually between the first two chapters and the third. Specifically, they assign the historical passages to Joel and the apocalyptic ones to another writer. However, there is a consistent theme that ties the whole book together, which is one reason most conservative interpreters believe that Joel wrote all three chapters.

Date

The date of Joel is its largest introductory problem, as is the case with Obadiah.[1] There are four most likely possibilities. First, some scholars advocate *an early pre-exilic date* during the reign of King Jehoshaphat (872-848 B.C.), or possibly his grandson, King Joash (835-796 B.C.). Arguments in favor of this period include the position of Joel in the Hebrew canon; it appears among other prophetic writings of this period. However, the order of the pre-exilic Minor Prophets is not strictly chronological, in both the Hebrew and the English versions. Also, the enemies of Israel that Joel named (Tyre, Sidon, Philistia [cf. 2 Chron. 21:16-17], Egypt [cf. 1 Kings 14:25-26], and Edom [cf. 2 Kings 8:20-22]; 3:2-7, 19) were enemies of Israel during this time. The prominence Joel gave to Judah's priests and elders rather than to her king—Joash was a boy king under the influence of Jehoiada, the high priest, early in his reign—is a further argument for this view. However, these conclusions are open to other interpretations.[2]

Second, some authorities believe *a mid-pre-exilic date* of composition, probably during the reign of Joash's grandson, King Uzziah (792-740 B.C.), fits the evidence best. Supporters of this view also claim the first two arguments cited in favor of the early pre-exilic view above. They argue, in addition, that the absence of references to Assyria, Babylonia, and Persia make a later date, when these nations were the major ancient Near Eastern superpowers, unlikely. Joel's reference to Greece in 3:6 may fit this period since the Ionian Greeks were at this time expanding their commercial influence in Asia Minor. Joel's reference to the Sabeans in 3:8 is appropriate for this period as well. Internal references and linguistic characteristics may also reflect Uzziah's times, and are similar to the writings of the other eighth-century prophets (i.e., Amos, Hosea, Micah, and Isaiah). However, again, much of the same evidence can fit other periods of Judah's history.[3]

Third, some interpreters opt for *a late pre-exilic date*. Statements in Joel could fit this period, and some of his statements are similar to those of Jeremiah and Ezekiel, and may reflect conditions before the destruction of Jerusalem, perhaps between 597 and 587 B.C. If true, Joel would have been a contemporary of Jeremiah, Habakkuk, and Zephaniah. Yet Joel 2:18-19 seems to imply that God had been merciful to Joel's generation, suggesting that the people had repented, but there is no record of this happening during this period.[4] A variation of this view is that Joel wrote either just before the Assyrian invasion of 701 B.C. or just before one of the Babylonian invasions: the 598 B.C. invasion, or the 588 B.C. invasion.[5]

The fourth view is that Joel wrote at *a postexilic date*, perhaps 515-500 B.C., or even as late as sometime in the 400s B.C. Interpreters who see Joel 3:1-2 and 17 as references to the destruction of Jerusalem and the Babylonian Captivity take the references to the temple in 1:9, 13 and 2:17

---

[1]See Tremper Longman III and Raymond B. Dillard, *An Introduction to the Old Testament*, pp. 411-14.
[2]Advocates of this view include Hobart E. Freeman, *An Introduction to the Old Testament Prophets*, p. 148; Gleason A. Archer Jr., *A Survey of Old Testament Introduction*, p. 305; E. J. Young, *An Introduction to the Old Testament*, pp. 271-72; C. F. Keil, *The Twelve Minor Prophets*, 1:169-70; Walter C. Kaiser Jr., *Toward an Old Testament Theology*, p. 188; Charles H. Dyer, *The Old Testament Explorer*, p. 737; Warren W. Wiersbe, "Joel," in *The Bible Exposition Commentary/Prophets*, p. 333; and Leon J. Wood, *The Prophets of Israel*, p. 268.
[3]Advocates include Richard D. Patterson, "Joel," in *Daniel-Malachi*, vol. 7 of *The Expositor's Bible Commentary*, pp. 231-33.
[4]Advocates include Wilhelm Rudolph, *Joel-Amos-Obadja-Jona*, pp. 14-15; and Arvid S. Kapelrud, *Joel Studies*, pp. 154-58.
[5]Douglas Stuart, *Hosea-Jonah*, pp. 224-26.

as applying to the second temple (completed in 515 B.C.). Yet all these texts could apply to earlier periods.[6] Generally, scholars who view apocalyptic writing as a late development in Judaism tend to date Joel quite late.

As should be obvious from this brief review, the dating of the book rests on interpretations of various verses that are not clear. No other Old Testament book mentions Joel. Consequently, dating the book amounts to guesswork, though some writers were quite dogmatic about their convictions. I prefer an early or mid-pre-exilic date, mainly because of Joel's position in the Hebrew canon among other writers of this period. I think he was probably one of the earliest writing prophets. John Calvin's word of caution bears repeating:

> ". . . as there is no certainty, it is better to leave the time in which [Joel] taught undecided; and, as we shall see, this is of no great importance."[7]

Place of Composition and Audience

Joel's frequent references to Judah and Jerusalem suggest that he lived and ministered in the Southern Kingdom (cf. 1:9, 13-14, 16; 2:1, 14-15, 17, 23, 32; 3:1-8, 12, 14, 17-21).

> "Joel was a man of vitality and spiritual maturity. A keen discerner of the times, he delivered God's message to the people of Judah in a vivid and impassioned style, with a precision and originality of thought that served as a veritable quarry out of which many subsequent prophetic building stones were to be hewn."[8]

Purpose

Joel wrote to warn his audience about a coming day in which God would judge His people. He compared this devastating judgment to a terrible locust invasion that had fairly recently swept through the land. What he said about this coming judgment has only seen partial fulfillment; some of it still lies in the eschatological future (i.e., the eschaton). God would send blessing as well as judgment, however, and this too has only come partially on the Israelites so far. The prophet warned his hearers that unless they repented of their empty formalism in worship and turned back to Yahweh wholeheartedly, devastating judgment would overtake them. If they repented, God would pardon them and restore His blessings to them abundantly.

Theology

The sovereignty of God and the inevitability of divine punishment for covenant unfaithfulness are dominant themes in Joel.

> "Joel's depiction of the absolute authority of Yahweh over all the peoples of the earth is among the strongest in the Old Testament."[9]

So is Yahweh's compassionate forgiveness in response to repentance. "The day of the Lord," for both judgment and blessing aspects, is also a prominent theme.[10] Thus the administration of God is a strong motif: how God exercises His sovereignty when His people sin. Another important theological contribution of Joel is his prediction of God pouring out the Holy Spirit in the last days (2:28-32).

> "Like all the canonical prophets, Joel depended on the Mosaic covenant of the Pentateuch for the basic points of his message: the covenant's curses must come as a result of national disobedience; but after a period of chastisement, God will restore his people and bless them in ways they had not yet experienced."[11]

Style and Text

Joel's literary style is rich, vivid, classical, clear, and beautiful. The Hebrew text of Joel presents no serious interpretive problems and is well preserved.

---

[6]Advocates include Robert B. Chisholm Jr., "Joel," in *The Bible Knowledge Commentary: Old Testament*, p. 1410; idem, "A Theology of the Minor Prophets," in *A Biblical Theology of the Old Testament*, p. 387; idem, *Handbook on the Prophets*, p. 368; Raymond B. Dillard, "Joel," in *The Minor Prophets*, pp. 240-42 (though see pp. 301-2); David A. Hubbard, *Joel and Amos*, p. 27; Thomas J. Finley, *Joel, Amos, Obadiah*, p. 8; and John Bright, *A History of Israel*, p. 417.
[7]John Calvin, *Joel, Amos, Obadiah*, 2:xv.
[8]Patterson, p. 230.
[9]Stuart, p. 229.
[10]See the four-part series of articles on "The Day of the Lord" by Craig A. Blaising in *Bibliotheca Sacra* beginning with 169:673 (January-March 2012).
[11]Stuart, p. 228.

Outline

I. Introduction 1:1
II. A past day of the Lord: a locust invasion 1:2-20
    A. An initial appeal 1:2-4
    B. A call to mourn 1:5-13
    C. A call to repent 1:14
    D. The significance of the plague 1:15-20
III. A near future day of the Lord: a human invasion 2:1-27
    A. The invading army 2:1-11
        1. The nearness of the army 2:1-2
        2. The destructive power of the army 2:3-5
        3. The relentlessness of the army 2:6-9
        4. The invincibility of the army 2:10-11
    B. A call to repentance 2:12-17
        1. An appeal for private repentance 2:12-14
        2. An appeal for public repentance 2:15-17
    C. The possibility of forgiveness and restoration 2:18-27
        1. The Lord's gracious response 2:18
        2. The Lord's promise of blessing 2:19-27
IV. A far future day of the Lord: another human invasion and deliverance 2:28—3:21
    A. Israel's spiritual renewal and deliverance 2:28-32
    B. God's judgment on Israel's enemy nations 3:1-17
        1. The announcement of judgment 3:1-8
        2. The description of judgment 3:9-17
    C. Israel's ultimate restoration 3:18-21

Message

The Book of Joel contains a threefold vision. The first part of Joel's vision concerned a locust plague that had recently swept over the Promised Land. Joel prophesied about this plague because of the desolation that it had produced. The second part of his vision concerned a coming invasion from a foreign army in the fairly near future. He used the recent locust plague to illustrate the devastating effect of the coming military invasion. The third part of his vision concerned another coming invasion, in the far distant future, that would also be like the recent locust invasion, only worse.

Joel described each of these devastations as "the day of the Lord." The term itself refers to a time when God had been or would be controlling events for Israel in an unusually direct way. It was "His day" in the sense that, at those times, Yahweh was and would be especially prominent in what happened. Thus this term referred to a past "day," a near future "day," and a far distant "day," from the prophet's perspective. "The day of the Lord" was the burden of his prophecy. God revealed His plans simply at first. God does not overload us with too much information all at once. In later prophetical books, we will get more detail.

The Book of Joel has two preeminent timeless values. It illustrates the basic *principles* by which Yahweh governs, and it reveals the basic *plan* of Yahweh through the ages. It is important for us to grasp these basic principles and this basic plan, because the other prophets reveal more about them.

First, Joel illustrates the principles by which Yahweh governs. This book does not reveal them in the sense of explaining them fully. Isaiah explains them more fully. Joel illustrates these principles briefly.

Joel viewed Yahweh as enthroned in heaven, controlling affairs on earth. Joel saw Him presiding patiently over all the situations through which His people pass. He saw Him pressing into His service all the processes of nature and human activity. He also saw Him achieving ultimate victory in "His day": "the day of the Lord." He had accomplished victory by judging His people recently with a locust invasion. He would accomplish victory by disciplining His people with an invasion from a foreign foe in the near future. And He would accomplish victory by restoring His people through a fresh outpouring of His Spirit in the distant future. So one major lesson of this book is that God is enthroned in heaven, ruling over the affairs of humanity.

A second illustration of the principles by which Yahweh governs is Joel's emphasis on grace. *Grace* is at the heart of God's government. Grace is the inspiration of His government. We see this in God's appeal to the Israelites through Joel to repent, to "rend your hearts rather than your garments" (2:13a). The locust plague was a wake-up call to repent. The Israelites' repentance would affect the imminent invasion they faced. God promised judgment, but He offered mercy, if the people would repent (2:13b-14). Grace is also evident in the promise of a far-distant future outpouring of God's Spirit—in spite of the unfaithfulness of His people. God rules with grace. He is gracious to humanity in the way He governs people.

When the locust invasion swept through the land, the people bemoaned the tragedy. The locusts had so stripped the grapevines that even the drunkards could not find grapes to make wine. The people had so little grain that they could not bring offerings to the temple. They could hardly make bread to eat. They viewed the devastation as a natural disaster. Joel reminded them that the locust invasion had come by the will and hand of God. The people had forgotten God, but God wanted to get their attention, so He sent the plague. He had allowed this to happen so the people would think of Him, and return to Him. When the invasion happened, it was His "day." It was God who had done this (1:1-14).

Joel went on to remind the people that, because they had forgotten about Him, He was going to bring a worse devastation on them that would make the recent locust plague seem tame by comparison. If they turned back to Him, they could avoid this worse fate, because God would be gracious to them (2:12-13). The coming invasion, by humans rather than by locusts, would also be a day in which the Lord acted prominently. Joel even said that the Lord would lead this army of invaders (2:11). This was probably fulfilled in the Assyrian invasion of Jerusalem in 701 B.C.

Yet in spite of future devastating judgment, God would act again, dramatically and definitely, for His people (3:28-32). He would bring restoration and blessing to them, even after they had suffered His chastening discipline. He would just as surely and personally do this for them as He would punish them. This, too, would be one of His "days." And it would be the ultimate illustration of His grace.

A second great timeless value of this book is its revelation of God's plan for His people Israel's future.

First, there would be coming judgment that the people could affect by their repentance (2:14). Had the Israelites repented, the Assyrian and Babylonian Captivities would not have overtaken them. When the Assyrians attacked Judah, the people of Judah did repent, and the Lord delivered them. But when the Babylonians attacked Judah 115 years later, the Judeans failed to repent, and suffered defeat and deportation. Joel could honestly say for God, "Return to Me with all your heart" (2:12). When the people failed to repent, judgment befell them.

Second, there would be even worse judgment in the distant future because the prophet foresaw that the people would continue to apostatize (3:1-17). This refers to the judgments on Israel during the Tribulation. Yet after that, the Lord promised to restore and bless His people (2:18-32). These are millennial blessings. It is in this context of millennial blessings that the promise of the outpouring of the Holy Spirit appears (3:28-29). That outpouring on Israel is still future from our position in history.

But what about what Peter said on the day of Pentecost? He said that the outpouring of the Holy Spirit then was what Joel prophesied (Acts 2:17-18). This has led many Bible students to conclude that God has fulfilled His promises to Israel in the church. This is the viewpoint of amillennial and postmillennial interpreters who believe that God has no special future plans for Israel. Others see a double or partial fulfillment on the day of Pentecost with the church, and a future fulfillment with Israel in the Millennium. This is the viewpoint of many premillennialists. A third view is that fulfillment will only be in the Millennium, and that what Peter meant was that what happened on the day of Pentecost was similar to or like what Joel prophesied.

I favor the second interpretation, as do many other premillennialists. Why? First, Peter did not say that what was happening fulfilled Joel's prophecy completely. What he said could just as easily mean that what happened then was in harmony with, or analogous to, what Joel had predicted would happen in the Millennium. The two events were similar but not identical. In the same way, we take Jesus' statement, "This is My body," metaphorically. There are hundreds, if not thousands, of metaphors in the Bible. The New Testament writers frequently spoke of fulfillment in an analogical sense (e.g., Matt. 2:15; Hos. 11:1). Second, it should also be clear that these events were not the same because in the middle of the section of Joel's prophecy that Peter quoted (3:28-32a), Joel mentioned the sun turning into darkness and the moon to blood (Acts 2:20). That did not happen on the day of Pentecost. It will happen in the Tribulation, just before God pours out His Spirit on all flesh (i.e., believing Israelites) in the Millennium (Matt. 24:29; Rev. 6:12; 8:12). Third, the context of Joel's prediction is Israel in the future, not the church, which began on the day of Pentecost and was not revealed in the Old Testament. Joel predicted the future of Israel, not the future of the church. The context of this prophecy is the Millennium and the judgments immediately preceding it. A cardinal rule of biblical interpretation is to pay careful attention to the people in view in the passage. Here it is the Jews. Fourth, other prophecies refer to an outpouring of God's Spirit on the Jews in the future (e.g., Isa. 32:15; 44:3-4; Ezek. 36:27-28; 37:14; 39:29; Zech. 12:10). This prophecy in Joel is one of them.

Joel gave revelation about important aspects of God's plan for the future. He referred to the upcoming invasion by a foreign power, which took place about 135 years after he prophesied, when Sennacherib invaded Judah in 701 B.C., during King Hezekiah's reign (2 Kings 18—19). Judah avoided being judged then by repenting, but the people apostatized again and fell prey to the Babylonians a century later. Joel also talked about a far-distant future time of judgment on Israel: the Tribulation. For that time he revealed great blessing for all types of Israelites, from the most lowly to the most exalted, including the restoration of Israel during the Millennium. Sin, judgment, and restoration to privilege and power, are what would mark Israel's future.

I would summarize the message of Joel this way. Though God will judge Israel for her apostasy with locust invasion-like devastation in the future, He will also later restore her to blessings greater than she has ever experienced, illustrating that He governs the world graciously. Remember that "Israel" is not synonymous with the modern State of Israel. "Israel," when used of God's chosen people in the Bible, refers to the physical descendants of Jacob: ethnic Jews.

When Joel wrote, it was man's day, not the day of the Lord. The Lord had acted in the locust invasion, and He would act in judgment and in blessing in the future. These would be His days. But when Joel prophesied, the people failed to see God at work because He was not active, as He was and will be on these great days when His presence was and will be manifest. We, too, live in man's day. Most people, including many Christians, conclude that God either does not exist or takes no active role in human affairs, because He is not *obviously* working. At least His working is not apparent to them, because what is happening can be explained as natural or chance phenomena. Thus we live in a day very similar to Joel's day.

Whether people recognize it or not, God is executing His plan for the world. He will break into human experience again in the future. Thus it is imperative that we sound the same warning that Joel did. Judgment is coming, but people can avoid God's judgment by repenting. "Whoever calls on the name of the Lord will be delivered" (2:32; Acts 2:21). Humanity as a whole will fail to repent, just as the apostate Israelites failed to repent (cf. 1 Tim. 4; 2 Tim. 3). In that day, a far worse fate will befall the unrepentant. Yet, God's plans for His people include incredible blessing, even though we fail Him. This evidence of God's grace should motivate God's people to repent and remain faithful to Him now. Thus, God's government of Israel and His plan for Israel serve as a paradigm for His dealings with all humanity.[12]

Exposition

I. INTRODUCTION 1:1

Yahweh's word (message) came to Joel (lit. "Yahweh is God"), the son of Pethuel. ("Elijah" also means "Yahweh is God.") Therefore, what follows demands careful attention and appropriate response. We do not know anything about Joel or Pethuel's personal backgrounds, not even when they lived. This title does not tell where they lived either, though references that follow suggest that Joel lived in Judah. Hosea, Micah, and Zephaniah introduced their prophecies similarly.

II. A PAST DAY OF THE LORD: A LOCUST INVASION 1:2-20

The rest of chapter 1 describes the effects of a severe locust plague that had recently destroyed the agriculture of the land.

A. AN INITIAL APPEAL 1:2-4

1:2-3   Joel called on everyone, from the most respected ruling elders of the land (cf. 1 Sam. 30:26-31; 2 Sam. 19:11-15; 2 Kings 23:1; Ezra 10:8; Prov. 31:23; Jer. 26:17; Lam. 5:12, 14) to the ordinary inhabitants, to pay attention to what he had to say. Nothing like what he was about to describe had happened in their lifetime or in that of their recent ancestors. He urged them to retell the devastating news to their descendants for generations to come. (cf. Deut. 6:1-2).

"Thus, the book of Joel has a didactic function."[13]

1:4   Several waves of locusts had consumed all the agricultural produce of the land. What one wave of these voracious insects had left uneaten, other subsequent waves had destroyed. The devastation of the land had been complete (cf. Amos 4:9). God had threatened locust plagues as punishment if His people proved unfaithful to Him (Deut. 28:38, 42).

Four different words for "locusts" appear in this verse (and in 2:25), but a total of nine occur in the Old Testament. These words have led some interpreters to conclude that four subspecies of locusts are in view, or that locusts in four stages of maturity are meant.[14] It seems better, however, to view the locusts as coming in four waves: gnawing, swarming, creeping, and stripping—as they devoured the vegetation.[15] Four waves of invasion picture a thorough devastation (cf. Jer. 15:3; Ezek.

---

[12] Adapted from G. Campbell Morgan, *Living Messages of the Books of the Bible*, 1:2:181-95.
[13] Finley, p. 19.
[14] E.g., J. A. Thompson, "Joel's Locusts in the Light of Near Eastern Parallels," *Journal of Near Eastern Studies* 14 (1955):52-55; idem, "Translation of the Words for Locust," *Bible Translator* 25 (October 1974):405-11.
[15] See H. W. Wolff, *Joel and Amos*, pp. 27-28; and Keil, 1:181-82. For eyewitness accounts of devastating locust plagues, see S. R. Driver, *The Books of Joel and Amos*, pp. 40, 89-93; G. A. Smith, *The Book of the Twelve Prophets*, 2:391-95; and John D. Whiting, "Jerusalem's Locust Plague," *National Geographic*, December 1915, pp. 511-50. For more detailed discussions of locusts and locust plagues, see Stanley Baron, *The Desert Locust*; L. V. Bennett, "Development of a Locust Plague," *Nature* 256 (1975):486-87; Lev Fishelson, *Fauna Palestina: Insecta*. Vol. 3:

14:21). Though the prophets sometimes used locusts as a figure for horses (e.g., Jer. 51:27), most interpreters have concluded that Joel described a real locust invasion rather than a military invasion by soldiers on horses.[16]

B. A CALL TO MOURN 1:5-13

Joel called on four different entities to mourn the results of the locust invasion: drunkards (vv. 5-7), Jerusalemites (vv. 8-10), farmers (vv. 11-12), and priests (v. 13). In each section, there is a call to mourn followed by reasons to mourn.

1:5-7 Joel urged the drunkards of the land to weep because the locusts had destroyed all the grapevines. There would be no grapes to produce sweet (the most favored) wine for them to drink (cf. Isa. 5:11-12, 22; 22:13; 28:1, 7; 56:12; Hos. 4:11-19; 7:5, 13-14; Amos 2:6-8; 6:6; 9:13; Mic. 2:11; Acts 2:13, 15).

> "*Sweet wine* ('*asis*) was made by drying the grapes in the sun for a short time and then allowing the juice to ferment for five to seven days instead of the more usual nine."[17]

Normally drunkards laugh, with no concern for what goes on around them, but now they should wail. The locusts had invaded the land like a hostile army. The teeth of these invaders were like lions' teeth in that they destroyed their prey. They had stripped the vines and fig trees so thoroughly that their branches stood bare. The vine and the fig tree were symbols of God's blessings on Israel and symbols of Israel itself, so Joel probably also meant that the locusts had left the whole nation bare.

> "All that remained of shady, fruit-laden bowers were skeletonized wrecks of trees with their barkless branches gleaming white."[18]

1:8-10 The next entity called to mourn appears to be Jerusalem. The gender of "Wail" is feminine (singular), and Jerusalem is often compared to a virgin daughter in the Old Testament (e.g., 2 Kings 19:21; Lam. 1:15; cf. Joel 2:1, 15, 23, 32). This "virgin" (Heb. *bethulah*) was to weep in "sackcloth," clothing appropriate for such an occasion, as though she had lost her "bridegroom" in death. The Hebrew word suggests that this virgin was a presently unmarried woman who anticipated union with her betrothed. The reason for Jerusalem's mourning was the locusts' destruction of grain, wine, and oil, blessings from God and the products needed to worship Him in the daily temple burnt offerings (cf. Exod. 29:38-42; Lev. 2; 6:14-18; 9:16-17; 23:18, 37; Num. 15:5; 28:3-8). Grain, wine, and oil represent the three major types of vegetation in Israel: grasses, shrubs, and trees. Used together, as they often are in the Old Testament, they stand for all agricultural products.[19] This appears to be a merism: a figure of speech in which selected prominent parts represent all parts—the whole. The grain offerings required flour and oil (Num. 28:5), and the drink offerings necessitated wine (Exod. 29:40; Num. 28:7).

> "These offerings spoke of the very heart of the believer's daily walk before God: the burnt offering, of a complete dedication of life; the meal offering, of the believer's service that should naturally follow; and the drink offering, of the conscious joy in the heart of the believer whose life is poured out in consecrated service to his God."[20]

The result was that the priests and the whole nation mourned. It was bad enough that the people did not have food and drink for their own enjoyment, but it was worse that they could not worship Yahweh.

1:11-12 Joel next turned from city-dwellers to country folk. He called for the farmers and vine growers, those most directly affected by the locust invasion, to despair—because the fruits of their labors had perished. These fruits included: wheat, barley, grapes, figs, pomegranates, dates, and apples (all the fruits of trees). These Israelites would not be able to rejoice in an abundant harvest, which every farmer and viticulturist anticipated (cf. Ps. 4:7). Not only the symbols of divine blessing, but also the joy of divine blessing, had departed.

1:13 The prophet turned again to the priests (cf. v. 9) and urged them to lament "in sackcloth," because the grain and wine used in their offerings were no longer available. Joel's second call to the priests underlines the tragedy of curtailed worship in Judah's life. Since there were no offerings to bring to the Lord, the nation could not approach Him—as He had directed—at the very

---

Orthoptera, Acridoidea; Ovid R. Sellers, "Stages of Locust in Joel," *American Journal of Semitic Languages and Literatures* 52 (1935-36):81-85; and Z. Waloft and S. M. Green, "Regularities and Duration of Regional Locust Plagues," *Nature* 256 (1975):484-85.
[16]Stuart, pp. 241-42, 243, 245, believed they were figurative of invading Mesopotamian armies.
[17]Hubbard, p. 44. Cf. Driver, p. 225.
[18]Leslie C. Allen, *The Books of Joel, Obadiah, Jonah and Micah*, p. 52.
[19]Dillard, p. 262.
[20]Patterson, p. 240.

time she needed Him most. This closing reference to priests in this section contrasts with the opening reference to drunkards (vv. 5-7), moving from the most ungodly to the most godly (ideally). This merism has the effect of including all the citizens of Judah in Joel's call. Joel's reference to "my God" and "your God" in this verse ties him closely to the priests; their concerns and their relationship to Yahweh were ideally the same.

C. A CALL TO REPENT 1:14

Joel called on the priests not only to mourn (v. 13), but also to assemble all the people at the temple for a "solemn . . . fast." Such fasts indicated national repentance in Israel's history (cf. 1 Sam. 7:6; Neh. 9:1-2; Jer. 36:9; Jon. 3:5). Here, as usual, fasting combined with praying to the Lord. The people would pray to Him for mercy and for renewed blessing, and would demonstrate their sincerity and urgency by going without food while they prayed.

D. THE SIGNIFICANCE OF THE PLAGUE 1:15-20

"This section moves much closer to the form of the descriptive lament found in the lamenting psalms than did the descriptions earlier in the chapter."[21]

We move, then, from summonses to lament, to a lament itself.

1:15   The locust plague had destroyed (Heb. *shadad*) the fields and fruits of Judah, but Joel announced that things would get worse. Another day of destruction (Heb. *shod*) would come from the Lord, the Almighty (Heb. *shadday*). A locust plague was not only an evidence of God's judgment (cf. Deut. 28), but in the past it had been a harbinger of future worse destruction. A locust plague had preceded the plagues of darkness and death in Egypt (cf. Exod. 10—11). Thus, rather than seeing the locust plague as the end of the people's troubles, Joel saw it as a prelude to something worse.

The day of the Lord is a term that appears frequently in the Old Testament, especially in the Prophets. It refers to a day in which the Lord is working obviously, in contrast to other days, the day of man, in which man works without any apparent divine intervention. Specifically, it is a day in which the Lord intervenes to judge His enemies. Gerhard von Rad argued that this term was originally associated with the Israelite concept of holy war,[22] but other scholars have disputed this etymology. Most agree, however, that it had early associations with battles and conquest. Here the day of the Lord is obviously one of destruction, though elsewhere it also refers to a day of blessing. The eschatological day of the Lord that the prophets anticipated includes both judgment (in the Tribulation) and blessing (in the Millennium and beyond). Here Joel spoke of an imminent day of the Lord; it was coming on Judah relatively soon (cf. Isa. 13:6; Ezek. 30:2-3; Amos 5:18-20; Zeph. 1:7-13).

The term "the day of the Lord" occurs prominently here in the prophetic writings, and it is a major theme of prophetic revelation (cf. Amos, Zephaniah). When used *generally*, this term refers to any period of time in which God is dealing with people in dramatic, direct ways. It usually describes God's dealings with Israel, but it is also used of His dealings with other nations: Edom (in Obadiah), and Assyria, and Babylonia (in Isaiah, e.g.). It is always associated with judgment and or blessing. It may refer to the past, the immediate future, or the distant (eschatological) future. The *technical* sense of the term is more common in the Prophets. As a technical term, it refers to Israel's eschatological future that will include both judgment and blessing. The Jews thought the period of judgment would precede Messiah's coming. It did precede His first coming, but it will precede His second coming as well. We know this by comparing what the prophets said with what was fulfilled at Jesus' first coming and what has yet to be fulfilled at His second coming (e.g., in Rev.).

1:16-18   Joel described the effects of the recent locust plague to encourage his hearers to gather for prayer and fasting. He suggested that similar conditions would accompany the day of the Lord that he had just predicted. The people's food supply, and therefore their occasion for rejoicing, had disappeared (cf. Deut. 12:7). Drought had followed the denuding of the land by the locusts. Seeds were not germinating due to the lack of moisture. Barns and silos had become empty and had fallen into disrepair, and domesticated animals were starving. Grazing cattle wandered aimlessly looking for vegetation, and even the sheep, which require less grass, were going hungry.

1:19-20   Joel cried out to Yahweh in prayer in the distress that he shared with his countrymen. Fire had burned the dried pastures and trees, or perhaps severe drought (like a fire) had done so. The brooks were dry, and even the wild animals panted for water. Joel could say they panted for Yahweh because the Lord was the provider of the water these animals sought (cf. Ps. 42:1). By panting for Yahweh, these animals were setting a good example for the people of Judah and Jerusalem.

---

[21]Allen, p. 59.
[22]Gerhard von Rad, "The Origin of the Concept of the Day of the Lord," *Journal of Semitic Studies* 4 (1959):97-108.

III. A NEAR FUTURE DAY OF THE LORD: A HUMAN INVASION 2:1-27

Joel had spoken briefly of a coming day of the Lord in 1:15, but now he said more about it.

The term "the day of the Lord" seems to have arisen from the popular concept, in the ancient Near East, that a really great warrior king could consummate an entire military campaign in one single day.[23] Thus, as the Israelites used the term in relation to Yahweh, it reflected His greatness and pointed to His swift and effective dispatch of His enemies on a given occasion. Sometimes the term refers to such a judgment in the near past or future, and sometimes it refers to one in the distant future (eschaton).[24]

A. THE INVADING ARMY 2:1-11

The Lord revealed that an army of human beings, rather than locusts, would soon assail Jerusalem. He described this army at length in order to stress the danger that His people faced, and to motivate them to repent.

Thomas Finley believed that this section is an extended metaphor describing the literal past locust invasion referred to in chapter 1.[25] I side with those interpreters who interpret the Hebrew imperfect verbs as describing something in the future.

1. The nearness of the army 2:1-2

The prophet ordered a trumpet (Heb. *shophar*, ram's horn) to be blown in Zion (Jerusalem), specifically on the temple mount, to sound an alarm (cf. Jer. 4:5-6; Ezek. 33:2-6). Sometimes "Zion" refers to Jerusalem in the eschaton, but other times it is simply a poetic synonym for Jerusalem. Joel used it in the latter sense here. This shophar was the ancient equivalent of an air raid siren. The day of the Lord was coming, and all the inhabitants of the city should tremble. That day would be a time of foreboding evil, symbolized by a very overcast sky. It is interesting that a plague of darkness followed a locust plague in Egypt (Exod. 10). Darkness and clouds are common figures for judgment and destruction in the Old Testament (e.g., Jer. 13:16; Ezek. 30:3, 18; 32:7-8; 34:12; Amos 5:18-20; Zeph. 1:15). They are often associated with Yahweh in His role of mighty, victorious warrior (cf. Deut. 4:11; 5:22-23; Ps. 18:9, 11; 97:2). Joel could see a gigantic army spread over the horizon like the dawn. (Was the attack coming from the east, the direction of the dawn?). He said there never had been "anything like" *this* "day," nor would there be after it—not even the plagues in Egypt. This may be hyperbole, or this day may refer to the Great Tribulation, when the Jews will experience their worst ever attack. Joel said this attack was near, either in the near future in his day, or relatively near from his perspective as a prophet (cf. 2 Pet. 3:8).

Many scholars take this passage as predicting an invasion of Jerusalem by some ancient enemy of Israel, such as Assyria or Babylonia, in the relatively near future.[26] Feinberg and Patterson argued for the army being that of Assyria.[27] In favor of such a view is the reference to the invasion being near (v. 1). Against it is the statement of its uniqueness in all of history (v. 2). Other interpreters view 2:1-11 as a further description of the locust plague that Joel described in chapter 1.[28] This seems unlikely since the locust plague of chapter 1 was past, but the attack in 2:1-11 was future. I think it probably refers to an attack by some enemy in Joel's day, in view of what follows.

2. The destructive power of the army 2:3-5

2:3   This huge army advanced like a forest fire, consuming everything in its path (cf. 1:19). Before the devastation, conditions were idyllic, but after it, there was nothing but a scorched-earth wilderness. Nothing escaped the advancing judgment (cf. Exod. 10:5, 15).

> "Joel is quite interested in 'before and after' descriptions, and they form a motif throughout the book."[29]

2:4-5   Joel compared this advancing army to "war horses" and "chariots," the war machines of his day. He heard the familiar sound of chariots in battle, which he likened to the crackling of fire as it rages up a mountainside, swiftly consuming everything in its path. The huge army that Joel saw appeared unstoppable.

It is interesting that locusts look like tiny armored horses, and they behave like them as well (cf. Job 39:19-20; Rev. 9:7). The Italian word for locust means "little horse," and the German word means "hay horse."[30] Thus, the correspondence between the

---

[23] See Douglas Stuart, "The Sovereign's Day of Conquest," *Bulletin of the American Schools of Oriental Research* 220/21 (December 1975, February 1976):159-64.
[24] See Chisholm, "Joel," pp. 1412-13; or Patterson, p. 256, for good, brief discussions of the term and its uses.
[25] Finley, pp. 33-34.
[26] E.g., Wolff, p. 42; Chisholm, "Joel," pp. 1411-12; Stuart, *Hosea-Jonah*, p. 250.
[27] Charles Lee Feinberg, *Joel, Amos, and Obadiah*, p. 19; Patterson, pp. 245-46.
[28] E.g., Allen, pp. 29, 64-76; and Driver, p. 28.
[29] Finley, pp. 44-45.
[30] Cf. Wolff, p. 45, n. 46; Driver, p. 52; Feinberg, p. 20; et al.

army of locusts that had recently swept through the land swiftly, and this future invading army, is unmistakable. Even their sounds were similar. However, the point of the comparison is probably because the horse is a symbol of power and might (cf. Isa. 31:1-3; Hos. 14:3; Mic. 5:10; Hag. 2:22; Zech. 9:10; 12:4; Rev. 9:7).[31]

3. The relentlessness of the army 2:6-9

2:6 — As this army advanced, all the people in and around Jerusalem felt terrified and turned pale with fear (cf. Isa. 26:17; Jer. 4:31; Mic. 4:10).

2:7-9 — The enemy soldiers ran with great stamina and climbed over walls, as locusts do. They were very disciplined in their attack, each one staying in his proper position and not crowding his fellow soldiers (cf. Josh. 6:5). Even when they broke through an obstacle they did not break ranks. They rushed on the city of Jerusalem, ran along its walls, and climbed into its houses like so many thieves. Again, the comparison with locusts is striking (cf. Exod. 10:5-6).

4. The invincibility of the army 2:10-11

2:10 — The earth trembles as this army advances. The heavens also tremble. The sun and the moon grow dark, and the stars fade from view. Cosmic disturbances like these are common in biblical descriptions of Yahweh waging war (cf. 3:16; Judg. 5:4; Ps. 18:7; 77:18; Isa. 13:10, 13; Ezek. 32:7; Zech. 14:6-7; Rev. 6—18).

2:11 — It now becomes clear that Yahweh is leading this army against Jerusalem. Normally the Lord fought *for* His people, but here Joel saw Him leading an army *against* them. He is the One who is directing the soldiers with His voice. His host is both numerous and strong. The day of this attack, the day of the Lord, is great and awesome, and no one can withstand it (cf. Mal. 3:2; 4:5).

> "Here we find one of the great principles of God's dealing with man throughout his history: God only inflicts punishment after great provocation, and when He does so, it is meant to draw man back from further and more severe visitations of the wrath of God."[32]

Some interpreters regard the description of the locust plague in 2:1-11 as simply another description of the same locust plague as the one described in chapter 1, or another locust plague in Israel's past history. Others take this description as an allegory picturing Israel's traditional enemies. Still others view it as picturing the eschatological day of the Lord, in which the Lord Himself will come with His heavenly army in holy war against evil.[33] Many amillennialists take this view. The view that seems best to me, and to many other commentators, is that it is a metaphor based on the past locust plague. Joel used the past locust invasion as a harbinger of an impending human invasion by an undesignated foreign foe.

B. A CALL TO REPENTANCE 2:12-17

Such an awesome prospect of invasion led Joel to appeal to the people of Jerusalem to repent. This would hopefully turn away God's judgment. He voiced two appeals, but, unusually, he did not say what the sins of the people were. Evidently they were known well enough at the time.

1. An appeal for private repentance 2:12-14

2:12-13a — Speaking for the Lord, Joel urged his hearers even now, even though judgment was threatened, to repent. However, he clarified that their repentance needed to be wholehearted, not just external. Fasting, weeping, and mourning would give evidence of the people's sincerity, but they had to rend their hearts, not merely their garments, as was customary in mourning. They needed to return to Yahweh their God (cf. 2 Chron. 7:14). This was a call to return to obedience to the Mosaic Covenant.

2:13b-14 — If they did, they could count on Him being gracious, compassionate, patient, loyal to them, and willing to withhold punishment (cf. Exod. 34:6; Neh. 9:17; Ps. 103:8; 143:8; Isa. 28:21; Jon. 4:2). Their genuine repentance might—Yahweh is still sovereign—move Him to turn from His previously intended course of action and bless them, rather than curse them (cf. Mal. 3:7).

> "Human repentance does not control God. People cannot force God to show them his forgiveness. They can only appeal to him for mercy in not meting out against them what they very well deserve. They may hope for his compassion, but they cannot command it (Zeph 2:3; Lam 3:29)."[34]

---

[31] Dillard, p. 274.
[32] Feinberg, p. 21.
[33] E.g., Dillard, p. 278.
[34] Stuart, *Hoses-Jonah*, p. 252.

Agricultural blessings would signal a reversal of His judgment in the recent locust invasion, and they would then be able to offer grain and wine to the Lord again (cf. 1:9, 13).

> "Some dismiss biblical references to God 'relenting' from judgment as anthropomorphic, arguing that an unchangeable God would never change his mind once he has announced his intentions. While it is true that God will not deviate from an announced course of action once he has issued a formal, unconditional decree (see Num. 23:19; 1 Sam. 15:29; Ps. 110:4), he is often depicted as 'changing his mind' in contexts where he has given only a warning or made a conditional statement about what he will do. Since Joel 2:13 lists God's capacity to 'change his mind' as one of his fundamental attributes (see also Jon. 4:2), one cannot dismiss this characteristic as anthropomorphic."[35]

God's graciousness is seen in His willingness to respond, even when people do not deserve it.[36]

2. An appeal for public repentance 2:15-17

Joel went beyond calling for personal heart-felt repentance, to urging the people to assemble for a corporate expression of their sincere contrition.

2:15-16   The prophet urged the blowing of the shophar in Zion again, but this time, to call a public assembly and a fast, rather than to announce the coming invader (v. 1; cf. 1:14). Fasting involved sacrificially going without food in order to devote oneself to a higher spiritual purpose. God's people needed to gather together and re-consecrate themselves to Him as a special and holy people. Everyone without exception should participate, from the oldest to the youngest. The "elders," in this context, probably refers to the leaders of the nation. Even newlyweds, who sometimes received a special exemption for being newly wed (Deut. 24:5), needed to attend this meeting.

It is interesting that the Jews will assemble in the Promised Land, having received encouragement from the Antichrist, during the first half of the Tribulation. Then the invader will descend on their land and the terrible prospect envisioned in verses 1-11 will take place, in the second half of the Tribulation. Antichrist will persecute them. They will not assemble then in repentance, however.

2:17   The priests should take the lead in this public expression of repentance. They should weep and pray for God to have mercy on His people, because they were His special inheritance, for the glory of His name. The pagans might conclude that He was unable or unwilling to defend His chosen people from their enemy if He allowed the invader to succeed.

> "They cannot hope that Yahweh will forget all about the invasion by ignoring the enforcing of his covenant. Their punishment is a foregone conclusion; they can only hope that his mercy will restore them soon (Deut 32:36, 43; Lam 3:31-32, 40-50)."[37]

C. THE POSSIBILITY OF FORGIVENESS AND RESTORATION 2:18-27

Joel next revealed the Lord's response and comforting words in view of the people's private and public repentance. It is unclear whether he meant that the Lord had responded or would respond. The problem is the Hebrew perfect verbs, which can be rendered in English with either past or future verbs. Several English translations (NASB, NIV, AV) interpreted the Lord's response as being conditioned on the people's repentance, and they translated the verbs in the future tense. It is equally possible that Joel meant that God had already responded positively because the people had repented, which the prophet did not record. I view this section as what God promised to do if the people responded to Joel's call to repentance. Sometime before the destruction of Jerusalem in 586 B.C., God told the Israelites that they had passed the point of no return and that captivity was inevitable (Jer. 7:16; 11:14; 14:11-12). Since repentance was still possible for the Israelites when Joel wrote, this prophecy evidently does not deal with that time.

> "Laments in the OT are sometimes followed by a divine oracle in which Yahweh, through a prophet, assures his people that their prayers will be answered (or sometimes rejected)."[38]

---

[35]Chisholm, *Handbook of . . .*, p. 372. See also idem, "Does God Change His Mind?" *Bibliotheca Sacra* 152:608 (October-December 1995):387-99; and Thomas L. Constable, *Talking to God: What the Bible Teaches about Prayer*, pp. 147-48.
[36]Finley, p. 54.
[37]Stuart, *Hosea-Jonah*, p. 253.
[38]Allen, p. 85. See 2 Chr. 20; Ps. 12:5; 60:6-8; Isa. 33:10-13; Jer. 4:1-2 (cf. 3:21-25); Hos. 14:4-7; and Mic. 7:11-13.

1. The Lord's gracious response 2:18

If the Israelites repented sincerely, Yahweh would be zealous to protect His chosen land from foreign invaders and have pity on His chosen people. This was His essential response.

> "Beginning in Joel 2:18, Israel ceases to be the object of God's judgment and becomes instead the object of His blessing. In a similar reversal the hordes (locust and human) cease to be the instruments of God's judgment on Israel and become instead the objects of God's judgment. This reversal was originally foretold by God through Moses in Deuteronomy 30:1-9."[39]

> "Between verses 17 and 18, we should presume that the invitation and commands of verses 12-17 have been accepted and obeyed."[40]

2. The Lord's promise of blessing 2:19-27

Having given His essential response to the people's repentance, the Lord now explained what He would do in more detail. This section is chiastic, with the focus of emphasis on verses 21-24. Verses 19 and 26-27 promise a restoration of crops and a cessation of shame. Verses 20 and 25 promise the elimination of enemies, and verses 21-24 urge courage and encourage rejoicing.

2:19   Joel had interpreted the Lord's response (v. 18), and now he relayed His instructions (vv. 19-27). Yahweh would restore all that the locusts had eaten: grain, wine, and oil (cf. 1:10). The people would enjoy plenty of these products in the future (cf. Deut. 6:10-11; 8:7-10; 11:13-15). Yahweh would also never again allow the nations to disparage His people, assuming that they would not apostatize again (cf. vv. 26-27). Another view, less acceptable from my viewpoint, is that this promise is unconditional and refers to Israel's eschatological future. The problem with this view is that the Jews will experience some antagonism at the very end of the Millennium (Rev. 20:7-10).

2:20   The prophet now revealed that this invader would come from the north. Both Assyria and Babylon, as well as all other eastern invaders, entered Israel from the north because of the impassability of the Arabian Desert to Israel's east. (This is probably the strongest verse in support of the view that a literal army is in view in chapter 2.[41])

> "If 'the northerner' is yet future (eschatological), the army is possibly the army in Joel 3:9, 12; Daniel 11:40; and Zechariah 14:2."[42]

Instead of leading this army against Jerusalem (v. 11), the Lord would drive it from Judah. He would drive its soldiers "into a parched and desolate land" (Arabia?), and into "the eastern (Dead) sea," and into "the western (Mediterranean) sea" (cf. Dan. 11:45). In other words, He would turn against them rather than leading them, and scatter them rather than uniting them against Jerusalem. The smell of the dead carcasses of the many soldiers would fill the air because they had done many "great things" (possibly meaning that they had arrogantly invaded the Holy Land—unprovoked—causing vast destruction and much death, i.e., atrocities). In short, they had tried to overthrow God's people (cf. the Egyptians drowning in the Red Sea). Masses of dead locusts also smell terrible, especially after dying in the sea and then being washed ashore.[43]

2:21-24   Joel called on the land, personified to represent its people, to rejoice because the Lord had done great things (in contrast to the enemy army, v. 20). The NIV interpreted the last line of verse 20 as referring to the Lord, but it probably refers to the invading army, as the NASB, AV, and RSV translated it. Specifically, He had delivered His people from a much larger and more powerful enemy invasion, assuming the Judahites' repentance. The animals, too, could stop fearing because God's blessing had returned to the land. Green pastures had replaced brown, and trees and vines had again become abundantly fruitful—rather than dry and lifeless (cf. 1:7, 10-12, 19). Fall and spring rains, signs of divine blessing (cf. Deut. 11:14), had replaced drought, so the Lord's people could again rejoice rather than grieving (cf. 1:5, 8, 11, 13, 20). The 1978 NIV translation "a teacher for righteousness" (v. 23) is better rendered "the autumn rains for your righteousness."[44] The threshing floors would be full of grain and the vats would overflow with new wine and oil (cf. 1:17).

2:25   The Lord further promised that He would make up to His people what they had suffered because of the locust invasion (cf. 1:4; Exod. 22:1; 2 Kings 4:7). The "years that the locusts had eaten" refers to the yield or produce of those years. Sin had resulted in covenant curses, but repentance would result in covenant blessings (cf. Deut. 28—29).

---

[39]Dyer, p. 742.
[40]Hubbard, p. 61.
[41]Finley, p. 62. Cf. Feinberg, p. 79.
[42]Chisholm, "Joel," p. 1419.
[43]Driver, pp. 62-63; Smith, 2:441.
[44]See Kapelrud, p. 116; or Patterson, p. 254.

2:26-27	The people would have plenty to eat and would feel satisfied physically. They would also be full spiritually and praise Yahweh their God for working wonders for them (cf. Exod. 3:15; 15:11; 34:10; Josh. 3:5; Jud. 6:13; Ps. 77:14). Then they would never be put to shame, again assuming that they continued in their attitude of humble trust and obedience (cf. v. 19). God's blessings would evidence His presence among them and the intimacy of their fellowship with Him (cf. Num. 11:20; 14:14; Deut. 7:21). They would realize in their experience that He is the only true God (cf. Exod. 6:7; 16:12; Deut. 4:35, 39), and they would abide in that shameless condition (as long as they remained faithful to Him).

". . . just as God's warnings of judgment are often conditional and can be averted by repentance, so his promises of prosperity are often contingent on their recipients remaining loyal to God (see Jer. 18:7-10)."[45]

IV. A FAR FUTURE DAY OF THE LORD: ANOTHER HUMAN INVASION AND DELIVERANCE 2:28—3:21

The preceding promises foreshadowed even greater deliverance and blessing for the Israelites in their far distant future. The clues to a leap to the distant future in the prophet's perspective are the words: "after this" (2:28), "in those days" (2:29), "the great and awesome day of the Lord" (2:31; cf. 2:11), "in those days and at that time" (3:1), and "in that day" (3:18).

Alva McClain organized and expounded the Old Testament revelation concerning this distant Day of the Lord fairly concisely.[46] He divided the events chronologically, according to the four periods of a normal 24-hour day, from the viewpoint of the Israelites: with the day beginning at sunset (darkness followed by light). Some of the predictions describe what will happen before the darkness sets in. Others describe what will happen during the period of darkness. Then there are events that will take place in the twilight period: just before the period of daylight begins. Finally, there are events during the light of that great day. His outline is as follows:

1. Preparatory events—before the Day of the Lord
   a. A court of judgment will be set in heaven.
   b. The voice of a prophetic messenger will be heard on earth.
   c. Internecine warfare and chaos will sweep the world.
   d. A blasphemous political ruler will rise to world power.
   e. There will be great geological and cosmic disturbances.
2. Penal events—during the darkness of the Day of the Lord
   a. Wrath will fall upon a great northern power.
   b. Wrath will fall upon the nation of Israel.
   c. Wrath will fall also on all the Gentile nations.
3. Transitional events—at the dawn of the Day of the Lord
   a. The glorious arrival of the Mediatorial King
   b. The destruction of the hostile armies
   c. The doom of the blasphemous "Little Horn"
4. Constitutive events—during the light of the Day of the Lord
   a. There will be a resurrection.
   b. There will be a repentance of Israelites in the land.
   c. There will be a regathering of dispersed Israelites.
   d. There will be a judgment of living Israelites.
   e. There will also be a judgment of living Gentile nations.

A. ISRAEL'S SPIRITUAL RENEWAL AND DELIVERANCE 2:28-32

2:28-29	"After this," namely, after the deliverance from the northern invader just described, God promised to pour out His Spirit on all the Israelites—without gender, age, class, or position distinctions. Other similar promises identify the Israelites as the recipients of the Spirit (e.g., Ezek. 36:27; 37:14; 39:29; Zech. 12:10), and here "your sons and daughters" (i.e., Israelites) are the object of this blessing. God never gave His Spirit to unbelievers, so believing Israelites are in view. Amillennialists believe that "all flesh" means all believers, namely: believing Jews and Gentiles in the church.[47] They change the meaning of what Joel said. Walter Kaiser believed that "all flesh" means "all mankind," because the gift of the Spirit extends to slaves, and the Israelites had Gentile slaves (Deut. 20:10-14; cf. 1 Chron. 2:34-35).[48] But the Israelites also had Israelite slaves (Exod. 21:1-11; cf. 2 Kings 4:1).

---

[45] Chisholm, *Handbook on . . .*, p. 373.
[46] Alva J. McClain, *The Greatness of the Kingdom*, ch. 16: "The Establishment of the Prophetic Kingdom," pp. 178-205. For more extended discussions, see John F. Walvoord, *The Millennial Kingdom*, pp. 256-334; and J. Dwight Pentecost, *Things to Come*, pp. 229-546.
[47] E.g., Dillard, p. 295. Cf. Hubbard, p. 73.
[48] Walter C. Kaiser Jr., *The Uses of the Old Testament in the New*, p. 97.

In Old Testament times, God gave His Spirit only to select individuals (cf. Num. 11:24-29; 1 Sam. 10:10-11; 19:20-24), but in the future, everyone (i.e., all Jewish believers) would prophesy and receive revelations from the Lord. "Prophesying" often describes *praising God* in the Bible (cf. 1 Chron. 25:1-3), so that may be in view here. "Visions" and "dreams" were God's customary ways of giving special revelations to people in Old Testament times (cf. Num. 12:6). Normally the absence of prophetic revelation indicated sin and divine judgment, but the presence of such revelation reflected divine blessing (cf. 1 Sam. 3:1; Amos 8:11). So a universal bestowal of the Spirit on Jewish believers indicates a time of unprecedented divine blessing. This would be the fulfillment of Moses' desire (Num. 11:29; cf. Isa. 32:15; 44:3-4; Ezek. 36:27-28; 37:14; 39:29; Zech. 12:10).

> "When Joel speaks of those who prophesy, dream dreams, and see visions, the language must mean more than simply that, as Walter Price says, 'everyone would be his own prophet. All would have a direct revelation from God.'[49] Rather, it denotes a new era of revelation with the Israelites preaching to each other or, perhaps, even to the entire world."[50]

> "The expression . . . (*bayyamim hahemma*, 'in those days') is another way the prophets indicate the end times when the Lord will intervene in history to deliver His people and set up His kingdom (cf. Jer. 33:15, 16; Zech. 8:23). Particularly important is the variety of terms Joel uses, as well as the way he gradually makes the time notices more explicit: 'after this' (2:28 [MT 3:1;]) 'in those days' (2:29 [MT 3:2;]) 'before the day of Yahweh, the great and awesome day' (2:31 [MT 3:4;]) 'in those days and at that time when I restore the fortunes of Judah and Jerusalem' (3:1 [MT 4:1;]) 'the day of Yahweh is near' (3:14 [MT 4:14; and]) 'in that day' (3:18 [MT 4:18.])[51]

2:30-31   The Lord also promised awesome displays of celestial phenomena before this great and terrible day of the Lord arrived. Awe-inspiring miracles ("wonders") would occur "in the sky" as well as "on the earth." The appearance of "blood, fire, and columns of smoke" suggests warfare, with God's hand at work behind the scenes (cf. Exod. 19:9, 16-18; Rev. 6:12-17). "The sun" would become dark and "the moon" would turn red ("become blood"). These are probably descriptions of how these heavenly bodies will look (language of appearance), not what will become of them, in view of other similar descriptions (e.g., vv. 2, 10; 3:15; Jer. 4:23-24; Ezek. 32:6-8; Amos 5:18-20; 8:9; Zeph. 1:15; Rev. 6:12-13).

> "The synonymous parallelism of the initial couplet . . . (sun . . . darkness, moon . . . blood) does not focus on the sun and moon separately, as if there were to be daytime and nighttime signs in the sky, but merely pairs moon with sun, the sign being darkness during the daytime (cf. 1:2; Josh 10:12-14)."[52]

This sign will precede the great and awesome day of the Lord—still future (cf. Matt. 24:29-31; Mark 13:24-27; Luke 21:25-28).

2:32   The promise continued: that whoever would call on the name of Yahweh would be delivered.

> "To 'call on the name of Yahweh' . . . means not merely to pray to him, but to worship him consistently and presumably exclusively (Gen 4:26; 12:8; 13:4; 1 Kgs 18:24; Ps 116:17; Zeph 3:9); the expression can also indicate open acknowledgement of one's faith in the midst of a hostile environment (Ps 105:1; Isa 12:4; Zech 13:9)."[53]

"The day of the Lord," described earlier in this chapter, involved God judging the enemies of His people, and this eschatological day of the Lord also involves divine judgment. Therefore, the deliverance in view must be from divine judgment (cf. Rom. 11:26). Specifically, there will be people on Mt. Zion and in Jerusalem who escape, even among the survivors of previous distresses whom Yahweh has chosen for deliverance (cf. Isa. 51:3; Zech. 13:8).

The Apostle Paul quoted this verse and applied it to spiritual salvation (Rom. 10:13). His usage does not fulfill what God promised here, namely: physical deliverance in the coming day of the Lord. Paul meant that, just as God will deliver all who call on Him in that future day of the Lord, so He will deliver all who call on Him for salvation from sin. *They* will avoid the terrible day (i.e., the Great White Throne Judgment day) when all unbelievers will suffer condemnation by their Judge (Rev. 20:11-15).

---

[49]Walter K. Price, *The Prophet Joel and the Day of the Lord*, p. 74.
[50]Finley, pp. 72-73.
[51]Ibid., p. 74.
[52]Stuart, *Hosea-Jonah*, p. 261.
[53]Ibid.

There are nine different New Testament contexts in which these important promises appear (Matt. 24:29; Mark 13:24-25; Luke 21:25; Acts 2:17-21, 39; 21:9; 22:16; Rom. 10:13; Titus 3:6; Rev. 6:12).

The Apostle Peter also quoted this passage (vv. 28-32) in his Pentecost sermon (Acts 2:14-36). He said that what the people of Jerusalem were witnessing, which they mistook for drunkenness, was what Joel had spoken of (Acts 2:16-21; cf. Acts 10:45). Many interpreters believe that Peter meant that Joel's prophecy was completely fulfilled on the day of Pentecost.[54] This can hardly be what he meant, however, because much of what Joel predicted in this passage did not occur on the day of Pentecost, specifically the celestial phenomena. The day of Pentecost was not the day of the Lord that Joel predicted.

Another interpretation of Peter's meaning is that part of what Joel predicted was fulfilled on Pentecost, and the rest awaits fulfillment in the future day of the Lord.[55] God poured out His Spirit on the church on the day of Pentecost, but He will also pour out the Spirit on Israel in the eschatological future. The problem with this view, is that the promises of the outpouring of the Spirit and the other miracles are so intertwined, that separating them by thousands of years seems unnatural. Moreover, Peter quoted the whole passage in Joel, not just the promise of the Spirit's outpouring. In contrast, Jesus only quoted part of Isaiah 61:1-3 when He said that that prophecy was fulfilled when He read it in the Nazareth synagogue (Luke 4:18-21).

A third possible interpretation is that Peter meant that what happened on Pentecost was similar to what Joel had prophesied God would do in the future day of the Lord.[56] He drew a comparison and pointed out an analogy, but he did not claim fulfillment. Similarly, Jesus said, "This is my body," in the Upper Room. Both expressions are metaphors, according to this view. This view sees the entire fulfillment of Joel's prophecy in the eschatological future. The outpouring on the day of Pentecost was simply a foreview of what the Lord will do in the future (cf. Gal. 3:28). The day of Pentecost was not the day of the Lord that the prophets spoke of here and elsewhere.

There is not much practical difference between views two and three. View two sees the outpouring on Pentecost as a partial fulfillment, and view three sees it as a foreview of the fulfillment.[57]

> "Peter quoted this passage in Acts 2 because (a) it related to the outpouring of God's Spirit (2:4, 15-16), (b) it stressed his theme of repentance (2:21, 37-39), and (c) it fit with his understanding that the Jews were about to enter the Day of the Lord, leading up to the return of Israel's Messiah, Jesus (1:6-8; 2:36; 3:19-21)."[58]

The day of the Lord that Joel predicted here begins with the Tribulation (cf. Dan. 9:24-27; Rev. 6—18), continues through the return of Christ and the Millennium (cf. Rev. 19—20), and culminates in the eternal state (cf. 2 Pet. 3:10-13; Rev. 21—22). The signs in view picture what the Book of Revelation describes further as occurring in the Tribulation, and the pouring out of the Spirit will occur at the beginning of the Millennium. Then all believers will possess the Spirit and will have the ability to receive fresh revelations from the Lord. Forgiveness of sins and the indwelling of the Holy Spirit are two of four great blessings of the New Covenant (Jer. 31:31-34; Ezek. 36:24-30).

> "Joel envisioned the outpouring of the Spirit as being confined to Jews, but in the progress of revelation and history, we discover that Gentiles are included as well, for they too are incorporated into the new covenant community."[59]

B. GOD'S JUDGMENT ON ISRAEL'S ENEMY NATIONS 3:1-17

God's judgment on unbelievers would accompany the spiritual renewal and deliverance of His own in the future day of the Lord. As God promised to wipe out the locusts for despoiling Judah, now He promised to do the same to the nations that had despoiled Judah (cf. Zeph. 3:8; Ezek. 38—39; Matt. 25:31-46).

> "Like a photographer, Joel has used a wide-angle lens for the overall picture in 2:30-32. Then he zooms in for a close look at the Day of the Lord, with its mixture of judgment and grace, in chapter three."[60]

> "No prophet of the Old Testament has a more important revelation of the end times than the one now before us in the third chapter."[61]

---

[54] E.g., Dillard, p. 295.
[55] E.g., Chisholm, *Handbook on . . .*, p. 374; Finley, p. 79; Kaiser, *The Uses . . .*, p. 97.
[56] E.g., Feinberg, pp. 26-29.
[57] For a fuller discussion of the views regarding Peter's use of this prophecy, see my notes on Acts 2:16-21.
[58] Dyer, p. 743. Cf. Wiersbe, p. 338.
[59] Chisholm, *Handbook on . . .*, p. 374.
[60] Hubbard, pp. 73-74.
[61] Feinberg, p. 32.

1. The announcement of judgment 3:1-8

3:1-3   When God would "restore the fortunes of Judah and Jerusalem" in that future day (cf. Deut. 30:3), He would gather the other nations to "the valley of Jehoshaphat" (lit. "Yahweh judges"). If this is a geographical location, this is the only passage in Scripture that names the site of this judgment (cf. Zech. 14:3-5). Its exact location is debatable, since no valley by this name appears elsewhere in Scripture (cf. vv. 12, 14). Many interpreters believe it is the valley of Megiddo, just north and east of the Mt. Carmel range. Others believe that it must be a site near Jerusalem.[62]

Another view, which seems preferable to me, is that Joel was referring, in a more general sense, to the place where God will judge the nations.[63] That is, the name is symbolic. In this case, "the valley of Jehoshaphat" would mean the place where Yahweh judges, without reference to a specific geographical site. The following clause ("Then will I enter into *judgment* with them there") seems to support this view. Valleys were often preferred locations for battles in biblical times, so "valley" is an appropriate word to use to describe the place where God will judge (defeat) Israel's enemies.

Later, Joel referred to this place as the "valley of decision" (v. 14).[64] There, God would judge the nations for scattering His covenant people, His inheritance, and for dividing up His land (cf. Lam. 5:2). They had thought so little of the Hebrews that they gambled for them. They had valued them no higher than the price of a prostitute or the cost of a drink.

3:4   The Lord addressed the Phoenicians and Philistines directly. They had no special relationship to Yahweh, as Israel did, and they had not been just in dealing with the Israelites. The Lord promised to repay them for their sins. Probably these nations are representative of all of Israel's enemies, since God later said that He would judge "all" of them (v. 12).[65]

3:5-6   Specifically, these Gentile nations had robbed God and had sold the children of His chosen people as slaves to the Greeks. These nations had stolen from the Israelites. Amos also referred to the Phoenician and Philistine slave trade (Amos 1:6, 9; cf. Ezek. 27:13, 19).

3:7-8   To pay back these nations, the Lord said He would revive the Israelites in the remote places to which they had been sold. The Israelites would grow strong there and would sell the descendants of these Phoenicians and Philistines to the Sabeans (cf. Ezek. 27:22-23). Thus He would pay them back in kind, which is His customary method of retribution (Gal. 6:7). This may have been fulfilled in the fourth century B.C., or the fulfillment may still be future. Allen saw Antiochus III's enslavement of the people of Sidon, in 345 B.C., and Alexander the Great's enslavement of the citizens of Tyre and Gaza, in 332 B.C., as a partial fulfillment, assuming Jews were involved in these transactions.[66]

Probably the fulfillment lies in the future, specifically toward the end of the Tribulation, since this whole section of Joel deals with what God will do in *that* "day of the Lord." Again, Phoenicia and Philistia probably represent all the enemies of Israel (cf. Isa. 25:10-12; Obad.), over whom Israel will eventually gain ascendancy.

2. The description of judgment 3:9-17

This pericope contains a call to the nations to prepare for war (vv. 9-11), a statement by the Lord (vv. 12-13), and a description of the battle site (vv. 14-16).

3:9-11   The Lord issued a call to war. The nations will evidently believe that God is calling them to do battle, but, ironically, it is really to hear His sentence of judgment against them. The nations should prepare for a great battle by beating their plowshares into swords and their pruning hooks into spears. At a later time, in the Millennium, they would do the reverse because Messiah will end war (cf. Isa. 2:4; Mic. 4:3). The weak should "psych" themselves up in preparation.

> "In the coming great war of judgment, even the weakling . . . will have to declare himself a soldier . . . This synecdochic formulation is a way of saying that all the enemy population will be judged."[67]

---

[62]Ibid.
[63]Hubbard, p. 74; Finley, p. 84.
[64]Cf. also "the valley of vision" (Isa. 22:1, 5).
[65]Chisholm, "Joel," p. 1422.
[66]Allen, p. 114.
[67]Stuart, *Hosea-Jonah*, p. 269.

The nations should hurry and assemble (cf. Zech. 12:9). Joel also called on Yahweh to bring down His mighty army of angelic warriors to engage the enemy of His people (cf. Deut. 33:2-3; 2 Kings 6:17; Ps. 68:17; 103:19-20; Zech. 14:5).

> "But, when the nations were assembled in the valley, fully equipped for battle, they would receive a shock; they would find there the Judge of all the nations, and in their hands they would be holding the incriminating evidence of their own history of violence."[68]

3:12-13   The Lord urged the nations to rouse themselves and to assemble in the valley of Jehoshaphat (cf. v. 2) because it was there that He would sit in judgment on them. He compared this judgment to harvesting grain with a sickle and to treading grapes in a vat (cf. Isa. 17:5; 63:1-6; Rev. 14:14-20). As grapes squirt juice when trodden, so the nations will give up the wickedness with which they have been full (cf. 2:24).

This scene of divine warfare corresponds to the battle of Armageddon at the end of the Tribulation (cf. Rev. 14:14-20; 16:16; 19:11-21). The judgment of the nations following Christ's second coming (Matt. 25:31-46) will not involve warfare.

3:14-16   The prophet viewed many multitudes in the valley, which he now referred to as "the valley of decision" because there God will make a decision concerning their fate. Like the reference to "the valley of Jehoshaphat" (v. 2), "the valley of decision" involves word play in Hebrew. The Hebrew word *harus* ("decision") sounds like *haras*, which means "to render judgment" or "moat" (cf. Dan. 9:25).

> "Many preachers have appealed to verse 14 for an evangelistic thrust; their audiences are addressed as 'multitudes in the Valley of Decision' who must decide their fate. There is a problem with that use of this passage: in Joel the hordes do not gather to make a decision, but to hear one; they will not be deciding their fate, for God has already decreed it. The time for decisions is now past."[69]

This day of the Lord was near from his perspective, which for the prophets was often deceiving due to their foreshortened view of the future. He saw the celestial phenomena again that signaled doom (cf. 2:10, 31). Lion-like, Yahweh roared from Zion announcing His attack on the nations, and everything trembled (cf. 2:10-11; Rev. 16:16, 18). For His own people, however, He proved to be a refuge and a stronghold.

> "The ancient hearer/speaker would not tend to think because of this language that the night would be unusually dark, too, but would see the whole verse [i.e., v. 15] as stressing the total darkness of the fateful day. On such darkness as curse fulfillment, see Deut 28:29."[70]

3:17   Yahweh's victory will demonstrate to His people that He is indeed Israel's covenant God, and that His special place of abode is Mt. Zion (cf. 2:27). After this battle, Jerusalem will truly be the holy city, set apart entirely for God's people and no longer defiled by pagan invaders.

C. ISRAEL'S ULTIMATE RESTORATION 3:18-21

3:18   Joel continued describing the future day of the Lord, but now he passed from the judgments of the Tribulation to the blessings of the Millennium. "The mountains" of Israel would be so full of grapevines that they could be described as dripping "with sweet wine." There will be so many milk-yielding animals feeding on the luxuriant hills, that "the hills" could be said to flow "with milk." Instead of the wadis that have water in them only a few days each year, "all . . . the streams of Judah" would "flow with" abundant, life-giving "water." All these descriptions recall conditions in paradise (cf. 1:5, 18, 20). A spring will flow out from the millennial temple that will water the valley of acacia trees ("Shittim"), evidently between Jerusalem and the Dead Sea (cf. Ezek. 47:1-12; Zech. 14:8).

Feinberg believed this valley lay on the border between Moab and Israel and was known for its dryness.[71] Finley believed "the valley of Shittim" refers to the lower stretch of the Kidron Valley.[72] The "spring" will also be a visual reminder that Yahweh is the source of all provisions and fruitfulness.

---

[68]Peter C. Craigie, *Twelve Prophets*, p. 116.
[69]Dillard, p. 309.
[70]Stuart, *Hosea-Jonah*, p. 269.
[71]Feinberg, p. 37.
[72]Finley, p. 101.

	"Jerusalem is the only city of antiquity that wasn't built near a great river. Rome had the Tiber; Nineveh was built near the Tigris and Babylon on the Euphrates; and the great Egyptian cities were built near the Nile. But in the kingdom, Jerusalem will have a river that proceeds from the temple of God."[73]
3:19-20	"Egypt" and "Edom," probably representative of Israel's enemies, will become deserts because they "shed innocent blood," presumably the blood of God's people ("sons of Judah"). But "Judah" and "Jerusalem" would be full of people for all generations to come (cf. Ezek. 37:25; Amos 9:15; Zech. 14:11).
3:21	God's final promise through Joel was that He would "avenge" the "blood" shed by these enemies of Israel, which He had "not" yet "avenged" in the prophet's day. He promised to do this because He dwelt "in Zion," that is, He had a special covenant relationship with Israel (cf. Ezek. 43:1-12; Zech. 2:10-13).

"Joel 3:1-21 [4:1-21] became the classic passage for the rest of the OT on God's final judgment on all nations. It also became the classic statement for the blessed result for the people of God."[74]

The prophecy of Joel unfolds in chronological sequence. It begins with reference to a severe locust invasion that had come as a judgment on the Judahites for their covenant unfaithfulness to Yahweh (1:2-20). Even though it is impossible to date this plague, it happened in the fairly recent past from Joel's perspective. The Lord used this severe judgment to call His people, through His prophet, to anticipate an even worse devastation coming in the near future, not from insects but from foreign invaders. He called on the Jews to repent, and promised that if they did, He would forgive them and save them from this invasion. This would be a day of deliverance in which they would learn that He was at work for them. This is what happened when the Assyrians under Sennacherib's leadership attacked Jerusalem unsuccessfully in 701 B.C. (cf. 2 Kings 18—19; Isa. 36—37). If this is the near invasion that Joel predicted, he must have written in the early pre-exilic period (ninth century B.C.). Yet another, similar day, was coming further in the future, in which they would again experience an invasion by foreigners who hated them (in the Tribulation). Nevertheless, Yahweh promised to deliver them in *that day*, and to restore them to *unprecedented blessing*—because He was, and will always be, their covenant-keeping God (in the Millennium).

---

[73]Wiersbe, p. 340.
[74]Kaiser, *Toward an* . . ., p. 190. The reference in brackets in this quotation appears in this book and represents the versification in the Hebrew (Masoretic) text. In this text, there are four chapters in Joel: 1:1-20; 2:1-27; 3:1-5; and 4:1-21.

Bibliography

Allen, Leslie C. *The Books of Joel, Obadiah, Jonah and Micah*. The New International Commentary on the Old Testament series. Grand Rapids: Wm. B. Eerdmans Publishing Co., 1976.

Archer, Gleason L., Jr. *A Survey of Old Testament Introduction*. Revised ed. Chicago: Moody Press, 1974.

Barker, Harold P. *Christ in the Minor Prophets.* New York: Loizeaux Brothers, n.d.

Baron, Stanley. The *Desert Locust*. New York: Scribner, 1972.

Bennett, L. V. "Development of a Locust Plague." *Nature* 256 (1975):486-87.

Blaising, Craig A. "The Day of the Lord: Theme and Pattern in Biblical Theology." *Bibliotheca Sacra* 169:673 (January-March 2012):3-19.

_____. "The Day of the Lord and the Seventieth Week of Daniel," *Bibliotheca Sacra* 169:674 (April-June 2012):131-42.

Bright, John. *A History of Israel*. Philadelphia: Westminster Press, 1959.

Calvin, John. *Joel, Amos, Obadiah*. Commentaries on the Twelve Minor Prophets, vol. 2. 14 vols. Translated by John Owen. Reprint ed. Grand Rapids: Baker Book House, 1981.

Chisholm, Robert B., Jr. "Does God 'Change His Mind'?" *Bibliotheca Sacra* 152:608 (October-December 1995):387-99.

_____. *Handbook on the Prophets*. Grand Rapids: Baker Book House, 2002.

_____. "Joel." In *The Bible Knowledge Commentary: Old Testament*, pp. 1409-24. Edited by John F. Walvoord and Roy B. Zuck. Wheaton: Scripture Press Publications, Victor Books, 1985.

_____. "A Theology of the Minor Prophets." In *A Biblical Theology of the Old Testament*, pp. 397-433. Edited by Roy B. Zuck. Chicago: Moody Press, 1991.

Constable, Thomas L. *Talking to God: What the Bible Teaches about Prayer*. Grand Rapids: Baker Book House, 1995; reprint ed., Eugene, Oreg.: Wipf & Stock Publishers, 2005.

Craigie, Peter C. *Twelve Prophets*. Vol. 1. Daily Study Bible series. Philadelphia: Westminster Press, and Edinburgh: Saint Andrew Press, 1984.

Dillard, Raymond Bryan. "Joel." In *The Minor Prophets: An Exegetical and Expositional Commentary*, 1:239-313. 3 vols. Edited by Thomas Edward McComiskey. Grand Rapids: Baker Books, 1992, 1993, and 1998.

Driver, S. R. *The Books of Joel and Amos*. The Cambridge Bible for Schools and Colleges series. Cambridge, Eng.: University Press, 1915.

Dyer, Charles H., and Eugene H. Merrill. *The Old Testament Explorer*. Nashville: Word Publishing, 2001. Reissued as *Nelson's Old Testament Survey*. Nashville: Thomas Nelson Publishers, 2001.

Feinberg, Charles Lee. *Joel, Amos, and Obadiah*. The Major Messages of the Minor Prophets series. New York: American Board of Missions to the Jews, 1948.

Finley, Thomas J. *Joel, Amos, Obadiah*. The Wycliffe Exegetical Commentary series. Chicago: Moody Press, 1990.

Fishelson, Lev. *Fauna Palestina: Insecta*. Vol. 3: *Orthoptera, Acridoidea*. Jerusalem: Israel Academy of Sciences and Humanities, 1985.

Freeman, Hobart E. *An Introduction to the Old Testament Prophets*. Chicago: Moody Press, 1968.

Hubbard, David Allen. *Joel and Amos: An Introduction and Commentary.* Leicester, Eng., and Downers Grove, Ill.: Inter-Varsity Press, 1989.

Kaiser, Walter C., Jr. *Toward an Old Testament Theology*. Grand Rapids: Zondervan Publishing House, 1978.

_____. *The Uses of the Old Testament in the New*. Chicago: Moody Press, 1985.

Kapelrud, Arvid S. *Joel Studies*. Uppsala, Sweden: A. B. Lundequistska Bokhandeln, 1948.

Keil, Carl Friedrich. *The Twelve Minor Prophets*. 2 vols. Translated by James Martin. Biblical Commentary on the Old Testament. Reprint ed. Grand Rapids: Wm. B. Eerdmans Publishing Co., 1949.

Longman, Tremper, III and Raymond B. Dillard. *An Introduction to the Old Testament*. 2nd ed. Grand Rapids: Zondervan, 2006.

McClain, Alva J. *The Greatness of the Kingdom, An Inductive Study of the Kingdom of God*. Winona Lake, Ind.: BMH Books, 1959; Chicago: Moody Press, 1968.

Morgan, G. Campbell. *Living Messages of the Books of the Bible*. 2 vols. New York: Fleming H. Revell Co., 1912.

The Nelson Study Bible. Edited by Earl D. Radmacher. Nashville: Thomas Nelson Publishers, 1997.

Patterson, Richard D. "Joel." In *Daniel-Minor Prophets*. Vol. 7 of *The Expositor's Bible Commentary*. 12 vols. Edited by Frank E. Gaebelein and Richard P. Polcyn. Grand Rapids: Zondervan Publishing House, 1985.

Pentecost, J. Dwight. *Things to Come*. Findlay, Ohio: Dunham Publishing Co., 1963.

Price, Walter K. The *Prophet Joel and the Day of the Lord*. Chicago: Moody Press, 1976.

Rudolph, Wilhelm. *Joel-Amos-Obadja-Jona*. Gütersloh: Gütersloher Verlagshaus Gerd Mohn, 1971.

Sellers, Ovid R. "Stages of Locust in Joel." *American Journal of Semitic Languages and Literatures* 52 (1935-36):81-85.

Smith, George Adam. *The Book of the Twelve Prophets*. 2 vols. Revised ed. New York: Harper & Brothers, n.d.

Stuart, Douglas. *Hosea-Jonah*. Word Biblical Commentary series. Waco: Word Books, 1987.

_____. "The Sovereign's Day of Conquest." *Bulletin of the American Schools of Oriental Research* 220/21 (December 1975, February 1976):159-64.

Thompson, J. A. "Joel's Locusts in the Light of Near Eastern Parallels." *Journal of Near Eastern Studies* 14 (1955):52-55.

_____. "Translation of the Words for Locust." *Bible Translator* 25 (October 1974):405-11.

von Rad, Gerhard. "The Origin of the Concept of the Day of the Lord." *Journal of Semitic Studies* 4 (1959):97-108.

Waloft, Z., and S. M. Green, "Regularities and Duration of Regional Locust Plagues." *Nature* 256 (1975):484-85.

Walvoord, John F. *The Millennial Kingdom*. Revised ed. Findlay, Ohio: Dunham Publishing Co., 1963.

Whiting, John D. "Jerusalem's Locust Plague." *National Geographic*, December 1915, pp. 511-50.

Wiersbe, Warren W. "Joel." In *The Bible Exposition Commentary/Prophets*, pp. 333-42. Colorado Springs, Colo.: Cook Communications Ministries; and Eastbourne, England: Kingsway Communications Ltd., 2002.

Wolff, Hans Walter. *Joel and Amos*. Translated by Waldemar Janzen, S. Dean McBride Jr., and Charles A. Muenchow. Philadelphia: Fortress Press, 1977.

Wood, Leon J. *The Prophets of Israel*. Grand Rapids: Baker Book House, 1979.

Young, Edward J. *An Introduction to the Old Testament*. Revised ed. Grand Rapids: Wm. B. Eerdmans Publishing Co., 1960.

Constable's Notes
on Amos

Introduction

Title and Writer
The title of the book comes from its writer. The prophet's name means "burden-bearer" or "load-carrier."

Amos was a "sheepherder" (Heb. *noqed*; cf. 2 Kings 3:4) or sheep breeder, and he described himself as a herdsman (Heb. *boqer*, 7:14). He was more than a shepherd (Heb. *ro'ah*). He evidently owned or managed large herds of sheep, and or goats, and was probably in charge of shepherds. Amos also described himself as a grower of sycamore figs (7:14). Sycamore fig trees are not true fig trees but a variety of the mulberry family, which produces fig-like fruit. Each fruit had to be scratched or pierced to let the juice flow out so the "fig" could ripen. These trees grew in the tropical Jordan Valley, and around the Dead Sea, to a height of 25 to 50 feet, and bore fruit three or four times a year. They did not grow as well in the higher elevations such as Tekoa, Amos' hometown, so the prophet appears to have farmed at a distance from his home, in addition to tending herds. Tekoa stood 10 miles south of Jerusalem in Judah. Thus, Amos seems to have been a prosperous and influential Judahite, but there is no indication that he was a priest, or had any connection with the royal family or the ruling classes in his land. Amos' natural surroundings had a profound effect on him and his writing (cf. 1:2; 2:9; 3:4-5; 5:19-20, 24; 6:12; 7:1-6; 8:1; 9:3-15).

PLACES MENTIONED IN AMOS

Date
Amos ministered during the reigns of King Jeroboam II of Israel (793-753 B.C.) and King Uzziah (Azariah) of Judah (792-740 B.C.), specifically two years before "the earthquake" (1:1). Zechariah also referred to a notable earthquake during the reign of Uzziah (Zech. 14:5). Josephus wrote that an earthquake occurred when Uzziah entered the temple and was struck with leprosy (cf. 2 Chron. 26:16-20).[1] However, this may be simply Jewish tradition. Archaeological excavations at Hazor and Samaria point to evidence of a violent earthquake in Israel about 760 B.C.[2] So perhaps Amos ministered about 760 B.C. This date may account for the omission of the name of King Jotham who ruled as coregent with Uzziah from 750-740 B.C. Thus Amos was a contemporary of the other eighth-century prophets: Jonah, Hosea, Isaiah, and Micah.

> "A flurry of prophetic activity was divinely inaugurated in the eighth century B.C., mainly to warn the northern kingdom of an impending destruction if she did not repent and reverse her way of life."[3]

Place of Composition
Since Amos lived in the Judean town of Tekoa, he was a prophet from the Southern Kingdom. His hometown served as a defensive warning outpost for the protection of Jerusalem from the south. Similarly, Amos' prophecies were a defensive warning for the protection of Israel from the south.

---

[1]Josephus, *Antiquities of the Jews*, 9:10:4.
[2]Y. Yadin, et al., *Hazor II: An Account of the Second Season of Excavations, 1956*, pp. 24, 26, 36-37; and Philip J. King, *Amos, Hosea, Micah— An Archaeological Commentary*, p. 21.
[3]Walter C. Kaiser Jr., *Toward an Old Testament Theology*, p. 192.

Amos ministered in the chief center of idolatry in Israel: Bethel, near the southern border of Israel. Amos was a southerner ministering a message of judgment to the northerners of his day.

Audience and Purpose

Amos prophesied against the Northern Kingdom of Israel (1:1). Yahweh raised him up to announce judgment on Israel because of her covenant unfaithfulness and rebellion against His authority. Amos announced the destruction of the Northern Kingdom, but he also predicted that the Lord would preserve a remnant that was repentant. He would restore this remnant to political prominence and covenant blessing, and through them, draw all nations to Himself. Amos announced a warning to the residents of the Northern Kingdom, but he also held out hope.

Amos emphasized God's righteousness; Hosea, his contemporary in the north, God's love. Amos' prophecies are more threatening; Hosea's are more tender. Amos' professional life is a subject of his prophecies; Hosea's home life is a subject of his.

Historical Background

These were times of political stability, material prosperity, and geographical expansion for both the Northern and the Southern Kingdoms (cf. 1:6; 6:2, 13; 2 Kings 14:23-29; 2 Chron. 26:1-15). Jeroboam II and Uzziah were two of the most competent and effective kings that their respective kingdoms enjoyed. They brought their nations to heights of success, second only to those in Solomon's golden age. Archaeologists have found hundreds of ivory inlays in the excavations of Samaria, proving the Northern Kingdom's prosperity.[4] The Northern Kingdom was at the height of its power during Jeroboam II's reign. Aram had not recovered from its defeat by Adad-Nirari III of Assyria in 802 B.C., and Assyria had not yet developed into the superpower that it became under Tiglath-Pileser III (745-727 B.C.).

> "Commerce thrived (8:5), an upper class emerged (4:1-3), and expensive homes were built (3:15; 5:11; 6:4, 11). The rich enjoyed an indolent, indulgent lifestyle (6:1-6), while the poor became targets for legal and economic exploitation (2:6-7; 5:7, 10-13; 6:12; 8:4-6). Slavery for debt was easily accepted (2:6; 8:6). Standards of morality had sunk to a low ebb (2:7)."[5]

> "In other words the prosperity of Israel was merely a thin veneer over a mass of poverty and misery."[6]

Religion flourished too. The Hebrews participated in the yearly festivals (4:4; 5:5; 8:3, 10) and offered their sacrifices enthusiastically (4:5; 5:21-23). They believed God was with them and considered themselves immune to disaster (5:14, 18-20; 6:1-3; 9:10). Yet they worshipped the native Canaanite deities along with Yahweh.

> "If the Prophet Amos were to come to our world today, he would probably feel very much at home; for he lived at a time such as ours when society was changing radically."[7]

Unity

Almost all scholars agree that the Book of Amos was originally a single book that the prophet Amos wrote. Comparison with the writings of the other eighth-century prophets, plus the consistently vivid and forthright style of Amos, make this conclusion virtually inescapable.[8]

Theology

Amos' descriptions of God remind the reader of the descriptions of Him in the first few chapters of Genesis. Amos stressed the sovereignty of Yahweh over history. He controls the movements of peoples (9:7) and the order of nature (4:13; 5:8). The prophet also affirmed the ability of people to submit to or reject the Lord's authority. He reminded his hearers of Yahweh's election of Israel (3:2), but repudiated the popular idea of his day that God would not punish His people.

> "Amos, more than any other prophet, urged the responsibility of elective privilege."[9]

> "Whereas Hosea was crushed with a sense of the unfaithfulness of Israel to the love of God, Amos was outraged at the violence they had done to the justice and righteousness of God. The note he strikes in his prophecy is the counterpart and corollary to the message uttered by [his contemporary,] Hosea."[10]

---

[4]See the *Encyclopedia of Archaeological Excavations in the Holy Land*, 4:1044-46; and D. W. Thomas, ed., *Archaeology and Old Testament Study*, pp. 69-70.
[5]Donald R. Sunukjian, "Amos," in *The Bible Knowledge Commentary: Old Testament*, p. 1425.
[6]H. L. Ellison, *The Prophets of Israel*, p. 64.
[7]Warren W. Wiersbe, "Amos," in *The Bible Exposition Commentary/Prophets*, p. 344.
[8]For further discussion, see the commentaries, especially T. E. McComiskey, "Amos," in *Daniel-Minor Prophets*, vol. 7 of *The Expositor's Bible Commentary*, pp. 270-74.
[9]Ibid., p. 276.
[10]*The New Scofield Reference Bible*, p. 932.

Like many of the other prophets, Amos spoke of the day of the Lord. He saw it as a time when God would judge sin, even in His own people (5:18-20). Another day would come, however, when David's kingdom would be restored and would include both Jews and Gentiles (9:13-15).[11]

Amos' emphases on man and sin emphasize idolatry and social injustice, frequent themes in the other writing prophets, but especially prominent in this book.

Structure and Style

Scholars have observed that Amos wrote in the covenant-lawsuit structure and style that was common in the ancient Near East in his day (the *rib* oracle).[12] His words are covenant-lawsuit addresses.[13] The Great King (God) is introduced in the third person (1:2), and then begins to speak in the first person (1:3). Amos' phraseology illustrates the covenant background against which it was written, namely, the Mosaic Covenant.[14] One writer called the genre of the entire book a covenant enforcement document.[15] Other stylistic features that Amos employed prominently include repetition (e.g., 1:3, 4, 5), summary quotation (e.g., 4:1; 6:13; 8:5-6; 9:10), and irony (e.g., 4:1).

> "Amos makes use of a wide range of literary devices in presenting his oracles: metaphors, simile, epithets, proverbs, short narratives, sarcasm, direct vituperation, vision, taunt, dialogue, irony, satire, parody—'a virtual anthology of prophetic forms' (Ryken 1993, 342)."[16]

> ". . . he is the author of the purest and most classical Hebrew in the entire Old Testament."[17]

Amos was probably an impressive and effective speaker, as well as a gifted writer, since his writing style is rhetorical. He used short, uncomplicated sentences. He often asked questions and provided explanations. He also knew the power of repetition. He illustrated his points well with figures of speech and lessons from nature. Perhaps after he finished preaching in Bethel, he returned to Tekoa and wrote down his prophecies on a scroll.

Outline

I. Prologue 1:1-2
    A. Introduction 1:1
    B. Theme 1:2

II. Prophetic messages that Amos delivered 1:3—6:14
    A. Oracles against nations 1:3—2:16
        1. An oracle against Aram 1:3-5
        2. An oracle against Philistia 1:6-8
        3. An oracle against Phoenicia 1:9-10
        4. An oracle against Edom 1:11-12
        5. An oracle against Ammon 1:13-15
        6. An oracle against Moab 2:1-3
        7. An oracle against Judah 2:4-5
        8. An oracle against Israel 2:6-16
    B. Messages of judgment against Israel chs. 3—6
        1. The first message on sins against God and man ch. 3
        2. The second message on women, worship, and willfulness ch. 4
        3. The third message on injustice 5:1-17

---

[11] For further discussion of Amos' theological emphases, see Billy K. Smith, "Amos," in *Amos, Obadiah, Jonah*, pp. 31-33.
[12] E.g., Jeffrey Niehaus, "Amos," in *The Minor Prophets*, pp. 317-26. See R. Campbell Thompson and Richard W. Hutchinson, "The Excavations on the Temple of Nabu at Nineveh," *Archaeologia* 79 (1929):103-48; R. Campbell Thompson and Max E. L. Mallowan, "The British Museum Excavations at Nineveh, 1931-32," *University of Liverpool Annals of Archaeology and Anthropology* 20 (1933):71-127; and Wilfred G. Lambert, "Three Unpublished Fragments of the Tukulti-Ninurta Epic," *Archiv für Orientforschung* 18 (1957-58):38-51.
[13] See Herbert B. Huffmon, "The Covenant Lawsuit in the Prophets," *Journal of Biblical Literature* 78 (1959):285-95.
[14] See a chart of the phrases that appear both in Amos and in the Pentateuch in Niehaus, p. 322.
[15] Stephen J. Bramer, "The Literary Genre of the Book of Amos," *Bibliotheca Sacra* 156 (January-March 1999):43-49.
[16] Tremper Longman III and Raymond B. Dillard, *An Introduction to the Old Testament*, p. 430. Their quotation is from Leland Ryken, "Amos," in *A Complete Literary Guide to the Bible*.
[17] George L. Robinson, *The Twelve Minor Prophets*, p. 50.

        4. The fourth message on unacceptable worship 5:18-27
        5. The fifth message on complacency and pride ch. 6
III. Visions that Amos saw chs. 7—9
    A. Three short visions of impending judgment 7:1-9
        1. The swarming locusts 7:1-3
        2. The devouring fire 7:4-6
        3. The plumb line 7:7-9
    B. An intervening incident 7:10-17
        1. The challenge 7:10-13
        2. The response 7:14-17
    C. Two more visions of impending judgment chs. 8—9
        1. The basket of summer fruit ch. 8
        2. The Lord standing by the altar ch. 9

Message

The Book of Amos is distinctive from the other prophetic books of the Old Testament in two respects.

First, the prophet Amos was not a prophet in the same sense that the other prophets were prophets. He was not recognized as a prophet among his contemporaries. He had not been to one of the schools of the prophets. He had not been discipled by another recognized prophet. He was what we would call today a "layman," and an untrained layman at that. The other prophets claimed to be prophets, but Amos claimed to be a farmer and shepherd. God burdens some Christians to leave "secular" employment to announce His messages. They can identify with Amos. This was his calling, too.

Second, the prophecy of Amos is not a prophecy in the same sense that the other prophetic books were prophecies. Amos' perspective was wider than most of the other prophets. An evidence of this is that he did not refer to God as the God of Israel, as the other prophets did. Instead, he thought of Him, and referred to Him, as the God of the whole earth. Moreover, Amos grouped Judah and Israel with Damascus, Gaza, Tyre, Edom, Ammon, and Moab. He saw Yahweh as sovereign over all these city-states and nations, not just over Judah and Israel primarily. Whereas Isaiah, Jeremiah, Ezekiel, and Daniel all recorded messages of judgment against foreign nations, they focused on Judah and Israel particularly in their books. Amos focused on Israel particularly, but he viewed Judah and Israel as two among many nations that God would judge for the same sins.

In Amos we see God as detached from the prophetic order, and from every nation, yet directing through a man uniquely chosen as His prophet, and directing over the affairs of all nations. I do not want to overemphasize this point, because these are more differences in degree than in kind.

There are at least three timeless values of the Book of Amos. It reveals the philosophy, the practice, and the promise of God's divine government.

Amos gives us the philosophy of the divine government in the comprehensiveness of its outlook. The prophet did not argue for God's universal sovereignty, nor did he even affirm it. He assumed it and applied it. In particular, he explained the standard by which God exercises His universal sovereignty, the principle by which He rules, and the patience that marks His governing.

The standard by which God measures nations is their treatment of other nations. God would judge the Arameans because they were cruel to their neighbors. He would judge the Philistines because they bought and sold other human beings. The Phoenicians traded in human lives, in spite of a covenant in which they pledged not to do so. The Edomites were unforgiving and took revenge. The Ammonites were cruel. The Moabites were violent and vindictive. The Judahites had despised the Lord's instruction regarding what their treatment of others should be. And the Israelites had oppressed the poor and needy, even within their own borders. These are all expressions of violations of human rights. All these nations violated the terms of the Noahic Covenant (Gen. 9:5-6).

The principle that lies behind this standard is that privilege brings responsibility. God's harshest judgment fell on His own people, who had the most light. The pagan nations were guilty of violating human rights, too, but their punishment would be less, because they did not have the privilege of having as much of God's revealed will as the Israelites did. We see the same principle in operation in Hosea and in Romans 1—3. All people are under divine wrath, because everyone has failed to respond positively to the light that they have. But those who have more light fall under more severe judgment, because they sin with a greater knowledge of God's will (cf. Luke 12:48). Similarly, national privilege determines national responsibility. The United States has had great privilege, and so has great responsibility to God.

The patience that marks God's sovereign governing of the world comes out clearly in Amos, too. The phrase "for three transgressions, yes, for four" reminds us that God does not judge nations for only one transgression. Every transgression will receive punishment from God, but judgment does not fall immediately. God could have judged these nations much sooner than He did, but He was patient and waited until they had sinned repeatedly. In Genesis we read, "The iniquity of the Amorite is not yet complete" (Gen. 15:16). God waited to judge all these nations until they had amassed so much sin that He could delay no longer to judge them. Fortunately, God deals with us the same way, or all of us would have died long ago. His dealings with groups of people—nations—depends on the conduct of the individuals in those groups.

If cruelty to other nations makes God angry, it is because His heart is set on kindness. If oppression stirs up His wrath, it is because He desires people to live in peace. If violations of human rights call down His judgment, it is because He longs that people experience happiness and well-being. His sovereign government always moves toward the best conditions for humanity, and He resists what disrupts those conditions. Amos closes with a picture of the world order that God desires and will bring to pass eventually. It is a picture of peace.

The second timeless value of this book is its presentation of Israel as a case study of Yahweh's government. No nation had so much light as Israel had, or a closer relationship to God than Israel did (3:1-2, 7). But in Israel, privilege had borne the fruit of sin and would end with judgment.

When God wanted to convict His people of their sins, He described the luxury and wantonness of Israel's women (4:1). John Ruskin, the English poet, claimed that war would cease when enough pure women demanded it. Amos pictured the depravity of the Israelites by describing the evil women of the nation promoting it. He also described it ironically this way: "Enter Bethel and transgress; in Gilgal multiply transgression! Bring your sacrifices every morning, and your tithes every three days" (4:4). The Israelites were going to places of worship to engage in sinful rituals, not to worship. A modern equivalent would be: "Let's go to church to meet someone of the opposite sex that we can sin with."

Israel had sinned in failing to yield to Yahweh's chastisement (4:6, 8, 9, 10, 11). None of God's judgments on His people had moved them to repent. The Israelites who longed to see "the day of the Lord" failed to realize that it would be a day of judgment for them (5:18-20). Those of them who never gave "the day of the Lord" a thought, and were at ease in Zion, needed to realize that this day was coming.

The terrible descriptions of Israel's sins in this book appear all the worse because of Israel's privileged position. These were His chosen people. He did nothing without revealing it to them through His servants the prophets (3:7). Yet the Israelites were guilty of the sins of wanton womanhood, of refusal to submit to discipline, of professing a desire for God to act, and of indifference to the fact that He *would* act in judgment.

In five visions, Amos pronounced judgment that would fall on the Israelites. These were: the visions of the locusts, the fire, the plumb line, the basket of summer fruit, and the altar of judgment. In all of them, Amos pictured divine judgment determined, temporarily restrained, and finally executed. These prophecies of coming judgment must have sounded strange to the Israelites, who were then living lives of ease and material prosperity under King Jeroboam II. After all, had not God said He would bless the godly with prosperity? How could Amos then say that the Israelites were such great sinners? Furthermore, Amos was a "nobody" in society, a despised Judahite, a rural dolt.

Because Israel's light had been clear, her judgment would be pervasive. She had failed to take advantage of her privileges and had lived selfishly. Consequently her ruin would be complete.

The third timeless value of this book is the promise of ultimate restoration that it contains at the very end. Restoration would come in three stages. First, there would be preliminary restoration. God would restore the Davidic dynasty to power (9:11). Then, progressive restoration of the nation would follow (9:12-14). Finally, there would be permanent restoration (9:15). These blessings will all come on the Jews after Jesus Christ returns to the earth at His second coming.

Amos, then, reveals the sovereign government of the God of all the earth. We discover His philosophy of government, we see a case study of His government, and we learn of the outcome of His government in this book.

The message of Amos is that God blesses people so they can be channels of blessing to others, not so they may simply squander His blessings selfishly. My prayer is often, "Make me a blessing to someone today." Christians sometimes sing, "Channels only, blessed Master, but with all Thy wondrous power flowing through us, Thou canst use us every day and every hour." We need to ask ourselves often, "How can I help someone today?" not "How can I get someone to help me today." Christians should be givers more than takers. God blesses us as we bless others.

This message is applicable mainly to national life, because national life is the primary focus of the revelation in Amos. But obviously Christians can apply the lessons of Amos to our individual lives as well.

God still rules over all nations, not just His chosen people. He still opposes nations that violate human rights, and He will judge them. The old order may pass away with the turning of the pages of the calendar, but the divine order does not change. God remains the same. God's methods change, His requirements for His people change, His dispensations (household rules) change, but His underlying attitudes toward people do not change. Cruelty is as hateful to God today as it ever has been.

Another major lesson of Amos is that people who have the light of God's truth live with greater responsibility than those who live in darkness. The light exposes our sins, and when we see our sins, we must humble ourselves under the mighty hand of God, or we will experience His judgment. Christians have a greater responsibility to judge themselves, "that we be not judged," than the unsaved. We may be judged, not with separation from God eternally, but with separation from much future blessing.

Amos charged Israel with injustice, avarice, oppression, immorality, profanity, blasphemy, and sacrilege: seven deadly sins. These same sins characterize believers today. We are in danger of doing what the Israelites in Amos' day of material prosperity did. We can wrongly conclude that our prosperity is a reward from God: that He is blessing us for our goodness. All the while we may be preparing ourselves for judgment. It is only as we turn from our sins, in profound repentance, that we can live. Yet if judgment comes, its purpose is not to destroy us, but to restore us to the Lord.

We must distinguish between secular nations and the church of Jesus Christ. Nevertheless, the principles that Amos reveals are applicable to both groups. The nations with greater light have greater responsibility. The church has greater light and has greater responsibility. When nations fail to take advantage of their light, they become degraded. When the church fails to take advantage of its light, it becomes degraded.

These principles are also applicable to individuals. God's people are greatly blessed people. Unfortunately, many Christians conclude that because "there is therefore now no condemnation in Christ Jesus," there is also no accountability to Christ Jesus. We must all stand before the judgment seat of Christ to receive payment for what we have done with the light that God has given us (Rom. 14; 1 Cor. 3; 2 Cor. 5). This is an awesome thought that should sober and humble us every day we live. We need to prepare for our "day of the Lord," when we will see our Savior, stand before Him, and give an account of our stewardship to Him. Amos spoke to the Israelites as the people of God. Christians are the people of God in our day, and we need to heed His strong words of warning as well.[18]

Exposition

I. PROLOGUE 1:1-2

The first two verses of the book constitute a prologue. They contain an explanation of what follows, an identification of the writer, the time of his writing, and his theme.

A. INTRODUCTION 1:1

What follows are the words (i.e., collected messages, cf. Prov. 30:1; 31:1; Eccles. 1:1; Jer. 1:1) of Amos (lit. burden-bearer), who was one of the sheepherders who lived in the Judean town of Tekoa, 10 miles south of Jerusalem. This town stood on a comparatively high elevation, from which its residents could see the Mount of Olives to the north, as well as the surrounding countryside in every direction. Amos' words expressed what he saw in visions that came to him from the Lord. These visions concerned Israel, the Northern Kingdom at the time when he wrote, namely, during the reigns of King Uzziah of Judah and Jeroboam II (the son of Joash), king of Israel. Here "Israel" must mean the Northern Kingdom rather than the combined people of Israel and Judah, as it often means in the prophets, because of the many references to people and places in the Northern Kingdom that follow. Specifically, Amos wrote sometime after the visions the Lord gave him "two years before the earthquake," which was perhaps about 762 B.C.[19]

> "In this [ancient Near Eastern] culture an earthquake would not have been viewed as a mere natural occurrence, but as an omen of judgment. Amos had warned that the Lord would shake the earth (see 8:8; 9:1, 5, as well as 4:12-13). When the earthquake occurred just two years after he delivered his message, it signaled that the Lord was ready to make the words of Amos a reality."[20]

This introductory verse has been called "the most complete superscription to be found in all of prophetic literature."[21]

> "The opening words make it clear that what follows is a covenant lawsuit commanded by Israel's suzerain, the Lord himself."[22]

B. THEME 1:2

This verse summarizes the message that Amos received from the Lord. Amos reported that Yahweh roared from Zion, as a lion roars before it devours its prey or as thunder precedes a severe storm (cf. 3:4, 8; Jer. 25:30; Hos. 5:14; 11:10; 13:7). Yahweh was about to judge. "Yahweh" is the first word in the Hebrew sentence—usually a verb comes first—and so is emphatic by position. The Lord spoke from Zion (Jerusalem, also emphatic by position) because that is where He manifested Himself in a localized sense to the Israelites of Amos' day. In Israel, the primary worship centers were Dan and Bethel (1 Kings 12—13). All the land would mourn, from the shepherds' pastures in the lowland to the summit of

---

[18]Adapted from G. Campbell Morgan, *Living Messages of the Books of the Bible*, 1:2:197-211.
[19]See my comments above under "writer" and "date" in the Introduction section of these notes.
[20]Robert B. Chisholm Jr., *Handbook on the Prophets*, p. 378.
[21]Shalom M. Paul, *Amos*, p. 33.
[22]Niehaus, p. 336.

Mt. Carmel (a merism), because the Lord would dry up the land. This was one of the promises of judgment if God's people proved unfaithful to His covenant with them, the Mosaic Covenant (Deut. 28:20-24; cf. Lev. 26:22; Deut. 32:24). "Yahweh" was God's covenant name, and it connotes holiness and power (cf. Exod. 3:5; 19:10-25). However, since oracles announcing judgment on neighbor nations, as well as on Israel, follow, the extent of God's judgment would go beyond Israel's territory and Israel's covenant (cf. Isa. 24:4-6; 26:20-21). The mention of Mt. Carmel, nevertheless, fixes the primary site in Israel. Most of this book records messages of judgment against Israel. The theme of the book is practical righteousness (cf. James).

II. PROPHETIC MESSAGES THAT AMOS DELIVERED 1:3—6:14

The Book of Amos consists of words (oracles, 1:3—6:14) and visions (chs. 7—9), though these sections also contain short sub-sections of other types of material.

A. ORACLES AGAINST NATIONS 1:3—2:16

An oracle is a message of judgment. Amos proceeded to deliver eight of these, seven against Israel's neighbors, including Judah (1:3—2:5), and one against Israel (2:6—6:14). The order is significant. The nations mentioned first were foreign, but those mentioned next were the blood relatives of the Israelites, and Judah was its closest kin. Upon hearing this list, the Israelites would have felt "a noose of judgment about to tighten round their [the Israelites' own] throats."[23] This is the "rhetoric of entrapment."[24]

> "The prophet began with the distant city of Damascus and, like a hawk circling its prey, moved in ever-tightening circles, from one country to another, till at last he pounced on Israel. One can imagine Amos's hearers approving the denunciation of these heathen nations. They could even applaud God's denunciation of Judah because of the deep-seated hostility between the two kingdoms that went as far back as the dissolution of the united kingdom after Solomon. But Amos played no favorites; he swooped down on the unsuspecting Israelites as well in the severest language and condemned them for their crimes."[25]

Each oracle follows the same basic pattern. First, Amos declared the judgment to come. Second, he defended the judgment by explaining the reason for it. Third, he described the coming judgment. Smith described this pattern, which occurs with some variations in the oracles to follow, as a "messenger speech."[26] It contains five elements: introductory formula, certainty of judgment, charge of guilt, announcement of punishment, and concluding formula.

> "All the things condemned by Amos were recognized as evil in themselves, not merely in Israel, but by all the nations of the western Fertile Crescent."[27]

Other major collections of oracles against foreign neighbors appear in Isaiah (chs. 13—17, 19, 21, 23, 34), Jeremiah (chs. 46—51), and Ezekiel (chs. 25—32). One might consider all of Obadiah and Nahum as oracles against foreign nations as well. In fact, all the prophetical books except Daniel and Hosea contain some condemnation of Israel's neighbor nations.[28]

1. An oracle against Aram 1:3-5

1:3 The expression "for three transgressions [Heb. *pesha'im*, rebellions, i.e., against the universal Sovereign; cf. Gen. 9:5-17] and for four" is one of Amos' trademark phrases (cf. vv. 6, 9, 11, 13; 2:1, 4, 6). It means *for numerous transgressions* (cf. Job 5:19; 33:29; Ps. 62:11-12; Prov. 6:16; 30:15-16, 18-19, 21-23, 29-31; Eccles. 11:2; Mic. 5:5-6). "Three transgressions" represents fullness, and the fourth, overflow. Amos cited just the last transgression, the one that "broke the camel's back" and made judgment inevitable, or possibly the representative one, for Israel's enemies.[29] The phrase may also be a poetic way of describing seven transgressions, symbolizing completeness.[30] Limberg observed that the number *seven* plays a significant role in the structure of the whole book and in the makeup of certain of the sayings.[31] This may have been a way Amos

---

[23] J. A. Motyer, *The Day of the Lion: The Message of Amos*, p. 50.
[24] R. Alter, *The Art of Biblical Poetry*, p. 144. Cf. Isa. 28.
[25] McComiskey, pp. 281-82.
[26] Smith, p. 44. See also F. I. Andersen and D. N. Freedman, *Amos*, pp. 341-69.
[27] Ellison, p. 72.
[28] See the chart of oracles against foreign nations in D. Stuart, *Hosea-Jonah*, pp. 405-6.
[29] J. Mays, *Amos: A Commentary*, pp. 23-24.
[30] Meir Weiss, "The Pattern of Numerical Sequence in Amos 1—2, A Re-examination," *Journal of Biblical Literature* 86 (1967):418.
[31] J. Limburg, "Sevenfold Structures in the Book of Amos," *Journal of Biblical Literature* 106 (1987):217.

certified that the whole book and each section in it was the Word of the Lord.[32] In the oracle against Israel, Amos cited seven sins (one in 2:6, two in 2:7, two in 2:8, and two in 2:12). Israel's panic would also be sevenfold (2:14-16).

> "Based on structural parallels with proverbial statements that use the 'three, even four' numerical pattern (see Prov. 30:15-16, 18-19, 21-23, 29-31), one expects to find a list of four specific sins in each oracle. But this never happens in the first seven oracles. After specifying one or two sins, the prophet breaks off the list, announces judgment, and then moves on to the next nation as if the real target of God's anger lies somewhere else. This stylistic device does not become a bad omen for Israel until the list of Judah's sins is left truncated, suggesting that another nation, which proves to be Israel, will follow."[33]

"Damascus" was the capital city of Aram (Syria), and it stands for the whole nation by metonymy. Similarly, the capitals Jerusalem and Samaria often represent their respective nations, Judah and Israel, by metonymy, in biblical literature. Yahweh promised that He would not turn back the punishment due Aram, because the Arameans had proved to be a scourge to the people of Israel. Threshing "Gilead," a Transjordanian part of Israel, with sharp iron implements ("sledges"), pictures the plowing up of that part of the nation militarily (cf. Isa. 41:15; Mic. 4:13; Hab. 3:12).[34] Israelite citizens and territory had suffered greatly during constant battles with the Arameans, especially in Transjordan (cf. 2 Kings 8:7-12; 10:32-33; 13:3-7). The Aramean rulers, Hazael and his son Ben-hadad III, had repeatedly invaded and conquered Israel between 842 and 802 B.C.

1:4   The Lord promised to send a consuming "fire" (judgment) on the "house" (dynasty) and "citadels" (fortified towns) of the Arameans. "Hazael" and "Ben-hadad," dynastic names, probably represent all the Aramean kings.[35] Another view is that the Hazael in view was the king of Damascus who ruled for most of the second half of the ninth century B.C., and "Ben-hadad" was his son and successor (2 Kings 13:3, 22-25).[36] The idea of sending fire on the walls of the main cities of the land recurs throughout these oracles (cf. vv. 4, 7, 10, 12, 14, 2:2, 5). It is a vivid metaphor for *consuming destruction*.

1:5   Yahweh would "also break the bar" that secured the gate of Damascus, making it impossible to defend (cf. 1 Kings 4:13). He would cut off the people who lived in "the valley of Aven" (lit. evil, perhaps Baalbek or the Biq'ah Valley in Lebanon), and Aram's ruler, who lived in Beth-eden (perhaps Bit-Adini, an Aramean state on the Euphrates River 200 miles to the north-northeast of Damascus).[37] These names mean "valley of wickedness" and "house of pleasure," but since the other names mentioned in the oracles are real locations, these probably were as well. The Arameans would go into exile to "Kir" in Mesopotamia, from which they had originated (9:7, precise location unknown). Thus, God would send them back where they came from after He obliterated all they had achieved.

> "Benjamin Franklin said it well at the Constitutional Convention, 'I have lived, Sir, a long time, and the longer I live, the more convincing proofs I see of this truth—that God governs in the affairs of men.'"[38]

The fulfillment of this prophecy came when Tiglath-Pileser III of Assyria captured Damascus and took the Arameans captive in 732 B.C. (2 Kings 16:7-9).[39]

2. An oracle against Philistia 1:6-8

1:6   "Gaza" was the chief city of Philistia, as Damascus was of Aram. The particular sin for which God would judge the Philistines was their capture and deportation of whole communities (or people at peace, Heb. *shelema*), possibly Israelites and or Judahites,"to Edom" as slaves (cf. Joel 3:4-8). During the reign of Israel's King Jehoram (852-841 B.C.), Philistines and Arabs had carried off the royal household (2 Chron. 21:16-17), plundered the temple (Joel 3:5), and sold the people into slavery (Joel 3:3, 6).

> "The concern of Amos seems to have been the freedom and dignity of persons regardless of their national origin. Sale of such captives for use as slave laborers was to treat precious humans made in the image of

---

[32]Ibid., pp 222-23.
[33]Chisholm, p. 379.
[34]See D. A. Hubbard, *Joel and Amos*, p. 131.
[35]H. W. Wolff, *Joel and Amos*, p. 156.
[36]Chisholm, p. 382.
[37]Paul, pp. 52-54; Andersen and Freedman, pp. 255-56.
[38]Wiersbe, p. 344. His quotation comes from Catherine Drinker Bowen, *Miracle at Philadelphia*, p. 126.
[39]Charles Lee Feinberg, *Joel, Amos, and Obadiah*, p. 43.

God (Gen 1:26-27) as mere commodities. The driving force behind these atrocities was nothing higher than the profit of the mighty.

> "Broken treaties have marred the pages of history from ancient to modern times. God has a low tolerance level for those who break treaties, who take away human freedom and dignity, and whose motive is material profit. Such people should brace themselves for the destructive judgment of God."[40]

1:7-8 "Fire" (destruction) would overtake the cities of the Philistines and affect everyone from the ordinary citizens to the rulers. Ancient Near Eastern armies commonly used fire to burn and weaken a city wall.[41] Amos mentioned four of the five major cities of Philistia, all except Gath, probably because it had already fallen to enemies (cf. 6:2; 2 Kings 12:17; 2 Chron. 26:6). Another writer argued that Gath had become more of a Canaanite city by this time than a Philistine city, and that is the reason Amos did not mention it.[42] Still another possibility is that Amos simply chose to refer to some, but not all, of the Philistine cities. Sovereign Yahweh ("Lord GOD") promised to cut off *even* "the remnant" of Philistines that remained in Amos' day. This title for God occurs 19 times in Amos, but only five times in the other Minor Prophets. It stresses both His Lordship and His covenant relationship with people. Sennacherib (705-681 B.C.) captured "Ekron" and killed its officials because of their disloyalty.[43]

This prophecy was initially fulfilled when the Judean kings Uzziah and Hezekiah invaded Philistia (2 Chron. 26:6-7; 2 Kings 18:8), and when a succession of Assyrian conquerors captured these towns.[44] It was completely fulfilled during the Maccabean period (169-134 B.C.) when the Philistines passed out of existence.

3. An oracle against Phoenicia 1:9-10

"Tyre" was apparently the leading city of Phoenicia at this time. The sin of the Phoenicians was the same as that of the Philistines. They had sold whole communities of people to the Edomites as slaves.[45] They also broke a covenant of brothers.

> "If Israel was the injured partner, the reference is probably to the pact between Solomon and Hiram (1 Kings 5) or perhaps to the later relations established through the marriage of Ahab and Jezebel (1 Kings 16:29-31)."[46]

Ironically, many Tyrians became captives and were sold as slaves when Alexander the Great destroyed Tyre in 332 B.C. (cf. Ezek. 26—28). Phoenicia declined as a major power in the ancient Near East—after that destruction—and never revived.

4. An oracle against Edom 1:11-12

Amos next moved from addressing chief cities to addressing countries, specifically countries with closer ethnic ties to the Israelites. Perhaps their closer relationship to Israel is why he mentioned countries rather than cities in the introductions to the later oracles.

Edom's overflowing sin—that brought divine wrath down on its people—was the way the Edomites had treated the Israelites. The Edomites had been very hostile to their "brother," Israel (cf. Gen. 25:29-30; Num. 20:14; Deut. 2:4; 23:7; Obad. 12). This hostility existed throughout the history of these two nations. This animosity even led the Edomites to attack the Israelites "with the sword" (cf. Obad. 10). Consequently, God would send destruction on Edom's chief southern region and a prominent northern city, even on the whole land (a merism). "Teman" was both a village and a southern region in Edom, but here the region is probably in view.[47] "Bozrah" was a northern city.

The Assyrians subjugated Edom in the eighth century B.C., and the Nabateans, an Arabian tribe, took it over in the fourth century B.C.

5. An oracle against Ammon 1:13-15

The Ammonites were descendants of Lot, Abraham's nephew (cf. Gen. 19:30-38). Ammon was in trouble with Yahweh because its soldiers brutally attacked and slew the Israelites, even "the pregnant women" and their unborn children, who lived in Gilead to the west of Ammon. This brutal slaughter terrorized and decimated the attacked populace. The Ammonites did this "to enlarge their borders" (territory) to the west, for

---

[40]Smith, pp. 51-52.
[41]Niehaus, p. 345.
[42]H. Kassis, "Gath and the Structure of 'Philistine' Society," *Journal of Biblical Literature* 84 (1965):259-71.
[43]Daniel D. Luckenbill, *The Annals of Sennacherib*, pp. 31-32.
[44]See James B. Pritchard, ed. *Ancient Near Eastern Texts Relating to the Old Testament*, pp. 282-88; and King, pp. 52-54.
[45]See Paul, p. 59.
[46]Sunukjian, p. 1429.
[47]Niehaus, p. 352.

materialistic advantage, not for self-preservation. Consequently Yahweh promised to destroy "Rabbah," the capital, and Ammon's walled cities ("citadels") in battle. The Ammonites' king and royal officials would go into exile.

This happened when Tiglath-Pileser III invaded Ammon in 734 B.C., but Ammon's final demise came when Nebuchadnezzar sacked Rabbah and took many of Ammon's citizens captive to Babylon around 586 B.C. The last reference to them is the Ammonites' defeat by Judas Maccabeus in the second century B.C. (1 Macc. 5:6-7).

> "In the Old Testament, as in the ancient Near East, theophanic imagery was used to indicate the active presence of a god in battles against those who refused his rule."[48]

6. An oracle against Moab 2:1-3

Yahweh promised not to revoke His punishment of "Moab," another nation descended from Lot (cf. Gen. 19:30-38), because of its brutal treatment of an Edomite king's corpse. Burning the bones of a dead person dishonored that individual, since there was then nothing substantial left of him. Burning the king's bones indicated a desire to completely destroy the peace and even the soul of Edom's king, for eternity. This was a despicable crime in the ancient Near East where a peaceful burial was the hope of every person. This treatment of a dead corpse reflected a lack of respect for human life, life made in the image of God.

> "Highly significant is the fact that Amos here pronounced the punishment of Yahweh on a social crime involving a non-Israelite. In his other oracles the crimes were, for the most part, against the covenant people. Amos understood that an aspect of God's law transcended Israel."[49]

Probably the Noahic Covenant provides the background for the Lord's indictment (Gen. 9:5-7; cf. Isa. 24:5).

> "All the things condemned by Amos [in all eight oracles] were recognized as evil in themselves, not merely in Israel, but by all the nations of the western Fertile Crescent."[50]

> "Crimes against humanity [not just against Israel] bring God's punishment. This observation is a powerful motivation for God's people to oppose the mistreatment and neglect of their fellow human beings."[51]

> "However dimly and falsely men may draw the boundary, there are such things as absolute right and wrong based on the nature of the Creator and Ruler of all."[52]

> "When a society acquiesces in and welcomes an evil, knowing it is evil, that society is doomed."[53]

Because of this sin, Moab would perish in the tumult of battle, and its leaders would die. "Kirioth" was a major city in Moab (cf. Jer. 48:24).

Nebuchadnezzar conquered Moab shortly after 598 B.C., which opened the way for Arab tribes to occupy its land.[54]

7. An oracle against Judah 2:4-5

God would treat "Judah" with the same justice that He promised Israel's other neighbor nations. Judah's overflowing sin was her failure to live by the Torah, the instruction that Yahweh had given her, including the Mosaic Covenant (cf. Rom. 2:12-15). Listening to false prophets and worshipping idols (Heb. *kazib*, a lie, something deceptive) had been major evidences of this apostasy (cf. Deut. 6:14; 7:16; 8:19; 11:16, 28).[55] So Yahweh promised to destroy "Judah" and "Jerusalem," just as He had promised to destroy her sinful neighbors.

> "Verses 4 and 5 of this chapter are directed against Judah, while the remainder of the Book of Amos is addressed to Israel."[56]

The fulfillment came with Nebuchadnezzar's destruction of Jerusalem in 586 B.C. (2 Kings 25:1-12).

---

[48] Ibid., p. 355.
[49] McComiskey, p. 291.
[50] Ellison, p. 72.
[51] Niehaus, p. 358.
[52] Ellison, p. 74.
[53] Ibid.
[54] Josephus, 10:9:7.
[55] See Andersen and Freedman, pp. 301-5, for defense of the false prophet interpretation.
[56] Feinberg, p. 49.

8. An oracle against Israel 2:6-16

The greater length of this oracle, as well as its last position in the group of oracles, points to its preeminent importance. Verse 10, by using the second person rather than the third, suggests that all these oracles were originally spoken to Israel.

There are four sections to this oracle: Israel's recent sins, God's past gracious activity on Israel's behalf, Israel's response, and Israel's punishment.

Israel's recent sins 2:6-8

Not all the sins that Amos identified appear in verses 6-8; two more appear in verse 12. Amos named seven sins of Israel all together rather than just one, as in the previous oracles, though he continued to use the "for three transgressions and for four" formula. Seven seems to be the full measure of Israel's sin. The idea of "the straw that broke the camel's back" carries over from the first seven oracles into the eighth with double force.

2:6 Israel's first sin was that the Israelites took advantage of "righteous," or "needy" people for their own personal, material advantage and sold them into slavery, perhaps into debt (cf. 2 Kings 4:1-7). They sold, for the price of what they owed, honest people who would have repaid their debts if given the opportunity. They would even sell into slavery someone who could not pay the small price of "a pair of sandals." Another interpretation is that they would take as a bribe as little as what a pair of sandals cost. The Israelites should have been generous and open-handed toward the poor (Deut. 15:7-11). Sin often results in the devaluation of human life.

2:7 Second, the Israelites were perverting the legal system to exploit the poor. The courts were siding with creditors against their debtors; they were "stepping on" the poor. This was as painful and humiliating as having one trample on one's head as it lay in "the dust." The oppressors longed to see the poor reduced to extreme anguish. They may have been so greedy that they craved even the dust that the poor threw on their heads in mourning. Or, perhaps they *chased* ("panted after") the poor to death, starving them by economic means—sometimes literally to death—since "dust" is metaphorical for the grave. The Mosaic Covenant called for justice in Israel's courts (Exod. 23:4; Deut. 16:19).

Third, fathers and sons were having sexual intercourse with the same women. The women in view may be temple prostitutes, servant girls taken as concubines, or female relatives (cf. Exod. 21:7-11; Lev. 18:8, 15). This showed contempt for Yahweh's holy character (cf. Exod. 3:13-15). The Law forbade fornication, including incest (Lev. 18:6-18; 20:11, 17-21).

2:8 Fourth, the Israelites failed to return "garments taken as pledges," the collateral for debts owed them. The Law specified that the Israelites could take a garment as a pledge, except the garment of a widow (Deut. 24:17), but they were to return it to the owner before nightfall (Exod. 22:26-27; Deut. 24:10-13; cf. Deut. 24:6; Job 22:6). The Israelites were even taking these garments with them and displaying them at the public feasts to honor whatever god they worshipped. Another possibility is that the Israelite men were using these pledged garments as blankets on which to have sex with the temple prostitutes.[57]

Fifth, the Israelites had worshipped other gods (cf. v. 4). They were using "the wine" that they had received as fines, or had extracted from the poor, to honor heathen gods. The proper course of action would have been to drink wine that the worshipper had paid for himself or present it in worship of the true God.

God's past grace 2:9-11

In this section, Amos reminded the Israelites of Yahweh's past blessings on them. This made the heinousness of their sins even clearer. Israel's treatment of the poor had been destructive, but Yahweh's treatment of the poor Israelites had been constructive. The other nations that God pronounced judgment against, in the previous oracles, had not enjoyed these special blessings.

2:9 The Israelites had committed the previous breaches of covenant—in spite of God having driven the giant Amorites out of the Promised Land for them (cf. Num. 13:22-33). These enemies had been as strong and tall as cedar or oak trees (cf. Num. 13:28-33; Deut. 1:26-28), but the Lord "destroyed" them completely, from "fruit above" to "root below."

> "Destruction of 'his fruit' left no possibility of future life from seed. Destruction of 'roots' left no possibility of future life from the tree. God is able to deal decisively with the enemies of his people."[58]

---

[57] Ronald Boyer, in an e-mail dated October 23, 2012.
[58] Smith, pp. 65-66.

	Here the Amorites, the most formidable of the native inhabitants, represent all of them, by metonymy (cf. Gen. 15:16). The defeat of these giants demonstrated Yahweh's superior power as well as His love for His people. By implication, if God drove the Amorites out of the land, He might also drive the Israelites out.
2:10	Going back even further in their history, Yahweh reminded His people that He had redeemed them from slavery in Egypt and had led them safely through the wilderness for 40 years. He had preserved them so they could take possession of the Promised Land, the land of the Amorites. By shifting to the second person, Amos strengthened the force of God's appeal.
2:11	In the land, God had raised up prophets and godly Nazirites from among the Israelites' sons. Prophets relayed God's messages to them, and Nazirites were examples of ordinary citizens who dedicated themselves completely to the Lord. These individuals were blessings to the nation because, by their words and deeds, they encouraged the people to follow the Lord faithfully. Yahweh asked—rhetorically—if this was not in fact what He had done.

The order of these blessings is not chronological. Evidently Amos arranged them in this order to highlight the Exodus, the central of the three blessings mentioned and the single most important event in Israel's history.

Israel's response to God's grace 2:12

Even though God gave His people prophets and Nazirites, the Israelites had encouraged the Nazirites to compromise their dedication to Yahweh, and had told the prophets to stop prophesying. These were the sixth and seventh sins of the Israelites that Amos enumerated. The people were uncommitted to God and unwilling to hear and obey His Word.

> "Even today we are sadly familiar with the preacher who preaches the whole Bible most faithfully but yet so that none of his hearers are ever shaken out of their sins. I myself have been told by a sincere Christian man, who was motivated, as he thought, purely by concern for my well-being, 'You mustn't say that kind of thing here, or you will not be invited again.' How many a man of God has been passed over when a minister has been wanted: 'He is not the man for *us*.' There are many ways of saying to the prophet *Prophesy not*, and one and all they are an abomination to God and bring judgment on God's people."[59]

Israel's consequent punishment 2:13-16

In the previous oracles, Amos consistently likened God's judgment to fire (1:4, 7, 10, 12, 14; 2:2, 5). In this one, he did not use that figure, but described the judgment coming on Israel with other images—especially images of panic in battle.

2:13	The Lord said He felt burdened by the sinfulness of His people, as heavy as a wagon "weighted down," filled to its capacity with grain.[60] Another interpretation understands Amos to be picturing Israel being crushed, like an object under the wheels of a heavily loaded cart.[61]
2:14-16	Running fast would not provide escape from His coming judgment, resisting would not enable the Israelites to withstand it, and outstanding leaders could not deliver them from it. Archers opposing God would not be able to prevent Him from advancing against them, quick runners would not be able to flee, and riding a horse could not remove them from the scene of judgment. When Yahweh judged the Israelites, even the bravest among them would prove fearful and ashamed. In the past, Israel's heroes had routed the Canaanites, but in the future they would not even be able to deliver themselves in battle, much less win a victory. This sevenfold description of Israel's panic balances the earlier sevenfold description of Israel's sin.

The fulfillment of this threatened judgment came when the Assyrians besieged and destroyed Samaria, Israel's capital, in 722 B.C., and carried many of the people of that land into captivity.

These oracles teach the modern reader that God is sovereign over all nations, and holds them accountable for their conduct toward other human beings, as well as for their response to special revelation (cf. Gen. 9:5-6). They also teach that God is patient with sinners and will only punish when the measure of human sin has overflowed His predetermined capacity. The oracles also teach that God is impartial in His judgment; He will punish sin in His own people, as well as sin in those with whom He has established no special relationship.

---

[59]Ellison, p. 76.
[60]Andersen and Freedman, p. 334.
[61]Sunukjian, p. 1432; McComiskey, p. 295; Smith, p. 68.

B. MESSAGES OF JUDGMENT AGAINST ISRAEL CHS. 3—6

After announcing that God would judge Israel, Amos delivered five messages in which he explained more fully why God would judge the Northern Kingdom. Appeals for repentance and explanations of how to avoid judgment appear within these messages. The first three begin with the word, "Hear" (3:1; 4:1; 5:1; cf. Prov. 8:32), and the last two begin with "Alas" (5:18) and "Woe" (6:1), both being translations of the Hebrew word *hoy*. The first message was explanation, the second accusation, and the third lamentation.[62]

1. The first message on sins against God and man ch. 3

Amos' first message explained that God would judge His people because they had oppressed others in spite of their uniquely privileged relationship with Yahweh. The prophet addressed this message initially to both Israel and Judah (vv. 1-2), but he focused it mainly on Israel (vv. 9, 12). The first two verses are a brief oracle that introduces the series of judgment pronouncements that continue through chapter 6.

Israel's unique relationship with Yahweh 3:1-2

Amos called on all the Israelites to hear a message from their Lord. He referred to them as those whom Yahweh had redeemed from Egypt, reminding them of the unique privilege they enjoyed. He also mentioned that the Israelites, among all the peoples of the world, had a special relationship to the Lord. "You only" is in the emphatic first position in the Hebrew sentence. This is an allusion to the covenant that God had made with the Israelites at Mt. Sinai (cf. Exod. 19:3-6; Deut. 28:1-14). God had chosen (known, Heb. *yada'*; cf. Jer. 1:5) the Israelites, in that He had made a commitment to them as His vassal in a covenant relationship.[63] He had also revealed Himself to the Israelites as He had done to no other people. God said He would punish His people for their "iniquities" because these sins were against His unusual blessings (cf. v. 14). Greater privilege always results in greater responsibility (cf. Luke 12:48). Verses 2 and 14 both contain promises that God would punish His people, forming an *inclusio* or literary envelope around the whole passage.

> "A similar injunction to hear what God has to say formerly introduced his commands in the Sinai covenant. Now, it introduces his covenant lawsuit against his rebellious people, who are in fact his family."[64]

Israel's inevitable judgment by Yahweh 3:3-8

Amos asked seven rhetorical questions in verses 3-6 to help the Israelites appreciate the inevitability of their judgment. In each one, the prophet pointed out that a certain cause inevitably produces a certain effect. The five questions in verses 3-5 expect a negative answer, and the two in verse 6 expect a positive one. Verses 7-8 draw the conclusion.

3:3	Two people do not travel together unless they first agree to do so. By implication, God and Israel could not travel together toward God's intended destination for the nation, unless the Israelites agreed to do so on His terms (cf. v. 2).
3:4	A lion does not roar in the forest unless it has found prey. Young lions do not growl in their dens unless they have captured something and are protecting it (cf. 1:2).
3:5	Birds do not get caught in traps unless there is bait in the traps that attracts them. Animal traps do not snap shut unless something triggers them. Israel had taken the bait of sin and had become ensnared.
3:6	People do not tremble at the news of some coming danger unless someone blows a trumpet to warn them. Calamities do not occur in cities unless God has either initiated or permitted them.[65]

> "The seven examples of related events began innocuously, but become increasingly foreboding. The first example (Amos 3:3) had no element of force or disaster about it. The next two (v. 4), however, concerned the overpowering of one animal by another, and the two after that (v. 5) pictured man as the vanquisher of animal prey. In the final two examples (v. 6), people themselves were overwhelmed, first by other human

---

[62]Wiersbe, p. 348.

[63]See H. B. Huffmon, "The Treaty Background of Hebrew *Yada'*," *Bulletin of the American Schools of Oriental Research* 181 (February 1966):31-37.

[64]Niehaus, p. 375.

[65]See Robert B. Chisholm Jr., "How a Hermeneutical Virus Can Corrupt Theological Systems," *Bibliotheca Sacra* 166:663 (July-September 2009):264-66.

instruments, then by God Himself. This ominous progression, to the point where God Himself is seen as the initiator of human calamity, brought Amos to a climactic statement (vv. 7-8)."[66]

3:7   A similar inevitable connection exists between two other events. God does nothing to His people unless He first warns them through one of His prophets (cf. Ps. 25:14; Jer. 23:18, 22).[67] Here God meant that He would do nothing by way of covenant-lawsuit judgment without first telling His people. Obviously God does many things without giving a special revelation to His people that He will do them.

3:8   Amos drew the final comparison by alluding to his previous illustrations. The message of judgment coming from the Lord that Amos now brought the Israelites was like the roaring of "a lion." Who would not fear such a Lion as the sovereign Yahweh? Indeed, how could the mouthpiece of the Lion not prophesy since Yahweh had spoken?

> ". . . if an untrained rustic farmer is preaching God's Word, *it means God has called him*."[68]

The two rhetorical questions in this verse introduce the following series of oracles.

Israel's unparalleled oppression from God 3:9-10

3:9   Amos called for announcements to be made to the large buildings (i.e., to the people living in them) of "Ashdod" in Philistia and to those in "Egypt." The Mosaic Law required two witnesses in cases involving the death penalty (Deut. 17:6). Here those witnesses were Ashdod and Egypt. Amos may have chosen these nations because they had previously oppressed the Israelites. People who lived in "citadels" were for the most part the wealthy and the leaders of their local cities, towns, or districts. A "citadel" (Heb. *'armon*) was almost any fortified building higher than an ordinary house (cf. Ps. 48:3; Isa. 34:13; Jer. 9:21). These structures became part of a city's defense system because they were high and easier to defend than ordinary houses. Usually important people lived in these larger buildings, and they were often attachments of the palaces of kings (cf. 1 Kings 16:18; 2 Kings 15:25). Here, because of the military terminology in the passage, their function as fortresses is particularly in view. These witnesses should come and stand on the mountains surrounding Samaria, the capital of the Northern Kingdom. There they would see great tumults, not the peace and order that should have prevailed, and oppressions within Samaria. The Israelites were assaulting and robbing one another; the rich were taking advantage of the poor.

3:10   Yahweh announced that the Israelites had plundered, looted, and terrorized each other so long that they no longer knew how to do right (Heb. *nekohah*, straightness). The Israelites were different from their aggressors because they plundered and looted their own fortresses rather than those of a foreign enemy. It was as though the Israelites hoarded up "violence and devastation" while others, and they themselves, hoarded material wealth. Now the wealthy foreigners, infamous for similar sins, would see that the Israelites behaved even worse in their own citadels.

Israel's coming catastrophe from Yahweh 3:11-15

Amos' announcement of Israel's coming judgment came in three waves (vv. 11, 12, and 13-15).

3:11   Sovereign Yahweh announced that an enemy that would surround the land of Israel would destroy and loot its impressive fortresses. That enemy proved to be Assyria, which besieged and destroyed Samaria and overran all Israel in 722 B.C.

3:12   Yahweh also predicted that only a small remnant of the people would survive. The situation would be similar to when a shepherd snatched a remaining fragment of a sheep, a couple of leg bones or a small piece of an ear, from the mouth of an attacking wild animal. It would be like when someone stole everything in a house and the owner could only hold onto a piece of his bed or a bedspread. Similarly, an overpowering enemy would steal away the people of Samaria, and only a few would escape. Evidently about 27,000 Israelites from Samaria suffered captivity.[69]

The figure of a shepherd represented Yahweh in Israel's literature (e.g., Ps. 23:1; et al.). The people would have seen Him as the One who would rescue the remnant, as well as the One who would allow the enemy to overpower them.

3:13   Sovereign Yahweh Almighty, the suzerain Warrior who led the most vast and powerful of all armies, urged Amos to hear His Word and to bear testimony "against the house of Jacob." The reference to Jacob recalls the devious nature of this ancestor whose character the present generation of Israelites mirrored. It also recalls God's gracious promises to Jacob. The Israelites, as bad as they were, were *God's* people, not just the people of King Jeroboam II.

---

[66]Sunukjian, p. 1433.
[67]For a list of examples of God doing this, see ibid., pp. 1433-34.
[68]Wiersbe, p. 349.
[69]Pritchard, p. 284; D. Winton Thomas, ed., *Documents from Old Testament Times*, pp. 58-60; Ellison, p. 159.

3:14	God now promised to destroy the pagan "altars" that Jeroboam I had erected at "Bethel" at the same time He destroyed the people of Israel (cf. 1 Kings 12:26-30). This altar, and the one at Dan, had taken the place of the one in Jerusalem for most of the Israelites. The one in Bethel was the most popular religious center in Israel. There the Israelites practiced apostate worship. "The horns" of this "altar," symbolic of the strength of its deity, would be "cut off," and would "fall to the ground," showing its impotence. The horns of an altar were also places of asylum in the ancient Near East (1 Kings 1:50), so their *cutting off* pictures no asylum for the Israelites when God's judgment came.
3:15	God also promised to destroy the Israelites' winter and summer homes. The fact that many Israelite families could afford two houses, and yet were oppressing their poorer brethren, proved that they lived in selfish luxury. They had embellished their great houses with expensive ivory decorations (cf. 1 Kings. 21:1, 18; 22:39; Ps. 45:8). The two great sins of the Israelites, false religion (v. 14) and misuse of wealth and power (v. 15), would be the objects of God's judgment. Even some ancient kings did not possess two houses.[70]

> "The enduring principle here is that God will destroy elaborate altars, expensive houses, and other accoutrements of an extravagant lifestyle when these items are acquired through oppression, fraud, and strong-arm tactics. The idolatry of the people led to their opulent lifestyles. Life apart from God may yield temporary material gain, but it will surely result in eternal loss."[71]

The eternal loss for a Christian will not be loss of salvation, but loss of reward, at the judgment seat of Christ (cf. 1 Cor. 3:15).

2. The second message on women, worship, and willfulness ch. 4

This message consists of seven prophetic announcements, each of which concludes: "declares the LORD" (vv. 3, 5, 6, 8, 9, 10, 11). Verse 12 is a final conclusion, and verse 13 is a doxology.

Economic exploitation 4:1-3

4:1	Amos opened this second message as he did the first (ch. 3), with the cry, "Hear this word." He addressed the wealthy women of Samaria, calling them "cows of Bashan." Bashan was a very luxuriant region of Transjordan, east and northeast of the Sea of Chinnereth (Galilee), where cattle had plenty to eat and grew fat (cf. Ps. 22:12; Jer. 50:19; Ezek. 39:18; Mic. 7:14). These women, along with their men, were oppressing (threatening) the poor and crushing (harassing) the needy. The women were even ordering their husbands to wait on them and bring them drinks. The Hebrew word *'adonim*, translated "husbands," means "lords" or "masters." By using it, Amos was stressing the role reversal that existed. The picture is of spoiled, lazy women ordering their husbands to provide them with luxuries, which the men had to oppress the poor in order to obtain (cf. Deut. 28:56-57; Isa. 32:9-13).

> "What is luxury? The word 'luxury' comes from a Latin word that means 'excessive.' It originally referred to plants that grow abundantly (our English word 'luxurious'), but then it came to refer to people who have an abundance of money, time, and comfort, which they use for themselves as they live in aimless leisure. Whenever you are offered 'deluxe service,' that's the same Latin word: service above and beyond what you really need."[72]

4:2-3	Sovereign Yahweh had not just said what He would do, but He had sworn that He would do it. When God swore, He provided an additional guarantee, in addition to His word, that He would indeed do something (cf. Gen. 22:16-17; Isa. 62:8; Jer. 44:26; Heb. 6:16-18). He made this solemn declaration in harmony with His holiness. As surely as God is separate from humankind and cannot tolerate sin, these women would surely suffer His judgment one day.
	An enemy would cart them off, as butchers carry beef with large meat hooks, and as fishermen carry fish with hooks. This description may imply that the enemy would tie them in lines with ropes and lead them away, since this is how fishermen strung their fish on lines. Carved reliefs that archaeologists have found show Assyrians leading people by a rope attached to a ring in the jaw or lip of their captives.[73] Alternatively, it may mean that their dead bodies would be disposed of as so much

---

[70]Pritchard, p. 655.
[71]Smith, p. 83.
[72]Wiersbe, p. 352.
[73]See Leonard W. King, *Annals of the Kings of Assyria*, pp. 116-20, 125-26.

meat.[74] The enemy would carry the bodies of these women (living or dead) off through breaches in Samaria's walls. The women would be carried off without any complications; each one would go straight ahead to captivity or to burial through any one of the many passageways made through the broken walls.

The enemy would take them to Harmon, perhaps an alternative spelling of Mt. Hermon. Some scholars believe the meaning of "Harmon" is uncertain, though it appears to be the name of some site. Mt. Hermon was to the north of Bashan, so these cows of Bashan would end up near Bashan. This is, in fact, the direction the Assyrians took the Israelite captives as they deported them to Assyria.

"Those who oppress the poor and crush the needy in order to support an extravagant lifestyle can expect God's harsh judgment to fall upon them."[75]

Religious hypocrisy 4:4-5

4:4   Ironically, the Lord told these sinful Israelites to go to "Bethel," but to "transgress," not to worship. Such a call parodied the summons of Israel's priests to come to the sanctuary to worship (cf. Ps. 95:6; 96:8-9; 100:2-4). Bethel was the most popular religious site in the Northern Kingdom, but the Lord looked at what the people did there as transgressing His law rather than worshipping Him. "Gilgal," another worship center, was evidently the Gilgal where the Israelites had entered the Promised Land and had erected memorial stones (Josh. 4:20-24). Other references to it indicate that it was a place that pilgrims visited and where they sacrificed in Amos' day (cf. 5:5; Hos. 4:15; 9:15; 12:11). At Gilgal (from Heb. *galal*, to roll) God had rolled away the reproach of Egypt from His people (cf. Josh. 5:9), but now they were bringing reproach on themselves again by their idolatry at Gilgal.

God—hyperbolically and ironically—urged the people to bring their sacrifices every morning, and their tithes every three days (rather than every three years as the Law required, cf. Deut. 14:28-29). Even if they sacrificed every morning and tithed every three days, they would only be rebelling against God. The people were careful to worship regularly, but it was a ritual contrary to God's will.

> "It's as though a pastor today said to his congregation, 'Sure, go ahead and attend church, but by attending, you're only sinning more. . . . Your heart isn't serious about knowing God or doing His will. Since it's all just playacting.'"[76]

4:5   "A thank offering" expressed gratitude for blessings and answers to prayer (Lev. 7:11-15). The Israelites made freewill offerings spontaneously out of gratitude to God (Lev. 7:16; 22:17-19). God permitted the people to present "leavened" bread in these offerings. The people loved to practice these acts of worship, but they did not love to obey sovereign Yahweh or care for their poor, oppressed neighbors. The Lord wanted their loving obedience, not their acts of worship. Loving religious activity is not the same as loving God.

Refusal to repent 4:6-11

4:6   The Lord had brought famine throughout the land to warn His people about their disobedience and His displeasure, but this judgment did not move them to repent (cf. 1 Kings 8:37-39). They had made an idol of the sacrificial system. Famine was one of the curses that God said He might bring if His people proved unfaithful to His covenant (Lev. 26:26, 29; Deut. 28:17, 48).

4:7-8   He had also sent drought when the people needed "rain" the most, "three months" before their "harvest." He had let rain fall on one town but not another, resulting in only spotty productivity (cf. 1 Kings 8:35). This too should have moved them to repent. Drought was also a punishment for covenant unfaithfulness (Lev. 26:19; Deut. 28:22-24, 48).

4:9   The Lord sent plant diseases and insects to blight their "gardens," "vineyards," and fruit "trees." Yet the Israelites did not return to Him (cf. 1 Kings 8:37-39). These were also threatened judgments in the Mosaic Covenant (Lev. 26:20; Deut. 28:18, 22, 30, 38-40, 42). "Many gardens" is another indication that the Israelites were affluent.

---

[74] J. H. Hayes, *Amos*, pp. 140-41.
[75] Smith, p. 86.
[76] Wiersbe, p. 353.

4:10	Wars had brought various plagues on the Israelites, and many of their soldiers had died (cf. 1 Kings 8:33, 37). The plagues on the Israelites should have made them conclude that God was now judging them. God had plagued His people as He formerly had plagued the Egyptians. The "stench" of dead bodies should have led the people to repent, but it did not (cf. Lev. 26:16-17, 25, 31-39; Deut. 28:21-22, 25-27, 35, 49-52, 59-61; 29:23-28).
4:11	Even the overthrow of some Israelite cities did not move the Israelites to repent (cf. Deut. 28:62). Comparing these overthrown cities to "Sodom and Gomorrah" indicates their proverbial complete destruction (cf. Isa. 1:9; 13:19; Jer. 50:40; Zeph. 2:9), not necessarily the method of their destruction. God had rescued His people like burning sticks from a conflagration, as He had formerly extracted Lot and his daughters from Sodom (Gen. 19). The Assyrian kings customarily sowed the ground of a conquered area with salt so nothing would grow there.[77]

In all, Amos mentioned seven disciplinary judgments that God had brought on the Israelites: famine (v. 6), drought, (vv. 7-8), plant diseases (v. 9), insects (v. 9), plague (v. 10), warfare (v. 10), and military defeat (v. 11). God sometimes permits His people to suffer so they will turn back to Him (cf. Heb. 12:6), but the Israelites had not done that.

The inevitable outcome 4:12-13

4:12	The Israelites should "prepare to meet" their "God," because they had failed to repent (cf. Exod. 19:10-19; 2 Cor. 5:10). He would confront them with even greater punishments (cf. 3:11-15). They should prepare to meet Him, not in a face-to-face sense, but as they would encounter a powerful enemy in battle. The prophet's call was a summons to judgment for covenant unfaithfulness, not a call to repentance or an invitation to covenant renewal.[78] The absence of a stated punishment makes the summons even more foreboding.
4:13	Their enemy was the most formidable one imaginable. It was not another nation or army, but sovereign Yahweh of armies—"the LORD God of Hosts.". It was He who forms tangible and stable mountains, creates the intangible and transitory wind, reveals His thoughts to people, turns dawn into darkness, and steps on the hills of Israel like a giant approaching Samaria. They could not escape His judgment, so they better prepare for it (cf. Mic. 1:3-4).

> "In one bold sweep, this hymn shows the sovereignty of God—from his creation of the world to his daily summoning of the dawn, from his intervention in history to his revelation of mankind's thoughts. Every believer can take comfort in the fact that, while sometimes it seems that God does not interfere in human affairs, the world is never out of his control. His sovereignty extends to every aspect of human experience."[79]

The description of God here (and in 5:8 and 9:5-6) is a divine royal titulary. This is a genre that was common in the ancient Near East, and it appears occasionally in the writing prophets.[80] A titulary combines the name of the god or king with epithets that describe him.

3. The third message on injustice 5:1-17

The structure of this message is chiastic, which focuses attention and emphasis on the middle part.

A   A description of certain judgment vv. 1-3
    B   A call for individual repentance vv. 4-6
        C   An accusation of legal injustice v. 7
            D   A portrayal of sovereign Yahweh vv. 8-9
        C'   An accusation of legal injustice vv. 10-13
    B'   A call for individual repentance vv. 14-15
A'   A description of certain judgment vv. 16-17

Another structural feature stresses the solidarity between Yahweh and His prophet, namely: the alternation between of the words of Amos (vv. 1-2, 6-9, 14-15) and the words of God (vv. 3-5, 10-13, 16-17).

---

[77]Niehaus, p. 402.
[78]Paul, p. 151.
[79]McComiskey, p. 308.
[80]Niehaus, p. 323.

A description of certain judgment 5:1-3

5:1   This message begins as the previous two did, with a call to hear the Lord's Word. However here, Amos announced that what follows is "a dirge" (Heb. *qinah*) against the house of Israel. A dirge was a lament that was sung at the funeral of a friend, relative, or prominent person (e.g., 2 Sam. 1:17-27; 3:33-34; 2 Chron. 35:25). The prophets used the dirge genre to prophesy the death of a city, people, or nation (cf. Jer. 7:29; 9:10-11, 17-22; Lam.; Ezek. 19; 26:17-18; 27:2-32; 28:12-19; 32:2). Amos announced Israel's death, the fall of the Northern Kingdom, at the height of its prosperity under Jeroboam II.

> "To his listeners, hearing this lament would be as jarring as reading one's own obituary in the newspaper."[81]

5:2   Amos announced that the virgin Israel, in the prime of her beauty and vigor, had fallen fatally. "Fallen" in funeral songs usually means "fallen in battle" (cf. 2 Sam. 1:19, 25, 27; 3:34; Lam. 2:21). She would never rise to her former position again. No one came to her aid, even Yahweh (cf. Judg. 6:13; 2 Kings 21:14; Isa. 2:6). She lay forsaken in her land.

5:3   Israelite cities that had sent 1,000 soldiers against Israel's enemy saw only 100 survive, and smaller towns that sent out only 100 soldiers saw only 10 come home alive. No nation could survive such devastating defeat in war.

> "We have described for us, then, the utterly prostrate and helpless condition to which the northern kingdom was to be reduced by the Assyrian foe."[82]

A call for individual repentance 5:4-6

This pericope is also chiastic (Bethel, Gilgal, Beersheba, Gilgal, Bethel).

5:4-5   Yahweh invited the Israelites to seek Him so they might live. Even though national judgment and death were inevitable, individuals could still live. Announcements of impending judgment almost always allow for the possibility of individual repentance (cf. Jer. 18:1-10). The Israelites should not seek the Lord at the popular Israelite shrines at Bethel, Gilgal, or Beersheba in southern Judah, however. All these worship centers stood at cites that were important in Israel's earlier history, but God had commanded His people to worship Him at Jerusalem. There is a play on words regarding Bethel. "Bethel" means "house of God," but it would become "Beth-aven," meaning "house of nothing." "Aven" (nothing) often referred to the powerless spirits of wickedness (cf. Isa. 41:22-24, 28-29).

> "During my years of ministry, I've been privileged to speak at many well-known conference grounds in the United States, Canada, and overseas. I've met people at some of these conferences who actually thought that their physical presence by that lake, in that tent or tabernacle, or on that mountain would change their hearts. They were depending on the 'atmosphere' of the conference and their memories of them, but they usually went home disappointed. Why? Because they didn't seek God."[83]

5:6   Amos, as well as the Lord (v. 4), invited the Israelites to seek the Lord by doing good and refraining from evil so they might live (cf. vv. 14-15). The alternative would be God's judgment breaking forth and unquenchably consuming the whole house of Joseph (i.e., the Northern Kingdom, whose main tribe was Ephraim, a son of Joseph).

> "Fear of judgment may not be the highest motive for obeying God, but the Lord will accept it."[84]

An accusation of legal injustice 5:7

The reason for Yahweh's consuming judgment of Israel was that the Israelites were turning sweet justice into something bitter, and were throwing righteousness to the ground with disrespect. These figures picture their total contempt for what was right (cf. Prov. 1:3; 2:9; 8:20; 21:3; Isa. 1:21; 5:7; 28:17). Right conduct was the proper action, and justice was the result, but the Israelites had despised both in their courts. Instead of the judicial system functioning like medicine, healing wrongs and soothing the oppressed, the Israelites had turned it into poison.

---

[81]Sunukjian, p. 1438.
[82]Feinberg, p. 76.
[83]Wiersbe, p. 357.
[84]Ibid.

A portrayal of sovereign Yahweh 5:8-9

Since Yahweh made the Pleiades and Orion, constellations of stars, He could bring His will to pass on earth too. The rising of the Pleiades before daybreak heralded the arrival of spring, and the rising of Orion after sunset signaled the onset of winter.[85] Since Yahweh brings light out of darkness in the morning, and darkens the day at night, He could change the fate of Israel from prosperity to adversity. Since He calls the waters of the sea to form clouds and then empties them on the land, He can pour out judgment on the land as well. Yahweh is the name of this God, the covenant God of Israel. Israel's pagan neighbors attributed all these activities to their idols, and many of the Israelites worshipped them, but Yahweh was the only God who could do these things. The One who would flash forth like lightning from heaven, striking the strong oppressors with destruction and bringing an end to their fortresses on earth, was Yahweh.

Another accusation of legal injustice 5:10-13

This pericope is also chiastic. Intimidation and abusive treatment flank an announcement of covenant violation.

5:10   Amos cited other reasons for the coming judgment. The Israelites hated judges who reproved evildoers in the city gate, where the court convened, as well as witnesses who spoke the truth. When influential people in a society despise the truth, there is little hope that it will remain stable and secure.

5:11   They imposed high rents and taxes of grain on the poor iin order to keep them tenants on the land (cf. Exod. 23:2, 6).

> "The small farmer no longer owns his own land; he is a tenant of an urban class to whom he must pay a rental for the use of the land, a rental that was often a lion's share of the grain which the land had produced."[86]

The oppressors used this illegally obtained income to build themselves luxurious homes. The Lord promised that He would make it impossible for these evil people to live in their fancy houses and enjoy the fruits of their vineyards.

5:12   Yahweh knew the many "transgressions" of His covenant and the "great sins" that these perverters of justice committed. They had distressed the righteous by their unrighteous conduct, accepted bribes from the wealthy, and made it impossible for the poor to get fair treatment in the courts. God was looking for justice (in their relationships to one another) and for righteousness (in their relationship to Him). This dual emphasis on justice and righteousness runs throughout the Book of Amos.

5:13   Life had become so corrupt that keeping quiet about these abuses of power had become the only prudent thing to do. If a person spoke out against them, he could count on feeling the wrath of the powerful.

Another call for individual repentance 5:14-15

5:14   Again the prophet urged the Israelites to seek good rather than evil so they could live (cf. vv. 4-6). Then the sovereign, Almighty Yahweh would truly be with them, as they professed He was even as they practiced their injustice (cf. Num. 23:21; Deut. 20:4; 31:8; Judg. 6:12; Isa. 8:10; Zeph. 3:15, 17). He would become their Defender rather than their Prosecutor.

5:15   They should "hate evil," "love good," and "establish justice in the gate" (a metonym for the courts). Perhaps then, sovereign, Almighty Yahweh would be gracious to the faithful remnant in the Northern Kingdom and deliver them.

Another description of certain judgment 5:16-17

This message concludes by returning to a further description of conditions when Yahweh would judge Israel (cf. vv. 1-3). The sovereign Yahweh of armies, Israel's master, announced wailing in all the open plazas of the Israelite towns and in their streets. There would be many funerals. Everyone would bewail the conditions of divine judgment, not just the professional mourners, but even the poor farmers who would have to bury their oppressors. The vineyards, often places of joy and merriment, would be full of mourning, as would the streets. Yahweh promised to pass through the midst of His people, not to bless them but to blast them with punishment. Earlier, God had passed through Egypt with similar devastating results (cf. Exod. 11:4-7; 12:12-13).

4. The fourth message on unacceptable worship 5:18-27

This lament also has a chiastic structure. It centers on a call for individual repentance.

---

[85] Sunukjian, p. 1439.
[86] Mays, p. 94.

A	A description of inevitable judgment vv. 18-20	
	B	An accusation of religious hypocrisy vv. 21-22
		C A call for individual repentance vv. 23-24
	B'	An accusation of religious hypocrisy vv. 25-26
A'	A description of inevitable judgment v. 27	

A description of inevitable judgment 5:18-20

5:18   The prophet began his message by crying, "Alas" (Heb., *hoy*, woe, oh). This word announced coming doom, and another funeral lament (cf. v. 1). Many Israelites in Amos' day were looking forward to a coming "day of the LORD." Former prophets had spoken of a day in which Yahweh would conquer His enemies and the enemies of His people, and establish His sovereign rule over the world (e.g., Deut. 33:2-3; Joel 3:18-21, and perhaps Isa. 24:21-23; 34:1-3, 8). The Israelites knew that this was going to be a time of great divine blessing, but Amos informed them that it would first be a time of divine chastisement. It would be a time of "darkness" rather than "light" (cf. Jer. 46:10; Joel 3:1-17; Zeph. 3:8; Zech. 14:1-3). God would judge His people before He blessed them.

5:19   The coming day of the Lord would mean inescapable tragedy for Israel. The Israelites may have thought they had escaped one enemy, but they would have to face another. They might think they were secure and safe in their homeland, but deadly judgment would overtake them in that comfortable environment. There would be no safe haven from God's coming judgment, even though they frequented the temple.

5:20   Rhetorically, Amos stated that the coming day of the Lord would be a day characterized by "darkness" and "gloom" (despair), rather than by bright light (joy; cf. Joel 2:1-2, 10-11; Zeph. 1:14-15).

A brighter day of the Lord was also coming (cf. 9:11-15; Jer. 30:8-11; Hos. 2:16-23; Mic. 4:6-7; Zeph. 3:11-20), but first a dark one would appear. The Israelites wanted to hasten the good day of the Lord, but they wanted to forget about the bad one. This prophecy found fulfillment when the Assyrians overran Israel and took most of the people into exile in 722 B.C. The later Tribulation period for Israel, which will precede her millennial day of blessing, will be similar to what Amos predicted here, but I think it was not what God was foretelling here.

An accusation of religious hypocrisy 5:21-22

5:21   The Israelites enjoyed participating in the religious "festivals" and "assemblies" in which they professed to worship Yahweh. God had commanded the Israelites to observe several feasts and one fast each year, and these are probably the festivals in view. The feasts were Passover, Unleavened Bread, Firstfruits, Pentecost (also called Harvest or Weeks), Trumpets, and Tabernacles (also called Booths or Ingathering). The fast was the Day of Atonement. The first four feasts took place in the spring, and the last two and the Day of Atonement were fall festivals. It is not certain, however, how faithfully the apostate residents of the Northern Kingdom observed these special days. Yahweh hated the Israelites' worship assemblies, however, because the people were not worshipping Him from their hearts (cf. v. 15; Isa. 1:13-14). They were only going through the motions of worship. The repetition of "I hate," "I reject," and "Nor do I delight," stresses how much He detested this type of worship. Notice also, "I will not accept," "I will not look," and "I will not listen," in verses 22 and 23.

> "The presence of the poor and oppressed . . . witnessed to their failure to please God. The neglected widow and the poor child in dirty rags were theological statements condemning the attitudes of the oppressors. Amos viewed the sacrifices as objects of God's hatred because they furthered the spiritual ignorance of the people by giving them a false sense of security."[87]

5:22   "Burnt" and "grain (meal) offerings" were voluntary, and expressed the worshipper's personal dedication to Yahweh and the dedication of his or her works to the Lord (Lev. 1—2). Peace offerings were also voluntary and expressed appreciation for the fellowship that God had made possible for His redeemed people with Himself and with one another (Lev. 3). All three of these offerings were sweet-smelling to the Lord, and were primarily offerings of worship, rather than offerings to secure atonement for sins committed. These three offerings also represent all the worship offerings in another sense. The burnt offering was totally consumed on the altar. The grain offering was partly burned up and partly eaten by the offerer. And the offerer, the priest, and God shared the peace offering. God said He would not accept (lit. smell) or take any notice of any of these offerings, which represent all the others (cf. 4:4-5). In verses 21 and 22 of the Hebrew text, the plural pronouns "you" and "your" indicate that God was addressing the whole nation.

---

[87]Niehaus, p. 431.

A call for individual repentance 5:23-24

5:23   In verses 23 and 24, the singular pronoun "your" indicates that the call is for individuals to repent. God told His people to take away the songs that they sang when they worshipped Him because they were only so much noise in His ears. He would not even listen to the musical accompaniment. He would shut His ears as well as His nostrils (v. 21, vivid anthropomorphisms).

> "Today people will pay high prices for tickets to 'Christian concerts,' yet they won't attend a free Bible study class or Bible conference in their own church. Christian music is big business today, but we wonder how much of it really glorifies the Lord. What we think is music may be nothing but noise to the Lord."[88]

5:24   Instead of feasts and fasts, instead of offerings and sacrifices, instead of singing and playing musical instruments, the Lord said He wanted justice and righteousness (cf. v. 7). Instead of a constant stream of blood flowing from sacrifices, and an endless torrent of verbal and ritual praise from His people, He wanted these ethical qualities to flow without ceasing from them. The Israelites were inundating Him with rivers of religiosity, but He wanted rivers of righteousness.

> "Only when the personal concern of the law is incorporated into their social structure and 'rightness' characterizes their dealings with others will their worship be acceptable. A token practice of justice and righteousness will not do."[89]

This is the key verse in the book, since it expresses so clearly what God wanted from His people. It is a clear statement of the importance of moral and ethical righteousness over mere ritual worship. Amos' concerns boil down to justice toward man and righteousness toward God.

> "With Hos 6:6 and Mic 6:8 this text stands as one of the great themes in prophetic literature with regard to the nature of sacrifices and true religion. God is not pleased by acts of pomp and grandeur but by wholehearted devotion and complete loyalty."[90]

Another accusation of religious hypocrisy 5:25-26

5:25   The Lord now returned to explain further what He did *not* want (vv. 21-23). With another rhetorical question (cf. v. 20), the Lord asked if His people really worshipped Him with their animal sacrifices and grain offerings when they were in the wilderness for 40 years. Animal sacrifices and grain offerings represent the totality of Israel's Levitical offerings. As He clarified in the next verse, they had not. Their hypocritical worship was not something new; it had marked them from the beginning of their nation (e.g., the golden calf incident, Exod. 32).

> "Today, there are those who are more in love with the church than with Christ, people who are more preoccupied with choir robes and candle holders [and with worship styles and worship teams?] than with an encounter with the living God. Can we imagine that the God who is the same yesterday, today, and forever will wink at this misdirected love?"[91]

5:26   During the wilderness wanderings, the Israelites had also carried shrines of their "king." This may refer to unauthorized shrines honoring Yahweh or, more probably, shrines honoring other deities (cf. Acts 7:42-43). "Sikkuth, your king," probably refers to Sakkut, the Assyrian war god also known as Adar. "Kiyyun, your images," probably refers to the Assyrian astral deity also known as Kaiwan or Saturn. Amos evidently ridiculed these gods by substituting the vowels of the Hebrew word for "abomination," (*shiqqus*) in their names.[92] "The star of your gods [or god]" probably refers to the planet Saturn, that to them represented Kiyyun. Stephen's quotation of this verse in Acts 7:42-43 was from the Septuagint, which interpreted these names as references to pagan idols. The worshippers may have carried pedestals for their images of various idols including astral deities. Many scholars believe the Israelites conceived of the golden calf as a representation of that on which Yahweh rode, a visible support for their invisible God. Another view is that the golden calf represented Yahweh Himself. The bull in Egyptian iconography was a symbol of strength and power. Jeroboam I had erected bulls at Dan and Bethel in Israel, and had revived

---

[88]Wiersbe, p. 354.
[89]McComiskey, p. 316.
[90]Smith, p. 115.
[91]Niehaus, p. 433.
[92]Andersen and Freedman, p. 533.

this idolatrous form of worship. Amos pointed out that Israel had always mixed idolatry with the worship of Yahweh, so Israel's worship of Him had been hypocritical throughout her history. Certainly, at times, the Israelites worshipped God exclusively and wholeheartedly, but throughout their history there had been these instances of syncretistic hypocrisy. Do we still carry our idols around with us?

Another description of inevitable judgment 5:27

Because of this hypocritical worship, Yahweh, the God of armies, promised that the Israelites would go into exile beyond Damascus. They *did* go into exile in Assyria, to the northeast of Damascus, after 722 B.C. (cf. 4:3).

> "The horror of 'exile' was more than the ruin of defeat and the shame of capture. For Israel, it meant being removed from the land of promise, the land of God's presence. Exile, in effect, was excommunication."[93]

5. The fifth message on complacency and pride ch. 6

In this lament, Amos announced again that Israel would fall under God's judgment.

The boastful complacency of Israel's leaders 6:1-3

6:1 The prophet began this message by announcing coming "woe" (Heb. *hoy*, cf. 5:18). Those who felt "at ease in Zion" (Jerusalem) and "secure in . . . Samaria" were the subjects of his message. Those who felt comfortable in Samaria, partially because it stood on a high hill that was easily defensible, were the distinguished men. They regarded Israel, and Judah, as the foremost of the nations of their day. They were the men to whom the rest of the house of Israel (the people of the Northern Kingdom) came for advice and or justice.

> "With masterly irony, Amos addressed the self-satisfied rich, secure in their affluence (v. 1; cf. Luke 6:24-25; 12:13-21)."[94]

> "God doesn't look at the talent of national leaders, the extent of a nation's army, or the prosperity of its economy. God looks at the heart, and the heart of the two Jewish kingdoms was far from the Lord."[95]

This is the last reference to the people of Zion in this message; from now on Amos spoke only of the Northern Kingdom. Perhaps he referred to the Judean leaders because they were also guilty of the same sins (cf. Isa. 32:9-11), but God had not decreed destruction against them yet.

6:2 Amos challenged these proud leaders to visit other cities that had once considered themselves great. "Calneh" (or Calno, Isa. 10:9) and "Hamath" were city-states in northern Aram. Shalmaneser III of Assyria had overrun them in 854-846 B.C., but Israel controlled them in Amos' day. Gath had been a notable city in Philistia, but it had fallen before King Hazael of Aram in 815 B.C., and again to King Uzziah of Judah in 760 B.C. Presently Judah controlled it. Samaria was no better than those city-states, and their territories were larger than Samaria's. Yet they had fallen to foreign invaders. What had happened to them could happen to Samaria—even though the people of Israel believed that Yahweh would protect it.

6:3 The leaders of Samaria dismissed the possibility that calamity would overtake their city. But they were really hastening the day of terror (or seat of violence) by refusing to acknowledge and repent of their sins. Amos raised the possibilities as questions, but the answers were obvious.

The 31 years following King Jeroboam II's reign saw increasingly worse conditions for Israel (cf. 2 Kings 15:8—17:6). Six kings reigned, three of whom seized power by political coup and assassination. Fear and violence marked this period (cf. 2 Kings 15:16).

The luxurious indulgence of the Samaritans 6:4-7

6:4-6 Amos described the luxury and self-indulgence that characterized the leaders of Samaria during his day. They reclined on very expensive beds inlaid with "ivory." They "sprawled," implying laziness or drunkenness, "on their couches." They ate the best, most tender meat obtainable.

---

[93] Sunukjian, p. 1442.
[94] McComiskey, p. 317.
[95] Wiersbe, p. 360.

"Ordinary citizens probably ate meat only three times a year, at the annual festivals."[96]

They imitated great King David by composing and improvising songs and inventing musical instruments, but they entertained themselves rather than praising God. They consumed wine by the bowlful rather than in cups (cf. Phil. 3:19). And they spent much time and money anointing their bodies with oils and lotions to preserve and enhance their appearance. Instead, they should have been mourning over the moral weakness and decadence of their nation that would lead to its ruin.

"Too many Christians are laughing when they should be weeping (James 4:8-10) and tolerating sin when they should be opposing it (1 Cor. 5:2)."[97]

6:7   Amos announced that these luxuriant leaders would go into captivity "at the head of" the people of Israel. Their banquets would cease, and they would lounge on their soft couches no longer.

"Those who were first in prominence and sin will be the first in punishment and captivity."[98]

Money and material possessions are not wrong in themselves, but the love of them leads to all types of evil (1 Tim. 6:9-10; James 5:1-6).

The complete devastation of Samaria 6:8-14

6:8   The prophet announced further that sovereign Yahweh of Hosts, even He, had "sworn by Himself" (cf. 4:2; 8:7). This was a solemn warning because God can swear by no one greater than Himself (cf. Heb. 6:13-14). He loathed the pride of Jacob. "Jacob" here refers to the Northern Kingdom (cf. 3:13), and "the pride of Jacob" is probably the city of Samaria.[99] In their self-confidence, these leaders resembled their forefather Jacob. The Lord also hated their fortified mansions from which they oppressed the poor and needy (cf. 3:9-10).

"The mighty fortress is their god. Its security and power make God's protection and blessing irrelevant crutches in the real world of economic and political influence."[100]

Therefore, Yahweh would fight against them, and deliver up Samaria and all it contained to an enemy.

6:9-10   So thorough would be the overthrow, that even if 10 men took refuge in one house, they could not preserve their own lives. If the uncle of one of the dead rulers came to bury his nephew, or if a less interested undertaker did so, those still alive and hiding in the house would beg him not to reveal their presence. "Undertaker" is literally "one who burns him." Since cremation was not acceptable in ancient Israel, the reference may be to burning corpses during a plague that would accompany the destruction of Samaria. They would beg him not even to mention the name of Yahweh in anger, lament, or praise, because to do so might draw His attention to them and result in their deaths. As bad as the situation was, they could not bring themselves to seek the Lord for help.

6:11   Yahweh was going to command the utter destruction of all houses in Samaria, small and great. Not only would the people of the city die (vv. 9-10), but the houses of the rich and poor would also perish.

6:12   It was as unnatural for Israel's leaders to live as they did, as it was for horses to run on rocky crags, or for oxen to plow rocks. Horses normally ran on rock-free ground, and oxen plowed fields from which farmers had removed the rocks. Yet these leaders had replaced justice with corrupt courtroom decisions that had killed the defendants—just as though they had taken "poison." "Righteousness" in the rulers should have resulted in grace for the dependent, that would have been sweet to their taste—but the treatment they received was instead bitter to their souls.

6:13   The leaders felt very proud and confident because under Jeroboam II, Israel had recaptured some territory that it had formerly lost to Aram (cf. 2 Kings 14:25). This included the town of Lo-debar in Transjordan (cf. 2 Sam. 9:4; 17:27). Amos, however, cleverly made light of this feat by mispronouncing the city "Lo-dabar," which means "not a thing." They had taken nothing of much value. The people were also claiming that they had taken the town of Karnaim (lit. a pair of horns, symbols of strength)

---

[96]Smith, p. 118.
[97]Wiersbe, p. 362.
[98]Feinberg, p. 88.
[99]See Hayes, p. 188.
[100]G. Smith, *Amos: A Commentary*, p. 207.

by their own strength. It was not they but Yahweh, however, who had strengthened them to achieve this victory over a symbolically strong town. Actually, Karnaim was quite insignificant.

6:14   The Almighty, sovereign Yahweh, announced that He would raise up a nation against the Northern Kingdom. He was the *really* Strong One. Once again, God's people would fall under the control of a foreign oppressor, as they had done in the past (cf. Exod. 3:9; Judg. 2:18; 4:3; 6:9; 10:11-12; 1 Sam. 10:17-18). This enemy would "afflict" the Israelites throughout the length and breadth of their nation, from "Hamath" in the north to "the brook (or sea, cf. 2 Kings 14:25) of the Arabah" in the south (the Dead Sea). This nation, of course, proved to be Assyria.

In summary, the reasons for Israel's coming judgment that Amos identified in these five messages, were: legal injustice, economic exploitation, religious hypocrisy, luxurious self-indulgence, and boastful complacency. These sins involved unfaithfulness to Yahweh, the supreme, all-powerful Lord of Israel—with whom the Israelites lived in covenant relationship. Though national judgment was inevitable, individuals who repented could escape punishment.

III. VISIONS THAT AMOS SAW CHS. 7—9

Amos next recorded five visions that he received from the Lord that described the results of the coming judgment of Israel, plus one historical incident (7:10-17). Throughout this section of the book, two phrases stand out: "sovereign Yahweh" (7:1-2, 4 [twice], 5-6; 8:1, 3, 9, 11; 9:8) and "My people" (7:8, 15; 8:2; 9:10). They are constant reminders that Yahweh has authority over all nations and individuals, and that He still recognized Israel's special covenant relationship with Himself. The whole section builds to a terrifying climax of inevitable judgment for Israel. Some scholars believe these visions formed Amos' call.[101]

A. THREE SHORT VISIONS OF IMPENDING JUDGMENT 7:1-9

The three visions in this section are similar and may have followed one another in quick succession. The first two describe methods of divine judgment from which Amos persuaded God to turn aside, and the last one the method He would not abandon to judge Israel.

1. The swarming locusts 7:1-3

7:1   Sovereign Yahweh showed Amos a mass of locusts swarming in the springtime after the first harvest and before the second. The Lord was forming this swarm of locusts. Ideally, the very first crops harvested in the spring went to feed the king's household and animals (cf. 1 Kings 18:5). The crops that the people harvested later in the spring fed their animals and themselves. If anything happened to prevent that second harvesting, the people would have little to eat until the next harvest in the fall. The summer months were very dry and the Israelites had nothing to harvest during that season of the year.

The *swarming* of locusts indicated that they were about to sweep through an area and destroy all the crops. There was no way to prevent this in Amos' day. Locust invasions were a perennial threat, and they were a method of discipline that God had said He might use if His people proved unfaithful to His covenant with them (Deut. 28:38, 42; cf. Joel 1:1-7; Amos 4:9).

7:2   In his vision, Amos saw the locusts strip the land of its vegetation. Then he prayed and asked the sovereign Lord to pardon Jacob (Israel) for its covenant unfaithfulness. Jacob was only a small nation, and could not survive such a devastating judgment—if the Lord allowed it to happen as Amos had seen in his vision.

Amos' view of Israel, as small and weak, stands in contrast to that of Israel's leaders, who believed it was strong and invincible (cf. 6:1-3, 8, 13; 9:10). Israel occupied a large territory under Jeroboam II, second only in its history to what Solomon controlled, but it was still small in relation to the larger empires of the ancient Near East. Amos may have meant that Israel was small in the sense of helpless. God had promised to take care of Jacob when that patriarch encountered Yahweh at Bethel, now a center of apostate worship in Israel (cf. Gen. 28:10-22). Perhaps that is why Amos appealed to God with the name of Jacob (cf. 3:13; 6:8; 7:5; 8:7; 9:8).

7:3   In response to Amos' prayer, the Lord relented and said He would not bring a completely devastating judgment on Israel, at least then. He would be merciful and patient and would grant Israel more grace (cf. Exod. 32:14).

The prayers of righteous individuals, like Amos, can alter the events of history (cf. James 5:16-18). Some things that God intends to do are not firmly determined by Him; He is open to changing His mind about these things. However, He has

---

[101]E.g., Ellison, p. 65.

decreed other things and no amount of praying will change His mind about those things (cf. Jer. 7:16; 11:14; 14:11-12; Acts 1:11; Rev. 22:20). It is important, therefore, that we understand, from Scripture, what aspects of His will are fixed and which are negotiable. The same distinction between determined choices and optional choices is observable in human interpersonal relations. Good parents, for example, will not permit their children to do certain things no matter how much the children may beg, but they do allow their children to influence their decisions in other matters.[102]

2. The devouring fire 7:4-6

7:4 — Sovereign Yahweh also showed Amos a vision of a great fire that was burning up everything. Like a great drought it consumed all the water and all the farmland (or people) in Israel (cf. 1:9-10). What he saw may have been a scorching heat wave that resulted in a drought.

The "great deep" is a phrase that refers to subterranean waters that feed springs (cf. Gen. 1:2; 7:11; 8:2; 49:25; Deut. 8:7; Ezek. 31:4). So intense was the fire that Amos saw that it dried up even these underground water reservoirs. Great heat with consequent drought was another of the punishments that the Lord warned of for covenant unfaithfulness (Deut. 28:22).

7:5-6 — Amos prayed virtually the same prayer again, asking the sovereign Lord not to send such a judgment because Jacob was small (cf. v. 2). Again the Lord relented, and determined that it would not come then (cf. v. 3). He would not discipline Israel with a locust plague or with a raging "fire."

3. The plumb line 7:7-9

7:7 — Amos saw a third vision. The Lord was standing beside a vertical wall with a plumb line in His hand. The wall was probably a city wall rather than the wall of a house.[103] Niehaus believed Amos saw a wall of tin, symbolic of Assyria's power, and the Lord standing above the wall judging it.[104] A plumb line was a string with a weight on the end. People used it, and still use it, to determine if a vertical structure is completely straight. God was testing something by a true standard; His judgment is not arbitrary.

7:8 — The Lord asked the prophet what he saw, and Amos replied that he saw a plumb line. Then the Lord explained that He was about to test Israel as a builder uses a plumb line. The true standard by which He would judge Israel was undoubtedly the Mosaic Law, the covenant that He had given her by which God measured her uprightness (cf. Exod. 19:6). The Lord further announced that He would not spare the Israelites from His judgment any longer; Amos' prayers for Israel would not turn away His punishment as earlier (vv. 3, 6). The nation was so far out of plumb that God would tear it down.

7:9 — The method of judgment God would use would not be by locust invasion or by fire, but by the sword. An enemy would invade Israel (cf. Deut. 28:49-50). This enemy, as Yahweh's agent, would destroy the outdoor high places on the hilltops, and the temple sanctuaries at Dan and Bethel, where the people worshipped God and idols, namely: all their worship centers.

Amos probably used "Isaac" simply as a synonym for "Jacob" and "Israel." Another view follows:

> "Amos seems to have in mind the special veneration for Isaac which members of the Northern Kingdom displayed in making pilgrimages south to Beersheba (cf. 5:5; 8:14), Isaac's birthplace."[105]

The "house of Jeroboam" probably refers to the dynasty of Jeroboam II, but it could refer to the nation of Israel as headed by Jeroboam I. Jeroboam II's dynasty came to an end with the assassination of his son and successor, Zechariah (2 Kings 15:8-10).

> "There is no intercession from the prophet here, for the patience of God is at an end."[106]

These three visions appear to have come to Amos in close succession. The final compiler of Amos' prophecies, probably Amos himself, undoubtedly grouped them because of their similarity. They are obviously alike, and together present a picture of judgment, mercifully deferred

---

[102]For further discussion of this issue, see Thomas L. Constable, *Talking to God: What the Bible Teaches about Prayer*, pp. 149-52; idem, "What Prayer Will and Will Not Change," in *Essays in Honor of J. Dwight Pentecost*, pp. 99-113; John Munro, "Prayer to a Sovereign God," *Interest* 56:2 (February 1990):20-21; and Robert B. Chisholm Jr., "Does God 'Change His Mind'?" *Bibliotheca Sacra* 152:608 (October-December 1995):387-99.

[103]George Adam Smith, *The Book of the Twelve Prophets Commonly Called the Minor*, 1:114; Ellison, p. 66.

[104]Niehaus, p. 456. See also Chisholm, *Handbook on . . .*, pp. 397-98.

[105]Hubbard, p. 210.

[106]Feinberg, p. 97.

twice but finally brought on Israel. They clarify the method of Israel's punishment, namely, defeat by an enemy's invading army, and they show that judgment would come after God's patience with the nation had been exhausted.

B. AN INTERVENING INCIDENT 7:10-17

The event described in this pericope evidently followed and grew out of the preceding visions that Amos announced (vv. 1-9). Certain key words occur in both sections of the book but not elsewhere in it: Isaac (vv. 9, 16) and sanctuary (vv. 9-11). Also, the historical incident is a concrete example of God's plumb line in operation, but here it judged individuals. The prophet Amos passed the test, but one of the priests of Bethel, Amaziah, failed the test.

1. The challenge 7:10-13

7:10   Amaziah, who was one of the apostate priests who served at the Bethel sanctuary (cf. 1 Kings 12:26-33), felt that Amos was being unpatriotic in what he was prophesying. So Amaziah sent a message to King Jeroboam II, charging Amos with conspiring against the king within the land. He felt that Israel could not afford to endure Amos' prophesying any longer. Previously, internal revolt against a king had sometimes followed a prophet's pronouncements (cf. 1 Sam. 16:1-13; 1 Kings 11:29-39; 16:1-13; 19:15-17; 2 Kings 8:7-15; 9:1-28; 10:9).

7:11   Amaziah reported that Amos was saying that the king would die by the sword, and that the Israelites would definitely go into exile. While we have no record that Amos said these exact words, they do represent fairly the message that Amos was announcing (cf. vv. 8-9). By claiming that Amos was predicting Jeroboam's death, the priest was personalizing the danger of Amos' ministry to the king and was emotionally inciting him to take action against the prophet. Amaziah regarded Amos' prophecies as simply the prophet's own words. He had no respect for them as messages from Israel's God, but viewed them only as a challenge to the status quo.

7:12-13   Amaziah then approached Amos, and told him to move back to Judah and to earn his living in his home country (cf. 1:1). By referring to Amos as a seer (another term for a prophet, cf. 1 Sam. 9:9; 2 Sam. 24:11; Isa. 29:10), Amaziah was probably disparaging the visions that Amos said he saw (vv. 1-9).[107] By telling him to eat (earn) his bread in Judah, he was hinting that Amos needed to get a "legitimate" job rather than living off the contributions he received for prophesying (cf. Gen. 3:19; 2 Kings 4:8; Ezek. 13:17-20; Mic. 3:5, 11). Amaziah told Amos to stop prophesying in Bethel (emphatic in the Hebrew text) because it was one of the king's sanctuaries (places of worship) as well as one of the king's residences (places of living). Bethel, of all places, was an inappropriate town in which Amos should utter messages of doom against Israel, from Amaziah's perspective. Amos had become an embarrassment to the political and religious establishment in Israel.

2. The response 7:14-17

7:14   Amos replied that he was not a prophet by his own choosing; he did not decide to pursue prophesying as a career. Neither had he become a prophet because his father had been one. In Amos' culture it was common and expected for sons to follow in their father's line of work, though this was not true of genuine prophets. It is possible that Amos meant that he was not the son of a prophet in the sense that he had not been trained in one of the schools of the prophets under the tutelage of a fatherly mentor (cf. 2 Kings 2:1-15; 4:1, 38; 5:22; 6:1-7; 9:1).[108] Rather, Amos had previously earned his living in a totally unrelated occupation. He had been a herdsman and a nipper of sycamore figs. The term "herdsman" refers to someone who *bred* livestock, not just a shepherd who looked after animals. A *nipper* of sycamore figs was one who pierced sycamore figs so they would be edible.

> "The fruit is infested with an insect (the *Sycophaga crassipes*), and till the 'eye' or top has been punctured, so that the insects may escape, it is not eatable."[109]

> "Or, the term may refer to the practice of slitting the sycamore-fig before it ripens—a process that ensures that it will turn sweet."[110]

Thus, Amos had a respectable agricultural business background before he moved to Israel to prophesy. He had not been a "professional" prophet like many of the false prophets. He had not always made his living by being a prophet but only functioned as a "called" prophet. Therefore, Amaziah should not think that Amos came to Israel to prophesy because that was the only work that he could do or to make money.

---

[107] See Stuart, p. 376; and E. Hammershaimb, *The Book of Amos: A Commentary*, p. 116.
[108] B. Smith, p. 139, n. 56.
[109] W. R. Smith, cited in Samuel R. Driver, *The Books of Joel and Amos*, p. 212.
[110] Niehaus, p. 463. Cf. Wolff, p. 314; *The Nelson Study Bible*, p. 1473.

7:15	Amos had come to Israel having been sent there by Yahweh to prophesy (cf, Num. 18:6; 2 Sam. 7:8; Ps. 78:70). The Hebrew text repeated the words "the LORD" for emphasis. God had given him a definite commission, and Amos had left his former occupation to obey that divine calling (cf. Acts 5:27-29). Amos' ministry and his location were God's choosing.
7:16-17	Amos then announced a prophecy from the Lord for Amaziah. Because the priest had told the prophet to stop doing what Yahweh had commanded him to do (cf. 2:12), Amaziah's wife would become a harlot in Bethel. She would have to stoop to this in order to earn a living, because she would have no husband or sons to support her. Her children would die by the sword. This may also imply the end of Amaziah's family line. Amaziah's land would become the property of others, presumably the Assyrians, and he himself would die in a foreign, pagan land. All these things would eventually happen when the foreign enemy destroyed Israel. Stifling the Word of God proved disastrous for Amaziah, as it still does today. Finally, Amos repeated that Israel would indeed go into exile, the message that Amaziah had reported that Amos was preaching (cf. v. 11).
	Amaziah had told Amos to stop prophesying, namely, to stop preaching (v. 16). "Preaching" is from a verbal root meaning "drip" (Heb. *natap*), as the heavens drip rain (Judg. 5:4; cf. Amos 9:13). The idea is that Amos should stop raining down messages from heaven on his hearers. True prophets were people who spoke fervently for Yahweh.[111]

"Amaziah's loyalty was to Jeroboam, who probably appointed him as priest at Bethel. Amos's loyalty was to God, who sent him to prophesy against Israel. Conflict between Amaziah and Amos was inevitable since their loyalties were in conflict. Primary loyalty to God in their service to Israel would have eliminated conflict between the king, the priest, and the prophet. The answer to conflict among God's people is always to place loyalty to God above all else."[112]

C. TWO MORE VISIONS OF IMPENDING JUDGMENT CHS. 8—9

Amos received two more visions from the Lord that he continued to preach to the Israelites—in spite of Amaziah's threats.

1. The basket of summer fruit ch. 8

The vision with which this chapter opens (vv. 1-3) gave rise to three prophetic oracles that follow and expound it (vv. 4-6, 7-10, 11-14).

The vision proper 8:1-3

8:1-2	The sovereign Lord showed Amos a basket of summer fruit. Amos saw what God enabled him to see. The Lord asked him what he saw (cf. 7:8), and the prophet replied that he saw a basket of ripe summer fruit (Heb. *qayis*). Normally this would have been a pleasant sight associated with the joys and provisions of harvest. Then Yahweh told him that Israel was also ripe (Heb. *qes*), but ripe for judgment. The Lord would spare the Israelites no longer. Like the fruit in the basket, Israel also needed to be consumed soon.

> "Just as the final fruit of the summer signaled the end of the harvest season, so God's 'end' for Israel was now at hand. God would judge the religious hypocrisy and greed of the people."[113]

> "The Lord takes into his confidence those whom he desires to understand his words and his works (cf. 3:7; Gen. 18:17-19)."[114]

8:3	When judgment came, the singing in the royal palace would turn to wailing and lamenting. There would be many dead bodies lying around from the enemy's slaughter, and those people who remained alive would dispose of them in silence because it would be such a terrible sight. Like so much rotten fruit, the dead Israelites would be thrown out.

The sins of the people 8:4-6

Non-visionary material followed the third vision (7:7-9), and non-visionary material follows the fourth vision (8:1-3).

8:4	Amos called those who oppressed the needy and tried to exterminate them to hear him (cf. 5:11). Israel's law called God's people to extend an open hand of generosity to the poor (Deut. 15:7-11; cf. Ps. 72:12-13), but the stingy Israelites were trying to eliminate them.

---

[111]Leon J. Wood, *The Prophets of Israel*, p. 63.
[112]B. Smith, p. 136.
[113]Charles H. Dyer, in *The Old Testament Explorer*, p. 760.
[114]Niehaus, p. 467.

8:5-6	These oppressors were eager for the monthly festivals and the weekly Sabbaths to end, so they could get back to work cheating their fellow countrymen in order to make big profits. These holidays were days of rest and worship, but the Israelite workaholics did not enjoy them, though they observed them as good religious people. They were anxious to enslave the needy in their debt so they could control them and use them for their own selfish ends (cf. 2:6). Archaeologists have found at Tirzah the remains of shops from the eighth century B.C. that contain two sets of weights: one for buying and one for selling.[115] Tirzah was the first capital of Israel (1 Kings 14:17; 15:21, 33; et al.).

> "These people regarded cereals and human beings equally as stock for sale. Their practices were both dishonest and inhumane."[116]

Merchandising was their priority, not worshipping. Profit was their god, and they willingly sacrificed more important things for it. People who focus intently on what they will do after worship is over do not engage in true worship or enter into the spirit of worship.[117]

The wailing of the sufferers 8:7-10

The following two passages (vv. 7-10 and 11-14) describe more fully the two results of God's judgment mentioned earlier, namely: wailing and silence (cf. v. 3).

8:7	For the third time in this book, Amos said that Yahweh took an oath (cf. 4:2; 6:8). This time He swore by "the pride of Jacob." This may be a reference to Samaria (cf. 6:8)—or to Israel's arrogant attitude.[118] Some interpreters take it as a reference to God Himself (cf. 1 Sam. 15:29).[119] The NIV capitalized "Pride" as a title of God. In this case, God vowed never to forget any of the sinful Israelites' unrighteous deeds.
8:8	Because of the sins just described, "the land" would "quake" from the Lord's approach and from the large enemy army that He would bring against Israel. Perhaps a literal earthquake did occur, but probably trembling with fear is in view (cf. 2 Sam. 7:10). All the inhabitants would mourn over the coming destruction. The waves of terror and destruction would be like the rising and falling of the Nile River.

> "Since the rise and fall of the Nile usually extended over a few months, some national upheaval lasting a considerable period of time is implied by the analogy. Sometimes the flooding of the Nile was highly destructive. Amos may have been comparing the destructiveness of social injustice, civil strife, economic exploitation, and religious shallowness in Israel to the destruction caused by the inundation of the Nile. The flooding of the Nile occurred repeatedly, as did the social, civil, economic, and religious problems of society."[120]

8:9	On the day of judgment, sovereign Yahweh would send darkness over the land. This may refer to an eclipse of the sun, or it may be a figurative description of the coming judgment as an unnaturally bad day. I prefer the metaphorical interpretation since this whole chapter contains many metaphors. The figure of "the sun" going "down at noon" was particularly appropriate, since Jeroboam's reign was the zenith of Israel's prosperity, power, and glory.
8:10	Then Yahweh would turn their festivals into funerals, and their melodious singing into mourning. The people would wear sackcloth and shave their heads as signs of their grief. "Mourning" would come because judgment had come. It would be as sad a time as the death of "an only son." The death of an only son meant the extinguishing of hope for the future and the losing of provision for one's old age. "The end" of that day would be *bitter* indeed.

The silence of Yahweh 8:11-14

The few remaining Israelites would be silent as they disposed of the corpses of their fellows (v. 3), but God would also be silent in that day of judgment.

---

[115] Mays, p. 144.
[116] Andersen and Freedman, p. 804.
[117] Wolff, p. 326.
[118] Chisholm, *Handbook on . . .*, p. 400.
[119] See Thomas J. Finley, *Joel, Amos, Obadiah*, pp. 302-3.
[120] B. Smith, p. 148.

8:11   As part of His judgment, God would withhold His words from His people. This would be like a famine, not of physical food and drink but of spiritual food. God's words provide spiritual nourishment and refreshment, so when they are not available, people suffer spiritually (cf. Matt. 4:4).

The Israelites had rejected the Lord's words to them (2:11-12; 7:10-13), so He would not send them to them any longer (cf. 1 Sam. 3:1; 28:6). This is a fearful prospect. If we do not listen to the Word of God, we may not be able to hear the Word of God (cf. Luke 17:22; John 7:34). This does not mean that God would remove all copies of His Word from them, but that when they sought a word of help, advice, or comfort from Him, they would not get it (cf. King Saul). Prophets would not bring God's words to them anymore.

8:12-13   The Israelites would grope all over the land for some word from Yahweh, a word of explanation, forgiveness, or hope, but they would not be able to find one. Even "beautiful virgins" and strong "young men" would "faint" from lack of spiritual refreshment. These types of individuals would have the greatest stamina and could look the hardest and longest, but even they would find nothing. Their deaths would also mean the cutting back of the nation since they could not provide children.

8:14   The apostate Israelites who swore in the name of their favorite pagan deities would fall, never to rise again, because their idols would not uplift them. Amos described the prominent idol in Samaria as "Samaria's guilt" or "shame." One of the idols they worshipped in Samaria was Ashimah (cf. 2 Kings 17:29-30), which Amos apparently alluded to here. From Dan to Beersheba, throughout the whole Promised Land, the Israelites would seek some word from Yahweh, but they would find none to meet their need. In view of other prophecies of Israel's restoration, the prediction that the Israelites would fall and not rise again must have a limited scope. That generation as a whole would not survive the coming judgment, but presumably individuals could repent and escape.

2. The Lord standing by the altar ch. 9

This final vision differs from the preceding four in some significant ways. First, there is no introductory formula that explains the divine enablement of the prophet. Second, in the first pair of visions Amos spoke more than the Lord, in the second pair he spoke only a few words, and in the last one he said nothing. He played no active part in this vision. This creates an impression of Yahweh being increasingly separate from people and ready to judge. However, as with the preceding two visions, oracles follow the brief vision.

Yahweh's inescapable punishment 9:1-4

9:1   In the final vision that Amos recorded, he saw Yahweh standing beside an altar. The altar at Bethel is probably in view, since Bethel was the worship site referred to in most of this book, and since Amos' encounter with Amaziah occurred there (7:10-17). Another possibility is that any and every Israelite shrine might be in view.[121] The Lord gave a command that someone (an angel?) would strike the capitals that supported the roof of the temple there with such force that its foundation stones would shake and the whole structure would fall down (cf. Judg. 16:29-30; Isa. 6:4; Ezek. 40:6). The Lord also said He would slay with the sword the rest of the priests and worshippers who survived being killed by the collapse of the temple. No one would escape with his or her life.

> "The temple was not a literal temple, for the collapse of such a building would affect only a few. Rather it represents the religion of the northern kingdom, which, in the end, brought about the destruction of its adherents. The decay of the social structure that resulted from their cold externalism could lead only to national ruin. The gross sin of idolatry could lead only to judgment."[122]

9:2-3   It would be impossible—for those whom the Lord chose to slay—to escape, even if they tried to dig into the earth or climb into the sky (cf. Ps. 139:7-8; Jon. 1—2).

> "If neither heights nor depths can separate people from the love of God (cf. Rom. 8:38-39), they are also unable to hide them from the wrath of God."[123]

---

[121]Ellison, p. 68.
[122]McComiskey, p. 327.
[123]G. Smith, p. 268.

9:4	The ancients conceived of Sheol as under the surface of the earth, so digging "into Sheol" meant hiding in the ground. Neither would hiding in the forests and caves of Mt. Carmel, one of the highest elevations in Israel, or trying to conceal oneself on the floor of the sea, be effective. The Lord would seek the guilty out and command His agents to execute them, even if that agent had to be a "serpent" in the sea (cf. 5:19; Job 26:12-13; Ps. 74:13-14; 89:9-10; Isa. 27:1; 51:9-10). Note the chiastic structure in these verses going from down, to up, and back down—signifying *all* places.
9:4	The Lord would even slay the Israelites whom their enemy led away into captivity. Yahweh would order "the sword" to "slay them" even "from there," though *there* they would presumably be under the protection of a strong foreign power. They would not be able to hide from His all-seeing eye. Normally, God watched over His people for their good, but here He promised to set His eyes on them "for evil." His purpose and intention for them was evil from their viewpoint. So thorough was the dispersion following the Assyrian invasion of Israel, that the exiles came to be known as the "lost tribes." They were not really lost, however, as later revelation makes clear (vv. 11-15; et al.).

The God who would punish 9:5-6

These verses describe the great God who would judge the Israelites. The section closes, "Yahweh is His name" (v. 6). What precedes that clause is a revelation of His person (name).

9:5	The Judge is sovereign Yahweh, who controls and leads armies: both heavenly armies of angels and earthly armies of soldiers. As sovereign, He is the One to whom all people and nations are responsible—not just Israel. He is the One who, simply with a touch, can cause the earth to melt—a figure that recalls the effect on ice when a human finger presses on it. He has the power to alter the course of human affairs as well so everyone mourns, if that is His choice. He causes the earth and human affairs to rise and fall, to ebb and flow, like the waters of the mighty Nile River.
9:6	He built His dwelling place "in the heavens" as a vaulted dome "over the earth." He "calls for the waters" to leave the seas, rise up and form clouds, and pour down on the land. Since He exercises this control over the whole planet, it is impossible to hide from Him or to escape His powerful hand. "His name" is Yahweh, the covenant keeping God, whose sovereignty spans the universe (cf. 5:8).

The justice of His punishment 9:7-10

9:7	Rhetorically, Yahweh asked if Israel was not just like other nations. It was, in the sense that it was only one nation among many others in the world, that lived under His sovereign authority. It was like them, too, in that it was full of idolaters. The Ethiopians (Cushites) were a remote people in Amos' day, living on the edge of the earth from an ancient Near Easterner's perspective, yet God watched over them. He had separated "the Philistines from Caphtor" (Crete; cf. Deut. 2:23) and the "Arameans (Syrians) from Kir" in Mesopotamia (cf. 1:5), just as He had led Israel from Egypt to the Promised Land. The Philistines and Syrians were Israel's enemies, but God had done for them what He had done for Israel. He could justly send the Israelites into another part of the world, since He had sovereignly relocated these other nations as well. The Israelites considered themselves superior because of their election, but really they were no better or less accountable than any other nation.
	By referring to the pagan nations at the end of the book, Amos came full circle, having begun with oracles against these nations. Thus, the emphasis on Yahweh's universal sovereignty brackets the rest of the contents like bookends.
9:8	As the sovereign Lord looked over all the kingdoms of the earth, He noticed those of them that were sinful—and He determined to destroy them because of their wickedness. He would do to Israel what He would do to any other sinful nation (cf. 3:1-2). Yet He promised not to destroy completely "the house of Jacob" (i.e., the Northern Kingdom, because of the covenant He had made with Israel; cf. 5:4-6, 14-15).
9:9	God would sift all the Israelites, among the other nations, to separate the people deserving judgment from the righteous few. He would allow the righteous person (true wheat) to slip through but would retain the unrighteous (a kernel, pebble, anything compacted, Heb. *seror*) for judgment. Another possibility is that those who do not pass through the screen represent the righteous remnant and all others are the sinful Israelites. He would separate the righteous from the sinful as He sifted through the Israelites. God determines just how much sinfulness makes His punishment inevitable; He determines the mesh of the sifting screen.
9:10	"All" the guilty Israelites would "die by the sword," the Lord promised. None of them who claimed that they would escape that calamity would get away.

The restoration of the Davidic kingdom 9:11-12

The rest of the book is quite different from what has preceded because of its positive message. As is true of other eighth-century B.C. prophets to Israel and Judah, Amos included hope in his prophecy (cf. Isa. 40—66; Hos. 1:10—2:1, 14-23; Mic. 2:12-13; 4:1-5).

9:11   In "that day" Yahweh would also restore "the fallen booth of David" that had suffered some destruction (cf. v. 1; Lev. 23:33-42; 2 Sam. 11:11; 1 Kings 20:12-16; Jon. 4:5). The booth (tent) of David is a reference to the dynasty of David, which acted as a shelter over the Israelites. When Amos prophesied, the tent of David had suffered major damage due to the division of the kingdom into two parts, though it had not yet collapsed completely. In the future, God would restore the Davidic house and rebuild it as in former days—when it was a united kingdom—with a descendant of David ruling over all Israel (cf. Jer. 30:3-10; Ezek. 37:15-28; Hos. 3:4-5). That day, still future from our point in history, will be a day of restoration as well as a day of judgment. The restoration will follow in the Millennium after the judgments of the Tribulation.[124]

9:12   When the house of David is again intact, Israel will exercise authority over all the nations of the world and will then be a source of blessing to them. This will include even the small number of Edomites alive then, people who had formerly been implacable enemies of the Israelites (cf. Obad. 19). Israel's blessing will extend even to them, representing all of Israel's former enemies. "All the nations" will become associated with the name of Yahweh then, and will enjoy His Lordship and protection (cf. Gen. 12:3; Isa. 9:1-7; 11:1-13; 42:1-7; 45:22-25; 49:5-7; 55:1-5).

Amos described three different groups as remnants: (1) a small group of the faithful within Israel in his day in contrast to all Israel (3:12; 4:1-3; 5:3; 6:9-10; 9:1-4), (2) a small group of faithful Israelites in the future (5:4-6, 15), and (3) a small group of Edomites and other neighbors of Israel who would benefit from the Davidic promise in the future (9:12).[125]

At the Jerusalem Council, the Apostle James quoted verses 11 and 12 to support his view that the Gentiles of his day did not need to submit to circumcision and the Mosaic Law, in order to obtain salvation or to live acceptably as Christians (Acts 15:13-21). He knew that the judgments of Israel were not yet over (cf. Matt. 24:1-22; Luke 21:5-24; Acts 1:6-7). He also knew, from this passage and others (Isa. 42:6; 60:3; Mal. 1:11), that when God restored the house of David, Gentiles would have a share in that rule as Gentiles. James concluded, therefore, that Gentiles did not need to become Jews to enter into these (millennial) blessings. He did not mean that the church fulfills the promises to Israel, but that since Gentiles will experience millennial blessings as Gentiles, they do not need to live as Jews in the church.

The blessings of the restored kingdom 9:13-15

9:13   In contrast to the images of judgment that Amos had painted throughout this book, days were coming when these terrible conditions would be reversed. The topsoil would become so productive that farmers planting seed for the next harvest would hurry the reapers of the same fields to finish their work so they could plant the next crop. Normally the Israelites plowed their fields in October and the reaping ended in May, but in the future reaping would still be going on in October because of the huge harvests. Wine-makers would similarly pressure the farmers to plant more vines. The grape harvest took place in August, and farmers planted new vines in November. Harvests would be so abundant that the gathering of one crop would not end before it was time to begin the new crop.

"The mountains" would be so full of fruitful grapevines that they could be described as *dripping* "with sweet (the best) wine." "All the hills" would "be dissolved," in the sense of flowing down with produce, perhaps even washing the soil away with grape juice. This verse pictures the reversing of the curse that God pronounced on the earth at the Fall (Gen. 3:17-19). Instead of drought and famine (1:2; 4:6-8), there would be abundant harvests (cf. Lev. 26:3-5; Deut. 28:4-5, 8, 11-12). Even though these may be hyperbolic images, the point is clear.

9:14   Yahweh also promised to restore the Israelites to the Promised Land following their captivity and exile from it. They would return to their land and re-establish life: characterized by security and joy, abundant food and drink, and beauty and blessing. Such conditions could not occur during wartime (vv. 1, 10; 2:13-16; 3:11, 15; 4:10-11; 5:2-3; 6:9-10; 7:17), but would be possible in peacetime, i.e., in the Millennium (cf. Lev. 26:6; Deut. 28:6).

9:15   Furthermore, the Israelites would put roots down in the Promised Land and never have to leave it again (cf. Gen. 13:14-15; 17:7-8; Deut. 30:1-5; 2 Sam. 7:10; Jer. 30:10-11; Ezek. 37:25; Joel 3:17-21; Mic. 4:4-7; Zech. 14:11). They would not fear exile (4:2-3; 5:5, 27; 6:7; 7:11, 17; 9:4) but would be secure from every foe (cf. Lev. 26:7-8; Deut. 28:7, 10). Yahweh, Israel's true God, promised this.

---

[124]See Kenneth R. Cooper, "The Tabernacle of David in Biblical Prophecy," *Bibliotheca Sacra* 168:672 (October-December 2011):402-12.

[125]Gerhard Hasel, *The Remnant*, pp. 393-94.

> "Let us summarize the remarkable prophecy of Amos to be fulfilled in the consummation of Israel's history: (1) the restoration of the Davidic dynasty, verse 11; (2) the supremacy of Israel over the nations, verse 12; (3) the conversion of the nations, verse 12; (4) the fruitfulness of the land, verse 13; (5) the rebuilding of their cities, verse 14; and (6) their permanent settlement in their own land after their return from captivity, verse 15."[126]

> "The pivot on which all this turns is CHRIST. As we have seen, He is brought before us in Amos:—(1) As Israel's Shepherd, rescuing a remnant from the lion's mouth [3:12]. (2) As Israel's Intercessor, beseeching God for them that at all events some might 'arise' (or 'stand,' R.V) [7:2, 5]. (3) As the One for whom Israel will mourn, and to whom their hearts will turn [8:10]. (4) As the true David, who will bring in the state of blessing and peace which God has from the beginning purposed for His people [9:11]."[127]

The end of the Exile saw only a dim foreview of the blessings Amos announced here. Blessings in the Church Age do not compare either. Amillennialists see the fulfillment in the Israelites' return from exile, in the Church Age in a spiritual sense (i.e., abundant spiritual blessings), or in heaven.[128] Fulfillment has yet to come when God restores the tent of David in Jesus Christ's millennial reign.

> "Amos' single prophecy of future blessing (9:11-15) details (1) the restoration of the Davidic dynasty (v. 11); (2) the conversion of the nations (v. 12); (3) the fruitfulness of the land (v. 13); (4) Israel's return from captivity (v. 14); (5) the rebuilding of the waste cities (v. 14); and (6) Israel's permanent settlement in the holy land (v. 15)."[129]

> "God's promises for the future are anchor points to keep us stable, and to give us hope in times of personal distress and difficulty. The more we understand what God has promised for the future, the more we can endure our problems today."[130]

---

[126] Feinberg, p. 119.
[127] Harold P. Barker, *Christ in the Minor Prophets*, p. 36.
[128] See Bruce K. Waltke, *An Old Testament Theology*, p. 835.
[129] *The New Scofield . . .*, p. 938.
[130] Dyer, p. 763.

Bibliography

Alter, Robert. *The Art of Biblical Poetry*. New York: Basic, 1985.

Andersen, Frances I., and David N. Freedman. *Amos*. Anchor Bible series. New York: Doubleday, 1989.

Barker, Harold P. *Christ in the Minor Prophets*. New York: Loizeaux Brothers, n.d.

Bowen, Catherine Drinker. *Miracle at Philadelphia*. Boston: Little, Brown, 1966.

Bramer, Stephen J. "The Literary Genre of the Book of Amos." *Bibliotheca Sacra* 156 (January-March 1999):43-49.

Bright, John. *A History of Israel*. Philadelphia: Westminster Press, 1959.

Chisholm, Robert B., Jr. "Does God 'Change His Mind'?" *Bibliotheca Sacra* 152:608 (October-December 1995):387-99.

_____. *Handbook on the Prophets*. Grand Rapids: Baker Book House, 2002.

_____. "How a Hermeneutical Virus Can Corrupt Theological Systems." *Bibliotheca Sacra* 166:663 (July-September 2009):259-70.

_____. "A Theology of the Minor Prophets." In *A Biblical Theology of the Old Testament*, pp. 397-433. Edited by Roy B. Zuck. Chicago: Moody Press, 1991.

Constable, Thomas L. *Talking to God: What the Bible Teaches about Prayer*. Grand Rapids: Baker Book House, 1995; reprint ed., Eugene, Oreg.: Wipf & Stock Publishers, 2005.

_____. "What Prayer Will and Will Not Change." In *Essays in Honor of J. Dwight Pentecost*. Edited by Stanley D. Toussaint and Charles H. Dyer. Chicago: Moody Press, 1986.

Cooper, Kenneth R. "The Tabernacle of David in Biblical Prophecy." *Bibliotheca Sacra* 168:672 (October-December 2011):402-12.

Dyer, Charles H., and Eugene H. Merrill. *The Old Testament Explorer*. Nashville: Word Publishing, 2001. Reissued as *Nelson's Old Testament Survey*. Nashville: Thomas Nelson Publishers, 2001.

Driver, Samuel R. *The Books of Joel and Amos*. 2nd ed. Cambridge Bible for Schools and Colleges series. Cambridge: Cambridge University Press, 1915.

Ellison, H. L. *The Prophets of Israel: From Ahijah to Hosea*. Exeter, Eng.: Paternoster Press, 1969. American ed., Grand Rapids: Wm. B. Eerdmans Publishing Co., 1974.

Encyclopedia of Archaeological Excavations in the Holy Land. Edited by Michael Avi-Yonah and E. Stern. Englewood Cliffs, N.J.: Prentice-Hall, 1978.

Feinberg, Charles Lee. *Joel, Amos, and Obadiah*. The Major Messages of the Minor Prophets series. New York: American Board of Missions to the Jews, 1948.

Finley, Thomas J. *Joel, Amos, Obadiah*. The Wycliffe Exegetical Commentary series. Chicago: Moody Press, 1990.

Hammershaimb, E. *The Book of Amos: A Commentary*. Oxford: Blackwell, 1970.

Hasel, Gerhard. *The Remnant*. Berrien Springs, Mich.: Andrews University Press, 1972.

Hayes, J. H. *Amos*. Nashville: Abingdon Press, 1988.

Hubbard, David A. *Joel and Amos*. Tyndale Old Testament Commentaries series. Downers Grove, Ill.: InterVarsity Press, 1989.

Huffmon, Herbert B. "The Covenant Lawsuit in the Prophets." *Journal of Biblical Literature* 78 (1959):285-95.

_____. "The Treaty Background of Hebrew *Yada'*." *Bulletin of the American Schools of Oriental Research* 181 (February 1966):31-37.

Josephus, Flavius. *The Works of Flavius Josephus*. Translated by William Whiston. London: T. Nelson and Sons, 1866; reprint ed. Peabody, Mass.: Hendrickson Publishers, 1988.

Kaiser, Walter C., Jr. *Toward an Old Testament Theology*. Grand Rapids: Zondervan Publishing House, 1978.

Kassis, H. "Gath and the Structure of 'Philistine' Society." *Journal of Biblical Literature* 84 (1965):259-71.

King, Leonard W. *Annals of the Kings of Assyria*. London: British Museum, 1902.

King, Philip J. *Amos, Hosea, Micah—An Archaeological Commentary*. Philadelphia: Westminster Press, 1988.

Lambert, Wilfred G. "Three Unpublished Fragments of the Tukulti-Ninurta Epic." *Archiv für Orientforschung* 18 (1957-58):38-51.

Limburg, J. "Sevenfold Structures in the Book of Amos." *Journal of Biblical Literature* 106 (1987):217-22.

Longman, Tremper, III and Raymond B. Dillard. *An Introduction to the Old Testament*. 2nd ed. Grand Rapids: Zondervan, 2006.

Luckenbill, Daniel D. *The Annals of Sennacherib*. Oriental Institute Publications 2. Chicago: University of Chicago Press, 1924.

Mays, J. *Amos: A Commentary*. Old Testament Library series. Philadelphia: Westminster Press, 1969.

McComiskey, Thomas Edward. "Amos." In *Daniel-Minor Prophets*. Vol. 7 of *The Expositor's Bible Commentary*. 12 vols. Edited by Frank E. Gaebelein and Richard P. Polcyn. Grand Rapids: Zondervan Publishing House, 1985.

Morgan, G. Campbell. *Living Messages of the Books of the Bible*. 2 vols. New York: Fleming H. Revell Co., 1912.

Motyer, J. A. *The Day of the Lion: The Message of Amos*. Downers Grove, Ill.: InterVarsity Press, 1974.

Munro, John "Prayer to a Sovereign God." *Interest* 56:2 (February 1990):20-21.

The Nelson Study Bible. Edited by Earl D. Radmacher. Nashville: Thomas Nelson Publishers, 1997.

The New Scofield Reference Bible. Edited by Frank E. Gaebelein, William Culbertson, et al. New York: Oxford University Press, 1967.

Niehaus, Jeffrey. "Amos." In *The Minor Prophets: An Exegetical and Expositional Commentary*, 1:315-494. 3 vols. Edited by Thomas Edward McComiskey. Grand Rapids: Baker Books, 1992, 1993, and 1998.

Paul, Shalom M. *Amos*. Hermeneia series. Minneapolis: Fortress Press, 1991.

Pritchard, James B., ed. *Ancient Near Eastern Texts Relating to the Old Testament*. 3rd ed. Princeton: Princeton University Press, 1969.

Robinson, George L. *The Twelve Minor Prophets*. Reprint ed. Grand Rapids: Baker Book House, 1974.

Ryken, Leland. "Amos." In *A Complete Literary Guide to the Bible*. Edited by Leland Ryken and Tremper Longman III. Grand Rapids: Zondervan, 1993.

Smith, Billy K., and Frank S. Page. *Amos, Obadiah, Jonah*. The New American Commentary series. N.c.: Broadman & Holman Publishers, 1995.

Smith, G. *Amos: A Commentary*. Grand Rapids: Zondervan Publishing House, 1989.

Smith, George Adam. *The Book of the Twelve Prophets Commonly Called the Minor*. 2 vols. Tenth ed. London: Hodder and Stoughton, 1913.

Stuart, Douglas. *Hosea-Jonah*. Word Biblical Commentary series. Waco: Word Books, 1987.

Sunukjian, Donald R. "Amos." In *The Bible Knowledge Commentary: Old Testament*, pp. 1425-52. Edited by John F. Walvoord and Roy B. Zuck. Wheaton: Scripture Press Publications, Victor Books, 1985.

Thomas, D. Winton., ed. *Archaeology and Old Testament Study*. Oxford: Clarendon Press, 1967.

_____. *Documents from Old Testament Times*. New York: Harper & Row, 1958.

Thompson, R. Campbell, and Richard W. Hutchinson. "The Excavations on the Temple of Nabu at Nineveh." *Archaeologia* 79 (1929):103-48.

Thompson, R. Campbell, and Max E. L. Mallowan. "The British Museum Excavations at Nineveh, 1931-32." *University of Liverpool Annals of Archaeology and Anthropology* 20 (1933):71-127.

Waltke, Bruce K., with Charles Yu. *An Old Testament Theology: an exegetical, canonical, and thematic approach*. Grand Rapids: Zondervan, 2007.

Weiss, Meir. "The Pattern of Numerical Sequence in Amos 1—2, A Re-examination." *Journal of Biblical Literature* 86 (1967):416-23.

Wiersbe, Warren W. "Obadiah." In *The Bible Exposition Commentary/Prophets*, pp. 371-75. Colorado Springs, Colo.: Cook Communications Ministries; and Eastbourne, England: Kingsway Communications Ltd., 2002.

Wolff, H. W. *Joel and Amos*. Hermeneia series. Philadelphia: Fortress Press, 1977.

Wood, Leon J. *The Prophets of Israel*. Grand Rapids: Baker Book House, 1979.

Yadin, Y., et al. *Hazor II: An Account of the Second Season of Excavations, 1956*. Jerusalem: Magnes, 1960.

Constable's Notes
on Obadiah

Introduction

Title and Writer

As is true of all the other prophetical books in the Old Testament, the title of this one evidently comes from the name of its writer. "Obadiah" means "servant of Yahweh" or "worshipper of Yahweh," depending on the form (vocalization) of his name in Hebrew, which is debated. There are 13 men who bear this name in the Old Testament, from Davidic to postexilic times, assuming the writer was not one of the other 12. It appears that he was not, since attempts to identify him with one of the others have proved unsatisfying. A few scholars have favored the view that this "Obadiah" was not the name of an individual but a symbolic title of the writer who was an unidentified servant or worshipper of the Lord. This seems unlikely since the other prophetical books bear the proper names of their writers. Some scholars believe that Malachi ("my servant") is also a title rather than a proper name.

Exactly who Obadiah was, remains a mystery. Keil believed that the Obadiah who served King Ahab and who encountered Elijah (1 Kings 18:3-16) was the writer.[1] Usually something about the writer accompanies his name at the beginning of each prophetical book, generally his father's name, some of his ancestors, and or his hometown. This descriptive information is absent in only two of the prophetical books: Obadiah and Malachi.

Whoever Obadiah was, he possessed significant literary talent. He employed the skills of imagery, rhetorical questions, irony, repetition, and various forms of parallelism in his brief prophecy.

Unity

Some scholars have contended that this small book, the shortest one in the Old Testament but not in the Bible, is a collection of prophecies that two or more unidentified prophets uttered. There are two reasons for this view. First, since the identity of Obadiah is obscure, some students of the book have concluded that "Obadiah" is a title that describes prophets in general, as servants of the Lord, rather than the name of one specific individual. Second, the content of the book may consist of from two to five oracles. Form critics have identified three types of oracles: oracles of judgment, oracles of repentance, and oracles of salvation.[2] This has led some scholars to posit two or more prophecies and two or more prophets.

However, since "Obadiah" was a common Hebrew name, and since the other prophetical books bear the names of their writers, it is more natural to assume that one prophet named Obadiah wrote the whole book. Furthermore, since many other writing prophets recorded several oracles, it is reasonable to assume that one prophet named Obadiah did the same in this book if, indeed, it consists of more than one oracle. The whole brief book fits together nicely as a single composition.[3]

Date

Since we do not know who the writer was, other than that his name appears to have been Obadiah, it is very difficult to date this book and to determine where it came from.

> "This shortest book in the Old Testament, consisting of only twenty-one verses, bears the distinction of being the most difficult of all the prophecies to date."[4]

There are three clues concerning when the prophet wrote it: references to historical events in the book, the book's place in the Hebrew canon, and possible quotations or allusions to the writings of other Old Testament prophets.

First, Obadiah referred to a time in the apparently recent past when the Edomites had gloated over a successful invasion of Jerusalem (vv. 10-14, 16). There are at least seven occasions during the ministry of the writing prophets when we know Jerusalem experienced invasion and suffered a defeat. One of these is probably the event he referred to.

1. During Rehoboam's reign (930-913 B.C.; 1 Kings 14:25-26; 2 Chron. 12:2-9)

---

[1] C. F. Keil, "Obadiah," in *The Twelve Minor Prophets*, 1:337.
[2] See Bruce K. Waltke, *An Old Testament Theology*, p. 828-32.
[3] For further discussion of the book's unity, see especially John D. W. Watts, *Obadiah: A Critical Exegetical Commentary*, pp. 9-10; Leslie C. Allen, *The Books of Joel, Obadiah, Jonah and Micah*, pp. 133-355; and Tremper Longman III and Raymond B. Dillard, *An Introduction to the Old Testament*, pp. 439-40.
[4] Gleason L. Archer Jr., *A Survey of Old Testament Introduction*, p. 299.

2. During Jehoram's reign (853-841 B.C.; 2 Kings 8:20-22; 2 Chron. 21:8-10, 16-17; cf. Amos 1:6)
3. During Amaziah's reign (796-767; 2 Kings 14:13-14; 2 Chron. 25:23-24)
4. During Ahaz's reign (732-715 B.C.; 2 Chron. 28:16-18)
5. During Jehoiakim's reign (609-598 B.C.; 2 Kings 24:1-4; 2 Chron. 36:6-7)
6. During Jehoiachin's reign (598-597 B.C.; 2 Kings 24:10-16; 2 Chron. 36:10)
7. During Zedekiah's reign (597-586 B.C.; 2 Kings 25:3-7; 2 Chron. 36:15-20; cf. Lam. 4:21-22; Ps. 137:7)

Of these, the invasions that seem to fit Obadiah's description of the Edomites' behavior were: the one in King Jehoram's reign, and the destruction of Jerusalem by Nebuchadnezzar and the Babylonians in 586 B.C.[5] Most scholars believe that one of these instances is in view, and most believe the destruction of Jerusalem in 586 B.C. is.[6] The second most popular view is that the invasion of Jerusalem during Jehoram's reign is what Obadiah referred to.[7] This would make Obadiah a contemporary of Elijah and Elisha (cf. 2 Chron. 21:12-15).

The second clue to the date of Obadiah's prophecy is the place of the book in the Hebrew canon. The Minor Prophets are called "minor," of course, because they are shorter than the Major Prophets. The Jews put all 12 of the Minor Prophets on one scroll, for convenience sake and to keep them from getting lost. The order in which they appear in the Hebrew Bible is basically chronological, and this order continued in later translations of the Old Testament, including English translations. This would lead us to conclude that the ancient Jews regarded Obadiah as one of the earlier prophetical books.

The order is not completely chronological. Hosea seems to have been put first because it is the longest of the pre-exilic Minor Prophets. The recurrence of similar themes and or words, also appears to have influenced the order, since Joel, rather than Amos, the second longest pre-exilic minor prophet, follows Hosea. Allen suggested that Obadiah may follow Amos because it "may have been viewed as a virtual commentary on Amos 9:12."[8] Stuart suggested that Obadiah follows Amos because Obadiah used the name Adonai Yahweh (v. 1), a rare name for God in the prophets, that Amos also used.[9]

> "In the arrangement of The Twelve in the Hebrew Bible the chronological principle which seems to have determined the overall order was as follows: (1) the prophets of the Assyrian period were placed first (Hosea to Nahum); (2) then followed those of the Babylonian period (Habakkuk and Zephaniah); (3) the series closed with the three prophets of the Persian period after the exile (Haggai, Zechariah and Malachi)."[10]

The third clue concerning the date of Obadiah is evidence that one prophet depended on another. There are similarities between Obadiah 1-6 and Jeremiah 49:9 and 14-17, and between Obadiah 10-18 and Joel 1:15; 2:1, 32; 3:3-4, 17, and 19.[11] There are also similarities between Obadiah 9, 10, 14, 18, and 19 and Amos 1:2, 6, 11-12, and 9:13. However, in all these instances it is really impossible to determine if Obadiah referred to the other prophets, if they referred to Obadiah, if they all depended on another common source, or if the Holy Spirit simply led each prophet independently to express himself in similar terms.

---

[5]For arguments that Jerusalem fell in 587 B.C., see Rodger C. Young, "When Did Jerusalem Fall?" *Journal of the Evangelical Theological Society* 47:1 (March 2004):21-38.

[6]E.g., Watts, pp. 8-9, 19, 27, 54; Allen, pp. 129-33; Douglas Stuart, *Hosea-Jonah*, pp. 403-4, 416; Thomas J. Finley, *Joel, Amos, Obadiah*, p. 340-42; Billy K. Smith, "Obadiah," in *Amos, Obadiah, Jonah*, p. 172; David W. Baker, *Obadiah, Jonah, Micah: An Introduction and Commentary*, p. 23; Carl E. Armerding, "Obadiah," in *Daniel-Minor Prophets*, vol. 7 of *The Expositor's Bible Commentary*, p. 337; Frank E. Gaebelein, *Four Minor Prophets [Obadiah, Jonah, Habakkuk, and Haggai]: Their Message for Today*, pp. 13, 28; G. Herbert Livingston, "Obadiah," in *The Wycliffe Bible Commentary*, p. 839; Roland K. Harrison, *Introduction to the Old Testament*, pp. 898, 902; John Bright, *A History of Israel*, pp. 356, 417; Robert B. Chisholm Jr., "A Theology of the Minor Prophets," in *A Biblical Theology of the Old Testament*, p. 418; idem, *Handbook on the Prophets*, p. 403; *The New Scofield Reference Bible*, p. 939; and Waltke, p. 845.

[7]E.g., Keil, 1:341-49; Walter L. Baker, "Obadiah," in *The Bible Knowledge Commentary: Old Testament*, p. 1454; Hobart E. Freeman, *An Introduction to the Old Testament Prophets*, p. 136; Archer, pp. 299-303; Leon J. Wood, *The Prophets of Israel*, pp. 262-64; Eugene H. Merrill, *Kingdom of Israel: A History of Old Testament Israel*, p. 382; Walter C. Kaiser Jr., *Toward an Old Testament Theology*, p. 186; Edward J. Young, *An Introduction to the Old Testament*, p. 277; Charles H. Dyer, in *The Old Testament Explorer*," pp. 765-66; and Warren W. Wiersbe, "Obadiah," in *The Bible Exposition Commentary/Prophets*, p. 371. See especially Jeffrey Niehaus, "Obadiah," in *The Minor Prophets*, pp. 496-502.

[8]Allen, p. 129. Cf. Smith, p. 180.

[9]Stuart, p. 416.

[10]Freeman, p. 135. See also Greg Goswell, "The Order of the Books in the Hebrew Bible," *Journal of the Evangelical Theological Society* 51:4 (December 2008):673-88.

[11]For defense of the priority of Obadiah to Jeremiah, see Niehaus, p. 501.

Unfortunately, none of these sources of information enables us to date the book with certainty. All things considered, I tend to favor an early date for Obadiah, about 850 B.C. However, those who prefer a date shortly after 586 B.C. could be correct. Fortunately, discovering the correct date of this prophecy is not crucial to understanding it.

Place of Composition and Audience
Since Obadiah's concern was the Edomites' rejoicing over an invasion of Jerusalem, it seems most probable that the prophet lived in the Southern Kingdom of Judah. Most of the scholars do agree on this.

Since Obadiah's concern was Jerusalem, and since it seems likely that he lived in Judah, the original people who received his prophecy were probably the residents of Judah.

Historical Background
The Edomites were the descendants of Esau, who displaced the Horites (a.k.a. Hurrians) that we read about in the Book of Genesis. The Horites and the Amorites were the original inhabitants of Palestine.

During the Monarchy, David captured Edom, stationed a garrison there, and made Edom a vassal state (1 Chron. 18:12-13). Solomon later developed the port city of Ezion-geber (Elath; 1 Kings 9:26-28). Hadad, a member of the Edomite royal family, opposed Solomon and set up a government in exile in Egypt (1 Kings 11:14-17). But Judah still governed Edom during the reign of King Jehoshaphat, who posted a governor in Edom (1 Kings 22:47-48). Edom gained her freedom from Judah, in 845 B.C., by rebelling against Jehoram, the son of Jehoshaphat (2 Kings 8:20-22; 2 Chron. 21:8-10, 16-17). King Amaziah of Judah partially recaptured Edom between 790 and 770 B.C. (2 Kings 14:7). King Uzziah of Judah recaptured the port of Ezion-geber (2 Kings 14:21-22). Aram (Syria) later took Ezion-geber from Judah (2 Kings 16:5-6). After that the Edomites revolted and attacked Judah a second time, during the reign of King Ahaz of Judah (2 Chron. 28:17). Finally, when King Nebuchadnezzar attacked Judah, the Edomites assisted the Babylonians (Ps. 137:7; Jer. 49:7-22; Ezek. 25:12-14; 35:1-15).

After the Babylonian invasion of Judah—and of their former ally against Judah, Edom—the Nabatean Arabs took over the capital city of Sela (Gr. Petra) and forced the remaining Edomites into southern Judah, where they settled. The Greeks named this area "Idumea," and its inhabitants Idumeans, following Alexander the Great's conquest of Palestine in the 4th century B.C. The Romans replaced the Greeks as the dominant power in Palestine and permitted the Idumeans to enjoy some sovereignty. King Herod the Great, who was in charge of Palestine when Jesus was born, was an Idumean. The Idumeans later joined the Jews in revolting against the Romans in 68-70 A.D. Their defeat resulted in their scattering, and they ceased to exist as a people. This was the fulfillment of Obadiah's prophecy of judgment on their nation. Edom's history of antagonism against Israel was long and consistent.

Purpose and Uniqueness
Obadiah wrote to announce coming divine judgment on Edom, and to give the Israelites hope by reminding them of the future that God promised them.

> "Prophetic oracles against foreign nations, though full of the language of doom, are also implicitly messages of hope for God's people. Such oracles look forward to a time when the predicted demise of the nation under attack will open the way for the restored, purified Israel to blossom once again as the flower of all God's plantings.
>
> "Obadiah's message fits this pattern and in some ways even typifies it."[12]
>
> "What would be a single oracle against a foreign nation in one of the other prophetic books has in Obadiah become an independent book."[13]

Most authorities see Edom as typical of all the forces arrayed against Israel and Yahweh.[14] Some scholars also see Edom as a type of *the flesh*, and Obadiah as a prophecy of its eventual destruction.[15]

> "In a sense Obadiah is a miniature profile of the message of all the writing prophets."[16]

---

[12]Stuart, p. 408. See also Kaiser, p. 187; and Finley, p. 351.
[13]Longman and Dillard, p. 438.
[14]E.g., Archer, p. 302. Cf. v. 15.
[15]E.g., Charles Lee Feinberg, *Joel, Amos, and Obadiah*, p. 124.
[16]W. Baker, p. 1453.

> "Edom . . . was tenaciously and rather constantly hostile from beginning, i.e., after the exodus, to end, i.e., after the exile. This factor would itself be enough to cause such a small nation to receive such regular, even prominent mention in prophetic oracles against foreign nations. But Edom's prominence as an enemy was additionally noteworthy because of its historical position as a brother nation to Israel (Gen 25). There are, then, at least three factors that made Edom so prominent among Israel's enemies that it could sometimes function virtually as a paradigm for all of them: (1) the sheer chronological length of its enmity as alluded to in Ezek 35:5; (2) the consistency and intensity of its enmity (as in Obad 10-14); (3) the 'treasonous' nature of its enmity (as in Amos 1:11). No other nation quite shared these characteristics.
>
> ". . . of the ancient non-superpowers (i.e., leaving aside Egypt, Assyria, and Babylon) Edom is the subject of more separate oracles against foreign nations (seven [i.e., Isa. 21:11-12; Jer. 49:7-22; Ezek. 25:12-14; 35; Amos 1:11-12; Obad.; Mal. 1:2-5]) and more brief or passing hostile references (four [i.e., Isa. 11:14; Jer. 25:21; Lam. 4:21; Joel 3:19]) in the prophetical books than any other nation."[17]

There are more references to Edom in the Bible than to any other hostile nation except the superpowers.

> "The Edomites played such a consistently adversarial role in Israel's history that the prophetic literary category of 'oracles against foreign nations' was bound to include predictions of judgments against Edom. Edom, indeed, becomes in the OT a kind of metonymy for 'hostile nations.'"[18]

Metonymy is a figure of speech in which the writer uses the name of one thing (Edom) for another that is associated with or suggested by it (all Israel's enemies).

Edom is the subject of the little Book of Obadiah as Assyria is of the larger Book of Nahum. Assyria is also the subject of the Book of Jonah, but Jonah focuses on the capital city, Nineveh, more than on the whole nation of Assyria.

The New Testament writers did not quote from or allude to the Book of Obadiah.

As with all the other prophetical books, references to God's covenants form an important background. People who lived in the ancient Near East were aware of the covenants that nations made with one another, the blessings of covenant faithfulness, and the curses that would come because of covenant unfaithfulness. This view of life is very prominent in all the prophetical books.

Outline

I. Edom's coming judgment vv. 1-9
   A. The introduction to the oracle v. 1
   B. The breaching of Edom's defenses vv. 2-4
   C. The plundering of Edom's treasures vv. 5-7
   D. The destruction of Edom's leadership vv. 8-9

II. Edom's crimes against Judah vv. 10-14
   A. The statement of the charge v. 10
   B. The explanation of the charge vv. 11-14

III. The restoration of Israel's sovereignty vv. 15-21
   A. The judgment of Edom and the nations vv. 15-18
   B. The occupation of Edom by Israel vv. 19-21

Many competent commentators believed that the Book of Obadiah follows the covenant-lawsuit form of address that was common in the ancient Near East.[19] In this type of message, which many of the other writing prophets also used, there are certain formulaic sections. These are, most basically, a description of the scene of judgment and then the speech by the judge. This speech typically includes an address to the defendant

---

[17]Stuart, p. 404. This writer provided a helpful table of all the nations that the writing prophets referred to and the locations of their prophecies against these nations on pp. 405-6. For a synopsis of the relations between Edom and Israel, see Finley, pp. 345-48. Most commentaries and Bible encyclopedias contain a summary of Edom's history.

[18]Stuart, p. 421. Cf. Judg. 5:4; Isa. 63:1-6.

[19]See, for example, Herbert B. Huffmon, "The Covenant Lawsuit in the Prophets," *Journal of Biblical Literature* 78 (1959):285-95.

(including reproach based on an accusation and a statement that the accused has no defense), the pronouncement of guilt, and the sentence. Niehaus outlined Obadiah on this basis as follows.[20]

I. Title (1a)
II. Description of the scene of judgment (nations arise for battle, 1b)
III. Speech by the Judge (2-21)
    A. Three sentences (2-9)
        1. First sentence (2-4)
        2. Second sentence (5-7)
        3. Third sentence (8-9)
    B. Three pronouncements of guilt (10-14)
        1. First pronouncement (10)
        2. Second pronouncement (11)
        3. Third pronouncement (12-14)
    C. Sentence on the nations (15-16)
    D. Promise of restoration (17-21)

Message

The very fact that this book consists of only one chapter should alert us to its importance. If it were unimportant, God would not have preserved it, and it would have disappeared long ago. Its shortness also simplifies our task of discovering its message. Like all the Bible books, this one has a message that is vital for us today, as well as for its original readers centuries ago.

Obadiah reveals the culmination of sibling rivalry and the national antagonism that developed between the descendants of Jacob and Esau: the Israelites and the Edomites. The conflict between these two boys and their respective descendants began before they were born. The infants struggled in the womb of their mother Rebekah (Gen. 25:22). Moreover, God loved Jacob, but He hated Esau (Mal. 1:2-3). The terms "love" and "hate" reflect God's elective purpose for both sons. When God said He loved Jacob but hated Esau, He meant that He chose to bless Jacob in a way that He did not choose to bless Esau. The statement expresses polar opposites to make the difference clearer. Often when God wanted to say He chose to bless someone, in the Old Testament, He said He *loved* that person. This was covenant terminology in the ancient Near East, and people in that part of the world at that time understood that loving and hating had these connotations.

The line of Jacob finally produced Jesus Christ. The line of Esau produced the Herods. Both Jesus and the Herods were "kings of the Jews." Jesus never spoke to Herod Antipas, even when questioned by him, though He did send him a message once (Luke 13:32), illustrating the antagonism that existed between them. This antagonism consistently marked the relationship between the Edomites and the Israelites.

Esau is in the foreground of the Book of Obadiah, and Jacob is in the background. Jacob and his descendants passed through suffering and chastisement, and their ultimate destiny is restoration and usefulness. Esau and his descendants were proud, rebellious, defiant, and their end was ultimate destruction. Jacob was the more unattractive personality originally, and Esau was more appealing. Yet God overruled what was natural, in order to produce what He wanted in the lives of both of these men, in view of their choices. Divine sovereignty and human choices are so intertwined that it is impossible for us to separate them. The Scriptures consistently present both as real and significant factors in the course of human affairs.

Obadiah tells the story of the destruction of Edom, the nation that descended from Esau. It also shows that God will destroy all that Edom stood for and represented. "Edom" is "Esau projected into national proportions." In Obadiah, we see the essential evil of Esau, the supreme manifestation of that evil, and the inevitable result of that evil. But we also see a ray of hope even for "the mount of Esau," Mt. Seir, the most notable geographical feature in Edom, that often represents the nation of Edom in the Old Testament (by metonymy).

The essential evil of Esau and Edom was pride. This comes through in verse 3: "The arrogance of your heart has deceived you, you who live in the clefts of the rock, in the loftiness of your dwelling place, who say in your heart, who will bring me down to earth?" The Edomites lived in a rocky, reclusive region around a town that later became known as Petra: ancient Sela. The Nabateans, the Arabians who later drove the Edomites out, actually carved Petra out of solid rock.

The habitation of the Edomites, who occupied this region before the Nabateans took it over, says much about them. They were self-reliant isolationists and fiercely independent. In some ways, they were like the "survivalists" of our own day. They preferred to be by themselves. They distrusted others. They wanted to control their own destiny. They took refuge in a part of the wilderness from which they thought they could defend themselves against all enemies. And they were very proud.

---

[20]Niehaus, p. 507.

Pride is one of those sins that is most difficult to deal with. It is much easier to deal with lying, stealing, adultery and other blatant sins. Pride, on the other hand, is something that we can practice without too many people discovering it, if we are clever enough. In fact, we may be proud and not even know it ourselves. Pride is a root from which many more overt sins grow. *Pride* is an attitude that says: "I (or We) can get along without God." The Edomites had their idols, and they did not bow to the true and living God. The Edomites thought they were invincible.

Esau had no use for the promises of God, and his descendants, too, thought they could get along quite well without God. The New Testament calls Esau a "profane person" (Heb. 12:16), literally a person "against the temple." A profane person cares nothing for spiritual things, because he or she glories in his or her own animal abilities, and lives to satisfy those appetites. An extremely proud person acts as though he or she were independent of God: never prays, never worships, never thinks of heaven. Christians can live like this, too, of course.

The Edomites built their nests high, like the eagles—so high they appeared to be among the stars (v. 4). The eagle is often a picture of deity in the Bible. In the Edomites' case, they had deified themselves and made themselves their god. They thought they could protect themselves from danger and enemies by building their homes high in the cliffs of the Edom wilderness. But God said that He would bring them down (v. 4).

If pride was Edom's essential sin, violence was the supreme manifestation of that sin. The Edomites not only protected themselves, but they did wrong to others, and rejoiced when they harmed others. Verses 10 and 11 say, "Because of violence to your brother Jacob you will be covered with shame and cut off forever. On the day that you stood aloof, on the day that strangers carried off his wealth, and foreigners entered his gate and cast lots for Jerusalem, you too were as one of them." When the Edomites saw their brother Israelites suffering, they not only complacently did nothing, but they even rejoiced and added to those sufferings.

The Israelites represented faith in Yahweh. They stood for this ideal, though admittedly they failed to be consistent in their witness. Nevertheless, they continued to believe in God and to follow Him. The Edomites' unnatural violence against the Israelites revealed their hatred for what the Israelites stood for, not just the Israelites themselves. So when the Israelites suffered, the Edomites rejoiced. Even though they were the Israelites' brothers according to the flesh, they consistently opposed them for what the Israelites stood for. For example, the Edomites refused to allow the Israelites to pass through their territory on the way to the Promised Land.

The result of such godless pride, which leads to violence against the people of God, is divine retribution. The Edomites thought they were secure (v. 4), but God said that He would bring them down (v. 4). "Will I not on that day, declares the LORD, destroy wise men from Edom and understanding from the mountain of Esau? Then your mighty men will be dismayed, O Teman, in order that every one may be cut off from the mountain of Esau by slaughter" (vv. 8-9). The God, whom the Edomites thought they could disregard, would visit and destroy them. God is higher than even the eagles. He is the One who formed the mountains in which the Edomites foolishly trusted for safety.

God would bring down the Edomites by overruling the plans the Edomites made. "All the men allied with you will send you forth to the border, and the men at peace with you will deceive you and overpower you. They who eat your bread [as covenant partners] will set an ambush for you" (v. 7). The Edomites also trusted in other nations for their security rather than in God. But the Lord would use the very objects of Edom's trust to destroy her. He often uses the false gods that people rely on, instead of Himself, to do this. Allies in ungodliness turn out to be enemies eventually. For example, criminals sometimes become witnesses for the prosecution of other criminals to shorten their own sentences.

As usual, God would deal with Edom in poetic justice, or talionic judgment. What they had sowed they would reap (cf. Gal. 6:7-8). Esau had sowed to the flesh, and in the end the flesh became the instrument of the Edomites' destruction. God said, "As you have done, it will be done to you" (v. 15).

But this prophecy does not end with promises of Edom's destruction. It ends with promises of Israel's final victory, and the vindication of Israel's God. Obadiah predicted that, first of all, despised Israel would be delivered from her proud enemy. "The house of Jacob will possess their possessions" (v. 18). "Deliverers will ascend Mount Zion to judge the mountain of Esau" (v. 21). Then "the kingdom will be the Lord's" (v. 21). The conflict between the people of the world and people of faith still continues, but the kingdom will eventually become the Lord's. This will happen when Jesus Christ returns to the earth and sets up His rule of righteousness. He will then put down all the proud, violent antagonists of His people, and all that they stand for.

The Edomites were the most "fleshly" enemies of Israel, to use a New Testament term. Therefore, this book shows us the ultimate destiny of all such enemies of God's people throughout history, as well as the Edomites. It is for that reason that we have this little book in our Old Testaments. The church has its Edomites. The Christian has his or her Edomites. This book gives us hope. God will eventually destroy all Edomite types, just as He has already destroyed the historic Edomites in fulfillment of Obadiah's prophecy.

This book also challenges Christian readers to examine their own hearts: What sort of person am I? Am I like Esau, or am I like Jacob? Jacob was far from perfect, but God transformed him into Israel: "a prince with God" eventually. The difference between these brothers, and the nations that followed them, was that Jacob valued God's promises concerning the future, but Esau preferred a pot of stew that made him feel good right away. Jacob valued the spiritual; Esau valued the physical. What does the way you live your life, the way you spend your time, the places you go, and the people you like to "hang out" with say about what you value? Are you living with eternity's values consciously in view, or are you simply living for the present?

God will take Jacobs to the woodshed, as He did with Jacob at the Jabbok, and as He did with Jacob's descendants throughout their history. But He will discipline us because He has a future for us, and intends to prepare us for it. He does not bother to train up the Esaus of this world. He may allow them to become materially successful, to build secure nests, to soar like eagles, to be their own gods, to snub their noses at and even violently persecute believers, but He will eventually destroy them.

A few Edomites abandoned the typical Edomite lifestyle, believed in Yahweh, and moved to Israel to become a part of the people of God. A few people from all of Israel's pagan neighbors did this. Ruth the Moabitess is an outstanding example. So there is hope for any individual. Judgment is not inevitable for individuals, as long as there is time to repent. Nevertheless, what the Edomites stood for as a nation fell under divine judgment, and they perished.

Many students of Obadiah have noted that this book is a summary of the essential message of all the prophetical books of the Old Testament. It deals with a major issue that lies behind all the prophetic writings, namely: pride. Pride is probably the biggest problem that every Christian has to deal with. We must remember how God views pride, and this book reminds us.[21]

Exposition

I. EDOM'S COMING JUDGMENT VV. 1-9

This section of the prophecy begins with an introductory statement and then describes Edom's destruction three ways.

A. THE INTRODUCTION TO THE ORACLE V. 1

This verse contains the title of the book, the shortest title of any Old Testament prophetical book, as well as a summary of the Lord's decree against Edom. This revelation came as a vision (Heb. *hazon*; cf. 1 Sam. 3:1; Isa. 1:1; Nah. 1:1) to the prophet.

> "The vision is to be sharply differentiated from common sight and things seen. It is the result of inspiration and is understood as having unique significance since it is given by God himself."[22]

The vision came to the prophet Obadiah ("servant of Yahweh" or "worshipper of Yahweh"). As mentioned in the introduction to this exposition, nothing is known about Obadiah other than his name. We must infer where and when he lived and ministered from various clues.

"Thus says the Lord GOD" is a common phrase in the Prophets. It is a strong claim that the corresponding oracle did not originate in the prophet's own imagination, but in the mind of God (cf. 2 Pet. 1:20-21). "Adonai (i.e., sovereign) Yahweh" (cf. Gen. 2:4; et al.) had made a pronouncement concerning the nation of Edom. This is an unusual titulary (combination title and name) for the Lord. It identifies the covenant God of Israel as sovereign of the world and history.

> "Yahweh was truly Lord. This entire prophecy gives one specific example of the exercise of his lordship."[23]

"Edom" was the nation that had grown out of the descendants of Esau, the twin brother of Jacob (cf. Gen. 36:1). The Edomites occupied the territory east of the Arabah between the Dead Sea and the Gulf of Aqabah south of the Zered River and north of Ezion-geber (Elath). Its eastern boundary was the Arabian Desert. Edom was also known as Seir after Mount Seir, the prominent tableland that occupied the northeastern part of Edom's territory.[24]

Those who had heard a report (message) from the Lord were God's people. Obadiah spoke to them and used an editorial "we." God was sovereignly and supernaturally summoning other nations against Edom, probably through "natural" means (i.e., the desire to defeat her and take over her territory). The "envoy . . . sent among the nations" is probably a personification of the desire God had placed in these nations to destroy Edom. That desire, from the spiritual viewpoint, was His messenger.

B. THE BREACHING OF EDOM'S DEFENSES VV. 2-4

Verses 2-9 contain three sections, which the phrase "declares the Lord" marks off (vv. 4, 8).

---

[21]Adapted from G. Campbell Morgan, *Living Messages of the Books of the Bible*, 1:2:213-25.
[22]Watts, p. 42.
[23]Ibid., p. 47.
[24]For maps of Edom, see Barry J. Beitzel, *The Moody Atlas of the Bible*; the Hammond *Atlas of the Bible Lands*; and Yohanan Aharoni and Michael Avi-Yonah, *The Macmillan Bible Atlas*, revised edition.

v. 2   Yahweh called Obadiah's hearers to see that He would make Edom, which was already despised because of her character, "small among the nations." He would humble her further.

v. 3   The outstanding mark of Edom's national character was pride. The Hebrew word for pride (*zadon*) comes from a verb meaning to boil up (*zid*). It pictures pride as water that boils up under pressure in a cooking pot. Similarly the proud person is like a bubble that thrusts itself up but is hollow. Interestingly, the same Hebrew word occurs three times in the account of Esau, the father of the Edomites, squandering his birthright (Gen. 25:27-34).

> ". . . the key that unlocks the central moral lesson of the book is found in these words in the third verse: 'The pride of thine heart hath deceived thee.'"[25]

> "It is possible for Christians also to fall into the sin of pride. One has only to dismiss God from the reckoning, one has but to slip into the habit of neglecting his Bible, one has merely to fail to be alone with God daily in prayer, and he too may fall into the sin of making decisions and living his life on a secular basis without placing God and His will foremost."[26]

The Edomites thought they were superior because they inhabited a lofty region: Mt. Seir. They thought they were secure because they occupied this militarily favorable location. In fact, they thought they were invincible.

> "Edom's natural defenses were imposing. Its main centers of civilization were situated in a narrow ridge of mountainous land southeast of the Dead Sea ... This ridge exceeded a height of 4,000 feet throughout its northern sector, and it rose in places to 5,700 feet in the south. Its height was rendered more inaccessible by the gorges radiating from it toward the Arabah on the west and the desert eastwards.

> "In addition to these natural fortifications, Edom was strongly defended by a series of Iron Age fortresses, particularly on the eastern frontier where the land descended more gradually to the desert."[27]

The "rock" (Heb. *sela'*) in view is the granite and sandstone that made up Mt. Seir. Though Sela was also the name of an Edomite town (cf. 2 Kings 14:7), here the mountain home of the whole nation seems to be in view. The Greek translation of *sela'* is Petra, the modern name of this town.

v. 4   Here the figure of an "eagle," that was also in view in the previous verse, becomes explicit. Even if the Edomites would build their "nest" as high as the "stars" (hyperbole), God would "bring" them "down." Hyperbole is overstatement for the sake of emphasis. King Sennacherib of Assyria and King Assurnassirpal II of Assyria both used the same figure to boast of their security in their respective annals.[28] The Edomites might have been humanly unassailable, but they were not divinely unassailable. They had proudly boasted, "Who will bring me down to the earth?" (v. 3), but Yahweh replied, "I will bring you down" (v. 4). He would burst their bubble. He Himself declared that He would.

---

[25]Gaebelein, p. 48.

[26]Ibid., p. 52. This writer's discussion of the sin of pride in the light of today (pp. 48-52) is worth reading.

[27]Armerding, pp. 342-43.

[28]See Daniel D. Luckenbill, *The Annals of Sennacherib*, p. 36; and Albert K. Grayson, *Assyrian Royal Inscriptions*, 2:122.

Malachi, who wrote some 400 years later, mentioned that the Edomites were still in existence then (Mal. 1:3-4). By 312 B.C. the capital of Edom was in Nabatean hands, and Edom had ceased to exist as a nation, though Edomites continued to live. They became known as Idumeans. Herod the Great was an Idumean.

C. THE PLUNDERING OF EDOM'S TREASURES VV. 5-7

vv. 5-6 — Thieves robbed houses and grape harvesters stripped vineyards, yet both left a little behind that they did not carry off. However, Yahweh's destruction of Edom would be so complete that nothing at all would remain of her (cf. Jer. 49:9-10). There would be no remnant of Edom left (in contrast to the remnant that Yahweh promised elsewhere to leave in Israel). The form of this assurance sounds like mourning in the presence of death. Concealed "treasures" of all kinds, human as well as material, would not escape Yahweh's omniscient eye (cf. v. 4).

v. 7 — Edom's allies would treacherously betray their friend. Thus, Edom would not only deceive herself, but her trusted allies would also "deceive" her. They would do what in the ancient Near East was most despicable, namely: break a covenant with a covenant partner (cf. Ps. 55:20; Amos 1:9). Edom's allies would prove to be the worst of enemies. They would fail to assist her in her hour of greatest need. Three parallel descriptions of covenant disloyalty in this verse picture the treachery as certain. Moreover, this disloyalty would completely surprise ("ambush") the Edomites.

> "Edom was a weak country militarily, its small population and its limited agricultural wealth precluding powerful armed forces. Therefore its ability to attack Judah's Negeb and help plunder Jerusalem had depended on its obsequious alliance with more powerful states, especially Babylon."[29]

This writer believed Obadiah wrote after the Babylonians defeated Jerusalem.

D. THE DESTRUCTION OF EDOM'S LEADERSHIP VV. 8-9

"Obadiah's discussion nicely interweaves the themes of divine intervention and human instrumentality."[30]

v. 8 — The repetition of "declares the Lord" (cf. v. 4) reemphasizes Yahweh's initiative in this judgment. "That day" points to a specific, though undefined, day when He would surely destroy Edom.

God would destroy Edom's famous "wise men" (cf. 1 Kings 4:30; Job 1:1; 2:11; 4:1; Jer. 49:7; Lam. 4:21; Baruch 3:23), and their "understanding," by allowing them to fail to detect the unfaithfulness of their allies (v. 7). They would also overestimate their own security (v. 3).

> "Because of its communication with Babylon and Egypt and because of the information gleaned through the caravans going to and from Europe and India, Edom had gained an enviable reputation for wisdom."[31]

The "mountain of Esau" (cf. v. 9) is Mt. Seir, the mountain God gave Esau and his descendants to inhabit (Deut. 2:5).

v. 9 — The "mighty men" of Edom may be a synonym for the wise men (v. 8) or the nation's warriors. Together with the wise men, the mighty men form a merism, a figure of speech in which two parts stand for the whole, in this case all the Edomites. Rather than feeling confident, the mighty men, a chief resource of the nation, would feel dismayed when they realized that their covenant partners had proved traitorous.

"Teman" was both a prominent town in central Edom (possibly modern Tuwilan),[32] and the region around the town (cf. Gen. 36:10-11). But its name stands for the whole nation (by metonymy). The end of all this deception and destruction would be the total termination of Edom.

II. EDOM'S CRIMES AGAINST JUDAH VV. 10-14

Verse 10 summarizes what verses 11-14 detail in the same way verse 1 did in relation to verses 2-9.

---

[29]Stuart, pp. 417-18.
[30]Finley, p. 362.
[31]Feinberg, p. 126.
[32]Yohanan Aharoni and Michael Avi-Yonah, *The Macmillan Bible Atlas*, map 155; *Student Map Manual: Historical Geography of the Bible Lands*, map 9-2.

A. THE STATEMENT OF THE CHARGE v. 10

Pride was not the only reason God would humble Edom. The Edomites had also *cursed* the people whom God had purposed to bless, the Israelites (cf. Gen. 27:40-41; Exod. 15:15; Num. 20:14-21; Deut. 2:4; Judg. 11:17-18; 1 Sam. 14:47-48; 2 Sam. 8:13-14; 1 Kings 11:15-16; 1 Chron. 18:11-13; Ps. 60; et al.). In doing this, they had incurred God's wrath (Gen. 12:3). "Violence" (Heb. *hamas*) includes both moral wrong and physical brutality. This violence was especially despicable since it was against Edom's "brother, Jacob" (i.e., the Israelites). Consequently, great "shame" would cover Edom (cf. v. 2), and God would "cut" her "off forever" (cf. v. 9).

B. THE EXPLANATION OF THE CHARGE vv. 11-14

v. 11   God cited one specific instance of Edom's violence against her brother, but as I explained in the introduction, which instance is unclear. Edom's treachery against Judah had taken place on a particular "day" in the past. Likewise, God's judgment would come on a particular "day" yet future (v. 8). "Day" does not always refer to a period of 12 or 24 hours in the Bible. It sometimes refers to a longer period of time but one that is distinguishable as a period of time (e.g., Gen. 2:4). The Edomites' sin was that they failed to help the Israelites in their hour of need (cf. Luke 10:31-32). Instead, they stood aloof and watched joyfully as Israel's invader plundered Jerusalem. Enemies passing though a city's gate signified the loss of its self-rule.[33] God considered the Edomites as guilty as Jerusalem's invaders—because the Edomites failed to help their brethren.

> "In the sight of God, who looks not on the outward appearance but on the heart, there is little distinction in moral accountability between overt sin and an inner bias toward that sin that permits it to go unchecked (cf. Matt 5:21-32)."[34]

> ". . . the Israelites are always commanded in the law to preserve a friendly and brotherly attitude towards Edom (Deut. ii. 4, 5); and in Deut. xxiii. 7 it is enjoined upon them not to abhor the Edomite, because he is their brother."[35]

vv. 12-13   God reinforced the seriousness of the Edomites' sin by condemning it in parallel terminology eight times (vv. 12-14). Compare the same parallel structure in verse 7 where there is a threefold positive reiteration. There is also a pun in the Hebrew text since the word for "disaster" (*'edam*) is similar to the word "Edom" (*'edom*). Hostile attitudes, more than physical violence, were Edom's sins against the Israelites on this occasion. Blood ties should have transcended even covenant ties. Edom's allies would break covenant ties with her (v. 7), but she had betrayed blood ties.

v. 14   Physical violence eventually came into play too. As the Judean fugitives from Jerusalem left the city, the Edomites met them at some fork in the road, and murdered them, rather than helping them escape from the invader. Other Edomites imprisoned fleeing Judahites instead of giving them refuge. This could be poetic hyperbole, but there is nothing in the text that indicates overstatement. All the other descriptions of Edom's actions seem to be literal.

Some English translations render verses 12-14 as referring to the future, while others have interpreted them as referring to the past. Most commentators take the time as past; God was describing something that had already happened.[36] A few take it as future, describing something that would take place in the future.[37] Since this is a judgment oracle, it seems more likely that God was announcing judgment on Edom for something she had already done rather than for something she would do in the future. As she had been proud (v. 2), she had also been violent (v. 10). Keil proposed that Obadiah referred to an event that had happened *and* to another that would happen again in the future—the past event being typical of future reoccurrences.[38]

The two most likely historical occasions that are in view are: first, the invasion by a coalition of Arabs and Philistines who carried off King Jehoram's family and his property during a period of tension with Edom (2 Kings 8:20-22; 2 Chron. 20:1-2; 21:8-17; 22:1). The second possible event was the destruction of Jerusalem by Nebuchadnezzar in 586 B.C. (2 Kings 24:13-16; 25:4-17; 2 Chron. 36:18, 20; cf. Ps. 137:7; Jer. 9:26; 25:21; 27:3; 40:11; Ezek. 25:12; 32:29; 35:3-9, 11-15; 36:2-7; Lam. 1:17; 2:15-17; 4:21-22). As discussed in the introduction to this exposition, I think there is slightly better evidence for the first occasion than for the second.

---

[33]Niehaus, p. 529.
[34]Armerding, p. 348.
[35]Keil, 1:360.
[36]E.g., Finley, p. 340.
[37]E.g., Gaebelein, pp. 5, 29.
[38]Keil, 1:363.

III. THE RESTORATION OF ISRAEL'S SOVEREIGNTY VV. 15-21

As is true of many of the prophetical books, this one also ends with a promise of Israel's restoration in the future.

A. THE JUDGMENT OF EDOM AND THE NATIONS VV. 15-18

References to the work and word of the Lord frame this section. Obadiah announced that a reversal of roles was coming for Edom and all the nations.

v. 15   "The day of the Lord" here is a future day in which God will reverse the fortunes of Israel and the nations (cf. v. 8). "The day of the Lord," a common term in the Prophets, refers generally to any time when God intervenes in human affairs to accomplish His will. The day that Obadiah announced will be the day when God establishes His rule in human affairs, namely, when Jesus Christ returns to rule and reign on the earth. Obadiah said *that day* was approaching. As Edom and the other nations had done to Israel, so God would pay them back with precisely the same judgment (*lex talionis*; cf. Lev. 24:20; Deut. 19:21; Gal. 6:7).

> "God shows not only his sovereignty over all people by not permitting unrequited wickedness, but also his justice by not permitting punishment to exceed crime."[39]

Edom's punishments that resulted in her demise as a nation—before the Second Coming—were part of God's judgment on her, but the prophet saw all God's judgments on Edom and the nations, which will culminate in the eschaton (end times). All the prophets had difficulty seeing the proximity of the future events that they predicted to one another (cf. 1 Pet. 1:11).

> "The opening line of v. 15 therefore constitutes the core of Obadiah's prophecy. It provides a theological framework for the preceding verses: the localized disasters befalling Edom and Jerusalem are not merely isolated incidents in a remote and insignificant theater of war, for they mark the footsteps of the Lord himself as he approaches to set up a 'kingdom that will never be destroyed' (Dan 2:44). And the following verses are essentially a commentary on the implications of that impending 'day.'"[40]

> "Edom is presented as the paradigm of all the nations."[41]

v. 16   Edom had her "day" on the Lord's holy mountain, Jerusalem, when she failed to help her brother, Israel. Likewise, all the nations would have their "day" dominating Jerusalem and the Jews, during "the times of the Gentiles" (Luke 21:24). We live in "the times of the Gentiles." This period of history began when Nebuchadnezzar removed Israel's sovereignty in 586 B.C., and will end when Jesus Christ returns to the earth and restores Israel's sovereignty. During "the times of the Gentiles" Israel is being "trodden down by the Gentiles" (Luke 21:24). Obadiah described Israel's enemies as drinking there in celebration of their dominion over the Israelites (cf. Exod. 32:6; 1 Sam. 30:16). Though they would celebrate to the point of delirium, God would destroy them, and they would become "as if they had never existed." They would drink the cup of His wrath (cf. Ps. 60:3; 75:8; Isa. 51:17-23; Jer. 25:17-26, 28-29; 49:12-13; Hab. 2:15-16).

> "The verse apparently precludes any trace of the nations remaining . . ., yet there will be a remnant of various nations in the Millennium (Isa. 2:2-4; Amos 9:12; Mic. 4:1-3; Zech. 14:16-19). How are these two ideas to be reconciled? The answer perhaps lies in the difference between the concept of nations before and during the Millennium. Before the golden age of Messiah's rule on earth the nations consider themselves sovereign and fight to maintain their individual rights. When Christ returns, however, only those from the nations who have called on the Lord's name will enter. Also, they will be under one King and no longer a threat to Israel's existence. Therefore, the nations as we presently know them will exist no more once the Millennium begins. In any case, Obadiah dwells only on the destruction of the old order as far as the nations are concerned."[42]

v. 17   The future of Israel (restoration) contrasts with the future of Edom (judgment). In that future time of judgment (the Tribulation), there "will be those who escape" from Jerusalem, namely, many Jews (cf. Zech. 13:8; Rev. 12:13-17). Some writers viewed

---

[39]D. Baker, p. 38.
[40]Armerding, p. 353.
[41]D. Baker, p. 39.
[42]Finley, p. 372.

this as taking place during the fall of Jerusalem in A.D. 70.[43] But Jerusalem did not become holy and the house of Jacob did not possess their possessions after that event, as this verse predicts. The city would eventually become "holy" (at the Second Coming), and "the house of Jacob," in contrast to the house of Esau, would then "possess" what God intended for them to have (in the Millennium).

v. 18   The Israelites would then "consume" the Edomites, as "a fire" burns up "stubble" (cf. Exod. 15:7; Isa. 10:17; Joel 2:5; Zech. 12:6; Mal. 4:1; Matt. 3:12; Luke 3:17). Fire is often a tool of divine judgment in Scripture (cf. Deut. 28:24; 32:22). There would be no Edomites left (cf. vv. 8-9; Num. 24:18; Isa. 11:13-14; Ezek. 25:13-14; Amos 9:12), though Israelites would escape from Jerusalem (v. 17).

> "Obadiah distinctly mentions the house of Joseph, *i.e.* of the ten tribes, in this passage and in this alone, for the purpose of guarding against the idea that the ten tribes are to be shut out from the future salvation."[44]

"The house of Jacob," in contrast, refers to the Southern Kingdom. This prediction will find ultimate fulfillment during the judgment of the nations after the Second Coming and before the messianic rule of Christ in the Millennium begins. Yahweh again guaranteed the accuracy of this prophecy with His own spoken word (cf. vv. 4, 8).

> "Some passages, like v. 18, speak of a military participation by Israel in the judgment of the nations just prior to the Millennium (Zech. 12:1-9; Mal. 4:3 [MT 3:21]), while others depict the Lord carrying out the judgment on behalf of His people (Joel 3:12 [MT 4:12]; Zech. 14:3-5; cf. Matt. 25:31-46). It is difficult to reconstruct the precise order of events. In any case much of the material is evidently not strictly chronological."[45]

The Edomites' fortunes ebbed and flowed for centuries following Obadiah's prophecy. The "Herods," including Herod the Great (Matt. 2:1-17), Herod Antipas (Luke 13:31-32; 23:7-12), and Herod Agrippa I (Acts 12:1-11, 23), were all of Edomite descent. But in the second century B.C., the Jews and other enemies virtually consumed the Edomites. It was then that the Edomites lost their national identity and autonomy, which they never regained. So the final destruction of the nation of Edom by Israel took place long before the eschaton.

> ". . . one could speak of a partial fulfillment of Obadiah's oracles when the Maccabeans and Hasmoneans reclaimed these areas for Israel."[46]

This took place in the second century B.C. However, Obadiah spoke of "all the nations" (v. 16), not just Edom. He foresaw the destruction of all Gentile powers that dominated the Israelites. Had the Jews accepted Jesus Christ as their Messiah, He would have begun to rule shortly after His crucifixion and resurrection. Since they rejected Him, the final judgment of the nations that the prophets predicted is still future.

B. THE OCCUPATION OF EDOM BY ISRAEL VV. 19-21

This pericope (section of text), as the former one, also has a framing phrase: "the mountain of Esau" (vv. 19, 21). This mountain, of course, contrasts with the Lord's holy mountain: "Mount Zion" (vv. 16-17).

vv. 19-20   Obadiah predicted that Jews living in various parts of Israel would possess parts of the Promised Land that other nations formerly occupied (cf. Isa. 66:8; Zech. 12:10—13:1; 14:1-9). These parts included Mt. Seir (Edom), Philistia, and territories to the north of Judah, including Ephraim and Samaria (the Northern Kingdom), and Transjordan (Gilead). Formerly exiled Israelites, living to the north near "Zarephath" (in modern Lebanon) and in "Sepharad" (perhaps Sardis in modern Turkey or a territory in Media or Spain[47]), would return and occupy the southern portions of the land: "the Negev." The location of Sepharad remains a mystery. Israel would again conquer the land, but this time she would subdue it completely and occupy all the territory God had promised Abraham (cf. Gen. 13:14-17; 26:2-5; 28:13-15; Deut. 1:7).

> "Was Obadiah's prophecy fulfilled? By Malachi's time (approximately 450 B.C.), Edom had suffered a devastating defeat (see Mal. 1:1-4), though not of the magnitude envisioned by Obadiah. Obadiah's description of Edom's judgment is probably to some degree stylized and exaggerated. However, the

---

[43]E.g., Armerding, p. 354.
[44]Keil, 1:370.
[45]Finley, p. 373.
[46]Ibid., p. 374.
[47]See *The New Bible Dictionary*, s.v. "Sepharad," by D. J. Wiseman; and Watts, p. 64.

	cosmic dimension of the prophecy transcends historical developments and points to an end-time judgment of worldwide proportions. When viewed in this larger eschatological context, Edom serves as an archetype for all God's enemies, who will be crushed by his angry judgment (see also Isa. 34 and 63:1-6)."[48]
v. 21	In summary, those who deliver the Jews to their divinely intended destiny "will ascend Mt. Zion" and will "judge" Mt. Seir (cf. Judg. 3:9, 15). Edom will not prevail over Israel, but Yahweh will prove to be sovereign (cf. v. 1). His "kingdom" will extend over the whole Promised Land, even the part that Israel's enemies formerly occupied, and over the people who formerly opposed them. The conquest of the land that Joshua began but did not finish will be complete then. Thus Obadiah's prophecy, this envisioned account of two mountains, ends on a climax with Yahweh's kingdom dominating all the nations, and with Yahweh as King of Kings and Lord of Lords (cf. Rev. 19:16; 20:4). The verse is clearly messianic.
	"None of the prophets has a more exalted close than this. . . . No man-ruled empire nor any nation of this world will endure forever. All will one day be merged into that eternal kingdom over which the Lord Jesus Christ will reign in solitary glory."[49]

Amillennial interpreters understand New Testament references to Israel as references to the church. They see the fulfillment of Obadiah's prophecy, not in the restoration of Old Testament Israel to future sovereignty in the Promised Land, but in the final victory of the church over all her enemies.[50] Premillennialists reject this "replacement theology" (the church replaces Israel in God's program) because we believe when God said "Israel" He meant Israel. It is incorrect, we believe, to conclude that because Christians are the spiritual seed of Abraham, the church is the spiritual seed of Israel.

As the nation of Edom opposed the Israelites, so the Edomites of Jesus' day (Herod the Great and his successors) opposed Jesus Christ and His followers. Our Lord Jesus Christ, who proved to be the fulfillment of all that the nation of Israel was to be, became the personal focus of Herod's hostility, who tried to kill Jesus in His infancy. Yet Herod was unsuccessful. Likewise, all the enemies of Israel, and of Israel's Messiah, will be unsuccessful in doing away with the Savior—and will experience destruction themselves for trying to do so.

---

[48]Chisholm, *Handbook on . . .*, p. 406.
[49]Gaebelein, pp. 46-47.
[50]E.g., Stuart, p. 422; Keil, 1:378; and Allen, p. 172.

Bibliography

Aharoni, Yohanan. *The Land of the Bible: A Historical Geography*. Revised ed. Translated by Anson F. Rainey. Philadelphia: Westminster Press, 1979.

Aharoni, Yohanan, and Michael Avi-Yonah. *The Macmillan Bible Atlas*. Revised ed. New York: Macmillan Publishing Co., 1977.

Allen, Leslie C. *The Books of Joel, Obadiah, Jonah and Micah*. The New International Commentary on the Old Testament series. Grand Rapids: Wm. B. Eerdmans Publishing Co., 1976.

Archer, Gleason L., Jr. *A Survey of Old Testament Introduction*. Revised ed. Chicago: Moody Press, 1974.

Armerding, Carl E. "Obadiah." In *Daniel-Minor Prophets*. Vol. 7 of *The Expositor's Bible Commentary*. 12 vols. Edited by Frank E. Gaebelein and Richard P. Polcyn. Grand Rapids: Zondervan Publishing House, 1985.

Atlas of the Bible Lands. Maplewood, N.J.: C. S. Hammond & Co., 1959.

Baker, David W. *Obadiah, Jonah, Micah: An Introduction and Commentary*. Tyndale Old Testament Commentaries series. Leicester, Eng., and Downers Grove, Ill.: Inter-Varsity Press, 1988.

Baker, Walter L. "Obadiah." In *The Bible Knowledge Commentary: Old Testament*, pp. 1453-59. Edited by John F. Walvoord and Roy B. Zuck. Wheaton: Scripture Press Publications, Victor Books, 1985.

Barker, Harold P. *Christ in the Minor Prophets*. New York: Loizeaux Brothers, n.d.

Beitzel, Barry J. *The Moody Atlas of Bible Lands*. Chicago: Moody Press, 1985.

Bright, John. *A History of Israel*. Philadelphia: Westminster Press, 1959.

Chisholm, Robert B., Jr. *Handbook on the Prophets*. Grand Rapids: Baker Book House, 2002.

_____. "A Theology of the Minor Prophets." In *A Biblical Theology of the Old Testament*, pp. 397-433. Edited by Roy B. Zuck. Chicago: Moody Press, 1991.

Dyer, Charles H., and Eugene H. Merrill. *The Old Testament Explorer*. Nashville: Word Publishing, 2001. Reissued as *Nelson's Old Testament Survey*. Nashville: Thomas Nelson Publishers, 2001.

Feinberg, Charles Lee. *Joel, Amos, and Obadiah*. The Major Messages of the Minor Prophets series. New York: American Board of Missions to the Jews, 1948.

Finley, Thomas J. *Joel, Amos, Obadiah*. The Wycliffe Exegetical Commentary series. Chicago: Moody Press, 1990.

Freeman, Hobart E. *An Introduction to the Old Testament Prophets*. Chicago: Moody Press, 1968.

Gaebelein, Frank E. *Four Minor Prophets (Obadiah, Jonah, Habakkuk, and Haggai): Their Message for Today*. Chicago: Moody Press, 1970.

Glueck, Nelson. *The Other Side of the Jordan*. Cambridge, Mass.: American Schools of Oriental Research, 1970.

Goswell, Greg. "The Order of the Books in the Hebrew Bible." *Journal of the Evangelical Theological Society* 51:4 (December 2008):673-88.

Grayson, Albert K. *Assyrian Royal Inscriptions*. 2 vols. Records of the Ancient Near East 1-2. Wiesbaden, Germany: Harrassowitz, 1972-76.

Harrison, R. K. *Introduction to the Old Testament*. Grand Rapids: Wm. B. Eerdmans Publishing Co., 1969.

Huffmon, Herbert B. "The Covenant Lawsuit in the Prophets." *Journal of Biblical Literature* 78 (1959):285-95.

Ironside, Harry A. *Notes on the Minor Prophets*. New York: Loizeaux Brothers, 1947.

Kaiser, Walter C., Jr. *Toward an Old Testament Theology*. Grand Rapids: Zondervan Publishing House, 1978.

Keil, Carl Friedrich. *The Twelve Minor Prophets*. 2 vols. Translated by James Martin. Biblical Commentary on the Old Testament. Reprint ed. Grand Rapids: Wm. B. Eerdmans Publishing Co., 1949.

Livingston, G. Herbert. "Obadiah." In *The Wycliffe Bible Commentary*, pp. 839-42. Edited by Charles F. Pfeiffer and Everett F. Harrison. Chicago: Moody Press, 1962.

Longman, Tremper, III and Raymond B. Dillard. *An Introduction to the Old Testament*. 2nd ed. Grand Rapids: Zondervan, 2006.

Luckenbill, Daniel D. *The Annals of Sennacherib*. Oriental Institute Publications 2. Chicago: University of Chicago Press, 1942.

Merrill, Eugene H. *Kingdom of Israel: A History of Old Testament Israel*. Grand Rapids: Baker Book House, 1987.

Morgan, G. Campbell. *Living Messages of the Books of the Bible*. 2 vols. New York: Fleming H. Revell Co., 1912.

The Nelson Study Bible. Edited by Earl D. Radmacher. Nashville: Thomas Nelson Publishers, 1997.

The New Bible Dictionary. 1962 ed. S.v. "Sepharad," by D. J. Wiseman.

The New Scofield Reference Bible. Edited by Frank E. Gaebelein, William Culbertson, et al. New York: Oxford University Press, 1967.

Niehaus, Jeffrey. "Obadiah." In *The Minor Prophets: An Exegetical and Expositional Commentary*, 2:495-541. 3 vols. Edited by Thomas Edward McComiskey. Grand Rapids: Baker Books, 1992, 1993, and 1998.

Smith, Billy K., and Frank S Page. *Amos, Obadiah, Jonah*. The New American Commentary series. N.c.: Broadman & Holman Publishers, 1995.

Stuart, Douglas. *Hosea-Jonah*. Word Biblical Commentary series. Waco: Word Books, 1987.

Student Map Manual: Historical Geography of the Bible Lands. Jerusalem: Pictorial Archive (Near Eastern History) Est., 1979.

Waltke, Bruce K., with Charles Yu. *An Old Testament Theology: an exegetical, canonical, and thematic approach*. Grand Rapids: Zondervan, 2007.

Watts, John D. W. *Obadiah: A Critical Exegetical Commentary*. Grand Rapids: Wm. B. Eerdmans Publishing Co., 1969.

Wiersbe, Warren W. "Obadiah." In *The Bible Exposition Commentary/Prophets*, pp. 371-75. Colorado Springs, Colo.: Cook Communications Ministries; and Eastbourne, England: Kingsway Communications Ltd., 2002.

Wood, Leon J. *The Prophets of Israel*. Grand Rapids: Baker Book House, 1979.

Young, Edward J. *An Introduction to the Old Testament*. Revised ed. Grand Rapids: Wm. B. Eerdmans Publishing Co., 1960.

Young, Rodger C. "When Did Jerusalem Fall?" *Journal of the Evangelical Theological Society* 47:1 (March 2004):21-38.

Constable's Notes
on Jonah

Introduction

Background

Jonah is the fifth of the Minor Prophets in our English Bibles. The Minor Prophets are called the Book of the Twelve in the Hebrew Bible. Jonah is unique among the Latter Prophets (in Hebrew: Isaiah through Malachi) in that it is almost completely narrative, similar to the histories of Elijah and Elisha (1 Kings 17—19; 2 Kings 2:1—13:21). As with these two predecessors, Elijah and Elisha, Jonah also ministered in and to Israel, as well as in Phoenicia and Aram. The exceptional section of this book, of course, is Jonah's psalm in 2:2-9 (cf. Hab. 3). Jonah is the only Old Testament prophet on record whom God sent to a heathen nation with a message of repentance. Nahum's later ministry to Nineveh consisted of announcing certain overthrow, although, had the Ninevites repented again, God might have relented. Jonah was Israel's foreign missionary, whereas Hosea was Israel's home missionary. Both of these prophets revealed important characteristics about God: Hosea, God's loyal love to Israel, and Jonah, His compassion for all people, specifically Gentiles.

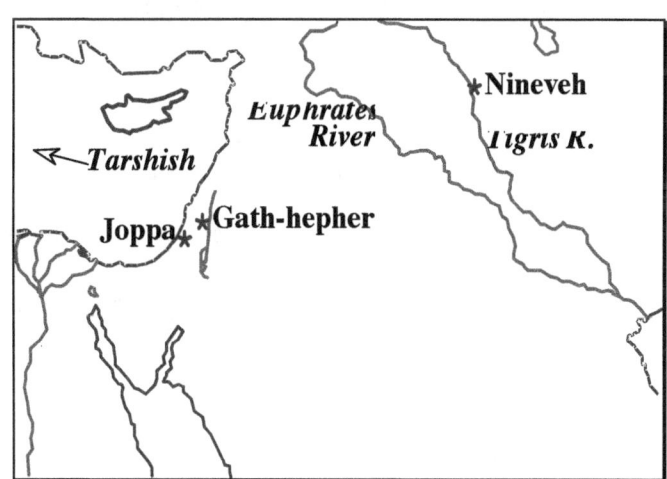

Jonah's hometown was Gath-hepher in Galilee (2 Kings 14:25; cf. Josh. 19:13). It stood north of Nazareth in the tribal territory of Zebulun. Jonah prophesied in the Northern Kingdom during the reign of Israel's King Jeroboam II (793-753 B.C.; 2 Kings 14:23-25). Second Kings 14:25 records that Jonah prophesied that Jeroboam II would restore Israel to her former boundaries, which the king did.

It is very probable that God sent Jonah to Nineveh, at this time a very significant city of the great Assyrian Empire, during the years when that nation was relatively weak. Following the death of King Adad-nirari III in 783 B.C., the nation was not strong again until Tiglath-pileser III seized the throne in 745 B.C. During this 37-year period, Assyria had difficulty resisting its neighbors to the north, the Urartu mountain tribes, who allied with their neighbors, the people of Mannai and Madai. These invaders pushed the northern border of Assyria south, to within 100 miles of Nineveh. This vulnerable condition evidently made the king and residents of Nineveh receptive to Jonah's prophetic message to them. Wiseman argued for a more specific time within this period, namely, during the reign of Assur-dan III (772-755 B.C.), when he held that Jonah visited Nineveh.[1] Dyer wrote that Nineveh became one of the capitals of Assyria during the reign of Sargon II (721-705 B.C.), and it became Assyria's sole capital during the reign of his son, Sennacherib (705-681 B.C.).[2]

Nineveh stood on the eastern bank of the Tigris River. It had walls 100 feet high and 50 feet thick, and the main one, punctuated by 15 gates, was over seven and one-half miles long.[3] The total population was probably about 600,000—including the people who lived in the suburbs outside the city walls (cf. 4:11). The residents were idolaters and worshipped Asur and Ishtar, the chief male and female deities, as did almost all the Assyrians. Assyria was a threat to Israel's security (cf. Hos. 11:5; Amos 5:27). This is one reason Jonah refused to go to Nineveh. He feared the people might repent and that God would refrain from punishing Israel's enemy (4:2).

Date and Writer

Many critical scholars date this prophecy in the postexilic period during the time of Ezra and Nehemiah. They base their opinion on linguistic features of the book and legendary descriptions, specifically: the size, population, importance, and king of Nineveh, plus late customs and audience.[4] Critics also point to the differences in style between Jonah and Hosea, another northern prophet. Many conservative scholars believe that these arguments do not outweigh the evidence for a pre-exilic date that many features of the book and the traditional Jewish commentaries present.

If the book records events that really happened, the record of them must have come from Jonah himself. However, the book nowhere claims that Jonah was its writer. It seems to argue against this possibility by relating the story in the third person rather than in the first. Therefore, some unidentified writer appears to have put the book in its final form. However, Jonah could have described himself in the third person. Daniel did this

---

[1]Donald J. Wiseman, "Jonah's Nineveh," *Tyndale Bulletin* 30 (1979):29-51.
[2]Charles H. Dyer, in *The Old Testament Explorer*, p. 772.
[3]See *International Standard Bible Encyclopaedia*, 1957 ed., s.v. "Nineveh," by A. H. Sayce; *Wycliffe Bible Encyclopedia*, 1975 ed., s.v. "Nineveh," by Elmer B. Smick; and *The New Bible Dictionary*, 1962 ed., s.v. "Nineveh," by D. J. Wiseman.
[4]For refutation of these objections, see T. Desmond Alexander, "Jonah," in *Obadiah, Jonah, Micah*, pp. 52-63.

in the Book of Daniel, which most conservatives believe Daniel wrote. The compilers of the Old Testament canon probably placed this book among the Minor Prophets because they believed that Jonah wrote it.[5] The title, however, honors the chief character in the narrative as much as its traditional writer.

One conservative scholar suggested that what we have is a version of the story that someone wrote for the nation of Judah. The writer supposedly did this to teach Judah's people the lessons that God earlier taught His prophet, the Ninevites, and the residents of Israel.[6] Such a message would have been appropriate when the weakened Southern Kingdom faced a threat from another formidable power to its north, namely, Babylonia. However, the arguments for the writer being Jonah are quite convincing.[7] Douglas Stuart argued that the writer was not Jonah because the story is so consistently critical of Jonah, more so than any other Bible book is critical of its writer.[8] This argument seems weak to me.

The events recorded in the book probably covered only a few months or years at the most. Jonah lived during Jeroboam II's reign over the Northern Kingdom of Israel (793-753 B.C.). Probably a date of composition somewhere in the neighborhood of 780 B.C. would not be far from the exact date.

> "From the death of Elisha to the prophesying of Amos nearly forty years must have elapsed, during which the only recorded prophetic voice is Jonah's."[9]

Historicity

Since the rise of critical scholarship in the nineteenth century, many writers and teachers now believe that the events recorded in this book were not historical.[10] They interpret this book as an allegory or as a parable.

The allegorical interpretation views the book as "a complete allegory in which each feature represents an element in the historical and religious experience of the Israelites."[11] This interpretation may have arisen because "Jonah" means "dove," and the Jews had long regarded the dove as a symbol of their nation (cf. Ps. 74:19; Hos. 11:11). Jonah indisputably brought peace to violent Nineveh as a dove. Those who adopt this interpretation see the book as teaching Israel's mission and failure in being God's missionary agent to the Gentiles. Jonah's flight to Tarshish represents Israel's failure before the Exile, and the great fish symbolizes Babylon. The disgorging of Jonah stands for Israel's second chance following her restoration to the land.

The parabolic interpretation also regards the book as not historical.[12] However, its advocates view it as simply a moral story designed to teach a spiritual lesson. Essentially, the lesson is that God's people should not be narrow and introverted, but outreaching and missionary in their love and concern for those outside their number who are facing God's judgment. The difference in these two interpretations is the amount of detail that its advocates press. The parabolic interpretation usually argues for one primary lesson in the story, whereas the allegorical interpretation finds meaning in its many details too.

Jewish and Christian interpreters believed that the Book of Jonah was historical until the rise of critical scholarship.[13] Jesus Christ referred to Jonah as a historical person and to his experience as real (Matt. 12:38-42; 16:4; Luke 11:29-32). Jonah is the only Old Testament character with whom Jesus Christ compared Himself directly.[14] Jesus did refer to other prophets, however, namely: Elijah, Elisha, and Isaiah—besides quoting and alluding to many others.

> "If the three days' confinement of Jonah in the belly of the fish really had the typical significance which Christ attributes to it . . . it can neither be a myth or dream, nor a parable, nor merely a visionary occurrence experienced by the prophet; but must have had as much objective reality as the facts of the death, burial, and resurrection of Christ."[15]

J. Vernon McGee argued that Jonah died and God raised him back to life on the basis of Jesus' words about him (Matt. 12:39-40).[16] Most conservative expositors believe that Jesus' prediction does not require that interpretation.

---

[5]See C. F. Keil, *The Twelve Minor Prophets*, 1:380.
[6]H. L. Ellison, "Jonah," in *Daniel-Minor Prophets*, vol. 7 of *The Expositor's Bible Commentary*, p. 362.
[7]See especially Gleason L. Archer Jr., *A Survey of Old Testament Introduction*, pp. 308-9.
[8]Douglas Stuart, *Hosea-Jonah*, p. 432.
[9]H. L. Ellison, *The Prophets of Israel*, p. 55.
[10]For discussion and refutation see Archer, pp. 309-15; Stuart, pp. 440-42; and Alexander, pp. 69-77.
[11]R. K. Harrison, *Introduction to the Old Testament*, p. 911.
[12]See the discussion in Tremper Longman III and Raymond B. Dillard, *An Introduction to the Old Testament*, pp. 444-45.
[13]See Josephus, *Antiquities of the Jews*, 9:10:2.
[14]For several comparisons and contrasts see Frank E. Gaebelein, *Four Minor Prophets*, pp. 122-24.
[15]Keil, 1:388.
[16]J. Vernon McGee, *Jonah: Dead or Alive?* pp. 21-27.

It is unlikely that the writer would have given us the name of Jonah's father if he was not a real person. Furthermore, the narrator presented Jonah as a real person, not a mythical or fictitious figure.[17]

The main argument against the book being historical is Jonah's surviving three days and nights in the fish's belly (1:17). However, various writers have documented many similar miraculous deliverances.[18] Since such a survival is physically possible, we should not dismiss the historical view, especially since Jesus endorsed Jonah's "resurrection."

Some interpreters, including myself, who hold to the historicity of the events—also believe that the book contains symbolic and typical teaching.

> "Whereas other prophets proclaimed in words the position of the Gentiles with regard to Israel in the nearer and more remote future, and predicted not only the surrender of Israel to the power of the Gentiles, but also the future conversion of the heathen to the living God, and their reception into the kingdom of God, the prophet Jonah was entrusted with the commission to proclaim the position of Israel in relation to the Gentile world in a symbolico-typical manner, and to exhibit both figuratively and typically not only the susceptibility of the heathen for divine grace, but also the conduct of Israel with regard to the design of God to show favour to the Gentiles, and the consequences of their conduct."[19]

> "Jonah's character and God's dealing with him foreshadow the subsequent history of the nation of Israel: outside the land, a trouble to the Gentiles, yet witnessing to them; cast out, but miraculously preserved; in future deepest distress calling upon the LORD as Savior, finding deliverance and then becoming missionaries to the Gentiles (Zech. 8:7-23). But chiefly Jonah typifies Christ as the Sent-One, raised from the dead, and carrying salvation to the Gentiles."[20]

What difference does it make if Jonah was not historical but fictional? The main effect is that, if Jonah was not a real person, then the force of Jesus' appeal to his experience would have been considerably weakened. If Jonah had not spent three days and three nights in a fish's belly, would Jesus' death have had to be literal? Perhaps Jesus was only talking about a spiritual or legendary experience similar to dying. Jesus based His sign of the prophet Jonah on the historicity of Jonah and his experience in the fish, which Jesus' contemporaries took literally.

Genre
The book is probably a sensational didactic prophetic historical narrative in its literary genre.[21]

> "The concern of a number of OT prophetic narratives is to trace the process whereby a divine oracle was fulfilled. This book, on the contrary, breaks the pattern surprisingly by showing how and why a divine oracle, concerning the destruction of Nineveh, was not fulfilled."[22]

Many commentators who deny the historicity of the book regard it as a parable or allegory and its literary tone as parody or satire.[23]

Purpose
The book is a revelation to God's people of His sovereign power and loving concern for all His creatures, even cattle (4:11). This revelation came first to Jonah personally, and then through him to the Jews. It was not primarily a revelation to the Ninevites. Their responsibility was simply to repent and humble themselves. This revelation should have moved the Israelites to respond as the Assyrians did, namely: with repentance and humility. They faced similar threats, first from the Assyrians and then from the Babylonians. Jonah's lack of concern for the Ninevites contrasts with God's concern for them that was to be the pattern for His people.

> "The main purpose of the book is to teach Israelites that God loves other nations than their own; or, in fact, to teach us that he loves other nations than *our* own. In service of this purpose, Jonah stands for most Israelites—or most of us—as he represents the typical attitude people tend to have toward nations they have no reason to love themselves."[24]

> "Jonah hopes all along that somehow God won't turn out to be consistent with his own well-known character (4:2). But God *is* consistent throughout, in contrast to Jonah's hypocritical inconsistency. What happens to Nineveh and to Jonah happens

---

[17]For additional evidence see Frank S. Page, "Jonah," in *Amos, Obadiah, Jonah*, pp. 217-19.
[18]See Harrison, pp. 907-8; A. J. Wilson, "Sign of the Prophet Jonah and Its Modern Confirmations," *Princeton Theological Review* 25 (October 1927):630-42; and George F. Howe, "Jonah and the Great Fish," *Biblical Research Monthly*, January 1973, pp. 6-8.
[19]Keil, 1:384.
[20]*The New Scofield Reference Bible*, p. 941.
[21]Stuart, pp. 435-38; Alexander, pp. 69-77. For further discussion of genre, see Ernst R. Wendland, "Text Analysis and the Genre of Jonah (Part 1)," *Journal of the Evangelical Theological Society* 39:2 (June 1996):191-206.
[22]Leslie C. Allen, *The Books of Joel, Obadiah, Jonah and Micah*, p. 175.
[23]See ibid., pp. 177-81; and Alexander, pp. 69-77, for further discussion.
[24]Stuart, p. 479. Cf. Dyer, p. 773.

precisely because of what God is like. The audience of the book is thus invited implicitly to revise their understanding of what God is like, if they have indeed shared Jonah's selfish views."[25]

"The overriding theme of the book is the sovereign God's grace toward sinners, illustrated in His decision to withhold His judgment from the guilty but repentant Ninevites."[26]

"God's grace was extended to the most hostile and aggressive of Israel's Gentile neighbors—the Assyrians. Surprisingly, they were even more responsive to God's messenger than was Israel, all to the chagrin of Jonah."[27]

"The Book of Jonah is one of the most relevant books for the present time."[28]

Canonicity

The earliest extra-biblical reference to this book is in Ecclesiasticus 49:10. There, Ben Sira, who lived no later than 190 B.C., referred to "the twelve prophets," namely, the writers of the Minor Prophet books, which includes Jonah. The Jewish rabbis never challenged the canonicity of this book.

Outline

I. The disobedience of the prophet chs. 1—2
    A. Jonah's attempt to flee from God 1:1-3
    B. Jonah's lack of compassion 1:4-6
    C. Jonah's failure to fear his sovereign God 1:7-10
    D. The sailors' compassion and fear of God 1:11-16
    E. Jonah's deliverance by God 1:17—2:1
    F. Jonah's psalm of thanksgiving 2:2-9
    G. Jonah's deliverance from the fish 2:10

II. The obedience of the prophet chs. 3—4
    A. Jonah's proclamation to the Ninevites 3:1-4
    B. The Ninevites' repentance 3:5-10
    C. Jonah's displeasure at God's mercy 4:1-4
    D. God's rebuke of Jonah for his attitude 4:5-9
    E. God's compassion for those under His judgment 4:10-11

The following outline points out some of the parallels in the story nicely.[29]

I. A Hebrew sinner saved (1:1—2:10 [11])
    A. Jonah's disobedience (1:1-3)
    B. Jonah's punishment; heathen homage (1:4-16)
    C. Jonah's rescue (1:17—2:10 [2:1-11])
        1. God's grace (1:17 [2:1])
        2. Jonah's praise (2:1-9 [2-10])
        3. God's last word (2:10 [11])

II. Heathen sinners saved (3:1—4:11)
    A. Jonah's obedience (3:1-4)
    B. Nineveh's repentance (3:5-9)
    C. Jonah's rebuke (3:10—4:11)
        1. God's grace (3:10)
        2. Jonah's plaint (4:1-3)
        3. God's last word (4:4-11)

---

[25]Stuart, p. 434.
[26]Robert B. Chisholm Jr., "A Theology of the Minor Prophets," in *A Biblical Theology of the Old Testament*, p. 432. See also Alexander, pp. 81-91.
[27]Walter C. Kaiser Jr., *Toward an Old Testament Theology*, p. 200.
[28]R. T. Kendall, *Jonah: An Exposition*, p. 11.
[29]Allen, p. 200. The verse numbers in brackets are those in the Hebrew text. See also Robert B. Chisholm Jr., *Handbook of the Prophets*, pp. 408-9, for a similar outline.

Message

The Book of Jonah does not contain the record of a prophet's message as much as the record of a prophet's experience. That feature makes Jonah distinctive among the prophetic books. This prophet's experiences are what we need to look at to learn the message of this book. That is also true of the Former Prophets books: Joshua, Judges, Samuel, and Kings. They, too, teach by recording selected experiences more than prophetic oracles.

There are many incidental features of this story, such as the ship, the storm, the fish, the gourd, the worm, the hot wind, and even Nineveh. They are important parts of the revelation, but they do not give us the message of the book. It is the major characters of the story that do that. The major characters are God and Jonah.

God's dealings with Jonah are even more important than His dealings with the Ninevites, from the standpoint of the book's revelation. These dealings reveal God's attitude and activity toward the nations, and toward His own people—for the nations' sake. We have here a revelation of Yahweh and a revelation of the responsibility of Yahweh's representatives.

One of the characteristics that marked the Israelites was their exclusivity. During the reign of Jeroboam II, when Jonah ministered, Israel was expanding geographically. She was forming alliances with her neighbor nations. However at the same time, she was more exclusive religiously than she ever had been. The Israelites believed that their privileged relationship with God needed guarding so the Gentiles would not take it from her, as they had taken so many other things. The Israelites projected their hostile attitude toward the Gentiles onto Yahweh. They thought of Him as hostile to their enemies too. Jonah epitomized that attitude. God gave His people this book to teach them that His attitude toward those outside the covenants and promises was quite different from theirs, and theirs should be different too.

The major revelation of Yahweh in this book comes through in His dealings with Nineveh and in His dealings with Jonah. Note, first, what this book reveals about the Lord from His dealings with Nineveh.

Rather than having a superior, exclusive attitude toward the Ninevites, God's attitude was compassion. We can see this attitude at the beginning of the book, when God commands Jonah to go to Nineveh. We see it again in God's patient persistence, as He brings His prodigal prophet to repentance. We see it again when He sends Jonah there a second time. The clearest revelation of God's attitude toward Nineveh, however, comes through in the last two verses of the book (4:10-11).

Jonah was probably the first of the eighth-century writing prophets (ca. 780 B.C.). Other eighth-century prophets who ministered to the Northern Kingdom of Israel, beside Jonah, were Hosea (760 B.C.), who emphasized the *love* of God, and Amos (760 B.C.), who emphasized the *righteousness* of God. Isaiah (740 B.C.) stressed the *holiness* of God, and Micah (735 B.C.) the *leadership* of God to the residents of the Southern Kingdom of Judah. Jonah reveals the *compassion* of God primarily. It is an important balancing revelation among these other prophetic messages.

The Hebrew word *hus*, translated "have compassion," in 4:10 and 11, means "to spare by sheltering." The idea is that of covering, and so shielding from danger. Jesus said, "O Jerusalem, Jerusalem, who kills the prophets and stones those who are sent to her! How often I wanted to gather your children together, the way a hen gathers her chicks under her wings, and you were unwilling" (Matt. 23:37). Jesus expressed the same attitude toward Jerusalem that God did toward Nineveh. We see God's attitude toward sinning cities: great groups of people. This is the attitude that has driven evangelists and missionaries throughout the ages. It is God's attitude of compassion.

All of God's activities in this book proceeded from this basic attitude. We might conclude that God sent Jonah to preach against Nineveh only because He was angry with it, because of its sin. Certainly it was under His judgment for its sins, but the last verse reveals the underlying motive of God: His compassion.

Seen in this light, the troublesome statement that God changed His mind in 3:10 becomes less problematic. The Hebrew word used here, *nacham*, carries the connotation of being relieved and comforted. We should hear God sighing in relief when we read this verse. When Nineveh repented, God saw that judgment would not be necessary, and this made Him very glad. When people turn from their sin, God turns from judging them. Of course, God's judgment of sin is a manifestation of His love, but we do not often appreciate that fact.

Turning to what this book reveals about God's dealings with Jonah, we see two things.

First, God needs messengers. In one sense, God needs no one and nothing because He is self-sufficient. However in another sense, He has chosen to send His messages through people. The New Testament expression of this truth is: "How shall they hear without a preacher?" (Rom. 10:14). God has chosen to use human messengers to carry most of His messages to other humans.

The second thing that we see, as we examine God's dealings with Jonah, is that because God needs messengers, He is persistent and patient with the messengers He selects. We see this in God not abandoning Jonah when he boarded the ship to go to Tarshish. We see it in God preparing a fish to preserve and transport him back to dry land. We see it in God re-commissioning Jonah. We see it in His providing a gourd to shelter the prophet. We see it in God's patient teaching when Jonah was burning up with heat and anger. We see it in God's attempts to bring

Jonah into sympathy with His merciful purpose. In all these instances, we see God lovingly persuading the prophet to share His fellowship by sharing His attitude.

What about the revelation of the responsibility of God's representatives in this book? Positively it is to represent God. Jonah did not rebel against God and become angry with God because He failed to appreciate God. He knew God quite well, as 4:2 makes perfectly clear. God sends people to represent Him who know Him. Jonah rebelled and became angry because he hated Nineveh. We should be able to appreciate this because all of us hate violence and cruelty when the wicked misdirect their wrath against people who do not deserve it.

To represent God, His servants must be obedient. His orders must take priority over their desires. God's purposes must override our prejudices and our preferences. If this does not happen, then the messenger experiences estrangement from God. However, there must be shared attitudes, as well as obedient actions, for true fellowship to exist. Jonah was not an acceptable representative until his attitude mirrored God's attitude, even though he had acquiesced to do God's will.

Jonah gives us the negative example in his attitude toward Nineveh. Jesus gives us the positive one in His attitude toward Jerusalem. Think of all the teeming cities of the world, where cruelty and corruption reign, and then remember that God has compassion on their inhabitants. Do we have more concern for plants than for people? I enjoy gardening, but I am learning to put people before plants and other projects. We will never have a missionary heart until we come into close fellowship with the God of compassion. When we not only know about Him, but walk with Him, then we will share His fellowship. When Jesus looked on Jerusalem, He wept over it.

This book teaches its readers how God feels about His people, as well as how He feels about the teeming masses who do not know Him. He needs us to take His message of compassion to the lost. God is always in need of messengers to stand in the gap. His Word must become incarnate before it becomes impressive. That was true in Jesus' case, and it is true in ours. It is good to send Bibles all over the world, but God's primary method always has been to send preachers with His Word. When people receive the witness of someone whose life God has persuaded to obey Him, the message of repentance becomes persuasive.

God still needs us, and He sends us (Matt. 28:19-20). Every Christian man, woman, boy, and girl can identify with God's call to Jonah to go to Nineveh. Why must we lift up our voices and cry against the Ninevehs of our day? Their wickedness has come up before the Lord, and it is damning them. God wants to save them. Judgment is forever God's unusual (strange) act (Isa. 28:21). What is usual for God is compassion, deliverance, and salvation. Therefore, we must announce God's judgment so people have an opportunity to repent.

Notice that when Jonah was disobedient to God, there was still much about him that was commendable. This is often true of us in our disobedience, and it often encourages us in our disobedience. Jonah went down to Joppa and found a ship waiting. Often when we disobey God we find that circumstances seem to accommodate us and cooperate with us. Jonah evidently paid his own fare. If he did, that was commendable responsibility. Nevertheless, all these circumstances that Jonah could have viewed as indications that he was doing right, clearly were not indicating that. He never reached Tarshish. God did not allow him to go that far. God gave him some freedom, but He eventually brought him up short. Likewise, God does not remind us at every turn that we are disobedient, but He will bring us to the point of acknowledging our disobedience (cf. 1:7). He will not take His hand off of us.

The church's failure in evangelism and missions is not due primarily to our failure to know God and His compassion. We know Him. We have even experienced His compassion in our own lives. Our failure is due mainly to our dislike for those under God's judgment: our Ninevites. Perhaps we need to admit that we really do not want to see the world saved. The evidence of this is that we are much happier enjoying the spiritual comforts of being God's chosen people than we are reaching out to the lost. Some Christians hate the lost, just as Jonah did. Why do we not reach out to the city in which we live? Perhaps it is because we do not like the people who live there.

How can we overcome this problem? We will not overcome it by trying to love those whom we hate. That is humanly impossible. What we must do is what Jonah did. We must begin by simply obeying God, by doing what He has told us to do, namely: go to them with the message of deliverance. In other words, we should love our Lord even though we may not love the lost. When we obey Him, as Jonah did, God will begin to deal with our attitude toward those under His judgment (cf. John 21).

The Book of Jonah deals with the problem of exclusivism: the sin of concluding that if we have received God's compassion, it is for ourselves alone. What we need to do is begin obeying the commission that God has given us. Hopefully our obedience will arise out of love for Him, but it may arise out of our learning that disregarding that commission can result in much pain for us. In any case, we need to obey. Then God will begin to teach us love for the unlovely. That, too, may be a painful learning process, but God will be very tender with us as He teaches us. We will also enter into true fellowship with our Savior, who wept over Jerusalem, because we will share His heart of compassion.

The message of Jonah then is that God will give us His heart of compassion for the lost as we execute the commission that He has given us.

Exposition

I. THE DISOBEDIENCE OF THE PROPHET CHS. 1—2

The first half of this prophecy records Jonah's attempt to flee from the Lord and His commission, when he found it personally distasteful, and the consequences of his rebellion.

A. JONAH'S ATTEMPT TO FLEE FROM GOD 1:1-3

The story opens with God commissioning His prophet and Jonah rebelling against His will.

1:1 The book and verse open with a conjunction (Heb. *waw*, Eng. "Now"). Several versions leave this word untranslated because it makes no substantial difference in the story. Its presence in the Hebrew Bible may suggest that this book was part of a larger collection of stories. About 14 Old Testament books begin with "And," and they obviously connect with the books that immediately precede them. However, what Jonah might have continued is unknown.

> "These books remind us of God's 'continued story' of grace and mercy."[30]

The expression "The word of the LORD came to" occurs over 100 times in the Old Testament.[31] The writer did not record how Jonah received the following message from the Lord. That is inconsequential here, though often in other prophetic books the method of revelation that God used appears. Likewise, the time of this revelation is a mystery and unessential to the interpretation and application of this story. God's actions are the most important feature in this prophecy.

Jonah's name means "Dove."

> "We associate the dove with peace and purity; however, this positive meaning is not the only possible association. A 'dove' could also be a symbol of silliness (see Hos. 7:11), a description that sadly applies to this tragicomical prophet."[32]

We do not have any knowledge of "Amittai" ("Truthful"), other than that he was Jonah's father. The recording of the name of an important person's father was common in Jewish writings, and the presence of Amittai's name in the text argues for the historical reality of Jonah.

There are several unbiblical Jewish traditions about Jonah's origin.[33] One held that he was the widow's son whom Elijah restored to life (1 Kings 17:17-24). Another held that he had some connection with the Jerusalem temple, even though he was from the north. Another credited him with a successful mission to Jerusalem similar to the one to Nineveh. None of these has any biblical support. They were apparently attempts to fit Jonah into other inspired stories and to glorify the prophet.

1:2 "Nineveh" was indeed a "great city," its history stretching back as far as Nimrod, who built it—as well as Babel and several other cities in Mesopotamia (Gen. 10:8-12).[34] The word "great" occurs frequently in this book (1:2, 4, 12, 16, 17; 3:2; 4:1, 6, 11). Nineveh occupied about 1,800 acres, and stood on the east bank of the Tigris River across from the modern Iraqi city of Mosul.

Jonah was to "cry against it" (NASB) or "preach against it" (NIV), in the sense of informing its inhabitants that God had taken note of their wickedness. He was not to identify their sins as much as announce that judgment was imminent. God apparently intended that Jonah's condition as an outsider would have made the Ninevites regard him as a divine messenger. The Lord did not send him to be merely a foreign critic of that culture.

1:3 "Tarshish" was the name of a great-grandson of Noah through Noah's son Japheth and Japheth's son Javan (Gen. 10:1-4). From then on in the Old Testament, the name describes both the descendants of this man and the territory where they settled (cf. 1 Kings 10:22; 22:48; 1 Chron. 7:10). The territory was evidently a long distance from Israel and on the Atlantic coast of

---

[30]Warren W. Wiersbe, "Jonah," in *The Bible Exposition Commentary/Prophets*, p. 378.
[31]Alexander, p. 97.
[32]*The Nelson Study Bible*, p. 1493.
[33]Ellison, "Jonah," p. 368.
[34]For further description of its greatness, see my comments on 3:3 and 4:11.

southwest Spain (cf. 4:2; Isa. 66:19).[35] It also contained mineral deposits that its residents mined and exported to Tyre and probably other places (Jer. 10:9; Ezek. 27:12). Since the Hebrew word *tarshishu* means "smelting place" or "refinery," the Jews referred to several such places on the Mediterranean coast by this name.[36] Similarly, several towns along the coastlands of English-speaking nations today bear the name "Portland." Therefore it is probably impossible to locate the exact spot that Jonah proposed to visit. The identification of Tarshish with Spain is very old, going back to Herodotus, the Greek historian, who referred to a Tartessus in Spain.[37] This site was about 2,500 miles west of Joppa. (Curiously, and inaccurately, Josephus believed that Jonah tried to flee to Tarsus in Cilicia.[38]) In any case, Jonah sought to flee by ship from Joppa, on Israel's Mediterranean coast, and to go to some remote destination that lay in the opposite direction from Nineveh. Joppa stood about 35 miles southwest of Samaria, the capital of the Northern Kingdom. Nineveh lay about 550 miles northeast of Samaria.

> "Jonah the believer is disgruntled with his calling. (Whoever thought a missionary would be disgruntled—except a fellow missionary!)"[39]

Why did Jonah leave Israel? He evidently concluded that if he ran away, God would select another prophet, rather than track him down and make him go to Nineveh. By going in the opposite direction from Nineveh, as far from Nineveh as was then possible, Jonah seems to have been trying to get as far away from the judgment he thought the Lord would bring on that city as he could. In short, he seems to have been trying to run away from the Lord's calling and to preserve his own safety at the same time. This is the only instance in Scripture of a prophet disobeying God's call (cf. Amos 3:8 for the typical response).

However, it was "the presence of the Lord" localized in the Promised Land, mentioned twice in this verse for emphasis, that Jonah sought to escape more than anything. Specifically it was God's influence over him. He probably knew that he could not remove himself from the literal presence of the omnipresent God.

> "To be a prophet was not necessarily to be a great theologian. God chooses whom he will, whether trained professional specialist or not (cf. Amos 7:14-15)."[40]

There is a chiasm in this verse. It begins and ends with references to going to Tarshish from the Lord's presence. In the center is another reference to going to Tarshish. This structure stresses the fact that Jonah defiantly repudiated God's call.

Perhaps we can appreciate how Jonah felt about his commission if we compare a similar, but hypothetical case. Suppose God called some Jew living during the Hitler regime to go to Berlin and prophesy publicly that God was going to destroy Nazi Germany unless the Germans repented. The possibility of the Germans repenting and God withholding judgment on them would have been totally repugnant to such a Jew. His racial patriotism would have conflicted with his fidelity to God—just as Jonah's did.[41]

> "In this brief introduction to the book the reader learns three central things: (1) who Jonah was; (2) what Yahweh wanted him to do; (3) Jonah's response. Thus are introduced the main characters of the story, i.e., Jonah and God; and the situation around which the story revolves, i.e., Jonah's unwillingness to carry out a divine commission which he finds odious."[42]

Many servants of the Lord throughout history have mistakenly thought that they could get away from the Lord and escape the consequences of His actions by changing their location. This book teaches us that that is not possible (cf. Ps. 139:7-10).

> "It's possible to be out of the will of God and still have circumstances appear to be working on your behalf."[43]

> "An officer in an army may resign the commission of his president or king, but an ambassador of the Lord is on a different basis. His service is for life, and he may not repudiate it without the danger of incurring God's discipline."[44]

---

[35] See the map in Alexander, p. 49.
[36] *The New Bible Dictionary*, 1962 ed., s.v. "Tarshish," by J. A. Thompson.
[37] Ibid.
[38] Josephus, 9:10:2.
[39] Joyce Baldwin, "Jonah," in *The Minor Prophets*, p. 543.
[40] Stuart, p. 466.
[41] Gaebelein, p. 72.
[42] Stuart, p. 452.
[43] Wiersbe, pp. 378-79.

B. JONAH'S LACK OF COMPASSION 1:4-6

1:4   Jonah subjected himself to dangers, when he launched out on the sea, that Israel and the entire ancient Near East viewed as directly under divine control. "The sea," to them, was the embodiment of the chaotic forces that humans could not control or tame (cf. Ps. 24:2; 33:7; 65:7; 74:13; 77:19; 89:9; 114:3, 5; Isa. 27:1; 51:10; 63:11; Jer. 5:22; 31:35; et al.). Jonah was desperate to get away from where he thought God might come after him (cf. Gen. 3:8). Nevertheless, God used the "wind" to bring the prodigal prophet to the place He wanted him to be (cf. Gen. 1:2).

> "It was gracious of God to seek out His disobedient servant and not to allow him to remain long in his sin."[45]

In the Hebrew text, the last part of this verse is literally: "the ship thought she would be broken in pieces"—a graphic personification.

1:5   The sailors were of mixed religious convictions. Some of them were probably Phoenicians, since Phoenicians were commonly seafaring traders. Phoenicia was a center of Baal worship then. The sailors' willingness to throw their "cargo . . . into the sea" illustrates the extreme danger they faced (cf. Acts 27:18-20).

Jonah's ability to sleep under such conditions seems very unusual. The same Hebrew word (*radam*) describes Sisera's deep sleep, that his exhaustion produced (Judg. 4:21), and the deep sleep that God put Adam and Abram under (Gen. 2:21; 15:12). Perhaps Jonah was both exhausted and divinely assisted in sleeping. His condition does not seem to have a major bearing on the story; it is probably a detail. The events that follow could have happened if he had been wide-awake just as well. What does seem unusual is his attitude of "careless self-security."[46] He seems to have preferred death to facing God alive. Not only did he flee to Tarshish, but he also fled to the innermost part ("the hold") "of the ship" (cf. Amos 6:10).

1:6   It took a presumably pagan sea captain to remind Jonah of his duty. The words the captain used are the same as the ones God had used ("Get up!", v. 2, Heb. *qum lek*). Jonah should have been praying, instead of sleeping, in view of the imminent danger that he and his companions faced (cf. Luke 22:39-46). The normal reaction to danger, even among pagans, is to seek divine intervention, but this is precisely what Jonah wanted to avoid. Jonah did not care if he died (v. 12).

> "It is well known how often sin brings insensibility with it also. What a shame that the prophet of God had to be called to pray by a heathen."[47]

What the captain hoped Jonah's God would do, He did. He is the only true God, and He does show concern for people (cf. 4:2, 11). This demonstration of Yahweh's concern for people in danger is one of the great themes of this book. God showed compassion for the Ninevites and later for Jonah, but Jonah showed little compassion for the Ninevites, for these sailors, or even for himself.

Whereas the first pericope of the story (vv. 1-3) illuminates the lack of compassion that characterized the prophet, this second one (vv. 4-6) reinforces it and implies, in contrast, that God is compassionate. Not only was Jonah fleeing from God's presence, but he was also displaying a character that was antithetical to God's. Such is often the case when God's people turn their backs on Him and run from His assignments.

C. JONAH'S FAILURE TO FEAR HIS SOVEREIGN GOD 1:7-10

The sailors interrogated Jonah about his reasons for travelling on their ship, but it was his failure to live consistently with his convictions that amazed them.

1:7   It appears to have been common among the heathen to "cast lots" to determine who was responsible for some catastrophe (cf. John 19:24). Saul resorted to this when he could not get a direct response from the Lord (cf. 1 Sam. 14:36-42). Casting lots was a divinely prescribed method of learning God's will in Israel (e.g., Lev. 16:8-10; Num. 26:55-56; 33:54; 34:13; 36:2-3; Josh. 14:2; 15:1; 16:1; et al.). However, as practiced by pagans, it was a superstitious practice. In this case, God overruled and gave the sailors the correct answer to their request (cf. Prov. 16:33).

> ". . . Jonah won the lottery—or lost it."[48]

---

[44] Gaebelein, p. 74.
[45] Charles L. Feinberg, *Jonah, Micah, and Nahum*, p. 15.
[46] Keil, 1:393.
[47] Feinberg, p. 16.
[48] Allen, p. 208.

1:8 The sailors proceeded to interrogate Jonah when they believed they had identified the culprit responsible for their calamity. Had Jonah been involved in some situation that had brought down a curse from someone else that resulted in the storm? Possibly the reason for their trouble had some connection with Jonah's occupation or hometown. His national or ethnic origin might also prove to be the key they sought. Finding the reason for their trouble was what they wanted. They did not ignorantly assume that doing away with Jonah would solve their problem.

1:9 It should have been no surprise to the sailors that Jonah was "a Hebrew," since they had taken him on board at Joppa, a major port in Israel. "Hebrew" is the name by which the Israelites' neighbors knew them (cf. 1 Sam. 4:6, 9; 14:11). Jonah probably identified himself as a Hebrew as a preamble to explaining that he worshipped Yahweh Elohim, the heavenly God of the Hebrews. The Phoenicians also thought of Baal as a sky god (cf. 1 Kings 18:24). It was the fact that this God made "the sea" on which they traveled, as well as "the dry land," that convinced the sailors that Jonah had done something very serious. It was obvious to them that Jonah's God was after him, and had sent the storm to put him in His hands. Ironically, what was so clear to these pagans was obscure to the runaway prophet. When God sovereignly selects someone for special service, that person cannot run and hide from Him. Jonah had not yet learned this lesson.

The title "the God of heaven" is common in the postexilic books (e.g., Ezra 1:2; 7:12; Neh. 1:4; Dan. 2:18-19, 37, 44; 5:21, 23). This fact has influenced some scholars to conclude that the Book of Jonah must also date from the same period. However, this title was a very old one in Israel's history (cf. Gen. 24:3, 7). Its use on this occasion was particularly appropriate since it expressed the supremacy of Yahweh to polytheistic pagans.

Jonah's confession is a central feature in the narrative. It is the center of a literary chiasmus that begins in verse 4 and extends through verse 16.[49]

1:10 The sailors' exclamation (rather than question, cf. Gen. 4:10) expressed their incredulity at Jonah's naïveté in trying to run away from the God who created the sea—by taking a sea voyage! Surely Jonah must have known, they thought, that Yahweh would make their journey perilous. Evidently Jonah had previously told them that he was "fleeing from . . . the LORD" (cf. v. 3, where "from the presence of the LORD" occurs twice), but they did not then understand that the Lord was the Creator of the sea. Had they known this, they probably would not have sold him passage. In the polytheistic ancient Near East, people conceived of a multitude of gods, each with authority over a particular area of life. A god of the mountains, for example, would have little power on the plains (cf. 1 Kings 20:23).

Before, the mariners had feared the storm, but now they feared the Lord, recognizing the Creator above the creation.[50]

> "This is the storyteller's ironic view of the person who thinks he can escape Yahweh. And yet this irony, with all its exaggeration, is slyly absurd rather than bitter."[51]

This pericope, like the previous two, builds to a climax that stresses Jonah's failure. He did not fear his God though, again ironically, the pagan sailors did. Jonah professed faith in a sovereign God, yet by trying to escape from the Lord he denied his belief in God's sovereignty. One cannot flee or hide from a sovereign God.

D. THE SAILORS' COMPASSION AND FEAR OF GOD 1:11-16

Rather than becoming God's instrument of salvation, Jonah became an object for destruction because he rebelled against God.

1:11 The sailors might have known what to do with Jonah, had he been a criminal guilty of some crime against persons, or if he had accidentally transgressed a law of his God. However, he was guilty of being a servant of his God and directly disobeying the Lord's order to him. They had no idea what would placate the Creator of the sea in such a case, so they asked Jonah, since he knew his God.

1:12 Jonah's answer reveals the double-mindedness of the prophet. He could have asked the sailors to sail back to Joppa, if he really intended to obey the Lord and go to Nineveh. His repentance surely would have resulted in God withholding judgment

---

[49]See Ernst R. Wendland, "Text Analysis and the Genre of Jonah (Part 2)," *Journal of the Evangelical Theological Society* 39:3 (September 1996):374-75, which also points out many other structural features of Jonah.
[50]Gaebelein, p. 79.
[51]Hans W. Wolff, *Obadiah and Jonah*, p. 139.

from the sailors, just as the Ninevites' repentance later resulted in His withholding judgment from them. Still, Jonah was not ready to obey God yet. Nonetheless, his compassion for the sailors led him to give them a plan designed to release them from God's punishment. It would also likely result in his death, which he regarded as preferable to obeying God. His heart was still as hard as ever toward the plight of the Ninevites, even though he acknowledged he knew God was disciplining him.

> "He pronounces this sentence, not by virtue of any prophetic inspiration, but as a believing Israelite who is well acquainted with the severity of the justice of the holy God, both from the law and from the history of his nation."[52]

Why did Jonah not end his own life by jumping overboard? I suspect that he did not have the courage to do so. Obviously, it took considerable courage to advise the sailors to throw him into the sea where he must have expected to drown, but suicide takes even more courage.

> "The piety of the seamen has evidently banished his nonchalant indifference and touched his conscience. By now he has realized how terrible is the sin that has provoked this terrible storm. The only way to appease the tempest of Yahweh's wrath is to abandon himself to it as just deserts for his sin. His willingness to die is an indication that he realizes his guilt before God."[53]

1:13   The sailors initially rejected Jonah's advice and compassionately chose to drop him off at the nearest landfall. They strained every muscle for Jonah's sake, literally digging their oars into the water. They demonstrated more concern for one man than Jonah had for the thousands of men, women, and children in Nineveh. When reaching land became impossible due to the raging sea, they prayed to Yahweh, something that we have no record that the prophet had done.

1:14   The sailors also voiced their belief in God's sovereignty, which Jonah had denied by his behavior. They requested physical deliverance and forgiveness from guilt, since they anticipated that Jonah would die because of their act. They believed that God's sovereignty was so strongly obvious that He might forgive them. Jonah's innocent death seemed inevitable to them, try as they did to avoid it. Still, they could not be sure that they were doing God's will, and feared that He might punish them for taking the life of His servant. From their viewpoint, Jonah was innocent (Heb. *naqi*) of death, because he had not committed any of the crimes for which people suffered death at the hands of their fellowmen. Yet nothing less than death was what he deserved for sinning against God (Ezek. 18:4, 20; Rom. 6:23).

1:15-16   The immediate cessation of the storm proved to the sailors that Yahweh really did control the sea (cf. Matt. 8:26). Therefore they "feared" (respected) Him, "offered a sacrifice" to Him (when they reached shore?), and "made vows" (perhaps to venerate Him, cf. Ps. 116:17-18).

> "The book of Jonah contains within its few pages one of the greatest concentrations of the supernatural in the Bible. Yet it is significant that the majority of them are based upon natural phenomena."[54]

These mariners were almost certainly polytheists, so we should not conclude that they abandoned their worship of other gods and "got saved" necessarily. However, their spiritual salvation is a possibility. The fact that they made vows to God may point to their conversion.

Note that these pagan sailors feared God more than the prophet did (v. 9). By their actions they gave Him the respect He deserves, but Jonah did not.

> "In this episode the sailors are a foil for Jonah. In contrast to Jonah, who preaches but does not pray, the sailors offer prayers to God. In contrast to Jonah, who says he fears God but acts in a way that is inconsistent with his claim, the sailors, who barely know Jonah's God, respond to him in genuine fear."[55]

> "Through the defection of Jonah a ship's crew acknowledges the Creator's power, comes to the point of worshiping him, and acknowledges him as Lord. If this is the outcome of Jonah's disobedience, what will God bring to pass as the result of Jonah's obedience?"[56]

---

[52]Keil, 1:396.
[53]Allen, pp. 210-11.
[54]Gaebelein, p. 83.
[55]Chisholm, *Handbook of . . .*, p. 411.
[56]Baldwin, pp. 563-64.

This story is full of irony.[57] When someone knows God but chooses to disobey Him, that person begins to demonstrate even less compassion for others, less faith in God's sovereignty, and less fear of Him than pagans normally do.

> "Above all, the story thus far extols the fact that sin does not pay and that, try as the sinner will to escape, he is God's marked man. The wages of sin are death."[58]

E. JONAH'S DELIVERANCE BY GOD 1:17—2:1

For the second time in this story, God took the initiative to move His prophet to carry out His will (cf. v. 1). This time Jonah turned *to* the Lord.

1:17   The identity of the "great fish" remains a mystery, since the only record of what it was is in this story, and that description is general. The Hebrew word *dag*, translated "fish," describes a variety of aquatic creatures. The text does not say that God created this fish out of nothing (*ex nihilo*), nor does what the fish did require such an explanation. There are many types of fish capable of swallowing a human being whole.[59] Two examples are the sperm whale and the whale shark. (Josephus called it a whale.[60]) Occasionally today we hear of someone who has lived for several days in a fish or in some other large animal and has emerged alive.[61] In spite of this, Jonah's experience has been one of the favorite targets of unbelievers in the miraculous, who claim that this story is preposterous (cf. Matt. 12:39-40). Some Bible students have faulted some commentators for documenting instances of large fish swallowing people who have survived, as if such suggested explanations slight God's power. They do *not* necessarily.

> "The numerous attempts made in the past to identify the sort of fish that could have kept Jonah alive in it are misguided. How would even Jonah himself have known? Can we assume that he caught a glimpse of it as it turned back to sea after vomiting him out on shore (v 1 [10])? How much could he have understood of what had happened to him when he was swallowed? These questions have no answer. To ask them is to ignore the way the story is told. What sorts of fish people can live inside is not an interest of the scripture."[62]

Significantly, God saved Jonah's life by using a fish, rather than a more conventional method, such as providing a piece of wood that he could cling to. Thus, this method of deliverance must have some special significance. The Jews were familiar with the mythical sea monster (Ugaritic *lotan*, Heb. *leviathan*), which symbolized both the uncontrollable chaos of the sea and the chaotic forces that only Yahweh could manage (cf. Ps. 74:13-14; 104:25-26). The Hebrews did not believe that leviathan really existed any more than we believe in Santa Claus. Yet the figure was familiar to them, and they knew what it represented. For Jonah to relate his experience of deliverance in this ancient Near Eastern cultural context would have impressed his hearers that a great God indeed had sent him to them. It is probably for this reason that God chose to save Jonah by using a great fish.

> "In the Book of Jonah, it [the Hebrew word *manah*, translated "appointed" or "prepared"] signifies 'to appoint' or 'to ordain,' and describes God's intervention in natural events to bring about His will. By *preparing* the fish [1:17], the plant [4:6], and the worm [4:7, and the wind 4:8], God made sure that Jonah's mission was not left to chance. God exercised sovereignty not only over the plant and animal world, but also over Jonah's life, using animals as [large as a great fish and as] small as a worm to teach Jonah about His great mercy (see Jon. 4:6-8)."[63]

Here God controlled the traditionally uncontrollable to spare Jonah's life. The God who is great enough to control it could control anything, and He used His power for a loving purpose. This is more remarkable since Jonah, as God's servant, had rebelled against his Master. God's method of deliverance therefore reveals both His great power and His gracious heart.

> "Men have been looking so hard at the great fish that they have failed to see the great God."[64]

> "It is the greatness of Israel's God that is the burden of the book."[65]

---

[57] See Edwin M. Good, *Irony in the Old Testament*.
[58] Allen, p. 213.
[59] See Wilson, pp. 631-32.
[60] Josephus, 9:10:2.
[61] See Harrison, pp. 907-8, or Keil, 1:398, for several such instances.
[62] Stuart, p. 474.
[63] *The Nelson . . .*, p. 1499.
[64] G. Campbell Morgan, *The Minor Prophets*, p. 69.
[65] Allen, p. 192.

Jonah was able to calculate how long he was in the fish only *after* he came out of it. Obviously he lost all track of time inside the fish.

Ancient Near Easterners viewed the trip to the underworld land of the dead as a three-day journey.[66] Original readers of this story would have concluded that the fish gave Jonah a return trip from the land of the dead to which Jonah, by his own admission, had descended (2:2, 6).

The three-day time was also significant because Jonah's deliverance became a precursor of an even greater salvation that took three days and nights to accomplish (Matt. 12:40). God restored Jonah to life so he would be God's instrument in providing salvation to a large Gentile (and indirectly Jewish) population under God's judgment for their sins. He raised Jesus to life so He would be God's instrument in providing salvation for an even larger population of Gentiles and Jews under God's judgment for their sins.

2:1   This is the first mention of Jonah praying (cf. 4:2). In both this verse and 4:2 the usual Hebrew word *hitpallel*, "to pray," appears. In 1:5 and 3:8 the Hebrew word *qara'*, "to call," occurs. Until now Jonah had been fleeing from God and hiding from Him. Now in his great distress he finally sought the Lord. Being willing to die by drowning was one thing (v. 1:12), but death by gradual digestion was something Jonah had not anticipated. We do not know how long Jonah struggled in the sea before the fish swallowed him. Perhaps that terror also contributed to his repentance. Some interpreters believe that Jonah's repentance is a type of the repentance of the Jewish remnant that will occur prior to the beginning of the Millennium.[67]

God often has to discipline His rebellious children severely before we turn back to Him.

F. JONAH'S PSALM OF THANKSGIVING 2:2-9

The following prayer is mainly thanksgiving for deliverance from drowning. It is not thanksgiving for deliverance from the fish or a prayer of confession, as we might expect. Jonah prayed it while he was in the fish. Evidently he concluded after some time in the fish's stomach that he would not die from drowning. Drowning was a particularly distasteful form of death for an ancient Near Easterner, such as Jonah, who regarded the sea as a great enemy. Jonah's ability to thank God in the midst of his black torture chamber, which must have pitched him uncontrollably in every direction, shows that he had experienced a remarkable change in attitude (cf. 1:3, 12).

Jonah could have composed the core of this psalm, which contains his prayer, while he was inside the great fish. He may have composed or polished the whole psalm sometime after he was safely back on dry land. It bears many similarities to other psalms in the Psalter. Clearly Jonah knew the psalms well, and he could have spent much time reflecting on them during his three days in the fish. One wonders, however, how anyone could think very coherently inside a fish.

This chapter corresponds to chapter one in its contents.[68]

	Ch. 1: The Sailors		**Ch. 2: The Prophet**
1:4	Crisis on the sea	2:3-6a	Crisis in the sea
1:14	Prayer to Yahweh	2:2, 7	Prayer to Yahweh
1:15b	Deliverance from the storm	2:6b	Deliverance from drowning
1:16	Sacrifice and vows offered to God	2:9	Sacrifice and vows offered to God

2:2   Jonah, as many others, called to the Lord out of a distressing situation asking for help, and the Lord responded to his cry with deliverance (cf. Ps. 3:4; 120:1). The second part of the verse is a parallel restatement of the first part. The prophet compared the fish's stomach to a burial chamber from which he could not escape. "Depth" is literally the "belly" of Sheol, the place of departed souls that the Hebrews conceived of as under the earth's surface. Jonah thought that he had gone to join the dead (cf. Ps. 18:4-5; 30:3).

---

[66]George M. Landes, "The 'Three Days and Three Nights' Motif in Jonah 2:1," *Journal of Biblical Literature* 86 (1967): 246-250.
[67]E.g., J. Dwight Pentecost, *Thy Kingdom Come*, p. 328; and Feinberg, pp. 28-29.
[68]John D. Hannah, "Jonah," in *The Bible Knowledge Commentary: Old Testament*, p. 1467.

2:3 — Jonah saw God's disciplinary hand behind the sailors, who had only been His tools in casting the prophet "into the deep," and the "heart of the" sea (cf. Ps. 88:6-7). He also acknowledged that the sea belonged to God ("*Your* breakers and billows," cf. 1:9). Evidently the waves overwhelmed him many times before the fish swallowed him (cf. Ps. 42:7).

2:4 — This condition made Jonah believe that God had turned His back on him (cf. Lev. 21:7; Ps. 31:22). Nevertheless he determined to seek God in prayer (cf. Ps. 5:7). Looking toward God's "holy temple" is a synonym for praying, the temple being the place of prayer in Israel.

> "He felt he was cast out from the special regard and care which God exercises over His own. Now he realized how dire a thing it is to be apart from the presence of the Lord."[69]

2:5 — Jonah sensed his hopelessness as he continued his downward plunge into "the deep." He seemed to be in death's grip rather than God's. Seaweeds (Heb. *suph*, reeds) bound his head as the water encased his body (cf. Ps. 69:1-2).

2:6 — The prophet "descended" in the sea to the "roots" (bases) of the mountains, their very foundations. There he felt caged as a prisoner unable to escape. However, even though human deliverance was hopeless, Yahweh, Jonah's strong God, lifted him up out of Sheol's pit (cf. Ps. 49:15; 56:13; 103:4).

> "Jonah's 'downward' journey from Jerusalem *down* to Joppa (1:3a) *down* into the ship (1:3b) *down* into the cargo hold (1:5) and ultimately *down* into the bottom of the sea, pictured as down to the very gates of the netherworld (2:7), does not end until he turns back to God who brings him 'up' from the brink of death (2:6-7)."[70]

> "When you turn your back on God, the only direction you can go is down."[71]

2:7 — As Jonah was feeling that his life was ebbing away, his thoughts turned to Yahweh (cf. Ps. 107:5-6; 142:3, 5-7). Even though he felt far from God, his prayer reached the Lord in His heavenly dwelling place.

> "As in 1:6, prayer is presented as the key to the salvation of the one who would otherwise have perished."[72]

2:8 — Jonah proceeded to philosophize a bit. Everyone who makes an idol his or her god abandons the source of his or her loyal love (Heb. *hesed*) by doing so. The source of loyal love is Yahweh. This is true of pagans, but the prophet himself had done the same thing. The "vain idols" (lit. empty vanities) in view are things that one puts in God's rightful place in his or her life (cf. Ps. 31:6; 1 John 5:21).

2:9 — Jonah's desperate condition had brought him to his senses. He would return to the source of loyal love and express his worship of Yahweh with a sacrifice. His sacrifice would have to be "thanksgiving," though, because he despaired of being able to offer an animal or vegetable offering. He also promised to "pay" his vow to God. This probably refers to his *commitment* to serve the Lord faithfully, from which he had departed, but to which he now returned (cf. Ps. 50:14; 69:30; 107:22).

The testimony that "salvation comes from Yahweh" was the expression of Jonah's thanksgiving that he promised God. The last declaration in this psalm is one of the great summary statements about salvation in the Bible. Salvation, either physical or spiritual, ultimately comes from Yahweh and only from Him, not from idols or people, including oneself (cf. Ps. 3:8; 37:39). It is in His power, and only He can give it. This statement also implies recognition of the fact that God has the right to save whom He will.

> "Ironically, however, it is this very same fact which fills Jonah with intense anger in the final chapter of the book."[73]

The end of this psalm shows Jonah doing what the sailors had done earlier, namely: offering a sacrifice and making vows (1:16).

---

[69] Feinberg, p. 25.
[70] The NET Bible note on 1:3.
[71] Wiersbe, p. 381.
[72] Allen, p. 218. Cf. Heb. 4:16.
[73] Alexander, p. 118.

"Jonah deserved death, not deliverance. And yet Yahweh graciously delivered him by special intervention so that Jonah could not but recognize the greatness of Yahweh's compassion, praise him for it, and recognize his reliance on Yahweh alone (c. 2 Cor 1:9, 10)."[74]

"The narrator by his inclusion of the psalm immediately after ch. 1 slyly intends his audience to draw a parallel between Jonah's experience and that of the seamen. Both faced a similar crisis, peril from the sea; both cried to Yahweh, acknowledging his sovereignty. Both were physically saved; both offered worship. Ironically Jonah is at last brought to the point the Gentile seamen have already reached. In his supreme devotion he is still only following in the wake of the heathen crew. He who failed to pray, leaving it to the pagan sailors, eventually catches up with their spirit of supplication and submission."[75]

Thus the prophet repented and returned to the Lord in his heart. Having experienced the precious gift of God's salvation in his own life, Jonah was now more favorable to announcing His salvation to the Ninevites. He now appreciated the condition of the heathen as he had not done before.

One writer outlined Jonah's prayer as follows. The prophet prayed for God's help (vv. 1-2), accepted God's discipline (v. 3), trusted God's promises (vv. 4-7), and yielded to God's will (vv. 8-9).[76]

G. JONAH'S DELIVERANCE FROM THE FISH 2:10

Again the writer glorified Yahweh by attributing control of this formidable sea creature to Him (cf. 1:17). The first and the second chapters both close on this note. The Hebrew text says, "The Lord spoke to the fish" (cf. 1:1). Unlike Jonah, the fish obeyed God and "vomited" the prodigal prophet "onto the dry land." Jonah had spoken to the Lord in confession (vv. 1-9), and now God responded by speaking to the fish in deliverance. Having gained a preview of Sheol (v. 2), Jonah was now prepared to go to the Ninevites—whose destiny was Sheol.

The Hebrew word for salvation is *yeshua*, here used in its intensive form. The Hebrew name Joshua means "Yahweh is salvation." The Greek name Jesus is the translation of Joshua. Thus we can see a close connection between what Jonah declared ("salvation is of the Lord") and what all Scripture declares, namely, that salvation is through Jesus Christ.

"This miracle has also a symbolical meaning for Israel. It shows that if the carnal nation, with its ungodly mind, should turn to the Lord even in the last extremity, it will be raised up again by a divine miracle from destruction to newness of life."[77]

"When Israel turns to the Lord, when the veil is removed from the heart, when they cry out in truth to the Lord from the midst of their distresses, the Lord will restore them not only to their own land but also to the commission of witnessing to the Lord [cf. Rev. 7:1-8]."[78]

We do not know where on the coast Jonah landed. Unfortunately, several interpreters have made applications based only on their speculations.

II. THE OBEDIENCE OF THE PROPHET CHS. 3—4

The second half of this book records Jonah's obedience to the Lord following his initial disobedience (chs. 1—2). However, he was not completely obedient in his attitudes even though he was in his actions.

A. JONAH'S PROCLAMATION TO THE NINEVITES 3:1-4

God gave Jonah a second chance to obey Him, as He has many of His servants (e.g., Peter, John Mark, et al.).

3:1   The writer did not clarify exactly when this second commission came to Jonah. It may have been immediately after Jonah reached dry land or it may have been sometime later. The writer's point seems to be that God gave the prophet a second commission, not when it came to him (cf. 1:1-2). God does not always give His servants a second chance to obey Him after they refused to do so initially. Often He simply uses others to accomplish His purposes. In Jonah's case, God sovereignly chose to use Jonah for this mission—just as He had sovereignly sent the storm and the fish to do His will. The sovereignty of God is a strong revelation in this book.

---

[74]Stuart, p. 479.
[75]Allen, p. 219.
[76]Wiersbe, pp. 380-82.
[77]Keil, 1:385.
[78]Feinberg, p. 38.

Nineveh was about 550 miles northeast of Samaria, the capital of the Northern Kingdom of Israel.

3:2   Another evidence of God's sovereignty is the Lord's instruction to "proclaim" the precise message that He would give Jonah. Those who speak forth a message from God (i.e., prophets) must communicate the Lord's words, not their own ideas.

> "The will of God will never lead you where the grace of God can't keep you and the power of God can't use you."[79]

Nineveh was a "great" (Heb. *gadol*) city in several respects. It was a leading city of one of the most powerful nations in the world then. It was also a large city (cf. v. 3, 4:11).

> "The point is that Nineveh was a city God was concerned for, one that was by no means insignificant to him."[80]

3:3   Having learned that he must fulfill the Lord's commission or suffer the most unpleasant consequences, Jonah this time obeyed and traveled east—to Nineveh—rather than west (cf. 1:3). For all he knew, he might end up impaled on a pole or skinned alive, which is how the Assyrians often dealt with their enemies. Nevertheless, such a fate was preferable to suffering divine discipline again.

The writer's description that Nineveh "was" a great city has led some interpreters to conclude that it was not great when the book was written. Some of them take this as evidence for a late date of writing, even during the postexilic period. However, it seems more likely that the writer was simply describing Nineveh as it was when God sent Jonah to it. Probably "was" implies that Nineveh had already become a great city when Jonah visited it. The Hebrew syntax favors this view. Roland de Vaux estimated that Israel's largest city, Samaria, had a population of about 30,000 at this time.[81] Nineveh was at least four times larger (4:11).

The meaning of "a three-days' walk" remains somewhat obscure. The Hebrew phrase is literally "a distance of three days," which does not solve the problem. It may mean that it took three days to walk through the city from one extremity to the opposite one, but the extent of Nineveh's ruins argues against this interpretation. It may also mean that it took three days to walk around the circumference of the city, though this seems unlikely (cf. v. 4). Whether the size refers to the area enclosed by the major eight-mile wall, which seems improbable, or includes the outlying suburbs, is also unclear. Apparently, at that time "Nineveh" referred to: (1) the city and (2) a complex of four cities including the city in question.[82] Probably the "three-days' walk" describes the time it took to visit the city and its outlying suburbs.[83] In any case, the description clearly points to Nineveh's geographical size as being large and requiring several days for Jonah's message to reach everyone (cf. 4:11).

Another explanation is that the literal meaning of the phrase, namely, "a visit of three days," describes the protocol involved in visiting an important city such as Nineveh. It was customary in the ancient Near East for an emissary from another city-state to take three days for an official visit. He would spend the first day meeting and enjoying the hospitality of his host, the second day discussing the primary purpose of his visit, and the third saying his farewells.[84] If Jonah was such an emissary, he went as a divine representative to Nineveh's king and other government officials, as well as to the people. This explanation suggests that Jonah's preaching may have started with the king, and then proceeded to the people, rather than the other way around. This view may account better for the king's repentance, and his decree to all the people to repent (Heb. *sub*; vv. 6-9), compared to the traditional view.

3:4   The traditional view holds that after Jonah arrived at the edge of the city, he proceeded into it and began announcing his message during his first day there.[85] Alternatively, he may have done his first day's preaching to the king and perhaps also to some of the people. The essence of his proclamation was that Nineveh would be overthrown in only "40 days." Periods of testing in Scripture were often 40 days long (cf. Gen. 7:17; Exod. 24:18; 1 Kings 19:8; Matt. 4:2). The Septuagint has three instead of 40, but there is no justification for changing the Hebrew text.

---

[79]Wiersbe, p. 383.
[80]Stuart, p. 487.
[81]Roland de Vaux, *Ancient Israel: Its Life and Institutions*, p. 66.
[82]See Keil, 1:390; T. D. Alexander, "Jonah and Genre," *Tyndale Bulletin* 36 (1985):57-58; and Hannah, p. 1468.
[83]Stuart, pp. 487-88; *The Nelson . . .*, p. 1498.
[84]Wiseman, "Jonah's Nineveh," p. 38. See also Stuart, pp. 487-88.
[85]Ellison, "Jonah," p. 381; Keil, 1:405.

Note that Jonah's message was an announcement of impending doom, not a call to believe in the God of Israel. Jeremiah 18:7-8 explains that prophecies of impending judgment assumed that those under judgment would not repent. If they repented, they might avoid the judgment (cf. Joel 2:12-14). Physical deliverance rather than spiritual salvation was what the people of Nineveh would have wanted. As noted in the introduction to this exposition above, hostile tribes to Nineveh's north threatened the city.

The same Hebrew word (*haphak*, overthrown, destroyed) describes the destruction of Sodom and Gomorrah in Genesis 19:25. Possibly Jonah expected God to destroy Nineveh as He had overthrown Sodom and Gomorrah.

The basic simplicity of Jonah's message contrasts with the greatness of Nineveh. The Word of the Lord is able to change even a complex and sophisticated urban population.

B. THE NINEVITES' REPENTANCE 3:5-10

Jonah's proclamation moved the Ninevites to humble themselves and seek divine mercy.

"Although Nineveh was not overturned, it did experience a turn around."[86]

3:5   The people "believed" and repented, apparently after only one day of preaching (v. 4), because of the message from God that Jonah had brought to them.[87] Fasting and wearing "sackcloth" involved self-affliction, which demonstrated an attitude of humility in the ancient Near East (cf. 2 Sam. 3:31, 35; 1 Kings 21:27; Neh. 9:1-2; Isa. 15:3; 58:5; Dan. 9:3; Joel 1:13-14). Sackcloth was what the poor and the slaves customarily wore. Thus, wearing it depicted that the entire population viewed themselves as *needy* (of God's mercy in this case) and *slaves* (of God in this case). This attitude and these actions marked all levels of the city's population (i.e., the chronologically old and young, and the socially high and low). The Ninevites did not want to perish any more than the sailors did (cf. 1:6, 14).

Some commentators believed that two plagues, a severe flood and a famine, had ravaged Nineveh in 765 and 759 B.C., plus a total eclipse of the sun on June 15, 763, and that these phenomena prepared the Ninevites for Jonah's message.[88] The Ninevites probably viewed these phenomena as indications of divine displeasure, a common reaction in the ancient Near East.[89] However, this providential "pre-evangelism" is not the concern of the text. It attributes the Ninevites' repentance to Jonah's preaching.

Some commentators have credited the repentance of the Ninevites at least partially to Jonah's previous experience in the great fish's stomach. They base this on Jesus' statement that Jonah was a sign to the Ninevites (Matt. 12:39-41; Luke 11:29-32). Jonah was a sign in a two-fold sense. His three days and nights in the fish foreshadowed Jesus' three days and nights in the grave (Matt. 12:40), and his ministry as a visiting prophet delivering an announcement of impending doom for repentance to an evil people under God's judgment previewed Jesus' ministry (Matt. 12:41; Luke 11:30, 32).

These commentators note that the Ninevites worshipped Dagon, which was part man and part fish.[90] They have also pointed out that the Assyrian fish goddess, Nosh, was the chief deity in Nineveh. Some of them have argued that Jonah came to the city as one sent by Nosh to proclaim the true God. However, the text of Jonah attributes the repentance of the Ninevites primarily to the message that God had given Jonah to proclaim. Whatever the Ninevites may have known about Jonah's encounter with the fish—the text says nothing about their awareness of it—the writer gave the credit to the word (spoken message) of the Lord, not to Jonah's personal background.

One writer saw this text as support for the historic evangelical doctrine of exclusivism in salvation and used it to argue against religious inclusivism (pluralism).[91]

---

[86] Alexander, p. 121.
[87] See Steven J. Lawson, "The Power of Biblical Preaching: An Expository Study of Jonah 3:1-10," *Bibliotheca Sacra* 158:631 (July-September 2001):331-46.
[88] Wiseman, "Jonah's Nineveh," p. 44; and Stuart, pp. 490-91.
[89] Ibid., p. 494.
[90] E.g., Feinberg, p. 33.
[91] Wayne G. Strickland, "Isaiah, Jonah, and Religious Pluralism," *Bibliotheca Sacra* 153:609 (January-March 1996):31-32.

"God delights to do the impossible, and never more so than in turning men to Himself. Instead, then, of denying on the grounds of its 'human' impossibility the repentance that swept over Nineveh, let us see it as an evidence of divine power. For this, not the episode of the sea monster, is the greatest miracle in the book."[92]

3:6   Verse 5 could be a general record of the response of the Ninevites, and verses 6-9 a more detailed account of what happened. Even "the king" responded by repenting. The "king of Nineveh" would probably have been the king of *Assyria*, since Nineveh was a leading city of that empire. Similarly, King Ahab of Israel was called the "king of Samaria" (1 Kings 21:1), King Ahaziah of Israel was called the "king of Samaria" (2 Kings 1:3), and King Ben-hadad of Aram was called the "king of Damascus" (2 Chron. 24:23). In any event, the writer described this man as "the king of Nineveh." The explanation may be that the focus of Jonah's prophecy was specifically Nineveh (v. 4), not the whole Assyrian Empire. His name, though of interest to us, was unnecessary to the writer.

Who was this king? He was probably one of the Assyrian kings who ruled during or near the regency of Jeroboam II in Israel (793-753 B.C.).[93]

Assyrian Kings Contemporary with Jeroboam II	
Adad-nirari III	811-783 B.C.
Shalmaneser IV	783-772 B.C.
Ashur-dan III	772-754 B.C.
Ashur-nirari V	754-746 B.C.

Of these perhaps Ashur-dan III is the most likely possibility.[94]

". . . the first half of the eighth century is one of the most poorly documented periods of Assyrian history."[95]

"There is something affecting in the picture of this Oriental monarch so swiftly casting aside such gorgeous robes and taking the place of the penitent. He had the virtue of not holding back in his approach to God."[96]

"It must be remembered that an Assyrian king, as a syncretist, would hardly wish automatically to deny the validity of any god or any prophet. And does not an outsider often command far more respect than those with whom one regularly deals—even in the case of prophets and other clergy (cf. Melchizedek and Abraham, Gen 14:17-24; Moses and Pharaoh, Exod 5—14; Balaam and Balak, Num 22—24; the Levite from Bethlehem and the Danites, Judg 17—18; etc.)?"[97]

3:7   This verse further describes how seriously the king and his nobles regarded their situation and to what extent they went to encourage citywide contrition. They did not regard their animals as needing to humble themselves but viewed them as expressing the spirit of their owners.

3:8   Clearly the Ninevites connected the impending judgment with their own conduct. They felt that by abandoning their wickedness they could obtain some mercy from God. The Hebrew word translated "violence" (*hamas*) refers to the overbearing attitude and conduct of someone who has attained power over others and misuses it (cf. Gen. 16:5). Assyrian soldiers were physically violent (Nah. 3:1, 3-4; cf. 2 Kings 18:33-35), but so were the Chaldeans (Hab. 1:9; 2:8, 17) and others who, because of conquest, could dominate others. Discrimination against minorities because they are less powerful manifests this sin. We must not forget the violence of our own times and society.

---

[92]Gaebelein, p. 103.
[93]See *The Bible Knowledge Commentary: Old Testament*, p. 1463.
[94]Stuart, pp. 491-97.
[95]Alexander, p. 123.
[96]Gaebelein, p. 106.
[97]Stuart, p. 491.

> "*Violence*, the arbitrary infringements of human rights, is a term that occurs in the OT prophets especially in connection with cities: urban conglomeration encourages scrambling over others, like caterpillars in a jar."[98]

This reference to violence recalls Genesis 6:11 and 13. God had previously destroyed the world in Noah's day because it was so violent. Now Jonah became the bearer of a message of judgment on another violent civilization.

Decorating horses and other animals has long been a popular practice. In the funeral of President John F. Kennedy a riderless horse added a poignant touch to the procession.

3:9   The Ninevites lived in the ancient Near East that viewed all of life as under the sovereign control of divine authority, the gods.[99] Even though they were polytheists and pagans, they believed in some deity of justice who demanded justice of humankind. They also believed that their actions affected their god's actions. This worldview is essentially correct as far as it goes. We should probably not understand their repentance as issuing in conversion to Jewish monotheism. It seems unlikely that all the Ninevites became Gentile proselytes to Judaism (cf. 1:16).

> "The Ninevites then assumed that one of their gods—it is ultimately immaterial which one they may have thought it to be, or if they found it necessary to make such an identification—was planning to compound their recent troubles by bringing disaster to the city."[100]

God turning and relenting (Heb. *niham*) would result from His compassion, which the Ninevites counted on when they repented.

> "Though generalities must always be used with caution, we may say that never again has the world seen anything quite like the result of Jonah's preaching in Nineveh."[101]

It is amazing that God brought the whole city to faith and repentance through the preaching of a man who did not love the people to whom he preached. Ultimately salvation is of the Lord (2:9). It is not dependent on the attitudes and actions of His servants, though our attitudes and actions affect our condition as we carry out the will of God.

> "The book is a challenge to all to hear God's appeal to be like the sailors and the Ninevites in their submissiveness to Yahweh."[102]

3:10   God noted the genuineness of the Ninevites' repentance in their actions. These fruits of repentance moved Him to withhold the judgment that He would have sent on them had they persisted in their wicked ways. Repentance is essentially a change in one's thinking. Change in one's behavior indicates that repentance has taken place, but behavioral change is the fruit of repentance and is not all there is to repentance (cf. Matt. 3:7-10). Nineveh finally experienced overthrow in 612 B.C., about 150 years later.

> "We may know the character of God only from what he does and the words he uses to explain his actions. When he does not do what he said he would, we as finite men can say only that he has changed his mind or repented, even though we should recognize, as Jonah did (4:2), that he had intended or desired this all along."[103]

> "That God should choose to make his own actions contingent—at least in part—upon human actions is no limitation of his sovereignty. Having first decided to place the option of obedience and disobedience before nations, his holding them responsible for their actions automatically involves a sort of contingency. He promises blessing if they repent, punishment if not (cf. Jer 18:7-10). But this hardly makes God dependent on the nations; it rather makes them dependent on him, as is the point of the lesson at the potter's house

---

[98]Allen, p. 225.
[99]Keil, 1:107.
[100]Stuart, p. 494.
[101]Gaebelein, p. 95.
[102]Allen, p. 189. Cf. 1:6, 14.
[103]Ellison, "Jonah," pp. 383-84. Cf. Feinberg, p. 37. See also Thomas L. Constable, "What Prayer Will and Will Not Change," in *Essays in Honor of J. Dwight Pentecost*, pp. 99-113; and Robert B. Chisholm Jr., "Does God 'Change His Mind'?" *Bibliotheca Sacra* 152:608 (October-December 1995):387-99.

in Jer 18:1-11, and the point of the mourning decree in Jonah 3:5-9. God holds all the right, all the power, and all the authority."[104]

"Helpful also is the analogy of the thermometer. Is it changeable or unchangeable? The superficial observer says it is changeable, for the mercury certainly moves in the tube. But just as certainly it is unchangeable, for it acts according to fixed law and invariably responds precisely to the temperature."[105]

Notice that in this section of verses (vv. 5-10), the name "God" (Heb. Elohim, the strong one) appears exclusively. However, the name "LORD" (Heb. Yahweh, the covenant keeping God) occurs frequently, both earlier, and later in the story. Jonah did not present God, and the Ninevites did not fear God, as the covenant-keeping God of Israel, but as the universal Supreme Being. Likewise, God did not deal with the Ninevites as He dealt with His covenant people Israel, but as He deals with all people generally. Thus the story teaches that God will be merciful to anyone, His elect and His non-elect, who live submissively to natural divine law (cf. Gen. (9:5-6).

If such a remarkable turnaround really did occur in Nineveh, why is there no other historical record of it?

"First of all, the extant records are comparatively few. There are large segments of undocumented history. Second, there was a serious, pronounced bias in recording history that gave only the most favorable of impressions."[106]

C. JONAH'S DISPLEASURE AT GOD'S MERCY 4:1-4

The reader might assume that the Lord's deliverance of the Ninevites from imminent doom is the climax of the story. This is not the case. The most important lesson of the book deals with God's people and specifically God's instruments, not humanity in general.

"Though Jonah hardly comes across as a hero anywhere in the book, he appears especially selfish, petty, temperamental, and even downright foolish in chap. 4."[107]

4:1   The whole situation "displeased Jonah" and made him "angry": the Ninevites' repentance and God's withholding judgment from them.

"Jonah finds that the time-fuse does not work on the prophetic bomb he planted in Nineveh."[108]

This is the first clue, after Jonah's initial repentance and trip to Nineveh, that his heart was still not completely right with God. One can do the will of God without doing it with the right attitude, and that is the focus of the remainder of the book. The repentance and good deeds of the Ninevites pleased God, but they displeased His representative. They made God happy, but they made Jonah unhappy. A literal translation might be, "It was evil to Jonah with great evil." Until now evil (Heb. *ra'ah*) described the Ninevites, but now it marks the prophet. Consequently Jonah now became evil in God's eyes and in need of punishment as the Ninevites had (cf. Rom. 2:1), but God showed Jonah the same compassion He had shown the Ninevites.

"The word but points up the contrast between God's compassion (3:10) and Jonah's displeasure, and between God's turning *from* His anger (3:9-10) and Jonah's turning *to* anger."[109]

Contrast the Apostle Paul's attitude in Romans 9:1-3. Why did Jonah become so angry? Who was he to complain? He had only recently been very happy that God had saved him from destruction (cf. Matt. 18:23-35). It was not primarily because his announced judgment failed to materialize and so raised questions about his authenticity as a true prophet (cf. Deut. 18:21-22). Almost all prophecies of impending doom in the Bible assume that those being judged will remain unmoved. Divine punishment is avoidable provided people repent (cf. Jer. 3:22; 18:8; 26:2-6; Ezek. 18:21-22, 30-32; 33:10-15).[110] Jonah undoubtedly became angry because he wanted God to judge the Ninevites and thereby remove a military threat to the nation of Israel. If he was aware of Hosea and Amos' prophecies, he would have known that Assyria would invade and defeat Israel (Hos. 11:5; Amos 5:27).

---

[104] Stuart, p. 496.
[105] Gaebelein, p. 111.
[106] Page, p. 265.
[107] Stuart, p. 502.
[108] Allen, p. 227.
[109] Hannah, p. 1470.
[110] Pentecost, p. 180.

> "Countless numbers of modern-day believers miss much of the joy of being involved in God's wonderful work because of self-centeredness."[111]

4:2   To his credit, Jonah told God why he was angry (cf. 2:1; Job). Many believers try to hide their true feelings from God when they think God will not approve of those feelings. Even though the prophet had been rebellious, he had a deep and intimate relationship with God.

Contrast this prayer with the one in chapter 2. This one is negative and defensive; the former one is positive and praiseful. This one focuses on Jonah, but the former one on God. This one contains no fewer than nine references to "I" or "my" in the Hebrew.

> "The heart of every problem is the problem of the heart, and that's where Jonah's problems were to be found."[112]

Jonah's motive in fleeing to Tarshish now becomes known. He was afraid that the Ninevites would repent and that God would be merciful to this ancient enemy of God's people. By opposing the Israelites, her enemies were also opposing Yahweh. This is why a godly man such as Jonah hated the Assyrians so much, and why the psalmists spoke so strongly against Israel's enemies.

> "Some dismiss biblical references to God 'relenting' from judgment as anthropomorphic, arguing that an unchangeable God would never change his mind once he has announced his intentions. But both Jonah 4:2 and Joel 2:13 list God's capacity to 'change his mind' as one of his fundamental attributes, one that derives from his compassion and demonstrates his love."[113]

Jonah's description of God goes back to Exodus 34:6-7, a very ancient expression of God's character (cf. Num. 14:18; Neh. 9:17; Ps. 86:15; 103:8; 145:8; Joel 2:13; Nah. 1:3). "Gracious" (from the Heb. *hen*, grace) expresses God's attitude toward those who have no claim on Him because they are outside any covenant relationship with Him.[114] *Compassion*, one of the themes of this story, is a trait that Jonah recognized in God but did not share with Him as he should have. "Lovingkindness" (Heb. *hesed*) refers to God's loyal love to those who are in covenant relationship with Him. The prophet was criticizing God for good qualities that he recognized in God. He wished God were not so good.

> "It was not simply the case that Jonah could not bring himself to appreciate Nineveh. Rather, to a shocking extent, he could not stand God!"[115]

> "Jonah sees the deferment of judgment on Nineveh as a weakness on God's part and disapproves strongly of sharing the Lord's compassion with the unlovely."[116]

Even the best of people, people such as Jonah, wish calamity on the wicked, but God does not (cf. 2 Pet. 3:9).

4:3   Jonah felt so angry that he asked God to take his life (cf. 1:12; 4:8, 9). Elijah had previously voiced the same request (1 Kings 19:4), but we must be careful not to read Elijah's reasons into Jonah's request. Both prophets obviously became extremely discouraged. Both evidently felt that what God had done through their ministries was different from what they wanted to see happen. Elijah had wanted to see a complete national revival, but Jonah had wanted to see complete national destruction. The sinfulness of people discouraged Elijah, whereas the goodness of God depressed Jonah. How could Jonah return to Israel and announce that God was not going to judge the nation that had been such an enemy of the Israelites for so long? God had to teach Elijah to view things from His perspective, and He proceeded to teach Jonah the same thing.

4:4   God did not rebuke Jonah nor did He ask what right he had to criticize God. Rather, He suggested that Jonah might not be viewing the situation correctly. God also confronted Job tenderly by asking him questions (cf. vv. 9, 11; Job 38—39). The Jerusalem Bible translation, "Are you right to be angry?" captures the intent of the Hebrew text. Jonah had condemned God for not being angry (v. 2), but now God challenged Jonah for being angry. Jonah was feeling the frustration of not understanding God's actions in the light of His character, which many others have felt (e.g., Job, Jeremiah, Habakkuk, et al.).

---

[111]Page, p. 276.
[112]Wiersbe, p. 385.
[113]Chisholm, *Handbook of . . .*, p. 414. See also Exodus 32:14; and 34:6-7.
[114]Ellison, "Jonah," p. 385.
[115]Stuart, p. 503.
[116]Baldwin, pp. 584-85.

When God's servants become angry because God is as He is, the Lord deals with them compassionately.

D. GOD'S REBUKE OF JONAH FOR HIS ATTITUDE 4:5-9

The Lord proceeded to teach Jonah His ways and to confront him with his attitude problem.

4:5 We might have expected Jonah to leave what so angered him quickly, as Elijah had fled from Israel and sought refuge far from it to the south. Why did Jonah construct a shelter and sit down to watch what would happen to Nineveh? The same Hebrew word for "shelter" (*sukka*) describes the leafy structures that the Israelites made for themselves for the Feast of Tabernacles (Lev. 23:40-42; Neh. 8:14-18; cf. Mark 9:5). Did Jonah think that judgment might fall anyway, or was he waiting for God to clarify His actions? Perhaps he hoped that the Ninevites' repentance would evaporate quickly and that God would then call him to pronounce the judgment that he so wanted to see. Jonah did not know if the Ninevites' repentance would be sufficient to postpone God's judgment (cf. Gen. 18:22-33). He evidently took up residence somewhere on the slopes of the mountains that rise to the "east" of Nineveh to gain a good view of whatever might happen. Perhaps he expected to witness another spectacular judgment such as befell Sodom and Gomorrah. His shelter proved to be a classroom for the prophet similar to what the town dump had been for Job.

4:6 God continued to manifest compassion for Jonah by providing him with a shading plant that relieved the "discomfort" (Heb. *ra'ah*) of the blistering Mesopotamian sun. This is the only time that we read that Jonah was "happy," and it was because he was physically comfortable. His anger grew out of his personal discomfort resulting from God's mercy on the Ninevites. The Hebrew word *ra'ah*, translated "discomfort" here, is the same word translated "evil" where it describes the Ninevites' evil (1:2; 3:8), and "displeased" where it describes Jonah's displeasure over God's decision to spare the city (v. 1). Jonah's attitudes were as evil in God's sight as the Ninevites' actions.

> "The reach of God's mercy to the undeserving is a theme that continued to elude Jonah even as he experienced it."[117]

It is impossible to identify the exact "plant" that God provided, and it is inconsequential. Some commentators speculate that it was probably the castor bean plant, which in Mesopotamia grows rapidly to 12 feet tall and has large leaves.

Notice again the shift in the name of *God*, from "Yahweh" to "Elohim," in this verse. This is one of the rare appearances of the compound name "LORD God" in Scripture (cf. Gen. 2; 3; et al.). Its use here may help make a transition. God dealt with Jonah as He deals with all humanity in what follows.

4:7 The stress on God's sovereignty continues. God had provided (Heb. *manah*, to appoint, provide, or prepare) a storm, a fish, a plant, and now a worm to fulfill His purpose. A different Hebrew word occurred in 1:4 describing the storm. He would next provide a *wind* (v. 8). Clearly God was manipulating Jonah's circumstances to teach him something. He uses large things such as the fish, and small things like the worm. There may be some significance in the chiastic arrangement of the things that God provided—beginning and ending with natural forces, then animals, with a vegetable (that made Jonah happy) in the middle.

4:8 The "scorching east wind" that God provided was the dreaded sirocco. The following description of it helps us appreciate why it had such a depressing effect on Jonah.

> "During the period of a sirocco the temperature rises steeply, sometimes even climbing during the night, and it remains high, about 16-22°F. above the average . . . at times every scrap of moisture seems to have been extracted from the air, so that one has the curious feeling that one's skin has been drawn much tighter than usual. Sirocco days are peculiarly trying to the temper and tend to make even the mildest people irritable and fretful and to snap at one another for apparently no reason at all."[118]

Why did Jonah not move into the city and live there? Apparently he wanted nothing to do with the Ninevites whom he despised so much. He probably still did not know if God would spare Nineveh or destroy it catastrophically. Earlier he had wished to die because, as God's servant, he was not happy with God's will. Now he longed for death because he was unhappy with his circumstances. Divine discipline had brought him to the place where even the loss of a plant affected him so deeply that he longed to die.

---

[117] *The Nelson . . .*, p. 1499.
[118] Dennis Baly, *The Geography of the Bible*, pp. 67-68.

"The shoe Jonah wanted Nineveh to wear was on his foot now, and it pinched."[119]

4:9　　God's question here was very similar to His question in verse 4. Was Jonah right—"having a good reason" or justification—"to be angry" about the plant, God asked? Jonah's reply was a strong superlative.[120] He felt that strong anger was proper. Evidently Jonah believed that God was not even treating him with the compassion that He normally showed all people, much less His chosen servants.

> "The double question in 4:4 and 4:9 . . . is unmistakably the key to the book's central message. The climax of the story comes here—not with the repentance of the Ninevites in chap. 3 or at any other point—when God challenges Jonah to recognize how wrong he has been in his bitter nationalism, and how right God has been to show compassion toward the plight of the Assyrians in Nineveh."[121]

In this pericope, God was setting the stage for the lesson that He would explain to His prophet shortly.

E. GOD'S COMPASSION FOR THOSE UNDER HIS JUDGMENT 4:10-11

The story now reaches its climax. God revealed to Jonah how out of harmony with His own heart the prophet, though obedient, was. He contrasted Jonah's attitude with His own.

> "In these last verses the great missionary lesson of the book is sharply drawn: Are the souls of men not worth as much as a gourd? Like Jonah, God's people today are often more concerned about the material benefits so freely bestowed upon us by God than about the destiny of a lost world."[122]

4:10　　"Compassion" (Heb. *hus*, concern [NIV], be sorry for [NEB], pity [RSV, RV]) is the key attitude. Jonah had become completely indifferent to the fate of the Ninevites. He knew His God well (4:2). Nevertheless, his appreciation for God's love for Israel had evidently so pervaded his life, that it crowded out any compassion for these people who lacked knowledge of, and relationship with, Yahweh. Furthermore, Jonah had announced that Israel's borders would expand under King Jeroboam II (2 Kings 14:25).

To reveal Jonah's lack of compassion to himself, God dealt with him as any ordinary person. He exposed him to the pleasures and discomforts that everyone faces, and made him see that his theology made him no more compassionate than anyone else. It should have. Knowledge of a sovereign, compassionate God whom He feared should have made Jonah more submissive to God's will, more compassionate toward other people, and more respectful of God.

4:11　　God had invested much work in Nineveh and had been responsible for its growth. This is why it was legitimate at the most elementary level for God to feel compassion for its people. Jonah's compassion extended only to a plant but not to people.

> "It is the choice between gourds or souls."[123]

God's "compassion" extended not only to plants but also to people. The "120,000" people—that God cited as the special objects of His compassion—were probably the entire populace that did not know how to escape their troubles. The expression "do not know the difference between their right and left hand" is idiomatic, meaning: lacking in knowledge and *innocent* in that sense (cf. 2 Sam. 19:35; Isa. 7:15-16).[124]

> "Not to be able to distinguish between the right hand and the left is a sign of mental infancy."[125]

It would be unusual if this referred only to chronological infants, however.

> "Their inability to discern 'their right hand from their left' must refer to their moral ignorance. Though responsible for their evil deeds and subject to divine judgment (see 1:2), the Ninevites did not have the advantage of special divine revelation concerning the moral will of God. Morally and ethically speaking they were like children."[126]

---

[119]Allen, p. 233.
[120]D. Winton Thomas, "Consideration of Some Unusual Ways of Expressing the Superlative in Hebrew," *Vetus Testamentum* 3 (1953):220.
[121]Stuart, p. 435.
[122]*The New Scofield . . .*, p. 942.
[123]J. H. Kennedy, *Studies in the Book of Jonah*, p. 97.
[124]Stuart, p. 507.
[125]Keil, 1:416.
[126]Chisholm, *Handbook on . . .*, p. 416. Cf. Wiseman, "Jonah's Nineveh," pp. 39-40.

We normally have compassion for those with whom we can identify most closely, but God also has compassion on people who are helpless. Spiritually they are those who do not know God, those who are "lost."

People naturally go to one of two extremes in their attitude toward animals. We either look down on them and treat them inhumanely, feeling superior, or we elevate them to the level of persons and grant them rights that they do not possess. The Society for the Prevention of Cruelty to Animals tries to guard us from the first attitude. The "animal rights movement" tends to promote the second attitude. God has compassion on animals as creatures living below the level of humans that need His grace. This should be our attitude to them too (cf. Gen. 1:26, 28; Ps. 8:6-8).

The reference to "animals" concludes the book, and is the final climax of God's lesson to the prophet, and through him to God's people in Israel and in the church. If God has compassion for animals, and He does, how much more should we feel compassion for human beings made in God's image, who are under His judgment because of their sins (cf. 3:8)! We must never let our concern for the welfare of God's people keep us from reaching out with the message of hope to those who oppose us.

> "It is possible of course, that the animals are mentioned because animals are *ipso facto* innocent and also lack intellectual prowess. Thereby Jonah and the audience would understand that the Ninevites, likewise, are innocent and stupid. But a more likely reason for the mention of animals is that they constitute the middle point in the worth scale upon which the argument of Yahweh is based. That is, the people of Nineveh are of enormous worth. They are human beings (*'dm*), and they are the citizens of the most important city of their day. The animals (*bhmh*) in turn are of less worth, but still significant in the economy of any nation or city. . . . The gourd, on the other hand, is of minor worth. . . . Jonah has furiously argued for the worth of a one-day-old plant (v 9b). He can have no good argument, then, against the worth of Nineveh, with all its people and animals."[127]

> "God's question captures the very intention of the book. The issue is that of grace—grace and mercy. Just as Jonah's provision was the shade of the vine he did not deserve, the Ninevites' provision was a deliverance they did not deserve based upon a repentance they did not fully understand."[128]

The book closes without giving us Jonah's response, but that is not the point of the book. Its point is the answer to the Lord's question in verse 11 that every reader must give. Yes, God should have compassion on the hopeless Ninevites, and we should have compassion on people like them too (cf. Luke 15:25-32; Matt. 20:1-16). Only two books in the Bible end with questions, and they both have to do with Nineveh. Jonah ends with a question about God's pity for Nineveh, and Nahum ends with a question about God's punishment of Nineveh.[129]

> "Every hearer/reader may have some Jonah in him or her. All need to reflect on the questions God asks, including the final, specific, 'Should I not spare Nineveh?' (4:11). Anyone who replies 'Why is that such an important question?' has not understood the message. Anyone who replies 'No!' has not believed it."[130]

> "It is not only the unbelievers in the Ninevehs of today who need to repent; it is also we who are modern Jonahs. For no one begins to understand this profound and searching little book unless he discovers the Jonah in himself and then repentantly lays hold upon the boundless grace of God."[131]

> "As so often, the effect of this OT book is to lay a foundation upon which the NT can build. 'God so loved the world' is its basic affirmation, which the NT is to conclude with the message of the gift of his Son.

> "Throughout the story the figure of Jonah is a foil to the divine hero, a Watson to Yahweh's Holmes, a Gehazi to Yahweh's Elisha. The greatness and the goodness of God are enhanced against the background of Jonah's meanness and malevolence. Look out at the world, pleads the author, at God's world. See it through God's eyes. And let your new vision overcome your natural bitterness, your hardness of soul. Let the divine compassion flood your own hearts."[132]

---

[127] Stuart, p. 508.
[128] Page, p. 286.
[129] Wiersbe, p. 386.
[130] Stuart, p. 435.
[131] Gaebelein, pp. 126-27.
[132] Allen, p. 194.

Does this book constitute a call to foreign missionary service? It records God's call of one of His prophets to this type of ministry. However, we must remember that this was a rare ministry in the Old Testament period. Typically, Israel was to be a light to the nations by providing a model theocracy in the Promised Land that would attract the Gentiles to her. They would come to Israel for the knowledge of God that they would take back home with them (e.g., Exod. 19:5-6; 1 Kings 10; Isa. 42:6; Acts 8:26-40).

In the Great Commission (Matt. 28:19-20), Jesus changed the basic missionary method by which people are to learn of God. Now we are to go into all the world and herald the gospel to everyone, rather than waiting for them to come to us for it. The Book of Jonah shows an Old Testament prophet, doing reluctantly, what Christians are now to do enthusiastically.

It was not God's plan that *all* Old Testament prophets, much less all Israelites, were to do what he did. Nevertheless they were to have a heart of compassion, for those outside the covenant community, and to show them mercy, as this book clarifies (cf. Boaz in the Book of Ruth). Christian missionaries can use the Book of Jonah, therefore, but they should do so by stressing its true message, not by making Jonah's call the main point.

> "This book is the greatest missionary book in the Old Testament, if not in the whole Bible. It is written to reveal the heart of a servant of God whose heart was not touched with the passion of God in missions. Does it strike home . . .? Are we more interested in our own comfort than the need of multitudes of lost souls . . . dying in darkness without the knowledge of their Messiah and Saviour, the Lord Jesus Christ? Are we more content to remain with the 'gourds,' the comforts of home and at home, than to see the message of Christ go out to the ends of the earth to both Jew and Gentile?"[133]

---

[133]Feinberg, p. 48.

Bibliography

Alexander, T. D. "Jonah." In *Obadiah, Jonah, Micah*, pp. 45-131. The Tyndale Old Testament Commentaries series. Leicester, Eng., and Downers Grove, Ill.: Inter-Varsity Press, 1988.

_____"Jonah and Genre." *Tyndale Bulletin* 36 (1985):35-59.

Allen, Leslie C. *The Books of Joel, Obadiah, Jonah and Micah*. New International Commentary on the Old Testament series. Grand Rapids: Wm. B. Eerdmans Publishing Co., 1976.

Archer, Gleason L., Jr. *A Survey of Old Testament Introduction*. Chicago: Moody Press, 1964. Revised ed. 1974.

Backus, William. *The Paranoid Prophet*. Minneapolis: Bethany House Publishers, 1986.

Baldwin, Joyce. "Jonah." In *The Minor Prophets: An Exegetical and Expositional Commentary*, 2:543-90. 3 vols. Edited by Thomas Edward McComiskey. Grand Rapids: Baker Books, 1992, 1993, and 1998.

Baly, Dennis. *The Geography of the Bible*. London: Lutherworth, 1957.

Block, Daniel I. "The Privilege of Calling: The Mosaic Paradigm for Missions (Deut. 26:16-19)." *Bibliotheca Sacra* 162:648 (October-December 2005):387-405.

Chisholm, Robert B., Jr. "Does God 'Change His Mind'?" *Bibliotheca Sacra* 152:608 (October-December 1995):387-99.

_____. *Handbook on the Prophets*. Grand Rapids: Baker Book House, 2002.

_____. "A Theology of the Minor Prophets." In *A Biblical Theology of the Old Testament*, pp. 397-433. Edited by Roy B. Zuck. Chicago: Moody Press, 1991.

Constable, Thomas L. "What Prayer Will and Will Not Change." In *Essays in Honor of J. Dwight Pentecost*, pp. 99-113. Edited by Stanley D. Toussaint and Charles H. Dyer. Chicago: Moody Press, 1986.

de Vaux, Roland. *Ancient Israel: Its Life and Institutions*. New York: McGraw-Hill, 1961.

Dyer, Charles H., and Eugene H. Merrill. *The Old Testament Explorer*. Nashville: Word Publishing, 2001. Reissued as *Nelson's Old Testament Survey*. Nashville: Thomas Nelson Publishers, 1999.

Ellison, H. L. "Jonah." In *Daniel-Minor Prophets*. Vol. 7 of *The Expositor's Bible Commentary*. 12 vols. Edited by Frank E. Gaebelein and Richard P. Polcyn. Grand Rapids: Zondervan Publishing House, 1985.

_____. *The Prophets of Israel: From Ahijah to Hosea*. Exeter, Eng.: Paternoster Press, 1969. American ed., Grand Rapids: Wm. B. Eerdmans Publishing Co., 1974.

Feinberg, Charles Lee. *Jonah, Micah, and Nahum*. The Major Messages of the Minor Prophets series. New York: American Board of Missions to the Jews, 1951.

Gaebelein, Frank E. *Four Minor Prophets: Obadiah, Jonah, Habakkuk, and Haggai*. Chicago: Moody Press, 1970.

Good, Edwin M. Irony in the Old Testament. Second ed. Bible and Literature series 3. Sheffield, Eng.: Almond, 1981.

Hannah, John D. "Jonah." In *The Bible Knowledge Commentary: Old Testament*, pp. 1461-73. Edited by John F. Walvoord and Roy B. Zuck. Wheaton: Scripture Press Publications, Victor Books, 1985.

Harrison, R. K. *Introduction to the Old Testament*. Grand Rapids: Wm. B. Eerdmans Publishing Co., 1969.

Howe, George F. "Jonah and the Great Fish." *Biblical Research Monthly*, January 1973, pp. 6-8.

International Standard Bible Encyclopaedia, 1957 ed. S.v. "Nineveh," by A. H. Sayce.

Josephus, Flavius. *The Works of Flavius Josephus*. Translated by William Whiston. London: T. Nelson and Sons, 1866; reprint ed. Peabody, Mass.: Hendrickson Publishers, 1988.

Kaiser, Walter C., Jr. *Toward an Old Testament Theology*. Grand Rapids: Zondervan Publishing House, 1978.

Keil, C. F. *The Twelve Minor Prophets*. 2 vols. Translated by James Martin. Biblical Commentary on the Old Testament. Reprint ed. Grand Rapids: Wm. B. Eerdmans Publishing Co., 1949.

Kendall, R. T. *Jonah: An Exposition*. Grand Rapids: Zondervan Publishing House, 1978.

Kennedy, J. H. *Studies in the Book of Jonah*. Nashville: Broadman, 1956.

Landes, George M. "The 'Three Days and Three Nights' Motif in Jonah 2:1." *Journal of Biblical Literature* 86 (1967): 246-250.

Lawson, Steven J. "The Power of Biblical Preaching: An Expository Study of Jonah 3:1-10." *Bibliotheca Sacra* 158:631 (July-September 2001):331-46.

Longman, Tremper, III and Raymond B. Dillard. *An Introduction to the Old Testament*. 2nd ed. Grand Rapids: Zondervan, 2006.

McGee, J. Vernon. *Jonah: Dead or Alive?* St. Louis: Miracle Press, 1969.

Morgan, G. Campbell. *Living Messages of the Books of the Bible*. 2 vols. New York: Fleming H. Revell Co., 1912.

_____. *The Minor Prophets*. Westwood, N.J.: Fleming H. Revell, 1960.

The Nelson Study Bible. Edited by Earl D. Radmacher. Nashville: Thomas Nelson Publishers, 1997.

The NET (New English Translation) Bible. First beta printing. Spokane, Wash.: Biblical Studies Press, 2001.

The New Bible Dictionary, 1962 ed. S.v. "Nineveh," by D. J. Wiseman.

_____. S.v. "Tarshish," by J. A. Thompson.

The New Scofield Reference Bible. Edited by Frank E. Gaebelein, William Culbertson, et al. New York: Oxford University Press, 1967.

Pentecost, J. Dwight. *Thy Kingdom Come*. Wheaton: Scripture Press Publications, Victor Books, 1990.

Smith, Billy K., and Frank S. Page. *Amos, Obadiah, Jonah*. The New American Commentary series. N. c.: Broadman & Holman Publishers, 1995.

Strickland, Wayne G. "Isaiah, Jonah, and Religious Pluralism." *Bibliotheca Sacra* 153:609 (January-March 1996):24-33.

Stuart, Douglas. *Hosea-Jonah*. Word Biblical Commentary series. Waco: Word Books, 1987.

Thomas, D. Winton. "Consideration of Some Unusual Ways of Expressing the Superlative in Hebrew." *Vetus Testamentum* 3 (1953):209-24.

Waltke, Bruce K., with Charles Yu. *An Old Testament Theology: an exegetical, canonical, and thematic approach*. Grand Rapids: Zondervan, 2007.

Wendland, Ernst R. "Text Analysis and the Genre of Jonah (Part 1)." *Journal of the Evangelical Theological Society* 39:2 (June 1996):191-206.

_____. "Text Analysis and the Genre of Jonah (Part 2)." *Journal of the Evangelical Theological Society* 39:3 (September 1996):373-95.

Wiersbe, Warren W. "Jonah." In *The Bible Exposition Commentary/Prophets*, pp. 377-88. Colorado Springs, Colo.: Cook Communications Ministries; and Eastbourne, England: Kingsway Communications Ltd., 2002.

Wilson, A. J. "Sign of the Prophet Jonah and Its Modern Confirmations." *Princeton Theological Review* 25 (October 1927):630-42.

Wiseman, Donald J. "Jonah's Nineveh." *Tyndale Bulletin* 30 (1979):29-51.

Wolff, Hans W. *Obadiah and Jonah: A Commentary*. Translated by Margaret Kohl. Minneapolis: Augsburg; London: SPCK, 1986.

Wycliffe Bible Encyclopedia, 1975 ed. S.v. "Nineveh," by Elmer B. Smick.

Constable's Notes
on Micah

Introduction

Title and Writer

The title, as usual in the prophetical books of the Old Testament, comes from the name of the traditional writer.

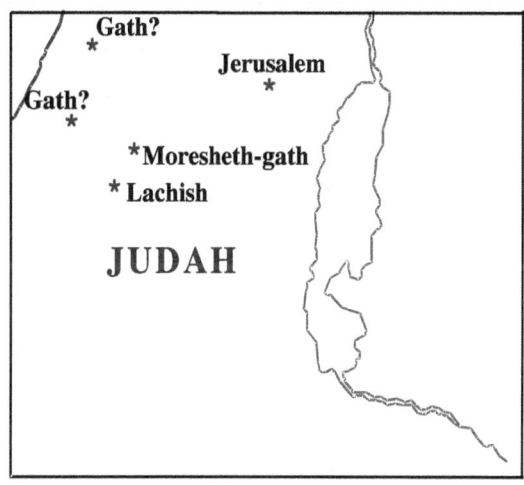

The name "Micah" is a shortened form of "Micaiah," which means: "Who is like Yahweh?" This was an appropriate name since Micah helped the people understand what Yahweh is like. There are many other Bible characters with the same name. Another Micaiah, the son of Imlah, served as a prophet in the Northern Kingdom during the reign of King Ahab of Israel (874-853 B.C., 1 Kings 22:8-28; 2 Chron. 18:3-27). Micah's hometown was Moresheth-gath, which stood about 25 miles southwest of Jerusalem in Judah (1:1), between Azekah and Marisa. It was called Moresheth-gath (1:14) because it was fairly close to the Philistine town of Gath. Moresheth-gath was also about six miles northeast of Lachish, an important Judean town in Micah's day, because it stood on an international trade route. Since Moresheth-gath stood only about a day's walk west of Tekoa, Amos' hometown, these prophets, who were roughly contemporary, may have known each other.[1] However, Amos' ministry may have been over by the time Micah began his. Amos prophesied during the reign of King Uzziah of Judah (Amos 1:1), and Micah prophesied during the reigns of Kings Jotham, Ahaz, and Hezekiah of Judah, who followed Uzziah (Mic. 1:1). This probably means that Micah was a younger contemporary of Hosea, Amos, and Isaiah.

Unity

Critics of the book have tried to prove that it is the product of several writers or editors (redactors). The reason for this view is its lack of apparent coherence. Chapters 4—7 have become the target of most critical attacks, yet the book is harmonious in its basic structure.[2]

Date and Place of Composition

Micah prophesied during the reigns of the Judean kings Jotham (750-732 B.C.), Ahaz (732-715 B.C.), and Hezekiah (715-686 B.C.; 1:1). This made him a late eighth-century B.C. contemporary of Isaiah, who also ministered in the Southern Kingdom of Judah (cf. Isa. 1:1), and Amos and Hosea, who ministered in the Northern Kingdom of Israel (cf. Amos 1:1; Hos. 1:1). These were years of economic affluence and international peace—but spiritual decadence—for both kingdoms, especially Israel.

Micah witnessed the fall of the Northern Kingdom to Assyria in 722 B.C. He also lived through the invasion of Judah by the Assyrians under King Sennacherib in 701 B.C. Leon Wood believed that Micah wrote between 735 and 710 B.C., because he did not cite Sennacherib's invasion of Judah.[3] However, Leslie Allen argued convincingly that 2:12-13 alludes to Sennacherib's blockade of Jerusalem in 701 B.C.[4] According to Sennacherib's own records he captured 46 of King Hezekiah's strong cities, walled forts, and countless small villages. He claimed to have taken captive over 200,000 Judahites plus innumerable animals. Two of the Judean cities taken were Lachish, second only to Jerusalem in importance, and Moresheth-gath, Micah's hometown. Micah referred to the distress that this foreign invasion produced in Judah (1:10-16; 5:6).

---

[1]Leon Wood, *The Prophets of Israel*, p. 310.
[2]See Tremper Longman III and Raymond B. Dillard, *An Introduction to the Old Testament*, pp. 451-52, for further discussion, or T. E. McComiskey, "Micah," in *Daniel-Minor Prophets*, vol. 7 of *The Expositor's Bible Commentary*, pp. 396-97; J. Mays, *Micah: A Commentary*, pp. 21-33; Leslie C. Allen, *The Books of Joel, Obadiah, Jonah and Micah*, pp. 241-52.
[3]Wood, p. 309.
[4]Allen, pp. 242, 244, and 301.

DATES OF SOME OLD TESTAMENT WRITINGS ACCORDING TO "NORMATIVE" BIBLICAL CRITICISM[5]	
EPOCH	LITERATURE
Pre-exilic (760-586 B.C.)	
Early	Amos
	Hosea
	First Isaiah (chs. 1—35)
	Micah
	Psalms of Zion (46, 48, 87)
Late	Jeremiah
EPOCH	LITERATURE
Exilic (586—539 B.C.)	
Early	Jeremiah
	Deuteronomist (Deuteronomy—2 Kings)
	Ezekiel
Late	Second Isaiah (chs. 40—55)
Post-exilic (516—?350 B.C.)	
Early	Zechariah
	Haggai
	Third Isaiah (chs. 56—66)
	Ezra, Nehemiah
Late	Malachi
	Joel

Audience and Purpose

Micah ministered to the people of Judah, the Southern Kingdom. He predicted the destruction of the Northern Kingdom of Israel by the Assyrians, and warned the Judeans that God would discipline them, too, for their sins. As in all the prophetical books, the standard by which God measured His people was the Mosaic Covenant. If they obeyed, they would enjoy blessing, but if they disobeyed, they could expect punishment (cf. Lev. 26; Deut. 28). Micah, too, pointed out how the Israelites had broken the covenant and that judgment was inevitable, but he also promised ultimate restoration in view of God's promises to the patriarchs. Micah never used the word "covenant" (Heb. *berit*), but it is clear from what he wrote that thoughts of the covenant were always in his mind.

Isaiah ministered in Jerusalem and had easy access to the court of the kings. He ministered to the kings and princes as well as the ordinary citizens. Micah ministered mainly outside Jerusalem among the ordinary Judahites. Micah was primarily a prophet of the poorer, ordinary Israelites and a friend of the oppressed. Micah's ministry was more rural, like Amos', and Isaiah's was more cosmopolitan. Micah was concerned with personal and social righteousness (contemporary issues), also like Amos, and Isaiah was concerned with more and larger issues covering the whole scope of history from his own day to the end times.

---

[5]From Bruce K. Waltke, "Micah," in *Obadiah, Jonah, Micah: An Introduction and Commentary*, p. 170

Micah's theme is *true religion* (cf. Amos; James 1:27). True religion is not conformity to external rituals but the practice of righteousness in personal and social life. His thesis is that God will discipline His own with judgment for their sins, but He will also fulfill His covenant promises in the future.

Structure and Emphases

The Book of Micah consists of three messages, each of which begins "Hear" (Heb. *shema*; cf. Deut. 6:4). They may have been messages that he preached, or probably condensations of several addresses he delivered during his ministry.[6] In each one the theme of judgment is prominent, but there is also mention of restoration and a remnant (2:12; 4:7; 5:7-8; 7:18).[7] Eventually God would restore the Israelites to a position of world prominence under their Messiah.

> "Much debate surrounds the structure of the book of Micah. Opinions vary radically. Some argue that the book has no overall structure but is simply a loose collection of prophetic oracles. Others identify extremely complex and sophisticated structures. A few points are certain: 1. Micah did not speak these oracles at one time. The book is best taken as an anthology of his prophetic messages over the years of his ministry. 2. Chronology is not the key to the structure of the book, though early in the book Micah does predict the capture of Samaria and Sennacherib's invasion, while at the conclusion of this book, he looks forward to the Babylonian captivity and the restoration. 3. The prophecy is roughly structured on the basis of alternating messages of threat and hope."[8]

Distinctive Characteristics

The main aspects of God that Micah emphasized were His sovereignty, self-consistency, and His leadership of all events and His people toward the fulfillment of all His ultimate plans and purposes for them.

Proportionately, this book has more prophecies about the advent and kingdom of Messiah, and Israel's future, than any other prophetic book. The future role of the Davidic dynasty, and its capital city, Jerusalem, receive greater attention in this prophecy than in the other eighth-century B.C. Minor Prophets (Jonah, Hosea, and Amos).

> "Like his contemporary Isaiah, Micah stressed God's incomparability."[9]

> "He had Amos' passion for justice and Hosea's heart of love."[10]

Like all the other eighth-century B.C. prophets, Micah also attacked the idolatry that accompanied the acceptance of Canaanite worship. However, his distinctive burden was the social injustice that marked the ruling class (2:1, 8-9; 3:11; 6:11; cf. Amos). He was a champion of civil rights. He has often been called, "the prophet of the poor," or, more accurately, the prophet of the oppressed middle class.[11]

Micah wrote about the coming Messiah. He predicted His birthplace, lineage, and origin (5:2), His future reign (4:1-7; 5:4), and he referred to Him as Israel's king (2:13) and ruler (5:2).

> "Micah's doctrine of the remnant is unique among the Prophets and is perhaps his most significant contribution to the prophetic theology of hope. The remnant is a force in the world, not simply a residue of people, as the word 'remnant' (*she'erit*) may seem to imply. It is a force that will ultimately conquer the world (4:11-13). This triumph, while presented in apparently militaristic terminology (4:13; 5:5-6), is actually accomplished by other than physical force [cf. Matt. 5:3-12]. By removing everything that robs his people of complete trust in him (5:10-15), the Ruler from Bethlehem will effect the deliverance of his people. The source of power for God's people in the world is their absolute trust in him and his resources."[12]

Like many of the prophetical books, Micah contains much poetry. One of the prominent features of Hebrew poetry is parallelism of thought, and this marks Micah. Micah used his native language as a craftsman. He utilized puns, wordplays, and probing questions. This book, like most of the other Prophets, is a collection of messages that Micah delivered.

---

[6] C. F. Keil, *The Twelve Minor Prophets*, 1:422.
[7] See Bruce K. Waltke, *An Old Testament Theology*, p. 837.
[8] Longman and Dillard, p. 452.
[9] Walter C. Kaiser Jr., *Toward an Old Testament Theology*, p. 201.
[10] J. M. P. Smith, cited by George L. Robinson, *The Twelve Minor Prophets*, p. 95. See also Henk Jagersma, *A History of Israel in the Old Testament Period*, pp. 152, 162.
[11] Bruce K. Waltke, "Micah," in *The Minor Prophets*, p. 594.
[12] McComiskey, p. 399.

There is one citation from Micah in the Old Testament and two in the New. The elders of Jerusalem in Jeremiah's day referred to Micah to support not persecuting Jeremiah for predicting judgment on Jerusalem (Jer. 26:17-19). Matthew quoted Micah 5:2 as predicting the birthplace of Messiah (Matt. 2:5-6), and he recorded Jesus' quotation of Micah 7:6 regarding conflict within families (Matt. 10:35-36). Micah drew on many other books of the Old Testament: Exodus, Numbers, Deuteronomy, Joshua, 2 Samuel, 1 Kings, Psalms, Proverbs, Amos, and Isaiah.

"In OT study Micah has tended to be overshadowed by Amos and Hosea and especially by his great contemporary Isaiah, whose prophetic material has been preserved in much greater quantity. Stylistically, to be sure, he sometimes has more of the qualities of an orator than of a poet. But his message is proclaimed with no uncertain sound, as with passionate forthrightness he attacks the social evils of his day. His stubborn refusal to float on the tide of his social environment, and his courageous stand for his convictions of God's truth, must commend Micah to believers in every age."[13]

"The church today needs men like Micah who can see the connection between the Western world's spurning of its Christian heritage and the international crises that surround it."[14]

The Hebrew text of Micah is fairly well preserved.

Outline

I. Heading 1:1

II. The first oracle: Israel's impending judgment and future restoration 1:2—2:13

    A. The judgment coming on Israel 1:2-7
    B. Lamentation over the coming judgment 1:8-16
        1. Micah's personal response 1:8-9
        2. Micah's call for the people's response 1:10-16
    C. The sins of Judah 2:1-11
        1. Sins of the wealthy 2:1-5
        2. Sins of the false prophets and the greedy 2:6-11
    D. A prediction of future regathering and leadership 2:12-13

III. The second oracle: the guilt of Israel's leaders and her future hope chs. 3—5

    A. Condemnation of Israel's leaders ch. 3
        1. The guilt of Israel's civil leaders 3:1-4
        2. The guilt of Israel's religious leaders 3:5-8
        3. The indictment of Israel's leaders 3:9-12
    B. Blessing for Israel in the future chs. 4—5
        1. The exaltation of Zion 4:1-8
        2. The might of Zion 4:9—5:1
        3. The King of Zion 5:2-5a
        4. The peace of Zion 5:5b-6
        5. The vindication of Zion 5:7-9
        6. The purification of Zion 5:10-15

IV. The third oracle: God's case against Israel and the ultimate triumph of His kingdom chs. 6—7

    A. The Lord's indictment against His people 6:1-5
    B. Micah's response for the Israelites 6:6-8
    C. The Lord's sentence of judgment 6:9-16
        1. Israel's sins 6:9-12
        2. Israel's punishment 6:13-16

---

[13]Allen, p. 241.
[14]Bruce K. Waltke, in *Obadiah, . . .*, p. 139. Since both of Waltke's commentaries on Micah that I cite in these notes bear the same title, "Micah," I will hereafter distinguish them by using the names of the two books of which they are parts.

        D.   Micah's lament over his decadent society 7:1-7
        E.   Micah's confidence in the Lord 7:8-20
                1.   Advice to the ungodly 7:8-13
                2.   Prayer for deliverance 7:14-17
                3.   Praise for forgiveness 7:18-20

Message

Micah directed all the nations to witness God's judgment of His Chosen People in these litigation speeches (*rib* [lit. lawsuit] oracles). He wanted the people of the earth to learn that Yahweh is sovereign by observing His dealings with Judah. If Israel had been faithful to God's purpose for her, all the nations would have learned how wonderful it can be to live under the government of Yahweh. But Israel had failed in her calling. Therefore, Micah pointed out—for the benefit of all people—that those who serve under God's government can expect judgment when they fail in their calling. As a police officer who breaks the law gets more severe treatment in court than the ordinary citizen, because of his calling, so the people of Judah got more severe treatment from the Lord, because of their calling.

Micah was very much aware of the throne in heaven, God's throne, that symbolized His eternal sovereignty over all people, including His chosen people. He was also aware of the failure of the throne on earth, the failure of King Ahaz of Judah.

Micah was a contemporary of Isaiah, and both of these prophets ministered in the Southern Kingdom during Ahaz's reign. But Micah's emphasis was different from Isaiah's. Isaiah focused on the throne in heaven. He saw the Lord high and lifted up above the earth, ruling in sovereign majesty and providing salvation for all people. Micah focused on the human rulers under the divine sovereign. He spoke of "the powers that be" that are ordained of God (Rom. 13:1). His eyes were on the earth. He saw the sin and corruption, the sighing and crying of the people, their agony and tears, and he traced these tragedies to misrule by people in authority in Judah.

The unique contribution of Micah is twofold: First, this prophet unmasked and denounced the false rulers. Second, he unveiled and proclaimed the true Ruler. The false rulers were the princes, priests, and prophets that surrounded him. The true Ruler was someone whom Micah saw coming in the future to rule and reign properly.

We see Micah's picture of false authority clearly in 3:11: "Israel's leaders pronounce judgment for a bribe, her priests instruct for a price, and her prophets divine for money." Micah identified all three major types of Judahite rulers as corrupt: civil leaders (the princes), religious leaders (the priests), and moral leaders (the prophets). The judges were judging according to who paid them best. The priests were teaching the people, but for what they could get out of it. The prophets were not really prophesying messages from the Lord but were divining messages from other sources. They were practicing sorcery and witchcraft for money and passing these revelations off as the word of the Lord. In every case, ministry was being conducted, but for selfish motives, for what the ministers could get out of ministering.

The judges (princes) were passing judgment in legal cases because they hated good and loved evil (3:1-3). They should have "known" judgment (3:1). That is, they should have practiced justice, ruled justly, and shown no partiality. Instead they were, as Micah described them, tearing the skin off the people, eating their flesh, and chopping up their bones like butchers (3:2b-3). They were robbing the people, like soldiers who took the spoils of war. They were not impartial. They did not represent God, the true Judge of His people. They were corrupt.

The priests were no better (3:11). When we think of Israel's priests, we probably think of them offering the sacrifices that the people brought to the temple. But one of the primary responsibilities of the priests in Israel was to teach the people the Word of God (Deut. 17:8-13). This was really a more important ministry than cutting up animals. This man-ward duty was more significant than their God-ward duty. God scattered the priests in Israel, rather than giving them one geographic region to inhabit, so they could teach the people God's will. Yet the priests in Micah's day were just telling the people what the Judahites wanted to hear, not what God had said. And they were doing it for money. They distorted their messages to get a favorable response to their messages.

The prophets claimed to have received fresh messages from the Lord for the people, but most of the prophets in Micah's day delivered favorable "words from the Lord" only if they received adequate compensation. If the people did not pay them well, they either gave a message of gloom and doom, or no message at all. They were getting messages for the people all right, but they were messages from the wrong source. Their "prophecies" amounted to sorcery and witchcraft. Micah wrote of them in 3:5: "When they have something to bite with their teeth, they cry, 'Peace.' But against him who puts nothing in their mouths, they declare holy war." The people had to pay for good prophecies. Otherwise they would get prophecies of disaster.

Many Christian ministers make ministry decisions primarily on the basis of money. I am not just referring to people who go into the ministry because they think it is a comfortable way to earn a living. I am also referring to evangelicals who are in the ministry because they love the Lord and want to serve Him. It is a temptation to evaluate opportunities for various ministries on the basis of financial remuneration. As you consider opportunities for ministry, let me encourage you not to make your pay a significant factor in your decision. If you go where the Lord wants you, He will take care of you. Try to discover where you can make the greatest contribution and go there, not where you can receive the best salary. It is also a temptation to expect, or even require, payment for some forms of ministry. When we view ministry that way, we are really viewing it as a job, not as sacrificial service. We have become hirelings, not ministers in the true sense of that word.

Wherever you find distressed and suffering people, the cause is usually their leaders. If the leaders are out of harmony with God, if they love evil and hate good, if they are selfish rather than servants, the people suffer. This is true no matter what form of government exists. Every form of government has the equivalent of princes, priests, and prophets: civil, religious, and moral leaders. Corrupt authorities rule for their own benefit, not for the benefit of the people. This is the opposite of "servant leadership."

Micah saw through the smog of his own day to a Ruler on the distant horizon beyond. He saw this One coming out of human obscurity, not out of a position of power. He would arise from the obscure town of Bethlehem in Judah, but His real origin was eternity (5:2). He would arise and shepherd His flock in the strength of the Lord (5:4). He would faithfully represent Yahweh and act in His strength. He would not serve Himself but Yahweh. He would not be a crooked judge but impartial. He would not pervert the truth to glorify Himself but would tell the truth, the whole truth, and nothing but the truth. He would not pass deceitful and destructive messages to the people, but only the true words of the Lord.

The result of His ministry would be peace, not distress and suffering (5:5a). The negative side of His rule would be the destruction of all the things the people's false rulers had encouraged them to trust in: horses, chariots, cities, strongholds, treaties, witchcraft, images, and idols. The strength of a nation is never in these things, but in its leaders. Israel would one day have a Leader who would provide adequate strength for her. He would not abuse her but glorify her.

The timeless value of Micah is that it reminds us that the test of authority is its motive. If the motive of leaders is self-aggrandizement, self-service, and self-glory, their leadership is corrupt and pernicious. The strength of leaders is in their recognition of Yahweh.

We see this clearly in that One whom Micah saw arising out of obscure human conditions, yet with the authority of eternity behind Him, to take the reigns of power and produce peace. When He came the first time, the obscurity of His human background so blinded the eyes of His contemporaries that they rejected Him and said: "We will not have this Man reign over us!" But when He comes the second time, no one will be able to resist His eternal authority, and He will reign over the whole world. He will provide the perfect civil, religious, and moral leadership that this world has longed for but has never yet enjoyed.

In the meantime, our duty is to obey Him because our eyes of faith have seen Him, and our hearts know Him. As His disciples, we must serve as He will serve, in whatever sphere of leadership or position of authority we may occupy. And we must eagerly await His return in power and great glory. Titus 2:13 says that we should be "looking for the blessed hope, even the appearing of the glory of our great God and Savior, Christ Jesus."

Micah is a great book because it contrasts imperfect leaders with the Perfect Leader. It uncovers present corruption, but it also gives us hope of future celebration. It assures us that God will replace selfish leadership with selfless leadership. It provides negative and positive leadership models for church leaders and individual Christians today. I believe that the aspect of God that Micah helps us appreciate most is His leadership.[15]

Exposition

I. HEADING 1:1

Prophetic revelation from Yahweh came to Micah concerning Samaria (the Northern Kingdom) and Jerusalem (the Southern Kingdom). These capital cities, by synecdoche, represent their respective nations and the people in them. These capital cities also, by metonymy, suggest the leaders of the nations, which Micah targeted for special responsibility. Micah "saw" these revelations (rather than "heard" them) because the Lord revealed them to him in visions and or dreams (Num. 12:6; cf. Isa. 1:1; Obad. 1; Nah. 1:1). Micah ("Who is like Yahweh?") was a resident of Moresheth-gath (v. 14), which was a Judean town in the Shephelah (foothills) of Judah, west and a bit south of Jerusalem. The mention of Micah's hometown, rather than his father's name, suggests that he had come to Jerusalem, and had become known there as "the Micah from Moresheth."[16] Normally, a man who was a longtime resident of a town, was described as "the son of so and so," rather than as being from a particular place. Micah received and delivered his prophetic messages during the reigns of three of the kings of his nation: Jotham, Ahaz, and Hezekiah. This dates his ministry between 750 and 686 B.C.[17] Similar full headings (superscriptions) begin the books of Isaiah, Hosea, Amos, and Zephaniah.

---

[15]Adapted from G. Campbell Morgan, *Living Messages of the Books of the Bible*, 1:2:243-55.
[16]Allen, p. 265
[17]See my comments on the writer and date in the Introduction section above.

II. THE FIRST ORACLE: ISRAEL'S IMPENDING JUDGMENT AND FUTURE RESTORATION 1:2—2:13

This is the first of three messages that compose the Book of Micah (cf. chs. 3—5; 6—7). Each of these messages gives evidence of containing other messages that Micah evidently preached and then compiled into the canonical form in which we have them. Each of the three main messages begins with the same imperative (Heb. *shm'*), translated "Hear" (cf. Deut. 6:4). In each one, promises of restoration follow predictions of ruin. Words of hope follow announcements of doom.

The first message deals with Israel's impending judgment and future restoration. The emphasis in this oracle is on the judgment coming on the Northern Kingdom, and Micah predicted the fall of Samaria (ch. 1). Then he gave reasons for divine judgment on both Israel and Judah, followed by a promise of future restoration and blessing (ch. 2).

A. THE JUDGMENT COMING ON ISRAEL 1:2-7

This opening pericope sets the tone and forms the backdrop for the rest of the book. All people were to hear God's indictment against His people (v. 2). Punishment was coming (vv. 3-4) that would be both reasonable (v. 5) and certain (vv. 6-7).

1:2   Micah shouted: "Hear ye, hear ye!" to the people of the earth, as a clerk summons a courtroom jury to pay attention to the testimony that will follow. Micah presented his message in the setting of a courtroom trial. This is the *rib* (lawsuit) oracle form, examples of which are quite common in the Prophets. Sovereign Yahweh was about to give His witness against His people ("you," Micah's audience; cf. Deut. 31:19-21, 26). This appeal assumes that those called on to listen will agree with the testimony to be given. The Lord would come out of "His *holy* temple" to give His testimony. The Hebrew word *hekal* literally means "palace" rather than "temple." It refers to the location of the throne of judgment. This appears to be a reference to God's *heavenly temple*, in view of the following verses (cf. Ps. 11:4; Isa. 3:13-14; Hab. 2:20).

> "What the peoples are supposed to hear serves not to increase their knowledge but to determine their lives."[18]

1:3-4   The Lord was about to intervene in the affairs of His people. He is not only transcendent above all, but immanently involved in the world—one of the most basic revelations in Old Testament theology. When He came, all the earth ("mountains") would "melt," "split," and quake before His awesome power (cf. Judg. 5:4-5). Since He could affect the physical creation so drastically, His people needed to fear Him. Treading on the "high places of the earth" (land), where the Israelites worshipped in idolatry (cf. 2 Chron. 33:17), probably also implies that He would crush pagan worship.[19]

> "If men would tremble before God, instead of before each other, they would have nothing to fear."[20]

1:5   The Lord's intervention was due to the Israelites' sins and rebellion against their Sovereign Lord. "Samaria" personified "the rebellion" of the Israelites, and "Jerusalem" had become "a high place" for idolatry rather than for holy worship. These capital cities had become leaders in wickedness rather than in holiness.

Micah liked to use "Jacob" as a title for all Israel (2:7, 12; 3:1, 8, 9; 4:2; 5:7, 8), though he also used it to describe the Northern Kingdom (here) and the patriarch Jacob (7:20). This name recalls the rebelliousness that marked the patriarch for most of his early life and that had subsequently marked his descendants. Micah used the name "Israel" to describe both the Northern and the Southern Kingdoms. Several of the prophets referred to the Southern Kingdom as "Israel," especially after the fall of Samaria in 722 B.C., because that kingdom represented the true Israel under the Davidic kings and the Aaronic priesthood. They generally referred to the Northern Kingdom as "Israel" in contrast to the Southern Kingdom of Judah.

1:6   Israel's capital, Samaria, stood atop a mountain, but Yahweh said He would make it a pile of "ruins" in a field. That is, He would both destroy and humiliate it. It would become a rural rather than an urban place, suitable for planting vineyards. He would topple the "stones" of its buildings "into the valley" below and expose their "foundations" by destroying their superstructures. The fulfillment came with the Assyrian overthrow of Samaria in 722 B.C. Even today the foundations of Samaria's buildings lie exposed.

1:7   God would smash Samaria's "idols," proving them incapable of defending themselves, much less helping others. He would burn the luxurious ornaments that the people offered as temple gifts in the conflagration that would accompany Samaria's overthrow. All the pagan "images" that the people had made would perish. The Lord viewed these physical treasures as the "earnings of a harlot"—Israel—who had been unfaithful to Him (cf. Hosea). The Israelites had committed adultery with temple

---

[18]Hans W. Wolff, *Micah*, p. 55.
[19]McComiskey, p. 404; John A. Martin, "Micah," in *The Bible Knowledge Commentary: Old Testament*, p. 1477.
[20]Waltke, in *Obadiah, . . .*, p. 152.

prostitutes, but the Assyrians would destroy the gifts that they had brought into their temples, and use them for their own idolatrous worship.

> "The reference is probably to the gold and silver plating on the images, melted down from the dirty money handed over for the use of religious brothels. Invading soldiers are to tear it off as loot and spend it as currency for further prostitution, as soldiers will."[21]

B. LAMENTATION OVER THE COMING JUDGMENT 1:8-16

"The judicial sentence against Samaria (vv. 2-7), fulfilled in 722/721 B.C., certifies the doom of idolatrous Judah (vv. 8-16), predicted in connection with Sennacherib's invasion of the Shephelah [Judean foothills] in 701 B.C."[22]

1. Micah's personal response 1:8-9

1:8   In view of this coming judgment, Micah said he felt compelled to "lament and wail." He would express his sorrow by going "barefoot and naked," a common way of expressing it in his culture (cf. 2 Sam. 15:30; Isa. 20:2; 22:12; Jer. 25:34). "Jackals" and "ostriches" (or owls) were nocturnal animals that lived alone, and were peculiar for their nocturnal hunting habits and their wailing sounds. Micah said he would mimic them.

> "Unlike some tub-thumping modern preachers of fire and damnation, Micah preaches judgment out of such love that he weeps for his audience."[23]

1:9   Samaria had a "wound" from which she could not recover, namely, a wound of punishment caused by her sin (cf. 1 Kings 20:21). This sin and its consequence had also infected Judah, even the capital city of "Jerusalem" (cf. Isa. 1:5-6). Jerusalem should have been especially holy because of the temple and God's presence there, but it was polluted. Punishment reached "the gate" of Jerusalem in 701 B.C., when Sennacherib attacked the city, but the Lord turned back the invader (cf. 2 Kings 18—19).

> "The problem with Samaria was that she was toxic; her infection had spread to Judah."[24]

2. Micah's call for the people's response 1:10-16

The prophet used several clever wordplays in this poem to describe the desolation that God would bring on Judah. He selected towns and villages near his own hometown, in Judah's Shephelah, whose names were similar to the coming devastations or to other conditions that he described. The known towns encircle Micah's hometown of Moresheth-gath.

> "Interestingly Sennacherib too used wordplays when recording *his* conquests."[25]

James Moffatt's paraphrase gives the sense of Micah's wordplays.

> "Tell it not in Tellington!
> Wail not in Wailing!
> Dust Manor will eat dirt,
> Dressy Town flee naked.
> Safefold will not save,
> Wallchester's walls are down,
> A bitter dose drinks Bitterton." Etc.[26]

> "He [Micah] turned around the meaning of a number of town names as a way of describing the world being turned upside down."[27]

---

[21]Allen, p. 274.
[22]Waltke, in *The Minor . . .*, p. 624.
[23]Idem, in *Obadiah, . . .*, p. 154.
[24]Warren W. Wiersbe, "Micah," in *The Bible Exposition Commentary/Prophets*, p. 391.
[25]Martin, p. 1479. See the map in Y. Aharoni, *The Land of the Bible*, p. 339, for the probable locations of the places mentioned in this passage.
[26]*The Old Testament, a new translation* by James Moffatt.
[27]*The Nelson Study Bible*, p. 1503.

1:10	Micah urged the Israelites not to report the Assyrian invasion of Jerusalem "in Gath" (cf. 2 Sam. 1:20), not even to indicate a crisis by weeping publicly. Why Gath? It was an enemy (Philistine) town, and news of Jerusalem's siege would encourage Israel's enemies. Specifically, "Gath" (*gat*) may have been chosen because of its similar sound in Hebrew to the verb "tell" (*taggidu*; cf. 2 Sam. 1:20).
	However, in the cities of Israel, like "Beth-le-aphrah" (Beth Ophrah, "house of dust"), the inhabitants should "roll . . . in the dust," expressing their distress (cf. Josh. 7:6; Job 16:15; Isa. 47:1; Jer. 25:34).
1:11	Residents of "Shaphir" ("beautiful," "pleasant") would become the opposite of their name, shamefully naked, when the invasion came. Inhabitants of "Zaanan," a town name that sounds like the Hebrew word translated "come out," would "not" be able to come out of their town to "escape." The people of "Beth-ezel" ("house of removal") would lament because the Lord would remove "its support."
1:12	Residents of "Maroth," which sounds like the Hebrew word translated "bitterness," would become "weak" as they waited for help that would not come. Their expectation would become bitter because God would send calamity to the gates of Jerusalem. Before Sennacherib besieged Jerusalem in 701 B.C., he defeated 46 other towns in Judah (2 Kings 18—19).[28]
1:13	Sarcastically, Micah urged the people "of Lachish" (Heb. *lakish*), a town known for its horses, to hitch a "team" (Heb. *rekesh*) of "horses" to a "chariot" to escape from the enemy. They would not be able to escape, however, because Lachish had led Jerusalem, as horses lead a chariot, into the sin of idolatry.
	"There is no record of this in the historical books of the Old Testament, although it has been suggested that the horses given to the sun (2 Kings 23:11) related to idolatry were kept there."[29]
1:14	Zion (Jerusalem) would give "Moresheth-gath" as a portion of a "parting gift" to the invader. "Moresheth" means "the possession of." The Davidic king would not be able to prevent the Assyrians from taking Moresheth-gath captive. The people of "Achzib" (Heb. *'akzib*), represented here by their "houses," would become deceitful (Heb. *'akzab*) "to the kings of Israel" because they could not fend off the enemy.
1:15	The Lord would bring on the inhabitants of "Mareshah" ("possessor") "one who" would take "possession" of them. "The glory of Israel," probably her leaders, would flee ashamedly for safety to "Adullam," as David had done earlier (1 Sam. 22:1).[30]
	"The point here may be that the situation would be so bad that the proper *heir* and *glory* of the nation—the members of the royal family—would have to flee in terror to remote hiding places."[31]
1:16	Micah called on the Judeans to "cut" their "hair" very short, as a sign of sorrow over the departure of their "children" (perhaps the nobles) "into exile." "The eagle" appeared to be bald because its head was white.

"This section (vv. 10-16) begins with words that recall David's lament at the death of Saul and ends with the name of the cave where David hid from Saul. These dark moments in David's life form a gloomy backdrop to the description of the fall of the towns Micah spoke of. Though he is never directly mentioned, the figure of David appears hauntingly in the tapestry of destruction—not a David standing tall in triumph, but a David bowed down by humiliation. It is as if Micah saw in the fall of each town and the eventual captivity of the two kingdoms the final dissolution of the Davidic monarchy. Like David, the glory of Israel would come to Adullam."[32]

C. THE SINS OF JUDAH 2:1-11

Micah identified the sins of the people of Judah, all of which violated the Mosaic Covenant. In view of these transgressions, divine punishment was inevitable and just.

---

[28]See D. W. Thomas, ed., *Documents from Old Testament Times*, p. 67, for Sennacherib's account.
[29]Charles Lee Feinberg, *Jonah, Micah, and Nahum*, p. 58.
[30]Charles H. Dyer, in *The Old Testament Explorer*, pp. 784-85, charted these place names, their meanings, and their significances helpfully.
[31]*The Nelson . . .*, p. 1503.
[32]McComiskey, p. 408.

In chapter 1 the sins of the people of both Northern and Southern Kingdoms seemed to be in view, but now Micah's audience, the people of Judah, appear to be the main subjects of his prophecy, in view of what he said. We should not draw this line too boldly, however, since the same sins that marked the people of Judah also stained the citizens of Israel.

1. Sins of the wealthy 2:1-5

Having spoken abstractly about rebellion and sin (cf. 1:5), Micah now specified the crime of the Israelites that had both social and theological dimensions.

> "The oracles against Samaria and Judah in the first chapter speak in general terms of their rebellion and sin and put the accent on immediate political destruction. This oracle indicts them for specific crimes and puts the accent on the eternal and theological punishment."[33]

> "It is in 2:1-5 that the prophet establishes the basis for the national crisis and the future collapse of the nation. It was not the imperialism of Assyria or the fortunes of blind destiny that brought the house of Israel to this critical stage. It was her disobedience to her God. How different is the prophetic view of history from that of the secular mind!"[34]

2:1   Micah announced that those who lay awake at night, plotting evil that they put into practice the next day, would experience "woe." Woe announces punishment coming because of guilt (cf. Isa. 3:9, 11; Jer. 13:27; Ezek. 13:3, 18; Hos. 7:13; Amos 5:18; Hab. 2:6; Zeph. 2:5). The people in view seem to be the rich because they had the ability to carry out their schemes. In times of affluence and peace, the rich and the poor in society normally become richer and poorer, and this was true in Israel and Judah in the late eighth century B.C.

> "This expectation of divine help and justice at morning (also in 2 Sam. 15:2; Job 7:18; Ps. 37:6; 73:14; 90:14; 143:8; Jer. 21;12; Hos. 6:3, 5; Zeph. 3:5) probably had to do in part with the king's practice of administering justice in the morning . . ."[35]

2:2   The plotting in view involved robbing others of their "fields," "houses," and "inheritance" (including land) through deception (cf. 1 Kings 21:3; Isa. 5:8). The wealthy not only violated the tenth commandment against coveting what belongs to a neighbor, but also the eighth commandment against stealing (Exod. 20:15, 17; Lev. 19:13; Deut. 5:19, 21; Col. 3:6-7). Furthermore, they broke the second greatest commandment, which said they should love their neighbors as themselves (Lev. 19:18; cf. Matt. 22:34-40).

> "They practiced the world's version of the Golden Rule: 'Whoever has the gold makes the rules.'"[36]

> "To *covet* is not just to have a passing thought; it is a determination to seize what is not one's own."[37]

2:3   Because they had done these things, Yahweh was plotting to bring "calamity" on the "family" of the Israelites that they would not be able to escape. They would be locked into it like a yoke holds the neck of an ox. The coming judgment would be a hard time for them that would humble them.

2:4   When God's judgment fell, other people would ridicule the Israelites. God's people would also lament—with *bitter* weeping—and mourn their complete destruction, as the victims of the rich Israelites' crimes just cited had mourned. They would bewail God's removal of His blessings, including their lands, from them—and His giving them to others that they considered apostate.

> "The situation envisaged seems to be the forced evacuation of the landed elite, who are marched away by the foreign invader while their estates are left to their erstwhile serfs, who are contemptuously spoken of as religious renegades."[38]

2:5   Evidently the Israelites set the boundaries between some land plots by casting lots (cf. Josh. 14:1-5; Ps. 16:6). No one would remain in the land who could do this "in the assembly" of Yahweh, namely, the covenant nation. The reason was that God would send His people into captivity and give their land to their captors.

---

[33]Waltke, in *Obadiah*, . . ., p. 156.
[34]McComiskey, p. 409.
[35]Waltke, in *The Minor* . . ., p. 636.
[36]Wiersbe, p. 392.
[37]*The Nelson* . . ., p. 1503.
[38]Allen, p. 291.

This is one of many examples of God's talionic justice. The Israelites would reap what they had sowed (cf. Gal. 6:7). They had taken land from their countrymen greedily and illegally, so God would take their land from them and let others occupy it.

2. Sins of the false prophets and the greedy 2:6-11

References to false prophets open and close this pericope (vv. 6-7, 11). In the middle, Micah again targeted the greedy in Judah for criticism (vv. 8-10). Apparently the false prophets condoned the practices of the greedy and took offense at Micah's antagonism toward their patrons.

2:6 The writer used another wordplay. False prophets were "speaking out" (lit. "dripping," Heb. *natap*) and telling Micah not to "speak out," not to announce the message of coming judgment for sin. These prophets were trying to silence him because they did not like his message (cf. Isa. 30:10; Amos 7:10-13). They were saying that Micah and his fellow true prophets, such as Isaiah, should not prophesy as they were doing. As long as they did, "reproaches" (i.e., disgrace for the sins they were charging the people with) would not leave the Israelites. This preferable interpretation sees the second and third lines of the verse as the words of the false prophets as well, as much as the first part of the first line. The NASB translation interpreted the last two lines as the words of Micah.

2:7 Micah reminded his audience that the false prophets were telling them that God would be patient with them, and that judgment was not His way of dealing with them. They evidently felt that it was inconsistent to say that Yahweh would allow His people to experience disaster since He had committed Himself to them (cf. Deut. 26:17-18). Theirs was a completely positive message. They failed to remind the people that God had also promised to punish them if they departed from His covenant (Deut. 28:15-68).

Micah affirmed that God would indeed bless those who do right (Deut. 28:1-14). One should not blame the continuing disgrace of the nation on his and his fellow prophets' pronouncements. After all, God provided blessing, when His people obeyed Him, as well as discipline, when they disobeyed. It was the people's obedience or disobedience, not Micah's prophecies, that was responsible for their condition. Preaching and teaching the whole counsel of God involves telling people how they fall short of God's requirements, so they can repent and enjoy His blessing, as well as affirming them for their good deeds.

"Spirit" could refer to the spirit or attitude of the Lord, or it could refer to the Holy Spirit. Either translation makes sense, but since the Holy Spirit executes the will of God in the world, He is perhaps in view here (cf. Gen. 1:2).

2:8 By failing to warn them of coming judgment for sin, the false prophets were really treating their fellow Israelites as their enemies; they were not doing them a service but a disservice. Micah proceeded to list more sins that the wealthy in Judah were practicing. They had taken the clothing of their fellow Israelites as payment for their debts, something their law forbade (cf. Exod. 22:26-27; Amos 2:8). They also did this to "unsuspecting" travelers who passed through their land, and to soldiers who had recently "returned from war."

It is possible that Micah had the false prophets in view here, and in the following verses, and not just the rich Israelites (cf. 3:5). However, "My people" seems to imply a larger group of Israelites than just the false prophets, probably the numerous wealthy oppressors among the people. They might as well have been the Assyrians or the later Babylonians in spoiling Israel.[39]

Waltke noted that in 1993, when he wrote, 35 percent of the wealth of the United States was concentrated in the hands of less than 1 percent of the people, many of whom functioned as patrons to the supposed representatives of the people.[40]

2:9 The rich Israelites also exacted payment from the dependent "women" of Israel, so much that they could no longer afford to live in their own houses (cf. Matt. 23:14; Mark 12:40). Their conduct affected the "children" as well, since these children would have to live out their lives in a foreign land as exiles (cf. Exod. 22:21; Ps. 146:9). The splendid heritage of the Israelites was the land Yahweh had given them (cf. Jer. 3:19).

2:10 Sarcastically, Micah told the rich oppressors to rise up and depart from the land (cf. Amos 4:4-5). They were wrong to be at rest in Israel when it had become an unclean place because of the people's sinfulness (cf. Deut. 12:9; Ps. 95:11). They should leave while they could because "painful destruction" was coming as punishment (cf. Lev. 18:24-28).

> "Their dirty conduct in illtreating their needy neighbors has rendered them unfit to tread Canaan's soil any longer."[41]

---

[39]Waltke, in *The Minor . . .*, p. 646.
[40]Ibid., p. 647.
[41]Allen, p. 298.

2:11 Micah bemoaned the fact that the Israelites had become so responsive to the false prophets that if one of them even spoke out (cf. v. 6)—promising alcohol galore—they would follow *him!* Any prophet who preached greater affluence and prosperity would have a receptive audience. In contrast, Micah's message of doom was unpopular. God's people would follow anyone whose prophetic fantasies blew with the wind, in contrast to being led by the Spirit (v. 7), or who lied to them by speaking falsehood.

"But we today need to deal with our sins of covetousness, selfishness, and willingness to believe 'religious lies.' We must abandon 'soft religion' that pampers our pride and makes it easy for us to sin. Why? Because 'our God is a consuming fire' (Heb. 12:29), and 'The Lord shall judge His people' (10:30). Remember, judgment begins in the house of the Lord (1 Peter 4:17)."[42]

"Unfortunately the evangelical church today is too closely associated with the business establishment, too usually motivated by serving self, not others, and too little concerned with the oppressed and needy, in spite of the clear teaching of the NT on this subject (Matt. 25:31-46; Mark 12:31; Acts 4:32-37; 1 Thess. 4:9-10; 1 John 1:6; 2:10; 3:16-18)."[43]

D. A PREDICTION OF FUTURE REGATHERING AND LEADERSHIP 2:12-13

The message of the false prophets was not completely wrong; it presented the positive aspects of God's promises to Israel—but omitted the negative. Micah's message had been mainly negative; the people needed to repent or they would experience divine chastening. Now Micah reminded his hearers that there were positive blessings ahead for Israel, but they would come later.

2:12 The Lord Himself would "assemble" the scattered "remnant" of "all" the Israelites ("Jacob" and "Israel"; cf. 1:5) following His dispersion of them in exile. The Assyrian and Babylonian exiles were only the first of several that the Jews have experienced. More recently, the Romans scattered them in A.D. 70, and since then most Jews have lived dispersed around the world, rather than in a homeland of their own. The return of many modern Jews to the State of Israel does not fulfill this prophecy, as is clear from what Micah and the other prophets said about that future regathering.

"The remnant" refers to the part of the people that would remain, following the dispersion of the majority. Yahweh would assemble them as a shepherd gathers "sheep in" a "fold," "in the midst of" a "pasture" (cf. 5:4; 7:14). This pictures the regathering of the Israelites in the Promised Land, which is similar to an island in the world. This pen "will be noisy" and crowded with people, because it will be a time and place of great rejoicing—like the city of Jerusalem was during one of Israel's annual feasts.

"That long-awaited time of blessing will come about for the nation of Israel in the Millennium. Some interpreters claim that this promise of blessing is being fulfilled now in the church, rather than in the future for Israel [i.e., covenant theologians]. However, if Micah 2:12 refers to spiritual blessing for the church, then Israel has been misled all these centuries since Abraham to think that she will inherit the land forever."[44]

2:13 As a shepherd ("the breaker") breaks through obstacles and barriers to lead his sheep into pleasant pastures, so Israel's Good Shepherd will clear the way for His sheep to return to the land (cf. Ps. 78:52-53; 80:1). They will "break out" of their former habitations, "pass through" the way ("the gate") He opens for them, and leave all parts of the world to return to the Promised Land.

Yahweh would not only function as their Shepherd but also as their (Davidic) King (cf. Isa. 6:5). He will lead them as a mighty conqueror and ruler (cf. Isa. 33:22; Zeph. 3:15; Zech. 14:9).

"If studied in isolation from the total context of the prophecy, the passage may be understood simply as a prediction of the return from the Captivity. But this is inadequate in view of the broader background of Micah's concept of the future."[45]

"Passages such as the one we have just contemplated are the strongest proof that God's heart yearns for a remnant in Israel."[46]

---

[42]Wiersbe, p. 393.
[43]Waltke, in *The Minor . . .*, p. 649.
[44]Martin, p. 1481.
[45]McComiskey, p. 415.
[46]Feinberg, p. 71.

III. THE SECOND ORACLE: THE GUILT OF ISRAEL'S LEADERS AND HER FUTURE HOPE CHS. 3—5

Micah's second oracle identifies the guilt of Israel's leaders and holds out hope for the future. Micah contrasted present conditions of injustice and corruption (ch. 3) with future blessings: Zion's exaltation, the Gentile nations' punishment, and Messiah's coming to put down idolatry (chs. 4—5).

In the first oracle, only the last two verses dealt with Israel's future blessings (2:12-13), while everything preceding exposed her sins and guilt. In this second oracle, the balance of emphasis is different. About one-third deals with present sins (ch. 3), and two-thirds with future blessings (chs. 4—5).

A. CONDEMNATION OF ISRAEL'S LEADERS CH. 3

This chapter consists of three sections. The first two point out the sinfulness of two groups of Israel's leaders, civil and religious, and the last one climaxes to assure their punishment. The leaders of God's people were not the only guilty individuals, of course, but they were particularly responsible and culpable because they affected so many other Israelites.

1. The guilt of Israel's civil leaders 3:1-4

3:1 This second oracle begins like the first and third ones, with a summons to hear the prophet's message (cf. 1:2; 6:1). The initial "And I said" ties this oracle to the preceding one and provides continuity. Micah asked rhetorically if it was not proper for Israel's rulers to "know" (practice) "justice" (fairness, equity). It was not only proper, but it was essential. Again, "Jacob" and "Israel" are a metonymy for all 12 tribes (cf. 1:5; et al.). A metonymy is a figure of speech in which something is named that is associated with or suggested by something else that is related to it.

3:2-3 Yet these rulers had stood justice on its head. They hated good and loved evil (cf. Prov. 8:13; Isa. 1:16-17; Amos 5:15). Tearing the flesh off the people, eating their flesh, and cooking their bones all represent abuse of their victims for their own selfish ends. The figure is of a hunter, and the implication is that the rulers regarded and treated the ordinary citizens as mere animals rather than as human beings. The rich stripped the poor of their money and property, and oppressed them unmercifully (cf. Zeph. 3:3)

> "Nothing short of new appetites, resulting from the new birth (Jn. 3:3-8) can remedy moral corruption."[47]

3:4 Because these rulers had turned deaf ears to the pleas of orphans and widows, they *themselves* would eventually "cry out to" Yahweh in prayer, asking Him for help. "But He" would "not answer" them (cf. Ps. 27:7-9; Prov. 21:13; Jer. 7:12-15). God hiding His face from them is an anthropomorphism that pictures God disregarding them and turning His back on them. God hears all prayers because He is omniscient, but He chooses not to respond to some of them.

2. The guilt of Israel's religious leaders 3:5-8

3:5 The Lord also had a message concerning the false prophets who were misleading His people. The false prophets gave benedictions to those who paid them, but people who did not give them anything received maledictions of doom and gloom (cf. Lam. 2:14; Jer. 6:14). Self-interest motivated these prophets, rather than the fear of the Lord (cf. 2 Tim. 4:3).

> "It was an ancient and respectable practice for a prophet to accept payment for services rendered to his clients. After all, as Jesus affirmed, 'the worker is entitled to his wages' (Luke 10:7). But with so apparently subjective a craft as prophecy there was ever a temptation. Why not make the message match the customer's pocket?"[48]

Even today, some ministers favor those who treat them well—and neglect, or worse, those who do not.

> "Few men are as pitiable as those who claim to have a call from God yet tailor their sermons to please others. Their first rule is 'Don't rock the boat'; their second is 'Give people what they want.'"[49]

---

[47]Waltke, in *Obadiah*, . . ., p. 162.
[48]Allen, p. 311.
[49]Wiersbe, p. 394.

3:6 — Because of this type of treatment, the Lord would withhold prophetic revelations from them. Rather than seeing the light, they would grope in the darkness. "The sun," a symbol of God who bestows blessings and favor, would set on their day, and they would have to live in the "darkness" of His disfavor.

3:7 — "Seers" and "diviners" would suffer embarrassment because they would not be able to come up with any word from the Lord when the people asked for it. Covering the face was a sign of mourning (cf. Lev. 13:45; Ezek. 24:17, 22).

> "Like unclean lepers they will go about with covered moustaches (*faces*, NIV; Heb., *shapim*) the very area of their abused gift (*cf.* Lv. 13:45."[50]

Seers received visions (v. 6), and diviners practiced divination (v. 6) to ascertain the future. The title "seer" is an old one describing a prophet (1 Sam. 9:9), but "diviners" sought knowledge of the future through illegitimate means, and they were outlawed in Israel (cf. Deut. 18:10). Thus, these two titles became derogatory terms for the false prophets.

> "True prophets had insight into Israel's history from a sympathy with God's kingdom perspective; false prophets could not discern the hand of God in history because they saw life through vested interests. True prophets conditioned the nation's well-being on its fidelity to the Lord, whereas false prophets arrogantly conditioned it on fidelity to themselves. True prophets seek the Lord's gain; false prophets their own."[51]

3:8 — In contrast to the false prophets who were full of greed (cf. Acts 5:3), Micah claimed to be full of spiritual "power" (not ecstasy) as a result of God's "Spirit." He virtually claimed that his prophecies were inspired. This statement also implies that Micah experienced continuous empowerment by the Holy Spirit as a prophet (cf. Ezek. 2:2; 3:12, 14). Whereas the Spirit empowered some Old Testament servants of the Lord only temporarily (cf. Judg. 3:10; 6:34; 11:29; 13:25; 14:6, 19; 15:14; 1 Sam. 16:14), He apparently empowered others, including most of the writing prophets, more or less continuously (cf. Num. 11:17; 1 Sam. 11:6; 16:13).[52]

Micah followed the will of God, and God's Spirit filled him (cf. Eph. 5:18). "Justice" marked his pronouncements (cf. vv. 1-3, 5), and "courage" his ministry (cf. vv. 4, 6-7; cf. Acts 4:13). These two words may be a *hendiadys*, meaning "courageous justice."[53] Micah did not tailor his prophecies to his honorarium, or fear what people might withhold from him if his message was negative (cf. 1 Thess. 2:2-6). His ministry was to declare the sins of the Israelites (as well as their future hope), and he fulfilled it faithfully and boldly.

> "In this eighth verse of our chapter we have a pen portrait of the preparation and equipment of the prophet of God."[54]

3. The indictment of Israel's leaders 3:9-12

3:9 — Micah proceeded to carry out his ministry (cf. v. 8). He called on all Israel's leaders to pay attention to what he had to say to them, they who despised (lit. utterly abhorred) "justice" and perverted right ways (cf. Isa. 5:20).

3:10-11 — He further described his audience of leaders as those who built Jerusalem by sacrificing the lives of innocent people. Micah used "Zion" and "Jerusalem" as synonyms to describe the same place (cf. v. 12; 4:2, 8; Ps. 149:2; Isa. 4:3; 40:9; Amos 6:1). However sometimes, as here, Zion carries theological overtones meaning not just the city but what the city represented, namely: the kingdom of God on earth.

The judges ("leaders") gave favorable verdicts to those who bribed them (cf. Exod. 23:8; Deut. 27:25), and the "priests" only taught "for a price." The "prophets" likewise only prophesied for those who would pay them (cf. Deut. 16:19). Yet they all claimed to trust in the Lord, and encouraged themselves with the false hope that since the Lord was among them, He would allow no evil to overtake them (cf. Ps. 46:4-5; Jer. 7:4).

---

[50]Waltke, in *Obadiah*, . . ., p. 163.
[51]Idem, in *The Minor* . . ., p. 663.
[52]See Wood, *The Prophets of Israel*, pp. 87-90.
[53]*The Nelson* . . ., p. 1505.
[54]Feinberg, p. 77.

3:12　　Micah announced a wholly different future for the Israelites. God would plow up (overthrow) Jerusalem like "a field," and tear down its buildings until they were only "ruins" (cf. 1:5-6). Even the temple mount, the most holy place in all Israel, would become like a hilltop in a forest: overgrown and neglected. This happened when the Romans destroyed Jerusalem in A.D. 70.[55]

Jeremiah, who lived a century later, quoted this portion of Micah's prophecy to assure the Jerusalemites of his day that the doom of their city was certain (Jer. 26:18). Jeremiah prefaced this quotation with, "Thus the LORD of hosts has said." He viewed Micah's prophecy as inspired of God (cf. 2 Tim. 3:16).

> "Micah's words, remembered for their shocking severity a hundred years later, deserve to be taken to heart by each generation of God's people. They challenge every attempt to misuse the service of God for one's own glory and profit. They are a dire warning against the complacency that can take God's love and reject his lordship. They are a passionate plea for consistency between creed and conduct. The Lord is content with nothing less."[56]

> "If Micah were ministering among us today, he would probably visit denominational offices, pastors' conferences, Bible colleges, and seminaries to warn Christian leaders that privilege brings responsibility and responsibility brings accountability."[57]

B. BLESSING FOR ISRAEL IN THE FUTURE CHS. 4—5

These chapters contain much revelation about the future kingdom of Messiah, to which almost all the writing prophets referred. This section contrasts conditions in Israel in the future with those the prophet just described in the present (ch. 3).

1. The exaltation of Zion 4:1-8

Micah mentioned several characteristics of the future kingdom of Messiah in this section. Verses 1-3 are similar to Isaiah 2:2-4. Scholars debate whether Isaiah borrowed from Micah or vice versa, whether they both drew from an older original source, or whether they each received their similar words directly from the Lord. There is no way to tell for sure.

Zion's positive future role 4:1-5

4:1　　Reference to "the last days" often points to the eschatological future in the Prophets, and it does here (e.g., Deut. 4:30; Ezek. 38:16; Dan. 2:28; 10:14; Hos. 3:5). This phrase usually refers to the Tribulation and or the Millennium. Some New Testament writers said that Christians live in the last days, namely, the days preceding Messiah's return to the earth and the establishment of His kingdom on earth (e.g., Heb. 1:2; 9:26; 1 Pet. 1:20).

"The mountain of the house of the Lord" is Mt. Zion where the temple, the Lord's house, stood in the past and will stand in the future (cf. Ezek. 40—43). In the future, Mt. Zion would become "the chief of" all "the mountains" on earth, rising above all other hills in its importance (cf. Gen. 12:3; Zech. 8:3). Some interpreters believe that this text projects a future change in the physical topography of Jerusalem (cf. Zech. 8:1-3; 14:1-11).[58] "Mountain" is also a figure for a *kingdom* in the Old Testament (e.g., Dan. 2:35, 44-45).

Here it probably has the double significance of literal Mt. Zion (Jerusalem) and the whole kingdom of Israel that Mt. Zion represents (by metonymy). "Peoples" (various ethnic groups) from all parts of the earth will migrate to it. This is quite a contrast from what Micah predicted about the immediate future of Jerusalem and the temple: its destruction and abandonment (cf. 3:12). Literal streams of water will flow from this millennial temple (Ezek. 47), but "peoples will stream to it."[59]

> "Year by year bands of pilgrims would make their way to Jerusalem to engage in festive worship, in the course of which they would receive instruction in the moral traditions of the covenant. This Israelite pilgrimage is here magnified to universal dimensions. Not merely Israel, but their pagan neighbors from all

---

[55] See Flavius Josephus, *The Wars of the Jews*, 7:2:1.
[56] Allen, p. 321.
[57] Wiersbe, p. 395.
[58] E.g., *The Nelson . . .*, p. 1506.
[59] Mays, pp. 96-97.

	around would one day wend their way to Yahweh's earthly residence, and there learn lessons which they would put into practice back in their own communities."[60]
4:2	"Many nations will" acknowledge the superiority of Israel by coming to the millennial Jerusalem to learn the Lord's ways from the Israelites. Israel will finally fulfill its function as a kingdom of priests, by mediating between God and the people of the world (cf. Exod. 19:6). Gentile people will want to obey His will, in contrast to the Jews of Micah's day who did not. Jerusalem will become the source of communication concerning the Lord and His will.

> "Imagine for a moment, if you will, Washington, London, Paris, Berlin, Moscow, and others proceeding to Jerusalem to learn the will of God! Could these things apply to our day? No, they will and must take place in the era of the personal and visible reign of the Messiah, the Lord Jesus Christ, on the throne of His father David."[61]

4:3	The Lord will serve as the global Judge, deciding disputes between many strong nations far removed from Israel geographically. The Jews of Micah's day did not want God telling them what to do and not to do, and their judges perverted justice (cf. 3:1-3, 9-11). In that future day, the Millennium, when Yahweh Messiah is reigning on earth, the nations will convert their implements of warfare into agricultural tools to promote life. They will never again engage in warfare or train for battle. Standing armies and stockpiles of armaments will be things of the past. In Joel 3:10, the reverse imagery is used in describing the Tribulation.
4:4	Peace will prevail worldwide. The figure of people sitting under their vines and fig trees describes them at rest, enjoying the fruits of their labors and God's blessings (cf. 1 Kings 4:25; Zech. 3:10). They will not fear. Perhaps because it is so hard to believe that these conditions will ever prevail on earth, Micah assured his audience that the very "mouth" of Almighty Yahweh had spoken these words. These promises came from Him, not just from the prophet. They were prophecies that were sure to come to pass, in contrast to those of the false prophets of Micah's day (cf. 3:5).

> "While the people of God who are the church have experienced peace in their hearts, it is difficult to limit this prediction only to Christians. The prophecy is national and even universal in scope and looks forward to a time when the nations will come so fully under the benign influence of God's Word that war will be no more."[62]

> "They will be safe living in the open fields. There will be no poverty, none to grasp property not his own, no war to dispossess or to terrify the even tenor of life. Though this seems beyond belief it is true, nonetheless, because God has said it."[63]

4:5	In Micah's day the Gentile nations, and many of the Israelites, followed other gods, but in the future they will all follow Yahweh. Consequently the Israelites needed to follow Him immediately. These promises encouraged Micah to make a fresh and lasting commitment for Israel to "walk" in the Lord's ways rather than in the ways of the gods of other nations (cf. 2 Pet. 3:11-12; 1 John 3:3). Walking "in the name of" Yahweh means living in dependence on His strength, which His attributes manifest.

Zion's future greatness 4:6-8

4:6	In "that day" the Lord also promised to "assemble" His people whom He had allowed the nations to abuse. This will occur when He turns the tide for Israel and begins to bless her, namely, at the beginning of the Millennium.

Some of the postexilic books of the Old Testament (i.e., Ezra, Nehemiah, Esther, Haggai, Zechariah, and Malachi) show that the tide did not really turn for Israel at the end of the Babylonian Captivity. The Jews continued to suffer under "the times of the Gentiles" (Luke 21:24), and will do so until Messiah returns to the earth (cf. Matt. 24:31). This includes suffering in the Tribulation to come (Dan. 7:25; Zech. 14:5). The Jews of Micah's day were weak morally and spiritually, and were about to go into captivity.

"The times of the Gentiles" are the times during which Gentiles control the affairs of the Jews, Israel having lost her sovereignty. These times began when Nebuchadnezzar destroyed Jerusalem and took the Jews into exile in 586 B.C., and they will end with the return of Jesus Christ to the earth at the Second Coming.

---

[60]Allen, p. 323.
[61]Feinberg, pp. 84-85.
[62]McComiskey, p. 422.
[63]Feinberg, p. 86.

4:7	The Lord promised to make these "lame outcasts" of the earth, the Jews, a surviving, "strong nation," and to "reign over them" personally from "Mt. Zion"—"forever" (cf. Ps. 146:10; Zeph. 3:19; Luke 1:33; Rev. 11:15). He will do this through the Messiah, Jesus Christ. His millennial reign will continue until the destruction of the present heavens and earth. Then it will continue on a new earth throughout eternity (2 Pet. 3:10-13).
4:8	Micah returned to contemplate again on Mt. Zion in the future (cf. v. 1). It would then become like a watchtower to "the flocks" of God's people, Israel, and a stronghold to her descendants. Israel's "former dominion" over her world—under David and Solomon—would return then, called here "the kingdom of the daughter (descendants) of Jerusalem."
	Only if we spiritualize the meaning of "the daughter of Jerusalem" to mean the church can we get away from the clear promise of Israel's restoration here (cf. Rom. 11:26). Reference to restoration of the glory of the former Davidic kingdom predicts the revival of the Davidic kingdom (cf. Isa. 9:7; Hos. 3:5; Amos 9:11).

One writer counted 11 characteristics of the future messianic kingdom in verses 1-8. These are: the global prominence of the temple (v. 1a) and its attraction of people worldwide (1b). Jerusalem will function as teacher of the world (2a) and as the disseminator of revelation (2b). The Lord will judge the world from Jerusalem (3a), and peace will be universal (3b). Israel will experience peace and security (4), spiritual sensitivity (5), regathering to the land (6), strength (7), and dominion (8).[64]

2. The might of Zion 4:9—5:1

One of the events that would occur before the realization of these great promises of blessing was Israel's exile, but the burden of this pericope is also future restoration.

4:9	Micah, speaking for the Lord, addressed the Jews in captivity. He was looking into the future, not as far as the restoration previously promised, but into the captivity. He asked, rhetorically, why the Israelites were crying out in "agony," like "a woman" in labor pains who can do nothing to relieve her misery. Did the Jews have "no king" leading them and providing counsel for them? This would be their condition during the captivity. The Babylonian Captivity is in view, primarily (v. 10).

> "The *now* has a certain width of reference, embracing both the Assyrian and Babylonian crises. Prophets saw the future not diachronically [consecutively] but synchronically [simultaneously]."[65]

4:10	The Israelites would leave Jerusalem as a woman in labor. They would have to live "in the field" (the countryside) temporarily until they arrived in "Babylon," but in Babylon "the LORD" would eventually rescue and "redeem" them. He would deliver them from captivity and return them to the land. This is one of the earliest references to the Babylonian Captivity in prophetic Scripture (cf. Isa. 39:1-7).
	This prediction of captivity in Babylon was unusual in Micah's day, because then Assyria was the great threat to the Israelites. The Babylonian deportations came a century later. In Micah's day, Babylon was part of the Assyrian Empire. Probably "Babylon" here has a double meaning: the historic Babylon of Nebuchadnezzar's day and the future Babylon, the symbol of Gentile power that has held Israel captive since Nebuchadnezzar (cf. Gen. 10:10; 11:4-9; Rev. 17—18).

> "God chose Babylon because in Micah's pagan world it functioned as the equivalent of Rome in the Middle Ages and of Mecca in Islam. The darkest land will become the place where the daylight of the new age dawns."[66]

Micah had just prophesied an eschatological redemption of Israel, and that future vision stayed with him (vv. 1-8).

4:11-12	In Micah's day, "many nations" desired to see Israel "polluted" and destroyed. However, they did "not understand" God's purposes for Israel or for themselves. They failed to see that He would gather the nations for judgment, as a farmer gathers "sheaves" of grain on a "threshing floor" in preparation for beating them out.

> "With many others we believe that the prophet has in mind a different siege from that of verse 9. From the contemplation of the Babylonian siege his mind is carried on by the Spirit of God to the last great attack of the nations of the world against Israel. The events are those of Joel 3, Zechariah 12 and 14, Ezekiel 38 and 39, and other prophetic portions of the Old Testament Scriptures."[67]

---

[64]Martin, pp. 1483-84.
[65]Waltke, in *Obadiah*, . . ., p. 178.
[66]Ibid., p. 179.
[67]Feinberg, p. 89.

4:13　In the future, Israel would be the Lord's instrument to "thresh" the nations. He will strengthen Israel to overcome ("pulverize") them, and to turn over ("devote") "their wealth" to Him, namely, to bring them into subjection to the sovereign Lord. Israel has not yet done this, so the fulfillment lies in the future, when Messiah returns to reign (cf. Zech. 14:12-15). Universal peace (in the Millennium, vv. 3-4) will follow this judgment of the nations.

> "Heathen conquerors used to set apart a portion of their spoils to the gods in their temples. Victorious Israel will devote the wealth gained from their triumphs to adorn the temple of the Lord."[68]

5:1　This verse is the last one in chapter 4 of the Hebrew Bible. It continues the theme of Zion's might.

Micah called on the Israelites to prepare for war, and reminded them that they had often engaged in war, by referring to them as a "daughter of troops." This expression means that Jerusalem was a city marked by warfare. Jerusalem's rich had been at war with the poor (2:8; 3:2-3, 9-10; 7:2-6), but now their external enemies would wage war against them. These enemies had "laid siege against" them (2 Kings 24:10; 25:1-2; Jer. 52:5; Ezek. 4:3, 7; 5:2), and would even "smite" Israel's "judge . . . on the cheek" (4:2-3)—a figure for humiliating him (cf. 1 Kings 22:24; Job 16:10; Lam. 3:30).

The judge in view appears to be King Zedekiah for the following reasons (cf. 2 Kings 25:1-7). First, according to this verse, the time of this smiting is when Israel was under siege. Second, verses 2-6 jump to a time in the distant future, whereas verse 1 describes a time in the near future (cf. "But," v. 2). Third, "judge" (Heb. *shopet*) is different from "ruler" (Heb. *moshel*) in verse 2, and probably describes a different individual. Micah may have chosen *shopet* because of its similarity to *shebet*, "rod." As noted earlier, Micah is famous for his wordplays. Waltke, however, believed the judge to be Messiah.[69]

3. The King of Zion 5:2-5a

"In chapter 5 the prophet repeated and expanded the major themes of 4:6-10, only in reverse order. This creates a chiastic structure for the central portion of the speech, which can be outlined as follows:

A　　The Lord strengthens a remnant (4:6-7a)
　B　　Dominion restored (4:7b-8)
　　C　　Zion and her king are humiliated (4:9-10)
　　　D　　Zion saved from the present crisis (4:11-13)
　　C'　Zion and her king are humiliated (5:1)
　B'　　Dominion restored (5:2-6)
A'　　The Lord strengthens a remnant (5:7-9)"[70]

This section introduces another ruler of Israel who, in contrast to Zedekiah, his *foil*, would effectively lead God's people.

"This royal oracle is obviously intended to be the central peak of the range of oracles in chs. 4 and 5. It presents a longer hope section than any other unit, and points to the fulfilment [sic] of royal promise as the key to the greatness of Jerusalem and Israel heralded in the surrounding pieces."[71]

5:2　In contrast to the humiliation of Israel's judge (king) Zedekiah, a greater "ruler" would emerge later in Israel's history (cf. 4:7). He would be Yahweh's representative (cf. John 17:4; Heb. 10:7), and would arise from the comparatively insignificant town of "Bethlehem" (House of Bread) "Ephrathah" (Fruitful). "Ephrathah" (also Ephrath) was an old name for the district in which Bethlehem of Judah lay, in contrast to other Bethlehems in the Promised Land (cf. Gen. 35:16-19; 48:7; Josh. 19:15; Ruth 4:11). Bethlehem was, of course, the hometown of David (1 Sam. 16:1, 18-19; 17:12), so the reference to it allows for the possibility of a familial connection with King David. As David had been the least notable of his brothers, so Bethlehem was the least honorable among the towns in Judah. The most insignificant place would bring forth the most significant person. This Ruler must be divine, since He had been conducting activities on Yahweh's behalf from long ago—even "eternity" past (lit. days of immeasurable time; cf. Isa. 9:6; John 1:1; Phil. 2:6; Col. 1:17; Rev. 1:8). The New Testament identifies this Ruler as the Messiah, Jesus Christ (Matt. 2:1, 3-6), though some of the Jews in Jesus' day did not know that Bethlehem was His birthplace (John 7:42).

This messianic prophecy not only gives the birthplace of Messiah, and thus assures His humanity, but it also asserts His deity. No mere human could be said to have been carrying out the will of Yahweh eternally.

---

[68]Ibid., p. 90.
[69]Waltke, in *Obadiah*, . . . , p. 181.
[70]Robert B. Chisholm Jr., *Handbook on the Prophets*, p. 422.
[71]Allen, pp. 340-41.

> "The preexistence of the Messiah is being taught here, as well as His active participation in ancient times in the purposes of God."[72]

5:3 Yahweh would give the Israelites over to chastening, until Israel had ended her painful period of suffering (like a woman in labor, 4:9), and she had brought forth a child. In view of previous revelation about Israel's continuing discipline by God until her Redeemer appeared (4:10), this seems to be a reference to the second coming of Messiah, not His first coming. This interpretation gains support from the promise in the last half of this verse. "Then the remainder" of the Redeemer's "brethren," the Jews, will experience a regathering (cf. 2:12; 4:6-7). They "will return" to the land and rejoin other Israelites.

5:4 This Redeemer "will arise and shepherd" Yahweh's flock (Israel) in Yahweh's "strength" and "majesty," in harmony with His character (cf. 2:12; 7:14; Zech. 10:3). Contrast the failure of Israel's leaders in Micah's day (3:1-11). The Redeemer will worship Yahweh as His God, another indication of His humanity. In the ancient Near East, kings frequently referred to themselves as the shepherds of their people.[73] It is the pastoral role of Israel's messianic King, leading and caring for His people, that is in view here. The Israelites "will remain" in their secure and glorious position because "*He* will be" so "great"; His greatness will guarantee His people's security (cf. Zech. 14:11). People throughout the world will acknowledge His greatness (cf. Mal. 1:11).

5:5a "This" Redeemer would also be responsible for—and the source of— the "peace" that God promised Israel that she would experience (in the Millennium; cf. 4:3-5; Eph. 2:14).

> "Whenever a prophet foretold the future, it was to awaken the people to their responsibilities in the present. Bible prophecy isn't entertainment for the curious; it's encouragement for the serious."[74]

4. The peace of Zion 5:5b-6

This pericope continues the emphasis on future peace.

5:5b Assyria was the main threat to the Israelites in Micah's day, but this prophecy predicts Israel's victory over the Assyrians. This did not happen in the history of Israel; Assyria defeated the Northern Kingdom and most of the Southern Kingdom. Thus, this prophecy must be a continuation of the vision of the distant future that God gave Micah (4:1—5:5a). When future Assyrians, representative of Israel's enemies (cf. 7:12; Isa. 11:11; Zech. 10:10), again invade the Promised Land and break down its mansions (cf. Zech. 12:9; 14:2-3), the Israelites will rise up against them. The expression "seven . . . and eight" means the same as "three . . . and four," a phrase that occurs often in Amos (cf. Amos 1:3; et al.). It implies completeness *and then some*. The Israelites will have more than enough leaders to defeat their enemy then.

5:6 Israel's leaders will then "shepherd" (lead and care for) "the land of Assyria with the sword"; they will bring it under Israelite control. The "land of Nimrod" is a synonym for Assyria (cf. Gen. 10:8-9; 1 Chron. 1:10), and "its entrances" imply the strategic areas of its territory. The Redeemer, and Yahweh behind Him, would deliver the Israelites from the Assyrian-like enemy that they would face in that day (cf. Zech. 14:3).

> "Only the most hyperliteral interpreter would suggest that a revived Assyrian Empire will reappear during the messianic era. Assyria is an archetype here. In terms that would have been very inspiring and meaningful to an eighth-century B.C. Israelite audience, Micah assured God's people that a time was coming, unlike their own day, when they would no longer be threatened by powerful, hostile nations. In other words, Micah's vision of Israel's future is contextualized so that his contemporaries might fully appreciate it. The essential point is that the new era will be one of peace and security for God's people where God's ideal king prevents the lionlike 'Assyrians' of the world from terrorizing helpless sheep."[75]

5. The vindication of Zion 5:7-9

5:7 In that day "the remnant of Jacob" will live all over the world, scattered among the other nations. "The remnant of Jacob" is one of Micah's favorite terms for the believing Jews living in the "last days" (cf. 2:12; 4:7; 5:8; 7:18), and here it refers to them after God judges the nations (vv. 5b-6). The presence of the Jews will be a divine gift to the other people of the world, as dew

---

[72]Feinberg, p. 95.
[73]*The New Bible Dictionary*, 1962 ed., s.v. "Shepherd," by R. A. Stewart.
[74]Wiersbe, p. 397.
[75]Chisholm, *Handbook on . . .*, p. 424.

and rain are to the earth (cf. Gen. 12:3). God will have sent them among the nations as He sends the dew and rain; their presence there will be due to His working, not the result of human choices or national policies ultimately.

5:8-9   The Israelites will be dominant and powerful over the other people of the world then, but in an irresistible rather than a ferocious sense (v. 7; cf. Deut. 28:13). They will have the upper hand, and their enemies will not be able to rise up against them. What a change this will be compared to the downtrodden and abused condition that the Jews have known since Nebuchadnezzar!

6. The purification of Zion 5:10-15

5:10-11   In that future eschatological day, the Lord also promised to remove the vain sources of security that had always tempted the Israelites, represented by: "horses," "chariots," "cities," and "fortifications" (cf. Deut. 17:16).

5:12-14   He would also remove the accouterments of pagan worship that had plagued His people. "Sorceries" involved seeking information from demonic sources (cf. 2 Kings 9:22; Isa. 47:9, 12; Nah. 3:4). "Fortune-tellers" cast spells by calling demonic spirits to influence other people (cf. Lev. 19:26; Deut. 18:10). "Carved images" were pagan idols (cf. Exod. 20:4). "Sacred pillars" and "Asherim" were stone and wooden symbols of the male and female Canaanite deities (cf. Deut. 16:21-22; 1 Kings 14:23; 2 Kings 17:10; 18:4; 23:14). Yahweh would free His people from these human inventions that had always oppressed them. "Cities" were infamous as places where spiritual impurity flourished (cf. 1:5), and God would "destroy" them, too. These were Israel's internal enemies whereas other nations were her external enemies.

> "Secular man more effectively manipulates life by his use of science than his ancestors did by magic, but no more than they can he secure eternal life for himself. By continuing to substitute the creation for the Creator, he individually deprives himself of eternal life and collectively hastens his eternal death."[76]

Occultism will continue into the Tribulation (Rev. 9:21), but the Lord will finally root it out in the Millennium.

5:15   Finally, the Lord promised to take "vengeance" angrily "on the nations" that "have not obeyed" His will (cf. Ps. 2:9; Rev. 12:5; 19:15). They are not responsible to keep the Mosaic Law, as Israel was, but they fail to acknowledge and worship Him as the only true God. "Vengeance" is "a legal term for the action of a royal suzerain against rebels who will not acknowledge his sovereignty."[77]

> "God is not a machine but a person, and some things need to be said and done with passion."[78]

IV. THE THIRD ORACLE: GOD'S CASE AGAINST ISRAEL AND THE ULTIMATE TRIUMPH OF HIS KINGDOM CHS. 6—7

The writer recorded a third round of messages that first announce judgment on the Israelites for their sins (ch. 6) and then promise future restoration (ch. 7). This third oracle lays out God's case against Israel and assures the ultimate triumph of His kingdom. Micah vindicated God's justice in this section. He justified God for punishing Israel and promised ultimate fulfillment of His promises in the future. All of this is certain because God is faithful. Chapter 6 explains the causes of judgment, and chapter 7 the coming glory.

A. THE LORD'S INDICTMENT AGAINST HIS PEOPLE 6:1-5

6:1-2   In this litigation speech, Micah called his audience to hear what Yahweh had told him to say. Yahweh had a "case" (lawsuit, Heb. *rib*) to bring against His people. The Lord was summoning Israel to defend herself in a courtroom setting. He addressed the "mountains," "hills," and "foundations of the earth" as the jury in this case (cf. Deut. 32:1; Isa. 1:2). The Lord called this jury, which had observed Israel's history from its beginning, to hear His indictment against the nation. Compare the function of memorial stones (Gen. 31:43-50; Josh. 22:21-28). If these jurors could speak, they would witness to the truthfulness of the Lord's claims.

6:3   The Lord called the Israelites, His people, to testify how He had caused them to be so weary of Him that they ceased to obey Him. His rhetorical questions were unanswerable; He had not given them reason to become dissatisfied with Him (cf. 1 Sam. 17:29; 20:1; 26:18; 29:8; Isa. 5:4). His questions convey a sense of pathos; rather than simply criticizing them, He asked how He had failed them. They had complained against Him very often, but He had given them no occasion to do so.

---

[76]Waltke, in *Obadiah, . . .*, p. 190.
[77]Allen, p. 360.
[78]Waltke, in *The Minor . . .*, p. 723.

6:4	Instead of wronging them, He had done nothing but good for them. Instead of letting them down, He had lifted them up. He had brought them from Egyptian bondage into the Promised Land of milk and honey. He had brought them out of "the house of slavery"—"Egypt"—which their Passover celebrated (cf. Exod. 12:3, 7, 12-13; Deut. 7:8; 9:26; 13:5; 15:15; 24:18). And He had given them capable leaders for their wilderness travels in "Moses, Aaron, and Miriam," a trio of siblings whom the Israelites respected throughout their history. Moses, the prophet, had given them their law (cf. Deut. 18:15-22). Aaron served them as their first high priest, and Miriam was a prophetess who led them in praising God for His goodness (Exod. 15:20-21).

> "The unforgettable act of God's goodness to them was His redemption of them from unbearable bondage in Egypt."[79]

6:5	Yahweh charged the Israelites to "remember" that "Balak, king of Moab," wanted God to curse His people, but "Balaam" revealed that God would never do that (Num. 22—24). God's intentions for His people had consistently been good. The events of their crossing the Jordan River and entering the Promised Land showed the same thing. "Shittim" was the Israelites' last camping place before they crossed the Jordan, and "Gilgal" was where they camped first after crossing (Josh. 3:1; 4:18-19). God had always done what was consistent with His covenant obligations to His people, never burdening them but always protecting, defending, and enabling them. He had lovingly led them from slavery, in a hostile foreign land, to settlement in their own comfortable country (cf. Josh. 24; 1 Sam. 12).

B. Micah's response for the Israelites 6:6-8

In this pericope, Micah responded to God's goodness, just reviewed, as the Israelites should have responded. His was the reasonable response in view of Yahweh's loyal love for His people (cf. Rom. 12:1-2).

6:6	The prophet, for his people, asked himself what offering he should bring to the exalted Lord in heaven that would be appropriate—in view of Yahweh's mercies to the Israelites throughout their history. Would "burnt offerings" of year-old "calves" be suitable, since they were the very best offerings and expressed the worshipper's total personal dedication to Yahweh (cf. Lev. 9:2-3; 22:27)?
6:7	Or would the Lord take pleasure if he offered Him "thousands of rams" and an extravagant amount of "oil," like Solomon and other kings had done (cf. Lev. 2:1-16; 1 Kings 3:4; 8:63; 2 Chron. 30:24; 35:7)? Neither the quality of a sacrifice nor its quantity was the important issue. Perhaps making the ultimate sacrifice and offering his "firstborn" son to atone for his sins would please the Lord. Micah, of course, did not believe that these sacrifices by themselves would please Him, but he used them as examples of ritual worship that the Israelites thought would satisfy God.
6:8	No, these sacrifices were not what the Lord wanted. He had already told the Israelites what would be "good" (beneficial) for them when they sinned (cf. Deut. 10:12, 18; 1 Sam. 12:24; Hos. 12:6). He wanted each of His people ("O man") to change his or her behavior. The address "O man" emphasizes the difference between God and man, particularly man's subordination under God. It also connects Micah's hearers, the people, not just the leaders, with the vain worshippers described in the two previous verses. Specifically, the Lord wanted His people to practice "justice"—rather than continuing to plot and practice unfairness and injustice toward one another (cf. v. 11; 2:1-2; 3:1-3). He also wanted them to "love kindness," and to practice loyal love (Heb. *hesed*), by carrying through on their commitments to help one another, as He had with them (cf. v. 12; 2:8-9; 3:10-11). And He wanted them to "walk humbly with" Him, to live their lives modestly trusting and depending on Him, rather than arrogantly relying on themselves (cf. 2:3). There is a progression in these requirements, from what is external to what is internal, and from human relations to divine relations. Doing justice toward other people demands loving kindness, which necessitates walking humbly in fellowship with God.[80]
	This verse contains one of the most succinct and powerful expressions of Yahweh's essential requirements in the Bible (cf. Matt. 22:37-39; 23:23; 1 Cor. 13:4; 2 Cor. 6:6; Col. 3:12; James 1:27; 1 Pet. 1:2; 5:5). It explains the essence of spiritual reality—in contrast to mere ritual worship. Though the Lord asked His people to worship Him in formal ways, which the Mosaic Covenant spelled out, His primary desire was for a heart attitude marked by the characteristics Micah articulated (cf. Ps. 51:16-17; Jer. 7:22-26).

---

[79]Feinberg, p. 104.
[80]Mays, p. 142. See also Waltke, in *Obadiah, . . .*, p. 197.

"No vital relationship with God is possible if one is unfaithful to the responsibilities arising out of his God-given relationships with his fellow men."[81]

C. THE LORD'S SENTENCE OF JUDGMENT 6:9-16

The Lord became specific about Israel's sins, as a prosecuting attorney, and then announced His verdict, as a judge.

1. Israel's sins 6:9-12

6:9   Micah announced that Yahweh would "call to the city" of Jerusalem; He would declare something important to the people of that town, Micah's audience of Judeans. They would be wise to "hear" Him and to "fear" Him because of *who He is* (cf. v. 1; 3:1; Prov. 1:7). The Lord summoned His people—the "tribe" of Judah—to hear Him because it was *He* who had sovereignly chosen them.

6:10   The Lord asked if there was still anyone in "the wicked house" of Judah who had "treasures (of wickedness)" (i.e., possessions) that he or she had accumulated through wicked behavior. For example, was there any seller who used a small ephah ("short measure"), a false measurement that was less than a true ephah? If so, this was evidence of not acting justly (v. 8; cf. Lev. 19:35-36; Deut. 25:13-16; Amos 8:5). The ephah was a basket that held about six gallons of dry produce. Using a slightly smaller basket robbed the buyer of some product that he was purchasing for the price of an ephah. The implication of the question is that this practice was common in Jerusalem.

6:11   Likewise, dishonest "scales" and inaccurate "weights," used in commercial transactions, were things God could not declare were all right. Ancient weights and measures were not as exact as our modern equivalents, varying as much as six percent.[82] Micah's contemporaries were stretching the limits beyond what was acceptable.

6:12   The "rich" people of Jerusalem practiced "violence" (lawlessness) in obtaining what they wanted from the weak. They lied to one another and practiced trickery and deception to obtain their desires. All of these dealings presented evidence of "injustice," which arose from a heart of unkindness toward others and lack of submission to God (v. 8).

2. Israel's punishment 6:13-16

6:13   Because of these sins, the Lord promised to make His people sick, downtrodden, and desolate.

6:14   They would continue to "eat," but their food would not bring them satisfaction (cf. Lev. 26:26). Their excessive accumulation of things would result in more garbage and waste products that they would have difficulty getting rid of. They would try to keep safe what they had bought, but they would not be able to do so, and what they did lock away would only become the property of invading soldiers eventually (cf. Lev. 26:16-17; Deut. 28:30). The Lord was restating the curses for covenant unfaithfulness listed in the Mosaic Code.

6:15   They would "sow" seed, but they would "not reap" a harvest, because the Lord would not bless the land with rain and cause the crops to grow (cf. Deut. 28:30). They would harvest and press their "olive" crops, but there would be so little product that they would not even be able to "anoint" themselves "with oil." Similarly, their "grape" harvests would be so small that they would produce too little "wine" to "drink" (cf. Deut. 28:39-40; Amos 5:11).

6:16   The people of Judah were living like their brethren in Israel who followed the instructions of the wicked Israelite kings: "Omri," "Ahab," and their descendants ("house"). This group of Israel's kings constituted some of the worst in the history of the Northern Kingdom, largely because of their idolatry and unjust oppression of the weak (cf. 1 Kings 16:21—22:40). Micah emphasized Israel's social sins more than idolatry, about which Isaiah had more to say, though there is a close relationship between both types of sin. Because of this wickedness, Yahweh promised to turn the residents of Jerusalem over to "destruction." Even though they were His people, they would become objects of horror and scorn ("reproach" or contempt, and "derision") by other nations.

"Loss of reputation is ever the final indignity which rubs salt into the wounds of suffering."[83]

D. MICAH'S LAMENT OVER HIS DECADENT SOCIETY 7:1-7

This section is an individual lament similar to many of the psalms (cf. 1:8-16).

---

[81]Robert B. Chisholm Jr., "A Theology of the Minor Prophets," in *A Biblical Theology of the Old Testament*, p. 403.
[82]*The New Bible Dictionary*, 1962 ed., s.v. "Weights and Measures," by D. J. Wiseman.
[83]Allen, p. 382.

7:1	Micah bewailed his own disappointment with Israel's situation. He compared himself to Israel's "fruit pickers" and "grape gatherers" who felt great disappointment over their poor harvests (6:15). Israel should have produced more spiritual fruit, but she did not (cf. Isa. 5:7; Mark 11:12-14, 20-22; John 15:1-8; Gal. 5:22-23).

> "He [Micah] is declaring that Israel is as lacking in good men as an orchard or vineyard after the fruit has been gathered with only gleaning left."[84]

7:2	The prophet, using hyperbole, said he could find no faithful "godly" (Heb. *hasid*, from *hesed*; cf. Hos. 4:1-2) or morally and ethically "upright" people (evidently rulers, cf. v. 3) in the land. Obviously there were some righteous, including Isaiah, but by overstating his case he made his point: there were very few. "All of them" seemed to "wait" for the opportunity to advance their own interests, even resorting to violence and "bloodshed" to do so (cf. 3:10; 6:12). They behaved like hunters waiting to snare unsuspecting birds in their nets.
7:3	They were so skillful at doing evil that it seemed they could do it equally well with either hand; they were ambidextrous when it came to sinning. Another view is that "'both hands' refer to 'the great man' and the officials next to him. . . . The king and his depraved minions flagrantly pervert the covenant . . ."[85] The leaders always had their hands out to receive "a bribe" (cf. 3:11). The powerful could expect to get the evil things they wanted because they pulled the necessary strings. These leaders formed networks of conspiracy, like a basket, to entrap the weak.
7:4	"The best" and most upright of the people were like briars and thorn hedges in that they entangled and hurt all who came in contact with them. As when the people posted a watchman to warn of coming danger, so the prophets, God's "watchmen," had announced coming "punishment" from Yahweh. Yet the people had not heeded their cries of danger. When captivity came, the result would be "confusion" among the people.
7:5-6	Micah warned the Judeans against trusting in their neighbors, friends, or even wives who reassured them that everything would be all right. They could trust no one because everyone was telling lies to gain their own advantage. They could not trust the members of their own families because everyone was after his or her own interests, and would stoop to betrayal to obtain them (cf. Matt. 10:35-36; Mark 13:12; Luke 12:53).

> "Man is so made that he finds security in a small group among whom he is accepted and receives support. At the heart of the concentric circles of people known to him there must ever be a stable core of friends, and usually family, if his psychological equilibrium is to be maintained. The prophet gradually penetrates to the center of these inner circles of familiarity: friend—best friend—wife. A man is now forced to go against his nature, retiring within himself and keeping his own counsel, if he is not to face betrayal."[86]

7:7	In contrast to the Israelites of his day, the prophet determined to "watch expectantly" and "wait" patiently "for the LORD" to act as He had promised (cf. 1 Sam. 4:13; Tit. 2:13). He would bring salvation to His people ultimately (cf. Isa. 59:20). This commitment gave him confidence that the Lord would "hear" his prayers.

The reason Micah did not succumb to utter pessimism—in view of the terrible conditions in his day—is that he determined to trust God. The same faith is much needed in our dark day (cf. Phil. 2:15-16).

E. MICAH'S CONFIDENCE IN THE LORD 7:8-20

This final section of the book is also in the form of a lament (cf. vv. 1-7). While Micah spoke as an individual, he spoke for the faithful remnant of Israelites in his day. His sentiments would have been theirs. Thus the lament is communal, but it gives way to glorious praise. Daniel, Ezra, Nehemiah, and many of the psalmists likewise prayed as spokesmen for the faithful as well as for themselves (cf. Dan. 9; Ezra 9; Neh. 9; Lam. 1:10-16, 18-22).

> "Micah concludes his book with a liturgical hymn, consisting of expressions of confidence, petition, and praise."[87]

---

[84]Feinberg, p. 113.
[85]Waltke, in *Obadiah, . . .*, p. 200.
[86]Allen, p. 388.
[87]Waltke, in *The Minor . . .*, p. 754. See Chisholm, *Handbook on . . .*, p. 426, for a structural analysis of this section.

1. Advice to the ungodly 7:8-13

7:8   When Micah's enemies saw him experience some discouraging situation, they rejoiced. He told them not to rejoice, because though he fell, God would raise him up. Though he appeared to be groping "in" the "darkness" (cf. Lam. 3:6), "the LORD" would be "a light" to him and illuminate the right path for him to take.

7:9   Micah identified with his people by confessing his guilt (cf. Dan. 9:5, 8, 11, 15). Though he had not personally committed the sins that he criticized his fellow Israelites of practicing, as a part of his nation he was with them in their guilt. He would have to bear the consequences of divine discipline as they did. Nevertheless, the Divine Advocate, whom we have seen indicting the Israelites in this book, would come to the prophet's defense. Micah would not suffer the same amount of punishment as the guilty in the nation. He would eventually come out of his dark circumstances into "the light" of God's presence, and he would behold God's "righteousness." That is, he would see God demonstrate His justice and faithfulness to His promises. God will vindicate the faithful.

7:10   Then Micah's enemies would see God's rightness and feel ashamed for accusing Yahweh of abandoning His watchman. Micah would also see these enemies humiliated and brought low, trodden down like mud in the street (cf. Josh. 10:24; Ps. 110:1).

7:11   "That day," when the Israelite critics of Micah and his prophecies would see they were wrong, would be when the "walls" around their vineyards would be rebuilt, and the boundaries of Judah "extended" (cf. Ezek. 47:13-23; Obad. 19-20). The word used here to describe walls, *gader*, elsewhere refers to the walls around vineyards (cf. Num. 22:24; Isa. 5:5), not walls around a city. In the Millennium, Jerusalem will have no walls (Zech. 2:4-5). This refers to the distant future when God will re-gather and reestablish Israel in her land, in the Millennium, not following the Babylonian Captivity. This is clear from what follows.

7:12   Israel's former enemies from all over the world, represented by "Assyria" and the "Euphrates" River on the northwest, and "Egypt" and its "cities" on the southeast, would "come to" the Israelites in their land (cf. Isa. 19:23-25; Amos 9:11-15). They would come from everywhere between the seas and the mountains, a synecdoche for everywhere on earth (cf. Ps. 72:8; Zech. 9:10). A synecdoche is a figure of speech that uses a part of something to represent the whole.

7:13   Before that, however, "the earth will become desolate" when God judges its "inhabitants" for their sinful "deeds" (cf. Isa. 24:1; 34—35). This will happen in the Tribulation and in the judgment of the nations that immediately follows the Lord's Second Coming (cf. Matt. 25:32-33, 46).

2. Prayer for deliverance 7:14-17

7:14   Micah prayed that the Lord would again take an active role as the Shepherd of His people Israel. Shepherding with His rod ("scepter," Heb. *shebet*) implies kingly leadership. This is a request for the promised descendant of David to appear and lead Israel. Presently the Israelites, the flock that Yahweh possessed uniquely (cf. Deut. 4:20), were isolated even though they inhabited the land that God had given them. Micah prayed that they might enjoy God's blessings, as when their flocks fed on the lush, grassy hills of "Bashan" and "Gilead" earlier in their history.

7:15   The Lord replied to Micah's prayer. He promised that He would "show" Israel "miracles" again, as when He sent the plagues on Egypt just before the Exodus (cf. Exod. 3:20; 15:11). The Jews' liberation from Gentile domination and return to their own land at the beginning of the Millennium will be another miraculous Exodus (cf. Hos. 9:3; 11:5, 11; 12:9).

7:16   The Gentile "nations" will observe this miracle, and feel "ashamed," because they will realize that "all their might" is inferior to God's power demonstrated in bringing Israel home (cf. v. 7; 3:7). They will not want to speak out against Yahweh or Israel—because of reverence and awe—or hear any more about what God is doing for His people, apparently because His power will be so overwhelming.

7:17   They will become as servile and humble as snakes. Licking the dust is a figure describing total defeat (cf. Gen. 3:14; Ps. 72:9; Isa. 49:23; 65:25). They will surrender to Yahweh, Israel's God, and "come . . . before" Him in fear and "dread" of what He will do to them (cf. Phil. 2:10).

3. Praise for forgiveness 7:18-20

Micah had prayed, he received the Lord's answer, and this answer moved him to worship (cf. Exod. 34:6-7). Modern orthodox Jews read verses 18-20 in their synagogues on the Day of Atonement following the reading of Jonah.

> "Few passages in Scripture contain so much 'distilled theology' as Micah 7:18-20."[88]

---

[88]Wiersbe, p. 402.

7:18	The prophet praised Yahweh as a God who is *unique* in that He pardons the rebellious sins of the surviving "remnant of His people." "Who is a God like You?" is another rhetorical question (cf. Exod. 15:11; Ps. 35:10; 71:19; 77:13; 89:6; 113:5), and it may be a play on Micah's name, which means, "Who is like Yahweh?" No one is just like Him! Pardoning such grave sins is contrary to human behavior, but Yahweh would "not retain His anger" against the Israelites "forever" (cf. Ps. 103:9). He will "pardon" them (cf. 1:5; 3:8; 6:7; Exod. 34:6-7) because He delights to be faithful to His "love" (Heb. *hesed*) for them (cf. v. 20).

"Here we have a description of God's grace unsurpassed in Scripture."[89]

7:19	Yahweh would "again have compassion" (tender, heartfelt concern, Heb. *rehem*) on the Israelites, as He had done so often in their history (cf. Ps. 102:13; 103:4, 13; 116:5; 119:156; Hos. 14:4; Zech. 10:6). He would subdue their "iniquities"—as though they were insects that He stepped on and obliterated. He would do away with "their sins," as surely as someone gets rid of something permanently by throwing it "into the . . . sea" (cf. Ps. 103:12). The use of three words for sin in verses 18 and 19 (iniquity, rebellious acts, and sins) gives added assurance of forgiveness. God will forgive all types of Israel's sins.

7:20	The basis of Micah's confidence was that God would be faithful to His promises "to Jacob," and loyal to His commitment (Heb. *hesed*) to bless "Abraham" (cf. Gen. 12:2-3; 13:15; 15:18-21; 17:7-8, 13, 19, 21; 28:13-14; 35:10-12; 48:4; et al.). These were ancient promises to their "forefathers," that God had sealed with His oath, vowing to fulfill them (e.g., Gen. 22:16-18; cf. Rom. 4:13; 2 Cor. 6:16; Heb. 4:1-10; 8:10; 1 Pet. 2:9; Rev. 1:6; 5:10; 21:3, 7).

"Like a day that begins with a dark, foreboding sky but ends in golden sunlight, this chapter begins in an atmosphere of gloom and ends in one of the greatest statements of hope in all the OT."[90]

---

[89]Feinberg, p. 121.
[90]McComiskey, p. 440.

Bibliography

Aharoni, Y. *The Land of the Bible*. Philadelphia: Westminster Press, 1967.

Allen, Leslie C. *The Books of Joel, Obadiah, Jonah and Micah*. The New International Commentary on the Old Testament series. Grand Rapids: Wm. B. Eerdmans Publishing Co., 1976.

Bright, John. *A History of Israel*. Philadelphia: Westminster Press, 1959.

Carlson, E. Leslie. "Micah." In *The Wycliffe Bible Commentary*, pp. 851-861. Edited by Charles F. Pfeiffer and Everett F. Harrison. Chicago: Moody Press, 1962.

Chisholm, Robert B., Jr. *Handbook on the Prophets*. Grand Rapids: Baker Book House, 2002.

_____. "A Theology of the Minor Prophets." In *A Biblical Theology of the Old Testament*, pp. 397-433. Edited by Roy B. Zuck. Chicago: Moody Press, 1991.

Dyer, Charles H., and Eugene H. Merrill. *The Old Testament Explorer*. Nashville: Word Publishing, 2001. Reissued as *Nelson's Old Testament Survey*. Nashville: Thomas Nelson Publishers, 2001.

Feinberg, Charles Lee. *Jonah, Micah, and Nahum*. The Major Messages of the Minor Prophets series. New York: American Board of Missions to the Jews, 1951.

Jagersma, Henk, *A History of Israel in the Old Testament Period*. Translated by John Bowden. Philadelphia: Fortress Press, 1983.

Josephus, Flavius. *The Works of Flavius Josephus*. Translated by William Whiston. London: T. Nelson and Sons, 1866; reprint ed. Peabody, Mass.: Hendrickson Publishers, 1988.

Kaiser, Walter C., Jr. *Toward an Old Testament Theology*. Grand Rapids: Zondervan Publishing House, 1978.

Keil, C. F. *The Twelve Minor Prophets*. 2 vols. Translated by James Martin. Biblical Commentary on the Old Testament. Reprint ed. Grand Rapids: Wm. B. Eerdmans Publishing Co., 1949.

Longman, Tremper, III and Raymond B. Dillard. *An Introduction to the Old Testament*. 2nd ed. Grand Rapids: Zondervan, 2006.

Martin, John A. "Micah." In *The Bible Knowledge Commentary: Old Testament*, pp. 1475-92. Edited by John F. Walvoord and Roy B. Zuck. Wheaton: Scripture Press Publications, Victor Books, 1985.

Mays, J. *Micah: A Commentary*. Old Testament Library series. Philadelphia: Westminster Press, 1976.

McComiskey, Thomas Edward. "Micah." In *Daniel-Minor Prophets*. Vol. 7 of *The Expositor's Bible Commentary*. 12 vols. Edited by Frank E. Gaebelein and Richard P. Polcyn. Grand Rapids: Zondervan Publishing House, 1985.

Morgan, G. Campbell. *Living Messages of the Books of the Bible*. 2 vols. New York: Fleming H. Revell Co., 1912.

The Nelson Study Bible. Edited by Earl D. Radmacher. Nashville: Thomas Nelson Publishers, 1997.

The New Bible Dictionary, 1962. S.v. "Shepherd," by R. A. Stewart.

_____. S.v. "Weights and Measures," by D. J. Wiseman.

The Old Testament, a new translation by James Moffatt. London: Hodder and Stoughton, Ltd., 1924.

Robinson, George L. *The Twelve Minor Prophets*. Reprint ed. Grand Rapids: Baker Book House, 1974.

Thomas, D. W., ed. *Documents from Old Testament Times*. New York: Harper & Row, 1958.

Waltke, Bruce K. "Micah." In *The Minor Prophets: An Exegetical and Expositional Commentary*, 2:591-764. 3 vols. Edited by Thomas Edward McComiskey. Grand Rapids: Baker Books, 1992, 1993, and 1998.

_____. "Micah." In *Obadiah, Jonah, Micah: An Introduction and Commentery*. Tyndale Old Testament Commenteries series. Leicester, Eng., and Downers Grove, Ill.: Inter-Varsity Press, 1988.

Waltke, Bruce K., with Charles Yu. *An Old Testament Theology: an exegetical, canonical, and thematic approach.* Grand Rapids: Zondervan, 2007.

Wiersbe, Warren W. "Micah." In *The Bible Exposition Commentary/Prophets*, pp. 389-403. Colorado Springs, Colo.: Cook Communications Ministries; and Eastbourne, England: Kingsway Communications Ltd., 2002.

Wolff, Hans W. *Micah: A Commentary.* Translated by Gary Stansell. Continental Commentaries series. Minneapolis: Augsburg/Fortress, 1990.

Wood, Leon J. *The Prophets of Israel.* Grand Rapids: Baker Book House, 1979.

Constable's Notes
on Nahum

Introduction

Title and Writer
The title of the book comes from the name of its writer.

We know nothing about Nahum ("compassion," "consolation," or "comfort") other than what we read in this book. His name proved significant since he brought comfort and consolation to the Judeans with his prophecies. He was "the Elkoshite" (1:1), so he evidently came from a town named Elkosh, but the location of such a town has yet to be discovered. Scholars have suggested that it stood near Nineveh, in Galilee, near Capernaum (City of Nahum?), east of the Jordan River, or somewhere in Judah. Since he was a Jewish prophet and evidently lived after the fall of Samaria in 722 B.C., a location in Judah seems most likely to me. Perhaps the Assyrians had carried his family away to Mesopotamia when they conquered the kingdom of Israel and large parts of Judah, and Nahum somehow managed to return to Judah later.[1] This may explain Nahum's familiarity with things Assyrian.

Unity
Some scholars have tried to prove that someone other than Nahum wrote sections of the book (1:1; 1:1—2:3; 1:2-10; 2:4—3:19), but their arguments are largely speculative. Jewish and Christian authorities have long held that Nahum was responsible for the whole work.

> "Every one of the forty-seven verses of this short prophecy has been attacked by higher critics as being spurious. Contemporary critical scholarship tends to hold that at least one-third of the material was written by someone other than Nahum."[2]

The canonicity of Nahum has never been seriously challenged, and the Hebrew text has been well preserved.

Date
Nahum mentioned the fall of the Egyptian city of Thebes (3:8), so we know he wrote after that event, which took place in 663 B.C. The Assyrian king Ashurbanipal conquered it. The prophet predicted the fall of the Assyrian capital, Nineveh, which happened in 612 B.C., so he must have written this book between 663 and 612 B.C. (Josephus wrote that Nineveh fell 115 years after Nahum's preaching.[3] But that seems incorrect.) Evidently, Nineveh fell to the Medes.[4]

> "There is some ambiguity in the Babylonian and later descriptions of the fall of Nineveh (Zawadzki 1988), but it appears to have been the Medes who actually destroyed the city. Indeed, the Babylonians were very careful in their records to distance themselves from the general looting of the city and especially the temples of this great city. However, it is clear that the Medes were either uninterested or unable to keep the city for a permanent possession, and it fell to their allies, the Babylonians, to possess it."[5]

There is some evidence that points to Nahum writing shortly after Thebes fell. First, Nahum's description of Nineveh (1:12; 3:1, 4, 16) does not fit the city as it existed between 626 and 612 B.C. when Ashurbanipal's sons, Ashur-etil-ilani (626-623 B.C.) and Sin-shar-ishkun (623-612 B.C.), ruled over it. Second, the Southern Kingdom of Judah was under the yoke of Assyria when Nahum wrote (1:13, 15; 2:1, 3), a condition that marked the reign of Manasseh (697-642 B.C.) more than that of Josiah (640-609 B.C.). Third, if Nahum wrote after 654 B.C., his rhetorical question in 3:8 would have had little or no force since Thebes rose to power again in that year.[6] Thus a date of composition between 663 and 654 B.C. seems most likely. This means he probably ministered during the reign of wicked King Manasseh of Judah (697-642 B.C.). Leon Wood dated Nahum a bit later, namely, about 630 B.C., during the reign of good King Josiah (640-609 B.C.).[7]

---

[1]Richard D. Patterson, *Nahum, Habakkuk, Zephaniah*, pp. 7-8.
[2]Ibid., p. 11.
[3]Flavius Josephus, *Antiquities of the Jews*, 9:11:3.
[4]See any good Bible dictionary or encyclopedia for the history of Nineveh.
[5]Tremper Longman III and Raymond B. Dillard, *An Introduction to the Old Testament*, p. 459. Their reference is to S. Zawadzki, *The Fall of Assyria and Median-Babylonian Relations in Light of the Nabopolassar Chronicle*.
[6]Walter A. Maier, *The Book of Nahum: A Commentary*, pp. 30, 34-37.
[7]Leon Wood, *The Prophets of Israel*, p. 316.

Nahum and Zephaniah both prophesied after Isaiah and Micah finished prophesying. Isaiah prophesied between about 740-680 B.C. Nahum prophesied from about 660-650 B.C. Zephaniah probably prophesied between 640 and 612 B.C. Jonah, Hosea (both from Israel), and Amos, Isaiah, and Micah (from Judah) were all eighth-century B.C. prophets. Nahum, Zephaniah, Habakkuk, and Jeremiah were all seventh-century B.C. prophets. The dating of Obadiah and Joel is debatable.

Place of Composition

No one knows for sure where Nahum was when he wrote the book, and our lack of knowledge of his hometown complicates the task of discovering the place of composition. However, traditionally Nahum lived and ministered in Judah, so most conservative scholars assume he wrote somewhere in that kingdom.

Audience and Purpose

Nahum was a Jewish prophet and wrote primarily for the Jewish people. While the main subject of his prophesying was Nineveh, his message was for the Jews. Similarly, Jonah wrote about Nineveh and Obadiah wrote only of Edom, but they also wrote for the Jews. Both Nahum and Obadiah probably served as preaching prophets in Judah, as well as writing prophets, as Jonah did in Israel.

> "Nahum's prophecy was the complement to Jonah, for whereas Jonah celebrated God's mercy, Nahum marked the relentless march of the judgment of God against all sinners world-wide."[8]

This book claims to be an oracle (1:1, an uplifting and or threatening prophecy). While most of the book threatens Nineveh with destruction, there are also words of comfort for the people of Judah (1:12, 15; 2:2). Nahum revealed that Yahweh would destroy Nineveh as punishment for the Assyrians' cruelty to many nations, including the Northern Kingdom of Israel, in 722 B.C., and Judah. This was a comforting message for the remaining Jews who were presently living under Assyria's shadow in Judah. Assyria had destroyed many Judean cities and had even besieged Jerusalem, unsuccessfully, in 701 B.C. The purpose of Nahum's book, then, was to announce Nineveh's fall and thereby comfort the Judean Jews with the assurance that their God was indeed sovereign and just.

> "God is a just governor of the nations who will punish wicked Nineveh and restore His own people."[9]

> "Even though God has chosen Assyria to act as his instrument of punishment against the rebellious and recalcitrant Israel (Is. 7:17; 10:5-6), he holds that nation corporately responsible for the excesses and atrocities committed in fulfilling this role (Is. 10:7-19; cf. Zp. 2:14-15)."[10]

Literary Form

Nahum contains a prophecy of the future destruction of a city that did fall. Critics of the Bible who do not believe that the prophets could possibly predict the future have tried to explain what Nahum wrote as a description of the fall of Nineveh after the fact. Some of them consider the book as a piece of liturgy written for the Israelites' annual "enthronement festival" in Jerusalem. This festival supposedly celebrated Yahweh's enthronement over His people, though there is no biblical evidence that it ever occurred. Other ancient Near Eastern nations conducted similar enthronement festivals. The Book of Nahum was, according to this view, a collection of writings of various literary types that an editor compiled to magnify Yahweh's greatness by reflecting on Nineveh's destruction.

While conservatives reject this low view of prophecy, it is obvious that the book does consist of several different types of literature, as do most of the other prophetical books. We believe that God guided Nahum to express the messages He gave him in a variety of ways using several different forms of expression.

> "Nahum, unlike many prophecies that are based on the structure of an anthology (such as Micah), has a well-delineated literary form."[11]

> "The main body of the prophecy, which is introduced with the words 'This is what the LORD says,' exhibits a chiastic structure:
>
> A   Assyrian king taunted/Judah urged to celebrate (1:2-15)
>   B   Dramatic call to alarm (2:1-10)
>   C   Taunt (2:11-12)

---

[8] Walter C. Kaiser Jr., *Toward an Old Testament Theology*, p. 221.
[9] Patterson, p. 53. See also Bruce K. Waltke, *An Old Testament Theology*, p. 840.
[10] David W. Baker, *Nahum, Habakkuk and Zephaniah*, p. 23.
[11] Tremper Longman III, "Nahum," in *The Minor Prophets*, p. 769.

```
            D       Announcement of judgment (2:13)
                E       Woe oracle (3:1-4)
            D'      Announcement of judgment (3:5-7))
        C'      Taunt (3:8-13)
    B'      Dramatic call to alarm (3:14-17)
A'      Assyrian king taunted as others celebrate (3:18-19)"[12]
```

Nahum was a poet. He has been called "the poet laureate among the Minor Prophets."[13] He wrote in a very vivid and powerful style.

"Nahum was a great poet. His word pictures are superb, his rhetorical skill is beyond praise."[14]

"None of the minor prophets . . . seem to equal Nahum in boldness, ardour and sublimity. His prophecy . . . forms a regular and perfect poem: the exordium is not merely magnificent, it is truly majestic; the preparation for the destruction of Nineveh, and the description of its downfall and desolation, are expressed in the most vivid colours, and are bold and luminous in the highest degree."[15]

"Nahum's poetry is fine. Of all the prophets he is the one who in dignity and force approaches most nearly to Isaiah. His descriptions are singularly picturesque and vivid . . .: his imagery is effective and striking . . .; the thought is always expressed compactly; the parallelism is regular."[16]

"His reverence for the almighty, trust in divine justice and goodness, condemnation of national iniquity, positive conviction that God will keep His word—these are qualities of true greatness. Add to that Nahum's mighty intellect, his patriotism and courage, his rare, almost unequaled, gift of vivid presentation, and he indeed looms as one of those outstanding figures in human history who have appeared only at rare intervals."[17]

The "Minor Prophets" were minor only in word count, compared with the longer "Major Prophets," not in their literary quality or theological relevance.

Outline

I.   Heading 1:1
II. Nineveh's destruction declared 1:2-14

    A.   The anger and goodness of Yahweh 1:2-8
    B.   Yahweh's plans for Nineveh and Judah 1:9-14

        1.   The consumption of Nineveh 1:9-11
        2.   The liberation of Judah 1:12-13
        3.   The termination of Nineveh 1:14

III. Nineveh's destruction described 1:15—3:19

    A.   The sovereign justice of Yahweh 1:15—2:2
    B.   Four descriptions of Nineveh's fall 2:3—3:19

        1.   The first description of Nineveh's fall 2:3-7
        2.   The second description of Nineveh's fall 2:8-13
        3.   The third description of Nineveh's fall 3:1-7
        4.   The fourth description of Nineveh's fall 3:8-19

---

[12]Robert B. Chisholm Jr., *Handbook on the Prophets*, p. 428. See also Gordon H. Johnston, "A Rhetorical Analysis of the Book of Nahum," (Ph.D. dissertation, Dallas Theological Seminary, 1992) for a thorough analysis of the book's structure.
[13]Patterson, p. 10.
[14]J. A. Bewer, *The Literature of the Old Testament*, p. 147.
[15]Robert Lowth, *Lectures on the Sacred Poetry of the Hebrews*, pp. 239-40.
[16]S. R. Driver, *An Introduction to the Literature of the Bible*, p. 336.
[17]Maier, p. 20. See also J. S. Cochrane, "Literary Features of Nahum" (Th.M. thesis, Dallas Theological Seminary, 1954), pp. 6-7.

Message

The story that Nahum told is a story of the utter and irrevocable destruction of a great city and a great people. Nahum told the story as prophecy, but what he predicted is now history. Nahum lived when Assyria was threatening Judah's existence. The prophet predicted that God would destroy the proud and cruel capital of the Assyrian Empire: Nineveh. So thorough was Nineveh's destruction that for centuries travelers passed over its ruins without knowing that this mighty and terrible city lay buried beneath their feet. Only in fairly modern times (1842, to be exact) have archaeologists laid bare its ruins.[18] Such was the literal and complete fulfillment of Nahum's prophecy.

The message of Nahum is quite compact. It is clear in statement, logical in argument, and definite in its declarations. In form, it is a vision, a vision of Yahweh, of Yahweh's anger, and of Yahweh acting in anger. Its permanent value is its unique picture of the wrath of God. The prophet begins the revelation of his vision by painting an angry Yahweh (1:2).[19] This is not an aspect of God's character that is popular in our day, but it is one that is prominent throughout the Bible.

Notice first the prophet's vision of God. All the prophets were impressed with a characteristic of God that shaped their prophecies. Isaiah saw God's holiness. Jeremiah saw God's judgment. Ezekiel saw God's glory. Micah saw God's leadership. And Nahum saw God's wrath.

Nahum used four words to describe God's anger that we could translate "furious," "avenging," "wrathful," and "angry." They all occur in a very brief passage, 1:2-3, heightening the solemnity of Yahweh's anger. The Hebrew word that I have translated "furious" presupposes love and expresses an emotional, subjective action. God's *jealousy* is not self-centered or petty, but instead it expresses His zealous concern for the welfare of those He loves. "Avenging," which occurs three times in these two verses, does not mean taking revenge, but rather the executing of retribution: paying back to someone what that one deserves. It expresses a volitional action, an objective rather than a subjective response.

"Wrathful" suggests a change in God's attitude. The word comes from a root meaning to cross over, and it was used to describe the Israelites crossing the Jordan River. This word suggests the idea that God crossed over from His typical attitudes of tenderness and compassion to an unusual attitude, for Him, of judgment. "Angry" has the idea of being flushed with anger, red in the face, if you will. It occurs in the dual form in Hebrew, suggesting the two nostrils that flare when one gets angry. So Nahum used four words for anger, and one of them three times, for a total of six expressions of God's anger, in these two verses alone.

Four Hebrew words that describe anger occur in this short description of Yahweh in 1:2-3. The total impression Nahum wanted to create was that of a very, very angry God. This was not, however, just a piece of rhetoric in which an extremely agitated prophet projected onto God feelings that were in his own heart. It is a careful and remarkable description of the character of God.

As the revelation unfolds, we move from a threefold description of the anger of God to an exposition of that threefold description. The name "Yahweh" appears three times in verse 2, and then it appears three more times in the next six verses. In verse 2, we have the proclamation describing what God is like. Then, in verses 3-8, we have the explanation. Consider first Nahum's proclamation concerning the character of God.

Yahweh is jealous and avenging (1:2a). The order of these aspects of God's anger indicates that His passion precedes His action. The second proclamation is that He is avenging and wrathful (1:2b). Here the order is reversed; God's action grows out of His passion. The third proclamation, that Yahweh takes vengeance on His adversaries and reserves wrath for His enemies (1:2c), reveals that God directs His passion and action discriminately, not carelessly or capriciously.

This is a very important revelation of God's anger, because it is the reverse of what usually characterizes human anger. People are often controlled by their anger, but God controls His anger. God's passion leads to action, but only against those whom God chooses to make the objects of His wrath.

The explanation of God's anger follows in verses 3-8. Verse 3a explains that Yahweh is a jealous and avenging God (cf. v. 2a). His passion precedes His action. "He is slow to anger and great in power, and will by no means leave the guilty unpunished." Verses 3b-6 explain that Yahweh is avenging and wrathful (cf. v. 2b). His action grows out of His passion. Verses 7-8 explain that Yahweh takes vengeance on His adversaries and reserves wrath for His enemies (cf. v. 2c). His anger is discriminating.

Often human anger is out of control. Anyone near it gets hurt, not just the object of one's anger. Human anger often results in other mistakes that the angry person makes: the fallout of his anger. That is never true of God's anger. He is slow to anger; He never "explodes" or "looses His temper." His anger is measured; He is never out of control. His anger is focused on the particular object or objects of His wrath. Innocent people never suffer because of His anger. He never makes mistakes because He is angry. He is always in full control of Himself and of everything that happens when He is angry.

---

[18]See Jack Finegan, *Light From the Ancient Past*, p. 211.
[19]See the Appendix "The Impassibility of God" at the end of these notes for a discussion of if and how human actions affect God.

We turn now from Nahum's vision of the anger of God to his vision of the vengeance of God. Nahum revealed: *why* God acts in vengeance—the *reason* for divine judgment; *when* God acts in vengeance—the *time* of divine judgment; and *how* God acts in vengeance—the *method* of divine judgment.

Why does God act in judgment? According to Nahum, there is a God-ward reason and a man-ward reason. In 1:11 we have the sin against God: pride. This was the fundamental sin of the Assyrians against God. We see it clearly in Sennacherib's invasion of Jerusalem (cf. Isa. 36). Pride, expressed in rebellion against God's sovereign control over His creation, was one of Nineveh's greatest sins. The other sin, for which God judges, is man-ward: cruelty. We see this in 3:1-4. The Assyrians were notorious for their oppression and cruelty toward their fellow men.[20] These were the two great sins of Assyria—Godward and manward—and they are the primary reason God gets angry and acts in judgment. It is interesting that these two sins almost always go together, as they did in Assyria. Where there is pride against God, there is usually cruelty toward other people. Jesus taught that the two greatest commandments were to love God wholeheartedly and to love our neighbors as ourselves (Matt. 22:37-39). When people do this, they are not proud or cruel. Why does God judge? He judges to punish pride and to protect people.

The second question about the judgment of God that Nahum answered was: *When* does God judge? What is the timing by which God judges? Again, we can look at the answer to this question from two viewpoints: God's and man's. God judges after He exercises long patience. A hundred years earlier, God had sent Jonah with a message of repentance to Nineveh. The people had repented, and God had relented. But then the people repented of their repentance. They returned to their former pride and cruelty. Now, after long waiting, God was about to avenge. From the human viewpoint, God judges when sin has become exceedingly sinful. He waits for people to repent, but if they do not, He steps in to judge (3:18-19; cf. Gen. 15:16; 1 Cor. 11:31; 2 Pet. 3:9).

How does God act in vengeance? The answer reveals God's method. He used natural and supernatural forces to destroy Nineveh. The Babylonians invaded the city through a breach in the wall that the flooding Tigris River opened up. God supernaturally controlled weather conditions so that the walls gave way. He then led human soldiers to storm through that opening and take the city.

We turn now to the abiding message of this book, for our own age and for every age.

One aspect of the message of Nahum is what it says about God. Nahum teaches the reader that to believe in God's love is to be sure of His wrath. If God is never angry, He does not really love. His anger grows out of His love. Can you look at sin, pride, oppression, and cruelty and not be moved? Then you do not love. Do you not care that Christians are being persecuted for their faith and are being killed daily in over 50 countries in the world? Do you not care that pride is keeping people from acknowledging their need for God in your country? Do you not care that women are being abused and children neglected by fathers who are so selfish that they think only of their own pleasures? If not, you are incapable of love. If God cannot burn with hatred, He is a God incapable of love. To believe in His love is to be sure of His wrath.

Henry Ward Beecher, the famous preacher said, "A person who doesn't know how to be angry doesn't know how to be good." Thomas Fuller wrote, "Anger is one of the sinews of the soul. He who lacks it has a maimed mind."[21]

A corollary to this revelation is another truth about God that Nahum reveals: God's love always interprets His wrath. Whenever we observe some instance of God's vengeance, we must remember that it springs from His love. We cannot always make the connection, and we may not be able to explain the connection to ourselves and others, but there is a connection. God's vengeance proves the depth of His love. Parents who love their children discipline them. Likewise, God disciplines because He loves.

The message of this book also concerns people. One sin against which God acts in vengeance is pride, which says: "I don't need Him. I am sufficient in myself. I am greater than others." If people persist in this sin throughout their lives and refuse to bow the knee to God, they will experience His eternal wrath. If believers lift themselves up in pride, God will bring them down in His hot anger.

Another sin that God judges is cruelty toward our fellowman. Fascination with violence reflects both pride and cruelty. Pride and cruelty are even worse, when, after people have turned from these sins in repentance, and then *repented of their repentance*, they return to practice them again with greater zeal than ever. These were the great sins of the ancient Assyrians, and they are the sins of modern man.

There is a message of hope in Nahum as well. It is the revelation that God's wrath is discriminating. God is absolutely just. He will not punish the innocent with the guilty (cf. Gen. 18:23-32). He will not lose control when He judges. Nahum 1:7 reminds us that "Yahweh is good, a stronghold in the day of trouble, and He knows those who take refuge in Him." The Book of Nahum was an encouragement to the Israelites, and God intended it to encourage all of His people.

I would express the message of the book this way: God's discriminating anger and vengeance against pride and cruelty arise from His great love for people.[22]

---

[20]See Erika Bleiblreu, "Grisly Assyrian Record of Torture and Death," *Biblical Archaeology Review* 17:1 (January/February 1991):52-61, 75.
[21]Cited by Warren W. Wiersbe, "Nahum," in *The Bible Exposition Commentary/Prophets*, p. 407.
[22]Adapted from G. Campbell Morgan, *Living Messages of the Books of the Bible*, 1:2:257-71

Exposition

I. HEADING 1:1

The writer introduced this book as an "oracle of (concerning) Nineveh." An oracle is a message from Yahweh that usually announces judgment. It is sometimes called a "burden," because it frequently contained a message that lay heavy on the prophet's heart, and came across as a "heavy" message. In this case it is a "war-oracle."[23] This book records "the vision" that "Nahum the Elkoshite" received from the Lord.

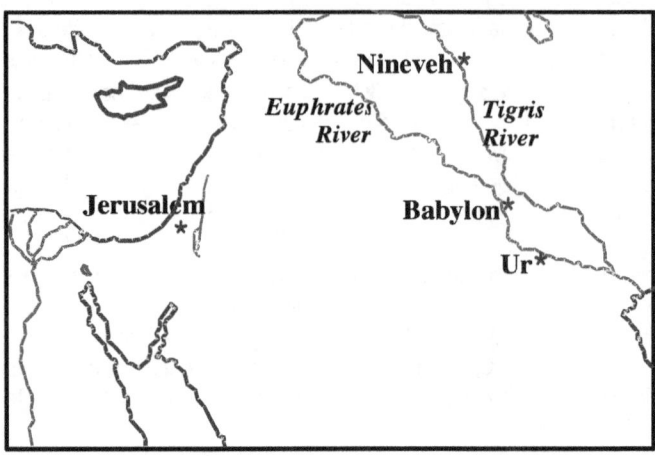

> "Having been founded by Nimrod (Gen. 10:8-12), Nineveh had a long history. It was located on the east bank of the Tigris River, which formed the western and southern boundaries of the city. A wall extended for eight miles around the northern and eastern boundaries. The section of the city within the walls was nearly three miles in diameter at its greatest width, and it held a population that has been estimated to have been as high as 150,000. The three days' walk required to traverse Nineveh (. . . Jon. 3:3) is no exaggeration."[24]

As noted above, the location of "Elkosh" is presently uncertain. The two most likely general locations are Mesopotamia or Canaan. I tend to think that Elkosh was in Judah, since all the other Old Testament prophets were from Canaan, and Nahum prophesied during the history of the surviving kingdom of Judah (ca. 650 B.C.).

Nahum evidently used "Nineveh," the capital of the Assyrian Empire, to stand for the whole empire in some places, as well as for the city in others. In some texts, the city is definitely in view, as is obvious from the fulfillment of the prophecy, but in others, all of Assyria seems to be in view. It is common, especially in prophetical and poetical parts of the Old Testament, for the writers to use the names of prominent cities to represent their countries. The most frequent example is the use of Jerusalem in place of Judah or even all Israel. This is an example of the common figure of speech called metonymy, in which a writer uses the name of one thing for that of another associated with or suggested by it.

II. NINEVEH'S DESTRUCTION DECLARED 1:2-14

The rest of chapter 1 declares Nineveh's destruction in rather hymnic style, and chapters 2 and 3 describe its destruction. Each of these major parts of the book opens with a revelation of Yahweh.

A. THE ANGER AND GOODNESS OF YAHWEH 1:2-8

> "The opening verses of Nahum form a prologue dominated by the revelation of God's eternal power and divine nature in creation (cf. Rom 1:20). As in Romans 1:18-32, this revelation is characterized preeminently by God's justice, expressed in retribution (v. 2) and wrath (vv. 2-3, 6) that shake the entire creation (vv. 3-6)."[25]

Armerding made much of the similarities between this section and the Exodus event, God's self-revelation at Mt. Sinai, His appearance to Elijah at Mt. Horeb, and parallels in Isaiah.

> "The seventh-century minor prophets focused on the justice of God as exhibited in powerful judgment on an international scale."[26]

---

[23] Longman, pp. 771, 786.
[24] Charles H. Dyer, in *The Old Testament Explorer*, p. 796.
[25] Carl E. Armerding, "Nahum," in *Daniel-Malachi*, vol. 7 of *The Expositor's Bible Commentary*, p. 460.
[26] Robert B. Chisholm Jr., "A Theology of the Minor Prophets," in *A Biblical Theology of the Old Testament*, p. 413.

"In the Book of Psalms there are three types of Divine Warrior hymns: those sung before a battle, calling on God's aid (Ps. 7); those sung during a battle, focusing on the Lord's protection (Ps. 92); and those celebrating the victory God has won for his people (Ps. 98). Nahum 1:2-8 bears a remarkable similarity to the last type of psalm, the original function of which was to sing the praises of Israel's Warrior God in the aftermath of a victory. What is significant, then, is the placement of Nahum's Divine Warrior hymn. The victory is celebrated before the battle is actually waged. The victory of God against Nineveh is certain. So much so, that the prophet could utter the victory shout years before the battle [cf. Rev. 5:9]."[27]

1:2   Nahum drew a picture of Yahweh as a God who is "jealous" for His chosen people (cf. Exod. 20:5; 34:14; Deut. 4:24; 5:9). That is, He greatly desires their welfare (cf. Deut. 6:15). He is also an "avenging" God who "takes vengeance" on all who violate His standards of righteousness (what is right), though not with human vindictiveness. Third, He is full of "wrath" against those who oppose Him and disregard His grace, those who set themselves up as His "adversaries" and "enemies" (cf. Deut. 32:35, 41). The repetition of avenging, vengeance, and wrathful in this verse creates a strong impression of an angry God. The word "wrath" (Heb. *hemah*) means "to be hot" and describes burning rage and intense fury. Why was God so angry? The rest of the oracle explains that it was the behavior of the Ninevites that had aroused His anger.

This is an unusual collection of anthropopathic descriptions of God (i.e., God described as having human feelings). Some students of Scripture have denied that God feels anything, and that descriptions of Him, like this one, only present God as exhibiting the appearance of anger. One example of this view follows.

"Now the mode of accommodation is for him to represent himself to us not as he is in himself, but as he seems to us. Although he is beyond all disturbance of mind, yet he testifies that he is angry toward sinners. Therefore whenever we hear that God is angered, we ought not to imagine any emotion in him, but rather to consider that this expression has been taken from our own human experience; because God, whenever he is exercising judgment, exhibits the appearance of one kindled and angered."[28]

I find this explanation unsatisfying, because it robs God of emotion, which is an essential component of personality. Significantly, Calvin excluded emotion from the faculties of the soul, believing that the soul consists only of understanding and will.[29] I believe that God does feel anger, as well as love and every other emotion, and that emotions are part of the image of God in man.

This is the first of several rhetorical allusions to uniquely Neo-Assyrian conquest metaphors in the book. The figure of a destroyer of mountains and seas continues through verse 6, and the figure of the self-predicating warrior extends through verse 8. Other metaphors are the raging storm and the overwhelming dust cloud in verse 3, the overwhelming flood and the uninhabitable ruin in verse 8, and the Assyrian yoke in verses 12-13. The metaphor of the mighty weapon appears in 2:1, and that of the consuming locust swarm in 3:16-17.[30]

"Verse 2 lays a foundation for the entire prophecy: all that follows is rooted in this revelation of the justice and burning zeal of the Lord exercised on behalf of his people."[31]

1:3   However, Yahweh was not out of control in His anger. His "anger" was "slow" in coming to the boiling point (cf. Exod. 34:6; Num. 14:18). He waited as long as possible to pour out His judgment (cf. 2 Pet. 3:9). About a century before Nahum prophesied, God sent Jonah to warn the Ninevites. This is an evidence of His being slow to anger. God's patience accounts for His allowing the Assyrians to abuse the Israelites for such a long time. Patience is sometimes a sign of weakness, but not so with the Lord. He is also "great in power," which makes the prospect of His releasing His anger terrifying (cf. Deut. 8:17-18). He will not pass over any guilty person and leave him or her unpunished, but will bring them to judgment eventually. Whirlwinds and storms manifest this angry aspect of God's character and His power (cf. Job 9:17). He is so great that the clouds are for Him what the dust on the ground is for humans (cf. 2 Sam. 22:10; Ps. 18:9). The great "clouds" overhead are "like dust" particles to the great God who resides in the heavens.

Verses 2 and 3 repeat "Yahweh" five times. This literary device has the effect of underlining the identity of Israel's covenant God. There should be no mistake whom Nahum was describing, even though he drew attention to characteristics of the Lord that were not the ones that His people liked to think about. Nahum frequently used Yahweh's name throughout the book.

---

[27]Longman, p. 788.
[28]John Calvin, *Institutes of the Christian Religion*, 1:17:13.
[29]Ibid., 1:15:7.
[30]See Gordon H. Johnston, "Nahum's Rhetorical Allusions to Neo-Assyrian Conquest Metaphors," *Bibliotheca Sacra* 159:633 (January-March 2002):21-45.
[31]Chisholm, "A Theology . . .," p. 462.

1:4   A simple word from Yahweh can cause the humanly uncontrollable "sea" and the "rivers" to "dry" up. The Lord had demonstrated this power when He parted the Red Sea and stopped the Jordan River from flowing (Exod. 14:21; Josh. 3:16). It can make "Bashan," "Carmel," and "Lebanon," which were normally lush, productive regions—wither away. The Lord had likewise sent many droughts on various parts of Canaan to encourage His people to return to Him (cf. 1 Kings 17—18). It is heat that causes bodies of water to dry up and bodies of land to wither away, but it is the heat of God's wrath in judgment that is sometimes behind this physical heat.

1:5   Yahweh produces earthquakes and landslides, other evidences of His awesome power. "Mountains" are the most stable physical features on this planet, yet God can move them. Mt. Sinai quaked when God revealed Himself there (Exod. 19:18). "His" very "presence" can cause the entire "earth" and "all" its "inhabitants" to convulse and upheave. The vast Assyrian Empire, therefore, was not too much for Him to overthrow.

1:6   No one can continue to exist if Yahweh is indignant with him or her. Nahum did not mean that the final destiny of God's enemies is annihilation. He meant that no one can survive His unchecked wrath. The Hebrew word translated "indignant," *za'am*, means to be enraged, like boiling water. *No one* "can endure" Yahweh's "burning . . . anger." Nahum made these points strongly by using two rhetorical questions.

> "Unlike a regular question, which is soliciting information, a rhetorical question assumes the answer is already known by both the asker and the asked. Instead of the statement which could have been used in its place, the rhetorical question forces the hearer to get actively involved in the discussion. . . . The technique is used elsewhere in Nahum (2:11; 3:7-8) and in other prophetic texts."[32]

The Assyrians should have learned this truth when God destroyed their army, as it surrounded Jerusalem, in one night (2 Kings 18—19). Yahweh's "wrath" pours out "like fire," and then even solid "rocks" break up (cf. 1 Kings 19:11). How much less will human flesh and manmade walls stand against His anger!

1:7   In contrast, Yahweh is also "good," not just angry and vengeful (cf. Rom. 11:22). He Himself is a more secure hiding place than any mountain, hill, or great city, like Nineveh, when people face trouble (cf. Ps. 27:1; 37:39; 43:2; 52:7). Furthermore, "He knows those who take refuge in Him" by drawing near to Him and resting their confidence in Him. He takes note of those who trust in Him—as well as those who incur His wrath. Whereas the previous revelations of God reflect His imminent dealings with the Assyrians, this aspect of His character (name) should have encouraged the Israelites to trust and obey Him.

1:8   Nahum returned to the wrathful aspect of God's character because that was the focus of his oracle. Without identifying Nineveh, the prophet described Yahweh destroying it totally and permanently, as with a tidal wave. Johnston showed that Nahum's maledictions are unique among the prophets, and probably imitate the Neo-Assyrian treaty curses, which were unusually brutal in the ancient Near East.[33] Nahum probably described an unrestrained army invasion (cf. Isa. 8:7-8; Jer. 47:2; Dan. 9:26; 11:40). Remarkably, when her enemies overthrew Nineveh, its rivers overflowed and washed away part of Nineveh's walls—a parallel and literal fulfillment of prophecy![34]

Using another figure, Yahweh said He would pursue His enemies until He caught up with them and killed them, even if it took all night. Normally battles ceased at nightfall and resumed at daybreak because fighting became so difficult at night. But the Lord would not let night stop Him from pursuing and slaying His enemies. They would not escape from Him simply because time passed. "Darkness" also has the metaphorical connotation of evil, spiritual lostness, and eternal judgment (e.g., Job 17:13; Ps. 82:5; 88:12; Prov. 4:19; 20:20; Isa. 8:22; 42:7; Jer. 23:12; Matt. 4:16; 8:12; John 3:19; Col. 1:13; 1 Pet. 2:9; Jude 6; Rev. 16:10).

The Lord is angry with those who abuse others, especially those who abuse His people, and He will punish them. This section stresses the justice, power, and goodness of Yahweh.

---

[32]Baker, p. 29.
[33]Gordon H. Johnston, "Nahum's Rhetorical Allusions to Neo-Assyrian Treaty Curses," *Bibliotheca Sacra* 158:632 (October-December 2001):415-36.
[34]*The New Bible Dictionary*, 1962 ed., s.v. "Nineveh," by D. J. Wiseman.

"We must keep in mind that the message of Nahum is not concretely applied to Assyria and Judah until later in the book. The psalm that occurs at the beginning of the book [1:2-8] presents a picture of God applicable for all times—he is the Warrior who judges evil."[35]

The first eight verses of Nahum are a partial acrostic.

"If an entire acrostic conveys completeness, half an acrostic may well be a prophetic way of indicating completeness with still more to come. Assyria faces imminent judgment, but only half of what is eventually in store for her."[36]

B. Yahweh's plans for Nineveh and Judah 1:9-14

Whereas the previous section assured Nineveh's doom, the primary focus of attention in it was the character of Yahweh and His ability to destroy His enemies. Now the focus shifts more directly to Nineveh. Three sections reveal Yahweh's plans for Nineveh (vv. 1-11, 14) and Judah (vv. 12-13) in chiastic form.

1. The consumption of Nineveh 1:9-11

1:9   Yahweh will frustrate and destroy all attempts to thwart His will. Even though they may appear to succeed at first, they will not endure. Sennacherib, the king of Assyria, had besieged Jerusalem once (1 Kings 18), but the Assyrians never did so a second time. Their plan to oppose God's people was actually opposition against *God Himself*, and He did not permit it to succeed. Once Nineveh fell, it was never rebuilt.[37]

1:10   "Tangled (Heb. *sebukim*) thorns" are tough to penetrate, but they are no match for fire. Likewise the Ninevites, as confused as they would be when their city was under attack, would be no match for the consuming fire of Yahweh's wrath (cf. v. 6). Many of the Ninevites were confused because they were drunk (Heb. *sebu'im*). Yahweh would destroy them as easily and quickly as fire burned up the dead stalks left in fields after harvest.

1:11   Since the Lord will destroy any plot against Him and His people (v. 9), the Assyrians were in trouble. "One of the Assyrians" had gone forth "who plotted evil" against Him. This is probably a reference to Sennacherib. He was "wicked" and worthless because He had opposed Yahweh (cf. 2 Kings 18).

2. The liberation of Judah 1:12-13

Emphasis now shifts from Assyria to Judah.

"In the form of an oracle (v. 12, *This is what the Lord says*) to two parties in a legal dispute, God pronounces his verdicts alternately to Judah, for her acquittal and hope (vv. 12-13, 15; 2:2), and to Assyria, for her destruction (v. 14; 2:1)."[38]

1:12   Yahweh declared that, even though the Assyrians were powerful and numerous, He would "cut" them "off," and they would pass off the stage of history. This must have been hard for many Israelites to believe, since the Assyrians had been their dreaded enemy for centuries. Even though the Lord had "afflicted" the Israelites, He would "afflict" them "no longer." Evidently He meant that He would not afflict them *with the Assyrians* any longer, since other nations *did afflict* them after Assyria passed off the scene. This is the only place in the prophecy where, "Thus says the LORD," occurs, guaranteeing that what He said would definitely happen. This verse is the clearest indication that Nahum ministered before the decline of Assyria as a military and political state.[39]

"In the context the expression 'quiet, and likewise many,' [AV; 'at full *strength*, and likewise many' NASB; 'unscathed and numerous' NIV] although a literal translation of the Hebrew, does not seem to make much sense. Actually the Hebrew here represents a transliteration of a long-forgotten Assyrian legal formula. Excavation in the ruins of ancient Nineveh, buried since 612 B.C., has brought to light thousands of ancient Assyrian tablets, dozens of which contain this Assyrian legal formula. It proves, on investigation, to

---

[35]Longman, p. 776. See idem, "The Divine Warrior: The New Testament Use of an Old Testament Motif," *Westminster Theological Journal* 44 (1982):290-307; and Kevin J. Cathcart, "The Divine Warrior and the War of Yahweh in Nahum," in *Biblical Studies in Contemporary Thought: The Tenth Anniversary Commemorative Volume of the Trinity College Biblical Institute 1966-1975*, pp. 68-76.

[36]Duane L. Christensen, "The Acrostic of Nahum Reconsidered," *Zeitschrift für die alttestamentliche Wissenschaft* 87 (1975):25.

[37]*The New Bible* . . ., s.v. "Nineveh."

[38]Baker, p. 32.

[39]Longman, "Nahum," p. 798.

indicate joint and several responsibility for carrying out an obligation. Nahum quotes the LORD as using this Assyrian formula in speaking to the Assyrians, saying in effect, 'Even though your entire nation joins as one person to resist me, nevertheless I shall overcome you.' As the words would have been equally incomprehensible to the later Hebrew copyists, their retention is striking evidence of the care of the scribes in copying exactly what they found in the manuscripts, and testifies to God's providential preservation of the Biblical text."[40]

1:13   The Lord promised to "break" Assyria's oppression of the Israelites, as when someone removed a "yoke" from the neck of an ox, or the chains ("shackles") that bound a prisoner. For years the Israelites had to endure Assyrian oppression—including invasion, occupation, and taxation (cf. 2 Kings 19:20-37; 2 Chron. 32:1-23; Isa. 37:27-38).

3. The termination of Nineveh 1:14

The subject reverts to Nineveh.

Yahweh had commanded His heavenly host to manage the world's affairs in such a way that Nineveh's "name" (or perhaps Nineveh's king's "name") would not continue forever. This does not mean that succeeding generations would be completely ignorant of Nineveh and its rulers. More is known about Assyrian literature than that of any other ancient Semitic people except the Hebrews.[41] But the residents, particularly the king, would have no surviving descendants (heirs).[42]

The Lord also promised to destroy Nineveh's idols and remove them from their temples. The Assyrians often carried off the idols of the nations they conquered, in order to demonstrate the superiority of *their* "gods" over those of the conquered, as did other ancient Near Eastern nations (cf. 1 Sam. 5). The conquering Medes, however, despised idolatry and did away with multitudes of images that existed in Nineveh.[43] Yahweh would "prepare" Nineveh's "grave," since He would likewise bury—metaphorically—the contemptible city. It was a great curse in the ancient Near East to have no descendants, and it was a great humiliation to have no gods, but both fates would befall Nineveh.

III. NINEVEH'S DESTRUCTION DESCRIBED 1:15—3:19

This second major part of Nahum contains another introduction and four descriptions of Nineveh's destruction. Having revealed general statements about Yahweh's judgment, Nahum next communicated more specific descriptions of Nineveh's demise. As in the previous section, he also gave promises of Israel's restoration.

> "Nahum portrays [the] siege, reproduces its horrors and its savagery, its cruelties and mercilessness, in language so realistic that one is able to see it and feel it. First comes the fighting in the suburbs. Then the assault upon the walls. Then the capture of the city and its destruction."[44]

The section begins, as the first major one did (cf. 1:2-8), with an emphasis on Yahweh—who contrasts with the human destroyer of Nineveh. Humans can destroy, but it takes Yahweh to deliver. This section is also chiastic, as was 1:9-14.

A. THE SOVEREIGN JUSTICE OF YAHWEH 1:15—2:2

1:15   This is the first verse of chapter 2 in the Hebrew Bible. It is a *janus*, a transition that looks back to what precedes and forward to what follows.

Nahum called his audience to give attention. Someone was coming over the "mountains" with a "good news" message of "peace." Consequently the people of Judah could "celebrate" their "feasts"; they had a future. They should "pay" their "vows" to the Lord, because He had answered their prayers. The "wicked" Assyrians would "never again . . . pass through" their land, as they had done in the past. The message was that they had been "cut off completely," like a piece of a garment, and so would be no threat in the future. The prophet spoke as if Nineveh had already fallen—and a messenger had just arrived with the news! The same statement appears in Isaiah 52:7, where the messenger announces the defeat of Babylon.

---

[40] *The New Scofield Reference Bible*, pp. 950-51.
[41] See Longman, "Nahum," p. 798.
[42] For a chart of the historical fulfillments of Nahum's prophecies, see *The Bible Knowledge Commentary: Old Testament*, p. 1495. Patterson, pp. 105-7, also catalogued some fulfillments.
[43] Charles Lee Feinberg, *Jonah Micah and Nahum*, p. 132.
[44] Raymond Calkins, *The Modern Message of the Minor Prophets*, p. 82.

> "So complete was its [Nineveh's] destruction that when Xenophon passed by the site about 200 years later, he thought the mounds were the ruins of some other city. And Alexander the Great, fighting in a battle nearby, did not realize that he was near the ruins of Nineveh."[45]

The Apostle Paul quoted the first part of this verse in Romans 10:15, in reference to those messengers who bring similar good news, namely: the gospel.

> "The message is one of peace, a peace from external oppression and a new kind of peace with the God who is the giver of all life."[46]

2:1   Nahum turned from addressing the people of Judah to the people of Nineveh. He used the Hebrew prophetic perfect tense, which predicts future events as though they were past, to heighten belief in their certainty. "One who scatters" would "come up against" Nineveh. "Scatterer" is a common figure for a victorious king (cf. Ps. 68:1; Isa. 24:1; Jer. 52:8). Consequently, the Ninevites should "man" their "fortress," "watch the road" for the coming invader, and "strengthen" themselves. These measures would prove futile because the Lord would destroy the city. Nahum was speaking sarcastically. This section has been called "a taunt song."[47]

> "Sennacherib had spent no less than six years building his armory, which occupied a terraced area of forty acres. It was enlarged further by Esarhaddon and contained all the weaponry required for the extension and maintenance of the Assyrian empire: bows, arrows, quivers, chariots, wagons, armor, horses, mules, and equipment (cf. Ezek 23:24; 39:9). The royal 'road' had been enlarged by Sennacherib to a breadth of seventy-eight feet, facilitating the movement of troops."[48]

Even though the Ninevites did all these things, they could not escape overthrow. The "invader" proved to be Cyaxares the Mede and Nabopolassar the Babylonian.[49] However, the "scatterer" behind them was Yahweh.

2:2   Turning back to Judah again (1:15), the prophet repeated that Yahweh would restore Israel to its former glory. Whereas a destroyer would destroy Nineveh (v. 1), Yahweh would restore Judah. Its fate would be the opposite of Nineveh's. Nineveh presently enjoyed great glory, but would suffer destruction, while Israel, having experienced devastation, would become splendid again. "Israel" was a name connected with Israel's glory, while "Jacob" recalls the perverse aspects of the nation's experience, reflecting its patriarch's names and life experience.[50] The invading Assyrians doubtless destroyed many of Israel's grapevines, but "vine branches" also symbolized the Israelites (cf. Ps. 80:8-16; Isa. 5:1-7). The devastators of Israel had been Assyria, and later the Babylonians. The promise probably looks beyond Israel's restoration, after the Assyrians' devastation, to her restoration after all her devastations throughout history. This restoration will take place in the Millennium.

B. Four descriptions of Nineveh's fall 2:3—3:19

The rest of the book contains four descriptions of Nineveh's fall that were evidently messages that Nahum delivered at various times in Judah.

1. The first description of Nineveh's fall 2:3-7

The first message sees the details of the siege of Nineveh taking place in the city when the enemy attacked, and it ends with the reaction of a segment of the populace (v. 7).

2:3   Nahum again focused on the destroyer (scatterer) of Nineveh (cf. v. 1). He described the siege and capture of Nineveh. "The shields" and uniforms of the soldiers who invaded Nineveh would be "red." This was, in fact, a favorite color of the Median and Babylonian armies (cf. Ezek. 23:14).[51] However, they may have been red with blood and or from the copper that they used to cover both shields and uniforms.[52]

---

[45]Elliott E. Johnson, "Nahum," in *The Bible Knowledge Commentary: Old Testament*, p. 1499.
[46]Peter C. Craigie, *Twelve Prophets*, 2:67.
[47]Longman, "Nahum," p. 801.
[48]Armerding, p. 472.
[49]For an ancient account of the battles that resulted in Nineveh's fall, see D. Winton Thomas, ed., *Documents from Old Testament Times*, p. 76; or James B. Pritchard, ed., *Ancient Near Eastern Texts Relating to the Old Testament*, pp. 303-5.
[50]See C. F. Keil, "Nahum," in *The Twelve Minor Prophets*, 2:19.
[51]Feinberg, p. 136.
[52]Johnson, p. 1500

> "These images speak of blood, violence, and warfare. Isaiah refers to the custom the Assyrians had of rolling their outer garments in blood before a battle (see Is. 9:5) to strike terror in the hearts of their opponents. Here the tables would be turned. While others would have 'shields,' 'chariots,' and 'spears,' the people of Nineveh would be bathed in blood—their own blood."[53]

Nahum saw the invading "chariots . . . flashing" with "steel." Scythed chariots were in use at this time in the ancient Near East, chariots with steel blades protruding from them and their wheels.[54] Spears made out of "cypress" (pine) were long and straight, and Nineveh's invaders would brandish them showing their readiness for battle.[55]

2:4   The invaders' "chariots" would "race" through Nineveh's "streets" and "squares." So gleaming with red and steel would they be, that they would look like "torches" or "lightning" darting to and fro. Since Nahum described the enemy advancing toward the city walls (v. 5), he may have seen these chariots darting through the suburban streets and squares outside the walls.[56]

2:5   The Assyrian king would call on his "nobles" to defend the city, but they would "stumble" in their haste to do so. They would "hurry" to Nineveh's walls to set up some type of protective shield ("mantelet") to deflect the attackers' arrows, spears, and stones.[57]

2:6   The Tigris River flowed close to the walls of Nineveh, and two of its tributaries, the Khosr and the Tebiltu, passed through the city. Virtually all of Nineveh's 15 gates also contained passages for the waters from one of these tributaries or its canals. They were called "gates of the rivers."[58]

Sennacherib had built a double dam and reservoir system to the north of the city to control the amount of water that entered it and to prevent flooding.[59] Nahum may have seen the invader opening these dam gates and flooding the city. However, ancient historians wrote that flooding from heavy rains also played a role in Nineveh's fall.

> "Diodorus wrote that in the third year of the siege heavy rains caused a nearby river to flood part of the city and break part of the walls (*Bibliotheca Historica* 2. 26. 9; 2. 27. 13). Xenophon referred to terrifying thunder (presumably with a storm) associated with the city's capture (*Anabasis*, 3. 4. 12). Also the Khosr River, entering the city from the northwest at the Ninlil Gate and running through the city in a southwesterly direction, may have flooded because of heavy rains, or the enemy may have destroyed its sluice gate."[60]

Other possibilities are that Nahum saw fortified bridges, the city gates that lay below the nearby Tigris River, sluice gates that emptied water into moats, other breaches in Nineveh's walls made by water, or floodgates that controlled the Khosr within the city.[61]

The "palace" the prophet saw washed away ("dissolved") was perhaps that of Ashurbanipal, which stood in the north part of Nineveh.[62] However, Nineveh contained many palaces and temples, and the Hebrew word *hekal*, used here, describes both types of structures. Assyria had ruined many enemy cities, palaces, and temples, but now this fate would befall Nineveh.

2:7   The Lord's judgment of Nineveh had been determined. The city would be "stripped" of its treasures, and they and their possessors would be "carried away" to other places. Even the slave girls, the bottom of the social scale, as well as the nobles (v. 5), the top, would lament the fall of the city. They would make mournful sounds and beat "their breasts" like "doves" that cooed and flapped their wings. Normally, one would expect slaves in a city to rejoice at its destruction, since that would mean their liberation. But life in Nineveh was good for some foreigners taken there as captives.

---

[53] *The Nelson Study Bible*, p. 1516.
[54] Feinberg, p. 136.
[55] See also Yigael Yadin, *The Art of Warfare in Biblical Lands*, pp. 4-5, 294-95, 452.
[56] Maier, p. 243.
[57] Yadin, p. 316.
[58] Armerding, p. 476.
[59] Maier, p. 253.
[60] Johnson, p. 1495.
[61] Ibid., p. 1500.
[62] Ibid., p. 1501.

2. The second description of Nineveh's fall 2:8-13

The second description of Nineveh's fall is more philosophical than the first one, and ends with a statement by Yahweh that gives the reason for its fall (v. 13).

2:8   "Nineveh" had been as placid as the waters around the city for most of her history. This is the first explicit reference to Nineveh since 1:1, yet because of 1:1 we know that the prophet's revelations of destruction dealt with Nineveh. Nahum now saw it *inundated* with water, and enemy soldiers and its inhabitants fleeing in panic, like water gushing from a broken dam. Someone might call to them "Stop, stop," perhaps to defend the city, but "no one" would turn back.

2:9   The prophet called the invading solders to "plunder" Nineveh, to take for themselves its vast "wealth" of "silver," "gold," and other valuable treasures. Nineveh had accumulated her wealth through centuries of conquests, taxation, and trading.[63] It was the richest city in the ancient Near East in the seventh century B.C.[64]

> "According to historical records, the Medes were the first to breach the defenses of Nineveh. Later, the Babylonians successfully attacked it. The Medes, however, were not interested in a long-term occupation of the area, but in a quick profit."[65]

2:10   The invaders would empty Nineveh of her treasures, and it would become a desolate wasteland. The Hebrew words in the first part of this verse sound like water flowing out of a bottle when read aloud, a literary device called onomatopoeia. Even the sound of the description of Nineveh's fall reinforced the prophecy. Hearts would melt and knees knock when people observed its overthrow. "Anguish" would grip "the whole body" of observers "and all their faces" would go "pale." If Nineveh could fall, would anything be secure?

2:11   After Nineveh's destruction, the people who remained would taunt the Assyrians by comparing Nineveh to a lion's "den" and nearby "feeding" grounds. They would also compare its inhabitants to "lions." Assyria's leaders were lion-like, and its youths like young lions, having plundered and preyed on others. But their once-secure haunts were now desolate.

> "Assyrian kings prided themselves in their ability to kill lions in lion hunts. And the kings likened their own ferocity and fearlessness to that of lions. For example, Sennacherib boasted of his military fury by saying, 'Like a lion I raged.' Lions were frequently pictured in Assyrian reliefs and decorations."[66]

2:12   Lions normally kill only what they need to eat, but the Assyrians "killed" innumerable enemies, not only to sustain their own needs, but just for the pleasure of conquest. They were unusually vicious toward their enemies, and notorious in the ancient world for being cruel.[67] Yet lions, while vicious, are not known for being excessively so.

2:13   Nahum closed this message with a word from Yahweh in which the Lord verbalized His antagonism toward Nineveh. What a terrible fate it is to have Almighty Yahweh say, "I am against you!" (cf. 3:5; Jer. 21:13; 50:31; 51:25; Ezek. 5:8; 13:8; 26:3; 28:22; 39:1; Rom. 8:31). He promised to destroy Nineveh's instruments of warfare. Invading armies would slay her "young lions" (men). She would no longer devour other peoples like a lion does its prey. And "messengers" would "no longer" leave Nineveh with threats and to demand submission and taxes (cf. 2 Kings 18:17-25; 19:22; Isa. 37:4, 6).

3. The third description of Nineveh's fall 3:1-7

This description explains further the "why" for Nineveh's fall, whereas the first two descriptions in the previous chapter gave more of the actual events, the "what" of it. There is much similarity between the descriptions of the siege in 2:3-4 and 3:2-3, however. This section has been called a woe oracle because it pronounces doom on Nineveh in typical woe oracle fashion (cf. Isa. 5:18-19; Amos 5:18-20; 6:1-7; Mic. 2:1-4).[68]

---

[63]See D. D. Luckenbill, ed., *Ancient Records of Assyria and Babylonia*, 1:181, 211, 263; 2:20, 133, 205; and Pritchard, ed., 274-301. For brief histories of Mesopotamia in the seventh century B.C., see Longman, pp. 767-68; and E. von Voightlander, " A Survey of Neo-Babylonian History" (Ph.D. Dissertation, University of Michigan, 1963).
[64]Armerding, p. 477.
[65]Longman, "Nahum," p. 807.
[66]Johnson, p. 1501. See also Gordon H. Johnston, "Nahum's Rhetorical Allusions to the Neo-Assyrian Lion Motif," *Bibliotheca Sacra* 158:631 (July-September 2001):287-307.
[67]See Pritchard, ed., p. 285; idem, ed., *The Ancient Near East in Pictures*, p. 373; Feinberg, p. 141; Hobart E. Freeman, *Nahum Zephaniah Habakkuk*, pp. 36-38; and Maier, pp. 281-83.
[68]See Patterson, pp. 81-82.

3:1	Nahum pronounced woe on Nineveh, a city characterized by bloodshed. Here, as often elsewhere (e.g., Isa. 3:9), "woe" announces impending doom. Sometimes "woe" is an expression of grief (e.g., Isa. 6:5), but that is only its secondary meaning here. As noted earlier, the Assyrians were notorious for their cruelty that included cutting off hands, feet, ears, noses, gouging out eyes, lopping off heads, impaling bodies, and peeling the skin off living victims.[69] Nahum saw the city as completely "full of lies" (cf. 2 Kings 18:31) and "pillage" (cf. 2:9). Nineveh always had "prey"; she was constantly on the prowl looking for other nations to conquer.
3:2-3	Again the prophet described the sounds and sights that would accompany the battle in which Nineveh would fall (cf. 2:3-4). Whips could be heard as soldiers urged their horses forward. Nahum heard the sound of chariot wheels and the hoofs of horses bearing cavalry soldiers clattering on the pavement. "Horsemen" were "charging," "swords" were "flashing," and "spears" were "gleaming" in the light. The large number of "corpses" on the scene of battle impressed Nahum. They seemed to be "countless," so many that they appeared to cover the ground completely. The living soldiers had trouble moving about because they kept tripping over dead bodies. This was a scene that someone might have seen had they visited the site of one of the Assyrian army's battles, but this one was taking place in Nineveh and the dead were mainly Ninevites.

> "God has allowed Nahum to witness the fall of Nineveh even though it is years, perhaps even decades, away."[70]

> "No passage of Hebrew literature surpasses this for vividness of description."[71]

3:4	This devastation was coming on Nineveh because of her wickedness. She had played the harlot often by luring unsuspecting nations and then harming them. For example, King Ahaz had been attracted to Assyria and had appealed for her to come and help Judah (2 Kings 16:7-18), but when she did, years later, she came to destroy rather than assist (cf. Isa. 36:16-17). The Ninevites were also practitioners of sorcery; they appealed to the spirit world for power to determine and control their destiny and that of their victims. The pagan worship of the Assyrians involved occultism, sexual perversion, and human degradation. Assyria had lured other nations, then, with immoral attractions and magical arts. These practices resulted in the enslavement of many nations and people groups; Nineveh sold them into slavery.
3:5	Almighty Yahweh repeated that He was "against" Nineveh (cf. 2:13). He would expose her shamefulness because of her shameless acts, as when someone lifted the skirt of a lady over her head so high that he covered her face with it (cf. Isa. 47:1-3; Jer. 13:26-27; Ezek. 16:37; Hos. 2:3-5; Rev. 17:15-16). "Nakedness" was a great shame in the ancient world. She who had enslaved the nations (v. 4) would have her own nakedness exposed to them.
3:6	As the Assyrians had made many other people detestable, the Lord would do the same to them. Nahum's picture is that of God covering Nineveh with human excrement and then lifting her up for all to behold, a disgusting sight indeed.
3:7	It is no wonder then that everyone who saw Nineveh would recoil from her and remark on her devastated condition. No one would grieve over Nineveh's destruction because all would be glad that she got what she deserved. Mourners over her demise would not be found, because all the people would rejoice, not sorrow, over her humiliation (v. 19). At least a few mourners would attend any funeral in the ancient Near East, even if relatives had to pay them to attend. But no one would agree to weep for Nineveh, even if paid to do so. This is hyperbole, but the point is clear: the world would rejoice when Nineveh fell.

4. The fourth description of Nineveh's fall 3:8-19

This section, evidently another message that Nahum delivered concerning Nineveh's fall, begins by comparing it to the fall of another great city. Nahum proceeded to use many figures of speech to describe how various segments of Ninevite society would respond to the coming invasion. The literary form of the section is that of a taunt song.[72]

3:8	Nineveh was similar to the Egyptian capital, "No-amon" ("city of [the god] Amon," Gr. Thebes). Thebes had been the capital of Upper (southern) Egypt and had stood at the site of modern Karnak and Luxor, 400 miles south of Cairo. Water from rivers, tributaries, canals, and moats surrounded this city, as it did Nineveh, and both were capitals of mighty kingdoms. However, Thebes had fallen to Ashurbanipal the Assyrian in 663 B.C. Jeremiah and Ezekiel predicted its fall (Jer. 46:25; Ezek. 30:14, 16). Just as Thebes' solid and liquid defenses did not protect that city, so Nineveh's defenses would not protect it, either.

---

[69]See Maier, p. 292.
[70]Longman, "Nahum," p. 813.
[71]Charles L. Feinberg, "Nahum," in *The Wycliffe Bible Commentary*, p. 867.
[72]See Patterson, pp. 93-94.

3:9	In contrast to Nineveh, Thebes had several allies. "Ethiopia" (Cush) was the country No-amon ruled over. It was a territory that included parts of modern southern Egypt, Sudan, Eritrea, and northern Ethiopia along the Red Sea. "Egypt" (Lower Egypt) in Nahum's day was a separate country to the north of Ethiopia, and Ethiopia was the stronger of the two powers. "Put" evidently lay farther to the south, reaching as far as present-day Somalia on the eastern tip of Africa, and "Lubim" (part of modern Libya) was to the west. Some references to Put in ancient literature seem to put it in the same area as modern Libya (cf. Gen. 10:6; 1 Chron. 1:8; Jer. 46:9; et al.), but the location described above seems more likely.[73] Thus Thebes' allies surrounded her for many miles, but that did not guarantee her security.
3:10	No-amon had become "an exile" and had gone "into captivity" to Assyria (cf. 2:7).[74] Instead of taking infants into captivity, however, the Assyrians simply slaughtered them where they found them, even at street corners (cf. Hos. 13:16). The "honorable men" of Thebes suffered the humiliation of being auctioned off as slaves and dragged away to Assyria in chains.
3:11	The same fate would befall Nineveh. It too would lose its powers of self-defense and self-control. This would happen through excessive wine drinking (cf. 1:10), but also in a metaphorical sense, because the Ninevites would imbibe a cup of wrath from Yahweh. They would vanish from the world.

> "The disappearance of the Assyrian people will always remain an unique and striking phenomenon in ancient history. Other, similar, kingdoms and empires have indeed passed away, but the people have lived on. Recent discoveries have, it is true, shown that poverty-stricken communities perpetuated the old Assyrian names and various places, for instance on the ruined site of Ashur, for many centuries, but the essential truth remains the same. A nation which had existed two thousand years and had ruled a wide area, lost its independent character."[75]

As noted above, the ancients could not find Nineveh after its destruction, and modern archaeologists, the Frenchman Botta and the Englishman Layard, first found physical evidence of Nineveh's existence in 1842. In the past, many people had sought to hide from the invading Assyrians, but when Nineveh fell, the Ninevites would try to hide.

3:12	Nineveh's "fortifications" would prove as weak as "fig trees" laden "with ripe fruit." Ripe figs fall off their trees of their own accord, and so easily would Nineveh's fortifications fall. Though the city's walls were large and impressive, they would crumble under their own weight when water eroded their foundations (cf. 2:6). The inhabitants, too, would drop like ripe fruit into the hands of their enemies.
3:13	The Ninevites would prove to be as defenseless, vulnerable, and fearful as "women"—in contrast to lion-like soldiers (cf. Isa. 19:16; Jer. 50:37; 51:30). Their "gates" would be so weak that they could have been left open, rather than bolted shut, because "fire" would consume them (cf. Isa. 10:16-17).
3:14	With irony (cf. 2:1), Nahum urged the Ninevites to "draw" plenty of "water" so they would have enough to drink, and so they could extinguish the fires that would burn their gates and city. They should "strengthen" their "fortifications," and make more bricks to build their walls and battlements higher and stronger, and "mortar" to fill in the holes the enemy would punch in them.

> "Nineveh's ruins include traces of a counter-wall built by the inhabitants to defend the city near places where the enemy had broken down some of the city's defenses."[76]

3:15	However, if the Ninevites did strengthen their defenses, "fire" would "consume" them wherever they went to draw water, and "the sword" would "cut" them "down" as they built. The walls of Nineveh would become the walls of her tomb rather than her defense.

> "There was no question about the clear traces of the burning of the temple (as also in the palace of Sennacherib), for a layer of ash about two inches thick lay clearly defined in places on the southeast side about the level of the Sargon pavement."[77]

---

[73]See Maier, p. 322; and Elizabeth Achtemeier, *Nahum-Malachi*, p. 25.
[74]See Armerding, pp. 484-85, for a short history of the fall of Thebes.
[75]J. B. Bury, et al., eds., *The Cambridge Ancient History*, 3:130.
[76]Johnson, p. 1503.
[77]R. Campbell Thompson and R. W. Hutchinson, *A Century of Exploration at Nineveh*, p. 77.

3:16	The city's destruction would be like a "locust" invasion. A hoard of invading soldiers would descend on Nineveh and leave nothing remaining (cf. Joel 1:2-13). Nahum ironically encouraged the Ninevites to multiply their numbers like locusts since they would have to face a swarm of invading locust-like soldiers.[78] Another interpretation is that Nahum was addressing the invading soldiers and encouraging them to increase their number so they would be successful. This seems less likely to me since the references to "yourself" are to the people of Nineveh in the context, and an ironical word to them makes sense.
3:16	Assyrian "traders," seemingly "more" numerous "than the stars," had increased their country's wealth. However, they would be like locusts when the invasion came, in that they would fly away in vast numbers rather than defending Nineveh.
3:17	Assyria's guards also reminded Nahum of locusts. There were huge numbers of them, but when the heat of battle came they would run away. Locusts do the same thing. They take their places on walls in the cool of the day, but when the hot sun beats on them they desert their posts and seek more comfortable surroundings.
3:18	Nahum addressed the king of Assyria who would rule after Nineveh's downfall (in 612 B.C.). This turned out to be Ashur-uballit, who tried for three years to hold the empire together from the city of Haran. The prophet told the king that Assyria's "shepherds" (leaders) and "nobles" were not providing leadership for their people. They were lying down on the job, asleep at the switch (cf. Isa. 5:26-27). The ordinary citizens were "scattered" all over, rather than being under the direction of the leaders, like sheep without shepherds. No one was available to re-gather them into the imperial fold.
3:19	Addressing Nineveh again, in conclusion, Nahum reiterated that the "breakdown" of Assyria would be impossible to repair. She had a fatal illness from which she would not recover. Everyone who heard about her demise would rejoice because her long practice of wickedness had touched everyone.
	Only two books in the Bible end with rhetorical questions, Jonah and Nahum, both of which focus on Nineveh. Jonah ends on a note of compassion for Nineveh, but Nahum ends with assurance that God's patience had run out and the destruction of Nineveh was now certain.

Is this book only about God's judgment on Nineveh and the Assyrians, or does it have a broader message? The reasons God brought Nineveh and the Assyrian Empire down are the same reasons He will humble any similar people. Any nation or city that lusts for conquest, practices violence and brutality to dominate others, abuses its power, oppresses the weak, worships anything but Yahweh, or seeks help from the demonic world—shares in Nineveh's sins and can expect her fate.

---

[78]Longman, "Nahum," p. 825.

Appendix

The Impassibility of God

Many theologians have held the doctrine of "divine impassibility" over many centuries. This doctrine is as follows. Nothing in the created universe, external to God Himself, can cause Him to suffer or to be affected at all. See, for example, William G. T. Shedd, *Dogmatic Theology* (Edinburgh: T. & T. Clark, 1889), 2:387.

This truth may raise questions in the minds of some concerning God's responses to His people's obedience, on the one hand, and our disobedience, on the other. Does man's obedience make God happy? And does our disobedience make Him sad? This is the impression that most people would draw just from reading the Bible.

Certainly the parable of the prodigal son (Luke 15) portrays God, as the father in the story, rejoicing over his younger son's repentance and return to home. It pictures a "happy" God. Likewise, the Flood account presents God as "sorry" He had made man (Gen. 6:6). These are only two of many examples of the biblical text presenting God as happy or sorry that human beings made certain decisions. They picture God as responding to human activity.

Yet because God is who He is, many theologians have concluded that He acts completely independent of any human influence. When Scripture describes God as responding to human actions, they say, it uses anthropomorphic expressions (i.e., descriptions of God in human terms even though He is not a human—apart, of course, from His incarnation in Christ). God was sorry He made man only in the sense that humankind's rebellion was an evil thing. It did not make Him sorry in the sense that man's action elicited a *response* of sorrow from God.

These theologians believe that when we read in the Prophets, for example, that the sins of the Israelites grieved God's heart, or that God was angry with people, we need to understand such statements as in no way contradicting His impassibility. They are simply descriptions of God as though He were a human responding. Actually, they say, He does *not respond*; in other words, He does not react to man's acts on the basis of or with emotion. His orientation toward sin is consistently negative, and His orientation toward righteousness is consistently positive, regardless of any human activity.

Other theologians view statements of God's responses to human actions as genuine responses. While there are admittedly many anthropomorphic descriptions of God in the Bible, these theologians believe some references to God responding, while anthropomorphic, are descriptions of how God really does respond. These texts indicate that He does respond to some human actions.

I tend to agree with the second position. I have found nothing in Scripture that tells the reader to understand God as not truly responding to human actions, including prayer. Rather I find much that leads the reader to conclude that God does indeed respond to some (not all) human activity. It seems to me that the doctrine of impassibility rests on a philosophical deduction concerning God, rather than on solid Scriptural revelation. Nowhere does God say in Scripture that He does not respond to human action, though, being holy, He is of course not *subject* to sin or sinful human beings. On the contrary, the writers of Scripture wrote repeatedly that He does respond to human activity.

Open theists take the fact that God responds to some human activity too far. They believe that there are things that God does not know until humans act. This view goes beyond the biblical revelation to the opposite extreme. It denies the omniscience of God and limits the sovereignty of God. Process theologians take this even further than Open theists. They believe that God is in the process of developing as a result of human activity.

(See also Walter C. Kaiser Jr.'s discussion of this subject in his commentary on Lamentations: *A Biblical Approach to Personal Suffering*, pp. 59-62.)

Bibliography

Achtemeier, Elizabeth. *Nahum-Malachi*. Interpretation series. Atlanta: John Knox Press, 1986.

Armerding, Carl E. "Nahum." In *Daniel-Minor Prophets*. Vol. 7 of *The Expositor's Bible Commentary*. 12 vols. Edited by Frank E. Gaebelein and Richard P. Polcyn. Grand Rapids: Zondervan Publishing House, 1985.

Baker, David W. *Nahum, Habakkuk and Zephaniah: An Introduction and Commentery*. Tyndale Old Testament Commentaries series. Leicester, Eng., and Downers Grove, Ill.: Inter-Varsity Press, 1988.

Bewer, J. A. *The Literature of the Old Testament*. 3rd ed. New York: Columbia University, 1962.

Bleiblreu, Erika. "Grisly Assyrian Record of Torture and Death." *Biblical Archaeology Review* 17:1 (January/February 1991):52-61, 75.

Bright, John. *A History of Israel*. Philadelphia: Westminster Press, 1959.

Bury, J. B.; S. A. Cook; and F. E. Adcock, eds. *The Cambridge Ancient History*. 12 vols. 2nd ed. reprinted. Cambridge, Eng.: University Press, 1928.

Calkins, Raymond. *The Modern Message of the Minor Prophets*. New York: Harper & Brothers, 1947.

Calvin, John. *Institutes of the Christian Religion*. The Library of Christian Classics series, volumes 20 and 21. Edited by John T. McNeill. Translated by Ford Lewis Battles. Philadelphia: Westminster Press, 1960.

Cathcart, Kevin J. "The Divine Warrior and the War of Yahweh in Nahum." In *Biblical Studies in Contemporary Thought: The Tenth Anniversary Commemorative Volume of the Trinity College Biblical Institute 1966-1975*. Edited by Miriam Ward. Somerville, Mass.: Greeno, Hadden, 1975.

Chisholm, Robert B., Jr. *Handbook on the Prophets*. Grand Rapids: Baker Book House, 2002.

_____. "A Theology of the Minor Prophets." In *A Biblical Theology of the Old Testament*, pp. 397-433. Edited by Roy B. Zuck. Chicago: Moody Press, 1991.

Christensen, Duane L. "The Acrostic of Nahum Reconsidered." Zeitschrift für die alttestamentliche Wissenschaft 87 (1975):17-30.

Cochrane, J. S. "Literary Features of Nahum." Th.M. thesis, Dallas Theological Seminary, 1954.

Craigie, Peter C. *Twelve Prophets*. 2 vols. Philadelphia: Westminster Press, 1985.

Driver, Samuel R. *An Introduction to the Literature of the Bible*. 11th ed. Edinburgh: T. & T. Clark, 1913.

Dyer, Charles H., and Eugene H. Merrill. *The Old Testament Explorer*. Nashville: Word Publishing, 2001. Reissued as *Nelson's Old Testament Survey*. Nashville: Thomas Nelson Publishers, 2001.

Feinberg, Charles Lee. *Jonah Micah and Nahum*. The Major Messages of the Minor Prophets series. New York: American Board of Missions to the Jews, 1951.

_____. "Nahum." In *The Wycliffe Bible Commentary*, pp. 863-69. Edited by Charles F. Pfeiffer and Everett F. Harrison. Chicago: Moody Press, 1962.

Finegan, Jack. *Light From the Ancient Past: The Archeological Background of Judaism and Christianity*. Second ed. Princeton, N.J.: Princeton University Press; and London: Oxford University Press, 1959.

Freeman, Hobart E. *Nahum Zephaniah Habakkuk*. Everyman's Bible Commentary series. Chicago: Moody Press, 1973.

Johnson, Elliott E. "Obadiah." In *The Bible Knowledge Commentary: Old Testament*, pp. 1493-1504. Edited by John F. Walvoord and Roy B. Zuck. Wheaton: Scripture Press Publications, Victor Books, 1985.

Johnston, Gordon H. "Nahum's Rhetorical Allusions to Neo-Assyrian Conquest Metaphors." *Bibliotheca Sacra* 159:633 (January-March 2002):21-45.

_____. "Nahum's Rhetorical Allusions to Neo-Assyrian Treaty Curses." *Bibliotheca Sacra* 158:632 (October-December 2001):415-36.

_____. "Nahum's Rhetorical Allusions to the Neo-Assyrian Lion Motif." *Bibliotheca Sacra* 158:631 (July-September 2001):287-307.

_____. "A Rhetorical Analysis of the Book of Nahum." Ph.D. dissertation, Dallas Theological Seminary, 1992.

Josephus, Flavius. *The Works of Flavius Josephus*. Translated by William Whiston. London: T. Nelson and Sons, 1866; reprint ed. Peabody, Mass.: Hendrickson Publishers, 1988.

Kaiser, Walter C., Jr. *A Biblical Approach to Personal Suffering*. Chicago: Moody Press, 1982.

_____. *Toward an Old Testament Theology*. Grand Rapids: Zondervan Publishing House, 1978.

Keil, Carl Friedrich. *The Twelve Minor Prophets*. 2 vols. Translated by James Martin. Biblical Commentary on the Old Testament. Reprint ed. Grand Rapids: Wm. B. Eerdmans Publishing Co., 1949.

Longman, Tremper, III. "The Divine Warrior: The New Testament Use of an Old Testament Motif." *Westminster Theological Journal* 44 (1982):290-307.

_____. "Nahum." In *The Minor Prophets: An Exegetical and Expositional Commentary*, 2:765-829. 3 vols. Edited by Thomas Edward McComiskey. Grand Rapids: Baker Books, 1992, 1993, and 1998.

Longman, Tremper, III and Raymond B. Dillard. *An Introduction to the Old Testament*. 2nd ed. Grand Rapids: Zondervan, 2006.

Lowth, Robert. *Lectures on the Sacred Poetry of the Hebrews*. Translated by George Gregory. London: Tegg, 1839.

Luckenbill, Daniel David, ed. *Ancient Records of Assyria and Babylon*. 2 vols. Chicago: University of Chicago Press, 1926-27.

Maier, Walter A. *The Book of Nahum: A Commentary*. St. Louis: Concordia Publishing House, 1959; reprint ed., Grand Rapids: Baker Book House, 1980.

Morgan, G. Campbell. *Living Messages of the Books of the Bible*. 2 vols. New York: Fleming H. Revell Co., 1912.

The Nelson Study Bible. Edited by Earl D. Radmacher. Nashville: Thomas Nelson Publishers, 1997.

The New Bible Dictionary. 1962 ed. S.v. "Nineveh," by D. J. Wiseman.

The New Scofield Reference Bible. Edited by Frank E. Gaebelein, William Culbertson, et al. New York: Oxford University Press, 1967.

Patterson, Richard D. *Nahum, Habakkuk, Zephaniah*. Wycliffe Exegetical Commentary series. Chicago: Moody Press, 1991.

Pritchard, James B., ed. *The Ancient Near East in Pictures*. Princeton: Princeton University Press, 1954.

_____, ed. *Ancient Near Eastern Texts Relating to the Old Testament*. 3rd ed. Princeton: Princeton University Press, 1969.

Thomas, D. Winton., ed. *Documents from Old Testament Times*. New York: Harper & Row, 1958.

Thompson, R. Campbell, and Hutchinson, R. W. *A Century of Exploration at Nineveh*. London: Luzac, 1929.

Voightlander, E. von. "A Survey of Neo-Babylonian History." Ph.D. Dissertation, University of Michigan, 1963.

Waltke, Bruce K., with Charles Yu. *An Old Testament Theology: an exegetical, canonical, and thematic approach*. Grand Rapids: Zondervan, 2007.

Wiersbe, Warren W. "Nahum." In *The Bible Exposition Commentary/Prophets*, pp. 405-10. Colorado Springs, Colo.: Cook Communications Ministries; and Eastbourne, England: Kingsway Communications Ltd., 2002.

Wood, Leon J. *The Prophets of Israel*. Grand Rapids: Baker Book House, 1979.

Yadin, Yigael. *The Art of Warfare in Biblical Lands*. New York: McGraw-Hill, 1963.

Zawadzki, S. *The Fall of Assyria and Median-Babylonian Relations in Light of the Nabopolassar Chronicle*. Delft, Holland: Eburon, 1988.

Constable's Notes
On Habakkuk

Introduction

Title and Writer
The title of the book is the name of its writer.

All we know for sure about Habakkuk is that he was a prophet who lived during the pre-exilic period of Israel's history. We know equally little about his seventh-century B.C. contemporaries Nahum and Zephaniah. The meaning of his name is questionable. It may come from the Hebrew verb *habaq*, which means "to fold the hands" or "to embrace." In the latter case, it might mean "one who embraces" or "one who is embraced." Luther thought it signified that Habakkuk embraced his people to comfort and uphold them. Jerome interpreted it to mean that he embraced the problem of "divine justice in the world," the subject of the book.[1] The simple designation, "the prophet," with no other identifying description, characterizes only two other prophetical books: Haggai and Zechariah. So Habakkuk is the only book so designated among the pre-exilic Prophets. The content of the book, which includes wisdom literature and a psalm of praise, indicates that Habakkuk was a poet as well as a prophet.

The New Testament writers told us nothing about the prophet. There are traditions about who Habakkuk was that have little basis in fact but are interesting nonetheless. Since the last verse of the book gives a musical notation similar to some psalms, some students concluded that he was a musician and possibly a Levite.[2]

> "The precise relationship of the prophets with the temple is one of the most debated elements in Old Testament study."[3]

The Septuagint addition to the Book of Daniel, the apocryphal *Bel and the Dragon*, mentions Habakkuk in its title as "the son of Jeshua of the tribe of Levi." It records a legend about him that is pure fantasy. Supposedly an angel commanded Habakkuk to take a meal to Daniel, who was in the lions' den a second time. When the prophet complained that he did not know where the den was, the angel picked him up by a lock of his hair and carried him to the spot (Bel vv. 33-39). According to rabbinic sources, Habakkuk was the son of the Shunammite woman whom Elisha restored to life (2 Kings 4). The basis for this theory is that Elisha' servant told the woman that she would "embrace" a son (2 Kings 4:16), and Habakkuk's name is similar to the Hebrew word for "embrace."

Unity
The major challenge to the unity of the book has come from liberal scholars who view psalmic material such as chapter 3 as postexilic. The commentary on Habakkuk found at Qumran does not expound this psalm, either. However, the continuity of theme that continues through the whole book, plus the absence of any compelling reasons to reject chapter 3, argue for the book's unity.[4]

Date
References in the book help us date it approximately, but make it impossible to be precise or dogmatic. The Lord told Habakkuk that He was raising up the Chaldeans (Neo-Babylonians), the fierce and impetuous people who were already marching throughout the whole earth, and that they would expand their territory even farther (1:6). The first of the Neo-Babylonian kings was Nabopolassar (627-605 B.C.). This reference points to a time before 605 B.C., when Babylon defeated the united forces of Egypt and Assyria at the battle of Carchemish, and became the major power in the ancient Near East. It may even point to a time before 612 B.C. when the Babylonians (with the Medes and Scythians) destroyed Nineveh. However, other references in the book, that describe conditions in Judah and the ancient Near East, support a date between 608 and 605 B.C. (cf. 1:7-11).[5] King Jehoiakim ruled Judah from 609 to 598 B.C., so it was apparently during his reign that Habakkuk prophesied (cf. 2 Kings 23:36—24:7; 2 Chron. 36:5-8). The background to Habakkuk is the decline of the Judean kingdom that began with the death of King Josiah in 609 B.C. Leon Wood dated this book more precisely at about 605 B.C.[6]

> "On the one hand, Habakkuk announced the Babylonians' rise to prominence as if it would be a surprise (1:5-6). . . . On the other hand, the prophecy seems to assume the Babylonians had already built a reputation as an imperialistic power (see 1:6-11, 15-17; 2:5-17). . . . Perhaps the best way to resolve the problem is to understand the book as a collection of messages from different periods in the prophet's career."[7]

---

[1] See J. Ronald Blue, "Habakkuk," in *The Bible Knowledge Commentary: Old Testament*, p. 1505.
[2] E.g., C. F. Keil, "Habakkuk," in *The Twelve Minor Prophets*, 2:49.
[3] Tremper Longman III and Raymond B. Dillard, *An Introduction to the Old Testament*, p. 463.
[4] See O. Palmer Robertson, *The Books of Nahum, Habakkuk, and Zephaniah*, pp. 212-14.
[5] See ibid., p. 37; and Charles Lee Feinberg, *Habakkuk, Zephaniah, Haggai, and Malachi*, pp. 11-12.
[6] Leon J. Wood, *The Prophets of Israel*, p. 323.
[7] Robert B. Chisholm Jr., *Handbook on the Prophets*, p. 433.

Another writer believed that some of the oracles date from before 605 B.C., while others came after 597 B.C., and that the final form of the book reflects Habakkuk's post-597 B.C. perspective.[8]

Place of Composition

Since the Chaldeans were on the rise when Habakkuk wrote, the prophet must have lived in Judah. The Northern Kingdom of Israel had passed out of existence in 722 B.C. with the Assyrian invasion. Thus Habakkuk was a prophet of the Southern Kingdom who lived in times of increasing degeneracy and fear.

Audience and Purpose

The people to whom Habakkuk ministered were Judeans who apparently lived under the reign of King Jehoiakim. During his reign the Israelites were looking for help in the wrong places, Egypt and Assyria, in view of growing Babylonian power. They should have been looking to the Lord primarily, and their failure to do so was one of the burdens of Jeremiah, Habakkuk's contemporary.

Habakkuk's concerns were more philosophical, however. What disturbed him was that the sovereign Lord was not responding to Habakkuk's evil generation and its internal injustices. He voiced his concern to Yahweh in prayer (1:2-4). The Lord replied that He was working. He was raising up a nation that would punish His people for their covenant unfaithfulness (1:5-11). This raised another problem for Habakkuk, which he also took to the Lord in prayer. How could He use a more wicked nation than Judah to punish God's chosen people (1:12—2:1)? The Lord explained that He would eventually punish the Babylonians for their wickedness too (2:2-20). The final chapter is a hymn of praise extolling Yahweh for His wise ways. The purpose of the book, then, was to vindicate the justice of God so God's people would have hope and encouragement.

> "Until the day God avenges the Babylonians and restores Jerusalem, the just live by faith (Hab. 2:1-4), waiting with confidence for the fulfillment of *I AM*'s unfailing promise that the wicked will be destroyed (2:5-19) and his legitimate claim to the whole world will be universally acknowledged (3:1-16)."[9]

Literary Form

This book employs a variety of literary forms. The first part of the book contains a dialogue between Habakkuk and his God that alternates between lament and oracle (1:2—2:5). The second part is a taunt or mocking song that the prophet put in the mouths of the nations that had suffered under Babylon's oppression. It consists of five "woes" (2:6-20). The third part is a psalm, complete with musical directions (ch. 3).

Distinctive Features

> "Habakkuk is a unique book. Unlike other prophets who declared God's message to people this prophet dialogued with God about people. Most Old Testament prophets proclaimed divine judgment. Habakkuk pleaded for divine judgment. In contrast with the typical indictment, this little book records an intriguing interchange between a perplexed prophet and his Maker."[10]

> "The prophet asked some of the most penetrating questions in all literature, and the answers are basic to a proper view of God and his relation to history. If God's initial response sounded the death knell for any strictly nationalistic covenant theology of Judah, his second reply outlined in a positive sense the fact that all history was hastening to a conclusion that was [as] certain as it was satisfying.

> "In the interim, while history is still awaiting its conclusion (and Habakkuk was not told when the end would come, apparently for him prefigured by Babylon's destruction), the righteous ones are to live by faith. The faith prescribed—or 'faithfulness,' as many have argued that *'emunah* should be translated—is still called for as a basic response to the unanswered questions in today's universe; and it is this, a theology for life both then and now, that stands as Habakkuk's most basic contribution."[11]

> "If Zephaniah stressed humility and poverty of spirit as prerequisites for entering into the benefits of the company of the believing, Habakkuk demanded faith as the most indispensable prerequisite. But these are all part of the same picture.

> "Whereas Zephaniah stressed Judah's idolatry and religious syncretism, Habakkuk was alarmed by the increase of lawlessness, injustice, wickedness, and rebellion."[12]

---

[8]J. J. M. Roberts, *Nahum, Habakkuk, and Zephaniah*, pp. 82-84.
[9]Bruce K. Waltke, *An Old Testament Theology*, p. 842.
[10]Blue, p. 1505.
[11]Carl E. Armerding, "Habakkuk," in *Daniel-Malachi*, vol. 7 of *The Expositor's Bible Commentary*, pp. 495-96.
[12]Walter C. Kaiser Jr., *Toward an Old Testament Theology*, p. 225.

Outline

I. Heading 1:1
II. Habakkuk's questions and Yahweh's answers 1:2—2:20
    A. Habakkuk's question about Judah 1:2-4
    B. Yahweh's answer about Judah 1:5-11
    C. Habakkuk's question about Babylonia 1:12-17
    D. Yahweh's answer about Babylonia ch. 2
        1. The introduction to the answer 2:1-3
        2. The Lord's indictment of Babylon 2:4-5
        3. The Lord's sentence on Babylon 2:6-20
III. Habakkuk's hymn in praise of Yahweh ch. 3
    A. The introduction to the hymn 3:1
    B. The prayer for revival 3:2
    C. The vision of God 3:3-15
        1. Yahweh's awesome appearance 3:3-7
        2. Yahweh's angry actions 3:8-15
    D. The commitment of faith 3:16-19a
    E. The concluding musical notation 3:19b

Message

Habakkuk is unusual among the prophetical books in that it tells a story. In this, it is similar to Jonah, which is also the record of a prophet's experience. Jonah gives the account of a prophet's failure to *sympathize* with God. Habakkuk gives the account of a prophet's failure to *understand* God. Jonah deals with a problem posed by *Nineveh*, and Habakkuk deals with a problem posed by *Babylon*. Habakkuk, like Jonah, also records one major event in the life of the prophet. Most of the other prophetic books record the messages and activities of a prophet over an extended period of years. Habakkuk does contain prophecies, so it is like the other prophetic books in this respect.

The key verse in the book is 2:4: "Behold, as for the proud one, his soul is not right within him; but the righteous will live by his faith." This verse suggests the difficulty that Habakkuk faced, and it contains his declaration following his struggle with faith.

Habakkuk is a book in which a man, the prophet, asked questions and received answers. Note, for example, 1:2, which voices the prophet's initial question. Then 3:19 gives his final affirmation, after having received answers. The contrast between these verses is startling. It is a contrast between a wail of despair and a shout of confidence.

> "From the affirmation of faith's agnosticism we come to the affirmation of agnosticism's faith."[13]

This is the story of Habakkuk. At the beginning, we hear a believer questioning God. The prophet's problem was why God was not doing what He promised to do, specifically: delivering His people from the violence with which the Babylonians were threatening them. Every believer faces the same problem sooner or later. Circumstances challenge the promises of God, and we wonder why God does not do something about the situation. Habakkuk wondered how God could use an *even more wicked* nation—Babylon—to discipline the wicked Judahites.

The key verse, 2:4, is similar to the constricted part of an hourglass. Everything that precedes it leads up to it, and everything that follows it results from it. It is like a doorway through which everything in the book passes. This verse contains two contrasting viewpoints on all of life. First, we have a swollen, proud, conceited person. Second, we have a person who is full of faith. The first is full of himself or herself, and the second is full of God. The difference is in attitude: great confidence in self, or in God. In both cases, we have something hidden and something manifest.

In the case of the proud, his soul or inner man is not straight or right within him. It is not upright or level, but crooked or twisted. His is an unnatural condition. While his inner, hidden condition is crookedness of soul, his outer, manifest condition is conceit or pride. He is wrapped up in himself, and being wrapped up in himself, he is wrapped up in a ball, so to speak—all twisted up on the inside. It is interesting that the verse says nothing about the outcome of the proud. We only have a description of him as swollen and twisted.

In the case of the righteous, his soul is right within him. His inner, hidden condition is straight. His outward manifestation of that condition is trust in God. It is interesting, in passing, that there is only one straightness, but there are many kinds of crookedness, perversity. If I asked a group of

---

[13] G. Campbell Morgan, *Living Messages of the Books of the Bible*, 1:2:274.

people to imagine a straight stick, everyone would visualize a stick that is free of any bends or curves. But if I asked them to imagine a crooked stick, everyone would visualize a different shape of crookedness. A crooked stick may be crooked in a hundred different ways, but there is only one way a straight stick can be straight. Goodness is basically simple, but evil is exceedingly complex. Goodness looks only one way, but evil can take many different forms and shapes.

The central affirmation of Habakkuk is the last part of 2:4: "the righteous will live by his faith." There are three key words in this affirmation: righteous, live, and faith. It is interesting that in the three places where this verse is quoted in the New Testament, in each case a different word receives the emphasis. In Romans 1:17, the emphasis is on "righteous." Paul's concern in Romans was with the righteousness of God and how people can obtain it. In Hebrews 10:38, the emphasis is on "live." The writer to the Hebrews stressed the importance of living by faith as a way of life, and not turning back to Judaism and living by the Law. And in Galatians 3:11, the emphasis is on "faith." Paul contrasted salvation by works and salvation by faith in Galatians. Thus, we can see that this statement is packed with meaning. In fact, many people believe that this verse expresses the central theme of the entire Bible. It has been called the John 3:16 of the Old Testament.

Now let us relate this to what Habakkuk saw that created a problem of faith for him. He saw the proud flourishing. He saw crookedness all around him in a hundred different manifestations of evil. He also saw the righteous, who were trusting in God, oppressed, threatened, and persecuted. Specifically, he saw the proud Babylonians, who did not acknowledge Yahweh, gaining more and more power. They appeared to be the ones truly alive. He saw the people of God, who were trusting in Yahweh, losing more and more power. They appeared to be headed for certain death and extinction. And, most disturbing of all, Habakkuk saw God doing nothing.

In the hour of his crisis of faith, God spoke to the prophet and gave him the great truth of 2:4. Faith is the principle that leads to life, in spite of all appearances, and pride is destructive, in spite of all appearances. Godless people and their plans seem so strong and invincible. Their enterprises, which are often in rebellion against God, seem so inevitable and sure to succeed. Nevertheless, the one whom God regards as righteous, because of his or her trust in Him, will live on.

What is God doing? He is causing things to work out in harmony with the principle set forth in 2:4, in spite of appearances. The Sovereign of the Universe, who often takes centuries to work out His plans—when we want Him to do it in years, if not months—holds everything in His grasp. He will fulfill His promises. He will reward faith. He will destroy the crooked and the proud.

The last part of the book, which follows 2:4, helps us to see the outcome of believing God's revelation in 2:4. Habakkuk reviewed many of the crooked manifestations of evil and announced the final destruction of them all. He also viewed the history of the Israelites as a testimony to the truth of the book's central affirmation, and he trembled as he projected forward what God had done in the past, to what He would do to the Chaldeans. The prophet, who started out thinking that God was doing nothing, ended by praying that Yahweh would remember mercy, when He poured out His wrath. He, who thought God had forgotten about the faithful, broke out into a song of praise as he realized that he could continue to trust God, in spite of appearances.

Habakkuk does not end with a wail, but with a song. It does not end with inquiry, but with affirmation. It does not end with frustration, but with faith: 3:17-18.

There are several lessons of timeless importance that Habakkuk teaches its readers.

One abiding lesson of this book is that people of faith sometimes have trouble continuing to trust God. If we look at what is happening in our world, we may come up with the same questions Habakkuk voiced at the beginning of the book. But if we continue to listen to the Word of God, we can have peace in our hearts and songs on our lips, while we wait for God to reward the righteous with life for their faith. This principle is true on two levels: justification and sanctification. The only way to obtain a proper legal standing before God (justification) is by trusting Him. And the only way to continue to live in that righteous standing before God (sanctification) is to continue to trust Him, in spite of appearances. We can do so because God has established a flawless record of faithfulness to His promises, and the Bible is the record of that faithfulness. Thus, we must live in the light of Scripture, rather than in the light of experience. God's promises and covenants are a better indication of reality than circumstances.

We also need to be careful that we do not fall into the category of the proud, who are wrapped up in themselves. We, too, quickly look to the proud of this world, who do not bow before God, for explanations. Rather, we should express our own righteousness by continuing to trust in God, in spite of appearances. Today, scientific explanations attract more faith than the simple statements of Scripture. Where will our trust be? We dare not join the ranks of the twisted and scoffing mockers whose end is not life, but destruction. It is interesting that now some of the so-called "assured facts" of science are being called into question by scientists themselves.

Notice, too, how Habakkuk handled his questions. He could have set up a schedule of speaking engagements all over Judah to point out how inconsistent God was in His government of human affairs. Fortunately, instead, he took his questions to God in prayer. God responded by giving him answers. The revelation of God came to Habakkuk. The prophet listened to the Word of God. We can say anything to God in prayer. The best place to take our questions is to God in prayer. And the best place to find answers from God is in His Word. Some people say that God does not speak as He spoke in days gone by. It is truer to say that people do not listen to God as they did in days gone by. Living by faith means becoming people of prayer and the Word.

Furthermore, the inner attitude always manifests itself in outward action. This is true whether the inner attitude is pride or faith. What is our outward action betraying about our inner attitude? Are we really trusting man or God? Where do we turn first for answers? Scripture? I hope so.

In 2:3, God said, "Though the vision tarries, wait for it, for it will certainly come." Part of being people of faith is that we wait for explanations, verbal or experiential, that will only come in the future. Someone has wisely said that Christians are people who do not live by explanations but by promises.[14] We must be content with God's promise that one day we will understand what is now obscure. How God will bring His will to pass is a mystery, in large measure. We only have the outlines of His actions in prophecy, though we have some remarkably specific details revealed here and there. Nevertheless for the most part, we must be willing to wait. The promise of God is life for those who *continue to wait* on God. Waiting is the hardest work of all, but like Habakkuk we will be able to sing as we wait if we keep talking to God and listening to God.[15]

Exposition

I. HEADING 1:1

The writer described this book as an "oracle" that "Habakkuk the prophet saw" in a vision or dream. This burden (Heb. *massa'*, something lifted up) was a message predicting judgment on Judah and Babylon.

> "Habakkuk's prophecy possesses a burdensome dimension from start to finish."[16]

We know nothing more about Habakkuk with certainty than that he was a prophet who also had the ability to write poetry (ch. 3).

> "Like Haggai and Zechariah in the books that bear their names (Hag. 1:1; Zech. 1:1) Habakkuk is called *the* prophet. This may mean that Habakkuk was a professional prophet on the temple staff . . ."[17]

These temple prophets led the people in worshipping God (cf. 1 Chron. 25:1).[18]

> "One of the functions of temple prophets was to give responses to worshipers who came seeking divine guidance: when the problem was stated, the prophet inquired of God and obtained an answer."[19]

II. HABAKKUK'S QUESTIONS AND YAHWEH'S ANSWERS 1:2—2:20

The prophet asked Yahweh two questions and received two answers.

A. Habakkuk's question about Judah 1:2-4

This section is a lament and is similar to many psalms of lament (e.g., Ps. 6:3; 10:1-13; 13:1-4; 22:1-21; 74:1-11; 80:4; 88; 89:46; cf. Jer. 12:4; Zech. 1:12).

1:2   While in prayer, the prophet asked Yahweh "how long" would he have to keep calling for help before the Lord responded (cf. 2:6; Exod. 16:28; Num. 14:11). God hears all prayers because He is omniscient, but Habakkuk meant that God had not given evidence of hearing by responding to his prayer. He had cried out to the Lord reminding Him of the violence that he observed in Judah, but the Lord had not provided deliverance (cf. Gen. 6:11, 13; Job 19:7). Normally where "justice" (Heb. *mishpat*) and "violence" (*hamas*) are in opposition in the Old Testament, as here, the wicked are Israelites unless they are clearly identified as being others (e.g., Exod. 23:1-9; Isa. 5:7-15). God had seemingly not heard, and He certainly had not helped the prophet.

> "Not hearing is equivalent to not helping."[20]

1:3   Habakkuk wanted to know why Yahweh allowed the "iniquity" and "wickedness"—that he had to observe every day—to continue in Judah. "Destruction," ethical wrong, "strife," and "contention" were not only common, but they were increasing. Yet Yahweh did nothing about the situation.

---

[14] See Warren W. Wiersbe, *The Bible Exposition Commentary/Prophets*, p. 95.
[15] Adaped from Morgan, 1:2:273-86.
[16] Robertson, p. 135.
[17] F. F. Bruce, "Habakkuk," in *The Minor Prophets*, p. 842. Johannes Lindblom, *Prophecy in Ancient Israel*, pp. 208, 254, advanced this view.
[18] On the subject of prophets who led the people in worship, see Aubrey R. Johnson, *The Cultic Prophet in Ancient Israel*.
[19] Bruce, p. 832.
[20] Keil, 2:56.

"Violence" (Heb. *hamas*) occurs six times in Habakkuk (1:2, 3, 9; 2:8, 17 [twice]), an unusually large number of times for such a short book. The Hebrew word means more than just physical brutality. It refers to flagrant violation of moral law by which someone injures his fellow man (e.g., Gen. 6:11). It is any ethical wrong, and physical violence is only one manifestation of it. By piling up synonyms for injustice, Habakkuk stressed the severity of the oppression.

> "This is not an instance of the earthen vessel finding fault with the potter who made it—an attitude rebuked by Isaiah and Paul. It is to the one who answers back in unbelief that Paul says, 'Who indeed are you . . . to argue with God?' (Rom. 9:20). But there are others who answer back in faith; their words, when they do so, are the expression of their loyalty to God."[21]

1:4   Since God had not yet intervened to stem the tide of evil, as He had threatened to do in the Mosaic Law, the Judeans were ignoring His law. They did not practice justice in their courts, the wicked dominated the righteous, and the powerful "perverted . . . justice." These conditions were common in Judah.

It is clear from the Lord's reply that follows, that others in the nation beside Habakkuk were praying these prayers and asking these questions. The prophet spoke for the godly remnant in Judah.

B. Yahweh's answer about Judah 1:5-11

Though God had not responded to the prophet's questions previously, He did eventually, and Habakkuk recorded His answer. The form of this revelation is an oracle.

> "The hoped-for response to a lament (*cf.* 1:2-4) would be an oracle of salvation, but here the response is an oracle of judgment."[22]

1:5   The Lord told Habakkuk and his people (plural "you" in Hebrew) to direct their attention away from what was happening in Judah, to what was happening in the larger arena of ancient Near Eastern activity. They were to observe something there that would astonish them and make them marvel. They would see that God was doing something in their days that they would not believe—*even if* someone had just told them about it!

> "The Apostle Paul, quoting from the LXX on this verse, applies the principle of God's dealings in Habakkuk's day to the situation in the church in his own day (Acts 13:41). No doubt God's work of calling the Gentiles into his church would be just as astonishing as his work of using the Babylonian armies to punish Judah."[23]

1:6   The Lord urged the prophet and his people to see that He was in the process of "raising up the Chaldeans" as a force and power in their world. The name "Chaldeans" derives from the ruling class that lived in southern Mesopotamia and took leadership in the Neo-Babylonian Empire. The last and greatest dynasty to rule Babylon was of Chaldean origin. Thus "Chaldean" was almost a synonym for "Babylonian." The Chaldeans were Semites, descendants of Kesed, the son of Abraham's brother Nahor (Gen. 22:22). Some modern Iraqis, especially those from southern Iraq, still identify themselves as Chaldeans. The Neo-Babylonian Empire began its rise to world domination with the accession of Nabopolassar to the throne of Babylon in 626 B.C. This aggressive king stimulated the Babylonians into becoming a ruthless and impetuous nation that—by this time—had already "marched throughout" the ancient Near East and conquered several neighboring nations (cf. Ezek. 28:7; 30:11; 31:12; 32:12). Thus, Babylonia would be the rod of God's punishment of Judah, as Assyria had been His instrument of judgment of Israel.

> "The seventh-century prophets depicted the Lord as the sovereign ruler over the nations."[24]

1:7   Many nations "dreaded and feared" the Babylonians, who were a *law unto themselves*. They lived by rules that they made up, rather than those that were customary at the time. Similarly, the Third Reich called error "truth," and right "wrong," to suit its own purposes.

> "If God's people refuse to fear him, they will ultimately be compelled to fear those less worthy of fear (cf. Deut 28:47-48; [sic] 58-68; Jer 5:15-22)."[25]

---

[21]Bruce, p. 844.
[22]David W. Baker, *Nahum, Habakkuk and Zephaniah*, p. 52.
[23]David W. Kerr, "Habakkuk," in *The Wycliffe Bible Commentary*, p. 873.
[24]Robert B. Chisholm Jr., "A Theology of the Minor Prophets," in *A Biblical Theology of the Old Testament*, p. 415.
[25]Armerding, p. 503.

The Jews of Habakkuk's day did not believe that God would allow the Gentiles to overrun their nation (cf. Jer. 5:12; 6:14; 7:1-34; 8:11; Lam. 4:12; Amos 6). Yet their law and their prophets warned them that this could happen (cf. Deut. 28:49-50; 1 Kings 11:14, 23; Jer. 4; 5:14-17; 6:22-30; Amos 6:14).

1:8   The military armaments of the Babylonians were state of the art. "Their horses," the implements of war in the ancient world, were the swiftest, faster even "than leopards" (hyperbole?), one of the fastest animals in the cat family. They were more eager to attack their enemies "than wolves" (cf. Jer. 5:6). Their mounted soldiers swooped down on their enemies, as fast and unsuspected as "an eagle" (or vulture), diving from the sky to devour a small animal on the ground (cf. Deut. 28:49; Jer. 5:17; Lam. 4:19). All three of these animals—that God used for comparison with the Babylonians—were excellent hunters, fast, and fierce.

1:9   The Babylonians loved "violence." The "faces" of their warriors showed their love for battle, as they moved irresistibly "forward" in conquest. They were as effective at collecting "captives" from other countries as the sirocco winds from the East were at driving sand before them (cf. Jer. 18:17; Ezek. 17:10; 19:12; Jon. 4:8). This enemy was advancing like a whirlwind, and gathering captives as innumerable as the grains of sand.

1:10 The "kings and rulers" of the lands they overran were no threat to them. They laughed at them and their fortified cities in contempt (cf. 2 Kings 25:7). They "heap(ed) up rubble" to "capture" fortifications. They did not need special machines, but used whatever materials they found, with which to build siege ramps to conquer them (cf. 2 Sam. 20:15; 2 Kings 19:32; Ezek. 4:2; 21:22; 26:8-9).[26]

1:11 The Babylonians would "sweep through" the ancient Near East like "the wind," and "pass on" from one doomed nation to the next. Yet Yahweh promised to hold them "guilty" because they worshipped power—as "their god"—instead of the true God. This is the reason God would judge them.

God may seem to be strangely silent and inactive in provocative circumstances. He sometimes gives unexpected answers to our prayers. And He sometimes uses strange instruments to correct His people.[27]

C. HABAKKUK'S QUESTION ABOUT BABYLONIA 1:12-17

This section is another lament (cf. 1:2-4). It expresses the problem of excessive punishment.

1:12 Power was not Habakkuk's god; Yahweh was. The Lord's revelation of what He was doing in the prophet's day brought confidence to his heart and praise to his lips. With a rhetorical question, Habakkuk affirmed his belief that Yahweh, his God, the Holy One, was "from everlasting" (or antiquity). The implication is that Yahweh is the only true God, and that history was unfolding as it was because the God who created history was in charge of events (i.e., sovereign).

Habakkuk believed the Judeans would not perish completely because God had promised to preserve them forever (2 Sam. 7:16). The prophet, furthermore, now understood that Yahweh had appointed the Babylonians "to judge" the sinful Judeans. The God who had been a Rock of security and safety for His people, throughout their history, had raised up this enemy "to correct" His people—not to annihilate them (cf. Deut. 32:4, 15, 18, 37.

1:13 Because Yahweh was the "Holy One" (v. 12), Habakkuk knew that He was "too pure" to look approvingly at "evil," nor could He "favor . . . wickedness." This was a basic tenet of Israel's faith (cf. Ps. 5:4; 34:16, 21). But this raised another, more serious, problem in the prophet's mind. Why did the Lord then look approvingly on the treachery of the Babylonians? Why did He not reprove them and restrain them when the Babylonians slaughtered people who were more righteous than they? Why did the godly remnant in Judah have to suffer with their ungodly Judean neighbors?

The prophet's first question (vv. 2-4) arose out of an apparent inconsistency between God's actions and His character. He was a just God, but He was allowing sin in His people to go unpunished. His second question arose out of the same apparent inconsistency. Yahweh was a just God, but He was allowing terrible sinners to succeed and even permitted them to punish less serious sinners. These questions evidenced perplexed faith rather than weak faith. Clearly Habakkuk had strong faith in God, but how God was exercising His sovereignty baffled him.

---

[26]See Yigael Yadin, *The Art of Warfare in Biblical Lands*, pp. 17, 20, 315.

[27]See D. Martyn Lloyd-Jones, *From Fear to Faith: Studies in the Book of Habakkuk and the Problem of History*, pp. 15-18.

> "It is one thing to face the problems that confront everyone who believes in a good and omnipotent God and ask why things are so, or how they can be so. It is something quite different to question the Divine goodness or justice, or the very existence of God, simply because one cannot answer these questions."[28]

1:14   Habakkuk asked the Lord why He had made people "like . . . fish" and other sea creatures that apparently have no "ruler over them."

> "This statement probably represents the prophet's most pointed accusation against the Almighty. In recognizing the sovereignty of God among the nations, he must conclude that God himself is ultimately behind this massive maltreatment of humanity."[29]

Big fish eat little fish, and bigger fish eat the big fish. The same thing was happening in Habakkuk's world. Babylon was gobbling up the smaller nations, and Yahweh was not intervening to establish justice.

1:15-16   Babylon was like a fisherman, who took other nations captive "with a hook" and "net," and rejoiced over his good catch. Earlier the prophet compared the Babylonians to hunters (v. 8). Babylonian monuments depict the Chaldeans as having driven a hook through the lower lip of their captives and stringing them single file, like fish on a line.[30] This was an Assyrian practice that the Babylonians continued. In another Babylonian relief, the Chaldeans pictured their major gods dragging a net in which their captured enemies squirmed.[31] The Babylonians even worshipped and gave credit to the *tools* they used to make their impressive conquests, rather crediting Yahweh (cf. v. 11). They had as little regard for human life as fishermen have for fish. That God would allow this to continue seemed blatantly unjust to Habakkuk.

> "Idolatry is not limited to those who bring sacrifices or burn incense to inanimate objects. People of position, power, and prosperity often pay homage to the business or agency that provided them their coveted status. It becomes their constant obsession, even their 'god.'"[32]

1:17   Habakkuk finished his question by asking the Lord if the Babylonians would continue to carry on their evil practices "without sparing" anyone. Yahweh's policy of not interfering with Babylon's wickedness baffled Habakkuk more than His policy of not interfering with Judah's wickedness. It was Yahweh's using a nation *that practiced such excessive violence* to judge the sins of His people, that Habakkuk could not understand.

D. YAHWEH'S ANSWER ABOUT BABYLON CH. 2

The Lord gave Habakkuk a full answer to his question about using Babylon to judge the Israelites.

1. The introduction to the answer 2:1-3

2:1   Habakkuk compared himself to a sentinel on a city wall, watching the horizon for the approach of a horseman (cf. Isa. 21:8, 11; Jer. 6:17; Ezek. 3:17; 33:2-3). He purposed to "watch" and wait expectantly for the Lord to reply to this second question, as He had the first, so he could report it to his people (cf. 3:16). He prepared himself for a discussion with the Lord about the situation, as well as for the Lord's answer that he expected in a vision or dream (cf. Job 13:3; 23:4).

> "Only by revelation can the genuine perplexities of God's dealings with human beings be comprehended."[33]

> "Yahweh's response to those who inquire of him is never automatic. They must be willing to wait in order to hear 'what God the LORD will speak' (Ps. 85:9 [8])."[34]

2:2   Yahweh did respond, and told the prophet to "inscribe" a permanent, easy-to-read "record" of "the vision"—which He would give him—"on tablets" (of clay, stone, or metal; cf. Exod. 31:18; 32:15-16; Deut. 9:10; 27:8). Having received and recorded the vision, Habakkuk, and other messengers, should then "run" to tell their fellow citizens what God's answer was.

---

[28]Kerr, p. 875.
[29]Robertson, p. 162.
[30]W. Rudolph, *Micha-Nahum-Habakuk-Zephanja*, p. 211.
[31]T. Laetsch, *Bible Commentary: The Minor Prophets*, p. 326.
[32]Blue, p. 1512.
[33]Robertson, p. 166.
[34]Bruce, p. 857.

"The matter was to be made so clear that whoever read it might run and publish it."[35]

"It [the interpretation of the Lord's command here] could involve passers-by, who will be able to read the message as they go by and then pass the message on informally to those they meet, or it could mean *a herald*, whose specific function will be to spread the message throughout the land (so NEB, NIV)."[36]

2:3   The vision Habakkuk was about to receive concerned events to take place in the future. Though it was a prophecy that would not come to pass immediately, it would materialize eventually. Habakkuk was to "wait" for its fulfillment, because it would indeed "come" at the Lord's "appointed time (cf. Dan. 12:4).

"The words simply express the thought, that the prophecy is to be laid to heart by all the people on account of its great importance, and that not merely in the present, but in the future also."[37]

The writer of the Book of Hebrews quoted this verse (Heb. 10:37). He used it to encourage his readers to persevere in their commitment to Jesus Christ, since what God had predicted will eventually come to pass, which in the context of Hebrews will be the Lord's return.

2. The Lord's indictment of Babylon 2:4-5

Having prepared the prophet for His answer, the Lord now gave it. What follows must be that revelation.

2:4   "Proud" Babylon was "not right" in doing what she did, but was puffed up with pride and evil passions. In contrast, the "righteous" one "will live by his faith" (cf. Gen. 15:6). By implication, Babylon, the unrighteous one, would not live because she did not live by faith (trust in God) but by sight and might. She sought to gratify her ambitions by running over other people rather than by submitting to God's sovereignty.

"A proud person relies on self, power, position, and accomplishment; a righteous person relies on the Lord."[38]

This verse appears three times in the New Testament. Paul quoted it in Romans 1:17 and emphasized "righteous." Faith in God results in righteousness for both Jews and Gentiles. He used it again in Galatians 3:11 but to stress "live." Rather than obtaining new life by obeying the Mosaic Law, the righteous person does so by faith. In Galatians, Paul was mainly addressing Gentiles. The writer of Hebrews also quoted this verse in Hebrews 10:38, but his emphasis was on "faith." It is faith that God will reward in the righteous. In this case, the original readers were primarily Jews. In all three cases, "live" has the broader reference to eternal life, but here in Habakkuk, it is mainly *physical life* that is in view. Thus, this verse is clearly a very important revelation in the Bible—even its essential message.

"It takes three books to explain and apply this one verse!"[39]

This is the key verse in Habakkuk, because it summarizes the difference between the proud Babylonians and their destruction, with the humble faith of the Israelites and their deliverance. The issue is trust in God.

"'The just shall live by his faith' was the watchword of the Reformation, and they may well be the seven most important monosyllables in all of church history."[40]

"The underlying theme of the book may be summarized as follows: A matured faith trusts humbly but persistently in God's design for establishing righteousness in the earth."[41]

Bruce stated the theme of the book as "the preservation of loyal trust in God in face of the challenge to faith presented by the bitter experience of foreign invasion and oppression."[42]

---

[35]Kerr, p. 876. Cf. Dan. 12:4.
[36]Baker, p. 59. Cf. Feinberg, p. 22; Keil, 2:69.
[37]Ibid., 2:70.
[38]*The Nelson Study Bible*, p. 1522.
[39]Warren W. Wiersbe, "Habakkuk," in *The Bible Exposition Commentary/Prophets*, p. 411.
[40]Ibid., p. 416.
[41]Robertson, p. 136. Italics omitted.
[42]Bruce, p. 831.

The Hebrew word *'emunah*, "faith," can also mean "faithful" or "steadfast." It can also mean "integrity."[43] Did the Lord mean that the righteous will live by his trust in God or by being faithful to God, by being a person of integrity? Scripture elsewhere reveals that both meanings are true: trust and integrity. However, in this context "faith" or "trust" seems to be the primary meaning, since the Babylonians did not trust God, whereas the Israelites did. Both the Babylonians and the Israelites, though, had been *unfaithful* (disloyal or disobedient) to God.

> "The discrepancy between 'faith' and 'faithfulness' is more apparent than real, however. For man to be faithful in righteousness entails dependent trust in relation to God (e.g., 1 Sam 26:23-24); such an attitude is clearly demanded in the present context of waiting for deliverance (2:3; 3:16-19)."[44]

> "This is the first of three wonderful assurances that God gives in this chapter to encourage His people. This one emphasizes God's grace, because grace and faith always go together. Habakkuk 2:14 emphasizes God's glory and assures us that, though this world is now filled with violence and corruption (Gen. 6:5, 11-13), it shall one day be filled with God's glory. The third assurance is in Habakkuk 2:20 and emphasizes God's government. Empires may rise and fall, but God is on His holy throne, and He is King of Kings and Lord of Lords."[45]

2:5   The Lord advanced the thought of verse 4 further. When a person drinks too much "wine," it leads him (or her) to reveal his pride publicly. Here, the "haughty man" is a personification of Babylon. The Babylonians were known for their consumption of wine (e.g., Dan. 5). "Wine" makes a person dissatisfied with his present situation and possessions, and he often leaves his home to find more elsewhere (cf. Prov. 23:31-32). The proud person is "never satisfied"—"like death" that consumes people every day and never stops. Here, "Sheol" is a personification of death. Babylon was similar, opening wide its jaws to consume all peoples. The proud person also seeks to dominate others, and this, too, marked Babylon. These were the evidences of Babylon's pride, and the basis for Yahweh's indictment of this nation (cf. 1:17).

> "*Sheol* is, in the O.T., the place to which the dead go. (1) Often, therefore, it is spoken of as the equivalent of the grave, where all human activities cease; the terminus toward which all human life moves (e.g. Gen. 42:38; Job 14:13; Ps. 88:3). (2) To the man 'under the sun,' the natural man, who of necessity judges from appearances, *sheol* seems no more than the grave—the end and total cessation, not only of the activities of life, but also of life itself (Eccl. 9:5, 10). But (3) Scripture reveals *sheol* as a place of sorrow (2 Sam. 22:6; Ps. 18:5; 116:3), into which the wicked are turned (Ps. 9:17), and where they are fully conscious (Isa. 14:9-17; Ezek. 32:21). Compare Jon. 2:2; what the belly of the great fish was to Jonah, *sheol* is to those who are therein. The *sheol* of the O.T. and *hades* of the N.T. are identical."[46]

3. The Lord's sentence on Babylon 2:6-20

The Lord pronounced taunts or mocking statements on the Babylonians, announcing that they would receive judgment for their sins. This taunt song consists of five stanzas of three verses each. Five woes follow. Baker entitled them "the pillager," "the plotter," "the promoter of violence," "the debaucher," and "the pagan idolator."[47] Each woe is "an interjection of distress pronounced in the face of disaster or in view of coming judgment (cf. Isa. 3:11; 5:11; 10:5; et al.)."[48]

Judgment for exploitation 2:6-8

2:6   Because of the Babylonians' sins, it was inevitable that the righteous would taunt and mock them. They would pronounce "woe" on them for increasing what was not theirs just to have more, and for making themselves rich by charging exorbitant interest on "loans." "How long" would this go on?—they asked themselves (cf. 1:2). When would God judge Babylon?

> ". . . the ode is prophetical in its nature, and is applicable to all times and all nations."[49]

2:7   Those from whom Babylon had stolen would surely "rise up" and rebel when they woke up to what was going on. Then they would turn the tables and Babylon would "become plunder for them." This happened when the Medes and Persians rose up (attacked) and overthrew Babylon in 539 B.C.

---

[43]Chisholm, *Handbook on . . .*, pp. 437-38.
[44]Armerding, p. 513.
[45]Wiersbe, p. 416.
[46]*The New Scofield Reference Bible*, p. 954.
[47]Baker, pp. 62, 64, 65, and 67.
[48]Blue, p. 1514.
[49]Keil, 2:77.

2:8   Babylon would suffer the same punishment it had inflicted on other nations (cf. Prov. 22:8; Gal. 6:7). Its survivors would "loot" it because it had "looted many" other peoples. Babylon's pillaging had involved "human bloodshed" and ethical wrong ("violence")—done to the land of Canaan and to the city of Jerusalem and its inhabitants.

Judgment for self-exaltation 2:9-11

2:9   Babylon used its unjust acquisitions to build a secure government for itself that it thought would be safe from all calamity (cf. Gen. 11:4; see also Obad.).[50] It built a strong and rich dynasty ("house") so it would be self-sufficient. Another interpretation is that the secure "nest" in view is the capital city.[51]

Saving to protect oneself from large future expenses is not wrong in itself, but to build a fortune so one will not have to trust in anyone else is saving with the wrong attitude (cf. James 5:1-6).

2:10   It was shameful for the Babylonians to destroy "many" other "peoples" (cf. vv. 5, 8). By doing so they were "sinning against" themselves. That is, they were doing something that would eventually bring destruction on themselves.

2:11   The stones and woodwork ("framework"), taken from other nations to build the Babylonians' fortresses and palaces, would serve as visual witnesses to the sinful invasions that brought them to Babylon. They would testify to the guilt of the Babylonians in the day that Yahweh would bring Babylon to judgment. Ostentatious buildings and cities make statements about their builders.

Judgment for oppression 2:12-14

2:12   The Babylonians could expect distress because they had built their cities at the expense of the lives of their enemies. We speak of "blood money" as money obtained by making others suffer, even shedding their blood. Babylon was built with "blood money" and the blood, sweat, and tears of enslaved people. It was a town founded on injustice; without injustice it could not have become what it had become.

2:13   This verse is the center of this taunt song structurally. It is significant that it focuses on Almighty Yahweh, the Judge. His assessment was that the Babylonians' hard work was in vain; all their labor would amount to "nothing." Their works would turn out to be fuel "for fire" that would burn them up, the fire of His judgment (cf. Jer. 51:58).

2:14   Rather than "the earth" being filled with the glory of Babylon, it will one day "be filled with the knowledge of" God's "glory," as comprehensively "as the waters cover the sea" (cf. Num. 14:21; Ps. 72:19; Isa. 6:3; 11:9; Jer. 31:34). This has yet to be. This prediction refers to the ultimate destruction of Babylon in the eschatological future (cf. Rev. 16:19—18:24).

The Babylon in view in the Book of Habakkuk was mainly the Neo-Babylonian Empire, but ever since Babel (Gen. 11:1-9), "Babylon" had a symbolic meaning as well as a literal one. Symbolically, it represented all ungodly peoples who rose up, in self-reliance, to glorify themselves and reach heaven by their own works. God destroyed the Neo-Babylonian Empire in 539 B.C., but *what Babylon represents* will continue until God destroys it—when Jesus Christ returns to the earth to set up His new order in the Millennium (cf. Rev. 17—18).

Judgment for rapacity 2:15-17

2:15   God would judge Babylon because the Babylonians had deceived their neighbor nations, with the result that they were able to take advantage of them. The Babylonians had behaved like a man who gets a woman "drunk" so she will lose her self-control, and he can then undress her. That the Babylonians took advantage of their victims sexually is implied in the illustration, as is their love for wine.

2:16   As they had made their neighbors drunk, so the Lord would give them a cup of judgment that would make them drunk. Yahweh's "right hand" is a figure for His strong personal retribution, giving back in kind what the person being judged had given (cf. Isa. 51:17-23; Jer. 25:15-17; Lam. 4:21; Matt. 20:22; 26:42; 1 Cor. 11:29). Having swallowed the cup's contents, the Babylonians would disgrace themselves, rather than honoring and glorifying themselves as they did presently. Their future

---

[50]Ibid., p. 83.
[51]Bruce, p. 867.

"disgrace" contrasts with Yahweh's future glory (v. 14). They would "expose" their "own nakedness," just as they had exposed the nakedness of others (v. 15). The Hebrew is more graphic and literally reads, "Drink, yes you, and expose your foreskin," namely, show yourself to be uncircumcised. Nakedness involves vulnerability as well as shame (cf. Gen. 9:21-25). The Lord pictured Babylon as a contemptible, naked drunk who had lost his self-control and the respect of everyone including himself.

2:17   Babylon's "violence" (ethical and moral injustice) would come back to cover ("overwhelm") him, because he had rapaciously stripped "Lebanon" of its vegetation and animals. However, "bloodshed" in Lebanon's main "town," and the slaughter of its "inhabitants," was an even more serious crime. "Lebanon" is probably a synecdoche for Israel, as it is elsewhere (cf. 2 Kings 14:9; Jer. 22:6, 23), and "the town" most likely refers to Jerusalem.

> "The Creator of the world has a concern for what is nowadays called ecology; the cultural mandate that he has given to the human race includes the responsible stewardship of plant and animal life."[52]

Judgment for idolatry 2:18-20

2:18   Habakkuk, like other prophets, saw through the folly of idolatry and exposed it (cf. Isa. 41:7; 44:9-20; 45:16, 20; 46:1-2, 6-7; Jer. 10:8-16). An "idol," "carved" by human hands, cannot help "its maker," because anyone who creates is always greater than his creation. Images in fact become teachers "of falsehood," since their existence implies a lie, namely: that they can help humans. An idol-carver "trusts in his" own "handiwork" by making it. Idols cannot even speak, much less provide help (cf. Rom. 1:22-25).

> "Modern people in their sophistications may regard themselves as free from the obvious folly of idolatry. What educated, self-respecting person would be deluded into expecting special powers to emanate from the form of an antiquated Idol? Yet the new covenant Scriptures make it plain that covetousness *is* idolatry (Eph. 5:5). Whenever a person's desire looks to the creature rather than the Creator, he is guilty of the same kind of foolishness. An insatiable desire for things not rightly possessed assumes that things can satisfy rather than God himself. Whenever a person sets his priorities on the things made rather than on the Maker of things, he is guilty of idolatry."[53]

> "Famous people are the 'idols' of millions, especially politicians, athletes, wealthy tycoons, and actors and actresses. Even dead entertainers like Marilyn Monroe, James Dean, and Elvis Presley still have their followers. People may also worship and serve man-made things like cars, houses, boats, jewelry, and art. While all of us appreciate beautiful and useful things, it's one thing to own them and quite something else to be owned by them. Albert Schweitzer said, 'Anything you have that you cannot give away, you do not really own; it owns you.' I've met people who so idolize their children and grandchildren that they refused to let them consider giving their lives for Christian service.

> "Social position can be an idol and so can vocation achievement. For some people, their god is their appetite (Phil. 3:19; Rom. 16:18); and they live only to experience carnal pleasures [including following their favorite sports?]. Intellectual ability can be a terrible idol (2 Cor. 10:5) as people worship their IQ and refuse to submit to God's Word."[54]

> "Idolatry begins with deception, encourages deception, and calls for a commitment to deception (see Is. 44:20)."[55]

2:19   The Lord pronounced "woe" on those who ignorantly tried to coax their dumb ("mute") idols—"wood" or "stone," perhaps "overlaid with gold" or "silver"—to speak (cf. 1 Kings 18:26-29). No matter what they looked like, or what material they were made out of, they were still *only lifeless objects* of art. How foolish it was to look to one of these as one's "teacher" or guide!

2:20   In contrast to lifeless idols stands the living and true God. Yahweh lived in His heavenly, "holy temple," not in the works of human hands. Therefore "all the earth," everything in it, should be quiet "before Him" out of respect and awe (fear; cf. v. 1; 3:16). There is no need to try and coax Him to come to life or to speak (cf. v. 19).

---

[52]Ibid., p. 872.
[53]Robertson, p. 209.
[54]Wiersbe, p. 418.
[55]*The Nelson . . .*, p. 1523.

"This contrasts with the frenetic activity of man to create 'speaking' gods, and the tumultuous cries of worshippers to make dumb idols respond. Lifeless idols approached in clamour are silent, while the living God, approached in silence and reverence, speaks."[56]

The implication of Yahweh's majestic sovereignty is that He would take care of Babylon; the Israelites did not have to concern themselves with that (cf. 3:16).

"God sometimes uses evil people to accomplish His larger purpose in life. But He never condones evil, and those who do evil He holds accountable for their actions."[57]

"The verse provides a bridge to the next major section of the prophecy in that it turns to the positive, looking at God, after the negative, attention to Babylon's sin."[58]

III. HABAKKUK'S HYMN IN PRAISE OF YAHWEH CH. 3

Having received the revelation that Yahweh would destroy Babylon, Habakkuk could understand that He was just in using that wicked nation to discipline Israel. Babylon would not go free but would perish for her sins. Israel's punishment, on the other hand, was only temporary (cf. 2 Sam. 7:16). This insight led Habakkuk to write the prayer of praise that concludes the book. It is "one of the most moving statements of faith and trust found in Scripture."[59]

This hymn is similar in language and imagery to Deuteronomy 33, Psalm 18:4-19, and Psalm 68. Its structure is chiastic, as indicated by the headings below.

A. THE INTRODUCTION TO THE HYMN 3:1

Habakkuk's prayer is hymnic in form, like many of the psalms (cf. Ps. 16; 30; 45; 88; 102; 142), and it apparently stood apart from the rest of the book at one time, as this title verse suggests. "Shigionoth" may be the title of the tune that the prophet, and later Israelites, used for singing this song. But the Hebrew word is the plural form of the same word used in the title of Psalm 7, but nowhere else. "Shiggaion" evidently means a poem with intense feeling: "a reeling song, *i.e.* a song delivered in the greatest excitement, or with a rapid change of emotion."[60] So another view is that the Israelites were to sing it enthusiastically. The intense feeling, in both contexts where the word occurs, is a vehement cry for justice against sin.

B. THE PRAYER FOR REVIVAL 3:2

The prophet acknowledged that he had received the Lord's revelation (cf. 2:1). It was essentially a revelation of Yahweh, His justice, sovereignty, and power, and it had filled him with awe. Reception of divine revelation resulted in the fear of the Lord, as it always should.

Habakkuk called on God to stir up ("revive") the "work" that He said He would do in judging Babylon, namely: to bring it to life.[61] He asked God to make it known to His people "in the midst of the years," namely, the years between Judah's judgment and Babylon's (cf. 2:6-20). God undoubtedly did this in part through the Book of Habakkuk. While God was preparing Babylon for His "wrath," Habakkuk asked Him to "remember" Israel by extending "mercy" to her, by shortening the period of her suffering. This verse contains the only petitions in Habakkuk's prayer: that God would preserve life, provide understanding, and remember mercy. Some readers have seen it as an encapsulation of the book's message. It also expresses the theme of the psalm.[62]

C. THE VISION OF GOD 3:3-15

Habakkuk moved from petition to praise in his prayer. He recalled God's great power and pardon in bringing the Israelites from Egypt, through the wilderness, and into the Promised Land. Since God had done this, Habakkuk was confident that He could and would deliver the Israelites from the Babylonians and reestablish them in the land.

---

[56]Baker, p. 68.
[57]Charles H. Dyer, in *The Old Testament Explorer*, p. 806.
[58]Baker, p. 68.
[59]Ibid.
[60]Keil, 2:93.
[61]Ibid., 2:94.
[62]Ibid., 2:92.

1. Yahweh's awesome appearance 3:3-7

3:3   The prophet pictured Yahweh as rising over His people, like the rising sun appearing over "Teman," a large town in Edom, and "Mt. Paran," the mountain opposite Teman (cf. Deut. 33:2-4). These locations were to the east of the Israelites as they exited Egypt. The idea is not that the Lord would rise over these eastern places, but that when He arose over His people, they would see Him as they saw the sun rising in the east—like they saw Him on Mt Sinai when He gave them the Law.[63]

The name for God used here, "Elohim," is in the singular—"Eloah"—perhaps stressing the essential unity of God who is "the Holy One." "Selah" is another musical notation meaning "to lift up" (cf. vv. 9, 13). It probably indicates a place where the singers of this song were to pause. This pause may have been to modulate the key upward, to increase the volume, to reflect on what was just said, to exalt the Lord in some other way, or to raise an instrumental fanfare.[64]

The Holy One's "splendor" covered "the heavens" like the sun after sunrise. The self-manifestation of His glory filled "the earth" with "His praise" (fame). "Glory" (Heb. *hod*) describes primarily kingly authority (e.g., Num. 27:20; 1 Chron. 29:25; et al.), and here it has particular reference to Yahweh's sovereignty over creation and history. This is evidently a description of the Lord's appearance on Mt. Sinai to the Israelites' forefathers. Moses used similar terms to describe His coming then (cf. Deut. 33:2).

3:4   The "radiance" of the Holy One's glory was "like the sunlight." "Power" seemed to flash from His fingertips as "rays" (lit. horns) of light stretch from the rising sun (cf. Exod. 34:29-30, 35). In spite of this, most of His power remained concealed.

3:5   As God moves through the earth, like the sun, He burns up what is in front of Him and chars what He leaves behind. "Pestilence" (lit. burning heat) and "plague" (i.e., devastation) are the accompaniments, the results and evidences of His searing holiness.

> "In the ancient Near East, important people were accustomed to being accompanied by attendants (*cf.* 1 Sa. 17:7; 2 Sa. 15:1)."[65]

3:6   Standing like the sun at its zenith, God "surveyed" the whole "earth." His downward look, like sunrays, caused the nations to tremble. His glance was enough to make the permanent mountains shatter and the ancient hills collapse. He always causes these repercussions since His ways are eternal. What a contrast He is to lifeless idols (cf. 2:18-19)!

3:7   Habakkuk saw the semi-nomadic Ethiopians and Midianites, who lived on both sides of Mt. Sinai, "trembling" with fear because they witnessed something of Yahweh's power. The terms "Midianite" and "Cushite" both described Moses' wife (Exod. 2:16-22; 18:1-5; Num. 12:1), so they may be synonymous here as well. Perhaps this is a reference to Yahweh parting the Red Sea. It is small wonder that these tribes trembled, since His glance can also cause mountains to melt (v. 6).

2. Yahweh's angry actions 3:8-15

Habakkuk now changed from describing the manifestation of God, and the inanimate and animate reactions to it, to a description of His acts on the earth.

3:8   With rhetorical questions, Habakkuk affirmed that Yahweh was not angry with the (Nile and Jordan) "rivers" and the (Red) "sea" when He transformed them. Another view is that the "rivers" refer to the rivers of the earth generally, and the "sea" refers to all the seas (cf. Nah. 1:4; Ps. 89:10; Job 38:8).[66] He was demonstrating His power for the "salvation" of His people, as a Divine Warrior riding His chariot.

> "In Canaanite mythology, Baal had confronted the personified god Yam (sea), alternatively called Judge River. Israel borrowed this motif but dropped any idea that natural phenomena are personified deities. Yahweh is presented as having engaged in combat with the sea at creation or at other unspecified periods (*cf.* Jb. 26:12-13; Pss. 29; 89:9-10)."[67]

---

[63]Ibid., 2:97-102.
[64]Blue, p. 1518.
[65]Baker, p. 71.
[66]Keil, 2:103.
[67]Baker, p. 72. See M. D. Coogan *Stories from Ancient Canaan*, pp. 75-115.

	"The horses and chariots of salvation upon which the Lord is pictured as riding are not the angels, but the elements—the clouds and the winds. See Psalm 104:4."[68]
3:9	He pulled His powerful "bow" out, and prepared to use it. He called for many arrows ("rods of chastisement") to shoot at His enemies (cf. Deut. 32:40-42). This is a notoriously difficult phrase to translate.
	"God had enlisted weapons and pledged them on oath for the destruction of his enemies."[69]
	"In the ancient Near East, warriors would sometimes empower their weapons with a magical formula. The Lord is depicted here as doing the same (see also Jer. 47:6-7)."[70]
	"Selah." (Think of that.)
	The prophet envisioned the "rivers" as God's instruments in dividing portions of "the earth."
3:10	Habakkuk personified "the mountains" and described them as shaking when they saw the Lord. Torrential rainstorms that resulted in flooding "swept by" Him (cf. Gen. 7:11, 19-20). The sea lifted up its waves like hands in response to His command (cf. Ps. 77:15-17, 19).
3:11	The "sun" and "moon stood" still at His word (cf. Josh. 10:12-13), and they paled when He sent forth flashes of lightning like arrows and shining spears (cf. Deut. 32:23, 42). Another view is that the "arrows" and "spear" do not refer to lightning, but simply to God's agents of judgment generally.[71]
3:12	The Lord had "marched throughout the earth" like a cosmic giant subduing Israel's enemies. He had "trampled" hostile "nations" as an ox does when it treads grain.
3:13	He had gone forth as a Warrior to save His "people" and to deliver His "anointed" one. This may refer to Moses in his battles with Israel's enemies, or it may refer to a coming anointed one: Cyrus (cf. Isa. 45:1), or Messiah (cf. Ps. 2:2; Dan. 9:26), or the Davidic kings generally, or more than one of these.
	"If the reference be to a past event (as a pattern) in the head out of the house of the wicked man, then allusion may be to one of the kings of Canaan. However, if the prophet is speaking of the future, and this is the more probable, then the king of the Chaldeans is meant."[72]
	"The first half of the verse provides the key to understanding the relationship of this chapter to the rest of the book. Rather than ignoring wrongdoing (1:2-4), or allowing oppression of his people to go unpunished (1:12-17), God remembers his covenant and acts on their behalf. The whole purpose of the psalm and of God's theophany is to indicate the continued presence of gracious care coupled with divine judgment. Here we have God's answer to Habakkuk's complaints (1:12-17)—his people will be saved."[73]
	The Lord had also destroyed the leaders ("struck the head") of many evil nations ("the house of evil") that opposed the Israelites, beginning with Pharaoh. He had disabled their nations as thoroughly as if someone had slit a body open from bottom to top, or tore a building off its foundation. "Selah." In the future, God would do this to the Chaldean dynasty.
3:14	The Lord used His enemies' own weapons to kill their leaders ("the head") in retribution (cf. Judg. 5:26). Israel's enemies had "stormed in(to)" the Promised Land with great enthusiasm "to scatter" God's people, like those who "devour" (destroy) "oppressed" people "in secret."
3:15	Yahweh had trodden down the Red Sea, as though He rode through it on cosmic horses, causing it to surge away and leave a dry road for His people to tread out of Egypt (cf. v. 8). This section closes with the motif with which it opened (3:8), namely: the crossing of the Red Sea.

---

[68]Feinberg, p. 35.
[69]Robertson, p. 234.
[70]Chisholm, *Handbook on . . .*, p. 442. See also R. D. Haak, *Habakkuk*, p. 95.
[71]Keil, 2:108-9.
[72]Feinberg, p. 37.
[73]Baker, pp. 74-75.

D. THE COMMITMENT TO FAITH 3:16-19A

3:16 Habakkuk "trembled" all over as he waited for the day of Babylon's invasion of Judah, "the day of" her "distress." He could do nothing but "wait" patiently for the Babylonians to grow stronger and for judgment to come on Israel. It is a terrible feeling to know that calamity is coming but that one can do nothing to prevent it. He could endure the prospect because he remembered that the omnipotent God of Israel had consistently defended her in the past—and promised to do so in the future. Earlier when the prophet heard about the powerful Babylonians, he wanted to talk with God (2:1). But now, having been reminded of the infinitely more powerful Yahweh, he had nothing more to say (cf. Job 42:1-6). God would handle the Babylonians. All Habakkuk had to do was wait.

> "Over the years, I've often leaned on three verses that have helped me wait patiently on the Lord. 'Stand still' (Ex. 14:13), 'Sit still' (Ruth 3:18), and 'Be still' (Ps. 46:10). Whenever we find ourselves getting 'churned up' within, we can be sure that we need to stop, pray, and wait on the Lord before we do some stupid thing."[74]

3:17-18 Even though everything would get worse in Judah, Habakkuk determined to praise Yahweh and to "rejoice in the God" who would save him (cf. Ps. 18:46; 25:5; Phil. 4:4, 10-19). The prophet pictured the worst of circumstances by using a variety of rural metaphors drawn from plant and animal life. Taken together they have the effect of saying that no matter what bad thing may happen, Habakkuk, and hopefully all Israel, would trust God. Even though the prophet felt weak physically, he was strong in faith spiritually. Thus he would live (cf. 2:4). Many of these bad conditions *did* typify Judah when the Babylonians overthrew the nation (cf. Lam. 2:12, 20; 4:4, 9-10; 5:17-18).

> "It is right and proper to voice appreciation of God's goodness when he bestows all that is necessary for life, health, and prosperity. But when these things are lacking, to rejoice in God for his own sake is evidence of pure faith."[75]

3:19a Sovereign Yahweh, Habakkuk's master, was the source of his "strength," even though the prophet's legs shook (v. 16). He enabled His servant to walk through the perilous valley he faced—as sure-footedly as the hoofs of a gazelle enabled it to navigate precipices (cf. Deut. 32:13; 33:29; 2 Sam. 22:34; Ps. 18:32-33, 39).

This statement of strong confidence sharply contrasts with the prophet's doubts and fears from which he spoke at the beginning of this book (1:2-4). A revelation from God, and Habakkuk's decision to believe what God revealed, turned his attitude around.

> "Habakkuk was about to 'go under' when he started this book. Destruction, violence, strife, conflict, injustice, and wickedness were all he could see. But he cried out to God and his cry did not go unheeded. The Lord not only answered his complaint but also provided the confidence needed to lift him from the quagmire. Habakkuk started in the pits, but ended on the mountaintop. His journey was not exactly an easy one, but it was certainly worth it."[76]

Essential elements in true prayer that are obvious in Habakkuk's prayer include humiliation, adoration, and petition.[77]

E. THE CONCLUDING MUSICAL NOTATION 3:19B

The final footnote to this book gives direction to "the choir director," who used this chapter as part of Israel's formal worship. Habakkuk specified the use of "stringed instruments" to accompany the singing, undoubtedly because they set the proper mood.

The book opened with a *dialogue* between Habakkuk and Yahweh, in which the prophet vented his fears and the Lord responded in love (ch. 1). Then it proceeded to a *dirge*, in which the Lord explained the wickedness of the instrument that He would use to judge Judah, the Babylonians, and promised their ultimate destruction (ch. 2). It closes with a *doxology*, in which Habakkuk praised God and recommitted himself to faith in, and faithfulness to, Yahweh—as he anticipated hard times to come (ch. 3).

> "Habakkuk teaches us to face our doubts and questions honestly, take them humbly to the Lord, wait for His Word to teach us, and then worship Him no matter how we feel or what we see."[78]

---

[74]Wiersbe, p. 422.
[75]Bruce, p. 893.
[76]Blue, p. 1522.
[77]Lloyd-Jones, pp. 58-67.
[78]Wiersbe, p. 422.

This book can be a great help to people who are discouraged about their present circumstances, and or can see nothing good coming in the future. It helps us adjust our attitude from one of pessimism, and even despair, to optimism and rejoicing. The crucial issue is whether we will listen to God and believe Him, namely: exercise faith.

Bibliography

Armerding, Carl E. "Habakkuk." In *Daniel-Minor Prophets*. Vol. 7 of *The Expositor's Bible Commentary*. 12 vols. Edited by Frank E. Gaebelein and Richard P. Polcyn. Grand Rapids: Zondervan Publishing House, 1985.

Baker, David W. *Nahum, Habakkuk and Zephaniah: An Introduction and Commentary*. Tyndale Old Testament Commentaries series. Leicester, Eng., and Downers Grove, Ill.: Inter-Varsity Press, 1988.

Blue, J. Ronald. "Habakkuk." In *The Bible Knowledge Commentary: Old Testament*, pp. 1505-22. Edited by John F. Walvoord and Roy B. Zuck. Wheaton: Scripture Press Publications, Victor Books, 1985.

Bright, John. *A History of Israel*. Philadelphia: Westminster Press, 1959.

Bruce, F. F. "Habakkuk." In *The Minor Prophets: An Exegetical and Expositional Commentary*, 2:831-96. 3 vols. Edited by Thomas Edward McComiskey. Grand Rapids: Baker Books, 1992, 1993, and 1998.

Chisholm, Robert B., Jr. *Handbook on the Prophets*. Grand Rapids: Baker Book House, 2002.

_____. "A Theology of the Minor Prophets." In *A Biblical Theology of the Old Testament*, pp. 397-433. Edited by Roy B. Zuck. Chicago: Moody Press, 1991.

Coogan, M. D. *Stories from Ancient Canaan*. Philadelphia: Westminster Press, 1978.

Dyer, Charles H., and Eugene H. Merrill. *The Old Testament Explorer*. Nashville: Word Publishing, 2001. Reissued as *Nelson's Old Testament Survey*. Nashville: Thomas Nelson Publishers, 2001.

Feinberg, Charles Lee. *Habakkuk, Zephaniah, Haggai, and Malachi*. The Major Messages of the Minor Prophets series. New York: American Board of Missions to the Jews, 1951.

Haak, R. D. *Habakkuk*. Vetus Testamentum Supplement 44. Leiden, Netherlands: Brill, 1992.

Johnson, Aubrey R. *The Cultic Prophet in Ancient Israel*. 2nd ed. Cardiff: University of Wales Press, 1962.

Kaiser, Walter C., Jr. *Toward an Old Testament Theology*. Grand Rapids: Zondervan Publishing House, 1978.

Keil, Carl Friedrich. *The Twelve Minor Prophets*. 2 vols. Translated by James Martin. Biblical Commentary on the Old Testament. Reprint ed. Grand Rapids: Wm. B. Eerdmans Publishing Co., 1949.

Kerr, David W. "Habakkuk." In *The Wycliffe Bible Commentary*, pp. 871-81. Edited by Charles F. Pfeiffer and Everett F. Harrison. Chicago: Moody Press, 1962.

Laetsch, T. *Bible Commentary: The Minor Prophets*. St. Louis: Concordia Publishing House, 1956.

Lindblom, Johannes. *Prophecy in Ancient Israel*. Philadelphia: Fortress, and Oxford, England: Blackwell, 1962.

Lloyd-Jones, D. Martyn. *From Fear to Faith: Studies in the Book of Habakkuk and the Problem of History*. London and Downers Grove, Ill.: Inter-Varsity Press, 1953.

Longman, Tremper, III and Raymond B. Dillard. *An Introduction to the Old Testament*. 2nd ed. Grand Rapids: Zondervan, 2006.

Morgan, G. Campbell. *Living Messages of the Books of the Bible*. 2 vols. New York: Fleming H. Revell Co., 1912.

The Nelson Study Bible. Edited by Earl D. Radmacher. Nashville: Thomas Nelson Publishers, 1997.

The New Scofield Reference Bible. Edited by Frank E. Gaebelein, William Culbertson, et al. New York: Oxford University Press, 1967.

Roberts, J. J. M. *Nahum, Habakkuk, and Zephaniah*. Old Testament Library series. Louisville: Westminster John Knox Press, 1991.

Robertson, O. Palmer. *The Books of Nahum, Habakkuk, and Zephaniah*. New International Commentaries on the Old Testament series. Grand Rapids: Wm. B. Eerdmans Publishing Co., 1990.

Rudolph, W. *Micha-Nahum-Habakuk-Zephanja*. KAT 13/3. 2nd ed. Gütersloh: Gerd Mohn, 1975.

Waltke, Bruce K., with Charles Yu. *An Old Testament Theology: an exegetical, canonical, and thematic approach.* Grand Rapids: Zondervan, 2007.

Wiersbe, Warren W. "Habakkuk." In *The Bible Exposition Commentary/Prophets*, pp. 411-24. Colorado Springs, Colo.: Cook Communications Ministries; and Eastbourne, England: Kingsway Communications Ltd., 2002.

Wood, Leon J. The *Prophets of Israel.* Grand Rapids: Baker Book House, 1979.

Yadin, Yigael. *The Art of Warfare in Biblical Lands.* New York: McGraw-Hill, 1963.

Constable's Notes
On Zephaniah

Introduction

Title and Writer
The title of the book comes from the name of its writer. "Zephaniah" means "Yahweh Hides [or Has Hidden]," "Hidden in Yahweh," "Yahweh's Watchman," or "Yahweh Treasured." The uncertainty arises over the etymology of the prophet's name, which scholars dispute. I prefer "Yahweh Hides."

Zephaniah was the great-great-grandson of Hezekiah (1:1), evidently King Hezekiah of Judah. This is not at all certain, but I believe it is likely. Only two other Hezekiahs appear on the pages of the Old Testament, and they both lived in the postexilic period. The Chronicler mentioned one of these (1 Chron. 3:23), and the writers of Ezra and Nehemiah mentioned the other (Ezra 2:16; Neh. 7:21). If he was indeed a descendant of the king, this would make him the writing prophet with the most royal blood in his veins, except for David and Solomon. Apart from the names of his immediate forefathers, we know nothing more about him for sure, though it seems fairly certain where he lived. His references to Judah and Jerusalem (1:10-11) seem to indicate that he lived in Jerusalem, which would fit a king's descendant.

Unity
Criticism of the unity of Zephaniah has not had great influence. Zephaniah's prediction of Nineveh's fall (2:15; 612 B.C.) led critics—who do not believe that the prophets could predict the future—to date the book after that event. Differences in language and style influenced some critics to divide the book up and identify its various parts with diverse sources. Yet the unity of the message and flow of the entire book, plus ancient belief in its unity, have convinced most conservative scholars to regard Zephaniah as the product of one writer.[1]

Date
Zephaniah ministered during the reign of King Josiah of Judah (640-609 B.C.; 1:1). Scholars debate just when during his reign Zephaniah wrote, before[2] or after[3] Josiah's reforms, which began about 622 B.C. There is support for both views.[4] Zephaniah made no explicit reference to Josiah's reforms, and the evidence is really insufficient to settle the debate.[5]

Zephaniah's reference to the future destruction of Nineveh (2:13) definitely fixed his writing before that event in 612 B.C. So the prophet ministered between 640 and 612 B.C. His contemporaries were Nahum, Habakkuk, and Jeremiah, though Jeremiah's ministry continued beyond the destruction of Jerusalem, which took place in 586 B.C.

Place of Composition
References to Jerusalem in 1:10-11 seem to indicate that Zephaniah knew Jerusalem well. Since he ministered to the Southern Kingdom, it is likely that he lived in Judah and probably in Jerusalem.

Audience and Purpose
The fact that Yahweh's word came to Zephaniah during Josiah's reign (640-609 B.C.), means that he could not have ministered to the Northern Kingdom, because it fell in 722 B.C. Thus, Zephaniah's audience consisted of the people of Judah: the surviving Southern Kingdom. He apparently ministered primarily to the upper echelons of society rather than to the average Israelites, as evidenced by his references to the princes, judges, prophets, and priests (1:8-9; 3:3-4).

The political situation in Judah during Josiah's reign was fairly peaceful. Following Assyria's capture of Samaria in 722 B.C., the Assyrian Empire began to decline. With its decline, Nabopolassar, the first of the Neo-Babylonian kings (626-605 B.C.), began to lead Babylonia forward. Assyria declined and Babylonia advanced until Babylonia, assisted by the Medes and Scythians, destroyed Nineveh in 612 B.C. and a few years later replaced Assyria as the dominant power in the ancient Near East. This happened in 605 B.C. when the Babylonians defeated the Assyrians and Egyptians at Carchemish. Judah benefited during this transitional period in Near Eastern politics. Josiah was able to get rid of some Assyrian

---

[1]For further discussion of the book's unity, see Richard D. Patterson, *Nahum, Habakkuk, Zephaniah*, pp. 290-92.
[2]E.g., ibid., p. 276; H. A. Hanke, "Zephaniah," in *The Wycliffe Bible Commentary*, p. 883; David W. Baker, *Nahum, Habakkuk and Zephaniah*, p. 91; Leon J. Wood, *The Prophets of Israel*, p. 320; Bruce K. Waltke, *An Old Testament Theology*, p. 839; et al.
[3]E.g., John D. Hannah, "Zephaniah," in *The Bible Knowledge Commentary: Old Testament*, p. 1523; et al.
[4]See Patterson, pp. 275-6, and Ralph L. Smith, *Micah-Malachi*, pp. 121-23, for other scholars who held each of these views.
[5]Tremper Longman III and Raymond B. Dillard, *An Introduction to the Old Testament*, p. 472.

religious practices, and he extended Judah's territory north into the tribal territory of Naphtali. Unfortunately, Josiah died prematurely in 609 B.C. (cf. 2 Chron. 35:20-27).

Josiah's evil predecessors, Manasseh (695-642 B.C.) and Amon (642-640 B.C.), had encouraged the people of Judah to depart from the Lord for over 50 years, so wickedness had become ingrained in them. In the eighteenth year of Josiah's reign (622 B.C.), Hilkiah the priest discovered the Law of Moses in the temple, and after Josiah read it, he instituted major reforms throughout Judah. Josiah's reforms were good because they were official. He eliminated much of the display of idolatry in the land and revived the celebration of the Passover, among other things. See 2 Kings 22:4-25 and 2 Chronicles 34:3—35:19 for lists of his extensive reforms. But unfortunately his reforms did not change the hearts of most of the people, as Jeremiah revealed in his earlier prophecies. So the people to whom Zephaniah ministered had a long history of formal religion without much real commitment to Yahweh.

God sent a prophetic word to Zephaniah because the Judeans of his day still needed to get right with Him in their hearts. The prophet announced that God was going to send judgment on Judah for her wickedness. He also assured the godly few in the nation, the remnant, that the Lord would preserve them and remain true to His promises concerning ultimate worldwide blessing for Israel in the future. Perhaps 1:7 summarizes what the book is all about better than any other single verse: "Be silent before the Lord God! For the day of the LORD is near."

> "In a sense, the history of the times has nothing to say about Zephaniah's message. Throughout the book there is a sense of distance from historical events. . . . Zephaniah is rooted in the flow of history . . ., but his concern is only with the goal—the eschaton—the day when calamitous human efforts to run the world will coincide in an awesome climax with the Lord's purposes of judgment and hope."[6]

> ". . . Zephaniah's purpose was to announce coming judgment on Judah in the Day of the Lord. However, he said that judgment would extend to all the nations of the earth, indicating that the Day of the Lord would also bring deliverance for Israel and the Gentiles."[7]

Literary Form

> "Zephaniah's style is chiefly characterized by a unity and harmony of composition plus energy of style. Rapid and effective alternations of threats and promises also characterize his style."[8]

> "All of Zephaniah is poetry with the exception of 1:1 and 2:10-11."[9]

> "Zephaniah can hardly be considered great as a poet. He does not rank with Isaiah, nor even with Hosea in this particular. . . . He had an imperative message to deliver and proceeded in the most direct and forceful way to discharge his responsibility. What he lacked in grace and charm, he in some measure atoned for by the vigour and clarity of his speech. He realised the approaching terror so keenly that he was able to present it vividly and convincingly to his hearers. No prophet has made the picture of the day of Yahweh more real."[10]

> "Literary genres used include judgment oracles (1:2-3, 4-6, 8-9, etc.), calls for response (1:7; 2:1-3; 3:8)—including a call to praise and a psalm of praise (3:14-17)—as well as salvation oracles (3:9-13, 18-20)."[11]

Distinctive Features

The Book of Zephaniah has been called "a compendium of the oracles of the prophets."[12] This is true for two reasons. First, Zephaniah's general message is similar to that of most of the other writing prophets. Second, he used the same terms as several of the other prophets (cf. 1:7 and Hab. 2:20; 1:7 and Joel 1:15; 1:7 and Isa. 34:6; 2:14 and Isa. 13:21; 34:11; 2:15 and Isa. 47:8).

> "Zephaniah reintroduced the message of Joel and Obadiah; however, for him the day of the Lord was both a day of world-wide judgment and a day when Judah would be punished."[13]

---

[6] J. Alec Motyer, "Zephaniah," in *The Minor Prophets*, p. 899.
[7] Charles H. Dyer, in *The Old Testament Explorer*, p. 809.
[8] Larry Lee Walker, "Zephaniah," in *Daniel-Malachi*, vol. 7 of *The Expositor's Bible Commentary*, p. 540.
[9] Smith, p. 127.
[10] J. M. P. Smith, *A Critical and Exegetical Commentary on Zephaniah and Nahum*, p. 176.
[11] Baker, p. 87.
[12] Walker, p. 539.
[13] Walter C. Kaiser Jr., *Toward an Old Testament Theology*, pp. 220-21.

"Obadiah, Joel, Amos, and Isaiah had all spoken of this day, but Zephaniah alone emphasized more strenuously than them all the universality of its judgment while also surprisingly predicting the conversion of the nations as one of its fruits."[14]

Zephaniah contains more references to "the day of the LORD" than any other Old Testament book. This phrase sometimes refers to the past, sometimes to the near future, sometimes to the distant future, and sometimes to the far distant, eschatological future. The phrase always refers to some period of time in which God is working in the world in a recognizable way. It usually refers to a time of blasting, but sometimes it refers to a time of blessing.

Zephaniah 1:14-18 has been called "emergent apocalyptic."[15] This pericope contains material that would one day become prominent in Jewish apocalyptic literature.[16]

Theologically, Zephaniah stressed the sovereign justice of Yahweh (1:2-3, 7, 14-18; 3:8) and His willingness to receive the repentant (2:3). He also emphasized the wickedness of man (1:3-6, 17; 3:1, 4). The theme of Yahweh's relationship to Jerusalem is prominent in Zephaniah as well (1:4-13; 3:1-7, 11-17).

Structurally, the book is a carefully crafted collection of oracles that compose one coherent message.[17]

"The Book of Zephaniah does not contain two or three prophetic addresses, but the quintessence of the oral proclamations of the prophet condensed into one lengthened prophecy . . ."[18]

"Zephaniah's prophecy has a more general character, embracing both judgment and salvation in their totality, so as to form one complete picture."[19]

Outline

I. Heading 1:1

II. The day of Yahweh's judgment 1:2—3:8

    A. Judgment on the world 1:2-3

    B. Judgment on Judah 1:4—2:3

        1. The cause for Judah's judgment 1:4-6
        2. The course of Judah's judgment 1:7-13
        3. The imminence and horrors of Judah's judgment 1:14-18
        4. A call to repentance 2:1-3

    C. Judgment on Israel's neighbors 2:4-15

        1. Judgment coming on Philistia 2:4-7
        2. Judgment coming on Moab and Ammon 2:8-11
        3. Judgment coming on Ethiopia 2:12
        4. Judgment coming on Assyria 2:13-15

    D. Judgment on Jerusalem 3:1-7
    E. Judgment on all nations 3:8

III. The day of Yahweh's blessing 3:9-20

    A. The purification of the nations 3:9
    B. The transformation of Israel 3:10-20

        1. Israel's purification 3:10-13
        2. Israel's and Yahweh's rejoicing 3:14-17
        3. Israel's regathering 3:18-20

---

[14]Ibid., p. 223.

[15]Duane L. Christensen, "Zephaniah 2:4-15: A Theological Basis for Josiah's Program of Political Expansion," *Catholic Biblical Quarterly* 46 (1984):682.

[16]For further discussion, see Patterson, pp. 285-88.

[17]See Motyer, p. 902, for a diagram of the chiasms, as he saw them.

[18]C. F. Keil, "Zephaniah," in *The Twelve Minor Prophets*, 2:121.

[19]Ibid., 2:122.

Message

The key to the Book of Zephaniah is the phrase "the day of the Lord." This phrase appears in most of the prophetic literature of the Old Testament. As the prophets used the phrase, "the day of the Lord" can be a past day, a day in the relatively near future, or a day in the far distant (eschatological) future. It is any day in which God is obviously at work in human affairs.

Wherever we find the phrase "the day of the Lord," it always suggests a contrast with the "day" of man. The day of man is any day when *man* appears to be in control of human affairs. It Is a day of God's patience. The day of the Lord is any day when *God* is clearly in control of human affairs. It is a day of God's judgment and or blessing. The phrase "the day of the Lord" is by no means unique to Zephaniah, but it is the key to the message of this book. Zephaniah used it more frequently than any other prophet. It was his burden, and he explained the meaning of this phrase more than any other prophet.

Zephaniah ministered during the reign of King Josiah of Judah (1:1). It is rather remarkable that the prophet did not refer to Josiah's reforms, which were his great spiritual contribution to the history of Judah. Perhaps the reason for the lack of mention is that Josiah's reforms were a result of his personal dedication to Yahweh, rather than the result of a revival of spiritual life among the Judahites generally. Huldah's prophecy reflects this difference (cf. 2 Kings 22:14-20; 2 Chron. 34:22-28). Zephaniah took no note of Josiah's good heart, but addressed the spiritual need of the Judahites. The contrast between this king and his subjects is striking.

The "day of the Lord" that Zephaniah predicted was an eschatological day in which God would judge the people of Judah and Jerusalem. This judgment will take place during the first part of the eschatological day of the Lord, the period we refer to as the Tribulation. Zephaniah also predicted restoration following judgment (ch. 3). This refers to the second part of the eschatological day of the Lord, the period we refer to as the Millennium.

But Zephaniah also had in mind an eschatological day of the Lord even after the Millennium. This seems clear from the extent of devastation he described, as well as the picture of restoration he painted. That "day of the Lord" will be the judgment of the Lord at the end of the Millennium, including the destruction of the present earth and heavens, which will be followed by the creation of *new heavens* and a *new earth*.

Other revelation helps us see that there are, in fact, two periods of future judgment followed by restoration, not just one, which we might conclude if all we had was Zephaniah's prophecy (cf. 2 Pet. 3; Rev.).

The timeless value of the Book of Zephaniah is its unveiling of the day of the Lord. The book does not reveal exactly when that day will come. The only chronological reference in the book is in the first verse, which locates Zephaniah's ministry in history. The book pictures God judging in the undefined future. This is not judgment through armies of invading soldiers, or through any human instrumentality. It is direct judgment from God Himself.

There are three things that this book reveals about this coming day of the Lord: its content, its extent, and its intent.

The content of the day of the Lord is clear from 1:2-3. God will visit earth with direct and positive retribution, not in the general administrative sense of bringing people to account eventually, but in the narrower sense of executing vengeance on humanity in cataclysmic judgment (1:14-16). This judgment will fall in spite of human unbelief (1:12). When people will be disregarding God, He will break into human history dynamically, supernaturally, to judge. Peter's description of the day of the Lord is remarkably similar (2 Pet. 3:1-10). People today are saying what these two prophets said they would say so long ago. They are saying that God will never intervene in judgment this way. The great statement of the Book of Zephaniah is that God will indeed do this in a day yet future.

What will be the extent of this judgment? Zephaniah reveals that it will be discriminating. His people Israel will be the special target of this judgment, though all humanity will also suffer (1:12). As we can see from this verse, the last stages of sin are complacency and indifference. It is an interesting fact of history that complacency and indifference have frequently preceded the destruction of great empires of the past. Assyria fell to Babylonia because she was complacent and indifferent (cf. Nahum). Remember the fall of the Babylonian Empire that we read of in Daniel 5. The Roman Empire fell to the Visigoths from the north because it had become complacent and indifferent. And earlier, the Northern Kingdom of Israel, and later the Southern Kingdom of Judah, fell to Assyria and Babylonia respectively for the same reasons. The spirit that produces these conditions is disregard for God and His Word (3:1-2). The result of such a spirit is that the leaders of the people forsake their proper servant role and turn to abusing the people to fatten themselves (3:3-4).

Reading Zephaniah is somewhat like watching a science fiction movie about a nuclear disaster, that leaves nothing but a sterile, uninhabited, windswept landscape with no life, no flowers, no fruit, and no beauty. What produces this horrible condition? The reason is the vast number of people who are complacent and indifferent, who disregard and ignore God. They do not obey God's voice, receive His correction, trust in Him, or draw near to Him. They are materialized, self-centered, living in luxury, and oblivious to their danger. So God steps in and turns their complacency into chaos, disorganizes their orderly lives, and purges them in their indifference. All that is left is a wind-swept desert (cf. the Flood).

What is the intent of this terrible activity? It is the creation of a new order, with God Himself enthroned among His creatures (3:17). Chapter 3 of this prophecy is such a different picture of the future, from what we have in chapters 1 and 2, that some commentators have said that a different person must have written it. Chapter 3 describes songs instead of sorrow, service instead of selfishness, and solidarity instead of scattering. That is the intent of this judgment. Marvelous restoration will follow devastating judgment.

The living message of this book is twofold. We can rejoice in the assurance of this coming judgment followed by restoration, and we have a responsibility in view of this coming judgment followed by restoration.

It is our privilege to "rejoice in the hope of the glory of God" that will be manifested at the end of God's judgment (cf. Rom. 5:2b). Even though the day of the Lord will involve the destruction of all things that destroy, it will also begin a new era of singing, service, and solidarity. That era will be the millennial reign of Christ first, and then the eternal state.

It is also our responsibility to live holy and godly lives as we anticipate the coming of "new heavens and a new earth in which righteousness will dwell" (2 Pet. 3:11-13). We need to be diligent to be found at peace with God, "spotless and blameless" in our lives (2 Pet. 3:14). We need to be on guard that we do not fall away from our own faithfulness because of the prevalent "error of unprincipled people" (i.e., complacency and indifference; 2 Pet. 3:17). And we need to continue to "grow in grace and in the knowledge of our Lord and Savior Jesus Christ" (2 Pet. 3:18). Rejoicing and responsible living: these characteristics need to distinguish the lives of people who anticipate the day of the Lord.

We could state the message of the book as follows: God will intervene in history, catastrophically, to judge humanity's complacency and indifference, and to restore His people to the conditions of blessing that He originally intended for them to enjoy.[20]

Exposition

I. HEADING 1:1

What follows is "the word" that Yahweh gave "to Zephaniah" during the reign of King Josiah of Judah (640-609 B.C.). This "word" includes all that the Lord told the prophet that He also led him to record for posterity (cf. Hos. 1:1; Joel 1:1; Mic. 1:1). This was a divine revelation that God gave through one of His servants the prophets.

Zephaniah recorded his genealogy, the longest genealogy of a writing prophet in any prophetical book. It goes back four generations to Zephaniah's great-great-grandfather, or possibly more distant relative, Hezekiah. As noted in the "Writer" section of the Introduction above, it is impossible to prove or to disprove that this Hezekiah was the king of Judah with that name. Chronologically, he could have been, since people married quite young during Israel's monarchy. I think *this* Hezekiah probably was *the king*, since the name was not common, and since it would make sense to trace the prophet's lineage back this far only if Hezekiah was an important person (cf. Zech. 1:1).[21] Normally the writing prophets who recorded their ancestors named only their fathers (cf. Jon. 1:1; Joel 1:1). We have no complete genealogy of King Hezekiah's descendants in the Old Testament.

II. THE DAY OF YAHWEH'S JUDGMENT 1:2—3:8

Zephaniah's prophecies are all about "the day of the LORD." He revealed two things about this "day." First, it would involve judgment (1:2—3:8), and second, it would eventuate in blessing (3:9-20). The judgment portion is the larger of the two sections of revelation. This "judgment followed by blessing" motif is common throughout the Prophets. Zephaniah revealed that judgment would come from Yahweh on the whole earth, Judah, Israel's neighbors, Jerusalem, and all nations. The arrangement of this judgment section of the book is chiastic.

A   Judgment on the world 1:2-3
      B   Judgment on Judah 1:4—2:3
            C   Judgment on Israel's neighbors 2:4-15
      B'   Judgment on Jerusalem 3:1-7
A'   Judgment on the all nations 3:8

A. THE JUDGMENT ON THE WORLD 1:2-3

Zephaniah presented three graphic pictures of the day of the LORD.[22] The first is that of a devastating universal flood.

---

[20]Adapted from G. Campbell Morgan, *Living Messages of the Books of the Bible*, 1:2:289-301.
[21]See ibid., p. 898; J. M. P. Smith, pp. 182-83; G. A. Smith, *The Book of the Twelve Prophets, Commonly Called the Minor*, p. 46; and Baker, p. 91.
[22]Warren W. Wiersbe, "Zephaniah," in *The Bible Exposition Commentary/Prophets*, pp. 426-27.

"These words not only introduce the particular judgment that would be pronounced upon Judah (v. 4), but they also speak of the final judgment that will usher in the kingdom of God on earth (see Rev. 19)."[23]

1:2   Yahweh revealed that He would "completely remove" everything "from the face of the earth" (cf. 2 Pet. 3:10-12). This is one of the most explicit announcements of the total devastation of planet Earth in the Old Testament (cf. Isa. 24:1-6, 19-23). While it may involve some hyperbole, it clearly seems to foretell a worldwide judgment.

"Its imminent reference, some think, was to the fact that the barbaric Scythians, who had left their homeland north of the Black Sea, were sweeping over western Asia and might be expected to attack Judah at any moment. The ruthless Scythians employed the scorched earth policy with fury and vengeance."[24]

1:3   This verse particularizes the general statement in verse 2 (cf. Gen. 1:1-2 and 3-31). The Lord will remove animal life, not that plants will survive—if animals die, plants will undoubtedly die too—but animal life was His focus of interest. This includes human beings, beasts of all types, birds, and fish, in other words, animal life on the land, in the air, and in the water. "Ruins" still standing from previous destructions, or perhaps from false religious practices that have caused people to stumble, would perish, as would the wicked. The Lord repeated that He would "cut off man" to make that fact indisputable. This would be a reversal of Creation (cf. Gen. 1:20-26) and a judgment similar to the Flood in its scope (Gen. 6:17; 7:21-23).

Does this prophecy refer to the judgments that will come during the Tribulation (Rev. 6—18) or at the end of the Millennium (2 Pet. 3:10; Rev. 20:11-15)? In view of what follows in this section describing judgment, especially 3:8, the parallel passage to 1:2-3, I think it refers to the Tribulation judgments.

B. THE JUDGMENT ON JUDAH 1:4—2:3

Zephaniah gave more particulars concerning the fate of Judah (1:4—2:3) and Jerusalem (3:1-7) than about the fate of the rest of humanity (1:2-3; 2:4-15; 3:8). He did this, both in the section of the book dealing with coming judgment, and in the section about blessing. In the section on blessing, he gave only one verse about the purification of the nations (3:9), but 11 about the transformation of Israel (3:10-20).

1. The cause for Judah's judgment 1:4-6

1:4   Yahweh announced that He would "stretch out" His "hand against Judah" and the people "of Jerusalem"—in judgment. "Stretching out the hand" is a figure of speech that implies a special work of punishment (cf. Exod. 6:6; Deut. 4:34; 2 Kings 17:36; Isa. 14:26-27; Jer. 27:5; 32:17; et al.). He promised to "cut off the remnant of Baal" worshippers who remained in Judah, or perhaps the temple (cf. Deut. 12:5, 11; 1 Kings 8:29-30; Ezek. 42:13), as well as the priests of Baal and the unfaithful priests of Yahweh. He would also terminate their reputations and the memory of them (cf. 2 Kings 23:5; Hos. 10:5).

This reference has suggested to some interpreters that Zephaniah wrote after Josiah began his reforms, since Josiah revived the worship of Yahweh and tried—unsuccessfully—to eliminate idolatry (2 Chron. 34:4). However, this verse may simply mean that the Lord would judge the idolaters in Judah, "Baal" being a figure (synecdoche) for all idolatry.

"Wherever excitement in religion becomes an end in itself and wherever the cult of 'what helps' replaces joy in 'what's true,' Baal is worshiped."[25]

1:5   The Lord would also judge those who worshipped "the host of heaven"—the sun, moon, stars, and planets—which the idolatrous Israelites did on their flat "housetops" (cf. Deut. 4:19; 2 Kings 21:3, 5; 23:4-5; Jer. 19:13). He would also punish the Judeans who worshipped both Yahweh and the pagan gods of the nations (cf. 2 Kings 16:3; 21:6; Jer. 32:35). "Milcom," (Molech, the god of Ammon; 1 Kings 11:33), probably represents all foreign gods. Swearing to and by a deity meant pronouncing an oath that called on that god to punish the oath-taker if he or she failed to do what he or she promised. Swearing by another god involved acknowledging its authority, which God prohibited in Israel.

1:6   Judgment would come, too, on all God's people who had apostatized, namely, departed from loving and following Yahweh, and had stopped praying to Him. They might not have participated in pagan idolatry, but if their love had grown cold, they were still guilty (cf. Rev. 2:1-7). The Lord commanded His people to love Him wholeheartedly (cf. Deut. 6:5). They may have forgotten Him, but He had not forgotten them.

---

[23] *The Nelson Study Bible*, p. 1526.
[24] Hanke, p. 884.
[25] Motyer, p. 912.

> "Sometimes it is the apathetic and indifferent who are more responsible for a nation's moral collapse than those who are actively engaged in evil, or those who have failed in the responsibilities of leadership."[26]

In this pericope, the prophet identified three types of idolatry: "the overtly pagan, the syncretistic, and the religiously indifferent."[27] Practitioners of all three would draw punishment from Yahweh.

How does this promise to judge the Israelites harmonize with the earlier prophecy that God would destroy the whole earth (vv. 2-3)? This is an example of a prophet's foreshortened view of the future, in which he could not see the difference in time between some events that he predicted (cf. Isa. 61:1-3; Dan. 11:35-36; et al.). God judged Israel when the Babylonians overran Judah and destroyed Jerusalem in 586 B.C. He will also judge the Israelites in the Tribulation (cf. Jer. 30:7; Rev. 6—18; et al.). Zephaniah described God's judgment of the people of Judah without specifying exactly when He would judge them. Most of what Zephaniah prophesied in this pericope found fulfillment, at least initially, in 586 B.C.

2. The course of Judah's judgment 1:7-13

Zephaniah's second picture of the day of the LORD is that of a great sacrifice.

1:7 In view of the inevitability of coming judgment for idolatry, it was appropriate for the Judeans to "be silent" or quiet before sovereign Yahweh (cf. Hab. 2:20).

> "This is a call to the people of Judah to cease every manner of opposition to God's word and will, to bow down in submissive obedience, in unconditional surrender, in loving service, to their Covenant God."[28]

This is Zephaniah's first reference to "the day of the LORD," to which he referred 24 times in this book.[29]

References to the day of the LORD as a time of judgment	References to the day of the LORD as a time of blessing
The day of the LORD 1:7, 14 (2)	That day 3:11, 16
The day of the LORD's sacrifice 1:8	That time 3:19, 20
That day 1:9, 10, 15	The time 3:20
That time 1:12	
A day of the LORD's wrath 1:18	
The day 2:2; 3:8	
The day of the LORD's anger 2:2, 3	
A day 1:15 (5), 16	

"The day of the LORD" was a time when God works, in contrast to *man's day*, in which he works.

> "As employed by the prophets, the Day of the Lord is that time when for His glory and in accordance with His purposes God intervenes in human affairs in judgment against sin or for the deliverance of His own."[30]

Here the prophet announced that the Lord's day was "near"; He was about to intervene in human history (e.g., the Flood). The Lord had prepared "a sacrifice," namely, Judah (cf. Isa. 34:6; Jer. 46:10), and He had set apart "guests" to eat it, namely, the Babylonians (cf. Jer. 10:25; Hab. 1:6). Another view is that the invited guests were the Judeans who, ironically, would also serve as the sacrifice.[31]

---

[26] Peter C. Craigie, *Twelve Prophets*, 2:114.
[27] Hannah, p. 1526.
[28] T. Laetsch, *The Minor Prophets*, p. 358.
[29] For a brief excursus on the day of the Lord, see Robert B. Chisholm Jr., "A Theology of the Minor Prophets," in *A Biblical Theology of the Old Testament*, pp. 417-18.
[30] Patterson, p. 310.
[31] Baker, p. 95.

1:8   When the Lord slaughtered Judah like a sacrifice, He would "punish . . . the king's sons," and those who wore foreign clothing. The king's sons, the future rulers of the nation, bore special responsibility for conditions in the land. Josiah's sons did indeed suffer Yahweh's punishment. Jehoahaz was taken captive to Egypt (2 Kings 23:34). Jehoiakim was defeated by Nebuchadnezzar and died in Jerusalem (2 Kings 24:1-6). Josiah's grandson, Jehoiachin, was taken captive to Babylon (2 Kings 24:8-16). The last son of Josiah to rule over Judah, Zedekiah, was blinded and also taken captive to Babylon (2 Kings 24:18—25:7). Wearing "foreign garments" evidently was a custom that expressed love and support for non-Israelite values, and so incurred God's wrath (cf. Num. 15:38; Deut. 22:11-12).[32] This reference to foreign garments may also imply that those who wore them were greedily practicing extortion against their neighbors and, possibly, participating in religious rites associated with exotic clothing.[33]

1:9   The Lord would also punish those who leaped over the thresholds of their neighbors in their zeal to plunder them, and who filled the temple with gifts taken through "violence and deceit."[34] Another view of "leaping over the threshold" is that this expression describes a superstition that anyone who walked on a building's threshold would have bad luck (cf. 1 Sam. 5:5).[35] In this passage, the temple in view might be the temple of Baal. "Their lord" is literally "Their Baal" (cf. v. 4).

1:10   When the Lord brought judgment on Judah, there would be crying out from various parts of Jerusalem—representing the total destruction of the city. The "Fish Gate" was the gate through which the fishermen normally entered the city with their catches. It was a gate that pierced Jerusalem's north wall close to the fish market (cf. 2 Chron. 33:14; Neh. 3:3; 12:39). It was probably through this gate that Nebuchadnezzar entered Jerusalem, since he invaded it from the north.

The "Second (or New) Quarter" was a district of Jerusalem northwest of the temple area (cf. 2 Kings 22:14; 2 Chron. 34:22). "The hills" may refer to the hills on which Jerusalem stood, or the hills surrounding the city, or both. In any case, the Babylonian army doubtless caused loud crashing on all the hills, in and around Jerusalem, as the soldiers destroyed the whole city and its environs.

1:11   Zephaniah called the "inhabitants of the Mortar," the market or business district of Jerusalem, to "wail" because judgment was coming. This section of Jerusalem may have received the name "mortar" (bowl) because it lay in the somewhat geographically depressed Tyropoeon Valley. The Canaanites who did business there would fall silent because business would cease. Or perhaps it was the Judeans, who were behaving like Canaanites, that were on Zephaniah's mind.[36] Those who weighed silver—i.e., who conducted commercial transactions—would also perish from the city.

1:12   The Lord would carefully search among the residents of Jerusalem then, as one searches by using a lamp (cf. Luke 15:8). He would punish the people whose love for Him had stagnated, like wine left undisturbed too long (cf. Rev. 3:15-16), and who concluded indifferently that He was complacent and would not act (cf. Isa. 32:9; Ezek. 30:9; Amos 6:1). *Their* complacency led them to believe that *He* was similarly complacent.

1:13   The treasures of the Jerusalemites, and all the Judeans, would "become plunder" for the enemy, and "their houses" would become vacant if not destroyed. They would "build houses"—but "not" be able to live in them—because the Babylonian invasion would come quickly. They would "plant vineyards"—but "not" be able to "drink their wine"—for the same reason (cf. Lev. 26:32-33; Deut. 28:30, 39; Amos 5:11; Mic. 6:15).

> "Rather than condemning the use of alcohol, as the passage could be understood (NEB), Zephaniah condemns apathy."[37]

3. The imminence and horrors of Judah's judgment 1:14-18

Zephaniah's third picture of the day of the LORD is that of a great battle.

1:14   Zephaniah reported that this "great day of the LORD" was "near," very near, and "coming very quickly." His hearers needed to realize that it would be a day in which Yahweh would act (cf. v. 12). When it came, warriors would cry out bitterly because that day would involve fierce fighting. The first deportation of Judeans to Babylon came in 605 B.C., not many years from whenever Zephaniah must have first announced this message.

---

[32] Keil, 2:131.
[33] *The Nelson . . .*, p. 1527.
[34] Keil, 2:132; Charles Lee Feinberg, *Habakkuk, Zephaniah, Haggai, Malachi*, p. 48.
[35] *The Nelson . . .*, p. 1527.
[36] Keil, 2:133.
[37] Baker, p. 98.

1:15-16	The prophet wanted to emphasize, even more strongly, the danger his complacent hearers faced. He described the effects of "the day of wrath" on people by using five synonymous word pairs. If would be a day marked by emotional "distress" and anguish ("trouble"), as well as physical "destruction" and devastation ("desolation"). The prophet described the terror as "darkness and gloom," and "clouds and" blackness ("thick darkness"). "Trumpet" blast "and battle cry" picture the tumult of that day. The "fortified cities" of Judah would face invasion, and the "high corner towers" of their walls would come under siege.
1:17	The Lord would "distress" His people so severely that they would grope around as though they were "blind." He would do this because they had sinned against Him (cf. Deut. 28:28-29). Their precious "blood" would lie all over the ground like common "dust," and their dead "flesh" would lie in the streets like putrid, decaying "dung."

> "Humans may categorize their sins into the serious, the mediocre, and the insignificant. To Zephaniah (see James 2:10-11) the mere fact of sin excited and merited the whole weight of divine rage. The simple statement 'they have sinned' is sufficient."[38]

1:18	The Judeans would not be able to buy themselves out of their trouble when the Lord poured forth His "wrath" (cf. Ezek. 7:19). He would devour the whole earth with "the fire" of His jealous rage, "jealousy" provoked by His people's preference for various forms of idolatry (vv. 4-6). He would destroy completely, and terribly, "all the inhabitants of the earth" (cf. vv. 2-3; cf. Joel 2:1-11).

The comprehensive nature of this judgment suggests that, at this point, the prophet's perspective again lifted to—what we can now see—will be the eschatological fulfillment of this prophecy. The Babylonian invasion only previewed it. Another possibility is that we should understand "all the earth" as referring only to the Promised Land. However, other descriptions of the worldwide extent of God's eventual judgment of sin and sinners, in this book and others, make this interpretation unattractive.

4. A call to repentance 2:1-3

This section of the book (1:4—2:3) concludes with an appeal to the Judeans to repent, and so avoid the punishment destined to come on them if they did not repent.

> "The prophet meant in that terrible description of approaching judgments not to drive the people to despair, but to drive them to God and to their duty—not to frighten them out of their wits, but to frighten them out of their sins."[39]

2:1-2	Zephaniah called for the shameless people of Judah to "gather . . . together," evidently in a nationwide public assembly, to repent (cf. 1:6; Joel 2:12-14). They needed to do so before the Lord's decree to punish them took effect, and His "burning anger" overtook them. Nineveh had repented at the preaching of Jonah, and the Lord relented from judging it. Perhaps He would do the same if the Judeans repented. That day was coming as swiftly as chaff blows before the wind, so they needed to act immediately.
2:3	The prophet urged his "humble" hearers, who had sought to be obedient to the Lord, to continue to seek Him in prayerful dependence. He was appealing to the faithful remnant in particular (cf. 3:12; Isa. 11:4; Amos 8:4; Matt. 5:3). They needed to continue to pursue righteous behavior, and to place themselves under the Lord's sovereign authority, by listening to Him and obeying Him. If they did this, the Lord might "hide" them when He poured out His "anger" on the unrepentant.[40] Here Zephaniah made a play on words with his own name: "Yahweh Hides." Repentance was open to anyone. God did indeed protect some Judeans from destruction when the Babylonians invaded (cf. 2 Kings 24:14-16). Zephaniah's exhortation appears to have been effective.

Zephaniah called on the "humble *of the earth*" to seek the Lord. While the Promised Land may be in view, this is probably a worldwide invitation. All people need to seek the Lord by repenting.

The Hebrew word *satar* is the root of the word translated "hidden." *Satar* is a synonym of *saphan*, which may be part of Zephaniah's name. If it is, "Zephaniah" probably means "Yahweh hides." Thus his name could have had connection with his message of preservation for the godly remnant.

C. JUDGMENT ON ISRAEL'S NEIGHBORS 2:4-15

Since all people need to seek the Lord (v. 3), Zephaniah revealed that judgment was headed for the nations around Judah as well as for Judah. He selected nations that lived in four directions from Judah to represent all the nations. Philistia lay west of Judah, Moab and Ammon east, Ethiopia south, and Assyria north.

---

[38]Motyer, p. 924.
[39]Matthew Henry, *Commentary on the Whole Bible*, p. 1168.
[40]See Wiersbe, pp. 433-35, for an excursus on "the company of the concerned."

> "He [God] would also judge nations that were near as well as nations that were far away. Those near would be plundered and possessed by Judah. Those far away would simply be destroyed by the Lord."[41]

Zephaniah prophesied to the people of Judah *about* these nations rather than *to* these nations themselves, though they might have heard about Zephaniah's prophecies. His prophecies about the nations reminded the Judeans that Yahweh was sovereign over all the earth, and that He was not just singling out Judah for punishment.

1. Judgment coming on Philistia 2:4-7

2:4   The prophet announced that destruction would overtake four of the five cities of the Philistine *pentapolis* (cf. Isa. 14:28-32; Jer. 47; Ezek. 25:15-17; Amos 1:6-8). He listed them from south to north. Gath had evidently declined already (cf. 2 Chron. 26:6; Amos 1:6-8; Zech. 9:5-7), or perhaps Zephaniah selected only four towns to preserve literary parallelism. Another option follows:

> "Uzziah and Hezekiah had kept Gath in subjection. 2 Kings 18:8 and 2 Chronicles 26:6."[42]

"Gaza" and "abandoned" sound similar in Hebrew, as do "Ekron" and "uprooted." Being "driven out at noon" may imply *an unexpected time*, since people normally rested during the hottest part of the day.

2:5   Zephaniah announced "woe" on the "Philistines" ("Emigrants") because destruction was coming on them. They inhabited the Mediterranean "seacoast," and they had come from Crete (cf. 1 Sam. 30:14; 2 Sam. 8:18; 20:23; 1 Chron. 18:17; Ezek. 25:16). Yahweh's powerful word was all it took to afflict them, and it would come against them. He promised to "destroy" them and their land, the coastal plain of Canaan, so no one would live there any longer. Pharaoh Neco II of Egypt (609-594 B.C.) initially fulfilled this prophecy (cf. Jer. 47).

2:6-7   The flat Philistine "seacoast" would become depopulated "pastures," and its "caves"—there are many in Judah and Mt. Carmel—would serve as refuges "for shepherds and folds for flocks" of sheep. After this destruction, the survivors from Judah would take possession of the coastal plain and pasture their sheep there. They would also take over the "houses" in "Ashkelon" and make them their homes, because Yahweh would "care for" this remnant "and restore their fortune" (cf. 3:20; Gen. 15:18-20).

2. Judgment coming on Moab and Ammon 2:8-11

2:8   Probably Zephaniah linked "Moab" and "Ammon" because both nations descended from Lot (Gen. 19:30-38), as well as because both lay to Judah's east. Both nations had "taunted" and reviled the Israelites from their earliest history. They had repeatedly lifted themselves up as enemies of God's chosen people (cf. Num. 22; 24:17; Judg. 3:12-14; 10:7-9; 11:4-6; 1 Sam. 11:1-11; 2 Sam. 10:1-14; 2 Kings 3).

2:9   Because of their hostility toward the Israelites, Almighty Yahweh, Israel's God, would definitely destroy these nations as He had "Sodom" and "Gomorrah" (cf. Isa. 15—16; Jer. 48:1—49:22; Ezek. 25:1-14; 35; Amos 1:11—2:3). God had completely destroyed these cities—that stood in the territory later occupied by Moab—shortly before either of these nations came into existence (Gen. 19:23-29). Sodom and Gomorrah had become a notorious perpetual desolation, a place of "salt pits" where nothing but "nettles" grew (cf. Jer. 48:9), and that would be what Yahweh would make of Moab and Ammon. The "remnant of" Israelites would "plunder" these neighbors and take over their territory as an inheritance from their God (cf. Isa. 11:14).

2:10   Yahweh of armies would bring this fate on these nations because of "their pride" and "arrogant" ridicule of His people Israel (cf. Isa. 16:6; Jer. 48:26, 29; Ezek. 25:5-6, 8).

> "The curse resting upon these lands will not be entirely removed till the completion of the kingdom of God on earth. This view is proved to be correct by the contents of ver. 11, with which the prophet passes to the announcement of the judgment upon the nations of the south and north."[43]

2:11   The Lord would terrify them. He would remove the inhabitants of these nations from the face of the earth so they would not be able to offer sacrifices to their pagan gods. As a result, these "gods" would "starve." What kind of a god needs the sacrifices of mortals to sustain it? People from "all" the "nations," pictured as living on "the coastlands" of the world, would worship Yahweh (cf. Mal. 1:11).

---

[41] Dyer, pp. 810-11.
[42] Feinberg, p. 55.
[43] Keil, 2:144.

"That the final fulfillment of these predictions is yet future to our day can be seen from the connection of verses 8 to 10 with verse 11."[44]

"After this statement of the aim of the judgments of God, Zephaniah mentions two other powerful heathen nations as examples, to prove that the whole of the heathen world will succumb to the judgment."[45]

3. Judgment coming on Ethiopia 2:12

Zephaniah's oracle against Ethiopia is very brief (cf. Isa. 18—20; Jer. 46; Ezek. 29—32). Patterson suggested that Zephaniah may have meant Egypt rather than Ethiopia.[46] Biblical Ethiopia occupied the territory now held by southern Egypt, Sudan, Eritrea, and northern Ethiopia. The "Ethiopians" were the southernmost (really southwestern-most) people known to the Judeans. God promised to send His "sword" against this nation. His instrument of judgment proved to be Nebuchadnezzar, who defeated Ethiopia shortly after overrunning all of Judah in 586 B.C. (cf. Ezek. 30:4-5, 9, 24-25). The prophet gave no reason for this overthrow, though it must be that Ethiopia shared the same disregard for Yahweh that the other nations He condemned held.

4. Judgment coming on Assyria 2:13-15

2:13   Zephaniah also prophesied the destruction of "Assyria" to Judah's north (really northeast), and her capital "Nineveh" (cf. Isa. 14:24-27; Nah.). Since Nineveh fell to the combined forces of Babylonia, Media, and Scythia in 612 B.C., Zephaniah must have uttered this prophecy before that date. The Lord would make Nineveh a "parched . . . desolation" (cf. Nah. 3). Until her fall, Nineveh had much water surrounding and circulating through it, but in the future she would be dry (cf. Nah. 1:8; 2:6, 8).

"Nineveh is part of Scripture's early-warning system."[47]

2:14   Beautiful Nineveh would become a dwelling place for wild animals ("beasts") and "birds," rather than populated with multitudes of sophisticated citizens. The very idea must have seemed incredible in Zephaniah's day because Nineveh was the greatest city in the ancient Near East.[48]

2:15   In Zephaniah's day, Nineveh was proud, carefree, and apparently impregnable. Its residents boasted of being citizens of the most important city in the world (cf. Isa. 10:12). Yet in the future, it would become a desolate "resting place for beasts" rather than barons. Passersby would ridicule the pride of Nineveh verbally, by reviling it, and bodily, by shaking their fists at it after its fall (cf. Nah. 3:19).

Motyer summarized five principles that Zephaniah taught in this section (2:4-15). First, the Lord is the God of all the earth. Second, the Lord plans for the spiritual needs of the world. Third, the Lord is in charge of the whole historical process. Fourth, the Lord's people are central to His world purposes. And fifth, the Lord is the fierce enemy of pride.[49]

D. JUDGMENT ON JERUSALEM 3:1-7

Having announced that divine judgment would come on the nations around Judah (2:4-15), the prophet returned to the subject of Yahweh's judgment on the Chosen People (cf. 1:4—2:3), but this time he focused more particularly on Jerusalem. Though he did not mention Jerusalem by name, it is clearly in view.

"Like Isaiah and Micah, he is a prophet of the city, open-eyed to its faults; unlike them, his focus is almost wholly civic and religious. But he draws the fundamental dividing line in the same place: whatever the basis on which the world is judged, the people of God are judged for turning from revealed truth (Amos 2:4) and for neglecting proffered spiritual privileges (Isa. 65:2).

"Like Amos, Zephaniah uses the rhetorical device of condemning surrounding nations, but all the while—unannounced to his hearers—bringing their own condemnation ever closer."[50]

---

[44]Feinberg, pp. 56-57.
[45]Keil, 2:146.
[46]Patterson, pp. 349-50.
[47]Motyer, p. 937.
[48]M. R. Wilson, "Nineveh," in *Major Cities of the Biblical World*, p. 186.
[49]Motyer, pp. 938-39.
[50]Ibid., p. 941.

3:1	Zephaniah pronounced another "woe" (cf. 2:5), this time on Jerusalem, which he described as "rebellious," "defiled," and "tyrannical." Rebels are those who refuse to submit to God's will. The defiled are those polluted by sinful practices. Tyrants disregard the rights of others, particularly those whom they can take advantage of.
3:2	There were four evidences that the people of Jerusalem had been rebellious against Yahweh (v. 1). They had been unresponsive to the prophets whom God had sent them. They were unteachable and refused to accept any correction. They "did not trust in" Yahweh, and "they did not draw near to . . . God" in repentance and prayer (cf. 1:6).
3:3	Evidence that they were oppressing the weak (v. 1): the greedy behavior of Jerusalem's civil rulers ("princes") and "judges." Like vicious "lions" and "wolves," they gobbled up all the possessions of vulnerable people that they could—as fast as they could (cf. 1:8; Ezek. 3:9-10; Mic. 2:1-3, 9-10).
3:4	Jerusalem's religious leaders, the (false) "prophets" and "priests," provided examples of the city's defiled condition (v. 1). The prophets were "reckless" in the way they announced their own advice as divine revelation, and "treacherous" in deceiving the people into thinking that their words were authoritative. The priests did not observe the laws of holiness that God had prescribed for worship, and they twisted the meaning of the Mosaic Law to suit their purposes (cf. 1:4-5).
3:5	In contrast to these crooked leaders, Yahweh was straight, and He was still in Jerusalem. He would "do no injustice," as the civil and religious leaders did. He performed "justice" every day, as faithfully as the rising of the sun. Yet the "unjust" leaders of Jerusalem knew "no shame" in the wickedness that they consistently practiced.
3:6	The Lord reminded the Jerusalemites that He had already destroyed other "nations." This probably refers to the nations around Judah that He had already allowed to fall to the Assyrians. He compared such a fallen nation to a city with strong "corner towers" that now lay in ruin because of the enemy's destruction. The "streets" of this representative "city" also lay deserted. The real "cities" of these already defeated nations were in ruins, without any inhabitants. Samaria was one such city, and the numerous towns of the former Northern Kingdom were others.
3:7	The Lord expected the people of Jerusalem to learn from the fate of the Northern Kingdom and other fallen nations. They should respect Him, since He was behind the destruction, and obey His word. They should have done this so He would not similarly judge them, as He had threatened to do. But they were more eager to pursue sinful self-indulgence, and to become thoroughly "corrupt" in "their deeds."

> "Great is the enticement of sin and great is the penalty it incurs, but man rushes headlong into it, nevertheless."[51]

E. JUDGMENT ON ALL NATIONS 3:8

The people of Jerusalem needed to "wait" a little longer. The Lord would soon "rise up" as a devouring animal to consume His prey. He had determined to "gather nations" and "kingdoms" that were wicked, including Judah, and "pour" His "burning anger," "indignation," and wrath on them. Yahweh's fiery "zeal" will devour "all" nations, because the world will again become thoroughly corrupt (as in the days of Noah, cf. Gen. 6:5-7; Zeph. 1:2-3). According to Charles Feinberg, this is the only verse in the Old Testament that contains all the letters of the Hebrew alphabet.[52]

The world is still waiting for the Lord to pour out His wrath on all nations. He has not done so yet because He is patient and is giving people time to repent (cf. 2 Pet. 3:9). Yet that day will surely come (2 Pet. 3:10). In view of its coming, Christians need to be holy in conduct and godly in character, looking for and hastening that day (by our prayers and preaching, 2 Pet. 3:11). The great outpouring of divine wrath on the earth predicted here will take place during the Tribulation, before our Lord returns to set up His kingdom (cf. 2:2; Zech. 14:2; Rev. 16:14, 16).

Zephaniah's final reference to the destruction of nations all over the world (v. 8) brings the section of his prophecy that deals with judgment (1:2—3:8) full circle.

```
A       Judgment on the world 1:2-3
    B       Judgment on Judah 1:4—2:3
        C       Judgment on Israel's neighbors 2:4-15
    B'      Judgment on Jerusalem 3:1-7
A'      Judgment on all nations 3:8
```

---

[51] Feinberg, p. 65.
[52] Ibid., p. 66.

III. THE DAY OF YAHWEH'S BLESSING 3:9-20

Having finished the revelation dealing with God's judgment of the world in a coming day (1:2—3:8), Zephaniah now announced that He would bring great blessing to all humankind after that judgment (3:9-20). As in the section of the book on judgment, he first briefly revealed God's plans for the Gentile nations, and then spoke extensively about His plans for Israel.

> "In what follows, the aim and fruit of the judgment are given; and this forms an introduction to the announcement of salvation."[53]

> "Why did the prophets consistently close their books with messages of hope? For at least three reasons. To begin with, hope is a great motivation for obedience, and the prophets wanted to encourage God's people to submit to God's will and do what He commanded. God's covenant blessings come to His people only when they obey His covenant conditions.

> "A second reason is the prophets' emphasis on the faithfulness of God. The Lord will keep His promises and one day establish the kingdom; and since God is faithful to keep His promises, we ought to be faithful obeying His Word. . . .

> "Finally, the closing message of hope was an encouragement to the faithful remnant in the land, who were true to God and suffered because of their devotion to Him. It's difficult to belong to that 'company of the committed' who stand true to the Lord and His Word no matter what others may do or say. Knowing that God would one day defeat their enemies and reign in righteousness would encourage the believers remnant to persist in their faithful walk with the Lord."[54]

A. THE PURIFICATION OF THE NATIONS 3:9

"Then" signals a major change in time, as well as in the focus of Zephaniah's prophecy. It is a hinge word that serves as a transition from judgment in the Tribulation to blessing in the Millennium. Then, after these judgments (1:2—3:8), the Lord promised to give the peoples of the world "purified lips" that would speak truth and grace, rather than lies and defiled speech (cf. Isa. 6:5-7).

> "Lip does not stand for language, but is mentioned as the organ of speech, by which a man expresses the thoughts of his heart, so that purity of the lips involves or presupposes the purification of the heart."[55]

Yahweh will effect this change in all the people of the world, so that they will worship Him (cf. Gen. 4:26) and serve Him as one united family of nations. This event has been seen as a reversal of Babel (Gen. 11:1, 6-7, 9).[56] This revelation indicates that everyone living on the earth at the beginning of the Millennium will be a believer in Jesus Christ (cf. Matt. 25:31-46).

B. THE TRANSFORMATION OF ISRAEL 3:10-20

Zephaniah had received from the Lord much more revelation about what He would do for Israel following the period of worldwide punishment. This section is also chiastic in its thought structure.

A   Israel's purification 3:10-13
        B   Israel's and Yahweh's rejoicing 3:14-17
A'   Israel's regathering 3:18-20

1. Israel's purification 3:10-13

3:10   The descendants of the Lord's "dispersed ones," the Jews, will bring Him offerings of worship from the farthest corners of the earth. "The rivers of Ethiopia," probably the Nile and its tributaries (the Atbara, the Astasobas, the Blue Nile, and the White Nile[57]), were at the edge of the known world in the prophet's day (cf. 2:12). The implication is that the Jews will come to Jerusalem, the city the Lord chose as the place where He would dwell among His people (cf. Deut. 30:1-10; Isa. 66:18, 20).

---

[53]Keil, 2:155.
[54]Wiersbe, p. 429.
[55]Keil, 2:156. Cf. Isa. 6:5-7.
[56]Craigie, 2:128.
[57]Feinberg, p. 67.

"We prefer with others to understand the words 'my suppliants, even the daughter of my dispersed' as the object of the verb and not the subject. In other words, the Lord's people dispersed in Ethiopia will be brought by the Gentiles to their homeland as an offering to the Lord."[58]

"The meaning is therefore the following: The most remote of the heathen nations will prove that they are worshippers of Jehovah, by bringing to Him the scattered members of His nation, or by converting them to the living God."[59]

3:11 "In *that* day," the day of blessing to follow the day of judgment, Zephaniah's hearers, the Jews, will not feel any more "shame" for all their previous rebellion against the Lord. This is because He will remove all the pride from their hearts (cf. Ezek. 20:34-38; Matt. 25:1-13). They "will never again" lift up themselves in haughtiness against Yahweh on His "holy mountain" Jerusalem (Ps. 2:6; Dan. 9:16; Joel 2:1; Obad. 16; et al.). A feeling of shame comes from an awareness of guilt, but they will not feel guilty any longer, because they will be humble rather than proud.

"The congregation, being restored to favour, will be cleansed and sanctified by the Lord from every sinful thing."[60]

3:12 The Israelites of that day will be "humble and lowly" in heart (cf. 2:3), and they will seek the Lord as their "refuge," rather than turning from Him to idols and self-exaltation. Seeking the Lord is an indication of humility, whereas forsaking Him, even by not praying, demonstrates a spirit of independence from God (cf. 1:6).

3:13 In contrast to their conduct since the Exodus, the Jews "will do no wrong," "tell no lies," and practice no deceit (cf. 3:1-4). They will resemble a flock of sheep at peace, grazing and lying down with nothing to disturb them (cf. Ps. 23; Mic. 4:4).

"When the Creator is worshipped and served as he ought to be, paradise is regained."[61]

2. Israel's and Yahweh's rejoicing 3:14-17

Zephaniah arranged this psalm of joy over salvation as another chiasm.

```
"A Zion singing (3:14a)
    B Israel's shouts (3:14b)
        C Jerusalem's joy (3:14c)
            D Yahweh's deliverance (3:15a, b)
                E Presence of Yahweh the king (3:15c)
                    F No more fear (3:15d)
                        G Jerusalem's future message (3:16a)
                    F' No more fear (3:16b, c)
                E' Presence of Yahweh the God (3:17a)
            D' The mighty deliverer (3:17b)
        C' God's joy (3:17c)
    B' Yahweh's silence (3:17d)
A' Yahweh's singing (3:17e)"[62]
```

3:14 In view of these wonderful prospects, Zephaniah called for the people of Jerusalem, and all the Israelites, to "shout for joy with all" their hearts.

"Although the command is aimed at the future Jerusalem, no doubt the message would not be lost on the godly worshipers of Zephaniah's own day."[63]

---

[58]Ibid., p. 68.
[59]Keil, 2:157.
[60]Ibid., 2:158.
[61]Baker, p. 117.
[62]Ibid., p. 87.
[63]Patterson, p. 377.

The phrase "daughter of" is a way of referring to the citizens of Zion (Jerusalem) as the children of the city. Children born in any city are the children of that city, in a metaphorical sense, as well as the children of their physical parents in a literal sense. Elsewhere, "daughters of Jerusalem" sometimes refers to the villages surrounding Jerusalem, those little communities that Jerusalem spawned.

3:15   The reason for rejoicing is that Yahweh will have removed His "judgments" and Israel's "enemies" from her presence and life (cf. vv. 8, 19). Yahweh, Israel's true and omnipotent King, will be in the "midst" of His people (in the person of Messiah, Jesus Christ, during the Millennium; v. 17; cf. Isa. 9:7; 44:6; Zech. 14:9). Consequently, they "will fear disaster no more" (v. 13).

3:16-17   "The battle cry on the day of judgment (1:14) will be replaced by the poignant hush of the reuniting of two lovers."[64]

"In that day" of blessing, the people of "Jerusalem" will have plenty of reasons not to fear. One reason is that Yahweh their God will be in their midst (v. 15). He will be "a victorious Warrior," having defeated all His enemies and all opposition worldwide (1:2-3; 3:8). Like a bridegroom, He will take "joy" in His people Israel, and they will rest quietly "in" the security of "His love" for them as His bride. Yahweh will even shout with joy over His beloved Israel!

"Most often the Lord's love is expressed by the Hebrew word *hesed*. This is the love that issues in commitment, the 'ever-unfailing' fidelity of love, love that lives in the will as much as in the heart. Here, however, the word is *'ahaba*, the passionate love of Jacob for Rachel (Gen. 29:20) and of Michal for David (1 Sam. 18:28), the fond love of Jacob for Joseph (Gen. 37:3), Uzziah's devotion to gardening (2 Chron. 26:10), Jonathan's deep friendship with David (1 Sam. 18:3), the devotee's delight in the Lord's law (Ps. 119:97). This too is the Lord's love for his people (Hos. 3:1), a love that delights him (Zeph. 3:17c), makes him contemplate his beloved with wordless adoration (v. 17d), a love that cannot be contained but bursts into elated singing (v. 17e)."[65]

"We can find hope in times of difficulty if we focus on God's power, God's deliverance, and God's love. He is our King (3:15), our Savior (3:16-17a), and our Beloved (3:17b)."[66]

3. Israel's regathering 3:18-20

3:18   In the past, Jews who lived far from Jerusalem were very sad because they could not travel to Jerusalem to observe Israel's annual "feasts." They suffered a certain criticism from their fellow Jews for living far away from Jerusalem. But in this time of blessing (the Millennium), the Lord will enable them to come to Jerusalem to celebrate the feasts. The feasts of Israel during the Millennium will be somewhat different from those that the Old Covenant specified, but there will be annual feasts in Jerusalem in the Millennium (cf. Ezek. 45:9—46:24).

"Why would the Lord restore religious practices that have now been fulfilled? Possibly as a means of teaching Israel the meaning of the doctrine of salvation through Jesus Christ."[67]

3:19-20   Having dealt with the Jews' "oppressors" (cf. vv. 8-15; 2:4-15; Gen. 12:3), the Lord will deliver even the weak ("lame") and dispersed ("outcasts") of His people, and give them a worldwide reputation for goodness (cf. Deut. 26:19). He will regather them in their land and give them a good reputation when He restores their fortunes (cf. v. 15; Gen. 12:1-7; 13:14-17; 15:7-21; 17:7-8; 2 Sam. 7:16; Ps. 89:3-4; Isa. 9:6-7; Dan. 7:27).

Zephaniah concluded his book by affirming that such was Yahweh's declaration. He would indeed "restore" His people.

"The whole message of Zephaniah is finally united in one grand inclusio, in that it begins and ends with Yahweh, Israel's just but caring covenant God, whose word (1:1) is spoken (3:20)."[68]

An *inclusio* is a repetition of key elements, either words or motifs, at the beginning and end of a literary unit.

---

[64]Baker, p. 119.
[65]Motyer, p. 958.
[66]Dyer, p. 812.
[67]Wiersbe, p. 432.
[68]Baker, p. 88.

Eight times in verses 18-20, in the NASB, the Lord said, "I will," "I am going to," or "When I." The future restoration and blessing of Israel in the world will be something that Yahweh Himself will accomplish "in that day" (i.e., the day of the LORD). No one but He *could* ever accomplish it, and no one but He *would* and *will!*

Bibliography

Baker, David W. *Nahum, Habakkuk and Zephaniah: An Introduction and Commentary.* Tyndale Old Testament Commentaries series. Leicester, Eng., and Downers Grove, Ill.: Inter-Varsity Press, 1988.

Bright, John. *A History of Israel.* Philadelphia: Westminster Press, 1959.

Chisholm, Robert B., Jr. *Handbook on the Prophets.* Grand Rapids: Baker Book House, 2002.

_____. "A Theology of the Minor Prophets." In *A Biblical Theology of the Old Testament*, pp. 397-433. Edited by Roy B. Zuck. Chicago: Moody Press, 1991.

Christensen, Duane L. "Zephaniah 2:4-15: A Theological Basis for Josiah's Program of Political Expansion." *Catholic Biblical Quarterly* 46 (1984):669-82.

Craigie, Peter C. *Twelve Prophets.* 2 vols. Philadelphia: Westminster Press, 1985.

Dyer, Charles H., and Eugene H. Merrill. *The Old Testament Explorer.* Nashville: Word Publishing, 2001. Reissued as *Nelson's Old Testament Survey.* Nashville: Thomas Nelson Publishers, 2001.

Feinberg, Charles Lee. *Habakkuk, Zephaniah, Haggai, Malachi.* The Major Messages of the Minor Prophets series. New York: American Board of Missions to the Jews, 1951.

Hanke, H. A. "Zephaniah." In *The Wycliffe Bible Commentary*, pp. 883-88. Edited by Charles F. Pfeiffer and Everett F. Harrison. Chicago: Moody Press, 1962.

Hannah, John D. "Zephaniah." In *The Bible Knowledge Commentary: Old Testament*, pp. 1523-35. Edited by John F. Walvoord and Roy B. Zuck. Wheaton: Scripture Press Publications, Victor Books, 1985.

Henry, Mattthew. *Commentary on the Whole Bible.* Edited by Leslie F. Church. Grand Rapids: Zondervan Publishing House, 1961.

Kaiser, Walter C., Jr. *Toward an Old Testament Theology.* Grand Rapids: Zondervan Publishing House, 1978.

Keil, Carl Friedrich. *The Twelve Minor Prophets.* 2 vols. Translated by James Martin. Biblical Commentary on the Old Testament. Reprint ed. Grand Rapids: Wm. B. Eerdmans Publishing Co., 1949.

Laetsch, T. *The Minor Prophets.* St. Louis: Concordia Publishing House, 1956.

Longman, Tremper, III and Raymond B. Dillard. *An Introduction to the Old Testament.* 2nd ed. Grand Rapids: Zondervan, 2006.

Morgan, G. Campbell. *Living Messages of the Books of the Bible.* 2 vols. New York: Fleming H. Revell Co., 1912.

Motyer, J. Alec. "Zephaniah." In *The Minor Prophets: An Exegetical and Expositional Commentary*, 3:897-962. 3 vols. Edited by Thomas Edward McComiskey. Grand Rapids: Baker Books, 1992, 1993, and 1998.

The Nelson Study Bible. Edited by Earl D. Radmacher. Nashville: Thomas Nelson Publishers, 1997.

Patterson, Richard D. *Nahum, Habakkuk, Zephaniah.* Wycliffe Exegetical Commentary sereis. Chicago: Moody Press, 1991.

Smith, John M. P. *A Critical and Exegetical Commentary on Zephaniah and Nahum*, International Critical Commentaries series. Edinburgh: T. & T. Clark, 1911.

Smith, George Adam. *The Book of the Twelve Prophets, Commonly Called the Minor.* Vol. 2. Revised ed. New York: Harper, 1928.

Smith, Ralph L. *Micah-Malachi.* Word Biblical Commentary series. Waco, Tex.: Word Books, Publisher, 1984.

Walker, Larry Lee. "Zephaniah." In *Daniel-Minor Prophets.* Vol. 7 of *The Expositor's Bible Commentary.* 12 vols. Edited by Frank E. Gaebelein and Richard P. Polcyn. Grand Rapids: Zondervan Publishing House, 1985.

Waltke, Bruce K., with Charles Yu. *An Old Testament Theology: an exegetical, canonical, and thematic approach.* Grand Rapids: Zondervan, 2007.

Wiersbe, Warren W. "Zephaniah." In *The Bible Exposition Commentary/Prophets*, pp. 425-36. Colorado Springs, Colo.: Cook Communications Ministries; and Eastbourne, England: Kingsway Communications Ltd., 2002.

Wilson, M. R. "Nineveh." In *Major Cities of the Biblical World*. Edited by R. K. Harrison. Nashville: Thomas Nelson, 1985.

Wood, Leon J. *The Prophets of Israel*. Grand Rapids: Baker Book House, 1979.

Constable's Notes
On Haggai

Introduction

Title and Writer

The title of this prophetic book is also the name of its writer. Haggai referred to himself as simply "the prophet Haggai" (1:1; et al.) We know nothing about Haggai's parents, ancestors, or tribal origin. His name apparently means "festal" or possibly "feast of Yahweh." This is appropriate since much of what Haggai prophesied deals with millennial blessings. His name is a form of the Hebrew word *hag*, meaning "feast." This has led some students of the book to speculate that Haggai's birth may have occurred during one of Israel's feasts.[1] Ezra mentioned that through the prophetic ministries of Haggai and Zechariah, the returned Jewish exiles resumed and completed the restoration of their temple (Ezra 5:1; 6:14; cf. Zech. 8:9; 1 Esdras 6:1; 7:3; 2 Esdras 1:40; Ecclesiasticus 49:11). Haggai's reference to the former glory of the temple before the Babylonians destroyed it (2:2), may or may not imply that he saw that temple. If he did, he would have been an old man when he delivered the messages that this book contains. In that case, he may have been over 70 years old when he prophesied. However, it is not at all certain that the reference in 2:2 implies that he saw the former temple.

Some editions of the Greek Septuagint and the Latin Vulgate versions of the Book of Psalms attribute authorship of some of the Psalms to Haggai and or Zechariah (i.e., Ps. 111—112, 125—126, 137—138, and 145—149). There is no other evidence that either prophet wrote any of these psalms. The reason for the connection appears to have been the close association that these prophets had with the temple where these psalms were sung.

Historical Background

The Babylonians, led by King Nebuchadnezzar, destroyed the city of Jerusalem, including Solomon's temple, in 586 B.C. and took most of the Jews captive to Babylon. There, the Israelites could not practice their formal worship (religious cult) as the Mosaic Law prescribed, because they lacked an authorized altar and temple. They prayed toward Jerusalem privately (cf. Dan. 6:10) and probably publicly, and they established synagogues where they assembled to hear their Law read and to worship God informally.

King Cyrus of Persia allowed the Jewish exiles to return to their land in 538 B.C. At least three waves of returnees took advantage of this opportunity. The first of these was the group of almost 50,000 Jews that returned under the leadership of Sheshbazzar, and Zerubbabel who replaced him, in 537 B.C. (Ezra 1:2-4). Ezra led the second wave of 1,700 men plus women and children (perhaps about 5,000 individuals) back to Jerusalem in 458 B.C., and Nehemiah led the third wave of 42,000 Israelites back in 444 B.C. Haggai and Zechariah appear to have been two of the returnees who accompanied Sheshbazzar, as was Joshua the high priest, though Haggai's name does not appear in the lists of returnees in the opening chapters of Ezra.

During the year that followed, the first group of returnees rebuilt the brazen altar in Jerusalem, resumed offering sacrifices on it, celebrated the Feast of Tabernacles, and laid the foundation for the reconstruction of the (second) temple. Opposition to the rebuilding of the temple resulted in the postponement of construction for 16 years. During this long period, apathy toward temple reconstruction set in among the residents of Judah and Jerusalem. Then in 520 B.C., as a result of changes in the Persian government and the preaching of Haggai, the people resumed rebuilding the temple.[2] Haggai first sounded the call to resume construction in 520 B.C., and Zechariah soon joined him. Zechariah's ministry lasted longer than Haggai's. The returnees finished the project about five years later in 515 B.C. (cf. Ezra 1—6). One way to calculate the 70-year captivity is: from the first deportation to Babylon in 605 B.C. to the year temple reconstruction began, 536 B.C. Another way is: to count from the destruction of the temple in 586 B.C to the completion of temple restoration in 515 B.C.

Date

Haggai delivered four messages to the restoration community, and he dated all of them in the second year of King Darius I (Hystaspes) of Persia (i.e., 520 B.C.). Ezekiel and Daniel had probably died by this time. Haggai's ministry, as this book records it, spanned less than four months, from the first day of the sixth month (1:1) to the twenty-fourth day of the ninth month (2:20). Haggai's ministry may have begun before 520 B.C. and continued a few years after it.[3] But that is speculation. In the modern calendar, these dates would have been between August 29 and December

---

[1] E.g., Joyce G. Baldwin, *Haggai, Zechariah, Malachi: An Introduction and Commentary*, p. 28; Richard A. Taylor and E. Ray Clendenen, *Haggai, Malachi*, p. 44. Taylor wrote the commentary on Haggai.
[2] For details concerning changes in the Persian government, see Robert L. Alden, "Haggai," in *Daniel-Minor Prophets*, vol. 7 of *The Expositor's Bible Commentary*, pp. 569-71; or Eugene H. Merrill, *An Exegetical Commentary: Haggai, Zechariah, Malachi*, pp. 5-9.
[3] Leon J. Wood, *The Prophets of Israel*, p. 365.

18, 520 B.C. This means that Haggai was the first writing prophet to address the returned Israelites. Zechariah began prophesying to the returnees in the eighth month of that same year (Zech. 1:1). Haggai was the most precise of all the prophets in dating his messages.

The precision in dating prophecies that marks Haggai and Zechariah reflects the *annalistic* style of history writing that distinguished Neo-Babylonian and Persian times.[4] Ezekiel, who was probably an older contemporary of these prophets, was the third most precise in dating his prophecies, and Daniel, another contemporary, also was precise but not as detailed. Likewise Ezra and Nehemiah, who wrote after Haggai and Zechariah, showed the same interest in chronological precision.

Probably Haggai wrote the book between 520 and 515 B.C., the year the returnees completed the temple. Lack of reference to the completion of the temple, while not in itself a strong argument for this view, seems reasonable—since mention of the completion of the temple would have finished off the book nicely.

Place of Composition

Haggai obviously preached and evidently wrote in Jerusalem, as is clear from his references to the temple in both chapters. Confirming this location is his reference to the nearby mountains (1:8, 11). There were no real mountains in the area of Babylonia where the Jewish exiles lived.

Audience and Purpose

Haggai was as specific about his audience as he was about when he prophesied. The first oracle was for Zerubbabel and Joshua, who were the Jewish governor of Judah and its high priest (1:1). The prophet delivered the second one to those men and the remnant of the people (2:1). The third oracle was for the priests (2:11), and the fourth one was for Zerubbabel (2:21). Obviously these oracles had a larger audience as well, namely, the entire restoration community and eventually the general population of the world.

> "Haggai is a prophetic history that intends to interpret the religious and theological significance of the historical events that it recounts."[5]

Haggai's purpose was simple and clear. It was to motivate the Jews to build the temple. To do this he also fulfilled a secondary purpose: he confronted the people with their misplaced priorities. They were building their own houses but had neglected God's house. It was important to finish building the temple because only then could the people fully resume Levitical worship as the Lord had specified. They had gone into captivity for covenant unfaithfulness. Thus they needed to return to full obedience to the Mosaic Covenant. Furthermore, in the ancient Near East, the glory of a nation's temple(s) reflected the glory of the people's god(s). So to *finish* the temple meant to glorify Yahweh.

> ". . . he also wrote to give the people hope by announcing that God's program of blessing would come 'in a little while' (Hag. 2:6) when God would again 'shake the heavens and the earth' (2:6, 21)."[6]

Theological Emphases

Central to Haggai's emphasis is the temple as God's dwelling place on earth, as a center for worship, and as a symbol of Yahweh's greatness. For him the temple was more important than the palace, and the priests were more important than the princes. There was no king of the Jews after the fall of Jerusalem in 586 B.C. Another theological emphasis was the relative importance of glorifying God compared to living affluently.

> "Governments work on the assumption that a healthy gross national product is the consequence of a proper industrial base, efficient management, skilled workers, and the due operation of market forces—in other words, that economic health depends on an effective economic system. Haggai, however, rose to challenge the view that economics can be left to the economists. Here, too, we live in God's world and unless he is given the central place and honor, the laws he created will work not for our blessing but for our bane. Thus Haggai speaks to our concern that world resources should meet world need and to our longing that not only will needs be satisfied but also that life will be satisfying. He addresses the problem of inflation more explicitly than any other prophet; his book is a tract for our times."[7]

> "The theological problem of this period was simply this: Where was the activity and presence of God to be found?"[8]

Other important themes are: holiness as a prerequisite for worship, the prophetic word as divine revelation, divine sovereignty, human responsibility, and a future for the Davidic dynasty.[9]

---

[4]For example, see D. J. Wiseman, *Chronicles of Chaldaean Kings (625-556 B.C.) in the British Museum*.
[5]Taylor, p. 56.
[6]Charles H. Dyer, in *The Old Testament Explorer*, p. 815.
[7]J. Alec Motyer, "Haggai," in *The Minor Prophets*, P. 963.
[8]Walter C. Kaiser Jr., *Toward an Old Testament Theology*, p. 250.
[9]See Taylor, pp. 73-83, for discussion of these themes.

Characteristic Features

Haggai is the second shortest book of the Old Testament, after Obadiah. The writer's literary style is simple and direct. The book is a mixture of prose and poetry, the introductory sections being prose, and the oracles, poetry. The book contains four short messages that Haggai preached to the returned Jews in less than four months of one year, 520 B.C. Haggai was clearly aware that the messages he preached to the Israelites were from God. He affirmed their divine authority 25 times. In contrast to almost all the writing prophets, Haggai was successful in that the people to whom he preached listened to him and obeyed his exhortations.

> "The truth is that few prophets have succeeded in packing into such brief compass so much spiritual common sense as Haggai did."[10]

> "Interestingly, Haggai's message has none of the elements so characteristic of the other biblical prophets. For instance, he wrote no diatribe against idolatry. He said nothing of social ills and abuses of the legal system, nor did he preach against adultery or syncretism. His one theme was rebuilding God's temple."[11]

> "Most of the other prophetic books consist of collections of prophetic sermons and oracles. Haggai, on the other hand, consists of direct address oracles set in a prose narrative framework (1:1, 3, 12, 15; 2:1, 10, 20) such that the book appears as more of a report on Haggai's utterances and the effect they had on the hearers . . ."[12]

This book and Hosea are the only inspired prophetical writings in the Old Testament that do not contain one or more oracles against foreign nations.

Unity and Canonicity

Critics have not seriously challenged either the unity or the canonicity of Haggai. Its place in the canon is chronological, leading the postexilic prophetical books and following the pre-exilic and exilic ones.

Text

There are only a few textual problems in the book (1:2, 9; 2:2, 5, 7, 9, 14, 16). In addition to these, the Septuagint made some additions to the Hebrew text (2:9, 14).

Outline

I. A call to build the temple ch. 1
   - A. Haggai's first challenge 1:1-6
   - B. Haggai's second challenge 1:7-11
   - C. The Israelites' response 1:12-15

II. A promise of future glory for the temple 2:1-9

III. A promise of future blessing for the people 2:10-19

IV. A prophecy concerning Zerubbabel 2:20-23

One writer saw a chiastic structure in the book.[13]

A   A pair of oracles delivered on the same day that stress the negative consequences of the unfinished temple followed by a double call to take the Lord's word to heart 1:1-11

    B   The promise of the Lord's presence that would energize the reconstruction of the temple 1:13-15a

    B'   The promise of the Lord's presence that would guarantee coming glory 1:15b—2:9

A'   A pair of oracles delivered on the same day that stress the positive consequences of the finished temple including a double call to take the Lord's word to heart 2:10-23

---

[10]Frank E. Gaebelein, *Four Minor Prophets [Obadiah, Jonah, Habakkuk, and Haggai]: Their Message for Today*, p. 199.
[11]Alden, p. 573.
[12]Tremper Longman III and Raymond B. Dillard, *An Introduction to the Old Testament*, p. 480.
[13]Adapted from Motyer, p. 968.

Message

Haggai is the first in the last group of prophetic Old Testament books. Along with Zechariah and Malachi, these books reveal life in the restoration community. The historical book of Ezra deals with the same time period and the same group of people. A remnant of the Israelites was back in the land following the Babylonian Captivity. The returnees remembered stories of the past glories of their nation, before the Captivity. But they also felt great shame since they returned to a land controlled by the Gentiles. They lived in difficult and discouraging times. Their hopes were very shadowy and uncertain in the short range. This was hardly the glorious return to the land that former prophets had promised.

Haggai had a single burden from the Lord. His passion was to motivate the returnees to rebuild their temple so they could resume life in obedience to the Mosaic Law. Zechariah helped him in this mission. Malachi lived some 90 years later and uttered the final warning from Yahweh to His people in the Old Testament.

About 18 years before Haggai ministered, in 538 B.C., about 50,000 Jews had returned from captivity under the leadership of Sheshbazzar and Zerubbabel. A year later they began to rebuild the temple. They had finished repairing the foundation and were starting on the superstructure when opposition from the native people of the land, the Samaritans, made them stop working. For about 17 years they did no work on the temple. Then the Lord led Haggai to challenge the people to resume temple reconstruction. He delivered four short messages, in 520 B.C., that got the people working again. The people went to work after hearing his first message, but then a difficulty arose and they stopped working. He delivered a second message, and the people got back to work. After a while, another difficulty arose and the people stopped working again. Haggai then delivered two messages on the same day, which moved the Jews to resume and finish their project.

The reason God preserved this book for all time and for all humanity is its permanent value, which is twofold. The Book of Haggai, first, is a revelation of the perils that often accompany a period of adversity. Second, it reveals the duty of people of faith in such a period and God's resources. In other words, Haggai exposes the perils that accompany times when there are discouraging circumstances and hope burns dim. And it helps us see what the duty of God's people should be in such times—and how God will help us.

Each of Haggai's four messages deals with one of these perils. The four perils are: misplaced priority, incorrect perspective, unrealistic expectation, and unnecessary fear.

The first peril was a problem of misplaced priorities. The people did not think that the time was right to proceed with the rebuilding of the temple (1:2). They seem to have been waiting for some indication from God that they should resume building, but they were busy building their own houses and had forgotten God's previous commands to rebuild the temple. They were very motivated when it came to building homes for themselves. They saw the need and proceeded to do something about it. But when it came to building a house that would honor Yahweh, enable them to worship Him as He had commanded, and exalt His reputation in their land, they were waiting. Seventeen years had passed. It was time to finish the unfinished temple structure, but the people put it on hold while they gave priority to what was more important to them.

The second peril was a problem of incorrect perspectives. When the workers began rebuilding again, some of the people started comparing the structure they were working on to the previous temple that the Babylonians had destroyed. They were saying that the present temple was nothing in comparison to Solomon's temple (2:3). Some of the older people, who had seen the former temple, could not help weeping when they compared the two structures. It looked as though all their work would amount to nothing significant, so they became discouraged and stopped working again.

The third peril was a problem of unrealistic expectations. The people thought that because they had taken on the project of rebuilding the temple, God would begin to bless them greatly. They looked at their external obedience as what God should bless (2:12). Haggai reminded them that it was wholehearted devotion to God that was necessary to obtain His blessing, not just piling stone upon stone.

The fourth peril was a problem of unnecessary fears. The people looked at the strength of the Gentile nations around them, and concluded that their small community would never amount to anything. Haggai had to remind them that God would judge the Gentile nations one day. They needed to look beyond the immediate future, and believe God's promises concerning Israel's ultimate restoration and exaltation over the nations (2:21-22).

God led Haggai to meet each one of these problems by reminding the people of their duty and their dynamic. They had a responsibility to do something different in each case, and then God would provide the enabling grace for them to succeed: the spiritual dynamic.

In regard to their problem of misplaced priorities, the people's duty was to get back to rebuilding the temple (1:8). They needed to give priority to what God said they should do, rather than to what they wanted to do. The dynamic that God would provide was His enabling presence with them. He would be with them and help them (1:13).

With regard to their problem of incorrect perspectives, their duty was to be strong and work. They should not compare the work that God had given them to do with the work that He had given their ancestors to do. They should simply give themselves to carrying out the will of God for them. The dynamic God promised to provide was, again, His own presence with them (2:4). He would help them to do what He had called them to do.

Regarding their problem of unrealistic expectations, their duty was to learn from their priests, who would remind them of the Lord's will from Torah, that blessing would come in response to genuine obedience. It was not enough simply to rebuild the temple. That was only part of God's will for His people, and not really the most important part. More important was that they should genuinely seek to exalt the Lord in their lives by following Him faithfully. The "dynamic" that Yahweh promised for such heartfelt obedience was *blessing* on their lives (2:19). He would bless them from the day the returnees turned their hearts to obey the Lord. But they should not expect much blessing if their obedience was only external.

Fourth, in regard to their problem of unnecessary fears, the people's duty was to be patient. They might not see a reversal of conditions in the immediate future, but eventually God would restore His people, as He promised. The dynamic that God promised them was His own acting, eventually, to reverse their fortunes (2:22-23). The Gentiles would not lord it over them forever. Their present leader, Zerubbabel, was only a foreview of a greater leader whom God would provide for them in the future. We know that the times of the Gentiles will come to an end when Jesus Christ returns to the earth to reign.

We are now in a position to point out the living message of this book. It is that whenever God's people face problems involving fulfilling His will, we should do our duty as the Word of God reveals it, with the assurance that when we do, God Himself will provide all that we need to succeed.

We often get our priorities out of order. We wait for direction from God to act when He has already told us what He wants us to do. While we wait, we may get involved in matters that require our energy and resources that are self-directed. What we should be doing is reading the Word, learning what God wants us to do, and then putting first things first. We need to make His agenda our agenda. When we do this, He will be with us and will provide all that we need to carry out His will successfully (cf. Matt. 6:33).

We also frequently lose the proper perspective on what God has called us to do. We may look at our part of the enterprise of fulfilling the Great Commission, and think to ourselves, "How insignificant this is. If only I was living when God was working—when Hudson Taylor, or some other greatly used servant of the Lord, lived—maybe then I could really change the world. Better yet, if only I lived in the days of the apostles." It is easy for many Christians to get so distracted, by looking at the great things that other Christians have done in the past, that they conclude that their little contribution is so insignificant that it is not worth the time and effort.

If that is *our* attitude, we need to remind ourselves that the same God, who enabled saints of old to succeed, has promised to be with us, and to enable us to succeed in our calling. We may indeed live in days of apostasy rather than in the glory days, when Christ was more greatly honored in the world. Nevertheless, our task in the will of God is just as important now as the task of other believers was in days gone by. We need to focus on what God has given us to do, not on what others did. We need to concentrate on serving faithfully.

We struggle with unrealistic expectations, too, like the postexilic community did. Why is our church not growing faster? Why are we not seeing more fruit in our ministry? Why do we not see more spiritual power in our lives? Ultimately all these blessings come by the will of a sovereign God who chooses to bless whom and how He will. We tend to underrate the importance of personal holiness and to emphasize activity, just like the returned exiles did.

Perhaps God is not blessing more because our commitment is superficial and shallow. If we expect His blessing simply because we are doing His work, we need to look deeper into ourselves and into His Word. God will bless if we follow Him wholeheartedly. We may not see the blessing this side of the grave, but since He has promised to bless those who follow Him sincerely, we can count on His blessing eventually.

Finally, *we* in the Church Age also struggle with unnecessary fears from time to time. The enemy looks so strong. We look or feel so weak. Things may not have changed much for a long time. But our duty is to be patient, to remember, and to believe the promises that the Lord will return and balance the scales of justice one day (cf. 2 Pet. 3:8-13). He will establish His kingdom on the earth. Our duty now is to be single-minded and to work.[14]

Exposition

I. A CALL TO BUILD THE TEMPLE CH. 1

This first main part of the book contains two oracles that warned the returnees of the consequences of allowing the temple to remain unfinished, two exhortations to act, and a promise of the Lord's help.

---

[14]Adapted from G. Campbell Morgan, *Living Messages of the Books of the Bible*, 1:2:303-15.

A. HAGGAI'S FIRST CHALLENGE 1:1-6

1:1   Like Ezekiel, Jonah, and Zechariah, the Book of Haggai contains no formal title. Yahweh sent a message to Zerubbabel ("born in Babylon" or "seed of Babylon," an allusion to his birthplace) and Joshua ("Yahweh saves") through "the prophet Haggai," though it went to all the Israelites too (vv. 2, 4). "Zerubbabel" was the political "governor" (overseer) of the Persian province "of Judah" who had led the returnees back to the land (Ezra 2:2; et al.). He was "the son of Shealtiel" ("I have asked of God," Ezra 3:2, 8; 5:2; Neh. 12:1; et al) and the grandson of King Jehoiachin (Jeconiah), one of the descendants of King David (cf. 1 Chron. 3:17-19; Matt. 1:12).

Zerubbabel apparently had two fathers (1 Chron. 3:17-19). Perhaps his other father, Pedaiah, was his uncle. If this was a levirate marriage (cf. Deut. 25:5-10), Pedaiah must have married a woman and then died. Shealtiel, Pedaiah's brother, would then have married the widow who gave birth to Zerubbabel in place of Shealtiel, Zerubbabel's physical father. Another possibility is that Shealtiel adopted Zerubbabel after Pedaiah died. A third option is that one of these men was actually a more distant ancestor of Zerubbabel, perhaps his grandfather.

"Joshua" was "the high priest" of the restoration community and a descendant of Aaron. He was "the son" of "Jehozadak," who had gone into Babylonian captivity in 586 B.C. (1 Chron. 6:15; cf. Ezra 3:2, 8; Neh. 12:1, 8).

The Lord gave Haggai this message on the first day of "the sixth month," "in the second year" that Darius I (Hystaspes) ruled as king over Persia. This was Elul 1 (August 29), 520 B.C.[15] When the Israelites returned from exile in Babylon, they continued to follow the Babylonian calendar and began their years in the spring rather than in the fall (cf. Exod. 23:16; 34:22). Each new month began with a new moon, and the Israelites commonly celebrated the occasion with a new moon festival (cf. Num. 28:11-15; Isa. 1:14; Hos. 2:11). This first prophetic revelation that God gave in the Promised Land, following the return from exile, came on a day when most of the Israelites would have been in Jerusalem. The meaning of Haggai's name (festal, or festal one) was appropriate, in view of when the Lord gave this first prophecy through him. The fact that the writer spoke of Haggai in the third person does not exclude Haggai himself from being the writer, since this was a common literary device in antiquity.[16]

In the historical books of the Old Testament, the writers usually dated the events in reference to a king of Judah or Israel, but the Jews had no king now. They were under the control of a Gentile ruler, in "the times of the Gentiles" (Luke 21:24; cf. Dan. 2; Zech. 1:1). "The times of the Gentiles" are the times during which Israel has lived under Gentile control. These times began when Judah lost her sovereignty to Nebuchadnezzar in 586 B.C., and they will continue until Messiah's Second Coming, when He will restore sovereignty to Israel.

1:2   Haggai announced that his message came from Yahweh of armies, Almighty Yahweh. This title appears 14 times in Haggai and 265 times in the Hebrew Bible. "Yahweh" occurs 34 times in the 38 verses of Haggai. The Lord told Zerubbabel and Joshua that the Israelites were saying that "the time" was not right to rebuild the temple. By referring to them as "this people," rather than "My people," the Lord was distancing Himself from them. Construction on the temple had begun 16 years earlier but had ceased, due to opposition from the Israelites' neighbors who were mostly Samaritans (Ezra 3:8-13; 4:1-5, 24). When the Jews considered resuming construction, most of them said it was not yet the right time. Contrast David's great desire to build a house for the Lord (2 Sam. 7:2). Their decision may have rested on the continuing threat from their neighbors. Or perhaps they felt that to finish the temple then would violate Jeremiah's prediction of a 70-year captivity (Jer. 25:11-12; 29:10). Another possibility is that they thought God Himself would finish it (Ezek. 40—48).[17]

> "To refuse to build the [Lord's] house was at best saying that it did not matter whether the Lord was present with them. At worst it was presuming on divine grace, that the Lord would live with his people even though they willfully refused to fulfill the condition of his indwelling that he had laid down."[18]

> "The need to rebuild is urgent, because temples in their world are the center for administering the political, economic, judicial, social, and religious life of the nation. In other words, rebuilding *I AM*'s temple would symbolize his rule over the life of his people and his prophesied rule of the world (cf. Zech. 1:14-17)."[19]

Today many Christians do not do God's will because they feel the time is not precisely right.

---

[15]R. A. Parker and W. H. Dubberstein, *Babylonian Chronology 626 B.C.-A.D. 75*, p. 30, established the equivalent modern (Julian) dates.
[16]Taylor, p. 52.
[17]See R. G. Hamerton-Kelly, "The Temple and the Origins of Jewish Apocalyptic," *Vetus Testamentum* 20 (1976):12.
[18]Motyer, p. 974.
[19]Bruce K. Waltke, *An Old Testament Theology*, p. 846.

> "Too often we make excuses when we ought to be making confessions and obeying the Lord. We say, 'It's not time for an evangelistic crusade,' 'It's not time for the Spirit to bring revival,' 'It's not time to expand the ministry.' We act as though we fully understand 'the times and the seasons' that God has ordained for His people, but we don't understand them (Acts 1:6-7)."[20]

1:3-4 Haggai then spoke to the people for the Lord, in this disputation speech, not just their leaders (v. 2). He rhetorically asked if it was proper for them to build their own houses but not rebuild His. They should have put the glory of their God ahead of their own comfort (cf. 2 Sam. 7:2; Phil. 2:21). Their priorities were upside down.

> "Their problem was not lack of goods but of good."[21]

"Paneled houses" apparently describes quite luxurious homes, though the Hebrew word *sapan* ("paneled") can mean simply houses with roofs. Wooden paneling or plaster that covered the walls and possibly the ceilings seems to be in view.

King Cyrus had provided the Jews with money to buy hardwood timber to rebuild the temple (Ezra 3:7; 1 Esdras 4:48; 5:54). It appears likely that the restoration Jews had used this superior wood to build their own homes rather than to rebuild the temple.

> "Many Christians are like those ancient Hebrews, somehow convincing themselves that economy in constructing church buildings [or financing God's work] is all-important while at the same time sparing no expense in acquiring their personal luxuries."[22]

> "Whereas the house of God today is no longer material but spiritual, the material is still a very real symbol of the spiritual. When the Church of God in any place in any locality is careless about the material place of assembly, the place of its worship and its work, it is a sign and evidence that its life is at a low ebb."[23]

1:5-6 The Lord called "the people" to evaluate what they were doing in the light of their present situation (cf. v. 7; 2:15, 18 [twice]). They were not experiencing God's blessings very greatly. They sowed much seed but harvested only modest crops (cf. vv. 10-11; 2:15-17, 19). The food and drink that they grew only met their minimal needs. They had so little fiber from which to make clothing, that their clothes were very thin and did not keep them warm. Their purses seemed to have "holes" in them, in the sense that the money they put in them disappeared before they could pay all their bills. This may be the first reference to coined money in the Bible. The Lydians in Asia Minor were the first to coin money, in the sixth century B.C., and there is archaeological evidence that there were coins in Palestine when Haggai wrote.[24] This was divine chastening for disobedience (cf. Lev. 26:18-20; Deut. 28:41). They should have put the Lord first.

> "An affluent generation of Christians that is wasting God's generous gifts on trivia and toys will have much to answer for when the Lord returns."[25]

B. HAGGAI'S SECOND CHALLENGE 1:7-11

1:7-8 Again the Lord called the people to reflect thoughtfully on what they were doing (cf. v. 5). He urged them to "go . . . to the mountains" where trees grew abundantly, to cut them down ("bring wood"), and to continue rebuilding "the temple" (cf. Ezra 3:7). The completed temple would please and glorify Him.

> "The important thing is not the size or magnificence of the house, but the *existence* of it—that they want the indwelling God among them."[26]

> "The hills of Judah were well wooded in Old Testament times, and from Nehemiah 8:15 we know that olive, myrtle and palm were available. It was customary to set layers of wood in stone walls to minimize earthquake damage (*cf.* Ezr. 5:8); this wood, and heavy timber, long enough to stretch from wall to wall of the Temple to support the roof, would probably have to be imported (Ezr. 3:7)."[27]

---

[20] Warren W. Wiersbe, "Haggai," in *The Bible Exposition Commentary/Prophets*, p. 441.
[21] Motyer, p. 977.
[22] Alden, p. 581.
[23] G. Campbell Morgan, *The Westminster Pulpit*, 8:315.
[24] See Ephraim Stern, *Material Culture of the Land of the Bible in the Persian Period 538-332 B.C.*, pp. 215, 236; and idem, *Archaeology of the Land of the Bible. Vol. II: The Assyrian, Babylonian, and Persian Periods, 732-332 BCE*, pp. 558-59.
[25] Wiersbe, p. 445.
[26] Motyer, p. 977.
[27] Baldwin, p. 41.

"When work is gladly done in order to please God it also brings Him glory."[28]

1:9 The Israelites had looked "for much" blessing from the Lord, but they had found very "little." When they brought their grain home, the Lord blew it away. Apparently their grain was so light and small that much of it blew away with the chaff when they threshed it. The reason was clear. They had neglected the temple and had given all their time and energy to providing for themselves by building their own houses.

There are six occurrences of the phrase "declares the LORD of hosts" in Haggai (1:9; 2:4, 8, 9, 23 [twice]) and six occurrences of the shorter phrase "declares the LORD" (1:13; 2:4 [twice], 14, 17, 23). This is unusual for a book as short as Haggai. Obviously the writer wanted to emphasize the divine origin of his message to the people.[29]

1:10-11 The hot weather and poor harvests that the returned exiles were enduring were due to their selfish behavior (cf. Lev. 26:19-20; Deut. 28:22-24). "Dew" was the only form of moisture that plants enjoyed during the hot summer months, besides artificial irrigation, but even that was unavailable. The Lord had called for drought, and it affected all their essential products and all aspects of the agrarian productivity of their lives ("all the labor of" their "hands"; cf. Deut. 28:38).

"Those who plan to give to God 'once they have enough for themselves' will never have enough for themselves!"[30]

C. THE ISRAELITES' RESPONSE 1:12-15

1:12 Haggai's preaching moved "Zerubbabel," "Joshua," and "all the remnant of the people" (Israelites) who had returned from captivity to obey the Lord. This demonstrated "reverence" for Him.

> "Haggai referred to the people as a **remnant** (here and also in v. 14 and in 2:2), not merely because they were survivors of the Babylonian Exile but also because they were becoming what the remnant of God's people should always be—those who are obedient within their covenant relationship to the Lord (cf. Isa. 10:21)."[31]

This term probably refers to the entire Judean population, consisting of both those who had returned from Babylon and those who had remained in the Promised Land (cf. Jer. 8:3; Ezek. 5:10; 9:8; 11:13).[32]

> "When times are prosperous, it may be easier to dismiss a word of prophetic rebuke; but hard times often expose raw nerves of the spiritual life that has grown insensitive to God's spirit. Frequently it is in the midst of exceptional human difficulty that God's word finds its greatest success."[33]

> "God whispers to us in our pleasures, speaks in our conscience, but shouts in our pains: it is His megaphone to rouse a deaf world."[34]

1:13 The people's obedient response resulted in the Lord sending another message to Haggai, His messenger. He reported that Yahweh was "with" them (cf. 2:4). This assurance of His divine enablement guaranteed their success as they continued obeying by rebuilding the temple. It is God's presence with us, more than anything else, that guarantees our success as we carry out His will (cf. Josh. 1:1-9; Matt. 28:19-20). Our loving obedience results in Him drawing close, but our disobedience leads Him to withdraw His presence.

1:14-15 The "LORD stirred up" the two leaders and the people to resume work on the temple (cf. 2 Chron. 36:22-23; Ezra 1:5). Work began again "on the twenty-fourth day" of that very month. Perhaps it took three weeks for the people to make their decision and make preparations, including chopping down trees and cutting (sawing and planing) wood (cf. v. 8). There was also a harvest of figs, grapes, and pomegranates in the month of Elul, which may have delayed them.[35]

---

[28]Ibid.
[29]Ibid., pp. 44-45, wrote an extended note on the name "the Lord of Hosts."
[30]Dyer, p. 816.
[31]F. Duane Lindsey, "Haggai," in *The Bible Knowledge Commentary: Old Testament*, p. 1540.
[32]See Taylor, p. 139.
[33]Ibid., p. 137.
[34]C. S. Lewis, *The Problem of Pain*, p. 81.
[35]P. A. Verhoef, *The Books of Haggai and Malachi*, p. 88.

II. A PROMISE OF FUTURE GLORY FOR THE TEMPLE 2:1-9

"God is not portrayed here as a divine puppeteer who manipulates people, but as a sovereign king who rewards obedience by giving it a boost."[36]

2:1   The Lord revealed another message, an oracle of encouragement, to Haggai almost one month later, "on the twenty-first" day of "the seventh month" (Tishri, modern October 17) of the same year, 520 B.C. This was the last day of the Feast of Tabernacles (Booths). Tishri was a month of celebrations for the Israelites. On the first of this month they celebrated the Feast of Trumpets, and on the tenth, the Day of Atonement. The Feast of Tabernacles lasted seven days, and the following day was a day of rest (Lev. 23:33-44).

2:2   The audience was the same as the one that received the first message: Zerubbabel, Joshua, and the entire Judean population.

2:3   The Lord asked if the older members of the restoration community who had seen Solomon's temple, which perished 66 years earlier, did not think the present temple was "like nothing in comparison" (cf. Zech. 4:10). The Lord's three questions forced the people to admit that the present temple was not as grand as the former one had been. The older returnees had made a similar negative comparison when the foundation of the temple was laid 16 years earlier in 536 B.C (cf. Ezra 3:8-13). The dedication of Solomon's temple took place exactly 440 years earlier, at the Feast of Tabernacles (1 Kings 8:2; 2 Chron. 7:8-10), so that was perhaps the reason the Lord gave this message to Haggai on this day.

> "To the devout and earnest Jew the second Temple must, 'in comparison of' 'the house in her first glory,' have indeed appeared 'as nothing.' True, in architectural splendour the second, as restored by Herod, far surpassed the first Temple."[37]

> "Though Zerubbabel's temple was leveled to the foundations by Herod when he renovated it, his temple was considered still the second temple."[38]

> "The Talmud expressly calls attention to this, and mentions as another point of pre-eminence, that whereas the first Temple stood 410, the second lasted 420 years."[39]

2:4   The Lord again encouraged Zerubbabel, Joshua, and the people to "work," and He promised again to be "with" them (cf. 1:13). David had given the same charge and promise to Solomon regarding the first temple (1 Chron. 28:10, 20). Comparisons can be discouraging when doing the Lord's work, so people involved in it need to remind themselves that He is with them (cf. Matt. 28:20; Mark 6:50).

> "The key to tackling despondency is found here: stop listening to ourselves and start listening to him and his word of promise."[40]

2:5   The Lord reiterated "the promise" He had made to the Israelites when they left "Egypt" in the Exodus. His "Spirit" would stay in their "midst," so they did "not" need to "fear" (cf. Exod. 19:4-6; 33:14). The returnees could identify with their forefathers who departed from Egypt, because they had recently departed from another captivity in Babylon. As the Lord had been with them in the cloudy pillar, so He was with them now. As David had encouraged Solomon to build the first temple with the promise that God would be with him (1 Chron. 28:20), so Haggai encouraged Zerubbabel and Joshua to build the second temple with the same promise.

> "There must have been those who were theologically naive and doubted that God could be with them if the temple and the ark in particular were not intact.

> "Undoubtedly fear gripped many of the returnees—fear that God had written an eternal 'Ichabod' over Jerusalem, fear that no amount of praying or piety would induce him to bless them again, fear that the whole endeavor was in vain, fear that the political enemies would in fact win, fear that all was lost."[41]

---

[36]Robert B. Chisholm Jr., *Handbook on the Prophets*, p. 452.
[37]Alfred Edersheim, *The Temple*, p. 61.
[38]Charles Lee Feinberg, *Habakkuk, Zephaniah, Haggai, and Malachi*, p. 90.
[39]Edersheim, f. 2.
[40]Motyer, p. 987.
[41]Alden, p. 585.

2:6	The basis of their confidence and lack of fear was a promise from Almighty Yahweh. He would do again, in the future, what He had done at the Exodus and at Mt. Sinai (Exod. 19:16, 18; Ps. 68:8; 77:16-18). Shaking "the heavens and the earth," including "the sea . . . and the dry land," describes an enormous earthquake, which was an evidence of the Lord's supernatural intervention (cf. Isa. 2:12-21; 13:13; Ezek. 38:20; Amos 8:8). This will occur when Christ returns to the earth (Joel 3:16; Matt. 24:29-30).

The writer of Hebrews quoted this verse in Hebrews 12:26. He then added that we who are in Christ have an unshakable kingdom that will endure the coming cosmic earthquake (Heb. 12:28-29). Haggai's prophecy still awaits fulfillment.

> "The New Testament writer sees in Haggai's language an implicit contrast between the transitory nature of the old economy and the abiding permanence of the new economy that was initiated by the mission of Jesus."[42]

2:7 At the same time, Almighty Yahweh would "shake all the nations"; His return will upset the political and governmental structures of the world (cf. Dan. 2:35, 44; Zech. 14:1-4; Matt. 21:44). "The nations" will bring their "wealth" to the Israelites, like the Egyptians gave their treasures to the departing Hebrews at the Exodus (cf. Exod. 3:21-22; 11:2-3; 12:35-36).

Some English translations have "the desire of all nations will come." This "desire" could be an impersonal reference to the wealth that the nations desire (cf. Isa. 60:5; Zech. 14:14).[43] Or this could be a personal reference. In this case it could be a messianic prophecy, which is why some translations capitalized "Desire."[44] Charles Wesley followed this second interpretation when he wrote the Christmas hymn "Hark! The Herald Angels Sing." "Come, Desire of nations, come! Fix in us Thy humble home. The Hebrew text does not solve the problem, which is interpretive. Perhaps the Lord was deliberately ambiguous and had both things in mind: the wealth of the nations and Messiah.[45]

> "It is well to remember . . . that from earliest days the majority of Christian interpreters followed the Jewish tradition in referring the passage to the coming of Israel's Messiah."[46]

The Lord also promised to "fill" the temple ("this house") "with glory." The temple in view must be the millennial temple, rather than the second (restoration) temple, in view of the context. This glory could be *the wealth* that the nations will bring to it (cf. Isa. 60:7, 13). Or the glory in view may be *the glory of God's own presence* (cf. Exod. 40:34-35; 1 Kings 8:10-11; Ezek. 43:1-12). Simeon referred to the infant Jesus as "the glory of your people Israel" (Luke 2:32). However, Jesus' presence in Herod's temple only prefigured the divine glory that will be present in the millennial temple.

2:8 This verse seems to support the view that impersonal wealth is in view in verse 7. The Lord reminded the people that He owned and controlled all "the silver" and "the gold" in the world, so He could cause the nations to bring it to the temple in the future.

> "The point may well be that because all such things are His and are therefore not of value to Him, His own glory is what is central."[47]

This reminder must have encouraged Haggai's contemporaries as they rebuilt the temple as well. God could easily bring more financial resources to them, so that they could some day glorify their presently modest temple.

2:9 Even though the present temple was less glorious than Solomon's temple, the Lord promised that the final ("latter") "glory" of the temple "will be greater than" its "former" glory. The Lord also promised to bring "peace" to the site of the temple, Jerusalem. Neither of these things has happened yet, so the fulfillment must be future (millennial). Lasting peace will only come when Messiah returns to rule and reign (cf. Isa. 2:4; 9:6; Zech. 9:9-10). Jesus Christ's adornment of the second temple, as renovated by Herod the Great, with His presence hardly seems to fulfill the exalted promises in this prophecy.[48]

---

[42]Taylor, p. 159.
[43]Robert B. Chisholm Jr., "A Theology of the Minor Prophets," in *A Biblical Theology of the Old Testament*, p. 421; idem, *Handbook on . . .*, pp. 452-53; Taylor, p. 161-65.
[44]Feinberg, p. 88.
[45]Herbert Wolf, *Haggai and Malachi*, pp. 34-37.
[46]Charles Lee Feinberg, "Haggai," in *The Wycliffe Bible Commentary*, p. 893.
[47]Merrill, p. 41.
[48]Chisholm, "A Theology . . .," p. 421.

The Lord used the occasion of the Feast of Tabernacles to encourage the builders of the temple in Haggai's day. This feast looked back to the Exodus, reminded the Israelites of their wilderness wanderings, and anticipated settlement in the Promised Land. This message also looked back to the Exodus, referred to the present temple construction, and anticipated the glory of the future temple.

III. A PROMISE OF FUTURE BLESSING FOR THE PEOPLE 2:10-19

2:10   Another prophecy came from the Lord "on the twenty-fourth" day "of the ninth month" of 520 B.C. (Kislev 24, December 18). This date holds particular significance because it was on this day, five years later, that the temple was rededicated. The Jews celebrated this event with the Feast of Chanukah (lit. Dedication), and still do. During the two months between this prophecy and the former one (vv. 1-9), Zechariah began his ministry in Jerusalem (Zech. 1:1).

2:11   Almighty Yahweh instructed Haggai to request "a ruling" from "the priests." The priests were the official interpreters of the Mosaic Law, and what follows deals with matters of ceremonial defilement. This is a didactic sermon, designed to teach an important lesson about religious impurity.

2:12   The question was, if someone "carries" consecrated food in "his garment" and touches other food of any kind with the garment, will that "food . . . become holy"? "Holy meat" was meat set apart for a particular sacrificial purpose (cf. Lev. 6:25; Num. 6:20). The answer the priests gave was "No," it would not become holy. The meat carried in the garment would make the garment holy, but the holiness would not be communicated beyond the garment to anything else (cf. Exod. 29:37; Lev. 6:27; Ezek. 44:19; Matt. 23:19). The people were apparently thinking that since they were working on the holy temple all that they contacted and did became holy. Another view is that the Lord sought to discourage His people from taking gifts from pagan rulers and using them to build the temple (cf. Ezra 6:8-10).[49]

2:13   A second question was, if someone who has become "unclean," for example by touching "a corpse," touches food of any kind, will the food "become unclean"? The answer was, yes, "it will become unclean." The Mosaic Law taught that moral uncleanness could be transmitted, but moral cleanness could not (cf. Lev. 6:18; 22:4-6; Num. 19:11-16). The same principle applies, by the way, in the area of physical health today. A sick person can transmit his or her illness to healthy people and make them sick, but a healthy person cannot transmit his or her health to sick people and make them well.

> "The long disobedience of the nation rendered their work unprofitable before God."[50]

2:14   Haggai then made an application of this principle to the people for the Lord. Their sacrifices and offerings were unacceptable to God because they were "unclean." They should not think that contact with something holy, such as the temple they were working to complete, made them acceptable to God. They had previously been unclean, so their present sacrifices were unacceptable to God.

2:15-16   The people needed to give careful consideration to something again (cf. 1:5, 7). They needed to remember that before they began to obey the Lord by rebuilding the temple (1:12), they had been disobedient to the Mosaic Covenant (cf. 1:5-11). The Lord's punishment for their covenant unfaithfulness had been greatly reduced harvests. Their grains had decreased by 50 percent and their grapes by 60 percent.

2:17   The Lord had used hot winds ("blasting wind" [blight, excessive drought]), "mildew" (excessive moisture), and "hail" to strike the people and what they had planted, but they still did not repent (cf. Amos 4:9). Hot winds posed problems for crops because of the dry heat, and mildew created other problems because of excessive moisture. Perhaps these conditions are a merism describing polar opposites that together mean all types of weather-related problems.[51] Hail, one of the plagues on Egypt (Exod. 9:13-35), caused severe damage to unprotected crops.

2:18-19   The people were to notice something on the "day" this prophecy reached their ears, "the twenty-fourth day of the ninth" month. They were to notice that from the day they started to rebuild the temple, their hardships had continued (cf. 1:14-15). They still suffered shortages of staples such as seed, grapes, and olives, and luxuries such as figs and pomegranates. However, the Lord revealed that He would now "bless" them, beginning that "very day," the twenty-fourth of the ninth month.

This oracle explained why agricultural blessing had not begun immediately after the people resumed reconstruction on the temple. Their present dedication and obedience did not wipe out their previous covenant unfaithfulness and its punishments. That punishment had to run its course, but now, as of the day of this prophecy, God would begin to bless the people with better harvests. This message surely must have encouraged the Jews to persevere in their obedience.

---

[49]See Merrill, pp. 45-46, 49.
[50]*The New Scofield Reference Bible*, p. 962.
[51]Taylor, p. 185.

God will bless His people for their obedience, but sometimes He will not erase the punishment that previous sins have made necessary. Sin always brings death (Rom. 6:23). Sometimes that punishment must run its course before blessing can begin.

IV. A PROPHECY CONCERNING ZERUBBABEL 2:20-23

"The final verses of his book reveal Haggai as the literary equivalent of an impressionist painter—he gives general tone and effect without elaborate detail."[52]

2:20   The Lord gave Haggai a "second" message on the same day as the previous message (v. 10), the "twenty-fourth day" of the ninth month (Kislev 24, December 18). This was an oracle of salvation.[53] Its purpose was to announce the Lord's intention to raise up a new leader for His people.

2:21   Haggai was to tell Zerubbabel that Yahweh was "going to shake the heavens and the earth." Again a divine judgment is in view (cf. v. 6). That "Zerubbabel"—not Joshua or the people—was the recipient, suggests that the message deals with a royal prediction.

2:22   The Lord announced that He would "overthrow" the rulers ("thrones") of the nations of the earth, and "destroy" the Gentile kingdoms' "power" (cf. Exod. 15:5; Dan. 2:34-35, 44-45). He would defeat ("overthrow") their armies ("chariots," "horses," and their "riders") by turning them against each other—"everyone . . . will go down . . . by the sword of another" (cf. Zech. 12:2-9; 14:1-5; Rev. 16:16-18; 19:11-21).

2:23   When He does that, the Lord promised to "make . . . Zerubbabel" His "servant." The title "My servant" is often messianic in the Old Testament (cf. 2 Sam. 3:18; 1 Kings 11:34; Isa. 42:1-9; 49:1-13; 50:4-11; 52:13—53:12; Ezek. 34:23-24; 37:24-25). Zechariah, Haggai's contemporary, used another messianic title to refer to Zerubbabel: the branch (Zech. 3:8; 6:12; cf. Isa. 11:1; Jer. 23:5-6; 33:14-16). The Lord would "make . . . Zerubbabel . . . like a signet" ring because He had chosen him for a special purpose. A signet ring was what kings used to designate royal authority and personal ownership (cf. 1 Kings 21:8; Dan. 6:17; Esth. 8:8). God had chosen Zerubbabel to designate royal authority and personal ownership, namely, the coming Messiah. God had revealed through Jeremiah that if Jehoiachin, Zerubbabel's grandfather, was His signet ring, He would take it off and give it to Nebuchadnezzar (cf. Jer. 22:24-25). Thus it is clear that this figure of a signet ring views "Zerubbabel"—figuratively—as the descendant of David and Jehoiachin through whom God would provide the victory promised in verses 21 and 22. He will do that, not through Zerubbabel personally, but through one of his descendants, namely: Jesus Christ (cf. Matt. 1:21).

The curse on Jehoiachin that none of his descendants would sit on David's throne or rule in Judah (Jer. 22:30) may have referred to his immediate descendants (i.e., children). However, *Jesus Christ* qualified as a *Davidic king* because He was the physical descendant of Nathan, one of David's sons, not Solomon. Jesus was the legal son of Joseph, who was a physical descendant of Solomon and Jehoiachin (cf. Matt. 1:12-16; Luke 3:23-31).

"God reverses to Zerubbabel the sentence on Jeconiah."[54]

Zerubbabel represents or typifies the Messiah here (cf. Joshua's similar role in Zech. 6:9-15). His name becomes a code name (atbash) for the promised Messiah.[55] The certainty of this promise is clear from the threefold repetition of "Yahweh," twice as "Yahweh of hosts."

". . . key events of the past (David's coming to power, Sodom, the exodus, Gideon) became symbols of the coming day, and the same is true of key people. David became so identified with what the Lord would yet do that not only was every successive king compared with him but the Messiah was even called David (Ezek. 34:23)."[56]

Other passages that speak of Messiah as David include Jeremiah 30:9 and Hosea 3:5.

---

[52]Motyer, p. 1000.
[53]See Claus Westermann, *Prophetic Oracles of Salvation in the Old Testament*.
[54]Edward B. Pusey, *The Minor Prophets*, 2:320. Cf. Chisholm, *Handbook on . . .*, p. 455; and Kaiser, p. 252.
[55]See Herbert Wolf, "The Desire of All Nations in Haggai 2:7: Messianic or Not?" *Journal of the Evangelical Theological Society* 19 (1976):101-2.
[56]Motyer, p. 1002.

> "By calling Zerubbabel His 'servant' and 'chosen' one God gave him the same status David had enjoyed (cf. 2 Sam. 3:18; 6:21; 7:5, 8, 26; 1 Kings 8:16). The comparison to a 'signet ring' indicates a position of authority and reverses the judgment pronounced on Zerubbabel's grandfather Jehoiachin (cf. Jer. 22:24-30).

> "The words of Haggai 2:21-23, though spoken directly to Zerubbabel, were not fulfilled in his day. How is one to explain this apparent failure of Haggai's prophecy? Zerubbabel, a descendant of David and governor of Judah, was the official representative of the Davidic dynasty in the postexilic community at that time. As such the prophecy of the future exaltation of the Davidic throne was attached to his person. As with the Temple (cf. Hag. 2:6-9), Haggai related an eschatological reality to a tangible historical entity to assure his contemporaries that God had great plans for His people. Zerubbabel was, as it were, the visible guarantee of a glorious future for the house of David. In Haggai's day some may have actually entertained messianic hopes for Zerubbabel. However, in the progress of revelation and history Jesus Christ fulfills Haggai's prophecy."[57]

> "Perhaps the prophecy should be taken at face value, but with an implicit element of contingency attached. The Lord may have desired to restore the glory of the Davidic throne in Zerubbabel's day, only to have subsequent developments within the postexilic community cause him to postpone that event, thereby relegating Zerubbabel to an archetype of the great king to come."[58]

> "Were these pronouncements actually fulfilled in Zerubbabel? Did he usher in a restoration of Israelite monarchy that was accompanied by the overthrow of Gentile nations in the fashion that Haggai describes? The history of this period provides no evidence that he did so. Haggai's promises did not come to fruition in the person of Zerubbabel. On the contrary, not long after this prophecy was given, Zerubbabel dropped into obscurity and passed off the scene. History is silent about what became of him or under what conditions he concluded his life."[59]

> "That Haggai himself necessarily expected a delayed fulfillment of his words is not likely. He had no way of anticipating the temporal distances that might exist between prediction and fulfillment."[60]

This final oracle promises a future overthrow of the Gentile nations that were, in Haggai's day, exercising sovereignty over Israel. A descendant of King Jehoiachin, and before him David, would be God's agent in that day. He would come from Zerubbabel's descendants and would be similar to Zerubbabel in that He would be the political ruler of God's people. Whereas God had withdrawn His signet ring (symbolic of divine selection and investiture with authority) from Jehoiachin (Jer. 22:24), He would give it back to a future descendant of Zerubbabel. This was an act of pure grace and faithfulness on sovereign Yahweh's part since the Israelites did not deserve such a future nor could they bring it about on their own. Such a message would have encouraged and motivated the returned exiles to complete the temple since there was still a glorious future for their nation in God's plans.

> "Haggai's sermons alternated between accusation and encouragement. (This is true of most of the prophets and in a sense should characterize all ministry.) The first sermon was basically negative. The second one aimed to encourage. [The third] . . . one is again essentially chiding and accusation. And . . . the last one is positive and uplifting."[61]

---

[57] Chisholm, "A Theology . . .," p. 422.
[58] Idem, *Handbook on . . .*, p. 455.
[59] Taylor, pp. 198-99.
[60] Ibid., p. 201.
[61] Alden, p. 588.

Bibliography

Alden, Robert L. "Haggai." In *Daniel-Minor Prophets*. Vol. 7 of *The Expositor's Bible Commentary*. 12 vols. Edited by Frank E. Gaebelein and Richard P. Polcyn. Grand Rapids: Zondervan Publishing House, 1985.

Baldwin, Joyce G. *Haggai, Zechariah, Malachi: An Introduction and Commentary*. Tyndale Old Testament Commentaries series. Leicester, Eng., and Downers Grove, Ill.: Inter-Varsity Press, 1972.

Bright, John. *A History of Israel*. Philadelphia: Westminster Press, 1959.

Chisholm, Robert B., Jr. *Handbook on the Prophets*. Grand Rapids: Baker Book House, 2002.

_____. "A Theology of the Minor Prophets." In *A Biblical Theology of the Old Testament*, pp. 397-433. Edited by Roy B. Zuck. Chicago: Moody Press, 1991.

Dyer, Charles H., and Eugene H. Merrill. *The Old Testament Explorer*. Nashville: Word Publishing, 2001. Reissued as *Nelson's Old Testament Survey*. Nashville: Thomas Nelson Publishers, 2001.

Edersheim, Alfred. *The Temple: Its Ministry and Services As They Were at the Time of Jesus Christ*. Reprint ed. Grand Rapids: Wm. B. Eerdmans Publishing Co., 1972.

Feinberg, Charles Lee. "Haggai." In *The Wycliffe Bible Commentary*, pp. 889-896. Edited by Charles F. Pfeiffer and Everett F. Harrison. Chicago: Moody Press, 1962.

_____. *Habakkuk, Zephaniah, Haggai, Malachi*. The Major Messages of the Minor Prophets series. New York: American Board of Missions to the Jews, 1951.

Gaebelein, Frank E. *Four Minor Prophets (Obadiah, Jonah, Habakkuk, and Haggai): Their Message for Today*. Chicago: Moody Press, 1970.

Hamerton-Kelly, R. G. "The Temple and the Origins of Jewish Apocalyptic." *Vetus Testamentum* 20 (1976):1-15.

Lewis, Clive Staples. *The Problem of Pain*. New York: MacMillan, 1947.

Lindsey, F. Duane. "Haggai." In *The Bible Knowledge Commentary: Old Testament*, pp. 1537-44. Edited by John F. Walvoord and Roy B. Zuck. Wheaton: Scripture Press Publications, Victor Books, 1985.

Longman, Tremper, III and Raymond B. Dillard. *An Introduction to the Old Testament*. 2nd ed. Grand Rapids: Zondervan, 2006.

Merrill, Eugene H. *An Exegetical Commentary: Haggai, Zechariah, Malachi*. Chicago: Moody Press, 1994.

Morgan, G. Campbell. *An Exposition of the Whole Bible*. Westwood, N.J.: Fleming H. Revell Company, 1959.

_____. *Living Messages of the Books of the Bible*. 2 vols. New York: Fleming H. Revell Co., 1912.

_____. *The Westminster Pulpit: The Preaching of G. Campbell Morgan*. 10 vols. London: Pickering & Inglis Ltd., n.d.

Motyer, J. Alec. "Haggai." In *The Minor Prophets: An Exegetical and Expositional Commentary*, 3:963-1002. 3 vols. Edited by Thomas Edward McComiskey. Grand Rapids: Baker Books, 1992, 1993, and 1998.

The New Scofield Reference Bible. Edited by Frank E. Gaebelein, et al. New York: Oxford University Press, 1967.

Parker, Richard A., and Waldo H. Dubberstein. *Babylonian Chronology 626 B.C.-A.D. 75*. Providence, R.I.: Brown University, 1956.

Pusey, Edward B. *The Minor Prophets: A Commentary, Explanatory and Practical*. 2 vols. 2nd ed. Grand Rapids: Baker Book House, 1950.

Stern, Ephraim. *Archaeology of the Land of the Bible. Vol. II: The Assyrian, Babylonian, and Persian Periods, 732-332 BCE*. Anchor Bible Reference Library series. New York: Doubleday, 2001.

_____. *Material Culture of the Land of the Bible in the Persian Period 538-332 B.C.* Warminster, Eng.: Aris & Phillipps; Jerusalem: Israel Exploration Society, 1982.

Taylor, Richard A., and E. Ray Clendenen. *Haggai, Malachi*. New American Commentary series. Nashville: Broadman & Holman Publishers, 2004.

Verhoef, Pieter A. *The Books of Haggai and Malachi*. New International Commentary on the Old Testaement series. Grand Rapids: Wm. B. Eerdmans Publishing Co., 1987.

Waltke, Bruce K., with Charles Yu. *An Old Testament Theology: an exegetical, canonical, and thematic approach*. Grand Rapids: Zondervan, 2007.

Westermann, Claus. *Prophetic Oracles of Salvation in the Old Testament*. Louisville: Westminster/John Knox Press, 1991.

Wiersbe, Warren W. "Haggai." In *The Bible Exposition Commentary/Prophets*, pp. 437-46. Colorado Springs, Colo.: Cook Communications Ministries; and Eastbourne, England: Kingsway Communications Ltd., 2002.

Wiseman, D. J. *Chronicles of Chaldaean Kings (625-556 B.C.) in the British Museum*. London: Trustees of the British Museum, 1961.

Wolf, Herbert. "The Desire of All Nations in Haggai 2:7: Messianic or Not?" *Journal of the Evangelical Theological Society* 19 (1976):97-102.

_____. *Haggai and Malachi*. Everyman's Bible Commentary series. Chicago: Moody Press, 1976.

Wood, Leon J. *The Prophets of Israel*. Grand Rapids: Baker Book House, 1979.

Constable's Notes
On Zechariah

Introduction

Title and Writer

The title of this book comes from its traditional writer, as is true of all the prophetical books of the Old Testament. The name "Zechariah" (lit. Yahweh remembers) was a common one among the Israelites, which identified at least 27 different individuals in the Old Testament, perhaps 30.[1] It was an appropriate name for the writer of this book, because it explains that Yahweh remembers His chosen people, and His promises, and will be faithful to them. This Zechariah was the son of Berechiah, the son of Iddo (1:1, 7; cf. Ezra 5:1; 6:14; Neh. 12:4, 16).

Zechariah, like Jeremiah and Ezekiel, was both a prophet and a priest. He was obviously familiar with priestly things (cf. ch. 3; 6:9-15; 9:8, 15; 14:16, 20, 21). Since he was a young man (Heb. *na'ar*) when he began prophesying (2:4), he was probably born in Babylonian captivity and returned to Palestine in 536 B.C. with Zerubbabel and Joshua. He became a leading priest in the restoration community succeeding his grandfather (or ancestor), Iddo, who also returned from captivity in 536 B.C., as the leader of his priestly family (Neh. 12:4, 16). Zechariah's father, Berechiah (1:1, 7), evidently never became prominent.

The Lord Jesus referred to a Zechariah, the son of Berechiah, whom the Jews murdered between the temple and the altar (Matt. 23:35). This appears to be how the prophet's life ended.[2] This would make Zechariah one of the last righteous people the Jews killed in Old Testament history.

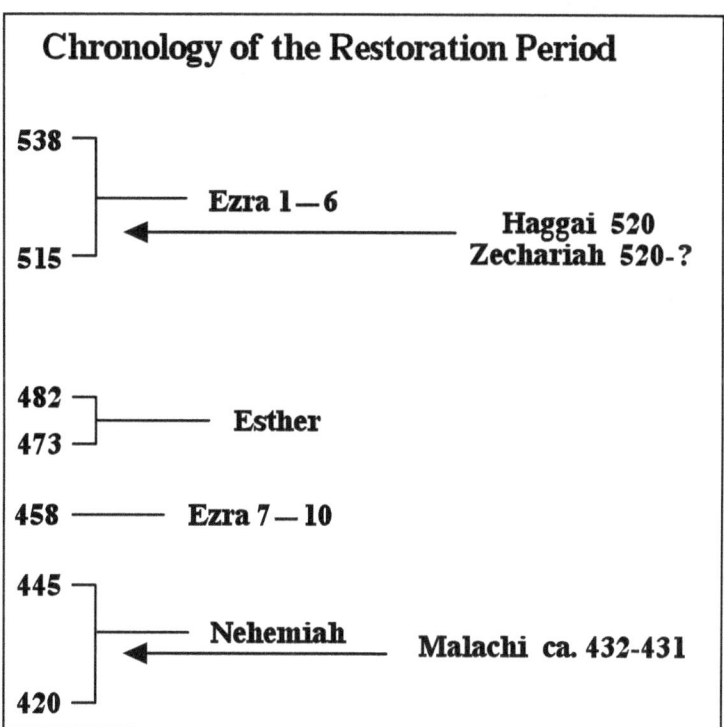

Some students of Scripture believe that the Zechariah to whom Jesus referred was the son of Jehoiada whom the Jews stoned in the temple courtyard (2 Chron. 24:20-22).[3] However, that man died hundreds of years earlier, before 800 B.C., and Jesus seems to have been summarizing all the righteous people the Jews had slain throughout Old Testament history chronologically. Zechariah ben Jehoiada was the last martyr in the last book of the Hebrew Bible, Chronicles, so Jesus may have been speaking canonically, the equivalent of "all the martyrs from Genesis to Revelation." Nevertheless that Zechariah was the son of Jehoiada, not Berechiah, and Jesus mentioned Berechiah as the father of the Zechariah He meant. "Son" sometimes means "ancestor," but there is no known Berechiah in the family line of the Zechariah of 2 Chronicles.

> "According to some ancient versions Zechariah was a poet as well as a prophet. His name is in the titles of Pss 137, 145—50 in the LXX; in the titles of Ps 111, 145 in the Vulgate; and in the titles of Pss 125, 145—48 in the Syriac."[4]

Date

Zechariah's inspired preaching began in the eighth month of 520 B.C. (1:1). His eight night visions followed three months later in 520 B.C. (1:7), when he was a young man (2:4). He delivered the messages in chapters 7—8 in 518 B.C. (7:1). Nehemiah mentioned Zechariah as the head of a priestly family when Joiakim, who succeeded Joshua, was high priest (Neh. 12:12, 16). This may have been as late as during the reign of Artaxerxes I (465-424 B.C.).[5] Some scholars believe Nehemiah wrote chapters 9—14 during this later period of his life.[6] The exact length of his life and ministry is guesswork, however.

---

[1] Robert Young, *Analytical Concordance to the Bible*, p. 1087. Cf. Ralph L. Smith, *Micah-Malachi*, p. 167.
[2] Gleason L. Archer Jr., *A Survey of Old Testament Introduction*, p. 425.
[3] E.g., Eugene H. Merrill, *An Exegetical Commentary: Haggai, Zechariah, Malachi*, p. 95.
[4] Smith, p. 168.
[5] See Joyce G. Baldwin, *Haggai, Zechariah, Malachi: An Introduction and Commentary*, p. 60.

Historical Background

Zechariah began ministering among the Jews who had returned from captivity in Babylon (i.e., the restoration community) two months after Haggai began preaching (1:1; 7:1; cf. Neh. 12:10-16; Hag. 1:1). In a sense, Zechariah's message supplements that of Haggai.[7]

> "Both prophets . . . contrast the past with the present and future, with Haggai stressing the rebuilt Temple as a sign and source of God's blessing and Zechariah emphasizing the role of repentance and renewal in achieving that end. The two prophets worked hand in glove, complementing each other's message."[8]

> "There is a marked contrast between Haggai and his contemporary Zechariah. If Haggai was the builder, responsible for the solid structure of the new Temple, Zechariah was more like the artist, adding colourful windows with their symbolism, gaiety and light. To make sure that their symbolism is rightly understood an interpreting angel acts as guide, adding in some cases a message that goes far beyond what could be deduced from the visions."[9]

Haggai and Zechariah's ministries followed those of Ezekiel and Daniel, who ministered during the Captivity in Babylon.

TABLE OF SOME POST-EXILIC EVENTS		
Cyrus issued his edict allowing the Jews to return home.	538 B.C.	Ezra 1
About 50,000 Jews returned under Zerubbabel and Joshua's leadership.	536 B.C.	Ezra 2; Neh. 7
The altar was rebuilt and sacrifices resumed.	536 B.C.	
Work on the temple began but then halted.	536 B.C.	Ezra 3:1-4
The Jews became occupied with rebuilding their own homes.	536-522 B.C.	Hag. 1—2
Cyrus died, and his son, Cambyses II, succeeded him and ruled Persia.	530 B.C.; 530-522 B.C.	
Smerdis ruled Persia.	522-521 B.C.	
Darius I, the Great (Hystaspes), rescued Persia from civil war and ruled Persia.	521-486 B.C.	
Darius confirmed Cyrus' decree and encouraged the Jews to continue rebuilding the temple.	520 B.C.	Ezra 6:1-14
Haggai preached his first three sermons.	520 B.C., 6th and 7th months	Hag. 1:1, 15; 2:1
Zechariah preached his first sermon.	520 B.C., 8th month	Zech. 1:1
Haggai preached his fourth and fifth sermons.	520 B.C., 9th month	Hag. 2:10, 20

---

[6]E.g., Kenneth L. Barker, "Zechariah," in *Daniel-Minor Prophets*, vol. 7 of *The Expositor's Bible Commentary*, p. 597; Merrill, p. 63; and Archer, p. 437.
[7]H. C. Leupold, *Exposition of Zechariah*, p. 3.
[8]Merrill, p. 62.
[9]Baldwin, p. 59.

TABLE OF SOME POST-EXILIC EVENTS (CONT.)		
Zechariah received his eight night visions.	520 B.C., 11th month	Zech. 1:7
Joshua, the high priest, was crowned.	520 B.C., 11th month	Zech. 6:9-15
The delegation from Bethel arrived, and Zechariah preached again.	518 B.C., 9th month	Zech. 7:1
The Jews completed the temple and dedicated it.	515 B.C., 12th month	Ezra 6:15
Xerxes I (Ahasuerus) reigned over Persia.	486-464 B.C.	Esth. 2:16
Artaxerxes I reigned over Persia.	464-424 B.C.	
About 5,000 Jews returned to Palestine under Ezra's leadership.	458 B.C.	Ezra 7:7
Artaxerxes I authorized Nehemiah to rebuild Jerusalem's walls.	445 B.C.	Neh. 2:1
Nehemiah led the third return to Palestine.	444 B.C.	Neh. 2:9
Malachi ministered.	ca. 432-431 B.C.	

Purpose and Themes

Zechariah ministered to the restoration community to motivate those Jews to finish rebuilding the temple and to rededicate themselves to Yahweh with the prospect of His blessing. The central theme of the book is encouragement and hope.[10] The key to this hope is the coming of Messiah and his overthrow of ungodly forces and establishment of His kingdom on earth.

> "The prophet is concerned to comfort his discouraged and pessimistic compatriots, who are in the process of rebuilding their Temple and restructuring their community but who view their efforts as making little difference in the present and offering no hope for the future."[11]

This prophet dealt with the future of Israel, and particularly its distant, eschatological future, to an extent that surpassed the other Old Testament prophets (cf. 12:1-3, 9; 14:1-5, 16-21). His revelations concerning a future day of the Lord are numerous.

> "What former prophets revealed at length, Zechariah epitomizes for us in terse sentences or even clauses."[12]

This book also contains many messianic prophecies (cf. 3:8-9; 6:12-13; 9:9-10, 14; 11:12-13; 13:7; 14:4, 9, 16).

> "Particularly prominent in the book is the Messianic element. With the exception of Isaiah, there is no other prophet whose book contains such a wealth and variety of this element, not only in proportion to the total amount of material offered, but also as a sum total of passages."[13]

> "Few books of the OT are as difficult of interpretation as the Book of Zechariah; no other book is as Messianic."[14]

Canonicity and Unity

This book is the second to the last of the Minor Prophets in the second (Prophets) division of the Hebrew Bible. Neither Jews nor Christians seriously challenged its canonicity. One reason for this is the fact that the New Testament quotes and alludes to Zechariah so often, about 41 times.[15] The Gospel evangelists cited chapters 9—14 more frequently in their passion narratives than any other portion of the Old Testament. The

---

[10] See Archer, pp. 423-24; Robert D. Bell, "The Theology of Zechariah," *Biblical Viewpoint* 24:2 (November 1990):55-61; and Robert B. Chisholm Jr., "A Theology of the Minor Prophets," in *A Biblical Theology of the Old Testament*, pp. 423-28.

[11] Merrill, p. 87.

[12] Charles L. Feinberg, *God Remembers: A Study of the Book of Zechariah*, p. 3.

[13] Leupold, p. 4.

[14] *The International Standard Bible Encyclopaedia*, 1949 ed., s.v. "Zechariah, Book of," by George L. Robinson, 5:3136.

[15] E. Nestle and K. Aland, eds., *Novum Testamentum Graece*, pp. 670-71.

Book of Revelation refers to the Book of Zechariah more frequently than to any other Old Testament book except Ezekiel. There are also few textual problems in the book; the text has come down to us well preserved.[16]

Until A.D. 1653, no one seriously questioned that Zechariah wrote the whole book. In that year, Joseph Mede suggested that Jeremiah may have written chapters 9—11, in view of Matthew 27:9. In succeeding years, other scholars proceeded to question the second part of the book (chs. 9—14), because of its differences in content and historical and chronological references as compared to the first part (chs. 1—8). Today almost all critical scholars regard this book as the product of two or three writers who wrote either before the exile or after Zechariah. Bruce Waltke, though conservative in most matters, dealt with this book by referring to "First Zechariah" and "Second Zechariah."[17] Similarly, critical scholars regard Isaiah as having two or three writers. Critics commonly divide Zechariah into chapters 1—8 and 9—14; or 1—8, 9—11, and 12—14. The presence of predictive prophecy in the last chapters of the book has encouraged those who deny the miraculous to relegate this part to a later time and writer(s).[18]

> "We maintain it is impossible to confine or restrict the Spirit of God in His revelatory purposes. If He cares to predict an event three centuries off, He is sovereign; and if it pleases Him to foretell the plan of God a millennium before its materialization, He is just as sovereign. We emphasize this because we believe it to be the *sine qua non* of reverent, acceptable interpretation of Biblical prophecy."[19]

Competent conservative scholars have refuted the arguments of the radical critics adequately.[20]

> "In the nature of the case it is not possible to prove conclusively who wrote chapters 9—14, but when every argument has been considered the fact remains that all fourteen chapters have been handed down to us as one book in every manuscript so far discovered. Even the tiny fragment of the Greek manuscript found at Qumran, which includes the end of chapter 8 and the beginning of chapter 9, shows no gap or spacing whatsoever to suggest a break between the two parts."[21]

Genre

Zechariah consists of a combination of poetry (chs. 9—10), exhortations (sermon material; 1:1-6), prophetic-apocalyptic visions (1:7—6:8), symbolic actions (6:9-15), and oracles (chs. 7—14), some of which concern eschatological salvation (chs. 9—14). Some of the oracles introduce or follow visions, and others do not. Along with Ezekiel, Daniel, and Revelation, Zechariah is one of the most apocalyptic books in the Bible.[22]

> "In the present writer's judgment, his [Zechariah's] book is the most Messianic, the most truly apocalyptic and eschatological, of all the writings of the OT."[23]

> "Apocalyptic literature is basically meant to encourage the people of God."[24]

> "Only apocalyptic could express the utter transcendence involved in the radical transformations that would accompany the irruption of the kingdom of YHWH and the consequent shattering of all human and earthly systems in its wake."[25]

> "The apocalyptic visions of Zechariah, though filled with symbolism, are not as complicated and bizarre as those of Ezekiel, but do require angelic interpreters, at least in chapters 1-6. He goes beyond Ezekiel and other early apocalyptists, however, in his declarations that what he envisions is as good as done, for it is only an earthly reflection of what has in fact come to pass in heaven."[26]

---

[16]See T. Jansma, "Inquiry into the Hebrew Text and the Ancient Versions of Zechariah ix-xiv," *Oudtestamentische Studiën* 7 (1950):1-142.
[17]Bruce K. Waltke, *An Old Testament Theology*, pp. 846-47.
[18]See Tremper Longman III and Raymond B. Dillard, *An Introduction to the Old Testament*, pp. 487-90, for further discussion.
[19]Feinberg, p. 10.
[20]See especially Baldwin, pp. 62-70; Leupold, pp. 6-13; Merrill F. Unger, *Unger's Bible Commentary: Zechariah*, pp. 13-14; R. K. Harrison, *Introduction to the Old Testament*, pp. 950-56; and Archer, pp. 425-30.
[21]Baldwin, pp. 69-70.
[22]For discussion of apocalyptic as a genre, see Ralph H. Alexander, "Hermeneutics of Old Testament Apocalyptic Literature" (Th.D. dissertation, Dallas Theological Seminary, 1968), p. 45; Elliott E. Johnson, "Apocalyptic Genre in Literary Interpretation," in *Essays in Honor of J. Dwight Pentecost*, p. 200; Merrill, pp. 69-74; and Baldwin, pp. 70-74.
[23]Robinson, 5:3136.
[24]Barker, p. 600.
[25]Merrill, p. 71.
[26]Ibid., p. 72.

Structure

"The 'shape' of a poem, the artistic arrangement of a book are instruments used by the Holy Spirit to convey His message."[27]

In the case of Zechariah, there are three large chiastic sections (1:7—6:15; 7:1—8:19; and chs. 9—14). These contain Zechariah's eight night visions and their accompanying oracles, his messages prompted by a question about fasting, and the two burdens (oracles) announcing the triumphant interventions of the Lord into history in the future. A brief section introduces the whole book (1:1-6).

Zechariah is the longest of the Minor Prophets. It contains 14 chapters with 211 verses, whereas Hosea, the second longest, has 14 chapters with 197 verses. Daniel, the shortest Major Prophet, contains 12 chapters with 357 verses.

Outline

I. Introduction 1:1-6
II. The eight night visions and four messages 1:7—6:8
    A. The horseman among the myrtle trees 1:7-17
        1. The vision proper 1:7-15
        2. The oracle about God's jealousy for Israel 1:16-17
    B. The four horns and the four smiths 1:18-21
    C. The surveyor ch. 2
        1. The vision itself 2:1-5
        2. The oracle about enemy destruction and Israelite blessing 2:6-13
    D. The cleansing and restoration of Joshua ch. 3
        1. The symbolic act 3:1-5
        2. The accompanying promises 3:6-10
    E. The gold lampstand and the two olive trees ch. 4
        1. The vision 4:1-5
        2. Two oracles concerning Zerubbabel 4:6-10
        3. The interpretation of the vision 4:11-14
    F. The flying scroll 5:1-4
    G. The woman in the basket 5:5-11
    H. The four chariots 6:1-8
III. The symbolic crowning of Joshua 6:9-15
IV. Messages concerning hypocritical fasting chs. 7—8
    A. The question from the delegation from Bethel 7:1-3
    B. The Lord's rebuke 7:4-7
    C. The command to repent 7:8-14
    D. Israel's restoration to God's favor 8:1-17
    E. Kingdom joy and Jewish favor 8:18-23
V. Oracles about the Messiah and Israel's future chs. 9—14
    A. The burden concerning the nations: the advent and rejection of Messiah chs. 9—11
        1. The coming of the true king ch. 9
        2. The restoration of the true people ch. 10
        3. The rejection of the true king ch. 11
    B. The burden concerning Israel: the advent and acceptance of Messiah chs. 12—14
        1. The repentance of Judah ch. 12
        2. The restoration of Judah ch. 13

---
[27]Baldwin, p. 74

3. The reign of Messiah ch. 14

Message

This is the second post-exilic prophetical book. The historical background and audience are the same as those for Haggai. As Zechariah's contemporaries looked back, they saw former glory and recent shame. As they looked forward, they saw difficulty and felt discouragement. Zechariah ministered to inspire hope in the heart of this discouraged remnant of Israelites. That was his purpose.

Zechariah delivered his first message between Haggai's first and second messages, and his purpose was the same as Haggai's: to motivate the restoration community to finish rebuilding the temple. Zechariah followed this first message with eight visions to inspire hope in his hearers. Why should they rebuild the temple if there was no future? Zechariah then explained that the present sorrowful fasts that the people were celebrating would give way to future glorious feasts. The final two oracles also provided hope for the future by predicting the coming of Messiah and His glorious kingdom. Note the 8—4—2 structure of this book. This structure makes it easier to remember what is in it.

Many writers on Zechariah have called this book the apocalypse (Gr. for "revelation") of the Old Testament, because it unveils so much of Israel's future, particularly Messiah's place in her future. The whole book is a revelation of the pervasive power and the persistent purpose of Yahweh. Zechariah revealed things about the future of the Jews that gave his discouraged contemporaries hope.

People experiencing adversity frequently see only things that are close at hand. Zechariah provided hope from visions that he saw, and from voices that he heard, that encouraged his audience to lift their eyes to behold the larger plans and purposes of their God. The permanent values of this book are, therefore, that it reveals the proper attitude and activity of God's people in all circumstances, as well as the pervasive power and the persistent purpose of Yahweh. To generalize, Haggai is more practical, and Zechariah is more theoretical.

The first three verses of the book stress the first of these values. The great appeal of the entire book appears in verse 3: "Return to Me that I may return to you, says the LORD of Hosts." Everything that follows illustrates and applies this promise.

As often is the case, the key to understanding a book of the Bible lies in the aspect of God that God stressed in revealing Himself to His people through its writer. The title "the LORD of Hosts" occurs for the first time in the Bible in 1 Samuel, when the people of Israel were concerned about armies, particularly the Philistine armies. This title rarely appears in the other historical books, but it is very common in the prophetical books. Zechariah used it more frequently than any other prophet: at least 35 times.

The word "hosts" in the Bible describes stars, angels, the people of Israel, and the armies of other nations. The title "the LORD of Hosts," then, describes Yahweh as the sovereign Lord and Master of the entire universe. As the prophets used it, they stressed Yahweh's sovereignty in action, not just in its abstract meaning. That is, they saw Yahweh as leading all armies—of stars, angels, and people. Zechariah lived when Israel had lost its army, had no military power, and had little political organization. Thus, by referring to Yahweh as "the LORD of Hosts," Zechariah was reminding his hearers of their God's abiding and active sovereignty.

The prophet referred to Yahweh as "the LORD of Hosts" three times in the opening paragraph of his book (vv. 1-3). The first reference (in v. 3) reminded the Israelites that their sovereign God had made His will known to His people; He had spoken (cf. 1:6). The Lord illustrated this truth in verse 4. The sovereign Lord had said, "Return to Me" (v. 3). This was the first part of Zechariah's prophetic burden. The second part was that Yahweh promised to return to His people (v. 3). He explained the work that He, as the Sovereign, would do to make this return possible. God Himself would provide the power necessary for the restoration of order, by coming to His people in His Son and by His Spirit.

Thus, Zechariah had a three-fold conviction. God reveals His will, He calls people back to Himself and provides the way for their coming, and He promises that if they will return to Him, He will return to them. God revealed His will to the returnees through the prophetic word. He promised to provide a way for people to return to Him through the "Branch," the second person of the Trinity (3:8). The revelation of this divine-human person occupies much of this book in proportion to its length. Second, God promised to return to people who return to Him through His Spirit, the third person of the Trinity. He would return "not by might nor by power, but by My Spirit," says the Lord (4:6).

The visions and oracles in Zechariah illustrate Yahweh's pervasive power. They draw attention to this.

In the first vision, God revealed the presence of His angel that was watching over His people in their depressed place. They knew about the depressed place, but the presence of the angel was news to them. The second vision revealed that forces would destroy the powers that opposed them. The people knew about these enemy powers, but they needed a reminder that God planned to destroy them. In the third vision, God revealed Jerusalem in its future large, secure condition. The people knew about Jerusalem; they were rebuilding it. But they were not sure about its future large and secure condition. The fourth vision revealed an adversary and an advocate. The people were aware of their adversary, but they were unaware of their divine advocate.

In the fifth vision, God revealed the people's responsibility to be lights in the world and their resource for doing so. The people knew their responsibility, but they did not fully appreciate that they had a supernatural resource that would enable them to fulfill their responsibility. The sixth vision revealed the purging of sin with divine revelation. The people were aware of the present sin, but they now learned that observing God's law would deal with it. The seventh vision illustrated ongoing evil and its final purging away. The people were aware of widespread evil, but they needed reminding that God would eventually remove it forever. The eighth vision revealed the need for divine control over present chaos and the provision of divine control. The people were very conscious of the need for divine control in their chaotic world, but they needed to remember that God would indeed exercise divine control in the world.

Each vision revealed an aspect of God's pervasive power to overcome what Zechariah's audience faced, and so gave them hope. Were they in a depressed place? God was watching over them. Were weapons being formed against them? He would break those weapons. Was the city they were rebuilding insecure? He would enlarge it even further and make it secure. Was their adversary going to be successful? God would be their Advocate. Was their responsibility heavy? He would prove to be a sufficient resource for them. Was sin present everywhere? He would give the power to overcome sin. Was evil ever going to end? He would end it. Would order ever come? He would bring it.

The two oracles in Zechariah 9—14 teach the same basic lesson: the pervasive power of "the LORD of Hosts." To summarize this briefly, the anointed King would be rejected initially, but He would return with the pervasive power of Yahweh.

The visions and oracles also illustrate the second major revelation of Zechariah: the persistent purpose of Israel's God.

The visions unfold God's dealings with Israel eschatologically, as well as contemporarily. While all the conditions of Israel described in the visions marked the restoration community, they will also mark the future of Israel. She was and would continue to be depressed among the nations. Enemies would attack her, but God would eventually defeat them. Jerusalem would be rebuilt and protected, and Israel would be cleansed to serve the Lord. Israel would fulfill her destiny as a light to the nations, and she would disseminate the knowledge of God in the world. Evil will be greatly constrained, and all of Israel's enemies will suffer defeat. All these predictions reveal the persistent purpose of God whereby He moves history toward His intended goal, despite human and Satanic opposition.

The oracles illustrate the same principle. Messiah's rejection would lead to His coronation. Some of Yahweh's purposes in salvation took place when Messiah came the first time, but the rest of His purposes in salvation will take place when He comes the second time.

What should be the attitude of God's people in view of these revelations? They should return to the Lord (1:3). They should believe these revelations, obey them, and work in view of them.

The people of God in Zechariah's day needed to complete the temple and reestablish right relations with Yahweh, even though they lived in a day of darkness and discouragement. They needed to abandon the fasts, that they had established to commemorate the destruction of Jerusalem, and prepare for feasts that would celebrate the glorious future that Yahweh promised and would provide.

Whereas Haggai called these people to be strong and to work, Zechariah revealed the secret of their strength. The Apostle Paul put it this way: "For momentary light affliction is producing for us an eternal weight of glory far beyond all comprehension" (2 Cor. 4:17). That is the message of Zechariah in New Testament language.

The proof of vision is strength. What do we see as we look out over the church? We may see only the discouraging things that the restoration Jews saw as they viewed their situation. We need to be aware of the unseen things that God has said He is doing, and will do, in order to persevere in the work of building His church, that He has called us to do (cf. Matt. 16:18; 2 Cor. 2:14—5:21)

The secret of strength is vision. If God's people say they see these positive, encouraging things and that they believe them but do nothing, it is hard to believe them. The person who is conscious, through all the appalling defeat of the hour, of the immediate, pervasive presence and power of God, is the person who grabs ahold of the piece of desolation nearest to him or her, and works on it until it blossoms like a garden. The true demonstration of vision is taking ahold of the present situation and doing something about it, trusting in the unseen presence and promises of God. In our day, visionaries are a dime a dozen. It is the visionaries who follow through that are rare and successful.

The writer of the Epistle to the Hebrews challenged his readers with words that are very appropriate in light of the message of Zechariah (Heb. 12:12-13). Some Christians seem to equate spirituality with pessimism. They consider others "visionary" who explore and deplore in great depth the difficulties of our days. We need to be realistic about our times, but we must also keep our eyes on the person of God and our ears open to His promises. We must also fall in line with His purposes and work in harmony with His principles of power. When we do this, we can rest assured that when the Rejected One is crowned, we will share in His triumph as we have shared in His travail.[28]

---

[28]Adapted from G. Campbell Morgan, *Living Messages of the Books of the Bible*, 1:2:317-32.

Exposition

I. INTRODUCTION 1:1-6

That this pericope introduces the whole book seems clear, since verse 7 introduces the eight night visions that follow it (1:7—6:8). Its content is also foundational to all that follows.

> "It strikes the keynote of the entire book, and is one of the strongest and most intensely spiritual calls to repentance to be found anywhere in the Old Testament."[29]

> "The initial six verses of the first chapter of Zechariah constitute a synopsis of a sermon of the prophet. Its theme strikes the keynote of the entire book and forms an indispensable introduction to it. The truth it enunciates is one which runs throughout the revealed ways of God with man; namely, *the appropriation and enjoyment of God's promises of blessing must be prefaced by genuine repentance*."[30]

> ". . . these introductory verses take the place of a call narrative [cf. Isa. 6; Jer. 1; Ezek. 1—2]."[31]

1:1   The writer identified the time when this first word from the Lord came to Zechariah, as well as his family origin. "The word of the Lord" is a technical term meaning the prophetic word of revelation. The eighth month of the second year of Darius was October-November of 520 B.C. Evidently Haggai began ministering two months earlier to the same audience and ended his prophetic ministry one month later (Hag. 1:1; 2:10, 20; cf. Ezra 5:1; 6:14). Since there was no human king of Israel then, the writer dated the prophecy in reference to Darius, a reminder that Israel was in "the times of the Gentiles" (Luke 21:24). "The times of the Gentiles" is the era of time when Gentiles control the destiny of Israel, namely, from the reign of Nebuchadnezzar until the future millennial reign of Christ. Zechariah's father was Berechiah, and his more prominent grandfather (or ancestor) was Iddo. Iddo was among the priests who returned from the Captivity with Zerubbabel and Joshua (Neh. 12:4, 16).

1:2-4   The Lord told Zechariah that He had been "very angry" with the Jews' forefathers. Therefore, the prophet was to preach repentance to his contemporaries as Yahweh's authoritative and faithful mouthpiece. If they turned back to the Lord (enabled by His grace), He would return to bless them (cf. Isa. 55:6-7; Jer. 3:12; Hos. 7:10; Joel 2:12-13; Amos 5:4, 6; Mal. 3:7). This is the clarion call that furnishes the background for this book's message of hope.[32] And this was the reassurance that the restoration community needed after the discipline of the Exile. They were to "return to" Yahweh, to a personal relationship and allegiance to Him, not simply to a formal obedience to His law and covenant. Zechariah was to warn the Israelites not to be like their (pre-exilic) forefathers who refused to respond to the preaching of earlier (pre-exilic) prophets who urged them to repent (e.g., Isaiah, Jeremiah, et al.).

> "It's one thing to ask God to bless us but quite another to be the kind of people He can bless!"[33]

1:5-6   Their ancestors had perished, and the former prophets who warned them were no longer alive to continue warning them. They would not have endless opportunities to repent. The punishments that the former prophets had warned the people about had overtaken them. The Lord had pursued and caught the evildoers like a hunter captures his prey. Then they acknowledged that the Lord had indeed done as He had warned them that He would do (cf. Deut. 28:15, 45; 2 Chron. 36:16). This would also be the experience of the contemporary Israelites if they, too, failed to heed Zechariah's exhortation (cf. 1 Cor. 10:11).

Even though the Israelites had failed God miserably in the past, this introductory message clarified that the Abrahamic Covenant was still in force. God promised to bless His people, but their enjoyment of that blessing in any given generation depended on their walking with Him in trust and obedience. "Repent" (Heb. *shub*) means "return." It presupposes a previous relationship with God from which His people had departed.

> ". . . Zechariah enumerates in his introductory address five great principles: (1) The condition of all God's blessings, verse 3. (2) The evil and peril of disobedience, verse 4. (3) The unchangeable character of God's Word, verse 6a. (4) God's governmental dealings with His people in accordance with their deeds, verse 6b ('according to our ways and according to our deeds'). (5) God's immutable purposes, verse 6b ('as Jehovah . . . determined . . . so did he with us')."[34]

---

[29] George L. Robinson, *The Twelve Minor Prophets*, p. 150. Cf. Walter C. Kaiser Jr., *Toward an Old Testament Theology*, p. 253.
[30] Unger, p. 20.
[31] Longman and Dillard, p. 491.
[32] Unger, p. 20.
[33] Warren W. Wiersbe, "Zechariah," in *The Bible Exposition Commentary/Prophets*, p. 449.
[34] Feinberg, p. 21.

II. THE EIGHT NIGHT VISIONS AND FOUR MESSAGES 1:7—6:8

Zechariah received eight apocalyptic visions in one night (1:7). As the text shows, they concerned God's purpose for the future of Israel, particularly Jerusalem, the seat of the Davidic dynasty and the site of the temple, and Judah. They deal with issues of more immediate concern to the restoration community, though none of them was fulfilled in Zechariah's day. The broad theme of this section is the coming of the King. The purpose of these visions was to encourage the returnees to persevere in their work of rebuilding the temple.

Certain features mark each of these eight visions: an introduction, an explanation of what the prophet saw, his request for clarification of its meaning, and the elucidation. Oracles accompany three of the visions, making their messages clearer (1:16-17; 2:6-13; 4:6-10). Some interpreters also connect the oracle in 6:9-15 to the vision in 6:1-8, but it seems to me, and others, that that oracle was separate from the preceding vision.

> ". . . The arrangement of the visions follows a chiastic pattern [abbccbba]. The first and last bear a strong resemblance to one another, the second and third, sixth and seventh are pairs, and the fourth and fifth, with their assurance of God-given authoritative leaders, form the climax. All eight visions are meant to be interpreted as one whole, for each contributes to the total picture of the role of Israel in the new era about to dawn."[35]

A	The horseman among the myrtle trees (1:7-17)			
	B	The four horns and the four smiths (1:18-21)		
		C	The surveyor (ch. 2)	
			D	The cleansing and restoration of Joshua (ch. 3)
			D'	The gold lampstand and the two olive trees (ch. 4)
		C'	The flying scroll (5:1-4)	
	B'	The woman in the basket (5:5-11)		
A'	The four chariots (6:1-8)			

A. THE HORSEMAN AMONG THE MYRTLE TREES 1:7-17

This first vision emphasizes that God was lovingly jealous of His chosen people, and would restore them, even though they were troubled at present, and the nations that oppressed them were at ease (cf. Habakkuk). In the vision, an angelic patrol reported on the state of the whole earth. This vision presents hope for dispersed and downtrodden Israel.[36]

1. The vision proper 1:7-15

1:7   Zechariah received another revelation from the Lord three months after his previous one in Darius' second year, 520 B.C. The "second year of Darius" was 520 B.C., but the "eleventh month" would have been January-February. In our modern calendar this would have been 519 B.C.

> "On the same day (24 Shebat), five months earlier, the rebuilding of the temple had been resumed (cf. Hag 1:14-15; see also 2:10, 18, 20). It was evidently a day in which God had special delight because of the obedience of his people."[37]

> "Also on that day two months previously Haggai had delivered a stern rebuke to the priests for their impurity and to the people for their delay in building the temple (Hag. 2:10-17). On that day, moreover, Haggai had received the far-reaching revelation (Hag. 2:20) of the destruction of Gentile world power previous to the establishment of millennial rule of the greater Zerubbabel-Messiah (Hag. 2:21-23)."[38]

1:8   The prophet saw a vision, and in his vision it was "night." He saw "a man" sitting "on a red (bay, reddish-brown) horse," among "myrtle trees in" a "ravine." He also saw "red, sorrel (Heb. *seruqim*, mixed color), and white horses behind" the man on the red horse. There were riders on these horses too (v. 11).

To Zechariah, who knew the Old Testament and who lived in a particular culture (Persian as well as Hebrew), the meaning of these symbols would have been more readily apparent than they are to the modern reader.

---

[35]Baldwin, p. 93.
[36]Unger, p. 25.
[37]Barker, p. 610.
[38]Unger, p. 26.

> "Viewed from the perspective of a literary type, symbolism has a unique force, impressing itself on the mind and touching the emotions with greater facility and power than prosaic literary types."[39]

"Night" had connotations of gloom, obscurity, and foreboding. The present was such a period for the Israelites. The light of joy, clear sight, and security was yet to break for them. The "riders" evidently represent some of the Lord's angelic army (host) that serve as His scouts and report world conditions to Him (v. 10). "Horses" were instruments of war and prestigious possessions (10:3; 1 Kings 10:26), and the colors of these horses apparently represent their mission. The colors doubtless implied something to Zechariah, possibly bloodshed, a mixed mission (of judgment and blessing), and victory (cf. 6:2; Isa. 63:1-6; Rev. 6:4). If their color was very significant, the angel probably would have commented on it. Some scholars believed the colors of the horses have no significance.[40] But if so, why did Zechariah mention their different colors?

> "Compare Rev. 6:4. The whole period of Gentile world power is characterized by the red horse, i.e. by the sword. Cp. also Dan. 9:26; Mt. 24:6-7."[41]

"Myrtle trees" were evergreens, used in the Feast of Tabernacles to picture future endless messianic blessings that would come to Israel (Neh. 8:15; Isa. 41:19; 55:13).[42] Here they represent Israel. "The ravine" may hint at Israel's present depressed position in Zechariah's day. One amillennialist took the myrtle trees as typifying "the Jewish Church."[43] Others take them as representing the church or God's people of all ages.

1:9   Zechariah asked the angel who was with him in his vision what the horsemen and the horses represented, and the angel said he would explain.

1:10 The angel, who looked like a "man" and who was standing in the grove of trees, said that the horsemen were Yahweh's representatives whom He had "sent to patrol the earth."

> "Like the Persian monarchs who used messengers on swift steeds to keep them informed on all matters concerning their empire, so the Lord knew all about the countries of the earth, including the great Persian state."[44]

1:11 The horsemen then reported to the angel that they had "patrolled the earth," and had found it "peaceful and quiet."

> "Darius boasted that in nineteen battles he had defeated nine rebel leaders and had subdued all his enemies. So the empire was again virtually quiet by 520 B.C."[45]

The description of the interpreting angel as "the angel of the LORD" can be understood in one of three ways. He was either the Lord Himself (i.e., the second person of the Trinity), or he could have been an angel sent from the Lord and responsible to the Lord, the Lord's special angel (cf. 3:1-2; Gen. 16:11, 13; 18:1-2, 13, 17, 22; 22:11-12, 15-18; 31:11, 13; Exod. 3:2, 4; Josh. 5:13; 6:2; Judg. 2:1-5; 6:11-12, 14; 13:3-23; Ezek. 43:6-7). The third interpretation is that "the angel of the Lord is a representation of Yahweh in a way that actualizes His immanence, but not in direct theophany."[46]

1:12 Then the angel of the Lord addressed sovereign Yahweh. Clearly they were separate persons. He asked the Lord "how long" He planned to remain bent on disciplining "Jerusalem and the cities of Judah" (i.e., the Israelites), which He had done in His indignation for the last "70 years" (i.e., the Captivity; cf. Jer. 25:11-12). That prophesied period was now over, but the Israelites were still oppressed and under foreign domination.

1:13 The Lord responded to the angel's question graciously and "with . . . comforting words." However, what He said Zechariah did not reveal, either because he did not hear it or because he chose not to do so under divine inspiration.

1:14 The angel then instructed Zechariah to proclaim that Yahweh was very "jealous for Jerusalem and Zion." Jealousy when used to describe God's attitude refers to His careful concern, specifically intolerance of rivalry or unfaithfulness, for the well-being of

---

[39] Thomas E. McComiskey, "Zechariah," in *The Minor Prophets*, p. 1012.
[40] E.g., Smith, p. 190.
[41] *The New Scofield Reference Bible*, p. 964.
[42] Leupold, p. 33.
[43] Charles L. Feinberg, "Zechariah," in *The Wycliffe Bible Commentary*, p. 898.
[44] Baldwin, p. 95.
[45] Barker, p. 612.
[46] McComiskey, p. 1038.

others. Often in Scripture it alludes to God as a husband wanting to keep His wife, Israel or the church, true to Himself.[47] God's jealousy has none of the negative connotations that we associate with selfish human jealousy. The double names for Jerusalem may be a case of poetic parallelism, or they could suggest Jerusalem of the past and Zion of the future. Zechariah's people evidently thought that the stability that the Persian Empire currently enjoyed indicated that God had turned from them to look favorably on the nations.

1:15   The Lord continued to explain that He was "very angry with the" Gentile "nations," which were presently "at ease." He was angry because they had compounded the punishment of Israel that God had inflicted on the Chosen People—by prolonging it (cf. Gen. 12:3).

2. The oracle about God's jealousy for Israel 1:16-17

This is the first of four oracles that appear within the visions that Zechariah saw. These were messages that the prophet was to deliver along with the revelation of the vision.

"The vision had lifted the veil which hides the unseen, spiritual world to show that God is in control and active in the earth, but it would not have been of specific comfort without the message in words given by the interpreting angel (verses 14b-17). This oracle is essential to elucidate the implications of the vision."[48]

1:16   Because the people of "Jerusalem" had experienced so much hostility, the Lord promised to "return" to them and show them "compassion." The sovereign Lord promised that the temple would be rebuilt there, and the city again would become a viable entity. The Jews finished the temple in 515 B.C., but the city walls were not complete until 444 B.C. (Neh. 7:4; 11:1). Measuring the city pictures its expanded restoration (cf. Jer. 31:38-40), the "measuring line" being a construction tool.[49]

1:17   God promised that His cities, the cities of Judah (v. 12), would "again overflow with" the benefits of "prosperity." He would "again comfort Zion" and "choose" (to bless) "Jerusalem" (cf. 1 Kings 8:44, 48; 2 Chron. 6:6, 34, 38).

"The distinctive features of comfort for Israel in this first vision are: (1) the presence of the Angel of Jehovah in the midst of degraded and depressed Israel; (2) His loving and yearning intercession for them; (3) the promises of future blessings. We may say, then, that the import of the vision is this: although Israel is not yet in her promised position, God is mindful of her, providing the means of His judgment on the persecuting nations, and reserving glory and prosperity for Israel in the benevolent and beneficent reign of the Messiah.

"The series of visions carry us through God's dealings with Israel from the time of their chastisement by God under the Gentile powers until they are restored to their land with their rebuilt city and temple under their Messiah King. The first vision gives the general theme of the whole series; the others add the details. . . . When the world was busy with its own affairs, God's eyes and the heart of the Messiah were upon the lowly estate of Israel and upon the temple in Jerusalem."[50]

B. THE FOUR HORNS AND THE FOUR SMITHS 1:18-21

The second vision elaborates the concept of comfort promised in the first vision (vv. 13, 17). Here we learn how God will execute His anger against the nations that excessively oppressed His people. The nations will meet with retribution, and Israel will triumph over her foes.

1:18   Verse 18 begins chapter 2 in the Hebrew Bible. Zechariah then saw another scene in his vision. He observed "four" animal "horns." Presumably they were on living animals since they could feel terror (v. 21), although there is no mention of animals. Horns were a common figure for power in biblical and ancient Near Eastern iconography, specifically, of a Gentile king or world empire (e.g., Deut. 33:17; Ps. 18:2; 75:10; 89:17; Dan. 2:36-44; 7:3-7, 24; 8:20-21; Rev. 17:12).

1:19   In response to the prophet's request for an interpretation, the assisting angel explained that they represented the powers that had "scattered Judah, Israel, and Jerusalem." Assyria took Israel into captivity, and Babylonia destroyed Jerusalem and took the Judahites captive. So perhaps the fact that there were four horns symbolizes that they represented nations from the four corners of the world, the totality of opposition.[51] Another view is that they stand for Babylonia, Medo-Persia, Greece, and Rome (cf. Dan. 2; 7).[52]

---

[47]See Baldwin, pp. 101-3.
[48]Ibid., p. 98. She understood the oracle as beginning with verse 14.
[49]See Baruch Halpern, "The Ritual Background of Zechariah's Temple Song," *Catholic Biblical Quarterly* 40 (1978):178, n. 51.
[50]Feinberg, *God Remembers*, p. 38.
[51]Smith, p. 193.
[52]Charles H. Dyer, in *The Old Testament Explorer*, p. 823; and Feinberg, "Zechariah," p. 900.

1:20	Then the Lord showed Zechariah "four" smiths (Heb. *harashim*, lit. workers in metal, "craftsmen"). Either the Lord Himself pointed them out, or the Lord did so through Zechariah's guiding angel.
1:21	Again in answer to the prophet's request for interpretation, the angel repeated that the horns represented the powers that had scattered the Israelites. Then he added that the four artisans had come "to terrify" these horns, and to overthrow them for attacking Israel and scattering the Israelites. These smiths evidently carried hammers with which they threatened to smash the horns. Probably the kingdoms of Medo-Persia, Greece, Rome, and Messiah are in view. Each of these kingdoms would destroy the preceding one, as Medo-Persia, the first one, had already defeated Babylonia (cf. Dan. 2:34-35, 44-45).

The four smiths		The four horns
Medo-Persia	destroyed	Babylonia
Greece	destroyed	Medo-Persia
Rome	destroyed	Greece
God's kingdom	will destroy	Rome

Another, less likely view, is that they describe kingdoms that had already destroyed Israel's enemies. A third possibility is that they will all appear in the future to take vengeance on Israel's end-times enemies. A fourth, less probable view, I think, is that the horns represent "the full extent of human cruelty, military might, political machinations, and lust for power ... which destroyed pre-exilic Judah."[53] A fifth view is that they represent the four judgments of Ezekiel 14:21: sword, famine, wild beasts, and plague (cf. Rev. 6:1-8).[54] The Ezekiel prophecy describes the destruction of Jerusalem by the Babylonians in 586 B.C., but similar judgments are predicted for the Tribulation in Revelation 6—19.

"Several features are noteworthy in this vision: (1) God takes account of every one that lifts his hand against Israel; (2) He has complete knowledge of the dejected condition of His people and the extent of their injury; and (3) He has already provided the punishment for every foe of His chosen ones."[55]

"As little as horns can hold their own before powerful smiths, so little can God's enemies lastingly prevail over God's people."[56]

C. THE SURVEYOR CH. 2

In the first vision (1:7-17), God promised comfort to Israel. In the second (1:18-21), He explained that He would bring this comfort by punishing the nations that had afflicted Israel. In this third vision (ch. 2), He guaranteed the future prosperity and expansion of Israel. Jerusalem has a divine protector. As will become clear, this future blessedness must extend beyond the restoration period to messianic times.[57] This third vision has a counterpart in vision six (5:1-4), in that they both deal with measuring, dimensions, and Jerusalem. This vision stresses the importance of Jerusalem, and vision six pertains to law within Jerusalem. This vision pictures Jerusalem in millennial glory.[58]

1. The vision itself 2:1-5

2:1-2	In the next scene of his vision, Zechariah saw "a man" (i.e., an angel who looked like a man) "with a measuring line in his hand" (cf. 1:11; 6:12; Ezek. 40:2-3). When the prophet asked him where he was going, he replied that he was going "to measure" the dimensions of "Jerusalem." This surveying would have been preparation for restoring and rebuilding the city. The restoration of Jerusalem in progress in Zechariah's day was only a foreview of a much grander future restoration to be described (cf. Jer. 32:15; Ezek. 40:3, 5; Rev. 11:1).
2:3-4	"Another angel," possibly the angel of the Lord (1:11-12), came forward to meet Zechariah's guiding angel as he was going out toward the "man" with the measuring line. He instructed him to tell "that young man," Zechariah, that Jerusalem would expand

---

[53]McComiskey, p. 1048.
[54]*The New Scofield . . .*, p. 965.
[55]Feinberg, *God Remembers*, pp. 42-43.
[56]Leupold, p. 51.
[57]See T. T. Perowne, *The Books of Haggai and Zechariah*, p. 74.
[58]Unger, p. 43.

2:5 — The Lord promised to be Jerusalem's defense ("a wall of fire")—instead of a physical wall—and to "be the glory in her," in contrast to any human glory. Such a promise must have been a great encouragement to the returnees from captivity. *Yahweh Himself* (emphatic in the Hebrew text) would provide security by His protection and presence (cf. 1:16; Ps. 24:7-10). Though God did protect the returnees, His promise has not yet found fulfillment. The "wall of fire" that Yahweh would be, recalls the pillar of cloud and fire by which God revealed His protecting presence at various times throughout her history (Exod. 13:21-22; 14:19-20; 40:34; Isa. 4:5-6).

beyond its walls because so many people and cattle would live in it (cf. Ezek. 38:11). Another interpretation is that the young man was the angel with the measuring line.[59] But it seems more probable that the other angel gave this revelation to Zechariah directly. During the restoration period, the Jews built walls around the city to make it secure, yet few people wanted to live in it (cf. Neh. 11:1-2; 7:4). This prophecy must have a future fulfillment, though it doubtless encouraged Zechariah's contemporaries to rebuild the city in their day.[60]

> "This anticipates the Lord's personal presence through the Messiah in his kingdom on earth (cf. 2:11-12; 14:9; Isa 60:19; Ezek 43:1-5; 48:35). So then the literal kingdom will be very spiritual."[61]

> "At a time when others such as Nehemiah were interested in rebuilding the walls of Jerusalem and excluding from the community those who had divorced their wives and married young foreign girls (Ezra 10:2-3), Zechariah sees a vision of the future Jerusalem as a broad, spreading metropolis with the wall of God's presence around her and the glory of his presence within her."[62]

Both the second and third visions guarantee the future safety of Jerusalem. Since Jerusalem has not been safe for millennia, it seems reasonable to expect a fulfillment in messianic times.

2. The oracle about enemy destruction and Israelite blessing 2:6-13

This message brings out the practical implications of the two visions just related. It is a section of poetry in the middle of the prose visions. The prophet now spoke for the Lord, first to the Jews still in exile (vv. 6-9), and then to the Jews in Jerusalem (vv. 10-13). The first part deals with the overthrow of enemies and so connects with the second vision. The second part declares Yahweh's sovereignty in Zion and reinforces the third vision.[63]

> "The future greatness of Zion is too important a subject to be quickly dismissed. Various aspects of it should yet be unfolded; therefore verses 6-13 follow, which are very much in place at this point, and for just this reason."[64]

The destruction of oppressing enemies 2:6-9

2:6-7 — The Lord called on His people to "flee from the land of the north" (cf. Jer. 3:18; 16:15; 23:8; 31:8) where He had scattered them "as the four winds" (cf. Isa. 43:5-6; 49:12). Most of the Israelite exiles had gone into captivity in Assyria, and most of the Judean exiles went into captivity in Babylon. However, there were many other Israelites who had been taken or had fled to Egypt (Jer. 43:7), Moab, Ammon, and Edom (Jer. 40:11-12), Persia, and many other nations. These were Jews who later constituted the Diaspora, those who did not return to Palestine but remained dispersed throughout the ancient world. The Lord called these people to "escape" from "Babylon" among whose "daughter" nations they lived. This was a call for the scattered Jews to return home in Zechariah's day and help rebuild their nation. But it is also, because of the context and lack of fulfillment, a prophetic call to those living in the end times to abandon the Babylon of their day (cf. Rev. 18:4-8).

> "Since Babylon in the post-exilic period epitomized all the suffering and indignity inflicted on Judah at the fall of Jerusalem and after, the name could stand for all lands of exile, and was not confined to the geographical area known as Babylon."[65]

---

[59]E.g., Leupold, p. 55.
[60]See Merrill, pp. 116-18, for defense of this "both in Zechariah's day and in the future" interpretation.
[61]Barker, p. 617. For a defense of the spirituality of the physical, earthly kingdom of Messiah, see Feinberg, *God Remembers*, p. 45.
[62]Smith, p. 197.
[63]Baldwin, pp. 107-8.
[64]Leupold, p. 57.
[65]Baldwin, p. 109.

2:8-9	They were to flee because the Lord purposed to send His representative to plunder "the nations" for afflicting (plundering) His people, "the apple" (lit. gate, the pupil, which is the most sensitive part) "of His eye" (cf. Deut. 32:10; Ps. 17:8; Matt. 25:34-45; Acts 9:1, 4-5). This would result in His "glory."

> "This statement ["after glory"] anticipates the New Testament revelation of the Father sending the Son to glorify Him, both in His first advent (John 17:4, cf. Isa. 61:1, 2; Luke 4:17-19) and in His second advent (Isa. 61:1, 2)."[66]

> "This will be fulfilled in the judgment of the Gentiles at Messiah's Second Advent (Matt. 25:31-46)."[67]

The person whom the Lord would send as His representative ("Me") could not be Zechariah, in view of what the following verses say He would do. He must be Messiah, the only one with sufficient power and authority to fulfill what God predicted here. He would simply "wave" His "hand" over these nations in a menacing gesture, and they would become "plunder" for the Israelites whom they had enslaved (cf. Esth. 7:10; Isa. 11:15; 14:2; 19:16; Gal. 6:7-8). "Then" God's people would "know" that Yahweh of armies had "sent" this One (cf. Isa. 61:3; John 17:4). This would be the sovereign Lord's doing, so the Jews should rejoice, return to the land, and prepare.

Yahweh's ultimate blessing of Israel 2:10-13

2:10-11	The Israelites in Jerusalem and elsewhere were to rejoice because the Lord promised to intervene for them and to dwell among them. His return to Jerusalem would prompt the nations to come there and acknowledge Him as sovereign (cf. Ps. 47:9; 96:1; 97:1; 98:4). "Many nations" will turn "to the LORD in that day" (the eschatological day of the Lord, cf. ch. 14; Isa. 2:12-21; 24—27; Joel 1:15; 2:28—3:21; Amos 5:18-20; 9:11-15; Zeph.) and become part of his family of believers (8:20-23; Gen. 12:3; 18:18; 22:18; Isa. 2:2-4; 60:3). They will resemble Him, as well as acknowledge Him (cf. Is. 56:6-8; 60:3, 21). He "will dwell" in the "midst" of His people (cf. 8:3, 20-23; John 1:14; 2 Cor. 6:16; Rev. 21:3), and they will "know" that Yahweh had "sent" this One. This is clearly a reference to Messiah's second advent, not His first advent.

> "In fulfillment of the great OT covenants, particularly the Abrahamic covenant, this section anticipates full kingdom blessing in the messianic era.... This language is ultimately messianic—indirectly or by extension from God in general to the Messiah in particular."[68]

2:12-13	The Lord will at that time "possess Judah" as His inheritance in the "holy land," and will "choose Jerusalem" for special blessing (cf. Isa. 19:24-25). This is the only occurrence of the term "holy land" in the Bible. Canaan would become holy (sacred, not common or ordinary) because it would be the site of the throne and habitation of God, who is holy, dwelling among His covenant people. "All" the people of the earth should be still (silent), because Yahweh will arouse Himself "from His heavenly habitation" and take action on the earth.
	The typical amillennial interpretation, represented by Leupold, sees "'Judah' and 'Jerusalem' as a designation of His people wherever they may be found. So also 'the holy land' is not specifically Palestine but every place where God manifests Himself."[69] McComiskey, another amillennialist, viewed the promise of land in both a territorial (a world conquered by Christ; Rom. 4:13) and a spiritual sense (the rest that those in Christ enjoy; Heb. 3—4).[70]

"The first vision introduced the judgment (or curse) and blessing motif (1:15-17). That motif is then developed in the second and third visions in an alternating cycle: judgment for the nations (1:18-21) but blessing and glory for Israel (2:1-5); judgment for the nations (2:6-9) but blessing for Israel—and the nations (2:10-13)."[71]

D. THE CLEANSING AND RESTORATION OF JOSHUA CH. 3

The Lord explained that Joshua and his friends were men who had prophetic significance (v. 8). As will become clear, Joshua, Israel's high priest, represents Israel in this vision, specifically Israel in her divinely appointed role as a kingdom of priests (Exod. 19:6). Similarly, Israel's high priest represented the nation each year on the Day of Atonement. In this vision and the next, Israel's standing before God and her resources are in view. This vision presents Israel's restoration as a high priestly nation.

---

[66]Unger, p. 49.
[67]F. Duane Lindsey, "Zechariah," in *The Bible Knowledge Commentary: Old Testament*, p. 1553.
[68]Barker, p. 619.
[69]Leupold, p. 61.
[70]McComiskey, pp. 1044 and 1096.
[71]Barker, p. 621.

"As the first three visions dealt principally with the material side of Israel's tribulation and restoration, the remaining five dealt pre-eminently with her moral and spiritual influence."[72]

This vision has two parts: a symbolic act (vv. 1-5) and accompanying promises (vv. 6-10).

1. The symbolic act 3:1-5

3:1 Zechariah's guiding angel next showed the prophet, in his vision, "Joshua" (lit. Yahweh saves), Israel's current "high priest" (6:11; Ezra 5:2; Neh. 7:7; Hag. 1:1), "standing before the angel of the LORD" (1:11-12). "The accuser" (lit. "the Satan," Heb. *hasatan*) was standing at Joshua's "right hand," prepared "to accuse him" before the angel of the Lord (cf. Job 1:6-12; 2:1-7; Rev. 12:10). The writer made a play on the Hebrew word in its noun and verb forms here translated "Satan" and "accuse."[73] Standing *at the right hand* was the traditional place where an accuser stood in Jewish life (cf. 1 Chron. 21:1; Ps. 109:6).

> "The term *satan*, when used without the definite article, usually refers to a human adversary. The one exception is in Num. 22:22, 32, where the angel of the Lord assumes the role of Balaam's adversary. In 1 Chron. 21:1, the term probably refers to a nearby nation, though some prefer to take the word in this context as a proper name, 'Satan.' When the term appears with the article, as it does here and in Job 1—2, it is a title for a being who seems to serve as a prosecuting attorney in the heavenly court."[74]

> ". . . sin exposes the sinner to satanic attack not only in the case of unbelievers (Matt. 12:43-45), but believers as well (I Cor. 5:5; I John 5:16)."[75]

Evidently the scene that Zechariah saw took place in the temple.

> "The first three visions brought the prophet from a valley outside the city to a vantage-point from which the dimensions of the original Jerusalem could be seen. In the fourth and fifth visions he is in the Temple courts, where the high priest officiated and had access to God's presence."[76]

> "Joshua is standing in a tribunal, where he is being accused of unfitness for the priestly ministry."[77]

Another view is that he was not on trial but simply ministering to the Lord.

3:2 "The LORD" then spoke to the accuser, citing His own authority as "the LORD (Yahweh) who had chosen Jerusalem." This is one indication that Joshua represented Israel, since God linked Joshua with Jerusalem. Joshua was secure from Satan's accusations because of the Lord's sovereign choice of Jerusalem (cf. 12:2; Rom. 8:33). "The Lord" may be distinct from "the angel of the LORD," but they seem to be synonymous. Most conservative commentators equate them, and believe "the angel of the LORD" is the second person of the Trinity. In other contexts, adversaries argue their cases before God, not before His representatives (e.g., Job 1—2). The Lord rebuked Satan twice, the repetition adding force to the initial rebuke (cf. Jude 9).

The Lord then referred to Joshua as a burning stick "plucked from the fire," evidently for His future use (cf. Amos 4:11). If Joshua represents Israel, then the fire must refer to the Babylonian Captivity from which Israel had emerged almost destroyed, and the stick refers to the surviving remnant. Israel had experienced another brush with extinction at the Exodus (Deut. 4:20; 7:7-8; Jer. 11:4), and she will do so again in the Tribulation (13:8-9; Jer. 30:7; Rev. 12:13-17).

3:3 Joshua stood "before the angel" of the Lord, dressed in excrement bespattered garments (cf. Isa. 4:4). He was ministering to the Lord in this extremely filthy—and ceremonially unclean—condition. This represented the unclean state in which Israel stood in Zechariah's day, as she ministered before Him like a kingdom of priests in the world (cf. Exod. 19:6).

3:4 The Lord then instructed others "who were standing before" Him, probably angelic servants, to "remove" Joshua's "filthy garments" (cf. Exod. 28:8-9, 41; Lev. 8:7-9; Num. 20:28). The Lord explained that these garments symbolized the high priest's (Israel's) iniquities, which He had forgiven. He promised to remove His representative's filthy robes and replace them with

---

[72]G. Campbell Morgan, *An Exposition of the Whole Bible*, p. 399.
[73]See Sydney H. T. Page, "Satan: God's Servant," *Journal of the Evangelical Theological Society* 50:3 (September 2007):449-65.
[74]Robert B. Chisholm Jr., *Handbook on the Prophets*, p. 460.
[75]Unger, p. 57.
[76]Baldwin, pp. 112-13.
[77]Merrill, p. 131.

"festal," stately "robes," the apparel of royalty and wealth—symbolic of God's righteousness (cf. Isa. 3:22). Thus God would restore Israel to her original calling as a priestly nation (cf. Exod. 19:6; Isa. 61:6).

> "Theologically, however, there also seems to be a picture here of the negative aspect of what God does when he saves a person. Negatively, he takes away sin. Positively, he adds or imputes to the sinner saved by grace his own divine righteousness (cf. v. 5)."[78]

Amillennialists contend that this is all that the vision means; it contains no special promises for Israel.[79]

3:5   Zechariah chimed in, suggesting that the angelic dressers also put "a clean turban on" Joshua's "head," which they did along with his other new garments. A plaque on the front of the high priest's turban read "Holy to the Lord" (Exod. 28:36; 39:30). This is what Israel will be in the future, a holy nation of holy priests. The Lord observed all that was happening, sovereignly approving and directing all the changes in Joshua's condition.

> "What is unique here is the command of a mere man to bring about a purpose of God."[80]

Similarly, prayer plays a part in the execution of God's will.

2. The accompanying promises 3:6-10

3:6-7   Then "the angel of the LORD" admonished Joshua. He promised, in the name of sovereign Yahweh, that if Joshua obeyed the Lord and served Him, Joshua would "govern" the temple, "have charge of" the temple "courts," and enjoy "free access" into the Lord's presence. He could come into the Lord's presence like the angels who stood before Him. Joshua's commission pertained to a priestly function within the framework of a covenant relationship.[81] As always, faithful, obedient service leads to further opportunities for service.

The Lord specified two conditions and promised three results. The first condition was Israel's practical righteousness; she had to walk in His ways faithfully with heart and hand (cf. Deut. 10:12-22; 28:9). Second, she had to carry out her priestly duties faithfully. If Israel did these things, she would govern God's house (people and temple; cf. Deut. 17:8-13; Jer. 31:7), have charge of His courts—keeping them pure (cf. Isa. 56:7; Jer. 31:23), and enjoy free access to God (cf. Exod. 19:6; Isa. 61:6; Heb. 4:16; 10:19-22).

> "In all this the person and work of Joshua's greater namesake, Jesus, was being anticipated. The faithful high priest of the pre-Christian era entered into God's presence as the Christian [believer priest] does 'by grace through faith'."[82]

3:8   Evidently, Zechariah also saw in his vision other priests—Joshua's friends—sitting in front of him. The Lord continued to address Joshua, identifying him as "the high priest." He called the friends, sitting in front of Joshua, "men" who were "a symbol" (sign; Heb. *mopheth*, token of future events, prophetic sign; cf. Isa. 8:18). It was not just Joshua individually who represented Israel, but the other priests also represented the priesthood within Israel.

> "The miracle, which is to be seen in Joshua and his priests, consists . . . in the fact that the priesthood of Israel is laden with guilt, but by the grace of God it has been absolved, and accepted by God again, as the deliverance from exile shows, and Joshua and his priests are therefore brands plucked by the omnipotence of grace from the fire of merited judgment. This miracle of grace which has been wrought for them, points beyond itself to an incomparably greater and better act of the sin-absolving grace of God, which is still in the future."[83]

The Lord also said that He planned to bring into the picture His Servant, "the Branch." This is a double title of Messiah (cf. 6:12; Ps. 132:17; Isa. 11:1; 53:2; Jer. 23:5; 33:15). As Yahweh's servant (Isa. 42:1; 49:3, 5; 52:13; 53:11; Ezek. 34:23-24), Messiah would come into the world to do His Father's will, including redeeming, cleansing, and restoring Israel to God's intended place for her.

> "As Branch, the Messiah is represented in the OT in four different aspects of his character (King, Servant, Man, and God). These aspects are developed in the NT in the four Gospels: (1) in Matthew as the Branch

---

[78]Barker, p. 624.
[79]See Leupold, pp. 74, 77.
[80]Merrill, p. 136.
[81]Ibid., p. 138.
[82]Baldwin, p. 115. Cf. Heb. 4:14-16.
[83]C. F. Keil, *The Twelve Minor Prophets*, 2:259.

	of David, i.e., as the Davidic messianic King (Isa 11:1; Jer 23:5; 33:15); (2) in Mark as the Lord's Servant, the Branch (Isa 42:1; 49:6; 50:10; 52:13; Ezek 34:23-24; Zech 3:8); (3) in Luke as the Man whose name is the Branch (Zech 6:12); and (4) in John as the Branch of the Lord (Isa 4:2)."[84]
3:9	Zechariah also saw in the vision a "stone . . . set" in front of Joshua. The stone, too, is a common figure of God and Messiah in the Bible (10:4; Exod. 17:6; Num. 20:7-11; Ps. 118:22; et al.). In the past, God had promised that the Stone would be a secure, never-failing refuge for His people (Isa. 28:16; 1 Pet. 2:6). When Messiah appeared, however, He proved to be a stone over which the Jews stumbled and an offensive rock to them (Ps. 118:22-23; Isa. 8:13-15; Matt. 21:42; 1 Pet. 2:7-8). Presently He is the foundation stone, the chief cornerstone of the church (Eph. 2:19-22). And in the future He will be the great stone that smites the nations (Dan. 2:35, 45).[85]

> "The reason two figures are used, one the Servant-Branch, the other the single Stone, is because one applies specifically to the first advent and the other centers in the second advent."[86]

Another view is that they represent Messiah as king and priest.[87] But this seems unlikely because of a lack of connection between the branch and the stone and the king and the priest.

The stone that Zechariah saw had "seven eyes" (Heb. *'ayin*), probably symbolizing its complete, divine intelligence (omniscience; cf. 1:10; 4:10; 2 Chron. 16:9; Isa. 11:2; Ezek. 1:18; 10:12; Col. 2:3, 9; Rev. 5:6). The "inscription" engraved on the stone remains unexplained, but many of the early church fathers and interpreters ever since have taken the engraving as a preview of Messiah's wounds.[88] The engraving may indicate that the stone is a commemorative one, since the Assyrian and Babylonian kings set such stones in the foundations of buildings to perpetuate their memories.[89]

> "The eyes on the stone would be the divine signature identifying YHWH as the real architect and builder of the structure."[90]

The Lord continued, saying that He would also "remove the iniquity" of "that land," the holy land (2:12), "in one day." He did that when Messiah died on the cross, but Israel will finally realize this benefit of His death when He returns to earth, at His Second Advent, and cleanses and forgives Israel as a whole (12:10—13:1; Rom. 11:26-27). The Day of the Lord is doubtless in view.

> "As the Servant of the Lord, Christ is the One who comes to do the will of the Father (Isa. 42:1; 49:3-4; 50:10; 52:13; 53:11). As the Branch of David, Christ is the Davidic Descendant who will rise to power and glory out of the humiliation into which the line of David had fallen (Isa. 4:2; 11:1; Jer. 23:5; 33:15; Zech. 6:12-13). As the Stone (cf. Ps. 118:22; Matt. 21:42; 1 Peter 2:6) He will bring judgment on the Gentiles (Dan. 2:44-45) and be a stone of stumbling for unbelieving Israel (Rom. 9:31-33)."[91]

3:10	"In that day," the Lord promised, the Israelites will all "invite" their (Gentile) neighbors to join them in enjoying their peace and prosperity. Israel would enjoy peace and security as never before, even under the reign of Solomon (1 Kings 4:25; cf. 2 Kings 18:31; Mic. 4:4). Then God will lift the curse that He imposed on the creation at the Fall, and there will be agricultural prosperity—as well as spiritual prosperity (Isa. 11:1-9; 35; 65:17; Dan. 7:13-14, 27; Mic. 4:1-4). Paradise lost will become paradise regained.

"In summary, vision four describes a day of redemption in which Joshua the high priest, typical or representative of Israel as a priestly people, will be cleansed of his impurities and reinstalled in his capacity as high priest. This presupposes a Temple in which this can take place, so Joshua will build such a structure. Again, this Temple is only the model of one to come, one whose cornerstone is YHWH Himself. That cornerstone contains the glorious promise of the regeneration of the nation, a mighty salvific event that will be consummated in one day (Isa. 66:7-9)."[92]

---

[84]Barker, p. 626. See also Feinberg, *God Remembers*, p. 64.
[85]See ibid., p. 65.
[86]Unger, p. 66.
[87]Smith, p. 201.
[88]See E. B. Pusey, *The Minor Prophets*, 2:359.
[89]Baldwin, p. 116.
[90]Merrill, p. 143.
[91]Lindsey, pp. 1554-55.
[92]Merrill, pp. 143-44.

E. THE GOLD LAMPSTAND AND THE TWO OLIVE TREES CH. 4

This vision would have encouraged the two leaders of the restoration community, Zerubbabel and Joshua, by reminding them of God's resources, and it would have vindicated these leaders in the eyes of the Israelites. Chapter 3 brought Joshua forward to encourage him, and chapter 4 does the same to Zerubbabel. The chapter contains the vision (vv. 1-5), two oracles concerning Zerubbabel (vv. 6-10), and the interpretation of the vision (vv. 11-14). It presents Israel as the light of the world under Messiah, her king-priest. The amillennial interpretation sees no fulfillment in the future for Israel, only in the church.

> ". . . after Israel as the priestly nation of God has been cleansed from all defilement and has entered into the restoration of her priestly calling, then she is prepared to fulfill God's original purpose in her as the bearer of light and truth to all the surrounding nations in their idolatry and paganism."[93]

> "Vision five forms a matching pair with vision four, both in terms of its juxtaposition to it and its subject matter. Both deal with cultic persons or objects (the high priest and the menorah respectively), both mention historical persons contemporary to the prophet (Joshua and Zerubbabel), both refer to temple building, and both reach their climax on a strong messianic note."[94]

1. The vision 4:1-5

4:1   Zechariah's guiding angel "roused" the prophet from his visionary slumber. Evidently when the last scene of his vision ended, Zechariah remained in a sleep-like condition. Even in an ecstatic state, human beings remain dull and obtuse to divine revelation, and must receive supernatural enlightenment.

4:2-3   The angel asked the prophet what he saw, and Zechariah replied that he saw a golden "lampstand" with a "bowl" above it. Lampstands generally, and the lampstands in the tabernacle and temple particularly, held removable lamps (Exod. 25:31; 1 Kings 7:49). Their purpose was to support these light-bearers. Symbolically a lampstand represents what supports whatever bears light (cf. Matt. 5:16; Rev. 1:20; 2:5). This seems to be the figure in view in 1 Timothy 3:15, where Paul called the church the pillar and support of the truth. The purpose of the church is to support individual Christians who bear the light of God's truth in a dark world (cf. Rev. 1:20). Ultimately the light is the Lord Himself (John 1:8-9; 1 Tim. 3:16). In the case of the present vision, the lampstand represents the temple and the Jewish community, which were to hold the light of Israel's testimony for Yahweh up to the rest of the world. The bowl on top of this lampstand contained oil that constantly replenished the lamps (cf. v. 12).

> "Lamp pedestals excavated from Palestine cities were . . . cylindrical in shape, hollow, and looked rather like a tree trunk. They were usually made of pottery, and had a hole in the side, into which a spout could have been fixed. . . . Zechariah's lampstand (*menora*) was probably just a cylindrical column, tapered slightly towards the top, on which was a bowl. Innumerable pottery versions of bowl lamps show how the rim was pinched together to form a holder for the wick, the better the light needed the more the places for wicks, seven being the most popular number. . . . The picture is of seven small bowls, each with a place for seven wicks, arranged round the rim of the main bowl. . . . What would be unusual would be such a lampstand in gold. With its seven times seven lights it would be both impressive and effective."[95]

The Hebrew text has "seven and seven pipes to the lamps." Most conservative commentators understood the number of pipes (spouts) connecting the large upper bowl to the individual lamps below to be distributive, indicating seven each for a total of 49 such pipes. This presents the picture of a somewhat "spaghetti-like configuration"[96] "with an excess of plumbing."[97] Nevertheless this interpretation seems to be truest to the text. Another view is that there were two pipes connecting the bowl to each of the lamps for a total of 14 pipes. The Septuagint simply omitted one of these sevens, resulting in one pipe connecting them, for a total of seven pipes. The large number of pipes probably stresses the abundant supply of oil from the reservoir to each lamp.

There were seven lamps, one resting on each of the seven branches of the lampstand, and each lamp had seven spouts (lips). Most such earthenware lamps that archaeologists have found had only one spout for a wick. Here the picture is of a full complement of lamps (seven) that manifested the full complement of light (seven flames from each lamp).

---

[93]Feinberg, *God Remembers*, p. 69.
[94]Merrill, p. 145.
[95]Baldwin, pp. 119-20.
[96]Merrill, p. 148.
[97]Leupold, p. 85.

There were also two olive trees, one standing on either side of the bowl. Human maintenance of the lamps was unnecessary, since the oil flowed from the trees, to the reservoir, to the lamps. This important feature of the vision stresses God's singular provision of the oil (cf. v. 6).

> "The two olive trees represent Joshua and Zerubbabel, whose witness in that day is the prototype of the two witnesses of Rev. 11:3-12. Actually no human being can be the real source of the power that actuates God's witness. It is only as Joshua, Zerubbabel, or any other human being represents Christ, the true Priest-King, that he fulfills this vision. In their fullest significance the two olive trees speak of Christ, the LORD's Priest-King (cp. Ps. 110:4)."[98]

The two olive trees played an important part in the founders' perception of the new State of Israel in 1948, in which "religion" and "state" and their respective dignitaries (the high priest and the prime minister) stand together to realize the Zionist dream in this official emblem.

4:4-5   Zechariah asked the angel for an explanation of what he saw. The angel asked if he did not understand what these things represented, and Zechariah admitted that he did not (cf. v. 13).

2. Two oracles concerning Zerubbabel 4:6-10

The writer inserted two oracles that Zechariah received from the Lord concerning Zerubbabel, at this point, because they help to clarify the meaning of the vision.

The first oracle 4:6-7

4:6   The angel announced "a word" of explanation from Yahweh that Zechariah was to pass on "to Zerubbabel," the descendant of David who became the leader of the first group of returnees from exile.[99] He was to tell him: "not by might [Heb. *hayil*] nor by power [Heb. *koah*], but by the Spirit [Heb. *ruah*] of Yahweh of hosts."

> "This principle is an elliptical sentence: 'Not by might, nor by power, but by My Spirit, says the Lord of hosts,' a kind of motto, as it were, to guide all endeavors and enterprises of the nation in these evil days. If we were to complete the ellipsis we might formulate the statement somewhat after the following fashion: If success is to be gained in the achievements of the people of God it will not be secured by what man can do but by the Spirit's work."[100]

Since Zerubbabel was leading the rebuilding of the temple and the restoration of the community, the Lord's word to him was a word of encouragement. These restorations would not need an army of workers, as Solomon's temple did (1 Kings 5:13-18), nor unusually strong laborers. The strength of the workers, in fact, failed because the work was so strenuous (cf. Neh. 4:10). The work would succeed because of the supernatural grace (help) that the Lord would provide by His Spirit (cf. Gen. 1:2; Exod. 15:8, 10; 28:3; 31:3; Num. 11:17-29; Judg. 3:10; 6:34; 11:29; 13:25; 14:6, 19; 15:14, 19; 2 Sam. 22:16; Ezek. 37:1-14). This is, of course, true of any work that seeks to carry out God's will in the world (cf. 2 Cor. 12:9).

4:7   A "great mountain" would become a "plain . . . before Zerubbabel." Mountains epitomize large obstacles (cf. Isa. 40:4; 41:15; 49:11; Matt. 17:20; 21:21; Mark 11:23; 1 Cor. 13:2). They are also symbols of kingdoms (cf. Isa. 41:15; Jer. 51:25; Dan. 2:35, 45; et al), but that is not the meaning here. The whole process of temple restoration seemed like a mountainous job to the few exiles who returned from captivity. In addition, there was much opposition to building (Ezra 4:1-5, 24), and the Israelites themselves proved unwilling to persevere in the task (Hag. 1:14; 2:1-9). Nevertheless, God would reduce this mountain to a flat plain by assisting the workers.

Furthermore, Zerubbabel would "bring forth the top stone," the final stone on the project, *with shouts of* "Grace, grace to it!" The joyful cry of the people, as they saw the last stone put in place, would voice their prayer that God's blessing would now rest on the beautiful structure that His grace had made possible.

> "There is nothing that makes the heart of God's people more ready to overflow with the truest joy than to witness success or the fulfillment of God's promises in the work of the kingdom."[101]

---

[98]*The New Scofield . . .*, pp. 966-67.
[99]See David L. Petersen, "Zerubbabel and Jerusalem Temple Reconstruction," *Catholic Biblical Quarterly* 36:3 (1974):366-72.
[100]Leupold, p. 87. See also Thurman Wisdom, "'Not by Might, nor by Power, but by My Spirit,'" *Biblical Viewpoint* 24:2 (November 1990):19-26.
[101]Leupold, p. 90.

The second oracle 4:8-10

4:8-9   Another word from the Lord also came to Zechariah about Zerubbabel. This appears to be another oracle that the writer inserted here because it is appropriate at this point. He promised that as Zerubbabel had "laid the foundation" of the temple (Ezra 3:8-11; 5:16), so he would also complete it (cf. Ezra 6:14-18). Construction began on the foundation of the temple in 536 B.C., and the last stone went in place in 515 B.C. The date of this oracle is unclear, but it probably came in 519 B.C. or perhaps shortly before that (cf. 1:7). Ezra 5:16 credits Sheshbazzar with laying the foundation, but Ezra 3:8 and Zech. 4:9 give Zerubbabel the credit for doing it. Probably Zerubbabel finished the work that Sheshbazzar had started. The Lord promised that when the temple was complete, the people would "know" that it was indeed "the LORD" who had "sent" the messenger who brought this message to Zechariah. The messenger in view appears to be the angel of the Lord (cf. 1:11-12; 2:8-9, 11; 3:1, 5-6).

4:10   The people would be ashamed that they had despised the rebuilding project as insignificant (cf. Ezra 3:12; Hag. 2:3).[102] The Lord Himself was "glad" to "see ... Zerubbabel" building with his "plumb line," as His omniscient eyes ("these seven") surveyed all that was happening in the world (cf. 3:9; 2 Chron. 16:9). The Hebrew words translated "plumb line" may mean "separated [i.e., chosen] stone." In this case, the idea would be that the Lord, in addition to His people, would rejoice when He *saw the capstone put in place* (cf. v. 7; Ezra 6:16-22). Now His people could serve Him as He purposed.

> "Bible history is the record of God using small things. When God wanted to set the plan of salvation in motion, He started with a little baby named Isaac (Gen. 21). When He wanted to overthrow Egypt and set His people free, He used a baby's tears (Ex. 2:1-10). He used a shepherd boy and a sling to defeat a giant (1 Sam. 17) and a little lad's lunch to feed a multitude (John 6). He delivered the Apostle Paul from death by using a basket and a rope (Acts 9:23-25). Never despise the day of small things, for God is glorified in small things and uses them to accomplish great things."[103]

3. The interpretation of the vision 4:11-14

Though some help understanding the vision came through the preceding oracles concerning Zerubbabel, Zechariah still had some questions about what he had seen in the vision. The angel helped him further.

4:11-12   Zechariah asked specifically for an explanation of the "two olive trees" that he had seen (v. 4). He also wanted to know the meaning of the "two branches" of these trees that emptied olive oil into "two golden pipes" (spouts) that carried the golden oil into the bowl atop the lampstand. "Golden oil" is literally "gold," but clearly olive oil, which is golden in color, is in view. However, it may be the pure quality and value of the oil more than its color that the gold connotes.[104]

4:13   Again the interpreting angel expressed surprise that Zechariah needed an explanation of these things (cf. v. 5). He did not want to give an interpretation if Zechariah could figure it out himself. Normally God does not provide additional information until we have done all we can to discover His meaning. To do so would discourage human effort Godward.

4:14   He then said that the two branches represented "the two anointed ones" who stood by the Lord of all the earth. It was their relationship to the Lord that equipped them for their tasks. "Anointed ones" is literally "sons of oil."

> "The phrase 'sons of oil' is typically interpreted to mean that the two individuals mentioned were anointed with oil as the Lord's special servants (see NIV). However, the word for 'oil' used here (Heb. *yitshar*) does not refer to anointing oil elsewhere (the Hebrew term for such oil is *shemen*) but to fresh oil that symbolizes a land's agricultural abundance.[105] It is more likely, then, that the individuals are called 'sons of oil' because under their leadership the Lord would restore agricultural prosperity to the land (see 3:10, as well as Hag. 2:19). These 'sons of oil' were, of course, the high priest Joshua and the governor Zerubbabel (see 3:1-10; 4:7-10; 6:9-15)."[106]

Nevertheless, the earlier reference to the Spirit's enablement (v. 6) presents these "sons of oil" as empowered by Him.[107]

---

[102]See Wayne O. McCready, "The 'Day of Small Things' vs. the Latter Days: Historical Fulfillment or Eschatological Hope?" in *Israel's Apostasy and Restoration: Essays in Honor of Roland K. Harrison*, pp. 223-36.
[103]Wiersbe, p. 456.
[104]Unger, p. 79.
[105]Footnote 299: See David L. Petersen, *Haggai and Zechariah 1—8*, pp. 230-31.
[106]Chisholm, *Handbook on . . .*, p. 462.
[107]For an edifying explanation of the similarities between oil and the Holy Spirit, see Feinberg, *God Remembers*, pp. 74-75.

Zerubbabel and Joshua point ultimately to the Messiah, who combined the royal and priestly offices and functions in one person, the Branch (3:8; 6:12; Isa. 11:1; Jer. 23:5; cf. Ps. 110; Heb. 7). Some of the Jews in Jesus' day (e.g., the Qumran community) expected two Messiahs, a princely one and a priestly one.[108] In the Tribulation, two other special witnesses will appear (cf. Rev. 11:3-12).

The point of this vision, and its accompanying oracles, was the Lord's ability to bring a seemingly impossible project to completion—successfully and gloriously—through His anointed servants (Messiah, and Zerubbabel and Joshua) and His supernatural enablement (cf. 2 Cor. 12:9). The lesson is applicable to any project that God has ordained and called His people to execute, including rebuilding the temple and building the church (Matt. 16:18).

F. THE FLYING SCROLL 5:1-4

The priests and the kings in Israel were responsible for justice in the nation (cf. Deut. 17:9; 2 Sam. 15:2-3), though neither group could prevent wickedness from proliferating. The sixth and seventh visions deal with the removal of wickedness. This sixth one deals with the elimination of lawbreakers, and the next one with the removal of wickedness from the land. What God promised in the preceding two visions required the purging predicted in these two visions.

"At this point the series of visions takes a sharp turn from that which heretofore has been comforting, to a stern warning that the Lord (Yahweh) is a holy God and cannot brook evil."[109]

". . . before the blessing of the first five visions will be actualized, there will intervene in the life of the nation a period of moral declension and apostasy. God must and will purge out all iniquity, though He has promised untold glory for the godly in Israel."[110]

5:1   The next thing Zechariah saw in his visions was an unrolled "scroll," "flying" through the air. This was a scroll that contained writing, the equivalent of a modern book.

> "A scroll (or roll), in Scripture symbolism, denotes the written word, whether of God or man (Ezra 6:2; Jer. 36:2, 4, 6, etc.; Ezek 3:1-3, etc). Zechariah's sixth vision is of the rebuke of sin by the Word of God. The two sins mentioned [in verse 3] really transgress both tables of the law. To steal is to set aside our neighbor's right; to swear is to set aside God's claim to reverence."[111]

5:2   The prophet replied to the interpreting angel, who asked him what he saw, that he saw a "flying scroll" that was 20 cubits long and 10 cubits wide (30 feet by 15 feet). Several commentators made connections between this scroll and the tabernacle, and the temple, since these were the dimensions of the holy place of the tabernacle (Exod. 26:8), as well as the porch in front of the holy place of Solomon's temple (1 Kings 6:3). But this correspondence seems to be coincidental. The scroll that Zechariah saw was open—and large—so that people could read it easily. During the restoration period, the returnees demonstrated an increased interest in the Mosaic Law, which was written on scrolls (cf. Neh. 8). No one could plead ignorance, because the scroll in Zechariah's vision was large enough for all to see and read.

5:3   The angel explained that the scroll represented the curses that God had decreed against the Israelites who stole and who swore falsely in the Lord's name (v. 4; cf. Deut. 28). According to what God had previously written in the Law, those who stole and profaned His name would die, thus purging the land of sin. The Hebrew word *ha'arets* can mean either "the earth" or "the land." Here, and in verse 6, the primary meaning seems to be "the land," namely, the land of Israel. Writing was on both sides of the scroll, as it had been on the stone tables that contained the Ten Commandments (Exod. 32:15). On one side there was a curse against Israelites who broke the eighth commandment (Exod. 20:15), and on the other side was a curse for breaking the third commandment (Exod. 20:7). These two commandments, from the first part of the Decalogue and the second part, which Zechariah's contemporaries were apparently breaking frequently, probably represent by synecdoche the whole Law (cf. James 2:10). Synecdoche is a figure of speech in which the writer uses a part, or parts, to represent the whole, or the whole to represent a part.

5:4   Yahweh then promised to cause His curse to seek out the guilty and to bring judgment on them. He personified the curse and pictured it going throughout the land, even into homes, to seek out law-breakers. God's Word still had its ancient power even

---

[108] See Helmer Ringgren, *The Faith of Qumran*, pp. 171-73.
[109] Unger, p. 83.
[110] Feinberg, *God Remembers*, p. 82.
[111] *The New Scofield . . .*, p. 967.

in post-exilic Judaism. Even the privacy of their homes would not afford protection from the judgment that the Lord would send on those of His people who broke His law.

In spite of the glorious promises of the future just revealed in the previous visions, the Israelites needed to realize that sin would still bring inevitable divine punishment on them. They needed to remain pure so they could avoid the Lord's curses and enjoy His promised blessings (cf. 2 Cor. 7:1). They were still under the Mosaic Law, including the Decalogue.

> "It is striking that this vision plays down any human activity."[112]

> "This whole passage is very valuable as a commentary on the nature of Christ's rule in righteousness in the millennial period as well as the severity of His dealing with sinners once the day of grace is ended and the day of wrath and judgment is ushered in with the opening of the seven-sealed roll of Revelation 5:1-9, loosing the seals, trumpets, and bowl judgments that dispossess Satan, demons, and the wicked men from the earth preparatory to the advent of the King of kings and Lord of lords to establish His rule and kingdom."[113]

Amillennialists hold that "there is no allusion in our vision to the millennial kingdom and its establishment within the limits of the earthly Canaan."[114]

G. THE WOMAN IN THE BASKET 5:5-11

The preceding vision described the future removal of individual sinners from the land through divine judgment, and this one pictures the eventual removal of all wickedness from the future "holy land" (2:12; cf. 3:9).

> "In line with the scope of all eight of Zechariah's night visions, the fulfilment [sic] of this likewise extends into the millennial kingdom. Nevertheless the immediate application of the vision to the prophet's time and to the conditions then prevailing is plain."[115]

5:5   The angelic guide next proceeded to instruct Zechariah to view something else that was happening in his vision.

> "So little is human nature capable of readily appropriating divine revelation that it is not only necessary for God to let the necessary visions appear but also to stimulate the recipient's attention step by step lest, overcome by the power of the heavenly, he fail to appropriate all that God desires to offer."[116]

5:6-7   The prophet asked what it was he was seeing, and the angel replied that it was an "ephah," a basket that held about a half bushel (or five gallons) of dry (or liquid) material (cf. 1 Sam. 1:24; Ruth 2:17). Some authorities contend that an ephah was slightly more than a bushel. The ephah was the largest dry measure among the Hebrews, and its use here suggests that Israel's sins had accumulated greatly in Zechariah's day.[117] The angel "lifted up" the "lead cover" on top of the basket and revealed "a woman sitting inside." A lead cover would be heavier than the customary stone cover, and would guarantee that what was inside would not get out. Either the ephah was oversized, like the flying scroll, or the woman was a miniature in Zechariah's vision. Perhaps God used an ephah in the vision simply because it was a standard container that people used to carry things in, similar to a barrel. Some commentators have seen in the ephah a particular allusion to commercial malpractice, since the ephah was used in commerce, but this may be over-exegeting the text.

> "The woman, made visible by the lifting of the lead cover, is still, like the evil she represents, mostly hidden from sight."[118]

The angel further explained that this is what the ephah and its contents would resemble as they went forth in all the earth.

> "As in the preceding vision, the earth (ha'arets) designates not merely Palestine, although this is the primary reference, and the removal of godless commercialism is first and foremost from 'the land,' which

---

[112]Merrill, p. 166.
[113]Unger, p. 89.
[114]Keil, 2:281.
[115]Unger, p. 91.
[116]Leupold, p. 103.
[117]*The New Scofield . . .*, p. 967.
[118]Baldwin, p. 128.

	will then be in reality 'the Holy Land' (Zech. 2:12 [16]); but more broadly the term points to the entire millennial earth."[119]
5:8	The angel explained that the woman personified wickedness. Some have interpreted the woman as covenant-breakers, a particular form of wickedness.[120] The angel picked her up, "threw her down into the middle" of the basket, and shut the lead cover over her (cf. 2 Thess. 2:6-8). Obviously some conflict was involved; "Wickedness" did not want to be restricted. Perhaps Zechariah saw a woman, instead of a man, because the word "wickedness" in Hebrew is feminine. It was not uncommon to represent wickedness as a woman (e.g., Prov. 7; Rev. 17; et al.). Here the woman represents the sum total of Israel's sins, wickedness being the opposite of righteousness (cf. Prov. 13:6; Ezek. 33:12). Another view is that she represents Babylon (Rev. 17—18), but this seems unlikely since she ends up in Babylon (v. 11).
5:9	The prophet next saw "two" other "women" flying through the air with "stork . . . wings." Perhaps they were women, and not men, because of the motherly attention they brought to their task.[121] Storks are strong, motherly birds that are capable of carrying loads a long distance in flight. They were commonly seen in Palestine in the spring months, while they were migrating to Europe (Jer. 8:7).[122] The word "stork" (Heb. *sida*) means "faithful one." These women would faithfully carry the ephah and its contents to God's appointed destination. Some believe they represent agents of evil, perhaps demonic forces.[123] If they were that, however, would they not try to help Wickedness escape? Storks were unclean birds for the Israelites (Lev. 11:19; Deut. 14:18), so these stork-like women were appropriate carriers of the contaminated basket. "They lifted up the ephah" into the air, flying off from earth to heaven with the divine assistance of "the wind" (Spirit, Heb. *ruah*).

> "The removal of Wickedness, like the removal of Joshua's filthy garments (3:4), was an act of free grace on the part of the covenant-keeping (*hasid*) God."[124]

5:10-11	When Zechariah asked the angel where the two flying women were taking the basket, his interpreter responded that they were taking the woman to "the land of Shinar" (Babylonia, cf. Gen. 10:10; 11:2; 14:1, 9).

> "Shinar, besides taking the theme of Babylon as antagonist back to the very beginning (Gen. 10:10), creating thereby a kind of 'historical inclusio,' lends a more trans-historical sense to the message."[125]

Leupold took Shinar as representing the world in contrast to the church.[126] These two women with storks' wings were God's agents carrying out His will (cf. Ps. 103:11-12; Jer. 32:39-40; Ezek. 36:25). At the appointed time, the woman Wickedness will sit atop a "pedestal" as an object of worship, an idol (cf. Rev. 17—18).

> "Thus where Judah had been exiled was a fitting place for wickedness to be worshipped, but not in the land where God had placed *his* name. The idolatry of Babylon must once and for all be separated from the worship of the God of Israel."[127]

"We understand the passage to speak of the heaping up of the full measure of Israel's sins prior to the time of God's separation of the wicked from the midst of the righteous remnant of the last days."[128]

"The two cleansing acts of this chapter are complementary, like the two goats on the Day of Atonement, Leviticus 16, of which the first must give its blood as an expiation before the Lord, while the second carries away the guilt of the people, and the

---

[119]Unger, p. 94.
[120]E.g., McComiskey, p. 1101.
[121]Merrill, p. 175.
[122]Smith, p. 211.
[123]E.g., Unger, p. 98.
[124]Baldwin, p. 129.
[125]Merrill, p. 178. Cf. Rev. 14:8; 17:1, 5, 18; 18:8, 10, 19, 21.
[126]Leupold, p. 108.
[127]David J. Ellis, "Zechariah," in *The New Layman's Bible Commentary*, p. 1034.
[128]Feinberg, *God Remembers*, p. 89.

impurity springing from it, to the region of the impure desert-demon. The cleansing judgment, despite the terror, is a benefit to the land, which is thus purified and fitted to receive the blessing pictured in the former visions."[129]

H. THE FOUR CHARIOTS 6:1-8

There are several similarities between this last vision and the first one (1:7-17), indicating a return to ideas introduced at the beginning of this chiastic series of revelations. Again there is a group of horses of various colors, but their order and colors are somewhat different. Zechariah mentioned a rider in vision one but no chariots, but in vision eight chariots without horsemen appear. There is a similar emphasis on the fact that Yahweh controls history and subdues the nations that oppress Israel.

> "This last of the eight [visions] shares so much in common with the first that the two, at least, must be viewed as book ends enveloping the whole series."[130]

6:1 The next thing Zechariah saw in his night visions was "four chariots" coming out from between "two . . . bronze . . . mountains." Due to the increasing repetition of "come forth" or "go forth" (Heb. *yasa'*) throughout the series of eight visions, the careful reader feels a developing sense of intensity in the activity being described, that reaches its climax in this vision (v. 8). Chariots were instruments of judgment, and bronze is a color that often carries this connotation in Scripture (cf. Exod. 27:2; Num. 21:9). William Kelly and others believed the four chariots represent the four great kingdoms in Daniel's prophecy (Dan. 2; 7).[131] This seems unlikely.[132]

"Bronze" was used to defend against attackers (Isa. 45:2; Jer. 1:18), so perhaps impregnability is also in view. Some interpreters believed the color bronze was due to the rising sun. This results, in the interpretations of some, in the first vision taking place at evening, and the last at sunrise.[133] Leupold referred to the commentators who take this view as letting "their fancy play at this point."[134]

Perhaps the mountains represent the gateway to heaven from which these agents of judgment come.[135] Another, more probable view, is that they were Mount Zion and the Mount of Olives, with the valley between being the Kidron Valley.[136] A third possibility is that they are the two parts of the Mount of Olives that will split apart when Messiah returns to the earth (cf. 14:1-8). Nevertheless they are "bronze."

> "Always in Scripture symbolism, they [chariots and horses] stand for the power of God earthward in judgment (Jer. 46:9-10; Joel 2:3-11; Nah. 3:1-7). The vision, then, speaks of the LORD's judgments upon the Gentile nations north and south in the day of the LORD (Isa. 2:10-22; Rev. 19:11-21)."[137]

6:2-3 The two horses pulling the "first chariot" were "red." "Black horses" pulled the "second chariot," "white horses" the "third," and "dappled horses" the "fourth." All of them were "strong." These horses evidently represent angels who facilitate the work of other angels, represented by the chariots (cf. v. 5). The colors of the horses may symbolize various aspects of judgment, perhaps war and bloodshed in the case of the red horses, famine and death for the black, victory and triumph for the white (cf. 1:8; Rev. 19:11, 14), and plague and disease for the dappled (spotted; cf. Rev. 6:1-8).[138]

6:4-6 In response to the prophet's request for interpretation, his angel guide explained that the chariots represented "the four spirits" (winds, Heb. *ruhoth*) of heaven (i.e., angels), which were going forth, having been in the presence of "the Lord of all the earth" (cf. 4:14). They were His messengers, the executors of His will (cf. Ps. 104:4). The chariot with the black horses went "north" from Jerusalem, the direction from which most of Israel's enemy invaders descended on the Promised Land (e.g., Babylonia; cf. Jer. 1:14; 4:6; 6:22; Ezek. 1:4). The chariot with the white horses went out next, and evidently followed the previous one—

---

[129]C. von Orelli, *The Twelve Minor Prophets*, p. 335.
[130]Merrill, p. 181.
[131]William Kelly, *Lectures Introductory to the Study of the Minor Prophets*, p. 461.
[132]See Feinberg, *God Remembers*, pp. 95-97, or Keil, 2:287, for refutation.
[133]See G. von Rad, *Old Testament Theology*, 2:287.
[134]Leupold, p. 110.
[135]Baldwin, p. 130; McComiskey, p. 1106.
[136]Barker, p. 636; Keil, 2:287; Unger, p. 101; Feinberg, *God Remembers*, p. 95; idem, "Zechariah," p. 903.
[137]*The New Scofield . . .*, p. 968.
[138]Unger, pp. 102-3.

north. The one with the dappled horses headed south. Egypt lay to Israel's south, and it was another implacable enemy. Presumably the red horses went south too.

Because of the geography of Palestine, all of Israel's enemies came against her from the north or from the south; the Mediterranean Sea on the west, and the Arabian Desert on the east, prohibited major foreign invasions from those directions. Since the chariots went in compass directions, we should probably understand their judgment to be universal (cf. 2:6; Jer. 49:36; Ezek. 37:9; Rev. 7:1). They went north and south out of Palestine, but they executed judgment in every direction. The total picture is of God executing His judgments against all nations that oppose Israel.

6:7   When these horses (angels) "went out" from between the bronze mountains, "they were eager to . . . patrol the earth"; they were anxious to carry out these judgments. The Lord gave them permission to patrol it, so they did.

> "From first to last (*cf.* 1:10) the affairs of the nations are under God's direction, not man's. It is this certainty that makes prophecy possible."[139]

6:8   The Lord then called out to Zechariah that the horses that had gone out into the north had "appeased" His "wrath in the land of the north." This probably represents judgment on Babylonia specifically, but it probably hints at the total destruction of all enemies of Israel. Babylon had fallen to the Persians 20 years earlier, in 539 B.C.

---

[139]Baldwin, p. 132.

| ZECHARIAH'S EIGHT NIGHT VISIONS ||||
Number	Reference	Subject	Lesson
1	1:7-17	The horseman among the myrtle trees	Yahweh's sovereignty over Israel's restoration
2	1:18-21	The four horns and the four smiths	The triumph of Israel over her enemies
3	ch. 2	The surveyor	Preparations for Israel's future restoration
4	ch. 3	The cleansing and restoration of Joshua	The renewal of Israel's priestly ministry
5	ch. 4	The gold lampstand and the two olive trees	Israel's testimony under Messiah as priest and king
6	5:1-4	The flying scroll	Judgment on Israel for covenant disobedience
7	5:5-11	The woman in the basket	The return of evil to Babylon
8	6:1-8	The four chariots	Judgment on Israel's enemies

III. THE SYMBOLIC CROWNING OF JOSHUA 6:9-15

The visions ended and Zechariah awoke from his dream-like state. What follows is a symbolic act that took place in Jerusalem at the Lord's command.

> "The position of this actual ceremony after the eight visions is significant. The fourth and fifth visions, at the center of the series, were concerned with the high priest [Joshua] and the civil governor in the Davidic line [Zerubbabel]. Zechariah here linked the message of those two visions to the messianic King-Priest. . . . Thus restored Israel is seen in the future under the glorious reign of the messianic King-Priest."[140]

> "Immediately following the overthrow of Gentile world power by the earth judgments symbolized by the horsed chariots (Zech. 6:1-8) occurs the manifestation of Christ in His kingdom glory (Zech. 6:9-15) typified by the crowning of Joshua the high priest. This is the usual prophetic order: first, the judgments of the day of the Lord; then full kingdom blessing (Ps. 2:5, cf. Ps. 2:6; Isa. 3:24-26, cf. 4:2-6; 10:33, 34, cf. 11:1-10; Rev. 19:19-21, cf. 20:4-6).

> "The eight night visions have ended, but the coronation of Joshua is closely connected with these revelations which extend in scope from Zechariah's day to the full establishment of Israel in blessing. The crowning of King-Priest Messiah is thus set forth symbolically by the coronation of Joshua, which is not a vision, but an actual historical act, which evidently took place the day following the night of visions."[141]

> ". . . this oracle serves as a comment on and climax to the night visions as a whole."[142]

Some commentators connect this oracle with the preceding vision, just as the other oracles in chapters 1, 2, and 4 connect with the visions in their contexts.[143] Nevertheless, even these writers acknowledge that this oracle was not originally part of the vision in 6:1-8, but it supplements the earlier mention of the Branch in 3:8.

> "Unlike vision one, number eight does not have its own oracle of response, though . . . the oracle that follows it (6:9-15) may serve it as such as well as bringing the whole series to an end."[144]

---

[140]Barker, pp. 638-39.
[141]Unger, pp. 109-10.
[142]Merrill, p. 193.
[143]E.g., Baldwin, p. 85.
[144]Merrill, p. 182.

The lesson that this symbolic act illustrated was that Messiah would appear as a king-priest and rebuild God's temple in the days of Israel's future restoration (i.e., the Millennium).

> "This is one of the most remarkable and precious Messianic prophecies, and there is no plainer prophetic utterance in the whole Old Testament as to the Person of the promised Redeemer, the offices He was to fill, and the mission He was to accomplish."[145]

6:9-10   The Lord's word came to Zechariah, instructing him to go and take part (or all) of an offering that certain of "the exiles" had brought from Babylon for the restoration of the temple. These recent returnees were "Heldai, Tobijah, and Jedaiah." The prophet was to meet these men "at the house of Josiah the son of Zephaniah," where they were evidently staying.

6:11   Zechariah was to make an ornate "crown" out of at least some of the "silver and gold" that had been donated, and to place it "on the head of Joshua the son of Jehozadak, the high priest" (3:1). The Hebrew text has "crowns," not "crown." The plural could indicate a composite crown (cf. Rev. 19:12), a superlative crown, and or a sacred crown.[146] One writer believed there were two crowns and a double crowning—of Joshua and Zerubbabel.[147] But I see no evidence of this in the passage. This crown was not the regular turban of the high priest (Heb. *nezer*), but a kingly crown with many parts (Heb. *'ataroth*; cf. Rev. 19:12). Zechariah was to crown the high priest as a king, not as a priest (cf. Ps. 110:4; Heb. 7:1-3).

> "Christ is now a Priest but is still in the holiest within the veil (Heb. 9:11-14, 24; cp. Lev. 16:15) and seated on the Father's throne (Rev. 3:21). He has not yet come out to take His own throne (Heb. 9:28)."[148]

6:12   Zechariah was then to announce, in the name of sovereign Yahweh, that those present should "behold" (take note of, recognize) Joshua, whom Zechariah would designate as "Branch" (lit. Sprout, Heb. *semah*, cf. 3:8; Isa. 11:1; 53:2; Jer. 33:15; Hag. 2:23). Joshua represented (was a type of) the coming messianic Branch. This name signified that the coming Shoot would shoot up from His humble place of origin (cf. Isa. 53:2; Mic. 5:2). "He will branch out from where He is" is a pun on the word "branch." It means, "The shoot will shoot up from beneath (where there is little promise of life)." His kingdom would be widespread. Furthermore, He would build the temple of Yahweh. Zerubbabel, not Joshua, was God's choice to build the restoration temple (4:9-10), but Messiah, whom Joshua prefigured, would build the future temple for Yahweh (cf. Isa. 2:2-4; 56:6-7; Ezek. 40—43; Mic. 4:1-7; Hag. 2:6-9). For amillennialists, the temple equals the church.[149]

> "How appropriate therefore that both the type (Joshua) and the antitype (Jesus) have a name meaning 'the Lord saves' (cf. NIV mg. at Matt 1:21)!"[150]

The Aramaic Targum, the Jerusalem Talmud, and a Midrash all regarded verse 12 as messianic. When Pilate said, "Behold, the man" (John 19:5), he was announcing to the Jews unwittingly that Jesus was the Branch promised in this verse.

6:13   Indeed, "He" (emphatic in the Hebrew text) would "build" the Lord's "temple." The Lord repeated this assurance for emphasis. The Branch would "bear the honor" of royal majesty (cf. Dan. 11:21; 1 Chron. 29:25), "sit" enthroned—Israel's priests never sat while ministering—and "rule" on David's "throne" (cf. 2 Sam. 7:16; Isa. 9:7; Luke 1:32). He "will be a priest," ruling as a king, and "peace" (Heb. *shalom*) will characterize His dual "offices."

Along with Psalm 110, this verse is one of the clearest statements in the Old Testament that the coming Davidic king would also be a priest (cf. Heb. 5:1-10; 7:1-25). Chisholm favored the view that Zechariah's audience would have understood that "the Davidic ruler, though not a priest as such, will enjoy the full support of the priesthood."[151]

6:14   The ceremonial "crown" that Zechariah made for Joshua was to remain in the restoration temple as "a reminder . . . to Helem" (strength; or Heldai, mole, v. 10), "Tobijah, Jedaiah, and Hen" (Josiah) "the son of Zephaniah." It would doubtless remind other Israelites as well, but they were the prominent men during this event. "Hen" means "gracious one" in Hebrew, and it was likely an honorary title for Josiah, who had been the host of this historic coronation (v. 10).

6:15   When the Branch appears, Gentiles from afar "will come" and help "build the temple" of Yahweh (cf. 2:11; 8:22; Isa. 2:2-4; 56:6-7; 60:1-7). The donors mentioned earlier (vv. 10, 14) were typical of future Gentiles who will come from afar—in the last

---

[145] D. Baron, *The Visions and Prophecies of Zechariah*, p. 190.
[146] Cf. Baldwin, p. 133.
[147] Merrill, pp. 197-201.
[148] *The New Scofield . . .*, p. 968.
[149] E.g., Leupold, p. 124.
[150] Barker, p. 639.
[151] Chisholm, "A Theology . . .," p. 425.

days—to help build the Lord's house (cf. Isa. 60:4, 6, 9). When this happens, the people "will know" that Yahweh "has sent" Messiah to His people (cf. 2:8-11; 4:9). Another view is that the fulfillment would vindicate Zechariah as the Lord's messenger. All these people could participate in the building of the future temple, by bringing gifts (Isa. 56:7), if they were faithful to obey the Lord by doing all that He commanded (cf. Deut. 28:1-2, 15; 30:1-10).

> "In the new covenant (Jer 31:33-34; Ezek 36:26-27), God personally guarantees that the people will ultimately obey; his Spirit will enable them to do so."[152]

What is the temple that the Branch will build? It appears to be a literal building in Jerusalem—where God will reside during the Millennium—that will bring great glory to Him (cf. Ezek. 40—46). There will be no temple in the New Jerusalem in the eternal state (Rev. 21:22). Whereas the church is now the temple of God (i.e., Christians corporately and local congregations of believers; 1 Cor. 3:16; 1 Pet. 2:5), the church is not in view here. The equality of Jewish and Gentile believers in one body (i.e., the church) was a mystery that was unknown until God revealed it later (Matt. 16:18; Eph. 2:11—3:11).

> "Here we have the end and consummation of all the prophetic Scriptures: the crowning of the Lord Jesus Christ. It is only after the dark night of world judgment and punishment is passed, that the glorious light of Christ's coronation day will follow. This is one of the sublimest passages in the Scriptures on the Person and work of the Messiah."[153]

The sequence of events in the eight night visions, and the crowning of Joshua, argues for the traditional dispensational interpretation: that Jesus will begin reigning as the Davidic King when He returns to the earth at His second coming. The progressive dispensational view, on the other hand, as well as the covenant premillennial and amillennial views, are that Jesus began ruling as the Davidic king at His first advent.

> "The fulness [sic] of this Messianic prophecy can better be seen if we but marshal the distinctive features in order: 1. The humanity of the Branch. 2. The place of His birth. 3. The building of the millennial temple by Him. 4. His fitness to bear the glory of God. 5. His reign on the throne of David. 6. His priestly ministry. 7. The issue of His blessed ministry—peace."[154]

This is the end of the apocalyptic visionary section of the book. Chapters 7—14 contain regular prophetic messages. Some scholars have tried to correlate the last eight chapters of Zechariah and the eight night visions, but these attempts seem strained.

IV. MESSAGES CONCERNING HYPOCRITICAL FASTING CHS. 7—8

A question posed by representative Israelites provided the occasion for God to give four messages that Zechariah collected in the text here. They all deal with the issue of empty ritualism, which the original question introduced.

> "As early as 1:3-6 it was clear that Zechariah was interested in the spiritual renewal of the postexilic community. Here he deals further with this problem. The purpose of chapters 7 and 8 is to impress on the people their need to live righteously in response to their past judgment and future glory."[155]

A. THE QUESTION FROM THE DELEGATION FROM BETHEL 7:1-3

7:1 A prophetic message came to Zechariah from the Lord in 518 B.C. The "fourth day of the ninth month" would have been in early December. "Chislev" is the Babylonian name of the month. This message, which comprises the following four messages in chapters 7 and 8, came to the prophet almost two years after he received the eight night visions (cf. 1:7), and about halfway through the period of temple reconstruction (520-515 B.C.).

7:2-3 Israelites who lived in "Bethel," about 10 miles north of Jerusalem (cf. Ezra 2:28; Neh. 7:32; 11:31), sent two representatives to ask the priests and prophets in the capital about how they should worship the Lord (cf. Mal. 1:9). The names of the two ambassadors were Babylonian, suggesting that they had been born in Babylonia during the Captivity. Another view is that a Jew living in Babylon named Bethel-Sharezar (lit. house of God-protect the king), whose title was Regem-melech (lit. king's friend), indicating his royal authority (from Darius), came with his men to pose the question.[156] A slightly different translation yields the view that Bethel-Sharezar sent Regem-melech and his men. Whoever these men were, they wanted to know if they should continue to "weep" and "abstain" from food (i.e., to fast), which had become traditional but which the Mosaic Law did not require. The only fast that the Mosaic Law prescribed was on the Day of Atonement (Lev. 16:29; 23:27-32).

---

[152]Barker, p. 641.
[153]Feinberg, *God Remembers*, p. 100.
[154]Ibid., p. 106.
[155]Barker, p. 643.
[156]Baldwin, pp. 142-43.

> "Coming as they did from a place long associated with apostate worship (1 Kings 12:29-33; 2 Kings 10:29; Jer. 48:13; Amos 3:14; 4:4; 7:13), these men would be particularly concerned to determine orthodox praxis on behalf of those who sent them."[157]

There were four fasts that the Jews in exile had instituted to commemorate various events connected with the destruction of Jerusalem in 586 B.C. (cf. 8:19). The one "in the fifth month" memorialized the destruction of the temple (cf. 2 Kings 25:8-10).[158] Since the temple was almost complete (cf. Ezra 6:16), did the Lord want His people to continue to fast? The people knew that the captivity would last 70 years (Jer. 25:11-12), and 68 of these had already past. It seemed to them that fasting over the destruction of the temple might be inappropriate, since the Lord had enabled them to rebuild the temple and reestablish worship. The question was a reasonable one.

> "What may have appeared to be an innocent question about the propriety of fasting was instead a question fraught with hypocrisy, as YHWH's response puts beyond any doubt. It therefore appears that the query to Zechariah by the Bethelites may not have been so much a matter of piety as it was of posturing. May it not be that the delegation was trying more to impress the prophet than to gain instruction from him?"[159]

B. THE LORD'S REBUKE 7:4-7

This is the first of four messages that Zechariah received from the Lord that bear on the question just raised. That there were four separate messages seems clear, since each one begins with the same preamble: "The word of the Lord came" (7:4, 8; 8:1; 18). The first two, in chapter 7, are negative, and the last two, in chapter 8, are positive.

7:4-5   The Lord spoke to Zechariah, and he proceeded to inform the messengers, "all the people in the land," and "the priests." The issue that the messengers had raised had widespread implications for the whole nation. The Lord asked—rhetorically—if the people had really observed the fasts that they had instituted in "the fifth and seventh months," for 70 years, for His benefit or for themselves. "Seventy years" is a round number for the length of the Captivity here, assuming the 70 years had not completely run their course yet. The fast in the fifth month, on the ninth of Ab, memorialized the destruction of Solomon's temple by Nebuchadnezzar. The fast in the seventh month, on the second of Tishri, commemorated the assassination of Gedaliah and his associates at Mizpah (2 Kings 25:25; Jer. 41:2).[160] Evidently the people had turned these events into occasions for self-pity over their physical condition, rather than engaging in prayer and genuine spiritual repentance.

7:6-7   Likewise, when the people ate and drank, they did it for themselves—rather than to please the Lord. They were simply perpetuating the selfishness for which "former prophets" had rebuked their ancestors. The prophets in view had lived before the captivity, when the whole land and its cities were still full of inhabitants (e.g., Isa. 58:3-9; Joel 1:14; 2:12). Now there were far fewer Israelites occupying the land. The "Negev" to the south of Beersheba, and "the foothills" (Shephelah) toward the Mediterranean coast, were grazing and agricultural areas in which the returnees had not yet settled.

> "Note that the inquiry put by the Bethel committee is not being answered directly. In fact, throughout chapters 7 and 8 no direct answer is offered. The reason is: the question is not an important issue. However, the attitude revealed by that question is of sufficient moment to receive exhaustive treatment."[161]

C. THE COMMAND TO REPENT 7:8-14

Having referred to the words of the former prophets (v. 7), Zechariah now summarized them as an exhortation to his own generation of Israelites.

7:8-10 Zechariah received another message from the Lord related to this inquiry. The sovereign Lord commanded His people to "dispense true justice" (Heb. *mishpat*), to exercise "kindness" (Heb. *hesed*) "and compassion" (Heb. *rahamim*) toward each other, "not" to "oppress" the weak and vulnerable among them, and "not" to plot "evil" against each other.

---

[157] Merrill, p. 208.
[158] *The Illustrated Family Encyclopedia of the Living Bible*, 8:93; Peter Ackroyd, *Exile and Restoration*, p. 207.
[159] Merrill, p. 209. Cf. McComiskey, p. 1125.
[160] *The Illustrated . . .*, 8:93.
[161] Leupold, p. 133.

"Here . . . is a concise yet comprehensive range of ethical teaching condensed into four pithy utterances."[162]

"Morality is certainly not piety, but the piety which does not include morality is a mere delusion. It mocks God and insults man."[163]

7:11-12   When the former generations of Israelites had heard these commands, "they refused to pay attention" to the Lord. They "turned" away from Him stubbornly like a rebellious ox, and they put their fingers in ("stopped") "their ears" so they would not hear Him. They hardened "their hearts" (minds and wills) like "flint" (Heb. *shamir*, diamond), so they could not hear the Law, or the Holy Spirit's messages, "through the former prophets" whom God had sent to them.

"This remarkable doctrine of the Holy Spirit as mediator of God's word to the prophets, who were themselves its mediators, has no parallels in the prophetic books. . . . Zechariah is the first to record this aspect of the doctrine of the Spirit."[164]

God had proceeded to dull the people's ears in discipline because they would not hear (cf. Isa. 6:10; Acts 28:27). Consequently great wrath had come from the Lord against them.

"One indispensable ingredient in true spirituality is a dogged attentiveness to familiar truths, but they did not 'pay attention.'"[165]

7:13-14   Since the forefathers refused to listen to the Lord's Spirit when "He called" to them (cf. Neh. 9:20, 30; 2 Pet. 1:21), the Lord refused to listen to them when "they called" to Him in prayer (cf. Jer. 11:11-14). Instead, He "scattered" them "among" many "nations," as though a windstorm had blown them off the Promised Land (cf. Deut. 28:36-37, 64-68; Hos. 13:3). As a result, "the land" had become "desolate"—with none of the Israelites returning to it during the Captivity (cf. Deut. 28:41-42, 45-52). This desolation of the formerly "pleasant land" of Israel was due to the sin of the people (cf. Ps. 106:24; Jer. 3:19; Dan. 11:16, 41).

". . . while Zechariah may well not have answered the original enquiry directly, he had nevertheless taken up the very essence of ritual in the heart of the worshiper, which was that the outward form of religious activity was useless and lifeless without an accompanying spirit of obedience, confession and repentance."[166]

D. ISRAEL'S RESTORATION TO GOD'S FAVOR 8:1-17

Chapter 8 not only contains two major messages from the Lord (vv. 1-17, 18-23), but 10 minor messages—"a *decalogue* of divine words"[167]—that make up the two major ones. Another writer believed there were seven oracles in this section.[168] "Thus says the Lord" introduces each of these minor messages (vv. 2, 3, 4-5, 6, 7-8, 9-13, 14-18, 19, 20-22, 23), each of which contains a promise of future blessing for Israel. These short sayings may have been the texts of different sermons that Zechariah had preached and later wove together because of their similar content.[169]

"In the preceding section [ch. 7] Israel was to repent and live righteously after the punishment of her captivity; here [in ch. 8] she is to repent and live righteously because of the promise of her future restoration."[170]

The whole chapter presents Israel's eventual restoration and participation in full millennial blessing.[171] The restoration from exile in Zechariah's day was only a precursor of greater future blessing and prosperity.

"Of a total of 36 occurrences of 'YHWH of hosts' in Zechariah, 15 are in this one oracle [ch. 8], the highest concentration of the phrase in the OT with the possible exception of Malachi. Even more remarkable, it occurs six times in the present passage

---

[162]Ellis, p. 1037. Cf. Mic. 6:8.
[163]J. P. Lange, ed., *A Commentary on the Holy Scriptures*, vol. 7: *The Book of Zechariah Expounded*, by Talbot W. Chambers, p. 58.
[164]Baldwin, p. 147.
[165]Barker, p. 647.
[166]Ellis, pp. 1037-38.
[167]Leupold, p. 141.
[168]Waltke, p. 846.
[169]Baldwin, p. 148.
[170]Barker, pp. 649-50.
[171]Unger, p. 132.

alone [8:1-8], a passage that focuses narrowly on eschatological restoration. So humanly impossible will that be, it can come to pass only by the resources of the Almighty One."[172]

I counted 16 occurrences of "the LORD of hosts" and four more of "the LORD" in this chapter.

8:1	The Lord's word came to Zechariah.

"The introductory formula lacks the words *to me* in the original, a fact which suggests that Zechariah was repeating words he had often spoken rather than expressing a new revelation."[173]

8:2	Almighty Yahweh had revealed that He was very "jealous" for the exclusive love and commitment of His people (cf. 1:14). His loving jealousy burned, "with great wrath," within Him.

". . . YHWH is a 'jealous God' (Ex. 20:5), one who tolerates no rivals real or imaginary and who is zealous to protect His uniqueness and maintain the allegiance of His people to Himself alone. He is also jealous for His people, that is, He is protective of them against all who would challenge them or claim to be elect alongside them. Therefore, He is zealous to safeguard their interests and come to their defense."[174]

The English word "jealous" derives from the Latin *zelus*, "zeal."

"The zeal with which God had carried through His chastisement of Israel and then of the nations (1:15, 21) was now burning to restore the covenant bond."[175]

8:3	Yahweh announced that He would "return to Zion" and reside among His people in "Jerusalem" again (cf. 1:16; 2:10). When He did, people would call Jerusalem the "City of Truth," and they would refer to the temple mount as the "Holy Mountain" (cf. 14:20-21). Finally the recurring cycle of apostasy followed by punishment would end.

"Jerusalem did not acquire this character in the period after the captivity, in which, though not defiled by gross idolatry, as in the times before the captivity, it was polluted by other moral abominations no less than it had been before. Jerusalem becomes a faithful city for the first time through the Messiah, and it is through Him that the temple mountain first really becomes the holy mountain."[176]

8:4-5	Then the elderly would feel secure enough to "sit in the" open "streets" again, and children would again play in the streets because they would be safe. During the destruction of Jerusalem, both of these groups of Israelites had suffered greatly (Lam. 2:21). In other words, Jerusalem would become a place of tranquility, long life, peace, prosperity, and security for even the most defenseless of her citizens (cf. Isa. 65:20-25). These conditions await the return of Jesus Christ at His second coming.

"In one of the most amazing and challenging statements about measurement of the health of society, Zechariah suggests that we look at the place the old and the young have in that society."[177]

8:6	Even though these blessings seemed impossible to the people of Zechariah's day, they were not to assume that they would be impossible for the Lord. His promises of blessing were as hard for the returned exiles to believe as His threats of judgment had been for their ancestors previously.
8:7-8	Sovereign Yahweh promised to deliver His people from the distant places in the world where He had scattered them, and to "bring them" back to live "in . . . Jerusalem" (cf. Isa. 11:11-12; Jer. 30:7-11; 31:7-8). Jerusalem stands for the whole land here (by metonymy), not "the true church of God."[178] It identifies the place where people would come to worship the Lord. There they would enjoy intimacy with Him, a relationship marked by truth and righteousness. This future Exodus depended on Yahweh's electing grace and His covenant faithfulness, just as much as the original Exodus did.

---

[172]Merrill, p. 220.
[173]Baldwin, p. 149.
[174]Merrill, pp. 220-21.
[175]Baldwin, p. 149.
[176]Keil, 2:312.
[177]Smith, p. 233.
[178]Leupold, p. 148. Cf. McComiskey, p. 1141.

"'They will be my people, and I will be ... their God' is covenant terminology, pertaining to intimate fellowship in a covenant relationship (cf. Gen 17:7-8; Exod 6:7; 19:5-6; 29:45-46; Lev 11:45; 22:33; 25:38; 26:12, 44-45; Num 15:41; Deut 4:20; 29:12-13; Jer 31:33; 32:38; Ezek 37:27; 2 Cor 6:16; Rev 21:3)."[179]

"This is one of the greatest and most comprehensive promises in reference to Israel's restoration and conversion to be found in the prophetic Scriptures."[180]

8:9 The Lord also told the people to gain strength from the "words . . . of the prophets" who had encouraged them to complete the rebuilding of the temple ever since they began the project (cf. Josh. 1:7; 2 Sam. 2:7; 16:21; Hag. 2:4). These prophets were Haggai, Zechariah, and perhaps others (Ezra 5:1-2). Probably the resumption of construction in 520 B.C. (Hag. 2:18) is in view, rather than the restoration of the foundation in 536 B.C. (Ezra 3:8). Between these dates the people did little work on the temple, especially between 530 and 520 B.C.

8:10 Before the returnees began to rebuild in earnest, there was severe unemployment, so there were no wages for many of the people (cf. Hag. 1:6). Even the animals were not earning their keep. "There was" also "no peace," because the "enemies" of the Jews oppressed them (cf. Ezra 4:1-5; Hag. 1:6-11; 2:15-19). The Lord Himself was ultimately responsible for the antagonism that existed then.

"This verse presents a contrast of the present, when they had begun to obey the Word of God, with the past, when they did not."[181]

8:11-12 The Lord promised to "treat the remnant of" His "people" differently in the future than He had in the past (cf. Hag. 2:19). "Peace" would prevail for the people as they sowed their seed: their fields would become productive (cf. Hag. 2:19), there would be abundant moisture so things would grow (cf. Hag. 1:10-11), and "the remnant" would enjoy the fruits of all these blessings. These were some of the things God had promised the Israelites for covenant obedience (Lev. 26:3-10; Deut. 28:11-12; cf. Ezek. 34:25-27).

8:13 Even though the Israelites had been "a curse among the nations" in the past (cf. Deut. 28:15-68; Jer. 24:9; 25:18; 29:22), the Lord would "save" them and make them "a blessing" to the world in the future.

"Not only the two tribes [of Judah] but the ten [of Israel]. This has never yet been fulfilled."[182]

One of the purposes of these promises was to remove the Jews' present "fear" and give them strength to complete the temple. "Let your hands be strong" is the exhortation that frames this sixth message of encouragement (cf. v. 9).

8:14-15 Yahweh of armies also promised that "just as" He had "purposed" to bring His people into difficult times because of their forefathers' sins (cf. Jer. 4:28; 51:12; Lam. 2:17), so He had "purposed" to bless ("do good to") "Jerusalem" in the near future. Covenant disobedience had brought divine discipline, but covenant obedience would bring divine blessing. As He had not relented from bringing the first promise to pass, so He would not go back on the second promise. His determination was equally strong in both instances. Therefore the people should "not fear" (cf. v. 13).

"These glorious eschatological promises illuminating the future of the Jews and setting before them their future national hope also came as an illustration to them of the blessing God had in store for them at that time. To describe this the prophet uses the expression **in these days** (v. 15). But the benefits that were immediate *did not exhaust the full scope* of these sweeping prophetic previews.

"Like Jonah out of God's will they have caused a storm among the Gentiles. Yet in a future day, after their great tribulation, like Jonah's experience in the fish, they shall be restored to faith and obedience to minister to the nations of the millennium, as Jonah did to the Ninevites."[183]

8:16-17 In view of this promise, the remnant should speak truthfully with each other. They should also practice justice and promote "peace" (Heb. *shalom*) in their community life. They should stop plotting to take advantage of one another and stop lying under oath—because the Lord hates these things (cf. Prov. 6:16-19; Mal. 2:16).

---

[179]Barker, p. 651.
[180]Baron, p. 237.
[181]Unger, p. 140.
[182]Perowne, p. 105. Cf. Jer. 31:1-31; Ezek. 37:11-28.
[183]Unger, p. 145.

"One theological rationale for ethics, then, is awareness that God hates attitudes and actions contrary to his character. We are to love what God loves and hate what he hates."[184]

Verses 14-15 explain God's part in the people's immediate restoration, and verses 16-17 explain theirs.

E. KINGDOM JOY AND JEWISH FAVOR 8:18-23

This final section of this part of the book (chs. 7—8) returns full circle to the theme with which it began, namely, the people's concern about fasting (cf. 7:1-7). These messages began after a few Bethelites came to Jerusalem (7:2-7), and they ended with the promise that multitudes of Gentiles representing all languages would come to Jerusalem. The fasting of the past would become feasting in the future.

8:18-19   Zechariah received another message from the Lord Almighty. He promised that in the future, the sorrowful fasts that the Jews had observed in captivity would give way to joyful "feasts." Thus at the end of this section of messages on hypocritical fasting (chs. 7—8), the Lord provided at least a partial answer to the question that the messengers from Bethel had asked about the traditional fasts (7:3). In addition to the fasts in the fifth and seventh months (7:3, 5), the exiles also had commemorated the breaching of the walls of Jerusalem (2 Kings 25:3-4; Jer. 39:2) in the fourth month and the beginning of the siege of Jerusalem (2 Kings 25:1; Ezek. 24:2) in the tenth month.[185] Strict modern Jews still observe these four fasts. They seemingly died out after the second (restoration) temple was finished, but after the destruction of this temple in A.D. 70, the observance of these fasts revived.[186]

> "The manifestation of the kingdom will be attended by such a fulness [sic] of salvation that Judah will forget to commemorate the former mournful events and will only have occasion to rejoice in the benefits of grace bestowed by God."[187]

The immediate practical application of this revelation was that the people should "love truth and peace" (cf. Lev. 19:18, 34; Deut. 6:5; Ps. 31:23; Amos 5:15). They could value these ideals in the present because they were sure to come in the future. Before mourning could become joy for them, the returnees would need to love truth and peace.

8:20-22   The Lord foretold that people from one of the world's cities would contact people from another of these cities, and would plan to go up to Jerusalem immediately to worship ("entreat the favor of") the Lord (cf. 7:2). They would do this eagerly, not out of a sense of duty or obligation (cf. 2:11; Isa. 2:1-5; Mic. 4:1-5). Many people, representing many nations from around the world, "will come" to "Jerusalem" to pray and worship Yahweh Almighty.

> "Jerusalem is no longer viewed simply as the heart of Judaism but as the centre of God's dealings with all nations, and as a glorious realization of the ancient promise given to Abraham (cf. Gen. 12:3)."[188]

> "With the Davidic kingdom established, Israel will be a medium of blessing to the entire globe."[189]

8:23   In this future time of Yahweh's blessing, many Gentiles from many nations and language groups will lay hold "of a Jew." In this case, as in many others, 10 is a round number suggesting completeness (cf. Gen. 31:7; Lev. 26:26; Judg. 17:10; Ruth 4:2; 1 Sam. 1:8; Jer. 41:8). They will do so, not to persecute him (as in times past), but to ask his permission to accompany him—because God's blessing would rest on the Jews so obviously.

> "The prophecy teaches, then, that Israel will be the means of drawing the nations of the earth to the Lord in the time of the Messiah's reign of righteousness upon earth."[190]

Amillennialists understand this promise as fulfilled by many Gentiles coming to salvation in the present age through Jewish influences (e.g., Messiah, the scriptures, etc.).[191]

---

[184]Barker, p. 653.
[185]*The Illustrated . . .*, 8:93.
[186]See Keil, 2:319.
[187]Unger, p. 148.
[188]Ellis, p. 1039.
[189]Unger, p. 148.
[190]Feinberg, *God Remembers*, p. 146.
[191]E.g., McComiskey, p. 1157.

> "By way of summary ... we can see the purpose of the Spirit through the prophet in answer to the question concerning fasting. It was a twofold objective: a present and a future one. For the time then present the Spirit pointed out the sham in the fastings, the need for reality and sincerity, the vivid warning from the past sins of the forefathers, and the imperative demand for righteousness in all the relationships of life. With reference to the future Zechariah was directed to point to a day of glorious promise for Israel when the Lord would dwell in her midst, when prosperity and peace would characterize her land, when her dispersed ones would be gathered back to their homeland, and ... when her fasts would be turned into feasts, the glory of the Lord being so manifest in Israel that all the nations would be drawn to Him through His people."[192]

Chapters 7 and 8 are a fruitful source for Christian preaching since there is empty ritualism in the church today.

V. ORACLES ABOUT THE MESSIAH AND ISRAEL'S FUTURE CHS. 9—14

This part of Zechariah contains two undated oracles that are almost entirely eschatological. They expand the eschatological vision in chapters 1—8, and modify its generally optimistic view, with emphasis on Israel's purification. The prophet may have composed these chapters after the temple was completed. The phrase "on that day" occurs 18 times and points to the distant future, as is clear from their contexts. The centerpiece of this section is the messianic King who will appear and bring both judgment and blessing.

> "Just as the eight night visions (chapters 1—6) and prophecies springing out of the question of the national fasts (chapters 7 and 8) all have their fulfillment in events leading *up to and into the kingdom* (without an exception), so chapters 9—14 likewise comprehend *the same great Messianic future of Israel.*"[193]

> "One must admit that once he begins a careful study of chapters 9—14 he is immediately made aware of the change of mood, outlook, style, and composition of this part of the book compared to the first eight chapters....

> "... the prophet in this section has entered another realm of thought and perspective, much as did Isaiah in the latter part (chaps. 40—66) of his work.... The perspective ... is primarily eschatological, it lacks any indisputable connection to contemporary persons or events, and it is dominated by cryptic allusions to cosmic, redemptive, and messianic themes that have no accompanying interpretation, contrary to the case in Zech. 1—8. In short, the prophet has broken free of the mold in which he cast the material of the first part and has created a new form in which to express the grand and glorious ideas that permeate his thinking in the second part."[194]

Many critics have concluded, therefore, that a different person wrote chapters 9—14. Lindsey, however, pointed out many thematic parallels between the eight night visions and the two oracles.[195]

> "The last six chapters are very different. Gone are the bold outlines, and instead there are enigmatic references to enemies of former days, grim battles, betrayal, bitter weeping, interspersed with assurances of peace, prosperity and ultimate victory. It is probably with these chapters in mind that Jerome wrote, '... that most obscure book of the prophet Zechariah, and of the Twelve the longest ...'.[196] Obscure though it is in places, chapters 9—14 are the most quoted section of the prophets in the passion narratives of the Gospels and, next to Ezekiel, Zechariah has influenced the author of Revelation more than any other Old Testament writer."[197]

> "In the first [burden] (chaps. 9—11), the judgment through which Gentile world-power over Israel is finally destroyed, and Israel is endowed with strength to overcome all their enemies, forms the fundamental thought and centre of gravity of the prophetic description. In the second [burden] (chaps. 12—14), the judgment through which Israel itself is sifted and purged in the final great conflict with the nations, and transformed into the holy nation of Jehovah, forms the leading topic."[198]

This section of the book is also chiastic (cf. chs. 1—6).

---

[192]Feinberg, *God Remembers*, pp. 146-47.
[193]Unger, p. 238.
[194]Merrill, pp. 239-40.
[195]Lindsey, p. 1561. See also McComiskey, p. 1017.
[196]Footnote 1: Quoted by P. Lamarche, *Zacharie i-xiv: Structure, Litteraire, et Messianisme*, pp. 8-9.
[197]Baldwin, p. 59.
[198]Baron, p. 285.

```
"A      God comes to protect and bless (chs. 9—10)
    B       The people reject God's shepherd (11:1-14)
        C       The worthless shepherd hurts the flock (11:15-17)
        C'      The nations come to destroy Jerusalem (12:1-9)
    B'      The people repent and turn to God (12:10—13:6)
A'      God comes to protect and bless (13:7—14:21)"199
```

A. THE BURDEN CONCERNING THE NATIONS: THE ADVENT AND REJECTION OF MESSIAH CHS. 9—11

In this first oracle there is much change. Judgment is coming on Israel's enemies (9:1-7), but Israel will enjoy deliverance (9:8). In the midst of much blessing (9:9—10:12), Israel will experience sorrow (ch. 11). The messianic King will come, but He will be rejected.

1. The coming of the true king ch. 9

This chapter reveals the destruction of nations, the preservation of Zion, the advent of Messiah, and the deliverance and blessing of Israel.

The destruction of nations and the preservation of Zion 9:1-8

The first four verses of this poem deal with the north and the last four with the south. The first two verses and the last two speak of salvation, and the middle four speak of judgment. The passage begins and ends with references to eyes: the eyes of men (v. 1), and the eyes of God (v. 8).

9:1-2   The Lord sent a burden (Heb. *massa'*, heavy pronouncement; cf. 2 Kings 9:25-26; Jer. 23:33) to Zechariah that announced judgment and blessing.[200] It concerned the lands of "Hadrach" (Hatarikka, near Hamath),[201] "Hamath" on the Orontes River (a city farther south in Aram, cf. Amos 6:2), "Damascus" (the capital of Aram, still farther south), and "Tyre and Sidon" (Phoenician cities between Aram and Israel, cf. Ezek. 26:3-14; 28:20-24). The order of these cities in the text is from north to south. Earlier prophets had seen enemies invading Israel from the north (Isa. 41:25; Jer. 1:14-15; Ezek. 26:7), but now Yahweh would take the same route, destroying Israel's enemies as He came.

> "Originally the Mediterranean coast had been designated Israel's territory (Nu. 34:5, 6) and yet it had never been possessed by Israel. Now at last the Lord will claim it."[202]

This revelation concerned a time when all the people of the world, especially the Israelites, would be looking toward Yahweh. Some translators believed the text means that the Lord has His eye on all people, just as He has His eye on the tribes of Israel.[203] As history would show, this later took place when Alexander the Great was rapidly moving south toward Egypt, after defeating the Persians at Issus in 333 B.C. The whole world was worried about what he would do next, especially the residents of the cities of Palestine that lay in his path. All these people would have their eyes on Alexander, but he was only the Lord's instrument, so Zechariah could say that they were really looking to Yahweh. The nations would have done so unwittingly, but Israel would have looked to Him for protection.

9:3-4   Tyre had trusted in physical fortifications for her defense, and in stockpiles of "silver" and "gold" for her security. She had built a 150-foot high wall around the city, which stood on an island just offshore, following Nebuchadnezzar's earlier unsuccessful 13-year siege (cf. Isa. 23:4; Ezek. 29:18), and she had gained great wealth through commerce. There is wordplay (paronomasia) in the Hebrew text. "Tyre" (Heb. *sor*, rock) was "a fortress" (Heb. *masor*, stronghold, rampart). Nevertheless, the Lord would "dispossess" Tyre and displace "her wealth," casting it into the Mediterranean Sea. The parts of the city that would not go down into the water would go up in flames. Alexander destroyed Tyre by building a causeway from the mainland to the island city, and then *leveling* it.[204]

9:5-6   The Philistine cities farther south along the Mediterranean coast would observe Tyre's fate and fear, especially "Ekron," the northernmost of the four cities mentioned. The fifth city of the Philistine pentapolis, Gath, had lost all significance by Zechariah's time, which probably explains its omission here (cf. 2 Chron. 26:6). God would also destroy these cities and

---

[199] Dyer, p. 827.
[200] For an excursus on the meaning of this rarely used Hebrew word, see Baldwin, pp. 162-63. For a more thorough study, see P. A. H. de Boer, *An Inquiry into the Meaning of the Term Massa'*.
[201] See J. B. Pritchard, ed., *Ancient Near Eastern Texts*, pp. 282-83.
[202] Baldwin, p. 157.
[203] E.g., ibid., p. 159.
[204] For accounts of Alexander's destruction of Tyre, see G. W. Botsford and C. A. Robinson Jr., *Hellenic History*, pp. 314-20; and A. A. Trever, *History of Ancient Civilization*, 1:456-59.

9:7   The Lord would also "remove" the "blood" that these pagans ate, which was forbidden in Israel, from their mouths. He would take the unclean, "detestable" food that they ate, from their mouths. Drinking blood and eating unclean food was part of Philistine pagan worship (cf. Isa. 65:4; 66:3, 17), so the judgment in view included punishment for idolatry. Some remaining Philistines would turn to the Lord and become like the Israelites in their faith in Yahweh. As the Jebusites became incorporated into Israel in David's day (cf. 2 Sam. 24:16; 1 Chron. 21:18), so would the Philistines in the future, from Zechariah's viewpoint.

(Continuing from previous page: populate them with a mixed group of citizens. Thus He would humble the pride of the Philistines. This too happened when Alexander swept south.[205])

9:8   The Lord promised to protect His people and land—as with a band of soldiers—since enemies would oppose them. "House" is probably a metonym for the whole land including its people. No enemy would oppress them ever again because the Lord had seen the plight of His people and would defend them (cf. 4:10; Exod. 3:7; Ps. 32:8). This promise of no more oppression anticipates the second advent of Messiah.

> "For their preservation at the time of Alexander and for their future deliverance from every oppressor, Israel is indebted to the providence of God which watched over them for good."[206]

This section is a prophetic description of Yahweh's march from the north, using Alexander the Great as His instrument, destroying Gentiles nations but preserving the Jews. Zechariah later predicted the coming Roman Empire (11:4-14) and the kingdom of Messiah (chs. 12—14).

> "As history shows, the agent of the Lord's judgment was Alexander the Great. After defeating the Persians (333 B.C.), Alexander moved swiftly toward Egypt. On his march he toppled the cities in the Aramean (Syrian) interior, as well as those on the Mediterranean coast. Yet, on coming to Jerusalem, he refused to destroy it."[207]

Josephus reported that Alexander had a dream and because of it decided to spare Jerusalem.[208]

> "The first section of this . . . part of the book establishes from the start two important facts: the Lord's victory is certain, and he intends to bring back to Himself peoples long alienated from Him. These truths underlie all that follows and culminate in the universal worship of the King, the Lord of hosts, in 14:16-19."[209]

> "One should not . . . anticipate a future scenario in which God will literally march from Hadrach to Jerusalem, establishing his dominion over all opposition. What is at hand is a formulaic way of asserting an unquestionably literal establishment of YHWH's kingship in the end times, a suzerainty to be achieved in the pattern well known to Zechariah and his fellow countrymen on the human level."[210]

The advent of Zion's King 9:9-10

> "This text is one of the most messianically significant passages of all the Bible, in both the Jewish and Christian traditions. Judaism sees in it a basis for a royal messianic expectation, whereas the NT and Christianity see a prophecy of the triumphal entry of Jesus Christ into Jerusalem on the Sunday before His crucifixion (Matt. 25:5; John 12:15). Thus, though the fulfillment may be in dispute, there is unanimous conviction that a descendant of David is depicted here, one who, though humble, rides as a victor into his capital city Jerusalem. The way will have been prepared by the imposition of universal peace, following which the king will exercise dominion over the whole world."[211]

> "We have pictured for us: (1) the Agent of peace, (2) the method of peace, and (3) the kingdom of peace."[212]

9:9   The Israelites should "rejoice greatly" because their King was "coming to" them (cf. Zeph. 3:15). The first part of this verse contains three figures of speech: Zechariah personified "Zion" and "Jerusalem" as daughters rejoicing and shouting, he named the city in place of its inhabitants (metonymy), and he used the city to represent the whole nation (synecdoche). Israel's King would be a just ruler who would bring salvation with Him.

---

[205]McComiskey, p. 1162.
[206]Unger, p. 160.
[207]Barker, p. 657.
[208]Flavius Josephus, *Antiquities of the Jews*, 11:8:3-5.
[209]Baldwin, p. 162.
[210]Merrill, pp. 247-48. Cf. Chisholm, *Handbook on . . .*, p. 468.
[211]Merrill, pp. 249-50. For further explanation of the Jewish view, see Joseph Klausner, *The Messianic Idea in Israel*, pp. 203-40.
[212]Feinberg, *God Remembers*, p. 163.

> "He is victorious, not in himself or anything that he personally commands, but by the grace, and in the might, of the God of Israel.... His triumph, therefore, is the triumph of the faith of the Servant of Yahweh."[213]

> "The world's peace depends upon a Savior and His salvation."[214]

The "king" would, therefore, be "humble," not proud and boastful. Zechariah pictured this humble king riding on a gentle "donkey colt" (cf. Gen. 49:11; Matt. 21:1-9; Mark 11:1-10; Luke 19:28-38; John 12:12-15). A donkey's colt was a purebred donkey, one born of a female donkey rather than of a mule.

> "It thus qualified to be a royal mount."[215]

In the ancient Near East, rulers commonly rode donkeys if they came in peace (Judg. 5:10; 10:4; 12:14; 2 Sam. 16:2; 1 Kings 1:33), but they rode horses into war. This verse gives one reason the Israelites should rejoice: the coming of the King. Alexander the Great's coming inspired fear, but Messiah's coming would inspire joy.

9:10

> "The entire age of the church fits between Zechariah 9:9 and 9:10, just as it does between Isaiah 9:6 and 7 and after the comma in Isaiah 61:2."[216]

This verse gives a second reason for rejoicing: the establishment of the King's kingdom. The Gospel writers believed Jesus was the coming King, but they said He fulfilled only verse 9, not verse 10, during His past earthly ministry (Matt. 21:5; John 12:15; cf. Rev. 19:11-16). The Lord would end war in Israel, and would establish peace in the world, with His sovereign proclamation (cf. Isa. 2:4; 9:5-7; 11:1-10; Mic. 5:10-15). Note the worldwide extent of Messiah's kingdom predicted here.

> "The chariot, the war-horse, and the battle bow represent the whole arsenal used in ancient warfare; so the passage implies the destruction of this whole arsenal."[217]

Yahweh would rule through this King over Israel, and His dominion would be worldwide, from the Euphrates River in the East to the ends of the earth (a merism; cf. Ps. 72:8-11; Isa. 66:18). In both of these verses, Messiah contrasts with Alexander the Great, the king who initially fulfilled verses 1-8.

> "One clue to the anticipation of a twofold event—a Palm Sunday as well as eschatological procession—lies in the clear difference in tone or emphasis between v. 9 and v. 10. In v. 9 the coming one, designated king to be sure, nevertheless is described as 'humble' or 'lowly,' a most inappropriate way to speak of one whose triumph is complete in every respect. Only in v. 10 is that triumph translated into universal dominion. The lowly one of v. 9, though victorious in some sense, does not achieve the fruits of that victory until v. 10.

> "Admittedly, exegesis of the passage apart from NT considerations would never uncover the distinction just suggested between the verses."[218]

This ambiguity resulted in some pre-Christian sects of Judaism, including the Qumran community, expecting two Messiahs.[219]

The deliverance and blessing of Zion's people 9:11-17

Before Messiah can reign in peace, He must destroy all enemies, and deliver and restore His people (cf. Ps. 110).

9:11   As for the Israelites (Zion), the Lord promised to set free those of them whom their enemies would hold prisoner. He pictured this as taking them out of a dry "cistern," where they were captives ("prisoners") like Joseph and Jeremiah (Gen. 37:24; Jer. 38:6-9).

---

[213]H. G. Mitchell, "Haggai and Zechariah," in *A Critical and Exegetical Commentary on Haggai, Zechariah, Malachi and Jonah*, p. 273.
[214]Feinberg, *God Remembers*, p. 165.
[215]Baldwin, p. 166.
[216]Wiersbe, p. 467.
[217]Barker, p. 663.
[218]Merrill, p. 250.
[219]See Klausner, p. 394.

> "God's people had been in the 'pit' of Babylonian exile, but they would find themselves in a worse predicament in the end of the age. From that pit God would again retrieve them according to His faithfulness to His covenant promises."[220]

"Blood" sacrifices ratified the Abrahamic Covenant (Gen. 15:9-11) and the Mosaic Covenant (Exod. 24:3-8; 29:38-46; cf. Mark 14:24).

9:12   The Lord instructed these former Israelite prisoners of the nations—who were now free—to "return" to their Stronghold, namely: Himself (cf. Ps. 18:2; 31:3; 71:3; 91:2; 144:2; Jer. 16:19; Nah. 1:7). He Himself promised to "restore" to them "double" of what He had allowed their enemy to take from them (cf. Job 42:10). A double restoration of joy pictures a complete restoration (by metonymy; cf. Job 42:12-13; Isa. 40:2; 51:19; 61:7).

9:13-14   Yahweh, as the Divine Warrior, would use Israel as a weapon to subdue the Gentiles. "Judah" would be His "bow," and "Ephraim" would be His arrow ("fill the bow"). The "sons" of "Zion" would be His "warrior's sword." He was in complete command of Israel's affairs. He would come against the nations, like an army called to advance with a "trumpet," and like the strong southern "storm winds" (cf. Exod. 24:9-10, 15, 18). This verse saw initial, partial fulfillment when the Jews overthrew the Greeks during the Maccabean revolts in the second century B.C. But final, complete fulfillment awaits Messiah's second coming.[221]

9:15-16   The Lord would "defend" Israel, and would cause His people to be victorious over their enemies. The death of these enemies would be a sacrifice to Him. However, the Israelites would experience deliverance and victory, like "a flock" of sheep protected by their Shepherd. They would be precious and beautiful ("sparkling") in the Lord's land, as jewels in "a crown" as they circled Jerusalem's hills. They would "trample on the sling stones" (v. 15) used in warfare, and would become precious "stones" in the King's "crown" (v. 16).

9:17   The Israelites would be very attractive then. They would all enjoy plenty of the best food and drink; they would "flourish" and prosper, having an abundance of all that human beings need.

An amillennial view that illustrates a spiritual, as contrasted with a literal, interpretation follows:

> "The citizens of Christ's kingdom as well as God's ancient people are a landed people. Hebrews 3 and 5 make this clear, affirming the believer's landedness in the gospel—'at-homeness in Christ.' Today, the fruit of the land that causes its citizens to flourish is the fruit of salvation."[222]

2. The restoration of the true people ch. 10

The first part of this oracle focused particularly on the true King who would come and exercise sovereignty over the nations (ch. 9). Now the emphasis changes to the people of the King, the Israelites, who will return to the Promised Land and rule with the King (ch. 10). Like the revelation in chapter 9, this chapter also has a near and a far fulfillment: the *near* being the revival of Israel's power under Judas Maccabeus in the second century B.C., and the *far* being the return and reign of Messiah.

> "Chapter 9 presents the victory of God's people from the positive side for the most part, showing how the true Israel shall be made strong by the Lord and shall prevail. Without abandoning this point of view, chapter 10 brings greater emphasis to bear upon the negative side of the victory, namely, how the enemies shall be brought low. Yet particular stress is at the same time laid upon the gathering of the scattered Israelites."[223]

10:1   The Lord urged His people, in the day of blessing just described, to "ask" Him to send "rain" when they needed it in the "spring," when they sowed their seed. He promised to send it, and it would cause their crops and other "vegetation in the field" to grow (cf. 9:11; Deut. 11:13-14). Asking *Him* is only reasonable, since He is the One who creates "storm clouds." The Canaanites gave credit to Baal for sending rain and producing fertility, but Yahweh was the true rainmaker (cf. Jer. 14:22; Amos 5:8). Since rain is often a symbol of many types of blessing in the Old Testament, spiritual as well as physical blessing is probably in view here (cf. 12:10; Isa. 55:10-12; Hos. 6:3; Joel 2:21-32). Many good commentators included this verse with 9:11-17 because of the continuation of thought. However, all of chapter 10 continues the thought of the previous pericope.

10:2   In contrast to the only true God, "*teraphim*" (household idols; cf. Gen. 31:19; Judg. 17:5, 14; 18:5; 1 Sam. 15:23; Hos. 3:4) only led people into "iniquity," and "diviners" saw misleading "visions" and "dreams" (cf. Deut. 18:9-14; Jer. 23:30-32; 27:9-10).

---

[220]Merrill, p. 258.
[221]See H. A. Ironside, *Notes on the Minor Prophets*, p. 394.
[222]McComiskey, p. 1174.
[223]Leupold, p. 189.

Their "comfort" was worthless. Consequently, the people who rely on these false indicators of God's will "wander like" shepherdless "sheep," and experience much needless trouble (cf. Mark 6:34).

> "A modern parallel is the renewed interest in magic, spiritism and other survivals of primitive times. The more widespread modern equivalent is to ignore God altogether and tacitly to assume that no problem is beyond man's unaided power to solve."[224]

10:3   The Lord was angry with these false "shepherds" (*rulers*, i.e.: kings, princes, nobles, prophets, and priests) and the other leaders who led His sheep astray like rams (cf. 1 Sam. 28:3-7; 1 Kings 16:31; 22:6-12; 2 Kings 1:2; 16:15; 21:6). The shepherds and rams may also include the foreign rulers under which the Jews had to live.[225] The Lord would visit "His flock," namely, the "house of Judah" (the Israelites), and He would make His people like the "majestic" war "horse" He rode "in battle" to defeat His enemies. In other words, He would empower the Israelites. The weak sheep would become as strong as horses. The battle of Armageddon is probably in view (cf. 12:1-9; 14:1-8).

10:4   From the house of Judah "will come the cornerstone" of the building (kingdom) He would build, namely: Messiah (cf. 3:9; Gen. 49:10; Ps. 118:22; Isa. 28:16; Jer. 30:21; Acts 4:11; Eph. 2:20; 1 Pet. 2:1-8). "The cornerstone" (Heb. *pinnah*) was a figure of a leader who would stabilize a nation and keep it from sliding down a slippery slope (cf. Judg. 20:2; 1 Sam. 14:38; Isa. 19:13). Messiah would also be like a "tent peg" (Heb. *yathed*), in that He would hold the tent (kingdom) firmly in place (cf. Judg. 4:21-22; Isa. 22:23-24; Acts 15:16). The Hebrew word also describes a peg inside a tent on which people hung beautiful things that glorified their homes (cf. 6:13; Isa. 22:22-24; Ezek. 15:3). Messiah would also be Yahweh's "bow of battle," by which He would destroy His enemies (cf. 9:13; Ps. 45:5; Rev. 19:11-16). All these figures picture the strong, stable, victorious, and trustworthy nature of Messiah's rule.

> "This verse constitutes one of the most far-reaching and meaningful Messianic prophecies in the Old Testament in which the seer summarizes a number of declarations by the former prophet [i.e., Isaiah], setting forth the character and ministry of Israel's Redeemer-King."[226]

From the house of Judah would also go forth (depart) "every" oppressing "ruler" (Heb. *noges*, cf. 9:8; Exod. 3:7; Isa. 3:12; 14:2; 60:17; Dan. 11:20).

> "Because the Messiah intervenes in the manner to be noted, every oppressor will depart from Judah. Cause and effect are clearly stated."[227]

10:5   These Israelites would be like "mighty men . . . in battle" (cf. David's mighty men). They would subdue the Lord's enemies in battle successfully because Yahweh would be "with them." The opposing adversaries would be defeated and shamed, even though they fought from positions of strength. The Lord's infantry would defeat the world's seemingly superior cavalry.

> "It is a great mistake to suppose that all will be accomplished by Jehovah single-handed."[228]

> "The scene is that of the *strengthening* of the Jews in Palestine at the time of the invasion from the North under 'the beast' (Dan. 7:8) in conjunction with the events of Armageddon (Rev. 16:14; 19:17-20)."[229]

10:6   The Lord "will strengthen," deliver ("save"), and restore ("bring back") "the house of Judah" and "the house of Joseph" (Ephraim), both the former Northern and Southern Kingdoms. He would do this simply because He "had compassion on them," not because they deserved His blessing. He would restore the Israelites to a condition similar to the one they enjoyed before He sent them into captivity, including sovereignty within their own homeland. He would do this because He is Yahweh, their God. He "will answer" their prayers for His help.

10:7   Then the Israelites, who previously had been weak from idolatry and apostasy, will be strong. They and "their children will rejoice in the LORD" when He saves them (Ps. 32:11; Phil. 4:4).

---

[224]Baldwin, p. 171.
[225]See Chambers, p. 78, in Lange's commentary.
[226]Unger, p. 177.
[227]Feinberg, *God Remembers*, p. 185.
[228]Kelly, p. 472.
[229]Unger, p. 180.

10:8	The Lord, the true Shepherd of His flock, "will" simply "whistle," and His people will follow Him because He had redeemed them (Exod. 12; Isa. 35:10; Mic. 6:4; John 10:11-16; 1 Pet. 1:18-19). They will again "be as numerous as they" had been in the days of their greatest prosperity.

> "Just as redemption, that is, election, theologically preceded the actual exodus escape from Egypt (Ex. 2:24; 3:7-8; 4:22-23; 6:2-8), so it is on the basis of an already effected redemption that YHWH's people will enter into the eschatological land of promise."[230]

10:9	When the Lord scattered His people like seed "among the" other "peoples" of the world, they would "remember" Him, even though they lived "far" from the Promised Land (cf. John 12:24; 1 Cor. 15:36). Not only would the Lord remember them (the meaning of Zechariah's name), but "they will remember" Him. "They" and "their children will live" (enter into new life) and return to the land. Sowing anticipates reaping a harvest and so connotes hope.

> ". . . even after Israel had been restored to the land after the Babylonian exile, the prospect of a regathered, reunited nation still appeared in Zechariah 10:9-12. The importance of this passage and its late postexilic date should not be lost by those who interpret the promise of the land spiritually or as a temporal blessing which has since been forfeited by a rebellious nation due to her failure to keep her part of the conditional (?) covenant. On the contrary, this hope burned brighter as Israel became more and more hopelessly scattered."[231]

10:10	Yahweh "will bring" the Israelites "back from the land of Egypt" (to Israel's south—where they had been slaves), and "from" the land of "Assyria" (to the north—where they had been exiles), namely: from all over the world (cf. Isa. 11:11-16; 19:23; Hos. 11:10). Probably Zechariah used Assyria as his example of a northern enemy, rather than Babylonia, because Assyria and Egypt were Israel's most persistent and hostile enemies historically. God "will bring them" back into the fruitful Promised Land, "into . . . Gilead" with its rich pastures east of the Jordan River, "and Lebanon" with its mighty forests west of the Jordan. Again, the whole land is in view.

> "The Lebanon . . . is referred to in the Old Testament as a symbol of strength, dignity and splendour (e.g., 2 Kings 19:23; Isa. 35:2), as are the mountains of Gilead. Hence the two are sometimes also mentioned together to denote power and pride . . . (Jer. 22:6). In our verse too this combination may be intended to demonstrate the future power and glory of the Messianic kingdom of Israel."[232]

Eventually there would be no more room because so many blessed Israelites would live there (cf. Isa. 49:19-21; 54:2-3).

10:11	Yahweh's representative, Messiah, "would pass through the sea" of His people's "distress" and banish it, as He had done to the Red Sea when the Israelites left Egypt in the Exodus (and as Jesus did when He calmed the Sea of Galilee). He would humble all of Israel's enemies, of which Egypt and Assyria were only representatives. The Gentile leaders of the world, symbolized by Egypt's "scepter," would no longer hold sway over Israel in the world.
10:12	Messiah "will" also "strengthen" the Israelites "in the LORD." "They will walk" all over the earth (exercise dominion over it) "in His name" (as His representatives and in harmony with His character). All of this was a promise from Yahweh.

3. The rejection of the true king ch. 11

Chapters 9 and 10 picture blessing and prosperity, but chapter 11 paints a scene of sin and punishment.

> "Preceding the fulfillment of the prophecies of blessing are the apostasy of Israel and their rejection of the Good Shepherd, their Messiah, with the consequent visitation of God upon them in dire punishment."[233]

Several shepherds are in view in this chapter: the wailing shepherds (vv. 1-3), the true Shepherd (vv. 4-14), and the false shepherd (vv. 15-17).

The announcement of doom 11:1-3

11:1	The prophet announced in vigorous poetic language that Lebanon's famous "cedars" would perish. The Israelites referred to the royal palace in Jerusalem as "Lebanon" because it contained so much cedar from Lebanon (Jer. 22:23; cf. 1 Kings 7:2).

---

[230] Merrill, p. 276.
[231] Kaiser, p. 255.
[232] *The Illustrated . . .*, 8:95.
[233] Feinberg, *God Remembers*, p. 197.

	The Talmud spoke of the second temple as "Lebanon" for the same reason.[234] The "second temple" refers to the temple that Ezra rebuilt, and that Herod the Great refurbished, which stood until A.D. 70. The cedar tree also became a symbol of the royal house of Judah (Ezek. 17:3-4, 12-13).
11:2	Likewise the "cypress" (juniper, pine) and "oaks of Bashan" should wail, because they too would perish in the coming devastation. Bashan was famous for its oak forests (cf. Isa. 2:13; Ezek. 27:6). Earlier, Zechariah combined Lebanon and Bashan to indicate the whole land (10:10). All these trees suggest the people of the land as well as the land itself. A judgment that would affect the whole land of Palestine and all its people, including its rulers, is in view.

> "Perhaps next in prominence to shepherd as metaphor for king is that of a plant, especially a tree [cf. Judg. 9:7-15; Isa. 10:33-34; Ezek. 31:3-18; Dan. 4:10, 23]."[235]

The cedar tree, in particular, is a metaphor for a king (cf. 2 Kings 14:9; Isa. 14:8; Ezek. 17:3; Amos 2:9).

11:3	The "shepherds" and "lions" (the rulers and leaders of Israel, cf. Jer. 25:34-38) would "wail" because a coming destruction would leave no pasture for their flocks, and no lairs or food for beasts.

> "The pride of the Jordan is not the river itself; this expression personifies it, referring to that in which the Jordan may take pride: the topography through which it flows—its beautiful valleys and hills—hence the land itself."[236]

In view of what follows in verses 4-14, verses 1-3 seem to be a description of the devastation of Palestine due to the rejection of the Messiah. Another view is that it is a lament over the destruction of the nations' power and arrogance described in chapter 10. This prediction had an initial fulfillment in the Roman destruction of Jerusalem and the scattering of the Jews in A.D. 70. Its complete fulfillment, however, lies in the future, specifically the destruction that will overtake the land and its people in the Tribulation.

The fate of the Good Shepherd 11:4-14

The reason for the devastation of the people and the land just described now becomes apparent. It is the people's rejection of the messianic Shepherd-King (cf. Isa. 42; 49; 50; 53). The Lord would graciously give His people another good leader (vv. 4-6), but they would reject the Good Shepherd that He would provide for them (vv. 7-14).

11:4	Yahweh, Zechariah's God, instructed the prophet to present himself as *a shepherd* assigned to care for ("pasture") a "flock *doomed* to slaughter." This may mean that the prophet was to act out a skit for his audience.[237] However, it seems more likely, in view of what follows, that Zechariah spoke for God, and sometimes as Messiah, as though *He* were the Shepherd. He seems to have been presenting an allegory that was the product of a visionary experience (cf. Jer. 1:10; 25:15-38).[238]
11:5	"Those who" bought the sheep would then "slay them" (Heb. feminine) and "go unpunished." This was bad because these were female sheep, ewes, intended for breeding and not for butchering. The butchers represent the foreign rulers who took over the Israelites, persecuted them, and had not paid the full penalty for their abusive treatment of them (Gen. 12:3). Those who sold the sheep were Israel's former rulers and leaders who, by their sins, had set the people up for divine judgment by foreigners.
11:6	The Lord's displeasure was the real reason for the Israelites' misery. He would "no longer" take "pity on them." He would cause the men of Israel to become dependent on "another's power" (kingdom: Roman Empire) and on "another king," evidently a foreign despot. This king and his followers would strike the land, but Yahweh would not deliver His people from them.

> "History demonstrates that these conditions did take place after Israel's rejection of their Messiah."[239]

The ruler in view was Caesar, and the striking took place in A.D. 70.

---

[234]Baron, pp. 378-79.
[235]Merrill, p. 285.
[236]McComiskey, p. 1189.
[237]E. Cashdan, "Zechariah," in *The Twelve Minor Prophets*, p. 314; Unger, p. 191.
[238]Leupold, p. 207; Feinberg, *God Remembers*, p. 201.
[239]Ibid., p. 204.

11:7	Zechariah proceeded to carry out his assignment from the Lord (v. 4). He spoke as a shepherd of the sheep "*doomed* to slaughter," "the afflicted" sheep of the "flock," and so represented Israel's Shepherd, Messiah. The two shepherd's staffs, that he named "Favor" (Heb. *no'am*, pleasantness, graciousness) and "Union" (Heb. *hobhelim*, binders, unifiers), represented God's blessing and the unity of the flock (Israel; cf. Ezek. 37:15-28).

> "The Eastern shepherd carried a rod or stout club hewed from a tree to beat away wild beasts attacking the sheep and a crooked staff for retrieving the sheep from difficult places [cf. Ps. 23:4]."[240]

11:8	Zechariah, as God's representative, did away with "three shepherds" that had been leading his flock within the first "month" that he took charge of the sheep. These appear to have been real shepherds and a real month. At the very least, Zechariah's action prefigured that of Messiah, in taking over the leadership of His flock from other leaders of Israel who did not appreciate His leadership. Who these shepherds were or will be has been the subject of much debate. Some commentators identified specific kings, either Jewish or Gentile, who failed the Lord and were set aside before or during the siege of Jerusalem in A.D. 70.[241] History records little about the Jews between 350 and 200 B.C. The three initial fulfillment shepherds could have lived then, but we may have no record of their activities. Other interpreters, including myself, believe the three shepherds refer to three classes of leaders, probably Israel's elders, chief priests, and scribes (cf. Luke 9:22).[242] The Luke 9:22 reference is particularly significant, since there Jesus named these three groups of leaders as those who would reject Him. Unger held that the one month was the time preceding the crucifixion of Jesus Christ, which sealed the fate of Israel.[243] Another view is that the shepherds represent all of Israel's unfaithful human leaders.[244] Many commentators remarked on the difficulty of this verse, which Baldwin called "probably the most enigmatic in the whole Old Testament."[245] Over 40 different interpretations of it appear in the commentaries.

It is also difficult to identify the antecedent of "them." Did Zechariah (Messiah) grow weary of the sheep (cf. Isa. 1:13-14), and did they detest him? Another interpretation sees the antecedent of "them" to be the three groups of leaders (kings). Perhaps "them" refers generally to both the leaders and the sheep.

11:9	Zechariah, as God's representative, turned "them" over to their fate, though that meant that some of them would die, suffer annihilation, and devour one another. The Jews did eat one another during the siege of Jerusalem in the first century A.D.[246] And they will evidently do so again during the Tribulation.

> "By withholding his leadership the shepherd abandoned the people to the consequences of their rejection of him: death, and mutual destruction. He simply let things take their course."[247]

11:10	Zechariah then chopped his staff "Favor" into pieces, picturing the end of the favorable pastoral care that he had provided. The covenant in view is none of the biblical covenants, since God never breaks His promises. It must refer to the security that He had been providing and the restraint that He had been exercising in relation to Israel thus far.

> "The term 'covenant' is here used in a looser sense, not as descriptive of a formal agreement entered into by contracting parties, but to indicate that, when the peoples round about Israel did her no harm, this was due to the fact that God had put them under as strong a restraint as might be exerted upon a nation by a covenant solemnly sworn to."[248]

11:11	The faithful Israelites who were listening to Zechariah, "the afflicted of" God's "flock" (cf. v. 7), realized that what he had done in breaking the staff was in harmony with "the word of the LORD." Another view is that the afflicted were a group within

---

[240] Unger, p. 194.
[241] E.g., Baron, p. 396, n. 1; Ellis, p. 1045; Mitchell, p. 307; and Merrill, p. 293.
[242] E.g., E. Henderson, *The Minor Prophets*, p. 442; Unger, p. 195; Feinberg, *God Remembers*, p. 206; idem, "Zechariah," p. 908; and Lindsey, p. 1565.
[243] Unger, p. 195.
[244] Baldwin, p. 183.
[245] Ibid., p. 181.
[246] Josephus, *The Wars of the Jews*, 6:3:3-4.
[247] Baldwin, p. 184.
[248] Leupold, p. 214.

Zechariah's society, not the whole postexilic community.[249] God had promised in the Mosaic Law that if His people apostatized—He would cast them off, temporarily, and allow the nations to punish them (cf. Matt. 23:13, 23-24, 33-39).

> "The 'poor of the flock' i.e. the 'remnant according to the election of grace' (Rom. 11:5), are those Jews who did not wait for the manifestation of Christ in glory but believed on Him at His first coming and subsequently. Of them it is said that they 'waited upon me,' and 'knew.'"[250]

11:12	Since Zechariah was terminating his protection of the flock, he asked the sheep to pay him his wages or, if they refused, to keep what they owed him.

> "He is more concerned about making the flock feel that he is done with it than he is about money."[251]

The sheep "weighed out 30" shekels "of silver" as his pay. This was the price of a gored slave in the ancient Near East (Exod. 21:32) and, though a substantial amount, was a pittance in view of all that the Shepherd had done for the sheep.[252] Their act was as shamelessly insulting as their general reaction to His ministry as a whole had been. To offer him this wage was far worse than simple outward rejection (cf. Matt. 26:15). It was the equivalent of telling the Shepherd that they could buy a dead slave who would be as useful to them as He had been. This response shows how unworthy the people were of His solicitude.

11:13	The Lord instructed Zechariah to "throw" the 30 shekels of silver "to the potter" since it was, sarcastically, such a handsome ("magnificent") price. His service had been worth far more than that. So Zechariah threw the 30 shekels of silver to the potter in the temple. Evidently the setting of Zechariah's visionary allegory was the temple courtyard. Throwing something to the potter was evidently a proverbial way of expressing disdain for it, since potters were typically poor and lowly craftsmen.[253]

> "The fulfillment of this prophecy in Matthew 27:3-10 is proof enough that the money was flung down in the temple and immediately taken up by the priests to purchase a field *of a potter* for a burying ground for the poor."[254]

Matthew attributed this prophecy to Jeremiah (Matt. 27:9-10). Probably Matthew was referring to Jeremiah 32:6-9, which he condensed, using mainly the phraseology of Zechariah 11:12-13 because of its similarity to Judas' situation. Joining (conflating) two quotations from two Old Testament books and assigning them to one prophet follows the custom of mentioning only the more notable prophet. Compare Mark 1:2-3, in which Isaiah 40:3 and Malachi 3:1 are quoted but are assigned to Isaiah.[255]

> "Like the earlier prophecy of the King (ix. 9), the prophecy of the Shepherd is remarkable for its literal fulfillment. The 'thirty pieces of silver' were literally the 'goodly price' paid for Him, 'whom they of the children of Israel did value.' 'The potter' was literally the recipient of it, as the purchase money of his exhausted field for an unclean purpose (Matt. xxvii. 5-10)."[256]

11:14	Zechariah then symbolically broke his second staff, "Union," indicating the end of the unity that bound the Jews together. Just before the destruction of Jerusalem in A.D. 70, the Jews broke up into parties that were very hostile to one another. This condition accelerated their destruction by the Romans.[257] Evidently fighting among the Jews will also be common in the

---

[249]McComiskey, p. 1194.
[250]*The New Scofield . . .*, p. 973.
[251]Leupold, p. 216.
[252]See E. Reiner, "Thirty Pieces of Silver," *Journal of the American Oriental Society* 88 (January-March 1968):186-90.
[253]Unger, p. 200; Leupold, p. 217.
[254]Unger, p. 200.
[255]For further discussion, see Hobart E. Freeman, *An Introduction to the Old Testament Prophets*, pp. 340-42.
[256]Perowne, p. 127.
[257]Chambers, p. 86, in Lange's commentary.

Tribulation. The order of events is significant, and it was historical: the breaking of God's favor on His people, their rejection of the Shepherd, and the breaking of their unity.[258] We know that this destruction will not be permanent, however, because of other promises that God will reunite and restore His people, and that He will not cast them off permanently (e.g., Rom. 11; et al.).

"Responsibility for human chaos lies squarely on human shoulders. God has offered men His shepherd, but they have rejected Him, to their own irreparable loss."[259]

The appearance of the bad shepherd 11:15-17

"The full fate of Israel is not recounted in the rejection of the good Shepherd God raised up to tend them. The complete tale of woe centers in their acceptance of the bad shepherd God will raise up to destroy them. The one dark episode centers in the events of Messiah's first advent and death, followed by the dissolution of the Jewish state (Zech. 11:1-14). The other tragic experience will occur in the events connected with Messiah's second advent and glory, and deals with the nation's final time of unparalleled trouble (Zech. 11* [sic] 15-17) previous to her entrance into kingdom blessing."[260]

11:15   The Lord next directed Zechariah to present himself as a "foolish" (worthless, v. 17, i.e., morally deficient, cf. Prov. 1:7) "shepherd," since his flock had rejected the Good Shepherd (cf. Ezek. 34:3-4).

11:16   In his new role, Zechariah represented one who would fail to do for the sheep all that a good shepherd would do. Instead he would be self-serving. Israel's preference for Barabbas over Jesus showed her willingness, many years later, to accept a bad individual in place of a good one.

"When one removes 'not' from the sentence, he has an enlightening description of a truly effective pastoral ministry in the church today. (1) 'care for the lost . . .' or . . . 'care for those in the process of being ruined or destroyed'; (2) 'seek the young . . . [or] 'the scattered'; (3) 'heal the injured,' and (4) 'feed the healthy.'"[261]

Tearing off the hoofs of the sheep probably represents the avaricious shepherd, searching for the last edible morsel that he can extract from his charges whom he has consumed.[262]

11:17   God pronounced judgment on "the worthless shepherd" for abandoning the flock (cf. Jer. 50:35-37). This condemnation applies to all the evil kings of Israel and Judah who had let their people down, but one particular individual is in view primarily. Yahweh would paralyze this man's power ("arm") and nullify his intelligence ("eye"), rendering him incapable of hurting others or defending himself.

Who is this bad shepherd? Some students of history have seen Bar Kokhba as at least a partial fulfillment. He led the ineffective Jewish revolt against the Romans in A.D. 132-135, and some in his day hailed him as the Messiah. Others see the fulfillment in "all those leaders of Israel, who, under the guise of shepherds, misled and harmed the poor flock . . . ever since Zechariah's day, especially since the time that the nation has rejected the Christ."[263] However, the ultimate fulfillment must be the Antichrist, who will make a covenant with Israel—but then break it and proceed to persecute the Jews (Ezek. 34:2-4; Dan. 9:27; 11:36-39; John 5:43; 2 Thess. 2:3-10; Rev. 13:1-8). Perhaps the whole collective leadership of Israel, from Zechariah's time forward—culminating in Antichrist—is in view.[264]

"The judgment here (vs. 17) brings to a close the cycle of prophecy which began with judgment (9:1). Judgment has gone from the circumference (the nations) to the center (Israel); Zechariah will yet reveal that in blessing the direction will be from the center (Israel) to the circumference (the nations) as in chapter 14."[265]

---

[258] See Feinberg, *God Remembers*, p. 211.
[259] Baldwin, p. 187.
[260] Unger, p. 202.
[261] Barker, p. 679.
[262] Unger, p. 204.
[263] Leupold, p. 219.
[264] Merrill, p. 303.
[265] Feinberg, *God Remembers*, pp. 213-14.

"With this climactic scene the first prophetic burden describing the first advent and rejection of Messiah, the Shepherd-King (chapters 9—11) comes to a close. The way is thus opened for the second burden and the second advent and acceptance of Messiah, the King (chapters 12—14)."[266]

B. THE BURDEN CONCERNING ISRAEL: THE ADVENT AND ACCEPTANCE OF MESSIAH CHS. 12—14

This last section of the book contrasts initial judgments on Israel with ultimate deliverance, restoration, and blessing.

"As a portion of the prophetic Scriptures it is second to none in importance in this book or in any other Old Testament book. It is indispensable to an understanding of the events of the last days for Israel—the time of the Great Tribulation and the establishment of God's kingdom on earth."[267]

The repetition of "in that day" and its equivalent 19 times in these three chapters sets these events quite clearly in the eschaton (end times).

"This prophetic time indicator is equivalent to 'the day of the Lord' and denotes precisely *that future period when the Lord will openly and publicly manifest His power in delivering Israel from her enemies and establishing her in millennial peace and prosperity.*"[268]

Two main events are in view in this oracle: the final siege of Jerusalem and the return of Messiah to the earth to defeat His enemies and establish His kingdom. The nations of the earth play a major role in what these chapters predict. These events follow in time Israel's acceptance of the evil shepherd predicted in 11:15-17.

"The major difference between the two oracles (chap. 11 excepted) is that 12—14 expands greatly on the themes of 9—10 and introduces a cosmic, universalistic motif that is not as clearly perceived in the latter. Moreover, 12—14 focuses on the messianic aspect of the eschatological redemption, going so far as to identify YHWH Himself as the messianic figure (12:10-14; 13:7-9)."[269]

1. The repentance of Judah ch. 12

This chapter consists of two parts: Israel's deliverance (vv. 1-9) and Israel's national conversion (vv. 10-14). These events will happen sequentially and very close together.

Israel's deliverance 12:1-9

12:1   "The burden . . . concerning Israel" introduces chapters 12—14 as "The burden . . . against the land of Hadrach" (9:1) did chapters 9—11. By describing Yahweh as the Creator of "the heavens," "earth," and "man," Zechariah reminded his audience of God's authority, and ability, to accomplish what He predicted, in this three-chapter oracle. He is the master over all things celestial, terrestrial, and human.

> "Here at the brink of a new age it is important to know that the same God who brought everything into existence in the first place is well able to usher in the new creation of a restored people in a renewed and universal kingdom."[270]

12:2   The Lord "will make Jerusalem" like "a cup" of strong wine to the nations ("all the peoples around"); when they try to consume Jerusalem (a metonymy for all Israel), it will cause them to reel. Jerusalem had previously drunk the cup of the Lord's wrath (Isa. 51:17, 22; Jer. 25:15-17, 28), but now it will be the nations' turn to drink it. Their "siege" of "Jerusalem" will extend to all the surrounding territory of "Judah." The time in view is after the Lord regathers the Israelites to their land (ch. 10).

12:3   "In that day" Jerusalem will also be like "a heavy stone" when the nations try "to lift" and carry it away; they will injure themselves when they try to do so. In that day, "all the nations of the earth will" gather together against Jerusalem (cf. 14:2; Joel 3:9-16; Rev. 16:16-21).

---

[266] Unger, p. 205.
[267] Feinberg, *God Remembers*, p. 218.
[268] Unger, p. 210.
[269] Merrill, p. 310.
[270] Ibid., p. 312.

> ". . . even if all the peoples of the earth should attempt to conquer Jerusalem, they will turn away, bloodied by their futile efforts."[271]

12:4 The Lord will cause the weapons that Israel's enemies used to destroy the city to be ineffective, and He will make the hostile soldiers crazy (cf. Deut. 28:28; Judg. 5:22). In this way, He "will watch over the house of Judah" (the Israelites; cf. Ps. 32:8; 33:18).

12:5 The leaders of Israel's groups outside Jerusalem will realize that Yahweh Almighty, "their God," is making the people of Jerusalem strong supporters of them.

12:6 "In that day," the Lord will not only preserve His people from the attacks of their enemies, but He will also make them effective as they aggressively attacked them (cf. Judg. 15:3-5; Esth. 9:1-28).

12:7 Yahweh will defend the outlying areas "of Judah first," so the people from David's line and the residents of Jerusalem would not conclude that they were more important in God's sight (cf. Jer. 9:23-24; 1 Cor. 1:29, 31; 12:22-26; 2 Cor. 10:17). All the Jews will see that it was "the LORD" who was responsible for their deliverance. This would evidently end their fighting among themselves (cf. 11:6).

12:8 As part of His defense of them, the Lord will strengthen the "feeble" among the people, so that they will be as strong as "David," the mighty warrior. The Davidic rulers will also receive supernatural strength and will be "like God," as "the angel of the LORD" who was going "before (in front of) them" (cf. Exod. 14:19; 23:20; 32:34; 33:2, 14-15, 22; 1 Sam. 29:9; 2 Sam. 14:17, 20; 19:27).

12:9 "In that day," the Lord "will set about" destroying "all" of Israel's enemies, and He will be successful.

> ". . . we place the entire passage in the time of the Great Tribulation and more specifically in the Battle of Armageddon, when the nations of the earth will make their last frantic effort to blot Israel out of existence, only to be met by the most crushing defeat at the hands of the Lord of hosts Himself."[272]

An amillennial explanation of the passage follows.

> ". . . it covers all time from that in which the prophet spoke to the end of days. What is said concerning Judah applies to the people of God of all times. The claims made for Jerusalem's future find their ultimate fulfillment in the true Zion of God—His church; in fact, they can be applied to Jerusalem only insofar as she for a time harbored the church of God. The whole passage speaks of God's sovereign care and protection of the church of the Old and the New Testaments through the ages and more particularly of the church's victory rather than the victory of Judah after the flesh."[273]

Israel's national conversion 12:10-14

The focus now changes from physical to spiritual deliverance (cf. Deut. 30:1-10).

12:10 The Lord also promised to "pour out on" the Davidic rulers and the inhabitants of Jerusalem, representing all the Israelites, a spirit of remorse. "Grace" will be the motive for this outpouring, and "supplication" to God (for what the Jews had done to their Messiah) will be the result. This God-given conviction will cause them to "mourn" when they look (in faith) *to* Him (better than *on* Him) "whom they" had formerly "pierced" (i.e., slain; cf. Num. 21:9; Isa. 45:22; 53:5; John 3:14-15; 19:34).

> "It is not so much a mourning for the act committed, but for the Person involved. Compare John 19:37; Revelation 1:7."[274]

> "The idea is that they will humble themselves and recognize that they were saved by another whom they pierced."[275]

---

[271]McComiskey, p. 1210.
[272]Feinberg, *God Remembers*, p. 228.
[273]Leupold, p. 234.
[274]Feinberg, *God Remembers*, p. 231.
[275]Smith, p. 277.

They would mourn as one mourns over the death of one's only (beloved, cf. Gen. 22:2; Jer. 6:26; Amos 8:10) son or his or her firstborn son.

> "It is a picture of penitence as vivid and accurate as any found anywhere in the Scriptures."[276]

The Jews will do this, either just before the Messiah returns to the earth, or when He returns to the earth (cf. Isa. 27:9; 59:20-21; Jer. 31:31-37; Amos 9:11-15; Rom. 11:25-27; Rev. 1:7). The "spirit" in view will be a result of the ministry of the Holy Spirit, who conveys *grace* (compassion; cf. Heb. 10:29) and calls forth *supplication* (prayer; cf. Isa. 32:15; 44:3; 59:20-21; Jer. 31:31, 33; Ezek. 36:26-27; 39:29; Joel 2:28-29). The coming of the messianic kingdom is contingent on Israel's repentance, God's sovereign control, and the Spirit's enabling grace.[277]

The unusual combination "they will look to *Me* whom they have pierced" and "they will mourn for *Him*" suggests two different individuals, but the deity of the Messiah solves this problem. Yahweh Himself would suffer for the people in the person of Messiah. The suffering could be figurative (they wounded His holiness) or substitutionary (He died in place of others). Other references to this text point to a substitute suffering (e.g., John 19:37; Rev. 1:7; cf. Isa. 53:5, 8).

> ". . . like Thomas their excruciating and inexpressibly penetrating cry of deepest contrition will be, 'My Lord and my God!' (John 20:28)."[278]

12:11   "In that day there will be great mourning in Jerusalem"—and undoubtedly elsewhere throughout Israel. Zechariah compared this mourning to "the mourning of Hadadrimmon in the plain of Megiddo," an event that scholars have had trouble identifying. "Hadadrimmon" is a compound of two Amorite or Canaanite divine names, "Hadad" being the storm god and "Rimmon" the thunder god.[279] Hadadrimmon may have been an important though presently unknown individual, a place near Megiddo (cf. 14:10; Josh. 15:32; 19:7),[280] or a pagan deity (cf. 2 Kings 5:18).[281] The devotees of the Canaanite god Baal mourned his "dying" each winter and then celebrated his "resurrection" each spring. Probably the place where King Josiah died, and or where the people mourned his premature death near there, as late as the writing of Chronicles, is in view (cf. 2 Chron. 35:20-27).[282]

12:12-14   All the Israelites, "the land," will mourn; this will be a national repentance. The repeated phrases "every family by itself" and "their wives by themselves" solemnize the mourning and underline its genuineness.

> "The wives are spoken of as mourning apart because in public lamentations the custom prevailed of separating into groups, also according to sex."[283]

> "The closest relationship is as nothing in [the] presence of sin and God as its judge. Each must be alone."[284]

This would not be a national media event staged by the leaders of Israel to make a show, but individuals everywhere throughout the nation would sincerely voice their remorse.

> "Individually and corporately, this is the experience of Leviticus 16 (the Day of Atonement) and Psalm 51 (a penitential psalm) on a national scale. . . . Isaiah 53:1-9 could well be their confession on the great occasion."[285]

The houses of "David" and of his son "Nathan" represent the political branches of the nation, though not just the kings, as reference to Solomon might have suggested (cf. 2 Sam. 5:14). Feinberg believed that this Nathan was the prophet of David's day, so he represents the prophets in Israel who will repent.[286] This is a minority view. The houses of "Levi" and of his

---

[276] Chambers, p. 94, in Lange's commentary.

[277] See Stanley D. Toussaint and Jay A. Quine, "No, Not Yet: The Contingency of God's Promised Kingdom," *Bibliotheca Sacra* 164:654 (April-June 2007):131-47.

[278] Unger, p. 217.

[279] Merrill, p. 323.

[280] Barker, p. 684; Merrill, p. 324; Unger, p. 219; Feinberg, *God Remembers*, p. 232; Leupold, p. 240; McComiskey, p. 1215.

[281] K. N. Schoville, *Biblical Archaeology in Focus*, p. 444.

[282] Feinberg, "Zechariah," p. 909.

[283] Leupold, p. 241.

[284] Kelly, p. 486.

[285] Barker, p. 685.

[286] Feinberg, *God Remembers*, p. 233. See pp. 233-35 for a history of the interpretation of this passage.

grandson "Shimei" represent the religious branches of Israel, though not just the main ones that reference to Gershon, Shimei's father, might have suggested (cf. Num. 3:17-18, 21). Perhaps the political and priestly families received mention because they were those chiefly responsible for Messiah's death. When these leading families mourned, all the other citizens would follow their example. The families of "Nathan" and of "Shimei" may have been the most prominent families of their kind in Zechariah's day. Zerubbabel came from Nathan's line (Luke 3:23-31), and the Shimeites presumably dominated the Levitical classes in the postexilic era.[287]

"Nothing can excite to repentance like a view of the crucified Saviour."[288]

The Battle of Armageddon, described in this section, will produce a great turning back to the Lord in Israel. When Jesus returns to the earth at His Second Coming, it will be at the climax of the Battle of Armageddon, when the nations of the world have gathered together to annihilate the Jews from the earth. Then the Jews will see Jesus coming from heaven and realize that He really is their Messiah. Compare Paul's Damascus Road experience. They will turn to Him in faith in such a large revival that Paul could say, "All Israel will be saved" (Rom. 11:26).

2. The restoration of Judah ch. 13

"The connection between chapters 12 and 13 is so close that a chapter division is really uncalled for. The same people, the same subject, and the same time are in view in both chapters. The relationship between 12:10-14 and 13:1-6 is not only logical but chronological as well. Once Israel is brought to a penitent condition and is brought face to face with her crucified Messiah, then the provision of God for cleansing will be appropriate."[289]

Israel's cleansing 13:1-6

13:1 "In that day," God will open "a fountain" for the complete spiritual cleansing of the Israelites, both for their moral sins and for their ritual uncleanness (cf. Ezek. 47). The figure of a fountain pictures abundant cleansing that would continue indefinitely. This will be the fulfillment of God's promise to forgive the sins of His people Israel in the New Covenant (3:4, 9; Jer. 31:34; Ezek. 36:25; cf. Rom. 11:26-27). "The blood of Jesus . . . cleanses us from all sin" (1 John 1:7). The cleansing is available now, but God will cleanse multitudes of Israelites in the future, after they turn to their Messiah in faith (12:10-14).

"The problem of sin is the central problem in the OT. It began in the garden of Eden and will not be eradicated until the final day of Yahweh."[290]

13:2 At that time the Lord also promised to remove idolatry, false prophets, and unclean spirits from the land. There would be external cleansing as well as internal. The Jews would "no longer ascribe supernatural powers to mere things, nor worship them as divine" (cf. 10:2-3; Jer. 23:30-32; 27:9-10; Ezek. 13:1—14:11).[291] False prophets, as is clear from the context, would not mislead the people (cf. Matt. 24:4-5, 11, 15, 23-24; 2 Thess. 2:2-4; Rev. 9:20; 13:4-15). The unclean spirits are the diviners, mediums, and demons who confused and afflicted the people in the past.

"The reference to the banishment of the unclean spirits out of the land . . . is the only passage in Scripture which explicitly refers to the imprisonment of demons during the kingdom age. But since Satan is remanded to the abyss (the prison house of evil spirits) during this era, as is clearly declared in Revelation 20:1-3, it is a necessary corollary that his demon aids shall also share the same fate."[292]

13:3 If anyone tries to play the part of a false prophet, then his own parents, those closest to him, are to put him to death. This was what God had commanded the Israelites to do to false prophets (Deut. 13:6-9). They "will pierce" the false prophets fatally, as they had formerly pierced the Messiah fatally (12:10).

13:4-5 This dangerous situation for the false prophets would lead them to hide their identity as "prophets." They will not identify themselves in traditional ways (cf. 2 Kings 1:8), but will deny that they were prophets. They will go so far as claiming to have been sold into slavery as field hands when they were only boys, so they could not possibly be prophets.

13:6 Sometimes false prophets cut themselves to arouse prophetic ecstasy, to increase ritual potency, or to identify themselves with a particular god (cf. Lev. 19:28; 21:5; Deut. 14:1; 1 Kings 18:28; Jer. 16:6; 41:5; 48:37). If someone saw such wounds on

---

[287]Merrill, p. 325.
[288]Feinberg, *God Remembers*, p. 233.
[289]Ibid., p. 236.
[290]Smith, p. 280.
[291]Baldwin, pp. 195-96.
[292]Unger, p. 225.

a false prophet's body in that future day, the false prophet might claim that he had received his injuries by accident in a friend's "house." The modern practice of claiming, "I walked into a door," to avoid telling the real reason for an injury, is similar.

Though some expositors believed this verse describes Messiah and His wounds, the preceding context and lack of any New Testament citation of the verse in relation to Messiah argue against this view.[293]

> "This verse is best understood as an evasive reply of a false prophet in the last days. It carries on and concludes the subject begun in v. 2. By no valid interpretation may it be referred to the Lord Jesus Christ. There is no clear change of subject between vv. 5 and 6 such as exists between vv. 6 and 7. Christ would not claim that He was not a prophet (cf. Dt. 18:15-18); He was not a farmer; He was not bought or sold from His youth. Verse 7 does speak of Christ, as Mt. 26:31 and Mk. 14:27 attest."[294]

"As is always the case with genuine conversion, there are both negative and positive aspects. The positive consists of the restoration to fellowship that takes place when sin has been forgiven (v. 1). The negative involves the removal of those habits and attitudes that occasioned the interruption of fellowship between God and His people in the first place (vv. 2-6)."[295]

The smiting of the Shepherd and the scattering of the sheep 13:7-9

13:7   Zechariah now returned—with a poem—to the subject of the Shepherd that he had mentioned in chapter 11. He also returned to the time when Israel would be scattered among the nations because of her rejection of the Good Shepherd.

Almighty Yahweh personified a sword, the instrument of violent death. Addressing it as "O sword," He commanded it to execute ("strike") His "Shepherd," the royal Good Shepherd of 11:4-14. This is a figure of speech called *apostrophe*: a direct address to an impersonal object as if it were a person. Yahweh further described this Shepherd as the Man who was very close to Him—even as "My Associate."

> "The expression 'who stands next to me' is used elsewhere only in Leviticus (*e.g.* 6:2; 18:12) to mean 'near neighbour'; similarly the shepherd is one who dwells side by side with the Lord, His equal."[296]

> "There is no stronger statement in the OT regarding the unimpeachable deity of Israel's Messiah, the Son of God."[297]

In 11:17 it was the worthless shepherd whom the Lord would strike, but here it is the Good Shepherd. The One doing the striking is evidently God Himself, since "strike" is masculine in the Hebrew text, and agrees with "the LORD of hosts." If so, Zechariah presented Messiah's death as God's activity (cf. Isa. 53:10; Acts 2:23) as well as Israel's (12:10-14).

The striking (death) of the Shepherd would result in the scattering of the Shepherd's sheep (i.e., Israel, 11:4-14). The Lord Jesus quoted this part of the verse, claiming the role of the Shepherd, when He anticipated the scattering of His disciples following His death (cf. Matt. 26:31, 56; Mark 14:27, 50).

The last line of the verse is capable of two different interpretations, both of which came to pass. Perhaps a double entendre was intended. God Himself would scatter even the young sheep and would extend mercy to them (cf. Mark 13:19, 24; Luke 2:35; Rev. 11:3-10). New Testament scholar R. T. France believed that this passage influenced the thinking of Jesus, regarding His shepherd role, more than any other shepherd passage in the Old Testament.[298]

> "The divine witness to the death and deity of the prophesied Messiah makes this verse one of the most significant in the entire Old Testament."[299]

---

[293]Ibid., pp. 228-30; and R. Jamieson, A. R. Fausset, and D. Brown, *Commentary Practical and Explanatory on the Whole Bible*, p. 865; were proponents of the messianic interpretation.
[294]*The New Scofield . . .*, p. 975. Cf. Feinberg, "Zechariah," p. 910.
[295]Merrill, p. 328.
[296]Baldwin, pp. 197-98. Cf. John 1:1-2; 14:9.
[297]Feinberg, "Zechariah," p. 910.
[298]R. T. France, *Jesus and the Old Testament: His Application of Old Testament Passages to Himself and His Mission*, pp. 103-4, 107-9.
[299]Unger, p. 232.

13:8-9 The scattering of the sheep would result in two-thirds of the flock dying, and one-third remaining alive. The Lord will "refine" the surviving one-third in the fires of affliction (cf. 3:2; Ezek. 5:1-12). This remnant must be the same group of Israelites, described in 12:10—13:1, who will turn to God in repentance. Evidently two-thirds of the Jews, the unbelieving, will perish during the Tribulation, and one-third will live through it and enter the Millennium. This surviving remnant, therefore, must include the 144,000 Israelite witnesses of Revelation 7:1-8 and 14:1-5. The one-third will call on the Lord's name in supplication for forgiveness (12:10). The Lord will respond to their cry by reaffirming His New Covenant relationship with them, and they will agree to it (cf. Ezek. 20:37).

3. The reign of Messiah ch. 14

"The cosmic, eschatological sweep of this last portion . . . is almost without compare in the prophetic literature of the OT for the richness of its imagery, the authority of its pronouncements, and the majestic exaltation of the God of Israel who will be worshiped as the God of all the earth."[300]

The final deliverance of Israel and the return of Messiah 14:1-8

14:1 The Lord announced through His prophet that "a day" was "coming for the LORD," i.e., coming primarily for His benefit, when the nations that had plundered Israel victoriously would divide their spoil between themselves in Jerusalem. This would be the Lord's day, in which He would do His will, in contrast to man's day, in which man conducts his affairs without divine interference.

> "The day of the Lord in prophetic literature designates any time when Yahweh steps into the arena of human events to effect his purposes."[301]

14:2 The Lord "will gather all the nations against Jerusalem" to fight against her (cf. Rev. 16:16-21, Armageddon). They will capture the city, plunder the houses, and rape the women. Half of the Jewish residents will depart as exiles, but the other half will remain. This will be one-half of the portion of the one-third of the Jewish population—that will be in Jerusalem—that had not died during the Tribulation (13:8). This has not yet happened.

> "The only [?] explanation is that this is an ideological conflict to remove a non-co-operative element that blocked the way to an international world order."[302]

> "This eschatological verse alone—with its statement that 'the city will be captured'—is sufficient to refute the notion popular in certain circles that 'the times of the Gentiles' (Luke 21:24) were fulfilled as of the rebirth of the modern state of Israel. According to Lucan theology, after 'the times of the Gentiles are fulfilled,' Jerusalem will be trampled on no more. Since Zechariah 14:2 clearly indicates that Jerusalem will be 'trampled on' again in the future, the 'times of the Gentiles' would seem to extend to the Messiah's second advent, when those 'times' will be replaced by the final, universal, everlasting kingdom of Daniel 2:35, 44-45."[303]

14:3 Yahweh will then take the role of the Divine Warrior, "and fight against those nations" for His people Israel (cf. 1:3; 9; 10:4-5; 12:1-9). He had done this previously in the Exodus and on numerous other occasions (cf. Exod. 14:13-14; Josh. 10:14; 23:3; Judg. 4:15; 2 Chron. 20:15).

> "In their quest for world peace, some denominations have removed the 'militant songs' from their hymnals, so that a new generation is growing up knowing nothing about 'fighting the good fight of faith' or worshiping a Savior who will one day meet the nations of the world in battle (Rev. 19:11-21)."[304]

---

[300]Merrill, p. 341.
[301]McComiskey, p. 1227.
[302]Baldwin, p. 200.
[303]Barker, p. 689.
[304]Wiersbe, p. 471.

"The actual order of events in this day peculiarly the Lord's is: (1) the nations assembled to war against Jerusalem (vs. 2); (2) the city captured and plundered, etc. (vs. 2); (3) the spoil of the city divided within its walls (vs. 1); (4) the Lord's intervention (vs. 3)."[305]

14:4 "In that day" Yahweh's "feet," in the person of Messiah (cf. Acts 1:9-12; Rev. 19:11-16), "will stand on the Mount of Olives" to "the east . . . of Jerusalem" (cf. Acts 1:11). This is the only place in the Old Testament where this name for this mountain appears (cf. 2 Sam. 15:30; Ezek. 11:23). Since people were east-oriented in ancient times, Zechariah described this mountain as "in front of" Jerusalem. The Lord will "split" this mountain in two (with an earthquake, v. 5), "so that half" of it will fall away "toward the north," and "the other half toward the south," leaving a large east-west valley down the middle (cf. Rev. 16:18-19). The earthquake will accompany Antichrist's invasion of Israel (cf. Dan. 7:8; Rev. 19:20).

"Words cannot express more plainly the personal, visible, bodily, literal return of the Lord Jesus Christ in power."[306]

14:5 The Israelites will "flee" for safety through this "valley," with mountains on either side (cf. 2 Sam. 15:16, 30; 2 Kings 25:4; Ezek. 11:22-25). Compare the Israelites' flight through the Red Sea during the Exodus. The "valley will reach" as far as "Azel" (lit. be joined to, or be at the side of, near; cf. Mic. 1:11), a site presently unknown but obviously some distance east of Jerusalem. They "will flee just as" they did during the great "earthquake" that happened during King Uzziah's reign over Judah (cf. Amos 1:1).[307] "Then the LORD will come," with all His "holy ones with Him," namely: Christians in heaven and angels (cf. Ps. 89:5, 7; Matt. 25:31; Col. 1:4, 12, 26-27; 1 Thess. 3:13; Jude 14; Rev. 19:11-16). Zechariah expressed his own relationship with the Lord, his faith in Him, and his wonder at this revelation by referring to Him personally: "O my God."

14:6 "In that day . . . the luminaries will dwindle" (lit. congeal), and there will be a reduction of light on the earth (cf. Joel 3:15-17; Amos 5:18).

"The meaning is that the loss of light is explained by the congealing of the heavenly bodies, their 'thickening' as it were to the point that they cannot shine [cf. Exod. 15:8; Job 10:10; Zeph. 1:12]."[308]

14:7 It will evidently be like twilight, "neither day nor night" (cf. Gen. 1:3-5). Even in the evening there will be more light than usual. It will be "a unique day" (time) in human history (cf. Jer. 30:7). This phenomenon will occur on a day that only Yahweh knows (cf. Matt. 24:36; Acts 1:7).

Other passages also predict cosmic phenomena in the Day of the Lord (Isa. 13:9-10; Joel 2:31; 3:15; Amos 5:18; Matt. 24:29-30; Rev. 6:12-14; 8:8-12; 9:1-18; 14:14-20; 16:4, 8-9). Bear in mind that this "day" is an extended period of time, not just a 12-hour or 24-hour period. Here, just the end of the Tribulation is in view—the entirety of which the prophets spoke of as "the Day of the Lord"—along with the Millennium.

14:8 Also, "in that day," life-giving water will flow rapidly "out of Jerusalem," half of it flowing east into the Dead Sea, and the other half west into the Mediterranean Sea. "Living water(s)" is a metaphor that pictures water as a living thing, flowing quickly and sparkling in its constant movement and shifting course (cf. Lev. 14:5-6, 50-52; 15:13; Num. 19:17). This water will flow all year round, even "in" the "summer" when most streams in Palestine dry up (cf. Ps. 46:4; Joel 3:18). The Israelites divided their year into two seasons instead of four: summer and winter (cf. Gen. 8:22; Ps. 74:17; Isa. 18:6).[309] Probably the water will be literal, but it certainly has symbolic significance as well (cf. Ps. 46:4; 65:9; Isa. 8:6; Jer. 2:13; Ezek. 47:1-12; John 4:10-14; 7:38; Rev. 22:1-2).

"There is no reason to take this [whole description] in any but a literal way, unless one is prepared to deny a literal coming of YHWH as well."[310]

---

[305]Unger, p. 245.
[306]Feinberg, "Zechariah," p. 910.
[307]See Josephus, *Antiquities of . . .*, 9:10:4.
[308]Merrill, p. 351.
[309]R. de Vaux, *Ancient Israel: Its Life and Institutions*, pp. 189-90.
[310]Merrill, pp. 343-44.

The security of Israel 14:9-11

14:9   "In that day," Yahweh will rule over the whole earth. He will be the only "king"; there will be no others. "His name" will be number "one" in all the earth; there will be no other so-called gods (cf. Deut. 6:4-5). This verse refers to Christ's millennial kingdom (cf. Ps. 2; Dan. 2:44-45; 7:27; Matt. 6:9-10).

> "Israelites for generations had been singing 'The Lord reigns' (Pss. 93; 97; 99), but it had been a declaration of faith. Once 'that day' comes He will be seen to be King over His world kingdom."[311]

> "Yahweh's kingdom will be complete, total, and real on earth as it is in heaven."[312]

14:10   The land around Jerusalem will become level, whereas Jerusalem itself will be elevated (apparently due to a great earthquake; cf. Isa. 2:2; Rev. 16:18-19). In view of the place names mentioned, this verse probably refers to the literal city and its topography. "Geba" stood about six miles north of Jerusalem (2 Kings 23:8), and the "Rimmon" south of Jerusalem stood about 35 miles southwest of it (Josh. 15:32; Neh. 11:29). The sites mentioned in Jerusalem were on the east, west, north, and south sides of the city, indicating its totality.[313]

14:11   People will live in millennial Jerusalem. From then on, Jerusalem will never again suffer depopulation by being put under the "curse" (or ban, Heb. *herem*). Canaanite cities placed under the ban were totally destroyed (Josh. 6:17-18). In other words, the city and those in it will enjoy "security," because Jerusalem will never again suffer destruction.

The destruction of Israel's enemies 14:12-15

Chronologically these verses describe what will follow verse 3.

14:12   The Lord will "strike" the nations that warred against Jerusalem (vv. 1-3) with a "plague" that will cause the people's flesh to "rot" off of them wherever they might be. They would not be able to see or speak (cf. Isa. 37:36). One wonders if nuclear warfare may be involved.

14:13   "Panic" will seize them "from the LORD . . . in that day," and they will fight one another (cf. Judg. 7:22; 1 Sam. 14:15-20; 2 Chron. 20:23). This will happen near Jerusalem.

14:14   The Israelites will also fight their enemies there, and will gather much spoil from the people they defeat. Thus there are three instruments God will use to defeat Israel's enemies: plague (v. 12), themselves (v. 13), and the Israelites (v. 14).

14:15   The "plague" that the Lord will send on Israel's enemies (v. 12) will also afflict their animals—precluding their escape (cf. Josh. 7:24-25).

The worship of the sovereign King 14:16-21

14:16   The remaining former enemies of Israel who have not died will bow to the sovereignty of Yahweh (cf. 8:20-23; Isa. 2:2-4; 45:21-24; 60:4-14; Ezek. 40—48; Phil. 2:10). They will be expected to make annual pilgrimages to Jerusalem to worship the one "King": Almighty Yahweh (cf. Ps. 24:10; Isa. 6:5; Rev. 11:15; 19:16), "and to celebrate the Feast of Booths." The Feast of Booths (or Tabernacles, Ingathering) commemorated the Lord's provision of agricultural bounty and the Israelites' redemption from Egyptian slavery. Strangers were welcome to participate in it in Israel's past history. It also anticipated entrance into the Promised Land and kingdom blessings (Lev. 23:34-43).

The Apostle Peter evidently concluded that the messianic kingdom had begun when he saw Jesus transfigured (Luke 9:33). He suggested that the disciples make three booths for Jesus, Moses, and Elijah. This indicates that the Jews in Jesus' day associated the Feast of Booths with the beginning of Messiah's kingdom, the same connection that Zechariah made here.

The Feast of Booths was the last of the three most important feasts on Israel's calendar, so it would be an appropriate one for these Gentiles to celebrate in Jerusalem yearly. This feast was a time of grateful rejoicing (Lev. 23:40; Deut. 16:14-15; Neh. 8:17). This may not be the only feast these people will celebrate, but it was the only one Zechariah mentioned, perhaps because it was so climactic.[314]

---

[311] Baldwin, p. 203.
[312] Smith, p. 289.
[313] Baldwin, p. 204.
[314] See de Vaux, pp. 495-502, 506.

> "There are many views as to why choice was made of the Feast of Tabernacles, but the most probable is that, speaking of the joys of the ingathering, it will celebrate the gathering of the nations to the Lord and especially His tabernacling among them [cf. Rev. 7:15-17; 21:3]."[315]

The Feast of Tabernacles is the only one of Israel's major feasts that will be unfulfilled until it is celebrated at this time.[316]

14:17-19   As punishment for not making the pilgrimage to attend this feast, the Lord will withhold rain (cf. Ps. 2:8-12; Rev. 2:27; 12:5; 19:15). This was also a curse for covenant disobedience under the Mosaic Law (Deut. 28:22-24). For example, if people from Egypt did not go up to Jerusalem, the Lord will withhold rain from Egypt. This will be His punishment on any nation that does not participate (cf. 9:11—10:1). Rain is a figure for spiritual blessing (cf. Ezek. 34:26), but both literal and spiritual blessing are probably in view here.

> "Egypt was an exception among the nations because it depended for water not on rainfall but on the Nile. As Egypt had experienced plagues at the time of the Exodus, and through them had been brought to acknowledge God's sovereignty, so *plague* was a fitting symbol of disaster in the new era."[317]

> "Zechariah portrays the Messiah as the complete and perfect King by applying all six royal functions [of ancient Near Eastern kingship] to him . . . : (1) mediating Servant (3:8); (2) Priest (6:13); (3) Judge (14:16-19); (4) Warrior (10:4; 14:3-4); (5) Shepherd (11:8-9; 13:7); and (6) 'Peace'-bringing King (3:10; 9:9-10)."[318]

14:20   "In that day," even the most common things will be as consecrated to God's glory as the gold plate on the high priest's turban that previously indicated his consecration (Exod. 28:36). This plate was to remind the Israelites of their holy calling as well. Finally, all the people will truly be consecrated to the Lord and will fulfill their holy calling (cf. Exod. 19:6; Jer. 2:3). The ordinary "cooking pots" in the temple will be as holy as "the bowls" used to sprinkle the sacrificial blood on the brazen altar had been. Distinctions between sacred and secular will no longer exist, since *everything will be holy*—set apart to God.

14:21   In fact, "every cooking pot" throughout the holy city will be set apart to honor Yahweh Almighty. People will even be able to use them to bring their sacrifices of worship to the Lord. Finally, there will be no more Canaanites in the temple of the Lord of Hosts in that day. The Canaanites throughout Israel's history represented people who were morally and spiritually unclean, reprehensible to Yahweh, and doomed to death (cf. Gen. 9:25; Isa. 35:8; Ezek. 43:7; 44:9; Rev. 21:27). Probably that is the significance of the name here, not just the ethnic Canaanites alone. There would be no more people like the Canaanites in the land because all would acknowledge Him as God and King.

> "There will be holiness in public life ('the bells of the horses,' v. 20), in religious life ('the cooking pots in the LORD's house,' v. 20), and in private life ('every pot in Jerusalem and Judah,' v. 21). Even common things become holy when they are used for God's service. So it is with our lives."[319]

Chapter 14 is the climax of this whole revelation: the reign of Messiah. Here we learn that God will deliver Israel through Messiah who will appear (14:1-8). Jesus will return to earth and touch down on the Mount of Olives, the same place from which He ascended into heaven (Acts 1:9). Messiah will then provide final security for the Israelites (14:9-11), destroy Israel's enemies (14:12-15), and the result will be universal worship of sovereign Yahweh (14:16-21). All of these benefits will occur after Messiah appears and sets up His kingdom on the earth.

---

[315] Feinberg, *God Remembers*, pp. 260-61.
[316] Unger, p. 265.
[317] Baldwin, p. 207. Cf. Feinberg, "Zechariah," p. 911.
[318] Barker, p. 664.
[319] Ibid., p. 697. For a synopsis of the future of Israel, see Louis A. Barbieri Jr., "The Future for Israel in God's Plan," in *Essays in Honor of J. Dwight Pentecost*, pp. 163-79.

Bibliography

Ackroyd, Peter. *Exile and Restoration*. Philadelphia: Westminster Press, 1968.

Alexander, Ralph H. "Hermeneutics of Old Testament Apocalyptic Literature." Th.D. dissertation, Dallas Theological Seminary, 1968.

Archer, Gleason L., Jr. *A Survey of Old Testament Introduction*. 1964; revised ed., Chicago: Moody Press, 1974.

Baldwin, Joyce G. *Haggai, Zechariah, Malachi: An Introduction and Commentary*. Tyndale Old Testament Commentaries series. Leicester, Eng., and Downers Grove, Ill.: Inter-Varsity Press, 1972.

Barbieri, Louis A., Jr. "The Future for Israel in God's Plan." In *Essays in Honor of J. Dwight Pentecost*, pp. 163-79. Edited by Stanley D. Toussaint and Charles H. Dyer. Chicago: Moody Press, 1986.

Barker, Kenneth L. "Zechariah." In *Daniel-Minor Prophets*. Vol. 7 of *The Expositor's Bible Commentary*. 12 vols. Edited by Frank E. Gaebelein and Richard P. Polcyn. Grand Rapids: Zondervan Publishing House, 1985.

Baron, David. *The Visions and Prophecies of Zechariah*. Third edition. London: Morgan & Scott, 1919.

Bell, Robert D. "The Theology of Zechariah." *Biblical Viewpoint* 24:2 (November 1990):55-61.

Botsford, George Willis, and Charles Alexander Robinson Jr. *Hellenic History*. 4th ed. New York: Macmillan, 1956.

Bright, John. *A History of Israel*. Philadelphia: Westminster Press, 1959.

Cashdan, Eli. "Zechariah." In *The Twelve Minor Prophets*, pp. 266-332. Edited by A. Cohen. London: Soncino, 1948.

Chisholm, Robert B., Jr. *Handbook on the Prophets*. Grand Rapids: Baker Book House, 2002.

_____. "A Theology of the Minor Prophets." In *A Biblical Theology of the Old Testament*, pp. 397-433. Edited by Roy B. Zuck. Chicago: Moody Press, 1991.

de Boer, Peter A. H. *An Inquiry into the Meaning of the Term Massa'*. Leiden, Netherlands: Brill, 1948.

de Vaux, Roland. *Ancient Israel: Its Life and Institutions*. Translated by John McHugh. London: Darton, Longman and Todd, 1961.

Dyer, Charles H., and Eugene H. Merrill. *The Old Testament Explorer*. Nashville: Word Publishing, 2001. Reissued as *Nelson's Old Testament Survey*. Nashville: Thomas Nelson Publishers, 2001.

Ellis, David J. "Zechariah." In *The New Layman's Bible Commentary*, pp. 1025-50. Edited by G. C. D. Howley, et al. Grand Rapids: Zondervan Publishing House, 1979.

Feinberg, Charles L. "Daniel." In *The Wycliffe Bible Commentary*, pp. 897-911. Edited by Charles F. Pfeiffer and Everett F. Harrison. Chicago: Moody Press, 1962.

_____. *God Remembers: A Study of the Book of Zechariah*. New York: American Board of Missions to the Jews, 1965.

France, R. T. *Jesus and the Old Testament: His Application of Old Testament Passages to Himself and His Mission*. London: Tyndale Press, 1971.

Freeman, Hobart E. *An Introduction to the Old Testament Prophets*. Chicago: Moody Press, 1968.

Halpern, Baruch. "The Ritual Background of Zechariah's Temple Song." *Catholic Biblical Quarterly* 40 (1978):167-90.

Harrison, R. K. *Introduction to the Old Testament*. Grand Rapids: Wm. B. Eerdmans Publishing Co., 1969.

Henderson, E. *The Minor Prophets*. Andover, Mass.: Warren F. Draper, 1860.

The Illustrated Family Encyclopedia of the Living Bible. 14 vols. Chicago: San Francisco Publications, 1967.

The International Standard Bible Encyclopaedia, 1949 ed., S.v. "Zechariah, Book of," by George L. Robinson, 5:3136.

Ironside, Harry A. *Notes on the Minor Prophets*. New York: Loizeaux Brothers, 1928.

Jamieson, Robert; A. R. Fausset; and David Brown. *Commentary Practical and Explanatory on the Whole Bible*. Revised ed. Grand Rapids: Zondervan Publishing House, 1961

Jansma, T. "Inquiry into the Hebrew Text and the Ancient Versions of Zechariah ix-xiv." *Oudtestamentische Studiën* 7 (1950):1-142.

Johnson, Elliott E. "Apoclayptic Genre in Literary Interpretation." In *Essays in Honor of J. Dwight Pentecost*, pp. 197-210. Edited by Stanley D. Toussaint and Charles H. Dyer. Chicago: Moody Press, 1986.

Josephus, Flavius. *The Works of Flavius Josephus*. Translated by William Whiston. *Antiquities of the Jews. The Wars of the Jews*. London: T. Nelson and Sons, 1866.

Kaiser, Walter C., Jr. *Toward and Old Testament Theology*. Grand Rapids: Zondervan Publishing House, 1978.

Keil, Carl Friedrich. *The Twelve Minor Prophets*. Translated by James Martin. Biblical Commentary on the Old Testament. Reprint ed. Grand Rapids: Wm. B. Eerdmans Publishing Co., n.d.

Kelly, William. *Lectures Introductory to the Study of the Minor Prophets*. Third edition. London: W. H. Broom and Rouse, n.d.

Klausner, Joseph. *The Messianic Idea in Israel*. London: Allen and Unwin, 1956.

Lamarche, P. *Zacharie i-xiv: Structure, Litteraire, et Messianisme*. Paris: Gabalda, 1961.

Lange, John Peter, ed. *A Commentary on the Holy Scriptures*. 25 vols. New York: Charles Scribner, 1865-80; reprint ed., Grand Rapids: Zondervan Publishing House, 1960. Vol. 7: *Ezekiel, Daniel, and the Minor Prophets*, by W. J. Schröder, Otto Zöckler, et al.

Leupold, H. C. *Exposition of Zechariah*. N.c.: Wartburg Press, 1956; reprint ed., Grand Rapids: Baker Book House, 1971.

Lindsey, F. Duane. "Zechariah." In *The Bible Knowledge Commentary: Old Testament*, pp. 1545-72. Edited by John F. Walvoord and Roy B. Zuck. Wheaton: Scripture Press Publications, Victor Books, 1985.

Longman, Tremper, III and Raymond B. Dillard. *An Introduction to the Old Testament*. 2nd ed. Grand Rapids: Zondervan, 2006.

McComiskey, Thomas Edward. "Zechariah." In *The Minor Prophets: An Exegetical and Expositional Commentary*, 3:1003-1244. 3 vols. Edited by Thomas Edward McComiskey. Grand Rapids: Baker Books, 1992, 1993, and 1998.

McCready, Wayne O. "The 'Day of Small Things' vs. the Latter Days: Historical Fulfillment or Eschatological Hope?" In *Israel's Apostasy and Restoration: Essays in Honor of Roland K. Harrison*, pp. 223-36. Edited by Avraham Gileadi. Grand Rapids: Baker Book House, 1988.

Merrill, Eugene H. *An Exegetical Commentary: Haggai, Zechariah, Malachi*. Chicago: Moody Press, 1994.

Mitchell, Hinckley G. "Haggai and Zechariah." In *A Critical and Exegetical Commentary on Haggai, Zechariah, Malachi and Jonah*, pp. 1-362. International Critical Commentary series. Edinburgh: T. & T. Clark, 1912.

Morgan, G. Campbell. *An Exposition of the Whole Bible*. Westwood, N.J.: Fleming H. Revell Company, 1959.

_____. *Living Messages of the Books of the Bible*. 2 vols. New York: Fleming H. Revell Co., 1912.

Nestle, Eberhard, and Kurt Aland, eds. *Novum Testamentum Graece*. New York: American Bible Society, 1950.

The New Scofield Reference Bible. Edited by Frank E. Gaebelein, et al. New York: Oxford University Press, 1967.

Page, Sydney H. T. "Satan: God's Servant." *Journal of the Evangelical Theological Society* 50:3 (September 2007):449-65.

Perowne, T. T. *The Books of Haggai and Zechariah*. Cambridge, Eng.: Cambridge University Press, 1886.

Petersen, David L. *Haggai and Zechariah 1—8*. Old Testament Library series. Philadelphia: Westminster Press, 1984.

_____. "Zerubbabel and Jerusalem Temple Reconstruction." *Catholic Biblical Quarterly* 36:3 (1974):366-72.

Pritchard, James B., ed. *Ancient Near Eastern Texts*. 3rd ed. Princeton: Princeton University Press, 1969.

Pusey, E. B. *The Minor Prophets*. 2 vols. Reprint ed. Grand Rapids: Baker Book House, 1950.

Reiner, Erica. "Thirty Pieces of Silver." *Journal of the American Oriental Society* 88 (January-March 1968):186-90.

Ringgren, Helmer. *The Faith of Qumran*. Philadelphia: Fortress Press, 1963.

Robinson, George L. *The Twelve Minor Prophets*. N.c.: Harper & Brothers, 1926; reprint ed., Grand Rapids: Baker Book House, 1974.

Schoville, Keith N. *Biblical Archaeology in Focus*. Grand Rapids: Baker Book House, 1978.

Smith, Ralph L. *Micah-Malachi*. Word Biblical Commentary series. Waco, Tex.: Word Books, Publisher, 1984.

Toussaint, Stanley D., and Jay A. Quine. "No, Not Yet: The Contingency of God's Promised Kingdom." *Bibliotheca Sacra* 164:654 (April-June 2007):131-47.

Trever, Albert A. *History of Ancient Civilization*. 2 vols. New York: Harcourt, Brace and World, 1936.

Unger, Merrill F. *Zechariah*. Grand Rapids: Zondervan Publishing House, 1963.

von Orelli, C. *The Twelve Minor Prophets*. International Critical Commentaries series. Edinburgh: T. & T. Clark, 1893.

von Rad, Gerhard. *Old Testament Theology*. 2 vols. Translated by D. M. G. Stalker. New York and Evanston, Ill.: Harper & Row, 1962, 1965.

Waltke, Bruce K., with Charles Yu. *An Old Testament Theology: an exegetical, canonical, and thematic approach*. Grand Rapids: Zondervan, 2007.

Wiersbe, Warren W. "Zechariah." In *The Bible Exposition Commentary/Prophets*, pp. 447-76. Colorado Springs, Colo.: Cook Communications Ministries; and Eastbourne, England: Kingsway Communications Ltd., 2002.

Wisdom, Thurman. "'Not by Might, nor by Power, but by My Spirit.'" *Biblical Viewpoint* 24:2 (November 1990):19-26.

Wood, Leon J. *The Prophets of Israel*. Grand Rapids: Baker Book House, 1979.

Young, Robert. *Analytical Concordance to the Bible*. Twenty-second American edition. Revised by Wm. B. Stevenson. Grand Rapids: Wm. B. Eerdmans Publishing Co., n.d.

Constable's Notes
On Malachi

Introduction

Title and Writer

The name of the writer is the title of this book. "Malachi" means "my messenger." We know nothing of the prophet's parentage, ancestral or tribal roots, geographical origin, or other vocation. All we know is that he received and communicated the word of Yahweh to the Jews of his day.

Some scholars have tried to prove that "Malachi" was not the name of a prophet but the title of an anonymous prophet. None of the references to this book in the New Testament mention Malachi by name (cf. Matt. 11:10; Mark 1:2; Luke 7:27). The arguments for anonymity rest on four points.[1] First, "Malachi" is a title rather than a name in its form. The Septuagint translators rendered it "my messenger" in 1:1. However, it could be a short form of a name such as *Malachiyyah*, "messenger of Yahweh." There are several other shortened forms of names similar to this in the Old Testament (e.g., *'abi* in 2 Kings 18:2, cf. *'abiyyah* in 2 Chron. 29:1; and *'uri* in 1 Kings 4:19, cf. *'uriyyah* in 1 Chron. 11:41).

Second, the Targum did not consider Malachi the writer but ascribed this book to Ezra. The Targum is an ancient Aramaic translation and paraphrase of the Old Testament. The Talmud credited Mordecai with writing it. The Talmud is a Jewish interpretation of the Old Testament compiled between 450 B.C. and 500 A.D. But there is little other support for Ezra or Mordecai's authorship of this book. Third, "Malachi" appears in 3:1 as an anonymous designation meaning "my messenger," so it may mean the same thing in 1:1. However, the Malachi in 3:1 seems clearly to be wordplay on the name of the prophet in 1:1. Fourth, this book was the third of three oracles (Heb. *massa'*, 1:1) in the postexilic books, the other two being in Zechariah 9—11 and 12—14 (cf. Zech. 9:1; 11:1). Yet Malachi introduced his oracle differently from the way Zechariah introduced his.[2] Furthermore, other prophets introduced their books by calling them oracles (cf. Nah. 1:1; Hab. 1:1).

If Malachi is not the prophet's name, this would be the only prophetic book in the Old Testament that is anonymous, which seems very unlikely.

Date

> "Haggai and Zechariah . . . are noteworthy for the chronological precision with which they related their lives and ministries to their historical milieu. This is not the case at all with Malachi. In fact, one of the major problems in a study of this book is that of locating it within a narrow enough chronological framework to provide a *Sitz im Leben* [situation in life] sufficient to account for its peculiar themes and emphases."[3]

Malachi referred to no datable persons or events in his prophecy, so we must draw our conclusions from implications in the text and traditional understandings of it. Malachi's place at the end of the twelve Minor Prophets in the Hebrew Bible and modern translations argues for a late date. The Talmud grouped Malachi with Haggai and Zechariah as postexilic prophets.[4]

Malachi's reference to "your governor" (1:8) indicates that he wrote after 538 B.C. when Cyrus the Persian allowed the Jews to return to their land, which was under Persian control. The word translated "governor" is *pehah*, a Persian title (cf. Ezra 5:3, 6, 14; 6:6-7, 13; Dan. 3:2-3, 27; 6:7). Zerubbabel bore this title (Hag. 1:1, 14; 2:2, 21), as did Nehemiah (Neh. 5:14; 12:26). Malachi must have written after the temple had been rebuilt, since he referred to worship there (1:6-14; 2:7-9, 13; 3:7-10). This would force a date after 515 B.C., when temple restoration was complete.

Since Malachi addressed many of the same matters that Nehemiah tried to reform, it is tempting to date Malachi during Nehemiah's governorship. Both Malachi and Nehemiah dealt with priestly laxity (Mal. 1:6; Neh. 13:4-9), neglect of tithes (Mal. 3:7-12; Neh. 13:10-13), and intermarriage between Israelites and foreigners (Mal. 2:10-16; Neh. 13:23-28). Some have conjectured that Malachi ministered while Nehemiah was away from Jerusalem.[5] In the twelfth year of his governorship, Nehemiah returned to Persia for an unknown period of time (Neh. 5:14; 13:6). Malachi probably wrote during the years Nehemiah served (445-420 B.C), and perhaps between 432 and 431 B.C., the years when Nehemiah was away from Jerusalem.

---

[1]Craig A. Blaising, "Malachi," in *The Bible Knowledge Commentary: Old Testament*, p. 1573. See also Douglas Stuart, "Malachi," in *The Minor Prophets*, pp. 1246-47.
[2]See Brevard Childs, *Introduction to the Old Testament as Scripture*, pp. 489-92.
[3]Eugene H. Merrill, *An Exegetical Commentary: Haggai, Zechariah, Malachi*, p. 371.
[4]*Yoma* 9b; *Sukkah* 44a; *Rosh Hashannah* 19b; *Megillah* 3a, 15a, et al.
[5]E.g., Robert L. Alden, "Malachi," in *Daniel-Minor Prophets*, vol. 7 of *The Expositor's Bible Commentary*, pp. 701-2.

Commentators have suggested a wide range of dates. For example, Craig Blaising suggested a date between 450 and 430 B.C.[6] Eugene Merrill preferred a date between 480 and 470 B.C.[7] Douglas Stuart believed Malachi wrote about 460 B.C.[8] R. K. Harrison and John Bright estimated a date close to 450 B.C.[9] Gleason Archer Jr. and Ray Clendenen concluded that Malachi wrote about 435 B.C.[10] Hobart Freeman was more specific: shortly after 433 B.C.[11] And Leon Wood was quite general: during the last half of the fifth century B.C., though contemporaneously with Nehemiah.[12]

Historical Background

Malachi was one of the three postexilic writing prophets along with Haggai and Zechariah, and he was quite certainly the last one chronologically, even though we cannot be dogmatic about an exact date for his writing.

The first group of almost 50,000 Jewish exiles returned from Babylonian captivity under Sheshbazzar and Zerubbabel's leadership in 537 B.C. Ezra 1—6 records their experiences. Haggai and Zechariah ministered to these returnees in 520 B.C. and urged them to rebuild the temple. Zechariah's ministry may have continued beyond that year. The events recorded in the Book of Esther took place in Persia between 482 and 473 B.C. A second group of about 5,000 Jews returned in 458 B.C. under Ezra's leadership. Ezra sought to beautify the temple and institute reforms that would purify Israel's worship (Ezra 7—10). Nehemiah led a third group of about 42,000 back in 444 B.C., and the events recorded in his book describe what happened between 445 and 420 B.C., including the rebuilding of Jerusalem's wall. Malachi probably ministered in Jerusalem during that period.

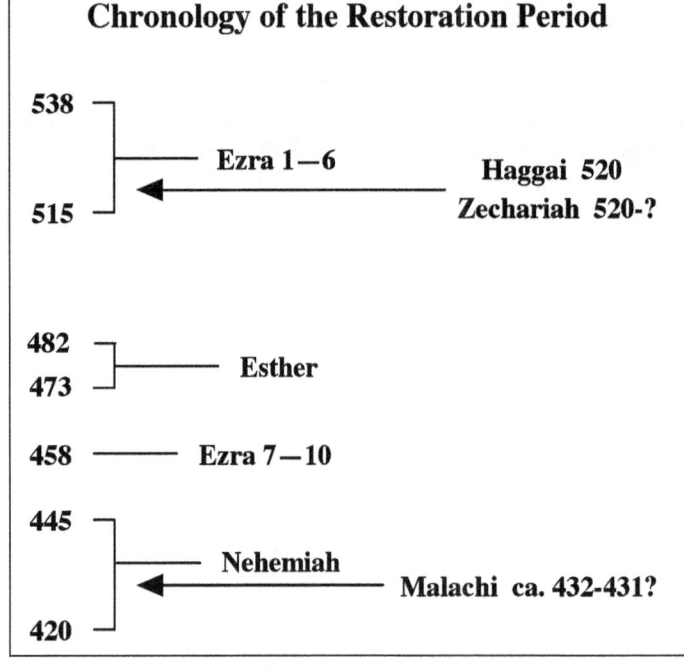

> ". . . Malachi's concerns are much different from those of either Ezra or Nehemiah, for he was almost wholly transfixed by concerns about the cult [formal worship]."[13]

Life was not easy for the returnees during the ministry of the fifth-century B.C. restoration prophet. The people continued to live under Gentile (Persian) sovereignty even though they were back in their own land. Harvests were poor, and locust plagues were a problem (3:11). Even after Ezra's reforms and Nehemiah's amazing success in motivating the Jews to rebuild Jerusalem's wall, most of the people remained cold-hearted toward Yahweh. Priests and people were still not observing the Mosaic Law as commanded, as is clear from references in the book to sacrifices, tithes, and offerings (e.g., 1:6; 3:5). Foreign cultures had made deep inroads into the values and practices of God's people. The Israelites still intermarried with Gentiles (2:11), and divorces were quite common (2:16). The spiritual, ethical, and moral tone of the nation was low.

---

[6]Blaising, p. 1573.
[7]Merrill, p. 378.
[8]Stuart, p. 1252.
[9]R. K. Harrison, *Introduction to the Old Testament*, p. 961, and John Bright, *A History of Israel*, p. 356.
[10]Gleason L. Archer Jr., *A Survey of Old Testament Introduction*, p. 431; and E. Ray Clendenen, *Haggai, Malachi*, p. 207.
[11]Hobart E. Freeman, *An Introduction to the Old Testament Prophets*, pp. 349-50.
[12]Leon J. Wood, *The Prophets of Israel*, pp. 374, 377.
[13]Merrill, p. 378.

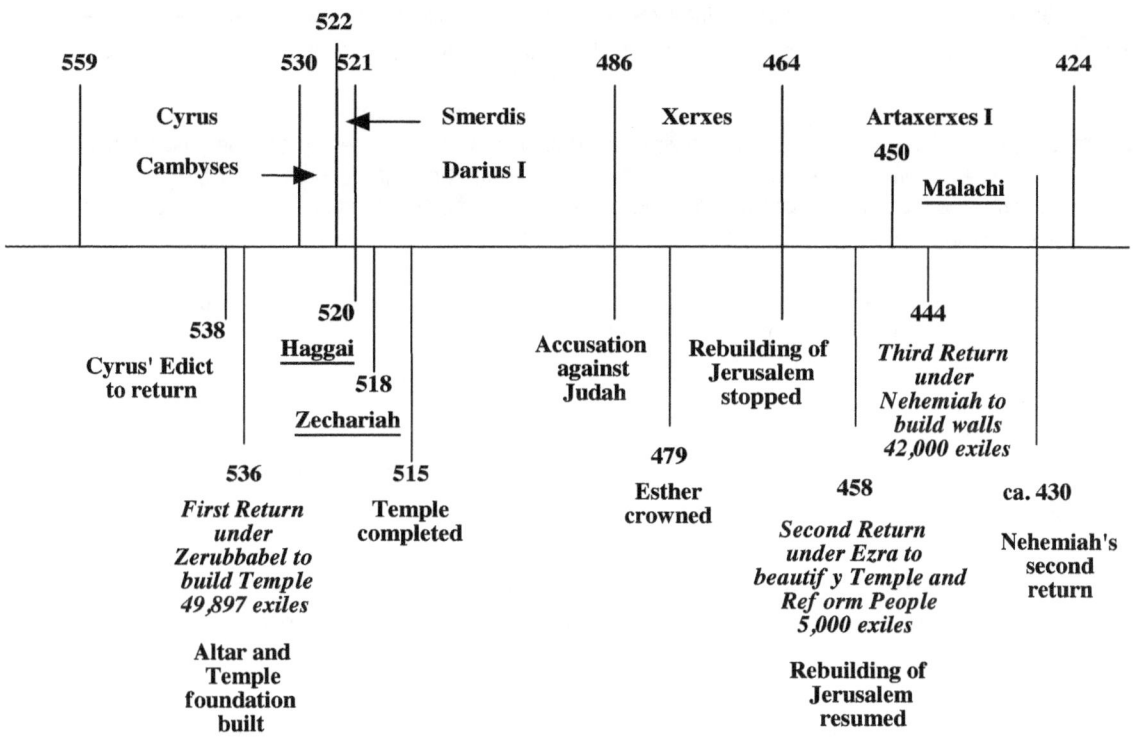

". . . Malachi and his contemporaries were living in an uneventful waiting period, when God seemed to have forgotten His people enduring poverty and foreign domination in the little province of Judah. . . . True the Temple had been completed, but nothing momentous had occurred to indicate that God's presence had returned to fill it with glory, as Ezekiel had indicated would happen (Ezk. 43:4). . . . Generations were dying without receiving the promises (*cf.* Heb. 11:13) and many were losing their faith."[14]

Place of Composition
Malachi evidently ministered in Jerusalem, as seems clear from his numerous references to practices that were current in that city and throughout Judah.

Audience and Purpose
The prophet addressed the restoration community of Israelites that had returned to the land from Babylonian captivity. His purpose was to confront them with their sins and to encourage them to pursue holiness.

"Malachi's prophecy indicts the religious leadership of the day and chides God's people for their spiritual apathy and their skepticism and cynicism concerning God's plan for their future. It also calls the people to correct their wrong attitudes of worship by trusting God with genuine faith as living Lord. Furthermore, it warns the people of their immoral behavior toward one another and calls for their repentance lest they be terrorized at the coming of the Lord."[15]

"The task of a prophet is not to smooth things over but to make things right."[16]

Theological Emphases
Like all the writing prophets, Malachi's chief revelation was the person and work of Yahweh. He presented Israel's God as sovereign over Israel, and the whole world, and as very patient with His wayward people.

---

[14] Joyce G. Baldwin, *Haggai, Zechariah, Malachi: An Introduction and Commentary*, p. 211.
[15] Clendenen, p. 231.
[16] Eugene Peterson, *Run with the Horses*, p 69.

Malachi also used the Mosaic Covenant as the standard by which he measured Israel's conduct. He pointed out instances of covenant unfaithfulness and urged return to the covenant. He also reminded the Israelites of Yahweh's faithfulness to His covenant promises—including promises of future blessing. Thus he sought to motivate his hearers to return to the Lord, by convicting them of their sins and converting them to love for their Savior.

> ". . . Israel's ethics grew out of (1) the nature of *God* and their relationship to him, (2) their identity as a *people* and their relationships and responsibilities to one another, and (3) their relationship to the *land*, which represented their material environment and possessions. The parallel with Malachi is that these are the exact themes found in the three discourses [in the book] and in the same order—God, people, and land."[17]

Malachi's notable messianic prophecy deals with Messiah's forerunner (3:1; 4:5). He would be like Elijah and would call the Israelites to repentance (cf. Matt. 11:14; 17:12-13; Mark 9:11-13; Luke 1:17).

Literary Form and Characteristics

Malachi's style is quite different from that of any other writing prophet. Instead of delivering messages to his audience, he charged them with various sins, six times in all. He employed a very confrontational style of address. After each charge, he proceeded to back it up with evidence. Malachi's rhetorical disputation speech form contains four components: assertion, questioning, response, and implication.[18]

> "Even a casual reading shows Malachi's use of rhetorical questions. Seven times he put them into the mouths of his audience (1:2, 6, 7; 2:17; 3:7, 8, 13, and perhaps 2:14). In addition he asked the people several rhetorical questions (e.g., 1:6, 8, 9; 2:10, 15; 3:2).

> "The format of 1:2 is typical of Malachi's style. First there is God's statement: 'I have loved you.' Then follows the popular objection that questions the truth of God's statement—viz., 'How have you loved us?' Finally there is the justification for God's statement."[19]

> "The most striking and creative aspect of Malachi's style is its disputational form . . ."[20]

Malachi used the question and answer method extensively. This method became increasingly popular, and in the time of Christ the rabbis and scribes used it frequently, as did the Lord Jesus. They also used rhetorical questions as a teaching device (cf. Matt. 3:7; 11:7-9; 12:26-27; Luke 14:5; John 18:38; Rom. 3:1-4; 4:1-3; 6:21; 7:7; 1 Cor. 9:7-13; Gal. 3:21; Heb. 1:5, 13-14).

This book consists of several short paragraphs on various themes. There are no long oracles against foreign nations (cf. 1:2-5), or any extended burden against Israel. There are no personal experiences to which the prophet referred, yet his style is straightforward, easy to understand, and beautifully designed.

> "Debate has centered on whether Malachi is a prosaic or poetic composition (compare W. Kaiser [*Malachi: God's Unchanging Love*] and B. Glazier-McDonald [*Malachi: The Divine Messenger*]). The most commonly used Hebrew Bible (BHS [Biblia Hebraica Stuttgartensia]) puts it in poetic format, while the most commonly used English versions of the Bible consider the book to be in prose. That such a discussion even takes place is testimony to the difficulty of defining what constitutes poetry in biblical Hebrew and also to the close connection between these two modes of discourse . . ."[21]

At least one commentator believed Malachi constructed his work in a chiasm.[22]

---

[17] Clendenen, p. 232.
[18] Stuart, p. 1248.
[19] Alden, p. 704.
[20] Tremper Longman III and Raymond B. Dillard, *An Introduction to the Old Testament*, p. 500.
[21] Ibid.
[22] Stuart, p. 1250. See also G. B. Hugenberger, *Marriage as Covenant*, p. 25.

A Superscription (1:1): Yahweh has a message for Israel.
 B First Disputation (1:2-5): God distinguishes between the good and the wicked. The proof of His love is His sparing the righteous and condemning the wicked.
  C Second Disputation (1:6—2:9): Condemnation of improper, begrudging offerings, promise of reversal of blessing, and the greatness of Yahweh's name among the nations.
   D Third Disputation (2:10-16): The Lord is witness to marital fidelity, and Judah is unfaithful.
   D' Fourth Disputation (2:17—3:6): The Lord is witness to marital fidelity, and Judah is unfaithful.
  C' Fifth Disputation (3:7-12): Condemnation of improper, begrudging offerings, promise of reversal of blessing, and the greatness of Yahweh's name among the nations.
 B' Sixth Disputation (3:13—4:3): God distinguishes between the good and the wicked. The proof of His love is His sparing the righteous and condemning the wicked.
A' Summary challenge (4:4-6): Yahweh has a message for Israel.

Essentially, the Israelites disputed God's love, His name, and His will concerning: marriage and divorce, His justice, His demands regarding stewardship, and His service.

Ray Clendenen challenged the view that Malachi is a series of "disputation speeches," a term coined by Herman Gunkel and applied to Malachi by E. Pfeiffer in 1959. Many commentators adopted Pfeiffer's view. Clendenen analyzed Malachi as monologue interspersed with exchanges between the Lord and His audience, and believed Malachi is a prophecy composed of three hortatory addresses. Hortatory addresses in ancient Near Eastern literature contain three elements: situation, change, and motivation, and all of these are present in the speeches that Clendenen identified in Malachi.[23]

> "Identifying paragraphs or subparagraphs as expressing either situation, command, or motivation (on the basis of the grammatical structure of the paragraph) uncovers a pattern of inverted repetition or chiasm. Whereas such chiasms are often identified on the basis of repeated words, here the chiasm appears in the semantic structure. There are three such chiasms in the book, identifying three divisions, addresses, or embedded discourses."[24]

Unity, Canonicity, and Text
Most scholars view the book as the product of one writer, and there is no textual support for viewing some verses as later additions. The general structure and dialogue pattern that appear throughout the book argue for its unity. Malachi's canonicity has never been challenged, because it appears in all the authoritative lists of canonical books, and is also quoted in the New Testament. The text is well preserved.

Outline
I have provided two outlines of the book below. The first represents the popular "disputation speech" approach represented well by Stuart and others.

I. Heading 1:1
II. Oracle one: Yahweh's love for Israel 1:2-5
III. Oracle two: The priests' illicit practices and indifferent attitudes 1:6—2:9
 A. The priests' sins 1:6-14
  1. Disrespectful service 1:6-7
  2. Disqualified sacrifices 1:8-10
  3. Disdainful attitudes 1:11-14
 B. The priests' warning 2:1-9
IV. Oracle three: The people's mixed marriages and divorces 2:10-16
V. Oracle four: The problem of God's justice 2:17—3:6
VI. Oracle five: The people's sin of robbing God 3:7-12
VII. Oracle six: The arrogant and the humble 3:13—4:3
 A. The people's arrogance 3:13-15
 B. The remnant's humility 3:16
 C. The coming judgment of Israel 3:17—4:3

---

[23]See Clendenen, pp. 218-26, for a full discussion of Malachi's literary style.
[24]Ibid., p. 230. See the outline of the book below.

VIII. A concluding promise and warning 4:4-6

The second outline expresses the "hortatory discourse" approach to Malachi advocated by Clendenen. In the notes that follow, I have followed this second outline of the book.[25]

I. Introduction 1:1
II. The priests exhorted not to dishonor the Lord (the theological angle) 1:2—2:9
    A. Positive motivation: the Lord's love 1:2-5
    B. Situation: the priests' failure to honor the Lord 1:6-9
    C. Command: stop the pointless offerings 1:10
    D. Situation: the priests' worship profaning the Lord's name 1:11-14
    E. Negative motivation: the results of disobedience 2:1-9
III. Judah exhorted to faithfulness (the social angle) 2:10—3:6
    A. Positive motivation: spiritual kinship among Israel 2:10a
    B. Situation: faithlessness against a covenant member 2:10b-15a
    C. Command: stop acting faithlessly 2:15b-16
    D. Situation: complaints of the Lord's injustice 2:17
    E. Negative motivation: the coming messenger of judgment 3:1-6
IV. Judah exhorted to return and remember (the economic angle) 3:7—4:6
    A. First command: return to the Lord with tithes 3:7-10a
    B. Positive motivation: future blessing 3:10b-12
    C. Situation: complacency toward serving the Lord 3:13-15
    D. Motivation: the coming day 3:16—4:3
    E. Second command: remember the Law 4:4-6

Message

Malachi prophesied during the times of Nehemiah. The dates of Nehemiah's ministry were about 445-420 B.C. Possibly Malachi ministered during the time when Nehemiah returned to Babylon following the completion of Jerusalem's walls and Nehemiah's term as governor of Judah (432-431 B.C.). This is only a guess, but it seems likely that God might have moved this prophet to minister when their godly leader was absent from them. I think Malachi probably wrote about 432 B.C. He was the only fifth-century B.C. writing prophet.

The conditions described in this last prophetical book are the same as those described in the last historical book of the Old Testament. Chronicles may have been written shortly before or after Nehemiah. Nehemiah deplored the defiled and corrupt priesthood, and Malachi's central charge was that the priesthood had corrupted the covenant (cf. Neh. 13:29 and Mal. 2:8). Nehemiah dealt with the mixed marriages and the evil that resulted from this condition, and Malachi spoke against the same evil (cf. Neh. 13:23-25 and Mal. 2:11-12). Nehemiah charged the people with neglecting the support of the priests, forcing them to return to farming (and thus plowing, a laborious life for anyone—but especially priests) their fields to support themselves. Malachi addressed the same condition and its underlying spiritual cause (cf. Neh. 13:10-11 and Mal. 3:8-10).

Ezra and Nehemiah had sought to correct certain external conditions, as well as certain internal conditions, that characterized the Jews who returned from Babylonian captivity. The external conditions that needed correcting were: the rebuilding of the altar of sacrifice, the temple, and the walls of Jerusalem. They were successful in changing these external conditions, but they were less successful in changing the internal conditions of the people. It is these conditions that Malachi addressed.

Malachi charged the Jews with seven specific sins. In each case, his contemporaries responded by challenging his criticism. They said, "How have we done that?" (cf. 1:2, 6; 2:14, 17; 3:7, 8, 13). Their response indicated hardness of heart, a resistance to deal with the internal conditions in their hearts that needed correcting. Malachi revealed the sensitivity of Yahweh to their condition and the insensitivity of the people to it. They believed that since they were serving God as He had directed, then He must be pleased with them. Malachi said that their hearts were not right with God, and He was *not* pleased with them. The people had a form of godliness, but they were devoid of the power of godliness.

---

[25]Bruce K. Waltke, *An Old Testament Theology*, pp. 846-47, divided the body of the book into three parts differently: God's faithful covenant love for Israel affirmed (1:2-5), Israel's unfaithfulness rebuked (1:6—2:16), and *I AM*'s coming announced (2:17—4:16).

Malachi is different from Haggai and Zechariah, the other two postexilic prophets. Haggai's mission was to stimulate the returnees to finish the temple reconstruction. Zechariah's mission was the same, but also to reveal the future to give them hope that would inspire them to work. Malachi's mission was to motivate the returnees to get back into fellowship with their God. Haggai focused on the material, Zechariah on the material and the spiritual, and Malachi on the spiritual.

Specifically, Malachi revealed three things to the physically restored Jews to motivate them to spiritual restoration: the unfailing love of Yahweh, their failures, and the secrets of strength in an age of failure.

First, Malachi revealed the unfailing love of Yahweh for His people. This is the master theme that recurs throughout the book. It is like the main melody that keeps coming back in a great piece of music. We find this theme introduced at the very beginning of the book (1:2a). We could render it: "I have loved you in the past, I love you in the present, and I will love you in the future." In other words, this is a revelation of the continual, unfailing love of Yahweh for His people.

His love for His chosen people was constant. This is a wonderful declaration, especially when we remember that it came to the Jews when they had no king, no high priest, and no spiritual power—only an outward form of worship in which the people trusted. Bear in mind, too, that this is the last prophetic message that came to the Jews before 400 years of silence from heaven, followed at long last by the provision of their Messiah.

God still loved His people as He always had, and as He always would. The dominant theme in this book is God's "I love you." As we hear the sub-themes of Israel's sevenfold spiritual failures, this major theme constantly keeps coming back and reminding us of God's love, in spite of His people's many sins. The mixing of these themes reveals that God was conscious of His people's sins and loved them anyway. So the book is not only a revelation of the constancy of God's love, but it is also a revelation of the constancy of His love in spite of His consciousness of their sins. The worst aspect of form without reality is that it hurts the heart of God, because it expresses a heartless response to God's love.

Second, Malachi reveals human failure. This book clarifies that no motive other than love for God can sustain a proper spiritual relationship with God (cf. John 21:15-17). It is possible to attend the place of worship, to go through the motions of worship, and even to make sacrifices of worship, and still not worship God—to have no fellowship with God. When these Jews lost their love for Yahweh, all their religious observances became as a noisy gong and as a clanging cymbal, noise but not music.

When true love departs, callousness sets in. We see this in the people's response to the Lord's reminder of His love for them. They replied: "How have You loved us?" (1:2). The attitude expressed in that question is the root of all sin (cf. Gen. 3). Since this is how these Jews felt, it is no wonder that, as Malachi pointed out, they failed God in so many other specific ways. The hour in which we begin to cease to love God is the hour in which we begin to wonder whether God really loves us. Then our worship of God, if we continue it, becomes only formal, not real. Then there is no real power in our lives, only a form of godliness.

Third, Malachi reveals the secrets of strength in an age of failure. We hear this theme clearly in 3:16. There was a smaller remnant among the remnant who returned from Babylon: the restoration community. This faithful remnant listened to and heeded the prophet's words. Notice what they did that led God to take note of them and honor them in a special way.

They feared the Lord. "Fear" is the term that throughout the Old Testament refers to someone's reverence for the Lord that arises from awareness of His love, on the one hand, and of His wrath, on the other. Some of Malachi's hearers, reminded of His constant love for them, *feared* Him. And they esteemed His name. That is, they gave some thought to the wealth of goodness that had flowed, was flowing, and would flow from Him. God's names reveal aspects of His character, for instance: "Yahweh Jireh" ("*The* LORD Provides"); "Yahweh Nissi" ("*The* LORD is My Banner"); "Yahweh Shalom" ("*The* LORD is Peace"); "Yahweh Tsidkenu" ("*The* LORD is Our Righteousness"); "Yahweh Shammah" ("*The* LORD is There"), etc.

As these people meditated on their God, as He had revealed Himself, they remembered how rich they were. Proverbs 18:10 says, "The name of the Lord is a strong tower; the righteous runs into it and is safe." These Jews had nowhere else to run. Their nation was no longer grand and glorious, their priests had corrupted the covenant, and the kings had passed away. All they had left was the name of their God, so some of them thought about that and remembered their spiritual wealth in their material poverty.

Notice that these remnant Jews who feared the Lord "spoke to one another" (3:16). Not only did they think on the name of the Lord individually, but they also shared their common thoughts with one another. That is the essence of fellowship. So a second resource for times when people fail to have fellowship with God, because of lack of love for Him, is fellowship with like-minded believers who *do* appreciate His name.

The result of this activity—fearing the Lord and having fellowship with the faithful—was that "the Lord gave attention and heard" (3:16). The word translated "gave attention" means "hearkened," as when a dog picks up its ears when it hears its master's voice. What these people did caught the Lord's attention. He hearkened to them, and He "heard" or listened attentively to what they said. God always listens carefully to the conversation of those who bind themselves together with other believers who genuinely fear Him, and who reflect on His great name.

The fourth secret of strength is hope (4:1-2). Malachi revealed that "the sun of righteousness shall appear." That is, righteousness will dawn on the earth like the rising sun. This will happen when Jesus Christ appears, bringing righteousness to the earth.

Then two things will happen. He will burn up, like the sun, what is dead and dry (i.e., dead works): those with only "dead works," whose relationship with God is only a formal one. But He will also provide healing for those whose relationship with Him is real: those who love to meditate on God and fear Him—and whose fruit endures. Thus, the same sun will burn some and heal others. This happened initially when Jesus came the first time, but it will happen also when He comes the second time.

The last word of the Old Testament is a reminder of the coming of this day of the Lord. So is the last word of the New Testament: the Book of Revelation. Therefore it must be very important that all people remember that this day is coming and live in the light of it. Let us, too, live by meditating on God and fearing Him, maintaining fellowship with others who do the same, with our eyes on the horizon of history, waiting for "the blessed hope and the glorious appearing of our great God and Savior, Jesus Christ" (Titus 2:13).

I would summarize the message of this book this way: Appreciating God's constant love is the key to revitalizing present spiritual life and assuring future divine blessing. The Lord's Supper helps Christians appreciate God's love.[26]

Exposition

I. INTRODUCTION 1:1

This title verse explains what follows as "the oracle" of Yahweh's "word" that He sent "to Israel through Malachi." The Hebrew word *massa'*, translated "oracle," occurs 27 times in the Prophets (e.g., Isa. 13:1; 14:28; Nah. 1:1; Hab. 1:1; Zech. 9:1; 12:1; et al.). It refers to a threatening message, a burden that lay heavy on the heart of God and His prophet. "Pronouncement" and "utterance" are good synonyms.

"The word of Yahweh" refers to a message that comes from Him with His full authority. "Yahweh" is the name that God used in relationship to Israel as the covenant-making and covenant-keeping God. What follows is evidence that Israel was in trouble with Yahweh because the Jews had not kept the Mosaic Covenant. Yahweh, of course, was completely faithful to His part of the covenant.

"Malachi" means "my messenger." The prophet's name was appropriate since God had commanded him to bear this "word" to the people of Israel. The prophet was not the source of the revelation that follows; he was only a messenger whose job it was to communicate a message from Yahweh (cf. 2:7; 2 Tim. 4:2; 2 Pet. 1:20-21). As many as 47 of the 55 verses in Malachi are personal addresses of the Lord.[27]

II. THE PRIESTS EXHORTED NOT TO DISHONOR THE LORD (THE THEOLOGICAL ANGLE) 1:2—2:9

> "Malachi's first address is governed by the ironic exhortation in 1:10, 'Oh, that one of you would shut the temple doors.' It is directed against the priests of the postexilic temple. Despite their responsibility under the covenant of Levi (cf. 2:4, 8) to be the Lord's messengers of Torah (2:7), they were dishonoring the Lord (1:6), particularly in their careless attitude toward the offerings (1:8). Failing to take their responsibilities to the Lord seriously, they had become political pawns of the influential in Israel who used religion to maintain respectability (2:9). The priests are here exhorted to stop the empty worship and to begin honoring the Lord with pure offerings and faithful service. As motivation the Lord declares his love for them (and for all the people; 1:2-5) and threatens them with humiliation and removal from his service (cf. 2:1-3, 9)."[28]

One's attitude toward, and his or her relationship with God, determine that person's health and wholeness as a child of God. They also determined Israel's national health and wholeness. This first address deals with this subject particularly: the theological issue of attitude toward and relationship with God.

A. POSITIVE MOTIVATION: THE LORD'S LOVE 1:2-5

1:2a   The Lord's first word to His people was short and sweet. He had "loved" them. He had told His people of His love for them repeatedly throughout their history (cf. Deut. 4:32-40; 7:7-11; 10:12-22; 15:16; 23:5; 33:2-5; Isa. 43:4; Hos. 11:1, 3-4, 8-9). Yet they were now questioning His love and implying that there was no evidence of it in their present situation in life. This is the first of seven such dialogues in Malachi (cf. vv. 6, 7; 2:14, 17; 3:7b-8, 13b-14). Yahweh had promised them a golden age of blessing, but they still struggled under Gentile oppression and generally hard times (cf. v. 8; 2:2; 3:9, 11). Their question revealed distrust of Him and hostility toward Him, as well as lack of appreciation for Him. Israel should have responded to Yahweh's love by loving Him and keeping His commandments (Deut. 6:4-9).

---

[26]Adapted from G. Campbell Morgan, *Living Messages of the Books of the Bible*, 1:2:335-49.
[27]Clendenen, p. 205.
[28]Ibid., p. 244.

1:2b-3　　In replying to the people's charge, the Lord asked them if "Esau" was not "Jacob's brother." Yet God had "loved Jacob," the younger, and "hated Esau," the older. The evidence of God's hatred for Esau was that He had "made" the ("his [Esau's]) mountains" of Seir, the inheritance that God gave Esau and his descendants, a desolate "wilderness." Unstated is the fact that God had given Jacob a land flowing with milk and honey for his inheritance, which proved His love for that brother. Some interpreters understand that God simply loved Jacob more than He loved Esau.

> "It was not a question of selecting Jacob for heaven and reprobating Esau to hell."[29]

Other interpreters believe that God predestined Jacob for salvation and Esau for reprobation.[30]

It is remarkable that God loved Jacob in view of the person Jacob was, and it is equally remarkable that God hated Esau, because in many ways he was a more likeable individual than his brother.

> "Someone said to Dr. Arno C. Gaebelein, the gifted Hebrew Christian leader of a generation ago, 'I have a serous problem with Malachi 1:3, where God says, "Esau I have hated." Dr. Gaebelein replied, 'I have a greater problem with Malachi 1:2, where God says, "Jacob, I have loved."'"[31]

Normally in the ancient Near East the father favored the eldest son, but God did what was abnormal in choosing to bless Jacob over Esau. God's regard for individuals does not depend ultimately on their behavior or characters. It rests on His sovereign choice to bless some more than others (cf. Rom. 9:13). This is a problem involving His justice, since it seems unfair that God would bless some more than others. However, since God is sovereign, He can do whatever He chooses to do (cf. Rom. 9).

Another problem that these verses raise concerns God's love. Does not God love the whole world and everyone in it (John 3:16)? Yes, He does, but this statement deals with God's choices regarding Jacob and Esau, not His affection for all people. When He said here that He hated Esau, He meant that He did not choose to bestow His favor on Esau to the extent that He did on Jacob (cf. Ps. 139:21). He made this choice even before they were born (Gen. 25:21-34; Rom. 9:10-13). To contrast His dealings with the twins, God polarized His actions toward them in this love-hate statement (cf. Luke 14:26). God loved Jacob in that He sovereignly elected him and his descendants for a covenant relationship with Himself (Gen. 29:31-35; Deut. 21:15-17), as His special possession (cf. Deut. 4:37; 5:10; 7:6-9). Often in Scripture to love someone means to choose to bless that person. Not to love someone means not to bless him or her.

> "Modern studies of covenant language have shown that the word 'love' (. . . *'aheb*, or any of its forms) is a technical term in both the biblical and ancient Near Eastern treaty and covenant texts to speak of choice or election to covenant relationship, especially in the so-called suzerainty documents."[32]

The fact that God gave Mt. Seir to Esau as "his inheritance" shows that He *did* love him to that extent. But He did not choose to bless Esau as He chose to bless Jacob, namely, with a covenant relationship with Himself. Similarly, a man might love several different women including his mother, sisters, daughters, and aunts. But when he enters into the covenant of marriage and sets his love on his wife, his love for her might make it seem like he hated the others, relatively speaking. Again, eternal destiny is not in view here; God was speaking of His acts in history toward Jacob and Esau and their descendants.

Did not God choose to bless Jacob because Jacob valued the promises that God had given his forefathers, whereas Esau did not (cf. Gen. 27)? Clearly Jacob did value these promises and Esau did not, but here God presented the outcome of their lives as the consequences of His sovereign choice rather than their choices. Clendenen believed God's love and hatred of Jacob and Esau was His response to their respective regard and disregard of His covenant promises.[33] Their choices were important, but the choice of God before and behind their choices, that resulted in the outcome of their lives, was more important (cf. Eph. 1; Rom. 9).

---

[29]Harry A. Ironside, *Notes on the Minor Prophets*, p. 187.
[30]E.g., John Calvin, *Institutes of the Christian Religion*, 3:21:6.
[31]Warren W. Wiersbe, "Malachi," in *The Bible Exposition Commentary/Prophets*, p. 479.
[32]Merrill, p. 391. See also Stuart, p. 1284; William L. Moran, "The Ancient Near Eastern Background of the Love of God in Deuteronomy," *Catholic Biblical Quarterly* 25 (1963):77-87; and J. A. Thompson, "Israel's Haters," *Vetus Testamentum* 29 (1979):200-205.
[33]Clendenen, p. 251.

Some of God's choices, the really important ones (His decree), determine all that takes place to bring those choices to reality. If this were not so, God would not be all-powerful; man could override the power of God with his choices. Some of God's choices are stronger than others, as reflected, for example, in the words "will," "counsel," or "purpose" (Gr. *boule*); and "desire," "wish," or "inclination" (Gr. *thelema*). In some matters, God allows people to influence His actions, even to cause Him to relent or change His mind from a previous course of action to a different one. Even so, in the really important things that He has determined, no one can alter His will.[34] Yet God's choices do not mean that man's choices are only apparently real. Human beings have a measure of freedom, and it is genuine freedom. We know this is true because a just God holds human beings responsible for their choices. How humans can be genuinely free, to the extent that we are free, and how God can still maintain control is probably impossible for us to comprehend fully.

The bottom line is that God chose to bless Jacob to an extent that He did not choose to bless Esau. This decision lay behind all the decisions that these twin brothers made. They were responsible for their decisions and actions, but God had predetermined their destinies (cf. Eph. 1:3-5; Rom. 8:28-30).

1:4 Even though the Edomites, Esau's descendants, determined to rebuild their nation after it had suffered destruction by the Babylonians, they would not be able to do so. They could not because Almighty Yahweh would not permit it. He would "tear down" whatever they rebuilt, so much so that other people would view them as a "wicked" land (cf. the holy land, Zech. 2:12), and the objects of Yahweh's perpetual indignation. The "holy" land was holy—sanctified—because God had set it apart for special blessing, as He had the nation of Israel. "Edom," on the other hand, was called "wicked," because God had not set it apart for special blessing.

> "Israel needed to consider what her lot would have been if she, like Edom, had not been elected to a covenant relationship with Yahweh. Both Israel and Edom received judgment from God at the hands of the Babylonians in the sixth century (Jer. 27:2-8). Yet God repeatedly promised to restore Israel (because of His covenant promises, Deut. 4:29-31; 30:1-10), but He condemned Edom to complete destruction, never to be restored (Jer. 49:7-22; Ezek. 35)."[35]

> "The Judeans had Persian permission and support in their rebuilding campaign (Ezra 1:1-11; 4:3; 6:1-15; 7:11-28; Neh. 2:7-9; 13:6). That was God's doing. The Edomites had no such help, which was also God's doing and which sealed Edom's fate as a people forever."[36]

1:5 Observing Yahweh's dealings with Edom, the Israelites would learn of His love for Israel and His greatness that extended "beyond . . . Israel" (cf. vv. 11, 14; 3:12; 4:6). They would eventually call on other people to appreciate Him too.

> "While Edom does not have the most space devoted to prophecies against it in total number of verses (Egypt has that honor, thanks to Ezekiel), it has the widest distribution among the prophetic books. From Isaiah 34 in particular it is clear that Edom can be used by the prophets to stand as a synecdoche for 'all the nations' (Isa. 34:2)."[37]

The point of this section was to get the Jews of the restoration community, who were thinking that God had abandoned them and forgotten His promises to them, to think again. Even though they seemed to be experiencing the same fate as their ancient enemy, the Edomites, God would restore them because He had entered into covenant relationship with them. He would keep His promises, both to the Israelites and to the Edomites, for better and for worse respectively. This reminder of the Lord's love provided positive motivation for the priests to return to the Lord, and it should have the same effect on all God's people who read these verses.

B. SITUATION: THE PRIESTS' FAILURE TO HONOR THE LORD 1:6-9

The preceding section ended with a statement of Yahweh's greatness. The second one opens with a question about why Israel's priests did not honor Him. The theme of honoring or fearing the Lord appears several times in Malachi, making it one of the major themes in this book (cf. 1:11, 14; 2:2, 5; 3:5, 16; 4:2). The first disputation (1:2-5) is the simplest, and this one (1:6—2:9) is the most complex.

---

[34]See Thomas L. Constable, "What Prayer Will and Will Not Change," in *Essays in Honor of J. Dwight Pentecost*, pp. 99-113.
[35]Blaising, p. 1576.
[36]Stuart, p. 1289.
[37]Ibid., pp. 1281-82. For a list of oracles against foreign nations in the Prophets, see ibid., p. 1281.

". . . God inspired Malachi to produce an excoriation of the priests, in the same overall disputation format that governs all the passages of the book, but incorporating terminology and themes from a famous blessing closely associated in everyone's mind with the priests [i.e., Num. 6:23-27]."[38]

1:6   This pericope begins like the first one, with a statement by Yahweh and a challenging response (cf. Isa. 1:2-3). The priests were responsible to teach the other Israelites the Law, to mediate between Yahweh and His people, and to judge the people.

Almighty Yahweh asked the priests of Israel why they did not "honor" Him, since sons normally honor their fathers (Exod. 20:12; Deut. 5:16), and He was their Father (Exod. 4:22; Isa. 1:2; 63:16; 64:8; Hos. 11:1). Since servants "respect" their masters, why did they not fear Him since He was their Master (Isa. 44:1-2)? Even though they were blind to His love, they should at least have given Him honor.

Speaking for the priests, Malachi gave their response. They denied having despised His name. The "name" of Yahweh was a common substitute for the person of Yahweh from early biblical times (cf. Exod. 23:21; Deut. 12:5, 11, 21; 16:2, 6; et al.). It became a virtual title for Yahweh by the end of the biblical period, and increasingly so after that.[39] By asking how they had despised His name, rather than saying, "We have not despised your name," the priests were claiming ignorance as to how they were doing this. However, their question also carried a challenge; they resented the suggestion that they had despised His name.

"Intimate familiarity with holy matters conduces to treating them with indifference."[40]

1:7   The Lord responded through Malachi that the priests had "despised" the Lord by presenting "defiled" sacrifices to Him (cf. Lev. 22:2, 17-30, 32). Defiled sacrifices were sacrifices that were not ritually clean or acceptable, as the Law specified. By offering these, they defiled (made unclean) both the "altar" of burnt offerings and the Lord *Himself!* The Law referred to the offerings as food for God (Lev. 21:6), though obviously He did not eat them. The use of "food" for "sacrifice" and "table" for "altar" continues the human analogies already begun in verse 6. Moreover, these terms also connote covenant relationships, because covenants were usually ratified when the participants, typically a king and his vassals, ate a meal together.[41]

"What does this say to professed Christians who spend hundreds of dollars annually, perhaps thousands, on gifts for themselves, their family, and their friends, but give God a dollar a week when the offering plate is passed?"[42]

1:8   Furthermore, the priests were offering "blind," "lame," and "sick" animals as sacrifices. These were unacceptable according to the Law (Lev. 22:18-25; Deut. 15:21). The Lord asked them if this was not evil. Of course it was. They would not dare to offer such bad animals to their "governor," for fear of displeasing him, but they *did* dare to offer them to their King. The governor in view would have been one of the Persian officials who ruled over the territory occupied by Judah. Nehemiah held this position for a while, but others preceded and followed him in it. The Book of Malachi seems to date from Nehemiah's leadership of Israel, but Nehemiah refused to receive offerings from the people (Neh. 5:14, 18). So the governor in view here was probably not Nehemiah. Elnathan, Yeho'ezer, and Ahzai were evidently the governors of Judah between Zerubbabel and Nehemiah.[43]

Anything second-rate that we offer to God is inappropriate in view of who He is. This includes our worship, our ministries, our studies, physical objects, anything. The Lord is worthy of our very best offerings to Him, and we should give Him nothing less. To give Him less than our best is to despise Him. Shoddiness is an insult to God. Shoddy holy is still shoddy.

1:9   How foolish it was to pray for God to bestow His favor on the priests when they were despising Him in these ways.

"This is irony. God will not hear the prayers of those who dishonor him."[44]

"Over the years, I've participated in many ordination examinations, and I've looked for four characteristics in each candidate: a personal experience of salvation through faith in Jesus Christ; a sense of calling from the Lord; a love for and knowledge of

---

[38]Ibid., p. 1297. On this page Stuart also showed the similarities between the two passages in a side-by-side chart. On page 1316 he did the same comparing Num. 25:11-13 and Deut. 33:8-11 with Mal. 1:6—2:9.
[39]See Walther Eichrodt, *Theology of the Old Testament*, 2:40-45.
[40]Alden, p. 711.
[41]See Paul Kalluveettil, *Declaration and Covenant*, pp. 10-15, 120-21; and Dennis J. McCarthy, *Treaty and Covenant*, pp. 163-64.
[42]Wiersbe, p. 480.
[43]N. Avigad, "Bullae and Seals from a Post-exilic Judean Archive," *Qedem* 4, p. 34.
[44]Burton L. Goddard, "Malachi," in *The Wycliffe Bible Commentary*, p. 915.

the Word of God; and a high respect for the work of the ministry. Whenever we've examined a candidate who was flippant about ministry, who saw it as a job and not a divine calling, he didn't get my vote. Whether as a pastor, missionary, teacher, choir member, or usher, being a servant of God is a serious thing, and it deserves the very best that we can give."[45]

C. COMMAND: STOP THE POINTLESS OFFERINGS 1:10

The Lord ironically wished the priests would "shut" the temple "gates," and stop offering sacrifices, since they had so little regard for Him. He was displeased with them and would not accept any offerings from them. They might continue to offer them, but He would have no regard for them. Obviously the Lord had ordained the offering of sacrifices under the Law, but He preferred that the priests not offer them, than to have them offer meaningless sacrifices, simply as an obligation. "I am not pleased with you" is the opposite of "Well done, good and faithful servant" (Matt. 25:21).

This verse is the chiastic center and the heart of the first hortatory discourse dealing with the importance of the priests honoring the Lord (1:2—2:9).

D. SITUATION: THE PRIESTS' WORSHIP PROFANING THE LORD'S NAME 1:11-14

This is the second section that describes how the priests were dishonoring the Lord's name (cf. 1:6-9). It is one of the bookends that flanks the central command to stop the pointless sacrifices (1:10).

1:11   It was particularly inappropriate for Israel's priests to despise Yahweh, because the time would come when people from all over the world would honor His "name" (i.e., His person; cf. Isa. 45:22-25; 49:5-7; 59:19). "Incense" accompanied prayers (cf. Rev. 5:8), and "grain offering(s)" were offerings of praise and worship (cf. Heb. 13:15-16). In that day, people from many places will offer "pure" offerings. This refers to worship in the Millennium (cf. 3:1-4; Isa. 11:3-4, 9; Dan. 7:13-14, 27-28; Zeph. 2:11; 3:8-11; Zech. 14:9, 16).

> "Others argue that this verse legitimizes sincere pagan worship as really being directed to the one true God. However, such a notion is antithetical to the militant monotheism that permeates Israel's Yahwistic theology."[46]

1:12   The priests of Malachi's day were treating Yahweh's reputation as common. The proof of this was their statements that the altar was "defiled," and the offerings on it were "despised." Their attitude and their actions were wrong.

> "Whenever we disregard or circumvent the Lord's instructions and requirements, such as his requirements for elders and deacons, we profane his name and desecrate his worship."[47]

1:13   They were also saying that it was "tiresome" and distasteful to worship the Lord. Their worship should have been passionate and joyful instead of boring and burdensome (cf. Col. 3:16-17). They would "disdainfully sniff at it" as something they "despised," and were bringing as offerings what they had stolen, as well as "lame" and "sick" animals (cf. 2 Sam. 24:24). Did they expect Him to "receive" such sacrifices from them? How could He?

> "God is most glorified in us when we are most satisfied in him."[48]

1:14   The people also were playing the old bait and switch game; they were swindling God. They vowed to offer an acceptable animal as a sacrifice, but when it came time to present the offering they substituted one of inferior quality. How totally inappropriate this was, since Yahweh was "a great King," the greatest in the universe—truly the ultimate royal suzerain! His "name" would "be feared among" all "the nations," yet His own people and their spiritual leaders were treating it with contempt.

> "Missions is not the ultimate goal of the church. Worship is. Missions exists because worship doesn't. Worship is ultimate, not missions, because God is ultimate, not man. When this age is over, and the countless millions of the redeemed fall on their faces before the throne of God, missions will be no more. It is a temporary necessity. But worship abides forever."[49]

---

[45]Wiersbe, p. 481.
[46]Robert B. Chisholm Jr., *Handbook on the Prophets*, p. 478. See also Baldwin, pp. 227-28.
[47]Clendenen, p. 281.
[48]John Piper, *Let the Nations Be Glad! The Supremacy of God in Missions*, p. 26.
[49]Ibid., p. 11.

"All of history is moving toward one great goal, the white-hot worship of God and his Son among all the peoples of the earth. Missions is not that goal. It is the means. And for that reason it is the second greatest human activity in the world."[50]

Lack of true heart for the Lord and His service marked these leaders of God's people. They evidently thought He did not notice their actions and attitudes, but Malachi confronted them with their hypocrisy. The prophet's words should also challenge modern servants of the Lord, and leaders of His people, to examine their hearts.

E. NEGATIVE MOTIVATION: THE RESULTS OF DISOBEDIENCE 2:1-9

Whereas the emphasis in Malachi's argument shifts at this point somewhat from the sins of the priests (cf. 1:6; 2:1) to their possible fate, there is a continuing emphasis on their sins. In the preceding sections (1:6-14), the cultic activity of the priests (i.e., offering sacrifices) was prominent, but in this one (2:1-9), their teaching ministry is. As with the second hortatory discourse (2:10—3:6), this first one begins with positive motivation (1:2-5) and ends with negative motivation (2:1-9).

2:1-2   Malachi announced an admonition to the "priests" from the Lord. If they did not pay attention to His rebuke and sincerely desire to honor Yahweh's name, the Lord would "curse" them (cf. Deut. 27:15-26; 28:15-68). He would cut off their "blessings"; troubles would plague their lives. Blessing was their business, and by cursing their blessings the Lord would render their pronounced blessings vain. This curtailment of blessing may also include their income from the people, in addition to spiritual blessings. In fact, He had already begun to do so.

> "The inevitable result of covenant unfaithfulness was the imposition of the curses that were always spelled out in covenant texts (cf. Lev. 26:14-39; Deut. 27:11-26; 28:15-57)."[51]

> "No single prophetic book contains all twenty-seven types of curses or all ten types of restoration blessings. The shorter books normally contain few of either. Malachi, on the other hand, contains a fairly high proportion of both types relative to its length, confirming what readers of the book have long noticed: the Book of Malachi is closely concerned with fidelity to the covenant and the consequences (thus curses and blessings) of keeping or breaking the law of Moses."[52]

Notice the importance of the priests taking to heart what the Lord was saying, repeated twice in verse 2 for emphasis.

> "The word 'heart' (*leb/lebab*) denotes in Hebrew what may be called the command center of a person's life, where knowledge is collected and considered and where decisions and plans are made that determine the direction of one's life. In view of the 814 occurrences of the word in the Old Testament in reference to the human 'heart' ('the commonest of all anthropological terms'[53]) and the common usage of 'heart' in English of emotions, it is important to differentiate the Hebrew meaning from the English and so to 'guard against the false impression that biblical man is determined more by feeling than by reason.'[54]"[55]

2:3   Part of this curse involved rebuking the priests' "offspring" (Heb. *zera'*, physical descendants), and spreading (Heb. *zarah*) "refuse" from their feasts on their faces (cf. Zech. 3:3-4). The disgusting picture is of God taking the internal waste of the sacrificial animals and smearing it on the priests' faces. Consequently, both sacrifices and priests would have to be taken outside ("taken away," thrown out with the garbage, picturing excommunication) for disposal. This play on words communicates a double curse (cf. v. 2). The priests' descendants would not continue because the priests would cease to bear any or many children, and their inferior sacrifices would render them unclean. They would not, then, be able to continue to function in their office.

2:4   When these things happened, the priests would "know" that this warning had indeed come from the Lord. Its intent was to purify the priests so God's "covenant with Levi" could "continue" (cf. 3:3). This is the first of six explicit references to "covenant" in Malachi. The covenants in view are God's covenant with Levi (vv. 4-5, 8), the Mosaic Covenant (v. 10), the marriage

---

[50]Ibid., p. 15.
[51]Merrill, p. 405.
[52]Stuart, pp. 1260-61.
[53]Footnote 173: H. W. Wolff, *Anthropology of the Old Testament*, p. 40.
[54]Footnote 174: Ibid., p. 47.
[55]Clendenen, p. 288.

	covenant (v. 14), and the New Covenant (3:1). God had promised a continuing line of priests from Levi's branch of the Chosen People (Deut. 33:8-11; cf. Exod. 32:25-29; Num. 3:12; 25:10-13; Neh. 13:29; Jer. 33:21-22).[56]
2:5	The Lord's covenant with Levi was a covenant of grant. In this type of covenant one individual, and perhaps his descendants, received a promise of continuing blessing for a special service rendered. The special service that Levi and his descendants rendered to God involved serving as His priests. The covenant that God made with Levi and his descendants resulted in "life and peace" for them. God gave them these blessings because they respected Yahweh and feared His name (Num. 18:7-8, 19-21; cf. Num. 25:10-13).
2:6	Also in contrast to the present priests, Levi and his descendants had given the Israelites "true instruction" rather than perverted teaching (cf. Heb. 13:17; James 3:1). Levi, who here represents his faithful descendants, "walked with" the Lord "in peace (Heb. *shalom*) and uprightness, and he turned many" away "from iniquity."
2:7	"Priests" should speak true "knowledge," and should be reliable sources of instruction (Heb. *torah*), because they are messengers of Yahweh. Levi contrasts with the priests of Malachi's day, and Malachi ("my messenger") also contrasts with the priests of his day. Ezra was the great example of a faithful priest in postexilic Judaism (cf. Ezra 7:10, 25; Neh. 8:9).

> "As the life of a community depends upon the keeper of its water supply to guard that supply from loss or contamination, so the life of Israel depended upon its priests to preserve God's written word and effectively to dispense it when 'men should seek' it."[57]

2:8	The priests of Malachi's day had deviated from the straight path of truth, and had "caused many" people who followed them "to stumble" through *their* "instruction" (Heb. *torah*).

> "The definite article on . . . (*tora*), 'instruction,' suggests that here it is not just any teaching in general but indeed *the* instruction, namely, the Torah, the law of Moses. The defection of the priests is all the more serious, then, for they are actually creating obstacles to the people's access to the Word of God itself. To cause the people to 'stumble in the Torah' is to so mislead them in its meaning that they fail to understand and keep its requirements. There can be no more serious indictment against the man of God."[58]

The unfaithful priests had "corrupted" the Lord's "covenant" with "Levi," in the sense that they had put its continuance in jeopardy by their evil conduct.

> "To have an ill-prepared minister, an incompetent pastor, a hireling for a shepherd was bad enough; much worse was it to have a deceiver, a schemer, a wolf in sheep's clothing for a leader."[59]

Malachi referred to three covenants in this chapter: this covenant with Levi, the covenant of the fathers (2:10), and the covenant of marriage (2:14).

2:9	Since the priests had despised the Lord, the Lord had made them "despised" in the eyes of "all the people." They did not obey His will, but instead had told the people what they wanted to hear. Their penalty should have been death (Num. 18:32).

Thus ends the first hortatory discourse in Malachi. This one, addressed specifically to Israel's unfaithful priests, should challenge all God's servants to serve Him with heartfelt gratitude for His grace and with the awareness that He will punish unfaithful workmen.

III. JUDAH EXHORTED TO FAITHFULNESS (THE SOCIAL ANGLE) 2:10—3:6

The Lord addressed the entire nation of Israel in this address, not specifically the priests as in the former one. His concern, as expressed through His messenger Malachi, was the peoples' indifference toward His will. They were blaming their social and economic troubles on the Lord's supposed injustice and indifference to them (2:17). Furthermore, they were being unfaithful to one another, especially to their wives, whom the husbands were apparently abandoning for foreign women. These conditions profaned the temple and the Mosaic Covenant (2:10b-15a). The Lord's command, which lies in the center of the section (as in the first and third exhortations), was for the people to stop their treachery toward one another (2:15b-16). Thus the major emphasis of this second main section of Malachi is social responsibility (love for and relationship with people), whereas the major emphasis of the first major section was theological (love for and relationship with God). First positive and, later, negative motivations act as bookends surrounding the Lord's command (cf. 1:2-5; 2:1-9; and 3:10b-12; 3:16—4:3).

---

[56]For an excursus on the Levitical Covenant, see ibid., pp. 296-306.
[57]Ibid., p. 314.
[58]Merrill, p. 410.
[59]Alden, p. 715.

"The style of the third oracle [according to the "disputation speeches" division of Malachi] differs from the others. Instead of an initial statement or charge followed by a question of feigned innocence, this oracle begins with three questions asked by the prophet. However, as at the beginning of each of the other oracles, the point is presented at the outset."[60]

A. POSITIVE MOTIVATION: SPIRITUAL KINSHIP AMONG ISRAEL 2:10A

This message deals with the same social evils that Ezra and Nehemiah faced: intermarriage with unbelievers (vv. 10-12), and divorce (vv. 14-16; cf. Ezra 9:2; Neh. 13:23-28), plus hypocritical worship (vv. 12-13).

Malachi said, by asking rhetorical questions, that God was the "father" of all the Israelites (cf. 1:2, 6; Exod. 4:22; Hos. 11:1).[61] Another view is that Malachi was referring to Abraham or Jacob as the father of the Israelites.[62] He was not saying that God is the father of all human beings in the modern "universal fatherhood of God" sense. One true God had created all of them. Israel belonged to God because He had created the nation and had adopted it as His son. Therefore the Israelites needed to honor the Lord. Since God is the creator and redeemer of His people, we have an obligation to honor, love, fear, worship, and obey Him.

B. SITUATION: FAITHLESSNESS AGAINST A COVENANT MEMBER 2:10B-15A

2:10b   In view of their common brotherhood in the family of God, it was inappropriate for the Israelites to treat each other as enemies and "deal treacherously" with each other. They should have treated each other as brothers and supported one another (Lev. 19:18). By dealing treacherously with each other, they had made the covenant that God had made with their ancestors virtually worthless; they could not enjoy the blessings of the Mosaic Covenant.

> ". . . the Mosaic covenant was by Malachi's time understood as a quaint, archaic document too restrictive to be taken seriously and inapplicable to a 'modern' age—virtually the same way that most people in modern Western societies view the Bible today."[63]

2:11   The evidence of Judah's treachery was that the Israelites were profaning (making common) Yahweh's beloved "sanctuary." This sanctuary may refer to the temple or His people. They did this by practicing idolatry. They had "married" pagan women who worshipped other gods (cf. 2 Cor. 6:14-16). Yahweh's *son* (v. 10) had married foreign women that worshipped other gods, and, like Solomon, had become unfaithful to Yahweh (cf. Exod. 34:11-16; Deut. 7:3-4; Josh. 23:12-13; Ezra 9:1-2, 10-12; Neh. 13:23-27).

2:12   In a curse formula, Malachi pronounced judgment on any Israelite who married such a woman. The judgment would be that he would die or that his line would die out (be "cut off"). The difficult idiom translated "who awakes and answers" (NASB) evidently means "whoever he may be" (NIV). This curse would befall him, even if he brought offerings to Almighty Yahweh at the temple. Worshipping God did not insulate covenant violators from divine punishment then, and it does not now.

2:13-14   The people evidently could not figure out why God was withholding blessing from them, so Malachi gave them the reasons. Another sin involved "weeping" profusely over the Lord's "altar"—because He did not answer their prayers—while at the same time dealing "treacherously" with their wives (cf. 1 Pet. 3:7). "Weeping over the altar" must be a figurative way of describing weeping as they "worshipped" Yahweh (hypocritically). The marriage relationship is a covenant relationship (cf. Prov. 2:17; Ezek. 16:8, 59-62; Hos. 2:16-20), and those who break their vows should not expect God to bless them. God Himself acted as "a witness" when the couple made their "covenant" of marriage in their "youth." This sin may have in view particularly the Israelite men who were divorcing their Jewish wives to marry pagan women (cf. v. 12), or divorce in general may be all that is in view.

> "Although the designation of a wife as a 'partner' [NIV] does not negate the subjection of her marital role to that of her husband, it certainly counters the concept that she was to be viewed as a mere possession to be disposed of at will. Though more than a friend or companion, she was not to be regarded as less than that."[64]

2:15a   No individual Israelite, who benefited from even a small amount of the Holy Spirit's influence, would break such a covenant as the marriage contract. God Himself would not break His covenant with Israel. In both cases, godly offspring were a major

---

[60]Blaising, p. 1580.
[61]Charles Lee Feinberg, *Habakkuk, Zephaniah, Haggai, and Malachi*, p. 112.
[62]Baldwin, p. 237.
[63]Stuart, p. 1332.
[64]Clendenen, p. 347.

reason for not breaking the respective covenants. The welfare of the children is still a common and legitimate reason for keeping a marriage intact.

> "Too often do contemporary married couples think of children as an option; they regard their own personal happiness or fulfillment as the primary goal in marriage. This was never to be the case according to the biblical revelation. The first divine command given to the first human couple [and later repeated to Noah; Gen. 9:7] was to 'be fruitful and increase in number; fill the earth and subdue it' (Gen 1:28). God intended that a man's purpose in departing from his father and mother and in joining himself to a wife by covenant, thus becoming one with her in flesh (Gen 2:24), should be fruitfulness. By that means were God's people to spread his rule throughout the whole earth, producing and discipling children who would manifest the divine glory in their obedient lives and continue the process until the earth was full of his glory (Gen 22:17). Although sin interfered with the process, the purpose has not been superseded. Although couples can no longer be assured of bearing children (as the theme of barrenness in Genesis makes clear), they are still to 'seek' them and can reproduce themselves in other ways if necessary, through adoption and/or spiritual discipleship."[65]

C. COMMAND: STOP ACTING FAITHLESSLY 2:15B-16

This "command" section begins and ends with commands not to break faith. Instruction to "take heed to your spirit" immediately precedes each of these commands. Two quotations from Yahweh lie within this envelope structure. These commands from Yahweh constitute the turning point in this second chiastic hortatory discourse (cf. 1:10).

2:15b   The Israelites needed to be careful, therefore, that "no one" of them dealt treacherously with the wife he married in his "youth"—by breaking his marriage covenant and divorcing her. The man is the responsible (guilty) party in the text, because in Israel only husbands could conveniently divorce their wives, as the context implies. Wives divorcing their husbands was less common in Jewish patriarchal society.

2:16   The Israelites were not to break their marriage covenants, because a person who divorces his mate *to marry an unbeliever* brings disgrace upon himself ("covers his garment with wrong"). Divorcing for this reason constitutes covenant unfaithfulness, breaking a covenant entered into that God Himself witnessed (v. 14). As such, it is an ungodly thing to do—since Yahweh is a covenant-keeping God. He keeps His promises. To break a covenant (a formal promise) is to do something that God Himself does not do.

Divorcing for this reason constitutes covering oneself "with wrong." This is a play on a Hebrew euphemism for marriage, namely: covering oneself with a garment (cf. Ruth 3:9; Ezek. 16:8). One *covers himself with wrong* when he divorces his wife, whom he has previously *covered with his garment* (i.e., married). For these Jews, divorce was similar to wearing soiled garments; it was a disgrace. For emphasis, the Lord repeated His warning to "take heed" to one's "spirit," so he or she does "not deal treacherously" with his covenant partner (cf. v. 15).

There is some dispute among English translators whether the rendering, "I hate divorce," is correct. It is possible, and some English translators have so rendered it (AV, NKJV, RSV, NRSV, NASB, NIV, TNIV, NET), but it requires emending the Masoretic text.[66] The normal way of translating the Hebrew literally would be, "If [or "for"] he hates sending away [i.e., divorce], says Yahweh God of Israel, then [or "and"] violence covers [or "he covers/will cover with violence"] his garment, says Yahweh of hosts." One paraphrase that captures the literal meaning well is, "For the man who hates and divorces, says the LORD, the God of Israel, covers his garment with violence, says the LORD of hosts" (English Standard Version). Another good paraphrase is, "'If he hates and divorces [his wife],' says the LORD of Hosts" (Holman Christian Standard Bible). One writer expressed the spirit of the Lord's statement by paraphrasing it, "Divorce is hateful."[67]

> "The hatred of God is also expressed against the one who covers his garment with violence. The reference is to the old custom of putting a garment over a woman to claim her as wife. Note particularly Deuteronomy 22:30; Ruth 3:9; and Ezekiel 16:8. Instead of spreading their garments to protect their wives, they covered their garment with violence toward their wives. The garment symbolized wedded trust and protection."[68]

---

[65] Ibid., p. 356.
[66] Joe M. Sprinkle, "Old Testament Perspectives on Divorce and Remarriage," *Journal of the Evangelical Theological Society* 40 (1997):539.
[67] D. L. Petersen, *Zechariah 9—14 and Malachi*, pp.204-5.
[68] Feinberg, p. 116.

> "The passage [2:10-16] does not deal with the case of a man divorcing a wife who has already broken her marriage vows, so it also does not apply to the case of a woman divorcing her husband who has already broken his marriage vows. This is another reason the passage should not be understood as an absolute condemnation of divorce under any circumstances. In fact, according to Jer 3:8 the Lord himself had divorced the Northern Kingdom of Israel because of her adulteries (cf. Hos 2:2)."[69]

The fact that Ezra *commanded* divorce (Ezra 10) may appear to contradict God's prohibition of divorce here. (Nehemiah neither advocated divorce nor spoke out against it; Neh. 13:23-29.) The solution seems to be that Malachi was addressing the specific situation of Jewish men divorcing their Jewish wives *in order to* marry pagan women. Ezra faced Jewish men who had already married pagan women. Does this mean that it is all right to divorce an unbelieving spouse but not a believer? Paul made it clear that the Christian is to divorce neither (1 Cor. 7:10-20). Evidently it was the illegitimacy of a Jew marrying a pagan that led Ezra to advocate divorce in that type of case.

Even though God typically opposes divorce, and in that sense hates it, He permitted it (Deut. 24:1-4)—to achieve the larger goals of maintaining Israel's distinctiveness, so she could fulfill His purposes for her in the world (Exod. 19:3-6). His purposes for the church are not exactly the same as His purposes for Israel. Furthermore, the church is not subject to the Mosaic Law. Therefore, it is inappropriate to appeal to the Jews' action in Ezra as a precedent for *Christians who are married to unbelievers* to follow (cf. 1 Cor. 7:12-13).

In none of the other passages in which divorce appears to be required (Gen. 21:8-14; Exod. 21:10-11; Deut. 21:10-14), does God present divorce as a *good* thing. He only permitted it under certain circumstances created by sin (Matt. 19:9).

> "The prophet's concluding exhortation, 'So guard yourself in your spirit, and do not break faith' is a strong warning to every husband that he must be constantly on his guard against developing a negative attitude toward his wife."[70]

D. Situation: complaints of the Lord's injustice 2:17

Malachi recorded complaints—that the people were voicing—that gave further proof that they were acting faithlessly and needed to change (cf. 2:10b-15a). That another disputation is in view is clear from the question and answer format that begins this pericope, as it does the others. Verse 17 contains the question and answer, and the discussion follows in 3:1-6. The Israelites' changeability (2:17) contrasts with Yahweh's constancy (3:6).

> "The reader is introduced here for the first time in Malachi to three themes, all of which may be expressed, for convenience, as needs: the need for messianic intervention, the need for a day of judgment, and the need for social justice."[71]

Malachi announced to his hearers that they had "wearied" God "with" their "words"; He was tired of hearing them repeat certain phrases. Their response was again hypocritical incredulity. They believed He could hardly be tired of listening to them, since He had committed Himself to them as their covenant Lord (cf. Isa. 40:28).

This is another place where Scripture seems to contradict itself. On the one hand, God said He does *not grow weary* (Isa. 40:28), but on the other hand, He said He *was weary* (here). The solution, I think, is that in the first case, He was speaking about His essential character; He does not tire out like human beings do. In the second case, He meant that He was tired of the Israelites speaking as they did. In this second case, He used anthropomorphic language to describe how He felt—as though He were a human being, which, of course, He is not.[72]

The prophet explained that Yahweh was tired of the Israelites saying that He delighted in them, all the while saying that "everyone who" did "evil" was acceptable to Him. They seem to have lost their conscience for right and wrong, and assumed that because God did not intervene, He therefore approved of their sin. In fact, their question amounted to a challenge of God's justice. If they were breaking His law and He was just, He surely must punish them. Their return to the land indicated to them that He was blessing them, and He promised to bless the godly in the Mosaic Covenant (Deut. 28:1-14).

Contemporary people say the same thing. "If there is a just God, why doesn't He do something about all the suffering in the world?" "If God is just, why do the wicked prosper?" Scripture reveals that God blesses the wicked as well as the righteous—because He is good (Matt. 5:45; Acts 14:17); and the righteous suffer as well as the wicked—because of the Fall and sin (Gen. 3:16-19; Eccles. 2:17-23). Moreover, God allows Satan to afflict the righteous as well as the wicked (Job 1—2). God will eventually punish the wicked and bless the righteous, but not necessarily in this

---

[69]Clendenen, p. 359.

[70]Ibid., p. 368. Cf. Col. 3:19.

[71]Stuart, p. 1346.

[72]For extended discussion, see Clendenen, pp. 372-82.

life (cf. Job 21:7-26; 24:1-17; Ps. 73:1-14; Eccles. 8:14; Jer. 12:1-4; Hab. 1). Malachi's audience had forgotten part of what God had revealed on this subject, and, of course, they had not yet received New Testament revelation about it.

> "Disillusionment had followed the rebuilding of the Temple because, though decade followed decade, no supernatural event marked the return of the Lord to Zion."[73]

E. Negative motivation: the coming messenger of judgment 3:1-6

Like the first address (1:2—2:9), this one ends with more motivation. Unpleasant things would happen if the people failed to change in their dealings with one another. The warning centers around the coming of another messenger whose arrival would bring judgment in the future. This section contains four predictions (vv. 1a, 1b, 3, 5).

3:1　　The Lord's response to the cynical Israelites was to point them to the future. He predicted the coming of His "messenger" (cf. Isa. 40:3-5). There is no question about who this was, because Jesus identified him as John the Baptist (Matt. 11:10; cf. Mark 1:2; Luke 7:27). This future messenger would "clear the way" in preparation for Yahweh (cf. Isa. 40:3; John 1:23). Clearly, Jesus Christ is Yahweh, since John the Baptist prepared the way for Jesus.

> "Perhaps most intriguing of all the issues raised by the fourth disputation is its implicit identification of the 'messenger of the covenant' as Yahweh himself. No other passage in the Old Testament so clearly assigns divine prerogatives and nomenclature to the figure of the Messiah (though the term *masiah* is not itself employed by Malachi). When one examines how this disputation describes the identity and actions of the 'messenger of the covenant,' one can only conclude that he is divine."[74]

Then "the Lord," whom the Israelites were seeking, would "suddenly come to His temple" (cf. Ezek. 43:1-5; Zech. 8:3). Though Jesus entered the temple in Jerusalem many times during His earthly ministry, this sudden coming was not fulfilled then (cf. vv. 2-5). It will occur when He returns to set up His messianic kingdom.

> "The fact that he will come *suddenly* is ominous, for suddenness was usually associated with a calamitous event (*e.g.* Is. 47:11; 48:3; Je. 4:20, *etc.*)."[75]

"The messenger of the covenant" is another name for the Lord who would come following the appearance of the first messenger promised in this verse. He would be the divine Messiah. "Messenger" means "angel," and the Angel of the Lord is in view here.

> "We dare not miss the three undeniable proofs of the deity of the Messiah given here: (1) he is identified with the Lord: 'he shall prepare the way before me . . . saith the Lord of hosts'; (2) he is indicated as the owner of the temple: 'to his temple'; and (3) he is called 'the Lord' whom they sought."[76]

The "covenant" is probably the New Covenant that God promised to make with the Jews in the future (cf. Jer. 31:31-34; Ezek. 36:22-36; 37:26). Another view is that the covenant in view is the Mosaic Covenant and, behind it, the Abrahamic Covenant.[77] The Jews delighted in this Messenger, because His "coming" had been a subject of messianic prophecy, and an object of eager anticipation from early in Israel's history (Gen. 3:15; *pass.*). Sovereign Yahweh promised His coming again here. The Jews had been expressing disbelief that God would intervene and establish justice in the world (2:17), but God promised He would.

3:2-3　　When the Lord came suddenly to His temple, no one would be able to "stand" before Him. Elsewhere the prophets foretold that this time would be a day of judgment on the whole world marked by disaster and death (4:1; Isa. 2:12; Joel 3:11-16; Amos 5:18-21; Zech. 1:14-17). Here, Malachi said no one would be able to "endure . . . His coming," because He would "purify" the priesthood ("sons of Levi"), the people who stood closest to Him. As "a refiner's fire" purifies "gold and silver," so He would burn up the impurities of the priests, and as a laundryman's "soap," He would wash them clean (cf. Deut. 4:29; Isa. 1:25; Jer.

---

[73]Baldwin, p. 242.
[74]Stuart, p. 1347.
[75]Baldwin, p. 243. Cf. Rev. 1:1; 22:6.
[76]Feinberg, p. 121.
[77]Clendenen, p. 386; Feinberg, p. 121.

6:29-30; Ezek. 22:17-22; Zech. 3:5). The Levitical priests would then be able to offer sacrifices to Yahweh in a righteous condition, rather than a defiled one, as they were in Malachi's day (cf. 1:6—2:9; Isa. 56:7; 66:20-23; Jer. 33:18; Ezek. 40:38-43; 43:13-27; 45:9-25; Zech. 14:16-21). The multiple figures of cleansing, and the repetition of terms for cleansing, stress the thoroughness of the change that the Lord's Messenger would produce.

> "Christ's atoning death meant that the entire sacrifice-based system could be brought to an end, its assigned purposes having been fulfilled."[78]

3:4   After this cleansing of the priests, "Judah and Jerusalem" (i.e., all Israel) would be able to offer sacrifices that would please the Lord, in contrast to the present ones that did not (cf. 1:13-14). They would be acceptable, like the offerings the priests offered earlier in Israel's history, before the priesthood had become corrupt.

3:5   At that time, the Lord assured His people that He would "draw near" to them, but it would be "for judgment." He would quickly judge ("be a swift witness against") all types of sin that they practiced, whereas in Malachi's day, and now, He waits to judge (cf. 2 Pet. 3:9-10). The Levites would not be the only Jews He judged; all the Israelites living then would come under His judgment (cf. Ezek. 20:34-38). He would judge them for all types of activity forbidden for His people: sorcery; adultery; lying; oppression of employees, widows, and orphans; mistreatment of aliens; even all forms of irreverence for, and unbelief in, Him. This was His answer to their claim that He was unjust (2:17).

3:6   The Lord concluded by reminding His people of one of His character qualities that should have made them fear Him and have hope. He does "not change," and that is why they would "not" be "consumed" totally. He was faithful to His covenant promises in the Abrahamic and Mosaic Covenants; He would never destroy them completely but would chasten them and finally bless them. By calling the Jews "sons of Jacob," the Lord was connecting their behavior with that of their notorious patriarch. Promises are only as good as the person who makes them, so the fact that Yahweh does not change strengthens the certainty of their fulfillment (cf. Deut. 4:31; Ezek. 36:22-32). The Apostle Paul gave the same reason for expecting Israel to have a future (Rom. 3:3-4; 9:6; 11:1-5, 25-29).

The statement that Yahweh does not change (cf. 1 Sam. 15:29; Heb. 13:8) may seem to contradict other statements that the Lord changed His mind (e.g., Exod. 32:14). This statement that He does not change refers to the essential character of God. He is always holy, loving, just, faithful, gracious, merciful, etc. The other statements, that He changes, refer to His changing from one course of action to another. They involve His choices, not His character. If He did not change His choices, He would be unresponsive; if He changed His character, He would be unreliable.[79]

IV. JUDAH EXHORTED TO RETURN AND REMEMBER (THE ECONOMIC ANGLE) 3:7—4:6

The Lord had said that Israel's earlier history was a time when the priests and the people of Israel pleased Him (v. 4). Now He said that those early days were short-lived (cf. Exod. 32:7-9). In contrast to His faithfulness (v. 6), they had been unfaithful.

This third and last hortatory speech in Malachi differs from the previous two in its construction. Whereas the former two both began with positive motivation and ended with negative motivation, this one begins and ends with commands. Whereas the central section in each of them was a command surrounded by evidence for needed change, this one centers on the evidence that is flanked by motivations. Thus this speech, and the entire book, ends with a climactic command to remember the Law (4:4-6).

The focus of the first speech was on the people's relationship to God (spiritual responsibility), the focus of the second one was on their relationship to one another (social responsibility), and the third one is on their relationship to their possessions (economic responsibility).

A. First command: Return to the Lord with tithes 3:7-10a

3:7   From Israel's early history, the people had deviated from the straight path that Yahweh had prescribed for them to walk in the Mosaic Covenant. They had disobeyed covenant stipulations. The Almighty Lord called His people to "return" to Him, with the promise that if they did, He would "return" to them (cf. Deut. 4:30-31; 30:1-10). A command to "return" to the Lord, in 3:7, occurs at the beginning of this speech, and a promise that the Lord would "return" to them, in 4:6, ends the speech. The response of the people was that they did not know "how" to "return." The Mosaic Covenant specified how they were to return—by trusting and obeying Yahweh—so their question indicated a reluctance to change their ways.

---

[78]Stuart, p. 1354.

[79]See Thomas L. Constable, *Talking to God: What the Bible Teaches about Prayer*, pp. 145-46; Robert B. Chisholm Jr., "Does God 'Change His Mind'?" *Bibliotheca Sacra* 152:608 (October-December 1995):387-99; and Clendenen, pp. 404-8.

"'How should we return?' is not an earnest entreaty for information but a self-serving declaration of innocence. The people, in effect, are saying, 'What need do we have to return since we never turned away to begin with?'"[80]

"They were like the stereotypical husband who has failed to recognize that his relationship with his wife has deteriorated."[81]

3:8   The Lord proceeded to give some examples of repentance that the Israelites needed to apply. How absurd it is for human beings to "rob God." To rob Him one would have to be stronger and smarter than He. Yet that is what the Israelites were doing, because God was allowing it. They were thieves of the worst kind: robbers of God. They brazenly asked how they had robbed Him. They had withheld the tithes (Lev. 27:30, 32; Deut. 12:5-18; 14:22-29) and offerings (Num. 18:21-32) that the Law commanded them to bring to God.

"There were several kinds of tithes: (1) the tenth of the remainder after the first-fruits were taken, this amount going to Levites for their livelihood (Leviticus 27:30-33); (2) the tenth paid by Levites to the priests (Numbers 18:26-28); (3) the second tenth paid by the congregation for the needs of the Levites and their own families at the tabernacle (Deuteronomy 12:18); and (4) another tithe every third year for the poor (Deuteronomy 14:28, 29)."[82]

Standing beside "tithes" as it does here, "offerings" may refer to the tithe of the tithe that went to the priests (cf. Exod. 29:27-28; Lev. 7:32; Num. 5:9). The Levites were to receive a tenth from the people and then give a tenth of that to the priests. But the widows, orphans, and sojourners also benefited from the tithes (Deut. 14:28-29), so withholding it hurt them as well. Another possibility is that Malachi was distinguishing the mandatory "tithes" from the voluntary "offerings" that the Israelites brought. Or perhaps any other offerings beside the tithes are in view. In any case, tithes and offerings constitute a merism representing all their economic responsibilities to God.

Since God owned the land and its produce in the first place (cf. 1:12-14; Lev. 25:23), withholding tithes when He commanded the Israelites to give them amounted to robbing Him. Earlier, the Lord criticized the priests for offering an inferior quality of sacrifices (1:7-14), and now He criticized the people for offering an insufficient quantity of sacrifices (cf. v. 10). Failure to adequately support the priests and Levites resulted in the breakdown of priestly service (cf. Neh. 10:32-39; 13:10).

3:9   All the people were guilty of this offense. That is, it was widespread in "the whole nation," not that every individual Israelite was guilty necessarily. Robbing the priests and Levites of what was due them was actually robbing God, since they were His servants and representatives, and they maintained His house, the temple. They would receive "a curse" from the Lord for this covenant violation (v. 11; cf. 4:6).

3:10a   The people needed to bring "the whole tithe," not just part of what they owed, "into the storehouse," in the temple. There were special rooms in the temple devoted to storing the gifts the Israelites brought (cf. 1 Kings 7:51; Neh. 10:38; 13:12). Then there would be "food" in the Lord's "house"—for the priests and for Himself. The sacrifices were, in a figurative sense, food for the Lord (cf. 1:7). The Lord urged His people to put Him to a "test" by doing this.

There are several references to people tempting God in the New Testament that discourage this practice (e.g., Acts 5:9; 15:10; 1 Cor. 10:9; Heb. 3:9). It is always wrong to test God's patience by sinning and presuming on His grace. It is another thing to hold Him accountable to His promises, and so test His faithfulness, which God asked His people to do here.

B. POSITIVE MOTIVATION: FUTURE BLESSING 3:10B-12

Both motivational sections of this speech have a future orientation (cf. 3:16—4:6).

3:10b   The Lord had promised to bless the Israelites for obedience, so their obedience in bringing the full amount of tithes that the Law required would test (i.e., prove, demonstrate) His faithfulness to His promise. He promised to reward their full obedience with rain ("windows of heaven") and harvests abundant enough to satisfy their needs ("blessing" that "overflows"). His "storehouse" of blessings for them was full.

This verse has often been used to urge Christians to tithe. However, the New Covenant under which Christians live never specified the amount or percentage that we should give back to God of what He has given to us. Rather it teaches that we should give regularly, sacrificially, as the Lord has prospered us, and joyfully (cf. 1 Cor. 16:1-2; 2 Cor. 8—9; Phil. 4). In

---

[80]Merrill, p. 437.
[81]Clendenen, p. 413.
[82]Feinberg, pp. 123-24.

harmony with the principle of grace that marks the present dispensation, the Lord leaves the amount we give back to Him unspecified and up to us. Christians who sit under a steady diet of preaching that majors on God's grace often give far more than 10 percent. Since tithing preceded the giving of the Mosaic Covenant (Gen. 14:20; 28:22), many Christians regard giving 10 percent as our minimal responsibility. However, the examples of tithing that appear before the Mosaic Law are just that: examples, not commands (e.g., Gen. 14:20; 28:22). Examples are not binding on believers, but precepts (commands) are. Another example of this is the early Jerusalem Christians practicing communal living (Acts 2:44). Few people would say that this practice is binding on all Christians today.

This verse has also been used to teach "storehouse giving." Those who do so view the church building, or the church congregation, as the storehouse into which Christians should bring their gifts to the Lord. Some go so far as to say that it is wrong for Christians to give to the Lord in ways that bypass the local church, for example, giving directly to a missionary.

This viewpoint fails to appreciate the difference between Israel's temple and Christian churches. Israel's temple was a depository for the gifts that the Israelites brought to sustain the servants and work of the Lord throughout their nation. The Christian church, however, is different in that we have no central sanctuary, as Israel did, nor does the church have a national homeland. Christians live and serve throughout the world, in contrast to the Israelites, who were to fulfill their mission by serving God within their land. God told the Israelites to stay in the land and let their light shine from there (Exod. 19:5-6), but He has told Christians to go into all the world and let our light shine there (Matt. 28:19-20). Some Christians believe that each local church is a microcosm of Israel, so we should regard our church as Israel regarded its temple. Most Christians believe the church is not limited to a collection of local churches but includes the whole universal body of Christ (Eph. 1; 4). The whole is greater than any of its parts, or even all its parts combined.

3:11-12 Not only would God provide adequate harvests (v. 10), but He would also preserve the harvested crops ("fruits of the ground") from animals and diseases ("rebuke the devourer" to "not destroy")—that might otherwise destroy them. The Israelites' grapes would also develop fully on their vines rather than dropping off prematurely. "All" other "nations" will acknowledge divine blessing on the Israelites, because their "land" will be such a "delightful" place.

The Mosaic Covenant, with its promises of material blessing for obedience, is no longer in force (Rom. 10:4; Heb. 8:13). Obedience to God's will does not necessarily result in material prosperity now (Phil 1:29; 4:11-13). However, we do have promises that God will reward those who trust and obey Him in the next stage of our lives, after death, if not before (Acts 4:31-35; 1 Cor. 3:11-15; 2 Cor. 5:10; 9:6-12; Gal. 6:6-9; Phil. 4:14-19). And we enjoy many spiritual blessings now (cf. Rom. 5:1-11; Eph. 1:3-14).

"The issue in Mal 3:7-12 is not tithing but apostasy. Judah is charged here with abandoning the God who had chosen and blessed them and turning away from the statutes he had given them to test their loyalty and to mark the path of life he would bless. By retaining for themselves the tithes and other offerings they owed to God, the people showed their idolatrous hearts in placing themselves before God, and they showed their callous hearts in leaving the Levites and landless poor to fend for themselves."[83]

C. SITUATION: COMPLACENCY TOWARD SERVING THE LORD 3:13-15

Now the Lord identified the sinful attitude that lay behind the peoples' failure to tithe. This is the longest complaint speech by the Judahites in the book, and it shows the hardness of the peoples' hearts.

3:13 The people had spoken arrogantly against the Lord, yet when faced with their disrespect, they asked for proof: "What have we spoken against You?"

3:14 The Lord obliged them. They had said that serving the Lord and obeying Him did not benefit them, that it did not pay to serve Yahweh. When they mourned over their sins, their physical conditions did not improve.

> "Some of the people who made the complaint (3:14) were guilty of the myopic legalism that eventually led to Jewish pharisaism in the first century A.D. This legalism concentrated on performing certain rigorous activities and not doing other things as the means of vindicating themselves before God. But this actually stifled the full expression of inner righteousness required by God (Matt. 5:20-48; 23:1-36)."[84]

> "So-called good works that do not arise from genuine faith and gratitude to God are simply 'hot checks' drawn on an empty bank account. They may provide a temporary sense of self-satisfaction, but God

---

[83]Clendenen, p. 429. See also his excursus on tithing in the church, pp. 429-33.
[84]Blaising, p. 1586.

recognizes their true value—zero, and he will eventually bring to justice anyone who tries to live on them."[85]

"I hear this complaint from some believers about their churches. 'We're not getting anything out of it!' But a church is like a bank or a home: you don't get anything out of it unless you put something into it."[86]

3:15   It seemed better for them to become self-assertive, because then some good things would come their way. It was those who practiced "wickedness" who got ahead (were "built up") and grew stronger materially (cf. 2:17). For them life was all about material prosperity, so it seemed better to be wicked than righteous. Even though they tested the Lord's patience, and tried to provoke a reaction from Him by behaving as they did, they escaped His punishment only temporarily.

D. MOTIVATION: THE COMING DAY 3:16—4:3

In the first two hortatory speeches, the first motivation sections are positive and the second ones are negative. In this last speech, the first is mainly positive, but the second is a mixture of positive and negative, though mainly negative.

3:16   Upon hearing the Lord's rebuke through His prophet, some of Malachi's hearers who genuinely "feared the Lord" got together. Evidently they discussed Malachi's message and agreed among themselves that they needed to repent. They even wrote down their commitment on a scroll ("book of remembrance").

"Almost surely this was a scroll that contained their names as signatories to some sort of statement of their commitment to Yahweh in faith that they were disassociating themselves from the prevailing sins, that his promises were reliable, and that his covenant was to be kept. In other words, it was a covenant renewal document."[87]

Yahweh paid attention to their heart attitude and heard what they said.

"How can an individual remain faithful to God in a faithless world? Malachi gave three tips for developing a lifestyle of faithfulness.
•   Vow to be faithful to God, even if those around you are not. Consider writing your own 'scroll of remembrance.'
•   Surround yourself with a group of likeminded individuals for encouragement. This group 'talked with each other' (Mal. 3:16) as they encouraged each other to remain faithful (see Heb. 10:25).
•   Remember that God's day of reckoning will come someday. Keep a long-range perspective (1 Cor. 3:12-15)."[88]

3:17   Almighty Yahweh announced that, on the day He prepares His "own possession," He will honor those who fear Him as His own. This probably refers to "the day of the Lord" (cf. v. 2; 4:1, 3), when He will resurrect Old Testament saints and judge them (cf. Dan. 12:2). This will be when Jesus Christ returns to rule and reign on the earth. The faithful will receive a reward in His kingdom for their submission (Dan. 12:3). He also promised to "spare them as a man spares his own son." When Jesus Christ judges Old Testament saints, He will separate the sheep from the goats (Matt. 25:31-46). Here God described the sheep as His sons. He will spare them the humiliation and punishment that will be the lot of those who did not honor Him (vv. 14-15).

3:18   In that day, it will be clear who behaved righteously and who behaved wickedly, because Jesus Christ will reward the righteous and not reward the wicked among the Israelites. Then the true and the false servants of the Lord will be clearly known. In Malachi's day, and in ours, the true motives of God's people are not obvious, but in the future they will become clear for many to see.

4:1   The Lord now elaborated on "the day" to which He had just referred (3:17). There is no chapter division in the Hebrew Bible; all of chapter 4 appears as the end of chapter 3. This day of the Lord would be a day of judgment. The Lord compared it to a fiery "furnace," in which "all the arrogant" and "every evildoer" (a hendiadys meaning every arrogant evildoer) will burn like "chaff" (or stubble; cf. 3:2-3, 15). Fire language is common in connection with divine judgment and anger (e.g., Gen. 19:24-28; Ps. 2:12; 89:46; Isa. 30:27; Jer. 4:4; 21:12; Amos 1:4, 7, 10, 12, 14; 2:2, 5). That "day . . . will set them ablaze," in the sense that the Lord *Himself* will set them ablaze in that day. He will so thoroughly purge them, that they will be entirely consumed, like a shrub thrown into a hot fire is totally burned up: from "root" to "branch" (a merism of totality). The judgment of wicked unbelievers is in view (cf. Matt. 25:46). Later revelation clarified the time of this judgment, namely, the end of the Millennium

---

[85]Clendenen, p. 437.
[86]Wiersbe, p. 487.
[87]Stuart, p. 1382.
[88]Charles H. Dyer, in *The Old Testament Explorer*, p. 841.

(Rev. 20:11-15). Because God will deal with the unsaved wicked so severely, His people needed to repent—remembering that He will deal with *all* sinners (unbelievers) severely.

> "This verse gives no basis for the error of annihilationism. It describes physical death, not the state of the soul after death. The unsaved are in conscious eternal woe (Rev. 14:10-11; 20:11-15), as the saved are in conscious eternal bliss (Rev. 21:1-7)."[89]

4:2   In contrast, the Israelites who feared Yahweh (1:14; 3:5, 16-17) will experience a reign ("sun") of "righteousness" compared here to sunshine (cf. Isa. 60:1-3). The "sun" can blister, but it can also bless, and its blessing effect is in view here. The prophet evidently visualized the sunrays like the "wings" of a bird stretching over the earth. This righteous day would have a "healing" effect on the inhabitants of the earth, healing them, and the planet, from the harmful effects of past millennia of sin (cf. Isa. 53:5).

Some expositors have understood "the sun of righteousness" to be a messianic title.[90] But it seems best to view it as a description of the day of blessing that Messiah will bring, the Millennium. The New Testament never referred to Jesus Christ as "the sun of righteousness." The figure of vigorous "calves" cavorting in open pasture, after having been cooped up in a "stall," pictures the joy and freedom that the righteous will enjoy in that day (cf. Isa. 65:17-25; Hos. 14:4-7; Amos 9:13-15; Zeph. 3:19-20).

4:3   The righteous will also appreciate their superiority over ("tread down") "the wicked" in that day, the opposite of the situation in Malachi's day. "The wicked" will be as "ashes" (from the burning, v. 1) "under" their (the calves') "feet," in that the wicked will suffer judgment and offer no resistance (cf. Isa. 66:24; Matt. 3:12; Mark 9:48). Almighty Yahweh is "preparing" that "day," so it will inevitably come.

E. SECOND COMMAND: REMEMBER THE LAW 4:4-6

"Malachi began with an illustration from Genesis (Jacob and Esau) and spent most of the first half of the book reminding priests and people of the need to keep the Mosaic Law. Now, close to the end of his book, he gives another terse reminder of their continuing obligation to those laws."[91]

"As the motivation provided in 1:2-5 extends beyond the first address to the whole book . . ., this concluding section provides the book's climactic command. . . . Malachi begins by pointing to the past and ends by pointing to the future (4:5-6[Hb. 3:23-24]), thus appropriately grounding the ethical impact of the book in both redemption and eschatology."[92]

4:4   Moses' last words to the Israelites in Deuteronomy contain about 14 exhortations to remember the Law that God had given them. Malachi closed his book, and God closed the Old Testament, with the same exhortation. One writer identified nine connections between Malachi and the Book of Deuteronomy.[93] Although the Hebrew canon ends with Chronicles rather than Malachi, Malachi concludes the Prophets section of the Hebrew Bible. The Jews regarded "the Law and the Prophets" as comprising their entire Scriptures (cf. Matt. 5:17; 7:12; 11:13; 22:40; Luke 16:16; John 1:45; Acts 13:15; 24:14; 28:23; Rom. 3:21).

The Israelites had forgotten and disregarded God's law, and Malachi had pointed out many specific instances of that. Now he urged the people to recall and obey their Law. By calling Moses "My servant," the Lord was reminding Malachi's audience of how faithful Moses had carried out God's will. He was to be their model of obedience. The "Law of Moses" (i.e., the Pentateuch) was still God's Word to His people, after all that had happened to them. Every revival that had taken place in the history of Israel had been the result of returning to the Law of Moses (cf. 2 Chron. 29—31).[94]

4:5   The Lord promised to send His people "Elijah the prophet before" the "great and terrible day of the LORD" arrived. An angel later told John the Baptist's parents that their son would minister in the spirit and power of Elijah (Luke 1:17). Yet John denied that he was Elijah (John 1:21-23). Jesus said that John would have been the Elijah who was to come if the people of his day had accepted Jesus as their Messiah (Matt. 11:14). Since they did not, John did not fulfill this prophecy about Elijah coming, though he did fulfill the prophecy about Messiah's forerunner (3:1).

---

[89]*The New Scofield Reference Bible*, p. 982.
[90]E.g., Calvin, 2:9:1; 2:10:20; 3:25:1; Feinberg, pp. 133-34.
[91]Alden, p. 724.
[92]Clendenen, p. 454.
[93]Hugenberger, pp. 48-50.
[94]Alva J. McClain, *The Greatness of the Kingdom*, p. 117.

This interpretation has in its favor Jesus' words following the Transfiguration, which occurred after John the Baptist's death. Jesus said that Elijah would come and restore all things (Matt. 17:11). Whether the original Elijah will appear before the day of the Lord,[95] or if an Elijah-like figure, similar to John the Baptist, will appear—remains to be seen. Since Jesus went on to say that Elijah had come, and that the Jews had failed to recognize him—speaking about John (Matt. 17:12-13)—I prefer the view that an Elijah-like person will come.

What John did for Jesus at His first coming, preparing the hearts of people to receive Him, this latter-day "Elijah" will do for Him at His second coming. Evidently the two witnesses in the Tribulation will carry out this ministry (Rev. 11:1-13). Who the witnesses will be is a mystery. Evidently one of them will be an Elijah-like person. These men will do miracles as Elijah and Elisha did.

4:6 Malachi revealed only one future forerunner of Messiah before the "day of the Lord" in view, perhaps the more prominent of the two. Elijah was a very significant person in Israel's history, because he turned the Israelites back to God at the time of their worst apostasy—when Ahab and Jezebel had made Baal worship the official religion of Israel. Moses established the theocracy on earth, but Elijah restored it when it almost passed out of existence. Similarly, the eschatological Elijah will unite the hearts of the Jews to turn back and worship Yahweh.

At His first coming, Jesus said that because of Him, families would experience division. Some fathers would believe on Him but their sons would not, and daughters would disagree with their mothers over Him (Matt. 10:35-36; Luke 12:49-53; cf. Mic. 7:6). When *this* "Elijah" comes, he will cause the Jews to believe on their Messiah, as many did in Elijah's day. They will unite over belief in Him.

If the Lord will not send *this* "Elijah," and if *he* did not turn the hearts of the Jews back to God, the Lord would have to come (in the person of Messiah) and strike the earth "with a curse." Because the Jews will turn to Jesus Christ in faith (Zech. 12:10), blessing will come to the earth, not a curse (vv. 2-3; cf. Zech. 14:11; Rom. 11:26). This is another reference to millennial conditions.

The Jews of Malachi's day needed to remember their Law, and practice it, in order to prepare for the coming day of the Lord. As Jesus said, Moses wrote about *Him* (John 5:46). Had Malachi's audience and subsequent generations of Jews paid attention to the Law of Moses, they would have recognized Jesus for who He was at His *first* coming. This was the last revelation that God gave His people before the forerunner of Messiah, whom He promised in 3:1, appeared some 400 years later. They had plenty of time to get ready.

In Malachi's day, the people needed to return to the Lord, or He would "smite the land with a curse." This in fact happened, because they did not return to Him. The Israelites' problems in occupying the land God gave them—ever since the Babylonian Captivity—is evidence of their failure.

Fortunately for them, and for the whole world, God did not cast off His people Israel because they rejected His Son (Rom. 11:1). He will send another powerful prophet, like Moses, to His people in the end times. They will believe the message of *that* "Elijah," and will *turn* to Jesus Christ in faith when He returns to the earth (Zech. 12:10; Rom. 11:26). Then Messiah will initiate a righteous worldwide rule that will last 1,000 years (Rev. 20:1-6), rather than smiting the land with a curse.

> "Genesis reveals the entrance of the curse into the human family (Gen. 3); the last word of the O.T. shows the curse still persisting (Mal. 4:6); Matthew begins (1:1) with Him who came to remove the curse (Gal. 3:13; Rev. 21:3-5; 22:3)."[96]

> "The warning that ends the Old Testament is not absent at the end of the New (Rev. 22:10-15), but the difference is that there grace has the last word (verse 21)."[97]

---

[95]Feinberg, p. 136.
[96]*The New Scofield . . .*, p. 982.
[97]Baldwin, p. 253.

Bibliography

Alden, Robert L. "Malachi." In *Daniel-Minor Prophets*. Vol. 7 of *The Expositor's Bible Commentary*. 12 vols. Edited by Frank E. Gaebelein and Richard P. Polcyn. Grand Rapids: Zondervan Publishing House, 1985.

Archer, Gleason L., Jr. *A Survey of Old Testament Introduction*. 1964; revised ed., Chicago: Moody Press, 1974.

Avigad, N. "Bullae and Seals from a Post-exilic Judean Archive." *Qedem* 4. Monographs of the Institute of Archaeology series. Jerusalem: Hebrew University, 1976.

Baldwin, Joyce G. *Haggai, Zechariah, Malachi: An Introduction and Commentary*. Tyndale Old Testament Commentaries series. Leicester, Eng., and Downers Grove, Ill.: Inter-Varsity Press, 1972.

Blaising, Craig A. "Malachi." In *The Bible Knowledge Commentary: Old Testament*, pp. 1573-89. Edited by John F. Walvoord and Roy B. Zuck. Wheaton: Scripture Press Publications, Victor Books, 1985.

Bright, John A. *A History of Israel*. Philadelphia: Westminster Press, 1959.

Calvin, John. *Institutes of the Christian Religion*. The Library of Christian Classics series, volumes 20 and 21. Edited by John T. McNeill. Translated by Ford Lewis Battles. Philadelphia: Westminster Press, 1960.

Childs, Brevard. *Introduction to the Old Testament as Scripture*. Philadelphia: Fortress Press, 1979.

Chisholm, Robert B., Jr. "Does God 'Change His Mind'?" *Bibliotheca Sacra* 152:608 (October-December 1995):387-99.

_____. *Handbook on the Prophets*. Grand Rapids: Baker Book House, 2002.

_____. "A Theology of the Minor Prophets." In *A Biblical Theology of the Old Testament*, pp. 397-433. Edited by Roy B. Zuck. Chicago: Moody Press, 1991.

Constable, Thomas L. *Talking to God: What the Bible Teaches about Prayer*. Grand Rapids: Baker Book House, 1995; reprint ed., Eugene, Oreg.: Wipf & Stock Publishers, 2005.

_____. "What Prayer Will and Will Not Change." In *Essays in Honor of J. Dwight Pentecost*, pp. 99-113. Edited by Stanley D. Toussaint and Charles H. Dyer. Chicago: Moody Press, 1986.

Dyer, Charles H., and Eugene H. Merrill. *The Old Testament Explorer*. Nashville: Word Publishing, 2001. Reissued as *Nelson's Old Testament Survey*. Nashville: Thomas Nelson Publishers, 2001.

Eichrodt, Walther. *Theology of the Old Testament*. 2 vols. London: SCM, 1967.

Feinberg, Charles Lee. *Habakkuk, Zephaniah, Haggai, Malachi*. The Major Messages of the Minor Prophets series. New York: American Board of Missions to the Jews, 1951.

Freeman, Hobart E. *An Introduction to the Old Testament Prophets*. Chicago: Moody Press, 1968.

Glazier-McDonald, Beth. *Malachi: The Divine Messenger*. Society of Biblical Literature Dissertation Series 98. Atlanta: Scholars Press, 1987.

Goddard, Burton L. "Malachi." In *The Wycliffe Bible Commentary*, pp. 913-20. Chicago: Moody Press, 1962.

Harrison, R. K. *Introduction to the Old Testament*. Grand Rapids: Wm. B. Eerdmans Publishing Co., 1969.

Hugenberger, G. B. *Marriage as Covenant: A Study of Biblical Law and Ethics Governing Marriage Developed from the Perspective of Malachi*. Vetus Testamentum Supplement 52. Leiden, Netherlands: Brill, 1994.

Ironside, Harry A. *Notes on the Minor Prophets*. New York: Loizeaux Brothers, 1947.

Kaiser, Walter C., Jr. *Malachi: God's Unchanging Love*. Grand Rapids: Baker, 1984.

_____. *Toward an Old Testament Theology*. Grand Rapids: Zondervan Publishing House, 1978.

Kalluveettil, Paul. *Declaration and Covenant*. Rome: Pontifical Biblical Institute, 1982.

Longman, Tremper, III and Raymond B. Dillard. *An Introduction to the Old Testament.* 2nd ed. Grand Rapids: Zondervan, 2006.

McCarthy, Dennis J. *Treaty and Covenant.* Rome: Pontifical Biblical Institute, 1963.

McClain, Alva J. *The Greatness of the Kingdom, An Inductive Study of the Kingdom of God.* Winona Lake, Ind.: BMH Books, 1959; Chicago: Moody Press, 1968.

Merrill, Eugene H. *An Exegetical Commentary: Haggai, Zechariah, Malachi.* Chicago: Moody Press, 1994.

Moran, William L. "The Ancient Near Eastern Background of the Love of God in Deuteronomy." *Catholic Biblical Quarterly* 25 (1963):77-87.

Morgan, G. Campbell. An Exposition of the Whole Bible. Westwood, N.J.: Fleming H. Revell Company, 1959.

_____. *Living Messages of the Books of the Bible.* 2 vols. New York: Fleming H. Revell Co., 1912.

The New Scofield Reference Bible. Edited by Frank E. Gaebelein, et al. New York: Oxford University Press, 1967.

Petersen, D. L. *Zechariah 9—14 and Malachi.* Old Testament Library series. Louisville: Westminster Press, 1995.

Peterson, Eugene. *Run with the Horses.* Downers Grove, Ill.: Inter-Varsity Press, 1983.

Piper, John. *Let the Nations Be Glad! The Supremacy of God in Missions.* Grand Rapids: Baker Book House, 1993.

Sprinkle, Joe M. "Old Testament Perspectives on Divorce and Remarriage." *Journal of the Evangelical Theological Society* 40:4 (December 1997):529-50.

Stuart, Douglas. "Malachi." In *The Minor Prophets: An Exegetical and Expositional Commentary*, 3:1245-1396. 3 vols. Edited by Thomas Edward McComiskey. Grand Rapids: Baker Books, 1992, 1993, and 1998.

Taylor, Richard A., and E. Ray Clendenen. *Haggai, Malachi.* New American Commentary series. Nashville: Broadman & Holman Publishers, 2004.

Thompson, J. A. "Israel's Haters." *Vetus Testamentum* 29 (1979):200-205.

Waltke, Bruce K., with Charles Yu. *An Old Testament Theology: an exegetical, canonical, and thematic approach.* Grand Rapids: Zondervan, 2007.

Wiersbe, Warren W. "Malachi." In *The Bible Exposition Commentary/Prophets*, pp. 477-89. Colorado Springs, Colo.: Cook Communications Ministries; and Eastbourne, England: Kingsway Communications Ltd., 2002.

Wolff, H. W. *Anthropology of the Old Testament.* Philadelphia: Fortress Press, 1974.

Wood, Leon J. *The Prophets of Israel.* Grand Rapids: Baker Book House, 1979.